INTRODUCTION TO
PERSONALITY

INTRODUCTION TO
PERSONALITY

Third Edition

E. Jerry Phares

Kansas State University

HarperCollins*Publishers*

20 01002 450

SPONSORING EDITOR: Laura Pearson
PROJECT COORDINATION, TEXT AND COVER DESIGN: The Wheetley Company, Inc.
PHOTO RESEARCH: Rosemary Hunter
COVER ILLUSTRATION: "Inside Vision" © 1989 by Eve Olitsky.
PRODUCTION: Michael Weinstein
COMPOSITOR: Pam Frye Typesetting, Inc.
PRINTER AND BINDER: R. R. Donnelley & Sons Company
COVER PRINTER: New England Book Components

155.2

Introduction to Personality, Third Edition

Copyright © 1991 by HarperCollins Publishers Inc.

Library of Congress Cataloging-in-Publication Data

Phares, E. Jerry.
    Introduction to personality / E. Jerry Phares.—3rd ed.
        p.   cm.
    Includes indexes.
    ISBN 0-673-46424-5
    1. Personality.   I. Title
BF698.P48   1991
155.2—dc20   90-22710
                                                              CIP

92 93 9 8 7 6 5 4

CONTENTS

PREFACE

Readers of the third edition of *Introduction to Personality* will find a great deal of continuity from previous editions. Both the basic format and the goals remain unchanged. This book is a general introduction to the field of personality that requires little in the way of background beyond a first course in psychology. The topics, level of writing, and general mode of presentation should continue to make the book appropriate for students from the sophomore to the senior level. Also, this edition continues to focus on both theoretical conceptions and upon specific personality processes and research.

While the continuity across editions has been both calculated and visible, there have been numerous changes. The most obvious is the extensive updating. For example, 105 references have been deleted and 350 added (almost 50% of which are dated between 1987 and 1990).

Within specific chapters, several significant changes will be apparent. In Chapter 1, the old issues section has been replaced by a fairly extensive discussion of the biological and environmental determinants of personality. In Chapter 4, the discussion of the neo-Freudians has been shortened and object relations theory and the self-psychology of Kohut have been added. The research topics in Chapter 5 have been updated and tightened as well. Chapter 6 continues to focus heavily on Rogers and Kelly but a more explicit discussion of the self has been added while the topics of humanism and existentialism now have a reduced role. A major addition to this chapter is new material on information processing, especially as it applies to self-schema approaches. These general changes carry over into Chapter 7 as well. Chapters 9 and 10 have been broadened. The previous exclusive focus on the trait perspectives of Allport, Cattell, and Eysenck has been changed and dispositional material from Murray and McClelland added. Furthermore, the discussion of the roles of traits versus situations has been shortened and moved from Chapter 1 to Chapter 8. Chapters 10 through 14 have been shortened a bit, updated, and generally tightened. Chapter 15 has been extensively rewritten and given much more of a health orientation in addition to the traditional topics of anxiety and stress. The chapters on aggression, altruism, and gender have all been updated significantly.

An Instructor's Manual, complete with strategies for teaching the course and multiple-choice, true-false, and essay questions has been prepared by Betty Royster, Ph.D. of Bowling Green State University.

I would like to thank the following reviewers for their input in the third edition:

Joel Aronoff
Michigan State University

James F. Calhoun
University of Georgia

Amerigo Farina
University of Connecticut

Edwin Lawson
State University of New York-Fredonia

Charles Lord
Texas Christian University

E. Jerry Phares

1

AN INTRODUCTION TO THE STUDY OF PERSONALITY

P A R T 1

Part 1 provides a general introduction to the field of personality and to its study. Chapter 1 begins by presenting a general definition of personality that focuses on the elements of distinctiveness and stability or consistency. The chapter also outlines the field of personality by describing the themes around which this book is organized: theory, development, adjustment, change, assessment, and research. The chapter concludes with a fairly lengthy discussion of the two major perspectives from which we can approach personality: the biological and the environmental.

With Chapter 2, the focus shifts to a discussion of the three sets of tools we can employ to better understand personality: theory, research, and assessment. Familiarity with these general topics will better enable the reader to grasp the substantive material presented in subsequent chapters.

CHAPTER 1

INTRODUCTION TO PERSONALITY

It is difficult to find a concept as sturdy, resilient, or enduring as personality. Each year, scores of new books dealing with one or another facet of personality appear. But the whole story hardly resides in books. Early on, even the most primitive of our ancestors recognized that no two people are ever exactly alike. Yet they also surely recognized that in certain ways all people are the same. They harnessed this seeming paradox in the service of prediction and understanding so they could better cope with the demands, the pressures, and the challenges of a very complex world. In children, one of the benchmarks of their growing maturity is the ability to recognize the sameness in all human beings while also utilizing their knowledge of the differences among people to attain their ends (see Box 1-1). Our fascination with personality (which all too often is reflected in the stacks of "pop" psychology books everywhere about us these days) is, then, rooted in very practical considerations.

In the Western world technological development has proceeded so far that relatively few of us need worry about basic survival. Food, shelter, and protection from predators have been virtually assured. As a result, we have the time to turn our attention inward. The search for emotional security and personal insight has replaced the fight for survival. Then, too, in the process of assuring our material needs, we have become more and more dependent on social, governmental, and scientific forces that we understand and trust less and less. In the face of anxieties the ability to understand ourselves and others gives us a measure of control. For example, at the height of post–World War II apprehensions over atomic warfare, David McClelland (1951) pointed out that a search for security leads us to focus more on the personal dynamics of ourselves and others. Certainly this effect is no less true today even though the precise circumstances of our anxieties may be different.

Like any psychological concept, personality has been closely examined over the years to determine its real utility. Indeed, it might be said that there have been many assaults but no one has yet breached the fortress. For example, Burnham (1968) noted that in the middle of the nineteenth century, many felt that neither a science nor a theory of personality was possible. But perhaps that was not so bad since supposedly no one was interested in human nature then anyway! This was surely the low point in the history of our interest in personality.

More recently, some have argued that personality is at best superfluous and at worst a misleading concept. One of the leading psychologists of the twentieth century, B. F. Skinner, has so argued (see Chapter 10). Likewise, Walter Mischel (1968) seemed to assert that if we know in detail the nature of the specific situations in which individuals find themselves, information about personality characteristics (or human nature, if you prefer) is unnecessary in predicting their behavior.

But despite such assaults, the concept will not go away. And the understanding of human nature has been a rare and elusive prize. In classical Greece, Aristotle decided that the essence of the human being resided in the ability to reason and that human behavior is a proper subject for scientific study. In the same period of history, Theophrastus contended that people differ among themselves in the kinds of character they possess. These same Greeks talked about a person's soul. Today, these discussions continue but we have concepts such as reinforcement, ego, cognitive schema, or perhaps observational learning. For example, in the March 1989 issue of the *Journal of Personality* a few of the titles of the papers that typify current research interests were:

- Trait-specific versus person-specific moderators of cross-situational consistency

- Gender and sex-role influences on children's self-esteem

- The role of sympathy and altruistic personality traits in helping: A reexamination

- Reinterpreting the Myer-Briggs Type Indicator from the perspective of the five-factor model of personality

NATURE OF PERSONALITY

The basic search for understanding has spanned several thousand years and has been marked by vastly different methods of inquiry. Indeed, over the years, the best efforts of poets and philosophers as well as scientists have been enlisted in this search. But emerging from their ruminations is, again, the awareness that all people are alike in some ways and yet different in others. Thus:

- We all learn but we learn different things and in differing degrees

- We each think but they are often very different thoughts

- We all feel but in differing ways to the same stimulus

It is almost as if we all dance to the same music but we each do a different step!

Let us now turn to a more specific examination of how we may define personality as a concept and as a field. In so doing, we shall find that the concept of personality as basically staked out in the 1930s and 1940s by such scholars as Gordon Allport, Henry A. Murray, and Gardner Murphy has survived all attacks and continues to be alive and well in the 1990s.

Box 1-1
LEARNING THAT PEOPLE ARE ALL DIFFERENT YET ALIKE

Children begin learning very early that people differ from one another in many important ways. For example, little Ralph discovers to his chagrin one morning at day care that not all little girls are as placid as his sister Kim. Take, for example, that red-headed girl over there in the corner. She decked him when he tried to take her chocolate milk away from her. And what about Dorothy, his afternoon teacher? Unlike his mother, Dorothy promptly deposits him in "time-out" whenever he hits someone. Repeated over many different situations with many different people, Ralph imperceptibly but inevitably learns the lesson that to deal adequately with others you are going to have to learn to recognize and utilize the fact of individual differences. It is not enough to be in a situation where someone else's chocolate milk is available. You must also know whose chocolate milk you are confronting.

But that is not the only lesson Ralph will learn. He will also learn that in many important ways, everyone is alike. All human beings have certain things in common that set them apart from other objects in the environment. Everyone bleeds when you cut them but rocks do not. People need to eat but clouds do not. All his teachers seem to be larger, smarter, and stronger than he. Some of his peers will be pushovers and some will not. But all of his teachers will outsmart him nearly every time. He will have to discover both the sameness and the diversity in those people with whom he would interact.

Of course, if Ralph grows up in a hut in a remote countryside somewhere, tends his goats, and never comes into contact with other human beings, chances are good that he will not need to learn much about personality (although knowing something about the personalities of goats would be a real blessing). But Ralph will most likely not tend goats. He will exist in a complex network of human interactions from the very moment he appears upon the scene.

Defining personality

There have been many, many specific definitions of personality offered over the years. Box 1-2 presents a very brief sample of such definitions. In general, however, a definition of **personality** that is quite similar to many of those utilized by psychologists today would be as follows:

> Personality is that pattern of characteristic thoughts, feelings, and behaviors that distinguishes one person from another and that persists over time and situations.

We can further elaborate the two aspects of this definition.

People show distinct differences from one another and these differences are stable over situations and over time. Photograph Brent Jones.

Distinctiveness.

We have already noted the emphasis on distinctiveness or individuality. Thus your behavior or feelings are as idiosyncratic as your fingerprints. Other observers, however, emphasize that what is really unique is the *pattern* of each person's feelings, thoughts, and behavior. According to this view, people may possess differing degrees of intelligence, aggressiveness, or, say, sensitivity. But the critical feature is the unique way in which each person combines these traits. Of course, if we truly regard every person as a one-of-a-kind event, this can create problems in trying to study them scientifically. In searching for general principles that apply to all humans, how can we deal with uniqueness? We can study an individual separately and exhaustively and then develop principles of behavior that apply to that specific person. But if we do so, we would surely have difficulty generalizing to others what we have discovered about that person.

Stability and consistency.

The second property of many definitions of personality is stability or consistency. If people are unique, they must to some extent behave in recognizable ways over a variety of situations and over time. This is not to

CASE STUDY

The following is an excerpt from the case of Rick L.

I was 47 last month. I live with my wife and oldest daughter. My two younger sons are both married. One lives here in town, and the other has a job in California. My mother is in her sixties now and lives in an apartment several miles from here. My parents were divorced a long time ago, and both remarried.

Dad remarried right away, and although I used to visit them, I never really felt comfortable, and then after they had a kid of their own, I just kind of felt like I was intruding. Don't get me wrong. They were nice, but it was just a feeling I had.

My mother worked for an insurance company after the divorce. She was a real competent gal, to say the least, and pretty soon she was an underwriter. We were really close. After awhile I felt like I had to get away, so I got an apartment of my own. We always seemed to be arguing about something. Mainly it was because I wouldn't go to college. When I decided to get married to this girl I knew in high school, Mom really hit the ceiling.

Then Mom married an engineer from Delaware, and they moved there. I got a job with the telephone company. Gradually I worked myself up so I was in charge of customer relations. I've done pretty good, but I suppose I should have gone to college. I just don't feel at ease around the other executives. It's like they have something I don't.

Mom and the engineer split up about 10 years ago, and she moved back here. She still works part time in a clothing store. Since she moved back I have felt sort of uneasy. Maybe she spends too much time with us, I don't know. My wife—Emily—really clams up when she is around. Emily and I seem to be getting along pretty good these days. For awhile after we got married I was really happy. But when the kids started coming I felt . . . I know it sounds trite, but I felt trapped. I would see myself forever with the telephone company. We fought a lot I guess. She kind of lost interest in things, and those girls at the office started looking better and better. I played around a little, not much. Just enough to feel guilty as hell afterward. I don't think Emily ever realized what was going on. But Mom sure as hell did.

Well, everything has settled down now. The kids are all raised, and Mom isn't quite as demanding. I guess I have everything I should. The house is almost paid for, and we go to Colorado every summer for 2 weeks. We're thinking of buying a place out there. I don't get so mad at people anymore. In fact, things don't seem to bother me enough nowadays. I can just sit and stare at TV for hours. Sometimes I think I've mellowed, but at other times I think it's depression.

say there must be perfect consistency or that no one ever changes. There must, however, be a detectable degree of stability over time and consistency across situations such that we can say, for example, "Well, I haven't seen John in twenty-five years but he's still his old pessimistic self!" Or, "That's Mary all right; she's always there to help when she's needed!" As we shall see later in Chapter 8, a number of psychologists have been studying the extent of behavioral consistency and generality.

The field of personality

So far, we have examined some of the reasons personality has interested people, what some of its purposes are, and, in a general way, what it means. However, the field of personality is considerably broader than this. People who call themselves personality psychologists often specialize in specific subfields of personality, and there are books and advanced courses devoted to each of these specialties. The six aspects of the field, to be covered in the sections that follow, are themes around which this book is organized. These aspects are: **theory, development, adjustment, change, assessment,** and **research.** The case study of page 6 will help introduce these points.

Box 1-2
SOME DEFINITIONS OF PERSONALITY

1 Deceptive masquerade or mimicry

2 Superficial attractiveness

3 Social-stimulus value

4 The entire organization of a human being at any stage of development

5 Levels or layers of dispositions, usually with a unifying or integrative principle at the top

6 The integration of those systems or habits that represent an individual's characteristic adjustments to the environment

7 The way in which the person does such things as talking, remembering, thinking, or loving

8 The dynamic organization within the individual of those psychological systems that determine his or her unique adjustments to the environment (Items 1–8 were adapted from those collected by Allport, 1937, pp. 25–50)

9 A person's unique pattern of traits (from Guilford, 1959, p. 5)

10 . . . those characteristics of the person or of people generally that account for consistent patterns of behavior (from Pervin, 1989, p. 4)

Personality theory.   To study personality in an organized fashion, we must first decide on a language of description. For example, in the case of Rick L should we resort to a language of traits and describe him as possessing insecurity, guilt, depression, intelligence, and anger? But perhaps it is better to regard behavior or traits as determined by deep-seated, unconscious urges. If we make this choice, some form of psychoanalytic theory would be more appropriate than trait theory. One could certainly say Rick's concern with his mother seems a bit intense, which could reflect unresolved problems. Or maybe his outbursts of temper reflect some unconscious instinctual force. Then, again, maybe we should look to a modification of psychoanalytic theory and focus on his feelings of incompetence, which are possibly reflective of an inferiority complex.

There are many ways of conceptualizing people—existential, behavioral, social learning, to name a few—and we shall consider a number of them later. Our choice of concepts will have far-reaching implications and will affect every other aspect of personality with which we deal. What all this boils down to is that human nature in general (and Rick in particular) is not something that has been decided forever and about which everyone will agree. The nature of human beings has been debated since the dawn of civilization, and the controversy shows no signs of slackening. Whether Rick is a collection of traits, a storehouse of unconscious impulses, a chain of behaviors, or someone searching for the meaning of life will be answered differently by different observers depending upon their theoretical orientations.

Development.   If, as noted earlier, personality refers to stable, enduring characteristics, it becomes more than a matter of idle curiosity to understand how such characteristics develop. Most of us are not content merely to see ourselves as happy, dependent, insecure, and so forth. We want to know how we got that way. We know intuitively that our understanding of ourselves or others will never be complete until we find out what caused us to be what we are. In the case of Rick, what made him subject to outbursts of temper? Why did he and his mother argue so often? Was it simply his refusal to go to college, or were there deeper reasons? What was the real nature of his relationship with his father, and how did the divorce affect Rick's perceptions? No full understanding of Rick would be possible until some of the earlier events in his life, especially those of his childhood, were teased out. In addition, could we better understand Rick's development into old age if we were aware of some of his current problems, aspirations, and thoughts? Also, if we know the critical conditions for certain events, we can work to provide the kind of environment that will foster the outcomes we want for children. In addition, personality development takes place throughout life. Consequently, understanding development will help us to cope more effectively with problems that arise in any part of the life cycle.

If we know how personality develops, we will be in a stronger position to change it. Not everyone is satisfied with what he or she has become. In addition, there may be compelling social reasons to want to alter the behavior of seriously maladjusted individuals. In either case, knowledge about how personality develops, or about the conditions that lead to one outcome rather than another, is a good reason for studying personality development.

Adjustment.   Was Rick L maladjusted? How seriously should we consider his depression or his temper? Clearly, a case study of personality like Rick's has implications for adjustment. Most theories of personality have addressed the issue of what constitutes the adjusted personality. For the behaviorist, adjustment may be defined as a satisfactory repertoire of behaviors. The psychoanalyst will assert that adjustment can be achieved only when a person is free of the tyranny of the unconscious. A social learning theorist may claim that adjustment exists when needs and expectations of fulfilling them coincide. It is therefore important that we include under the banner of personality the implications for adjustment offered by each theoretical point of view.

Personality change.   Modifying personality and conducting psychotherapy are often associated with clinical psychology or psychiatry. To accomplish those ends, these professions depend heavily upon ideas from the field of personality. For example, psychoanalysis as a theory of personality and as a technique of therapy developed almost simultaneously in Sigmund Freud's consulting rooms. And the early client-centered counseling approaches of Carl Rogers carried along with them particular conceptions about human nature and personality. Thus, behavior- and personality-change techniques are not disembodied things that spring up spontaneously; they grow alongside personality conceptions (Phares, 1988).

Theories of personality not only have specific implications for adjustment, as previously noted, but also have specific implications or suggestions for accomplishing changes in personality. Again, we shall inevitably feel that our understanding is just that much more complete when we know how changes in behavior or personality can be brought about. In the case of Rick L we would feel more comfortable in our analysis were we able to recommend how his feelings of depression could be eliminated. A decrease in his discomfort around his fellow executives would be evidence that we really had a good grasp of his personality.

Personality assessment.   Where do personality psychologists get the information that enables them to describe people, determine their patterns of adjustment, understand how they have become what they are, or alter their current modes of adjustment? The material presented about Rick L was autobiographical data. But there are many more avenues available to the personality psychologist, including a variety of other life records and case history materials, numerous interview techniques, and an amazing number of psychological tests.

All of this implies that we must do more than passively receive information in order to make judgments about personality. Indeed, we must be able to use a measurement technology. The kinds of questions we have to answer and the particular personality theory to which we are committed will determine the kinds of interviews or tests we employ. The field of personality assessment is an extremely important one; without it, we would surely be more ignorant about the nature of people than we need be.

Personality research.   Without research we can never be certain how good our understanding of particular personality issues is. With empirical research we can go beyond mere theoretical speculation about how individual differences develop or how they affect behavior. We can put our speculations to the test. Also, we can study the specific conditions that give rise to behaviors such as aggression, sexual responses, helping, and the like. That is, aside from learning how one person comes to behave more aggressively than someone else in a wide variety of situations, we can determine how certain conditions or situations promote or retard aggressive behavior. In addition, research can help us understand how particular personality characteristics interact with certain situational or environmental conditions to produce a given behavior.

There are many methods of research. Some are experimental and may be carried out in the laboratory. Other research is of the case study variety. Some personality research involves testing a person for only a few minutes; other times, research means following the same person over a period of years. But whether research is in a laboratory or in the field, or whether it consists of a brief encounter or sustained contacts over years, it is a crucial activity.

We have considered how personality may be defined, and we have identified the major sectors in the field of personality. It is time to consider the two major determinants of personality that have captured the attention of investigators and observers over the years.

PERSONALITY DETERMINANTS

Over the years, long and heated debates have centered around the determinants of personality. Is the adult personality largely a product of nature and the biological and genetic factors that comprise it? Or, instead, are we nurtured by our own experiences that provide the foundation for learning to become what we are?

So, then, is our behavior determined by inherited, biological forces or by learning, experience, and environment? Obviously, the answer is "Both of the above." I cannot jump as far as a kangaroo, and no amount of training or motivation is going to change that. And how far I actually wind up jumping (and, indeed, whether I desire to jump at all) is heavily influenced by coaching, diet, and other environmental forces. So it is with many personality traits and characteristics. Biology and genetics surely play an important role, one complemented by culture and experience. But which is more important, biology or psychology? Well, the only proper answer is "It depends." It depends on what aspect of personality we are considering. For example, a preference for rock music over waltzes is most certainly determined by culture or learning. On the other hand, aggressiveness could be influenced heavily by biology; after all, it is much easier to be aggressive if you are a large person. Therefore, the question of how much of personality is biological and how much is psychological is really a pseudo-question. They are often considered separately for the sake of discussion, but as we shall see, they really operate in concert.

Later in this book, a variety of theoretical and research topics will be examined. In each instance it will be useful for you to consider how issues of biological and environmental determinants of behavior and personality are handled.

Adult personality is surely a joint product of both genetic and environmental factors.
Photograph A. Brilliant/
The Picture Cube.

The biological perspective

There has always been variation within the species so that those individuals who possessed adaptive characteristics lived long enough to pass them along to the next generation. Those who could think better, run faster, or resist the rigors of a sparse diet survived. There is no doubt that this evolutionary progression continues, although the process is a slow one. Therefore, it may not occur to us that intelligence, resistance to the effects of pollution, or the ability to survive in crowded, noisy urban centers is a part of this timeless yet creeping process.

This perspective seems so reasonable that psychologists have been prompted from time to time to search for the biological-genetic basis of personality. For example, is there some biological link between body type and personality? Is it really true, as some have claimed, that fat people are jolly whereas thin ones are reserved? Does the uneasiness that many individuals experience when crowded into stuffy, small apartments spring from some long-buried instinctual urge to be free to roam open spaces? Is the greater aggressiveness of many small boys as compared to girls a simple product of learned roles, or does this difference stem from the same biological roots that dictate that girls and boys be anatomically different?

There is no question but that the influence of biological-genetic factors on personality is more widely accepted now. There are striking reports of identical twins reared apart and separated for forty years who, when they finally meet, are wearing virtually identical clothing and have similar haircuts and the same occupations and hobbies (Bouchard et al., 1981). Indeed, evidence has now been offered for the inheritance of a variety of traits or so-called conditions including activity level, anxiety, alcoholism, dominance, criminality, locus of control, manic-depression, schizophrenia, sexuality, and yes, even political attitudes (Holden, 1987).

Still some personality theorists have an ideological distaste for biological determinants. They consider acceptance of hormonal or genetic factors akin to taking a rather pessimistic view of the possibility of bettering the human condition. To accept such factors is virtually to rule out the possibility of changes in a person's condition or social status. To remain "psychological"—that is, to reject any influence of biology or genetics—is to view the human being in more optimistic terms.

In addition, personality psychologists usually have little training in biology or genetics, and it is difficult for them to come to grips with the intricacies of the interactions between social and biological factors. Similarly, investigators trained in biology have difficulty dealing with social or learning factors.

With the foregoing constraints in mind, let us now briefly review some of the more important bridges between biology and personality. We will begin with two important characteristics—intelligence and mental illness. These topics have fascinated investigators for many years. It was in these research areas that many hoped some definitive answers would emerge, thus providing a model for future research on the genetics of personality.

Intelligence.   Francis Galton (1869), a half-cousin of Charles Darwin, investigated the hereditary basis of genius by studying a variety of family biographies and other descriptive accounts of eminent persons. He concluded that intelligence was inherited since outstanding mental ability was more likely to occur in the close relatives of eminent figures than in remote ones. Such an observation accords well with everyday experience, which tells us that brightness and achievement run in families—not always, but often enough to make many of us believers in the effects of heredity. Of course, the obvious flaw in Galton's work, as well as with our casual experience, is that it fails to inform us whether it is really heredity at work or whether the environment is responsible. After all, eminent people usually provide "eminent" environments for their children.

A more refined way to approach the issue of nature versus nurture is through the study of the mental ability of fraternal and identical twins. Here, the mental ability scores of monozygotic (identical) twins are compared with the scores of dizygotic (fraternal) twins. Identical twins carry identical sets of genes since they come from a single fertilized egg that separated into two identical parts during initial cell division. Fraternal twins, on the other hand, come from two fertilized eggs and are thus no more likely to be similar genetically than ordinary siblings. A great deal of research over the years has shown that the intelligence test scores for identical twins are much more alike than those for fraternal twins. However, not only are the genetic backgrounds of identical

"Evolution's been good to me."

© 1981 Saturday Review Magazine Co. Reprinted by permission.

twins more similar than those for fraternal twins, but also their environments. Once again, genetic similarity is confounded with environmental similarity.

Another approach to this problem involves the **co-twin method**—the study of identical twins reared apart. Because these twins have identical heredity, any subsequent differences in their behavior or personality can be ascribed to environmental influences. Of course, it is difficult to find such twin pairs, and it has sometimes been hard to prove that the twins are actually identical. Furthermore, in some instances the twins were not separated until fairly late in childhood, thus mitigating the operation of "pure" heredity. For all these reasons there has been little conclusive evidence. Nevertheless such twins often bear striking similarities to each other in both physical and personality characteristics. It seems that the environments for separated identical twins have to be radically disparate before any substantial differences are noted. R. S. Wilson (1972) has even observed that the patterns of development during the first two years of life are more similar for identical than for fraternal twins. As Tyler (1978) puts it, "There is no longer any argument about the statement that heredity plays a part in development of abilities" (p. 40). Indeed, one analysis of heredity-environment data suggests that up to 75 percent of the variance of IQ scores can be attributed to hereditary differences (Gourlay, 1979). However, Kamin (1980) suggests that we remain cautious in our conclusions because the effects of environmental factors have yet to be completely controlled in research such as this. And Angoff (1988) concludes that the debate over whether intelligence is largely genetically or largely environmentally determined is really irrelevant. The truly critical question is whether intelligence can be changed.

To bolster further the notion of a genetic basis for intellectual functioning, some cases of mental retardation have been shown to be determined by biomedical defects. For example, phenylketonuria involves an abnormal secretion of phenylpyruvic acid in the urine. It follows a classic Mendelian pattern of recessive genes, and without early detection and treatment (prior to six months of age) results in mental retardation. There is a problem, however, in getting carried away with these kinds of examples and thus assuming that intelligence (and, by implication, many personality traits) is determined by inheriting a single gene. This is a simplistic line of reasoning that ignores several facts. First, in the vast majority of cases of mental retardation the individual falls only a little below the traditional benchmark of IQ = 70. Thus most mentally retarded persons are not severely or profoundly retarded. They are not "suffering" from any mental defect in the sense of an illness or condition. An analogous line of reasoning would suggest that a student who receives Ds or Fs is suffering from a mental defect whereas one who gets Cs is not. Although intelligence is certainly determined in part by genetic factors, unusual cases of severe defect should be regarded as just that—rare cases in which a single gene may be responsible. In general, however, intelligence as well as other traits is determined by combinations of genes.

Mental illness.   Certain types of psychosis provide another example of how extreme cases or rare instances can confuse as well as enlighten. For instance, Kallmann (1953), in studying **schizophrenia,** determined the concordance rates among identical twins, fraternal twins, siblings, and half-siblings. This means that when he found a schizophrenic with a twin or sibling, he checked to see whether that twin or sibling was also schizophrenic. Typically, he found much higher concordance rates (percent of pairs of twins who are both diagnosed as schizophrenic) for identical pairs than for fraternal pairs. The rates were also higher for fraternal twins than for regular siblings or half-siblings. Kallmann's work has a number of methodological flaws (e.g., his method of determining that twins are identical is suspect) and does not rule out critical environmental influences since some of the twins shared the same environment for many years.

The real problem, however, is that Kallmann's work has been used as a model for the conceptualization of the influence of genetics on personality. The tendency is to view extremely maladjusted individuals as having a disease (schizophrenia, manic-depressive psychosis, etc.) and then to set about looking for some simple biochemical cause or an equally simple single-gene influence. This approach oversimplifies a complex set of processes and encourages lines of research unlikely to yield definitive results. Like intelligence, schizophrenia is not a unitary phenomenon. In fact, the label "schizophrenic" subsumes a heterogeneous group of individuals, such that it is unlikely that we can reasonably talk about the simple inheritance of schizophrenia.

In fairness to Kallmann, it should be pointed out that he does not consider various psychotic disorders to be inherited directly; rather, a person is *predisposed* by genetics toward a psychotic adjustment. Similarly, Meehl (1962) has adopted what has been

Separated at birth, the Mallifert twins meet accidentally.

Drawing by Chas. Addams: © 1981, The New Yorker Magazine, Inc.

called a **diathesis-stress** approach to schizophrenia. That is, certain people inherit a neural defect called **schizotaxia.** However, if they grow up in non-schizophrenic-producing environments, they will not become psychotic. This view regards psychosis as a complex interaction between heredity and environment.

Therefore, whether it be intelligence, psychosis, or just plain old personality traits, the general conclusions of Liverant (1960) appear to apply. Ideas of fixed characteristics that stem from the inevitable action of single genes are outmoded or apply as exceptions rather than as rules. No characteristic occurs as a sole function of either heredity or environment but rather as a complex interaction of the two. The occurrence of any specific characteristic is a function of genetic factors operating within a specific environment. There may be genetically fixed potentials for any given environment, but the net result is that, in practice, genetic potential becomes a function of all possible environmental variations. Likewise, the limits of environmental influences are moderated by genetic potentials or limits.

The point in the foregoing is not that genetic factors are unimportant in schizophrenia. Quite the contrary. As Davison and Neale (1990) indicate, the preponderance of data collected thus far suggests that genetic factors play an important role in the development of schizophrenia. Perhaps the words of Plomin (1987) best summarize the interaction between genetics and environment in the development of psychosis:

> If you were an identical twin and your co-twin was schizophrenic, your risk for schizophrenia would be incredibly high—45 percent, as compared to the base rate in the population of 1 percent. Although this suggests genetic influence, it's important to remember that 45 percent is a long way from 100 percent. A genetic clone of a schizophrenic has only a 45 percent risk of schizophrenia—that's the best evidence we have for the importance of nongenetic factors in schizophrenia! (p. 9)

Personality characteristics.   A number of investigators have found what they regard as a link between genetics and personality characteristics. In one study, 150 children were followed for nearly ten years after birth (Thomas, Chess, and Birch, 1970). From observations in the home and interviews with parents the investigators concluded that babies have different temperaments at birth and that these differences last into later life. Thus even-tempered infants are less likely to show behavior problems later. Likewise, "friendly, outgoing" infants tend to become friendly teenagers (Schaefer and Bayley, 1964). In addition, many mothers will tell you that some infants like to be held whereas others resist. In both cases certain parental reactions may be prompted, which themselves begin to affect development and subsequent characteristics.

Other evidence suggests that in the case of sociability and activity level, adopted children ranging in age from fourteen to thirty-six years resemble their biological parents more than their adoptive parents (Loehlin, Willerman, and Horn, 1985). Also, when parents provide ratings of sociability, activity level, and emotionality in pairs of identical and fraternal twins, the similarities are relatively greater in identical twins. It should be noted, however, that much of the evidence here is based on self-reports via questionnaires rather than on direct behavioral observations. In addition, little evidence appears during the first year of life that supports the role of genetics in individual differences in temperament (Loehlin, Willerman, and Horn, 1988). But as noted above, older individuals do provide evidence linking temperament with genetic factors.

Hans Eysenck (1967) has argued that people are endowed with tendencies to behave in certain ways. Although his work will be reviewed in detail in Chapters 8 and 9, some mention is appropriate here. Eysenck considers intelligence as well as tendencies to be extraverted and neurotic as greatly influenced by genetic factors. This is not to imply that environment plays no role. Nevertheless, he argues that the nervous systems of extraverts and introverts differ, as do those of neurotics and normals. In support of this speculation, he has found that extraverts have lower cortical arousal levels and, as a result, condition less rapidly than introverts (Eysenck, 1967).

Other investigators (Tellegen et al., 1988; Pedersen et al., 1988), in studies of identical and fraternal twins reared together and reared apart, have also concluded that personality traits are much more influenced by genetic factors than by shared family environments. However, Rose et al. (1988) studied extroversion and neuroticism scores on the Eysenck Personality Inventory from 14,288 adult Finnish co-twins. Their results suggest that, indeed, genetic factors are major influences on personality. But the investigators also argue that the same data challenge the widespread assumption that shared experiences have a negligible impact on sibling similarity in adult personality traits.

Children from 181 families in the Texas Adoption Project were recontacted after a ten-year interval (Loehlin, Willerman, and Horn, 1987). These individuals who were, on the average, seventeen years of age, completed several standard personality tests and a life events questionnaire. They were also rated by a parent on several trait scales. Some test scores were available from both adoptive and birth mothers. Statistical analyses of all these test scores and other data suggest that adopted children do not resemble their adoptive family members in personality traits even when they lived with them since birth. The children also showed a modest degree of similarity to their birth mothers (whom they never knew). Because this latter degree of similarity is so modest, some observers would suggest that nongenetic factors are also at work in shaping personality traits.

Others also believe that characteristics such as aggression or even altruism have definite inherited components. For example, five questionnaires that measure altruistic and aggressive tendencies were administered to 573 adult twin pairs of both sexes (Rushton et al., 1986). A comparative analysis of the responses of identical and fraternal twins suggested a genetic component. Recently, even religious interests are said to have a significant genetic basis (Waller, Kojetin, Bouchard, Lykken, and Tellegen, 1990).

The complexities of nature-nurture phenomena are highlighted by a program of research carried out by Scarr, Webber, Weinberg, and Wittig (1981). Families with adolescents adopted in infancy and families with biologically related adolescents were administered a variety of personality measures. Only a modest degree of personality resemblance was found among biological relatives, but it exceeded the similarities observed in adopted relatives. In explaining their results, Scarr et al. note that studies of twins typically exaggerate the degree to which personality differences are caused by genetic differences and underestimate slightly the importance of environmental factors.

In the final analysis, it is not an *either-or* choice between genetics and environmental factors. As shown in Box 1-3, the two sets of factors *interact*. There is even some evidence to show that early on, genetic factors are quite important. But as twins grow older, they tend to become less alike (McCartney, Harris, and Bernieri, 1990). This suggests the role of environment.

Body types and temperament.

Kretschmer (1925) believed that people could be divided into four distinct categories according to body type: (1) **asthenic** (slight, long-boned, slender persons with a predisposition toward a schizophrenic personality type), (2) **pyknic** (round, stocky, heavy individuals with a predisposition toward manic-depressive reactions), (3) **athletic** (strong, muscular, broad-shouldered people with a tendency more toward schizophrenic than manic-depressive responses), and (4) **dysplastic** (individuals exhibiting disproportionate physical development or features of several body types with personality predispositions similar to the athletic type). For Kretschmer, then, personality, temperament, and even mental aberrations (should they develop) could be predicted from body type.

Box 1-3
PERSONALITY AND PARENT-CHILD INTERACTIONS

According to Thomas and Chess (1977) some babies are cheerful and easy right away. They sleep regularly and adapt readily to new experiences and people. But other infants are difficult from the very beginning. They start out as fussy babies and go on to be overactive and even difficult to toilet train. These seem to be built-in tendencies. Consider the following examples adapted from Babledelis (1984) and Meichenbaum et al. (1989):

> A baby is born one fine day. From the very start he is active and energetic—even a bit hyperactive. But he is not cranky or irritable—just very active. He quickly learns to sit up and just as quickly is crawling all over the place. He is in to everything. No table, cupboard, or bookshelf is safe. He is delighted when he can manage to take things apart. Thus, disorder is his constant companion.

Given this brief description, how might his parents respond to him? Well, it all depends on the nature of the parents. But make no mistake. Their responses will ultimately affect that little boy's personality.

1 The Smiths are parents who do not like messes. They like an orderly house. They also believe that children should be obedient and they are quite definite as to what is proper behavior for little boys. So, punishment seems to follow their little boy everywhere. He is also constantly reminded that he is clumsy, disobedient, and a great bother to everyone.

2 The Martins are parents who can tolerate a mess. They are not exactly in love with disorder but they can tolerate it as part of the parenting price. But they do like what they perceive as their son's curiosity. They see this as a sign of an inquisitive mind. Maybe he will become an important scientist. As a result, their strategy becomes one of rewarding his curiosity and labeling him as good or smart even as they try to cut down a bit on the breakage.

What, then, is the likely outcome in these two scenarios? Although undoubtedly an oversimplification, the following are possibilities:

1 The Smiths could produce a son who develops into a tense, overcontrolled person who constantly tries to suppress his own wishes so as to gain approval from others.

2 The Martins could produce a son who develops feelings of competence, is open with others, and seeks approval by striving to achieve.

Had each set of parents been blessed with a child with a different temperament, personality development might have proceeded quite differently. At the same time, had each set of parents been able to respond differently to their child, his personality development would have followed a different course.

Building on Kretschmer's work, Sheldon (1940, 1942) developed procedures by which an individual is given a rating (on a seven-point scale) on each of three dimensions: (1) **endomorphy** (highly developed and massive visceral structure), (2) **mesomorphy** (predominance of musculature), and (3) **ectomorphy** (delicate, fragile, poorly muscled type) (see Figure 1-1). Sheldon developed reliable means for getting ratings on these body-type dimensions. However, he went farther, arguing that there are highly correlated temperaments for these somatotypes. Thus, ectomorphs were said to be **cerebrotonic** (restrained, inhibited, somewhat withdrawn). Mesomorphs were thought to be **somatotonic** (active, assertive, vigorous). And endomorphs were supposedly **viscerotonic** (relaxed, comfort loving, sociable).

Although Sheldon's views have never had a major impact on psychological theory, they crop up from time to time and are sometimes uncritically accepted by laypeople. Humphreys (1957) cogently attacked Sheldon's typology on both statistical and methodological grounds. For example, in Sheldon's studies the same person made the ratings of both body type and temperament, opening the door for biased judgments. Humphreys's criticisms aside, it remains to be demonstrated that there are any meaningful relationships between social behavior and body type. Furthermore, even should such relationships be demonstrated, their origin need not reside in constitutional factors. For instance, the strongly built individual may learn early that assertiveness and dominance

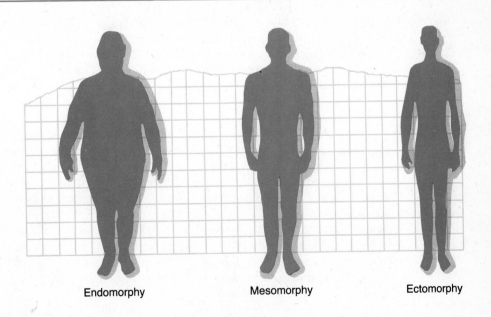

Endomorphy   Mesomorphy   Ectomorphy

FIGURE 1-1   Examples of three body types described by Sheldon.

are easily employed to gain his or her ends. The obese person may discover that humor and sociability are ready defenses against a fear of rejection. Or the ectomorph may soon realize that solitary pursuits are more likely to become a source of enjoyment than unsuccessful physical encounters with athletic peers. In any case, however, it would seem that human social behavior is so complex that mere assignment of people to simple typological categories will never be an adequate basis for prediction or explanation.

Biochemistry and personality.

There is a great deal of evidence that biochemical-hormonal factors are implicated in behavior. Thyroid secretions can directly affect sleeping, level of agitation, and so on. Disturbed insulin secretions from the pancreas can result in mental confusion. Some evidence even suggests the role of the adrenal glands in such emotional reactions as anger. Unfortunately the strongest evidence for relationships between hormones and behavior comes from animal research, and it is questionable how directly this research applies to humans, whose behavior is controlled so much more by learning and experience. And this is true even when we are discussing sexuality, aggressiveness, or emotion — three personality characteristics that seem most amenable to biochemical analysis. The demonstration of relationships between hormone functioning and behavior can be difficult indeed (Beach, 1975). Furthermore, when connections between personality functioning and biochemical factors are made, they often seem to apply best in the case of major behavior disorders. For example, one theory of schizophrenia suggests that it is caused by excessive activity of the neurotransmitter dopamine (Davison and Neale, 1990). This is suggested by the fact that one of the drugs that is effective in treating schizophrenia also lowers the person's dopamine level. Lowered dopamine levels are also known to produce Parkinson's disease (characterized by severe muscle tremors and other symptoms). Schizophrenics who receive dopamine treatment also often show side effects very much like Parkinson's disease. Obviously the trail from cause to effect here is a winding one — the kind of trail that is all too common when trying to link personality and biochemistry. (See Box 1-4 for a discussion of further research on the link between biochemistry and behavior.)

Another problem in determining the role of hormones in personality functioning is illustrated in the work of Schachter and Singer (1962). These researchers injected subjects with epinephrine (a hormone that produces sweating, flushing, rapid heart rate, etc.). Some of the subjects were told how epinephrine works; others were not. After being injected, one group of subjects was confronted by a confederate of the experimenter who behaved in a manner calculated to produce euphoria in the subjects. Other subjects were left with a confederate who engaged in a routine likely to make them angry. The results of the study showed that subjects who knew the effects of epinephrine attributed their increased sweating and heart rate to the hormone, whereas subjects who did not know described their physiological responses as either euphoria or anger, depending upon the experimental condition in which they had been placed. Although not everyone has been able to replicate these results, this study suggests that humans do not respond like simple physiological machines. Instead, the nature of one's emotional reactions is a complex interaction between biochemical events and the quality of the psychological situation.

Box 1-4
A RELATIONSHIP BETWEEN SENSATION SEEKING AND ENZYMES

Sensation seeking, the general tendency to seek stimulation, has been measured by a 40-item scale (M. Zuckerman, 1978). This scale contains four classes of items: (1) those related to physical risk taking (parachuting, skiing, etc.); (2) those reflecting an interest in new experiences through the mind and senses (music, art, certain drugs, traveling, etc.); (3) those that describe a hedonistic pursuit of pleasure (social drinking, sex, gambling, etc.); and (4) those involving an aversion toward routine activities, dull people, and the like. This is a reliable scale with behavioral correlates in sexual activity, drug use, volunteering for unusual activities, engaging in dangerous pursuits, and gambling.

An enzyme, MAO, is present in the brain and most other tissues. When drugs that inhibit MAO action are administered, a number of behavior changes often occur, among them euphoria, aggression, irritability, and hallucinations. In short, MAO appears to serve some dampening or regulatory role.

Several studies (e.g., Zuckerman, Buchsbaum, and Murphy, 1980) have shown negative correlations between MAO and sensation-seeking scores. That is, high sensation seekers tend to have low MAO levels, which may account for the greater activity levels, sociability, and so on, normally found in such individuals.

Assuming the reliability of such findings, what do they mean? What is cause and what is effect? Is the relationship between enzyme levels and sensation-seeking tendencies mediated by a third factor? Has an important link been forged between biochemistry and behavior, or is this just another blind alley? Perhaps time will tell.

Making your own environment.   It is possible that genetic factors may help determine the kinds of environmental influences to which the person is subjected. If so, this means that the roles of genetic factors and environment are inextricably intertwined. Scarr and McCartney (1983) have proposed that one's genes probably help determine those aspects of the environment that are experienced. For example, pleasant, happy babies tend to evoke pleasant, happy responses from parents and others in the immediate environment. In contrast, passive, even sober infants experience wholly different responses from environmental figures. Thus, what at first glance appears to be an exclusive environmental function turns out upon closer inspection to be a subtle outcome stemming ultimately from the genes. A different example of making your own environment relates to the body type of the individual. As noted earlier, people whose genes dictate that they shall be mesomorphs will be able to more easily select situations (e.g., sports) that will then determine in part what they learn over the course of their development. In addition, parents whose genetic body types impel them toward sports will more likely not only provide a sports environment for the child but also contribute the very genes that also make it more likely that the child can compete successfully.

Sociobiology.   While some would concede the heritability of such enduring qualities as intelligence or schizophrenia, others contend that even behaviors such as altruism or shyness are genetically influenced. Thus, **sociobiology** involves the study of relationships between biological factors and social behavior. In addition, the assumption is often made that much of our social behavior is an outcome of evolution and is maintained because of the adaptive advantages conveyed (Wilson, 1978).

In particular, many facets of altruistic behavior have been explained by sociobiologists as the result of genetics. For example, a bird may sacrifice itself to a predator and thereby lure that predator away from the nest. The result is that the individual bird dies but the several other birds in the nest survive. Although such altruism is surely hard on the heroic bird, it is good for the survival of the species (see Chapter 18 for a lengthier discussion of these phenomena). Likewise, in the case of human sexual behavior, some sociobiologists claim that, in general, males are more sexually promiscuous because their ultimate goal is to pass along as many genes as they can. In contrast, females can produce a relatively few offspring and each one takes an enormous amount of time to nurture and rear. The male is thus driven to select many partners and typically will marry younger women so as to enhance the likelihood of multiple births.

Although sociobiological explanations of some animal behaviors appear highly plausible, something often seems to get lost in the translation to human behavior. To pursue the sexual example above, how are we to explain the behavior of males who voluntarily choose sterilization? This certainly seems to violate the idea of evolutionary adaptiveness or survival of the species. Other critics simply argue that human social behavior is so complexly determined that it is folly to attribute it to some simple set of biological or evolutionary factors. Some also contend that sociobiological hypotheses are impossible to verify and that, coupled with the fact of reduced environmental emphasis, may inadvertently reinforce social systems that could justify even gender or racial prejudices. So it is that we could easily excuse male sexual promiscuity by attributing it to "adaptive" impulses that are buried deep in the genetic fiber of men. Sociobiology continues, then, to be controversial—especially among environmentally oriented personality psychologists. They will likely continue to reject many sociobiological explanations (e.g., those of Crawford, Smith, and Krebs, 1987) as much too biologically determinist in their orientations.

Conclusions.   The form of body structures, biophysical and biochemical factors, stimulation, environment, and developmental history are all important contributors to behavior. As Tyler (1978) puts it, "To ignore any of these factors (as psychologists have repeatedly done) is to come up with distorted and inadequate pictures of behavioral development" (p. 53).

But integrating biology and psychology is difficult. Currently the search for the biological bases of personality is being thwarted by at least two factors. First, the evidence for the role of behavioral genetics, hormones, and so forth is often internally contradictory and subject to numerous methodological flaws (e.g., the research on the relationship between women's presumed mood swings and hormonal changes during the menstrual cycle). As a result, what some see as striking evidence for the role of biology, others view as support for a more psychological explanation. And the beat goes on.

Also, it is difficult (some say impossible) to consider personality concepts in a framework of bone, muscle, neurons, or chemicals. For example, suppose I observe a person who repeatedly uses self-deprecating language or avoids competitive situations, leading me to attribute to that person a low expectancy for success. How, then, shall I deal with such expectancies as biochemical events or biological entities? Perhaps I am better off sticking to the psychological realm of explanation rather than trying to impose a rather foreign frame of reference.

Despite these difficulties, however, it hardly seems reasonable to argue that biological influences do not exist. Rather, both biologists and psychologists must accept that neither one of their current conceptual frameworks is powerful enough alone to account for human behavior in general, or personality in particular. A way must be found to integrate effectively the findings and methods of both perspectives. Furthermore the integration must not be at the level of clichés or vague generalizations but rather must prove to be specific, precise, and predictive.

Personality theorists and investigators vary markedly in how much attention they pay to biological variables. For some, it is as if flesh and blood do not exist. Others pay lip service, but that is about all. Still others recognize the importance of biology but have not found a satisfactory way to incorporate it into the field of personality. Because the biological perspective is potentially so important, you should try to evaluate how each personality theory or research area discussed later in this book incorporates biological factors (or at least has the potential for incorporation).

Environmental perspective

In contrast to the genetic and biological determinants of personality just discussed, most psychologists, as an article of faith, accept the critical role of environmental forces in shaping behavior. After all, to be human means ownership of a superior capacity for learning. And what is learning except the relatively permanent modification of behavior through the selective experiencing of environmental events? Whether we are talking about the psychoanalytic treatment developed by Sigmund Freud, the conditions of worth that Carl Rogers felt shape a person's self-esteem, or the ways in which Albert Bandura felt that observational learning affects behavior, we are really discussing the influence of the environment upon the person. Let us now consider a few of these environmental influences.

The physical world.   Speculations about the role of weather and its effects on human behavior have been around at least since Aristotle and Hippocrates. However, extremely forceful presentations of the effects of climate were made by Mills (1942) and Huntington (1945). The rise and fall of civilizations, development of racial characteristics, and even the origins of religions have been attributed to climatic factors. It has been argued, for example, that colder climates are more easily controlled and so it is easier to develop extensive educational systems under such conditions. These systems, in turn, have profound effects on both personality and behavior.

Climatic conditions directly affect how food is accumulated. For example, in the barren, ice-covered northern regions, the Eskimo becomes a hunter—growing food is not an alternative. In contrast, the Temne people of Sierra Leone are able to depend upon agriculture because of prevailing climatic conditions. But contrasting methods of food accumulation would also seem to require contrasting personalities in the people involved. For example, Barry, Child, and Bacon (1959) have contended that since the Eskimo culture relies on hunting and fishing, it requires individuals who are assertive, individualistic, and willing to take risks. As a result, there is leniency in disciplining children and individualism is encouraged so as to nurture the traits required in the adult. But the Temne people rely upon growing their food. Such reliance requires a more conscientious, compliant, and conservative adult. After all, a single crop is harvested each year and food is doled out carefully so that it will last until the next harvest. To produce such an adult, they seem to shower their infants with affection until weaning. At that point discipline is imposed severely and even toilet training becomes harshly applied. Little or no individuality is permitted.

Berry (1967) tested the foregoing analysis of the Temne and the Eskimo by presenting groups of subjects from each culture with a conformity task. This was a line-judging task in which subjects were subtly pressured to agree with the experimenter in making their judgments. As predicted, the Eskimo subjects virtually disregarded the experimenter's suggestions while the Temne accepted them. Berry (1967) described the contrast in subjects this way:

> . . . one Temne (in Mayola) did offer the following spontaneous comment: "When Temne people choose a thing, we must all agree with the decision—this is what we call cooperation." On the other hand, Eskimo subjects, although saying nothing, would often display a quiet, knowing smile as they pointed to the correct one. (p. 417)

Weather has long been known to affect the onset of criminal and aggressive behavior. In Chapter 17 we shall note the effects of heat upon aggression. But temperature also affects a number of interpersonal reactions including attraction. For example, Griffitt (1970) discovered that under high temperature-humidity conditions, interpersonal attraction responses were more negative than under normal temperature-humidity conditions.

Finally, considerable evidence has been accumulated detailing the stressful effects of the crowding, noise, and bureaucracy so characteristic of modern society. These effects will be reviewed later in Chapter 15.

Another example of the potent effects of the physical world comes from the field of gerontology. It sometimes happens that older persons are placed in various institutions for the elderly. Sometimes, this results in what Butler and Lewis (1982) have referred to as an **institutional neurosis.** This is marked by an erosion of the personality, overdependence, loss of interest in the outside world, and the like. Such responses can occur in hospitals, nursing homes, or prisons and are, therefore, not confined to elderly persons. In fact, whenever the individual must live in a rigid, isolated environment for a prolonged period of time, there is a real possibility for the development of an institutional neurosis. In fact, Lawton (1980) suggests that as an elderly person's cognitive competence decreases, factors in the external environment become more salient as determinants of both behavior and emotion. Thus, a very small change in the environment of a cognitively impaired elderly person may have large behavioral effects.

It was Gruenberg (1967) who first described a **social breakdown reaction.** This consists of a set of responses in which elderly persons come to see themselves as useless and helpless (see Figure 1-2). This is another example of how the arrangement of one's physical world can produce a host of either intended or unintended responses. Whether we are talking about institutions, offices, or grocery stores, the physical environment will be very important in keying our behavior. Indeed, it is not unfair to suggest that in predicting a person's behavior, the first thing you would want to know is where the individual is located. When you are in class you tend to behave like a student; when you are in a tavern you will likely behave quite differently. In short, one's behavioral setting can have a profound influence on behavior.

Sociocultural factors. We have already seen how climatic factors may indirectly influence child-rearing patterns. It is certainly true that each culture shapes its young by teaching them different things that, ultimately, make them all somewhat alike and yet different from those raised in other cultures. The classic studies of Margaret Mead (1949) in New Guinea are relevant here. She found two tribes who genetically were of essentially the same origins and who also lived in the same geographic region. But personality-wise, they were as different as night and day. Where the Arapesh were friendly, cooperative, and very peaceful, the Mundugumor were equally hostile, suspicious, and warlike. Since neither genetics nor geography could account for such differences, Mead attributed them to cultural factors that had influenced the way children were socialized.

Over the years, anthropologists have studied national character as an outgrowth of sociocultural processes. **National character** refers to the idea that there are distinct behavioral differences among people of differing nationalities. The point is that, for example, the average German has been said to be more authoritarian than the average Swede. Or the average Japanese is more industrious than the average American. Clearly, we are talking about presumed modal differences. And we would be hard-pressed to predict the behavior of a specific person knowing only the person's nationality. Still, the idea of national character persists and may have some merit (Etzioni, 1969).

But one need not go to New Guinea, Germany, or Sweden to verify the influence of culture. Cultures typically prescribe certain roles for their members. For example, sex roles clearly exist in our own culture. Although these roles may be in transition today, there are distinctly "masculine" and "feminine" roles (see Chapter 19).

Social class. Nearly every society is, in some fashion, divided into classes. Those in the upper classes have greater access to material goods and to personal recognition

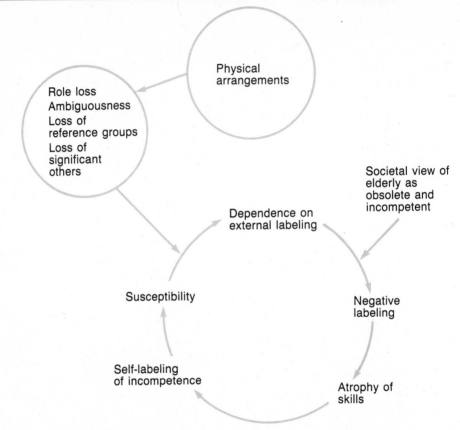

FIGURE 1-2   The social breakdown syndrome.

Adapted from Marguerite D. Kermis, *The Psychology of Human Aging: Theory, Research, and Practice*. Copyright © 1984 by Allyn and Bacon. Used with permission.

than do those at the lower levels. In general, these classes are separated by amount of education, occupational status, income, opportunity, and degree of personal control over their lives.

Particularly relevant here is the fact that psychopathology is significantly related to social class membership. As a generalization, it is clear that the incidence of mental illness is greater among individuals at the lower socioeconomic levels in the United States (Eron and Peterson, 1982). In the case of schizophrenia, the relationship is significant but in the case of some other disorders the relationship may be weak or nonexistent. Why these relationships occur is not always clear. However, two hypotheses are frequently offered. One possibility is that life for those in the lower socioeconomic classes is so stressful that psychopathology ensues. The poverty, the discrimination, the inaccessibility of jobs, and the difficulty in obtaining medical care and services all lead to the development of severe problems. It is also possible that all these factors combine not just to produce stress but also to create an inability to cope with stress (Kohn, 1973).

The second hypothesis about the relationship between social class and mental illness is that people who have severe psychological problems tend to drift down to the lower social classes. They may even produce children who are themselves disturbed. According to this notion, schizophrenia is less an effect than it is a cause. However, many feel that this is not a terribly plausible hypothesis.

A virulent cause of stress is lack of perceived control (see Chapter 16). It is also true that people in the lower socioeconomic classes often perceive themselves to be powerless (Phares, 1976). Small wonder that such a perception should exist given the lack of social mobility, opportunity, or material advantages of these individuals. Of course, as noted before, not every member of the lower social classes is disturbed or perceives a lack of personal control. And many deprived individuals go on to become great successes in life. But although wide individual differences do exist, the general relationships hold.

Another correlate of social class membership is the manner in which people discipline their children. Work by Waters and Crandall (1964) has suggested that lower-class mothers regulate their children more tightly while Feshbach (1973) has observed that a more negative approach to child rearing is taken by those same mothers.

Early deprivation.   Either being separated from one's parents or experiencing parental deprivation at an early age can have profound effects on personality and behavior. For example, Provence and Lipton (1962) compared institutionalized infants with those living with their families. By the age of one, the institutionalized infants showed pervasive disturbances in relationships with adults (e.g., few signs of attachment to an adult), marked retardation in speech along with emotional apathy, and the like. More recently, but in a similar vein, Burnstein (1981) has concluded that abandoned children are at risk for psychological problems and are also more likely to be aggressive and rebellious.

A similar story characterizes children who suffer parental deprivation (Ribble, 1944). Mothers who are rejecting, aloof, or punitive tend to produce tenseness and negativism very early in their children's development. More recent work continues to show that parental neglect and abuse can result in clearcut negative outcomes for children (e.g., Patterson, 1979; Yates, 1981). It is probably not far from the truth to assert that parental deprivation may be devastating for the child's development.

Child rearing.   It should come as no great surprise to find that psychologists regard child-rearing patterns as critical in determining subsequent personal development. Virtually every comprehensive theory of personality reviewed in this book has something to say about the child-rearing determinants of personality. Since this topic will be covered subsequently in this book, we shall only briefly touch on the subject here.

Methods of child rearing affect the development of personality as do sociocultural factors. Photograph M. Heron/Woodfin Camp.

In 1949, Percival Symonds published the book, *The Dynamics of Parent-Child Relationships.* In it he detailed the effects of many parental reactions including rejection, overindulgence, overprotection, overauthority, and overstrictness. Symonds (1949) concluded that:

> . . . the development of the child's personality is closely related to his relationships with his parents. This is a conclusion of the utmost importance. It means that one must consider parent-child relationships not only with respect to their influence in causing mental and emotional disorders and psychopathic states but also in connection with the development of normality, leadership, and genius. (pp. xii–xiii)

Little has transpired in the last forty years to challenge Symonds' statements. For example, Jenkins (1968) determined that overanxious children tended to have mothers who were overprotective and infantilizing in their responses to their children. Coopersmith (1967) showed that when parents do not care about anything as long as their children stay out of trouble, the results are lower needs for achievement and lower self-esteem in the child. When the child is overindulged by the parents, the outcome in that child is impatience, demanding and aggressive behavior, and poor frustration tolerance (Baumrind, 1975).

Severe discipline can also lead to problems as noted earlier in the discussion of social class. Often, when discipline is physical the result is increased aggressiveness (Patterson, 1979). Sometimes, discipline for aggressiveness tends to be highly inconsistent. When this occurs, it can become difficult to extinguish the behavior (Deur and Parke, 1970). In recent years, psychologists have come to the conclusion that thoughtful, consistent, and realistic discipline is helpful in generating a sense of competence in the child (Baumrind, 1975).

SUMMARY

- Personality is a sturdy, resilient concept that is embedded in the paradox that in some ways all people are alike and at the same time different from each other.

- Personality is commonly defined as that pattern of characteristic thoughts, feelings, and behaviors that persists over time and situations and distinguishes one person from another. This definition emphasizes the elements of stability and consistency.

- Personality as a field of study may be thought of as being composed of six subfields, each an important branch in its own right. These six subfields are theory, development, adjustment, change, assessment, and research. In sum, personality is a field that studies individual differences and their interaction with environmental conditions in order to help us predict and understand complex human behavior.

- In this chapter, two basic determinants of personality were briefly reviewed for their relevance to the field: biological determinants and environmental ones. The goal was to provide a basic orientation to these perspectives so that the theories and research presented later can be better evaluated.

- It is important to recognize that evolutionary, genetic factors likely play a significant role in personality. At the same time, their influence is so complex that all too often biologists and psychologists alike have trouble dealing with biological-psychological interactions.

- To illustrate the role of genetics, intelligence and mental illness were briefly described from a biological perspective. Some general findings along with a few methodological pitfalls were presented. In addition, links between certain personality characteristics and genetics were noted.

- Several studies linking personality characteristics to genetic factors were discussed. Traits such as introversion-extraversion, sociability, emotionality, and the like were illustrated.

- As an example of the difficulties in this area, the relationship between body type and temperament was discussed. It was concluded that, at best, the relationship is quite modest and that reliance on simple predictors such as body type is unwise.

- The role of biochemistry in shaping personality characteristics was briefly illustrated.

- It was also observed that genetic factors can affect the ways in which people construct their environments.

- A brief discussion of sociobiology, the study of relationships between biological factors and social behavior, was provided.

■ It was concluded that despite the difficulties in integrating the biological and personality perspectives, it is important that the goal of integration be pursued.

■ Several illustrations of how the environment affects personality were offered. These included the effects of climate and physical surroundings (e.g., institutions).

■ Both sociocultural factors and social class were discussed regarding their effects on personality development.

■ Finally, early deprivation and child-rearing practices generally were shown to directly influence personality.

CHAPTER 2

THE TOOLS OF UNDERSTANDING

To fully understand personality we need something more substantial than our own interest in the subject. We require some appreciation of the tools of understanding: theory, research, and assessment. The goal of this chapter, then, is an introduction to these important topics.

THEORY

We can begin our discussion with an analysis of the nature of theory. This is entirely appropriate since theory is the basic tool that serves our ability to understand the personality of the individual.

A diversity of theories

One of the things that most confuses people when they first begin their study of personality is that it can be described in so many different ways. Why is this? After all, is there not a correct way to describe the essence of a human being? In answering this question, consider an example offered many years ago:

> Suppose that three men, a realtor, a farmer, and an artist, are standing on a hilltop looking at the panorama of uncultivated land spread out below them. To the realtor, the scene represents an opportunity to develop a new housing project. To the farmer, the view suggests a chance to obtain arable soil for growing grain. To the artist, the vista is the embodiment of natural beauty. On descending, the realtor makes inquiries about the cost of the land, the availability of municipal utility services, and the supply of construction labor in the vicinity. The farmer takes soil samples for testing. The artist gets his easel and returns to the hilltop to paint a picture. All three men have "seen" the same thing, but each has responded in terms of a personal frame of reference, in terms of those aspects of the experience which were personally meaningful. (Shoben, 1954, pp. 42–43)

Depending on who you are or what your purposes may be, your understanding of people as well as real estate will be affected. Furthermore, this is true for famous personality theorists just as much as it is for realtors, farmers, or artists. Three of the most notable students of human nature have been Sigmund Freud, Carl Rogers, and B. F. Skinner. Each has made a contribution that is brilliant in its own way. But it would be hard to find three views of human nature that are so different from one another. Freud saw people as driven by sexual and aggressive impulses struggling for expression. Rogers, in contrast, saw within us a striving for self-enhancement and growth. Skinner seems to view humans as little different from animals in the way they respond to rewards and punishments. Looking at the backgrounds of these men, it is not hard to see how they arrived at such opposing pictures of personality. Freud worked in the late 1800s with inhibited patients who were discouraged by a Victorian society from expressing their sexuality. What is more, he was educated in a scientific world that emphasized the role of instincts in guiding behavior. On the other hand, Rogers grew up in a religious family and for a while attended a theological school. Later he worked not with severely maladjusted patients but with young college students who were intelligent and who had their entire lives stretching out ahead of them. And then Skinner spend a childhood designing everything from kites to perpetual motion machines. As a psychologist he worked with animals confined in a laboratory environment. Each of these theorists became, in a sense, the product of his own background and experience.

Theory in everyday life

It should come as no surprise that in a sense everybody is a theorist of sorts. This is illustrated by the term **implicit personality theory** coined by Bruner and Tagiuri (1954). The term refers to the fact that everyone develops a set of ideas (theory) to explain how other people's personality characteristics fit together. For example, some people believe that good-looking men are vain or that people with close-set eyes cannot be trusted. Still others are convinced that intelligent people are likely to be emotionally unstable. These ideas are impressions we have about one another, and they help us to make sense out of the world. Some of these impressions may turn out to be poor ones that subsequently cause us problems. Others are pretty simple, while others are complex. But they determine in many important ways how we think, feel, and act with respect to other people and events. Box 2-1 illustrates how a world leader's implicit theory related to his perceptions of other world leaders.

Nature of personality constructs

Essentially, a theory of personality is a collection of concepts and assumptions about how best to regard people and study them. As much as anything, these concepts and assumptions are the ground rules by which we understand and investigate personality phenomena. But the essence of a theory is contained in the concepts it employs—or as many choose to call them, **constructs.**

Box 2-1
HENRY KISSINGER'S
IMPLICIT THEORY
OF PERSONALITY

Henry Kissinger
UPI/Bettmann Newsphotos.

Henry Kissinger, it will be recalled, was Assistant to the President for National Security and Secretary of State in the Nixon administration. Swede and Tetlock (1986) used a quantitative method for extracting personality descriptions from Kissinger's 1979 book, *White House Years.* They carried out a content analysis that resulted in 3,759 trait descriptions of thirty-eight important world leaders based on Kissinger's words.

From this analysis there emerged five consistent personality themes: *professional anguish, ambitious patriotism, revolutionary greatness, intellectual sophistication,* and *realistic friendship.*

Using these themes or concepts, Kissinger differentiated among various leaders throughout the world. For example, he tended to believe that he, William Rogers, Melvin Laird, and Indira Gandhi were prone to experience *professional anguish.* Thus Kissinger said of himself:

> I did my best, if with frayed nerves. . . . I had been in motion for over two weeks
> . . . rarely getting more than four hours of sleep and riding an emotional roller coaster
> from hope to frustration, from elation to despair. (Kissinger, 1979, p. 1395)

He perceived Mao Tse-tung, Leonid Brezhnev, Chou En-lai, and Anwar Sadat as having *revolutionary greatness.* Of Chairman Mao, for example, Kissinger (1979) said

> that colossal figure, who challenged the gods in the scope of his aspirations (p. 1064);
> the titanic figure who made the Chinese Revolution. (p. 1065)

It was, then, through such implicit personality themes that Kissinger came to understand world figures. And it was through such understanding that he undoubtedly felt he could anticipate and interpret their behavior. As Swede and Tetlock (1986) put it, "These themes provide a potential key for understanding how Kissinger structured the extraordinarily complex political environment that he faced in the first Nixon administration" (p. 639).

How we understand complex human behavior is heavily determined by our theoretical perspective. Photograph G. Robert Bishop.

Constructs as descriptions. A construct is a way of describing a piece of reality. However, we should not confuse the construct with that part of reality it is meant to describe. If I describe someone as adjusted, this is not to say that adjustment is an inherent property of that person. Rather, it is a way I have devised to differentiate among people for some specific purpose. By observing many different people, I eventually construct in my head a notion of adjustment-maladjustment. But the person is just a person; the adjustment is a description I have created in order to better understand my world.

Constructs: reality vs. utility.   It may be obvious that those who are seeking reality or truth via theory are in for tough sledding. Where, for example, should I look in the brain to locate your self-concept? Is the superego at the top of the head or at the bottom? Are behavioral repertoires in the front of the cranium or in the back? The answer is that they are in *my* head, not yours. Psychoanalysts like to use descriptions such as superego, but when they do so they are really only asserting that such a concept has some purpose. Perhaps it helps the analyst understand why a patient keeps behaving in a self-destructive fashion. The superego has no existence, but it does have utility. The question becomes not, "What is John really like?" but "What is the best way to describe John for certain purposes?"

One of the reasons for avoiding reality as a criterion is that we have no one qualified to serve as the final judge of the nature of reality. We all view reality through the filter of our own past experience. One person likes vegetables and another regards them as virtually inedible. What is the reality of vegetables? Are rock groups "beautiful" or are they "abominable"? It surely depends on our past experience.

Constructs and their focus of convenience.   A big issue has just been made about utility versus reality. To carry this discussion one step farther, it must be emphasized that theories have what George Kelly (1955) called a **focus of convenience.** Concepts as well as entire theories do not have unlimited application. A theory's best use is restricted to a limited universe of situations or events. Theories of economics may work with some success in explaining inflation, but they are not much use in dealing with stomachaches. Sociologists have much to say about the structure of society, but they are notably silent about how to fertilize wheat. In less dramatic fashion the same is true of personality theories. They, too, have focuses of convenience. Freudian theory grew up in the context of hysterical disorders in Vienna at the turn of the century. It can be a helpful theory in explaining certain forms of neurosis. A theory of conditioning may be very helpful in teaching new skills to certain mentally handicapped persons but less so in explaining the identity crisis of an adolescent. One should not, however, decide that a theory is useless merely because it does not account for cosmic reality. We should build our theories, see how they work, and extend their applications as far as we can. But we should not be disappointed by their limited application. We should, however, have the good sense to discard them when something better comes along.

Value of personality theory

There is one overriding purpose for all theories of personality—"the organization of knowledge in a form that will make it usable and communicable" (Levy, 1970, p. 38). But what is meant by "communicable" and "usable"?

Communication.   Part of the charm of the implicit theories we all use is their relative inaccessibility to communication. We know what we know about people, but this knowledge is often chaotic, intuitive, and hard to explain. On the other hand, formal, scientific theories of personality are systematically formulated (ideally as assumptions, postulates, and corollaries) and organized. Such a structure enhances communication by helping ensure that we all understand what the theory is saying. This makes for reliability and utility. If everyone deduces contradictory things from a theory, the utility of that theory is irretrievably impaired. Contrast, for example, the following assertions:

- The reinforcement value of an external reinforcement may be ideally defined as the degree of preference for a reinforcement to occur if the possibilities of their occurring were all equal. (Rotter, 1954, p. 107)

- An individual's pitch at a certain moment determines in advance the choice, brightness, and coloring of his relationships to the world. (Boss, 1963, p. 41)

Which is more understandable? Which would better enable one to translate the assertions into specific behavioral consequences?

Framework for explanation.

The first aspect of "usability" noted previously involves explanation. Good theories offer a framework to help us account for behavior. We need a framework or system that will encourage us to organize what we know about people (or to seek additional specific information) so that their behavior can be predicted and understood. Without a systematic framework, our knowledge is in danger of turning into a catalog or a list of facts. We need a framework to help organize and select the facts that are important. For example, in predicting aggression in a given situation, what should we know about the potential aggressors? Their size, strength, or height? their expectancies for success? In short, there is a welter of facts available. Some are trivial, some not so trivial. But which is which?

Expansion of knowledge.

We never have enough knowledge. The more we know, the more we become aware of the gaps in our information. A theoretical point of view can be of enormous value in assisting us in the search for new knowledge by providing specific guidelines. In a very real sense, our theoretical orientation serves to direct both our research and assessment. Since we cannot know everything or pursue every question, a theory will give us a proper start. And, when evidence or data are lacking on a certain question, a theory can often provide hints.

Aid to consistent thinking.

Some students in courses that cover personality theory complain that theories are too confining. Or they feel that a theoretical commitment is analogous to a horse with blinders—it only sees what it is permitted to see! Their preference is eclecticism. That is, they want to take the "best" from each theory. Take a little self-concept, add a bit of superego and a pinch of reinforcement, mix them together in a bowl of humanism, and let simmer in a social learning pan. Well, the problem is that all too often the ingredients do not mix very well. Use of mixtures from an assortment of theories more often leads to inconsistencies and contradictions that hamper correct prediction.

Dimensions of personality theories

There are many different views, conceptions, and theories of personality. Hall and Lindzey (1978) devote 15 chapters to various personality theories, and several contain more than one theory. They also listed over twenty substantive dimensions along which personality theories may be compared. To simplify matters a bit, let us consider the six comparative dimensions offered by Julian Rotter (1967b).

Systematic vs. unsystematic.   Some theories are very systematic in the sense that they offer a set of interrelated postulates and assumptions. Other theories are so freewheeling that they are little more than loose collections of statements. In addition, systematic theories tend to be explicit documents that set forth their assumptions and propositions with clarity. At the other extreme are theories that are murky and difficult to grasp—whose statements are so ambiguous that contradictory deductions are commonplace.

Operational vs. nonoperational.   Other things being equal, better theories of personality are those that provide explicit methods for measuring their constructs. For example, the usefulness of asserting that "successful people will have actualized their potential in a more nearly perfect fashion" is significantly reduced if we have no agreed-upon means for measuring actualization (or potential, for that matter). The presence of explicit definitions of constructs greatly increases the likelihood that the theory will generate research and lead to testable hypotheses.

Content vs. process.   Some theories tend to focus on the elements or traits that characterize people. Others seem to emphasize the manner in which people acquire or change their particular patterns of behavior. For example, a theory may proclaim that personality is composed of Traits 1 through 141 but there is little in the theory to suggest how these 141 traits are acquired or altered. By contrast, other theories appear to tell us much about how people learn without devoting much attention to what it is they learn. A theory that stands high on both content *and* process would naturally be a desirable one.

Experience vs. heredity.   Here the question revolves around the usefulness of construing behavior as determined by experience or as related to hereditary characteristics, constitution, or physiological structure. Many personality theorists pay a certain amount of lip service to the importance of biology or structure but in practice largely ignore it and emphasize instead the role of learning. Others, like Sheldon (1940), have tried to relate body build to personality characteristics. There are many problems (as noted in Chapter 1) in trying to incorporate psychological and biological concepts into a common theoretical framework. Consequently contemporary theoretical approaches tend to emphasize one or the other set of determinants.

Generality vs. specificity.   Some theories tend to concentrate on a few reigning, superordinate concepts. Certain typological approaches (e.g., introvert vs. extravert) contain a few very broad constructs that are said to influence nearly everything an individual does. How one selects a mate, chooses clothes, decides on a major in college, or spends one's spare time is determined to a significant degree by one or a relatively few sovereign characteristics. Other more specific approaches contain many traits or characteristics, all of which function relatively independently to determine behavior. One important goal in personality theory today is settling upon a course of action that charts a position somewhere between the stark simplicity of the generality strategy and the confusion inherent in total specificity.

Internal vs. situational.   Related to the generality-specificity issue is the internal-situational dimension. Some theorists view behavior as determined by personality characteristics or, as it were, by internal determinants that people carry about with them from situation to situation. Others assert that behavior is determined by the nature of the specific situations in which individuals find themselves. Still others argue for a middle position that seeks the explanation for behavior in both sets of determinants.

Evaluation of theories

As has been noted, there are many ways to compare theories. But when all the comparisons are over, how are we to decide that one theory is better than another? Both Hall and Lindzey (1978) and Levy (1970) discuss several broad sets of criteria commonly applied to answer this important question.

Breadth, significance, and parsimony.   These criteria are admittedly a bit subjective and value oriented. In general, however, a theory that handles a broad range of events will be judged superior to one that deals with a narrow range. At the same time, one must consider the importance or significance of the events covered. But, in the final analysis, psychologists will differ among themselves in how broad and significant they believe the application of a theory to be. Parsimony is another subjective criterion that may be applied. That is, other things being equal, simple theories with an economical number of constructs are preferred. But again, reasonable psychologists may differ in their views of just how parsimonious a given theory is.

Formal constructions.   Good theories are theories whose assumptions and propositions are explicitly stated and also hang together in a logical, consistent fashion. Without doubt, theories that violate these characteristics will be less useful as a consequence.

Theories are not "writ in stone." They should be malleable, dynamic, changing instruments. As new data come in, the shape of a theory will change. Therefore, theories that are stated in vague, general terms typically generate hypotheses and data that cannot be judged as either supportive or nonsupportive of theory.

Utility.   When all is said and done, the only thing that really matters is whether a theory works. If the hypotheses deduced from a theory are verified more often than

Many personologists argue that behavior is determined not only by internal factors but also by the nature of the situation. Photograph AP/Wideworld.

not, we gain increasing confidence that the theory is useful. Furthermore, when the theory is applied to the events we consider important and it works (aids significantly in prediction and understanding), then that theory is a good one. Thus, the ultimate criterion is utility rather than correctness.

As we have seen, psychologists are not the only ones who have theories of personality. But what does make psychologists different is their commitment to the development and testing of those theories. The following sections on research and assessment will help make this clear.

RESEARCH

The second major topic of this chapter is the nature of personality research. Without research, the entire personality enterprise would be in danger of dying on the vine. As we shall see, it is research that gives theory its vitality.

The importance of research

If theory constituted the whole of the psychology of personality, a better term might be the "psychology of speculation and rumination." Research, whether it involves observation or experimentation, is the means by which we gather information or facts.

It also enables us to determine the relationships among events and to establish principles. Research not only helps us extend and modify our theories; it also is the road to determining the relative efficiency or utility of those theories. There is, then, an intimate relationship between theory and research—or at least there ought to be. Theory serves as both a stimulator and a guide for the speculation that precedes observation and experimentation. It helps glue together in a meaningful fashion the various facts that we have gleaned from our research. But there must be something to glue together; research provides that something.

The beauty of research is that it takes us out of the exclusive realm of argument, speculation, or appeal to authority. Things become settled in the arena of observation. Endless discussions give way to **empirical** test. This means that we determine by observation or experiment what the facts or relationships are. Not only that, but ideally our procedures are carried out in systematic, reliable ways so that others can verify them. This is the essence of the scientific method. This does not mean that empirical or scientific methods are fixed procedures that inevitably lead to truth. The scientific path is a tortuous one that involves as much perspiration as it does inspiration. There are many different methodological approaches that may be utilized in answering most questions, and the methods sometimes yield conflicting results. But over the long haul, empiricism, through its public and verifiable procedures, is better fitted to grapple successfully with our questions than is simple appeal to reason. How research can clarify speculation about the nature of certain events is illustrated in Box 2-2.

Observation

Observation is at once the most basic and pervasive of all research approaches. All research, whether it is experimental, naturalistic, or the study of individual cases, involves someone making observations of what someone else is doing or has done.

Unsystematic observation.   The ideas for much research begin with unsystematic observation. Simply observing one's own reactions or those of another may lead to the development of hypotheses. For example, one might casually observe two friends who, on separate occasions, each express a fear of dying. Intrigued, the observer notes that each is a rather self-centered, narcissistic individual. Could it be that self-love is associated with or even causes a concern about death? Such observations can provide the initial impetus to a more systematic and rigorous study of events.

Naturalistic observation.   Naturalistic observation is a more rigorous and systematic form of observation. Here, observations and measurements are made of various aspects of people's behavior. However, there is no control exerted by the investigator over the situations in which the behavior occurs. In effect, these are field studies. A good example is the work of Barker and Wright (1951), who followed a seven-year-old about for an entire day and systematically recorded every move he made. Another example comes from clinical psychology, where hospital personnel sometimes systematically observe and record the behavior of patients. In a specific case a given patient might be observed for one to three minutes every thirty minutes to help plan and understand the effects of treatment.

Box 2-2
RESEARCH ON EXPECTANCIES

A study from the 1950s on expectancies illustrates how research can help settle disagreements about the role of reinforcement in determining behavior. Although this issue may not appear particularly complicated today, its present clarity is at least partially attributable to the answers provided by that early research.

"If someone offers me a dollar today or five tomorrow, which should I choose?"

Based upon both animal and human research, the conventional wisdom was that immediate rewards are preferred over delayed rewards and that both rewards and punishment are less effective when their application is delayed. For example, given a choice between a small piece of candy that is offered now and a large one that will be provided two days hence, most children will choose the former. Obviously, delay does something to the *value* of immediate versus delayed rewards.

However, Mahrer (1956) believed that something was amiss here. Could it be that the crucial factor was the child's *expectancy*? That is, perhaps children choose the immediate but lesser reward because they have learned through experience that delayed rewards are less likely to occur than immediate ones. But rather than simply *offering* this revised argument, Mahrer *investigated* the problem empirically.

He did this by training groups of second- and third-grade children to have low, moderate, or high expectancies for receiving a toy promised by the experimenter. His data from the experiment supported the reasoning that, when the child trusts the promises of an adult, the child will choose a more valuable but delayed reward rather than an immediate but lesser one.

The point is that no matter how logical or intellectually impeccable one's reasoning may appear to be, that reasoning must be followed by systematic and reliable observation or experimentation. Without empirical research, we can never be sure.

Of course, naturalistic observations depend upon freely occurring events. For this reason alone, they can be quite cumbersome, and observers are often at the mercy of capricious events over which they have little or no control. A second problem is that observation is vulnerable to the biases and preconceived notions of the observer. Third, critics of this approach note that it is questionable how far one can generalize from one's observations of a few people or situations. Thus, findings may have very limited application. Finally, it is sometimes true that in the process of observing or recording, observers actually interfere with the events under study. For example, suppose you are observing family interactions to study the effects of dominance patterns. Can you really be sure that your presence is not a variable that subtly affects the family's interaction patterns?

Controlled field observations.   To deal with the foregoing criticisms, some investigators are making increased use of what might be called controlled field observations. In this approach, research is carried out in naturalistic settings but with more than passing attention to appropriate scientific controls. Such research attempts to combine several features of naturalistic observation and experimental research.

An example of this strategy is the work of Mathews and Canon (1975), who were interested in environmental noise level as a determinant of helping behavior. A hidden observer recorded the behavior of subjects who wandered into the following scenario. As a designated subject walked down the street, a confederate spilled a box of books all over the sidewalk. The behavior of interest was whether the subject would help the confederate pick up the books. At the same time, another confederate in an adjacent yard was either: (1) operating a very noisy lawn mower or (2) bending over a silent mower. What the observer noted was that 50 percent of the subjects helped the confederate when there was no lawn mower noise whereas only 12.5 percent helped in the noisy condition. Such a study has the distinct virtue of investigating questions in real settings, giving us increased confidence that the results can be generalized to other settings.

Case study methods

In case study methods, single individuals are examined qualitatively, and numbers and statistics usually take a back seat to the richness of detailed observation. Included are interviews, test responses, and even psychotherapy sessions, assuming that no systematic experimental variations were introduced. Also included would be first-person accounts such as letters, diaries, autobiographies, and the like. Third-person accounts—biographies, case history accounts, and so forth—would also qualify, as would certain naturalistic observations. For example, Rosenberg (1989) studied the organization of personality. He did so by analyzing the physical and psychological traits used by Thomas Wolfe to describe himself and others in the autobiographical novel *Look Homeward, Angel.*

A major value of case study methods is their richness as a source of hypotheses. They provide a basis for speculation that can later be translated into testable hypotheses and then subjected to careful scientific scrutiny. Sustained observation of real people and their productions is vital if for no other reason than as a prelude to scientific investigation. Computer simulation, statistical tables, and reviews of the literature are all useful, but we cannot afford to ever get completely away from looking at real people. If nothing else, analysis of case material and recourse to observation can serve to dampen the enthusiasm of those who deal exclusively on the one hand in theoretical speculation or, on the other, in laboratory research.

The experimental method

A major problem with observational and case study methods, or any other method that relies on naturally occurring events, is that we are often at the mercy of those events. Because we cannot control factors that might affect the events in which we are interested, it is always possible that causes other than those we have hypothesized may be operative. This is the fundamental reason why the experimental method has become so popular.

Let us consider the following hypothetical example. A great deal of evidence has suggested that aging individuals are cautious, have difficulty solving a variety of problems, show learning deficits, and so on (Botwinick, 1984). Some of this work has been done by having subjects complete tasks on small computers. Consequently, it has been argued that lack of experience on these computers is responsible for what appears to be learning deficits in the aging. Therefore, suppose we hypothesize that one aging group of subjects will take more trials to learn the stimulus material than will another group of aging subjects when the former are unfamiliar with computer equipment. Each group is treated in exactly the same way—that is, the stimuli are presented in the same fashion on the final test. Furthermore, we take some pains to match groups on IQ, educational background, and sex. The tasks are presented to all subjects on a computer screen, and subjects respond by pressing appropriate keys on the computer terminal. The only difference between the groups is that one is given some familiarization training and the other is not. There are fifty subjects in each group. The data analysis shows that, as predicted, the group with pretraining learned faster and also made fewer errors than did the other group.

The foregoing example illustrates several features of the experimental approach. We started with an **experimental hypothesis** developed from casual observation and from research—that is, a group of aging people with task familiarity are better learners than is a matched sample without such familiarity. We chose an **independent variable** that we could manipulate—in this case, the prior experience of the subjects. Finally, we examined the effects of this independent variable on the subjects' responses—the **dependent variable,** which in this example was responses to the stimuli appearing on the computer screen. In this hypothetical study, we followed good experimental procedure by controlling important variables (IQ, education, sex) in the situation and left free to vary only one aspect—task familiarity. Since the latter was the only thing different about the two groups, it must have been responsible for the observed performance differences between the groups.

In the previous example task familiarity was treated as the independent variable and it was manipulated through use of a **control group.** This is a group that serves as a baseline against which the performance of the experimental group can be compared. For example, suppose we wish to determine whether assertiveness training works. To do this we randomly select a group of people who are about to undergo such training and we measure in some fashion their initial level of assertiveness. Following their training we again measure their assertiveness level. Lo and behold, we find they are more assertive! Does this prove that the assertiveness training works? No, it does not. What we need is a matched control group that is measured before training but which, for example, is placed on a waiting list. After the same amount of time that characterized the training of the experimental group, they are measured again. Their before and after scores are then compared with the before and after scores of the experimental group to determine whether the training was effective. Without a control group one could just as easily argue that the real cause of the increase in assertiveness in the first group was their decision to undergo training rather than the training itself. Inclusion of a no-treatment control group increases our confidence that it really is the training and not some other set of factors that is causing the posttreatment improvement. Typically, the control group is matched on important variables with the experimental group, or else members of the total population under study are randomly assigned to either the control or the experimental group.

Historically, there have been five periods in the development of personality research methods: (1) the pre-identity era (the period before personality was really established as a field of study), (2) the pre-World War II era, (3) the post-World War II era, (4) the contemporary era, and (5) the current situation which is a part of the contemporary era (Craik, 1986). The laboratory and the use of personality scales are predominant, as Figure 2-1 illustrates.

Without doubt, the experimental approach to personality study has been dominant since the early 1960s, during which time personology (the study of individual differences) has virtually disappeared (Carlson, 1975). To be sure, work on a few popular individual-differences variables floated to the surface of the experimental sea. But even this research has been in the classical experimental mold that searched for general laws of behavior rather than focusing on the individual. Epstein (1979b) captured the essence of the trend when he remarked:

> In our zealous pursuit of rigorous, experimental research models we have somehow lost track of our subject matter. Instead of . . . studying individuals in breadth and depth, we have pursued a narrow vision of science, one in which method has become more important than substance. As a result, our journals are filled with studies describing laboratory manipulations of variables of little significance to the people in the experiments. (p. 649)

These are strong words. What they reflect is a growing dissatisfaction with the way personality research has been conducted over the past ten or fifteen years. Let us take a closer look at this problem.

Problems with the experimental method.   Where we used to talk about the fifty-minute therapy hour, we now have the fifty-minute experiment. This research approach leads to a concentration on isolated bits of behavior that often have not been integrated very well with the larger framework of a subject's personality. Thus, there is little awareness of the coherence of personality. Box 2-3 shows a specific example of what is being described here.

In addition, it is not unusual to discover that a laboratory finding cannot be replicated. How common this may be is uncertain since most studies are never replicated.

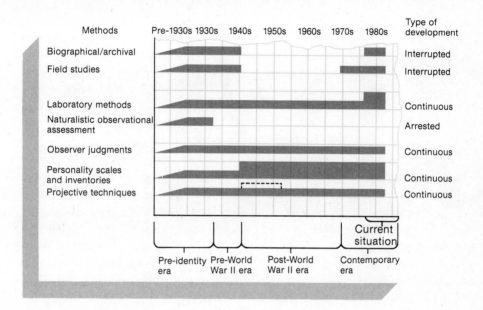

FIGURE 2-1 Historical trends in personality research.

From Kenneth H. Craik, "Personality Research Methods: An Historical Perspective," *Journal of Personality* 54:1, pp. 18–51, 1986. Copyright © 1986 by Duke University Press. Reprinted by permission.

Moreover, psychology journals do not routinely publish replication results unless there is some compelling theoretical reason to do so. Furthermore, many personality studies deal with a single behavior. But the expression of any specific behavior by a person is inherently unreliable. It depends upon so many things, including situational variables in the laboratory setting, experimenter characteristics, the subject's expectations, the relationship of the behavior to each subject's personality organization, and so on. All of this makes it hard to generalize a study's results to even a slightly different setting. In any case, questions about the reliability of the results of **nomothetic** (search for general laws by combining data from many individuals) studies are serious ones indeed. And reliability will not likely increase until we learn to solve problems involving representativeness of subject and situation samples, concentration on isolated bits of behavior, and the emphasis on brief encounters with subjects.

Furthermore, Lamiell (1981, 1987) has argued that conclusions based on studies that aggregate or add up the scores of individual subjects so as to provide a group mean do not really allow us to predict the behavior of a single subject. Just because, on average, forty subjects behave in a certain way does not tell us how *one* subject behaves. So, again, if we define personality in terms of distinctiveness, we are left hanging by traditional experimental approaches.

Box 2-3
THE FIFTY-MINUTE EXPERIMENT

The hypothesis of this study (Phares, 1962) was that when escape from a painful stimulus as a result of a subject's behavior is possible only on a chance basis, subjects will learn to recognize other stimuli associated with the stimulus less well than will subjects for whom escape is possible depending on their skill in learning to recognize the associated stimuli.

Three groups of subjects—fourteen skill, fourteen chance, and fourteen nonshock—were used. Tachistoscopic thresholds for twelve nonsense syllables were taken for all subjects. Following this, the skill group was given ten trials in which six of the syllables were always accompanied by shock and the other six were never accompanied by shock. By learning which shock syllable was associated with which button on their control panel, subjects could terminate the shock each time. Chance subjects were told that the correct button changed continuously so that no learning was possible, and thus that escape occurred only on a random basis. Chance subjects were matched with skill subjects with respect to number of escapes, syllables on which escape occurred, and sex. Following this procedure, thresholds were again taken for each of the twelve syllables. For nonshock subjects, the preexperiment and postexperiment thresholds were taken while, in between, the series of syllables was exposed for ten trials without shock.

Results indicated that, as predicted, threshold decrements were significantly greater for skill subjects than for chance subjects for both shock and nonshock syllables.

Several questions might be raised about this study:

1 Did subject selection have any influence? Subjects were paid volunteers, and all subjects fearful of electric shock were excused. Most subjects were college students.

2 How representative is the stimulus of electric shock? Are there specific qualities about shock that make it qualitatively different from other threatening stimuli?

3 Is learning nonsense syllables typical of learning in real-life situations? If so, how much so?

4 What were the needs that motivated the subjects, and were the needs possibly different from subject to subject? Was it money, a desire to please the experimenter, a wish to appear brave, a compulsion to achieve, etc.? Could each subject's results be replicated in another situation using different learning stimuli and different threats?

5 How significant was the overall laboratory setting to the subject? Would similar results be obtained in situations highly relevant to and typical of a subject's life?

6 Where, indeed, is the "personality" in this study? There are no measures of individual differences. Are all people, on the basis of this study, presumed to behave alike in all skill-chance settings? What about the subjects whose behavior did not follow the hypothesis?

Reasons for the popularity of experimental approaches. Many pressures have converged to make the experimental approach the preferred one currently. One reason has been the inadequacies of the **idiographic** (intensive study of individuals singly) method as commonly applied. For example, how do we know that what is true for one person provides an adequate basis for generalization to others since the idiographic approach imputes unique characteristics to each person.

Another reason has been the success of the biological and physical sciences. Some observers feel that psychology decided to mimic the rigorous methods of physical sciences as a way of gaining respectability. Apparatus, control groups, and sophisticated methods of data analysis became badges of scientific status. This is understandable in a discipline that was striving for acceptance and identity.

Another factor is the oft-proclaimed "publish or perish" syndrome in the academic-research establishment. Young investigators, learning early that promotions and salary increases are heavily dependent upon the rapid accumulation of an impressive list of publications, tend to design studies that can be carried out quickly and easily. In addition, variables chosen for study are straightforward—ones that can be easily manipulated. Little of this is done in an evil, Machiavellian fashion. In fact, this general approach has become so institutionalized that many investigators are unaware of the problem. Unfortunately, one effect of this approach may have been an overabundance of trivial findings.

A way out? It does not appear that the basic experimental methods of psychology are inherently a problem. Rather, it is the trivialization of these methods along with an overcommitment to them. The experimental method is a potent tool in our arsenal and we should continue to use it, but we also need to "rediscover" certain other approaches, for example, the longitudinal method. We should also become more adept at studying people in their natural habitat. Although naturalistic settings pose obvious difficulties in controlling variables, the gain is in using situations meaningful to subjects.

Indeed, there may likely be a return to strategies similar to those employed by Murray years ago (Bray, 1982; Epstein, 1979b; Rabin, Aronoff, Barclay, and Zucker, 1981). This will mean using a variety of measures on subjects over extended periods. Such an approach will help us to get a handle on the complexity of personality and permit us to deal with issues of the organization of personality. In support of the Murray strategy, no one should forget, for example, that the single most sweeping contribution to personality—Freudian theory—was based on case studies and idiographic research. The complementary nature of idiographic and nomothetic approaches (as illustrated in Box 2-4) may become part of the solution here.

The correlation method

In personality research we are often interested in whether one variable is related to another. Is anxiety related to performance? Do IQ scores relate to school achievement? Is there a relationship between obesity and unfulfilled needs for love and affection? In order to **correlate** two variables, we first obtain two sets of observations on each

Box 2-4
THE COMPLEMENTARY NATURE OF IDIOGRAPHIC AND NOMOTHETIC METHODS

Davis and Phares (1969) administered the 23-item I-E Scale. This is a forced-choice scale to determine the extent to which a person believes his or her own behavior is the determinant of rewards (internals) or that fate, luck, chance, or powerful others (externals) are crucial. College students were administered this scale along with a 192-item questionnaire designed to reveal various parental behaviors. Internals reported their parents as showing less rejection, hostile control, and withdrawal of relations and more positive involvement and consistent discipline as compared to externals.

Contrast these findings with the following quotation from R. W. White (1976):

> Bearing in mind that rejection involves interacting with the child as little as possible, it can be seen that such an attitude is not compatible with a real policy of close control and guidance. In his remarkable autobiography, John Stuart Mill describes in detail the manner in which his father, James Mill, undertook from the earliest years to control his education and preside over the forming of his mind. Clearly the elder Mill was committed to almost constant contact with his son in order to execute his strenuous plan for the shaping of character. The son describes studying his Greek lessons across the table from his father, who was writing a history of India, and interrupting him to ask the meaning of each new Greek word. He marvels that his father, naturally an impatient man, could have endured this constant breaking of his train of thought. It is indeed a marvel unless we assume that the son whose mind James Mill was shaping was in a true sense an object of love and esteem. The example makes it clear that high control need not imply rejection. Neither does low control necessarily signify love; it can go with indifference and with a desire to keep the child out of the way. (pp. 42–43)

Each of these disparate pieces, in its own way, contributes to our understanding of control. Each by itself is also quite incomplete as an analysis of the origins of control. Indeed, Hermans (1988) argues that psychology can only benefit from a combination of nomothetic and idiographic methods.

member of a group of subjects. For example, suppose we have ten subjects and each is given two tests: one that measures friendliness and one that measures how trusting a person is. These hypothetical paired scores are presented in Table 2-1. The resultant **correlation coefficient** is +.76, which suggests a strong positive relationship. Thus, as friendliness increases, so too does one's tendency to be trusting.

The **Pearson product moment correlation coefficient** is the statistical technique most commonly used to establish the degree of relationship between two variables. This is symbolized by *r*. An *r* may vary anywhere between -1.00 and $+1.00$. An *r* of $+1.00$ indicates that two variables are perfectly and positively related. An *r* of -1.00 indicates a perfect negative correlation. The *r* of .76 in Table 2-1 signifies a high positive correlation. A correlation of $-.76$ would mean a high negative relationship (i.e., as scores on Variable A increase, scores on Variable B decrease). A scatter plot of the two variables to be correlated will visually depict these relationships. For example, the data from Table 2-1 have been plotted in Figure 2-2. Each data point corresponds to one subject's scores on both friendliness and trust. Thus, the data point nearest the lower left-hand corner is Teresa's data (friendliness = 4; trust = 2).

Figure 2-3 presents scatter plots for several correlations. The more nearly perfect a relationship, the closer to a straight line will be the data points. When the *r* approaches .00, there is no relationship and the data points are scattered randomly around a straight line.

Statistical vs. practical significance.   In the case of both correlation and experimental methods, the data are subjected to a statistical analysis to determine whether they are significant. A correlation or a difference between an experimental group and a control group that could be expected to occur by chance less than 5 times out of 100 is traditionally considered to be statistically significant. The larger the correlation or the bigger the difference between groups, the greater the likelihood of significance. However, it is important to remember that when large groups of subjects are involved, even small differences between groups, as well as relatively small correlation coefficients, will be significant. For example, with data from 180 subjects, a correlation of .19 will be significant. But if only 30 subjects were involved, a correlation of .30 would not reach significance.

TABLE 2-1   *Hypothetical data for the correlation between friendliness and trust*

Subject	Friendliness Score	Trust Score
Mary	26	22
Betty	24	28
Grace	20	22
Dorothy	20	14
Nancy	16	18
Esther	12	22
Paula	12	6
Ann	10	14
Juanita	6	12
Teresa	4	2

Note: $r = +.76$ for the data above.

FIGURE 2-2

Scatter plot of data from Table 2-1.

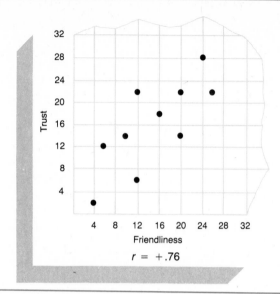

$r = +.76$

This raises the issue of practical versus statistical significance. An r of .19 really suggests a rather small relationship. For example, it might be true that size of income correlates to the tune of .15 with the amount of gasoline purchased each month in a sample of five thousand people. But even though the relationship is not a chance one, the actual relationship is very small. How important that relationship is may depend upon theoretical or value issues.

The problem of causality.   It is often very easy to assume that because two variables are correlated, one causes the other. No matter how "logical" this may appear, we cannot assert on the basis of a correlation alone that a cause-and-effect relationship holds. For example, we may find that in a third-grade class there is a correlation between IQs and teacher evaluations of intelligence. We might then assume that a child's intelligence is causing the teacher's evaluation (good or bad). But in a situation where the teacher is giving the IQ tests and also providing the evaluations, it may turn out that the evaluations predispose the teacher toward a biased administration or interpretation of the IQ test. Thus, it is the evaluation that is "causing" the IQ outcomes. Many years ago, a correlation was reported between the number of human births in Stockholm in a given year and the number of nests built by storks. What conclusion, pray tell, could we draw from this correlation? Although inferences about causality are not possible from correlation coefficients, this is not to say that cause-and-effect relationships do not exist in a given case. It only means that we must substantiate causal relationships by use of experimental methods rather than by correlational ones.

Evaluation of correlational methods.   The inability to infer causality from correlations represents their chief weakness. But there are tangible strengths as well. It is generally easier and less time-consuming to correlate than it is to construct elaborate experimental variations and manipulations. Therefore, if we can determine right off that no relationship exists between A and B, there is no point in experimentally investigating A as a cause of B. There is no question that knowledge about relationships can be quite practical. For example, everyone knows that cigarette smoking and lung cancer are correlated. The exact nature of any cause-and-effect relationship may be debatable, but few people would, on the basis of the correlation, advocate increased cigarette smoking.

Finally, correlational methods permit us to study variables that cannot practically or ethically be controlled. Variables such as sex, age, marital status, and birth order are not ones that can be manipulated experimentally. Nor can we ethically "train" someone to be a killer in order to study the effects of personality on crime.

Single-subject research

In recent years, single-subject research has come into vogue. It bears similarities to both experimental and case study methods. Like the experimental method, it allows for the manipulation of variables. The experimenter takes reliable, objective measures of a subject's behavior under several conditions that are controlled by the experimenter. This method has been most frequently used to evaluate the effectiveness of behavioral therapy. But since the research deals with a single subject, one cannot generalize and thus conclude that a principle has been established that will apply to an entire population. In this sense, it is much like the case study approach. But, as long as we are seeking to deal with only one specific individual or else are looking for leads that will allow us later to initiate a full-blown experimental study, the method has real merit.

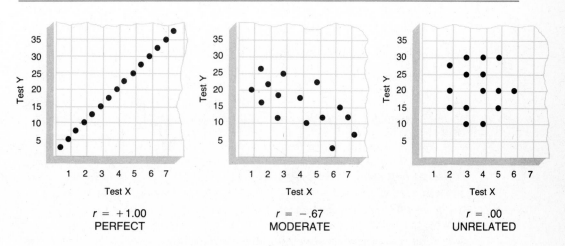

FIGURE 2-3 Scatter plots showing several different correlational relationships.

An example of this approach is the case of Robbie (Hall, Lund, and Jackson, 1968). Robbie was a very disruptive third-grader enrolled in an urban poverty-level school. He spent only about 25 percent of his time studying. The rest of the time he spent laughing, throwing things, and generally being a nuisance. This is shown graphically in Figure 2-4 as the Baseline period. During Reinforcement period I, the teacher paid a great deal of attention to Robbie, and it can be seen that his study behavior increased markedly. During the Reversal period, the teacher reverted to her old level of attention and Robbie's behavior deteriorated. With the reintroduction of attention by the teacher (Reinforcement period II), his behavior once again improved. The Reversal period, inserted as it was between the two reinforcement periods, effectively demonstrates a causal relationship between the teacher's behavior and Robbie's behavior.

ASSESSMENT

Regardless of one's commitment to a specific theory of personality or to a preferred research methodology, the need to systematically acquire information about people remains. In this section, we shall deal with the general topics of assessment.

Orientation to assessment

We can begin our discussion by considering three broad aspects of assessment.

A general issue in assessment.   Personality may be viewed in a very broad sense or in more narrow terms. Take the example of social interest, a concept which refers to an individual's willingness to be concerned with more than just self. This concern could be thought of as a broad, global tendency that cuts across nearly all areas of life (work, marriage, health, etc.). If so, the items on the scale designed to assess it would either sample a broad range of life situations or else be constructed so as not to refer directly to any specific situation. However, we could also decide to assess social interest separately in several different life areas. If the goal is to predict with considerable accuracy behavior in a specific, circumscribed set of situations, a very specific measure would be desirable. However, should the goal be one of predicting moderately well over a wide range of situations, then a general, more global measure would be appropriate (Rotter, 1975). This general versus specific assessment issue is illustrated in Box 2-5.

Test-taking attitudes and motives.   The psychologist always hopes that the person being assessed will respond in a straightforward, honest fashion. But this can be a vain hope. The point is, however, that regardless of what subjects' motives may be, the psychologist may not be aware of them. When this happens, the door is opened for interpretational error. Objective tests are very often subject to these problems. Suppose a subject is asked to answer "true" or "false" to the following item: "I have terrible nightmares nearly every night." It is not very difficult to figure out how

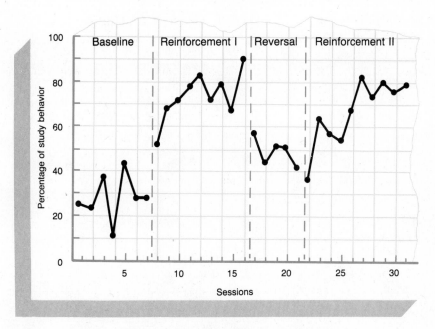

FIGURE 2-4 Robbie: The giving and withdrawal of reinforcement.

From "Effects of teacher attention on study behavior" by R. V. Hall, D. Lund, and D. Jackson, *Journal of Applied Behavior Analysis*, 1968, *1*, 1–12. Copyright 1968 by Society for the Experimental Analysis of Behavior. Reprinted with permission.

one should respond to create a good impression. Some objective tests have built-in detectors in the sense that certain items are designed to "trap" those being evasive or otherwise trying to "manage" their responses. But at best, these devices work imperfectly.

Other psychologists prefer projective tests—tests that are composed of ambiguous stimuli. Such tests make it more difficult for the subject to determine what is a correct or good response. But even here, ambiguous stimuli or not, the subject can, to some extent, manipulate the impression being conveyed. In short, the device has not yet been built that can totally defy a subject dedicated to misleading the examiner.

Inherent problems of measurement. In some instances, what we wish to measure is so poorly defined that measurement is inherently subject to difficulties. For example, if one can believe observers of the contemporary scene, a lot of us today are trying to "find ourselves" or looking to discover the "real me." But how can we measure this? What would those who have found themselves do or say on tests or in interviews that would distinguish them from those who are still looking? The problem lies in the fact that the constructs themselves are so vague and elusive that decent measurement is next to impossible.

Box 2-5
GENERAL VS. SPECIFIC TEST ITEMS FOR PREDICTING NARCISSISTIC BEHAVIOR

General

The following items (five-point agree-disagree scale) might be part of a scale that could be expected to predict moderately well over a number of different situations. Thus, the item content is not tied to specific situations but rather reflects general attitudes or beliefs.

1 If it feels right it is right.

2 Thinking of yourself first is no sin in this world today.

3 It's best to live for the present and not worry about tomorrow.

4 It seems impossible to imagine the world without me in it.

5 I believe everyone has the right to live any damn way they choose.

Specific

The following items (five-point agree-disagree scale) could compose part of a scale that could potentially predict well to the specific situations represented by the items but less so to other specific situations or to situations in general:

1 Having children keeps you from engaging in a lot of self-fulfilling activities.

2 When choosing clothes I usually prefer style over comfort.

3 Having a career that permits a great deal of leisure time is not very important.

4 I would be willing to participate in a program of wage controls.

5 One cannot truly achieve sexual gratification unless one's partner is also gratified.

Reliability

While there are many aspects of **reliability** (the extent to which a test yields consistent results), two major elements are of concern here. First, if we are dealing with a relatively stable factor of personality, our assessments on different occasions should agree with one another. This is commonly called **test-retest reliability**. If a subject were administered the same intelligence test four months ago and then again today, a reliable test would produce scores that are highly similar. This assumes, of course, that the testing conditions are comparable and that the subject has not undergone any serious changes in the meantime. Were the subject ill the second time or in the grip of an emotional crisis, or even tested by an unskilled examiner, the scores could easily vary. But the fault would lie not in the test but rather in changes in testing conditions. The second important aspect of reliability is the ability of different observers to agree among themselves when observing the same event. This is termed **interjudge reliability.** If different observers interpret an event differently, we have problems in deciding which observer to trust.

Validity

Even though an assessment technique is reliable, we still do not know whether it is valid. A valid test is one that measures what it purports to measure. A valid test of anxiety should measure anxiety. A valid intelligence test should predict those who will be good problem solvers and those who will not. There are several approaches to **validity**, and each has its particular utilities and shortcomings.

Content validity. **Content validity** is determined by observing whether the items of a given test appear to be sampling what is of interest. Does, for instance, a test of anxiety sample items congruent with our definition of anxiety? This is almost validity by inspection, and the difficulty, of course, is getting people of different theoretical persuasions to agree that the test items do indeed tap the construct in question. Content validity is only one step above **face validity,** which indicates that a test gives the appearance of being valid.

Criterion validity. **Criterion validity** is established by relating the scores on a test to some agreed-upon behavioral criterion. An example would be a test of creativity that predicted accurately creative accomplishments (music, art, writing, etc.) Criterion validity may be either of two kinds. The first is called **predictive validity.** This involves the ability of the test to predict to some criterion in the future. An intelligence test shows predictive validity when it accurately predicts later grades in school. **Concurrent validity** is evident when a test correlates significantly with another currently existing behavioral criterion. For example, when scores on an intelligence test are correlated with teachers' estimates of ability provided at the same time, concurrent validity exists. Of course, it is crucial that the teachers not have access to the scores. Otherwise, their judgments may be clouded or influenced by their knowledge, a situation called **criterion contamination.**

Construct validity. When the goal is simply to predict a specific behavior, the problem is a practical one and the foregoing kinds of validity would probably be pursued. But in other cases, the personality construct we wish to measure is derived from a specific theory of personality. Or we may be trying to establish the utility of a construct that is anchored in a theory of personality. With **construct validity,** the criteria are relative to what a specific theory says about the construct. An example of this approach is the work of Liverant (1958). From the point of view of social learning theory, Liverant wanted to measure certain need values. Since the theory dictated that need value be measured by a ranking procedure, he developed scales to measure need for love and affection by having subjects rank their preferences for the achievement of various kinds of goals. In this case, the theory dictated the measurement format and also defined the nature of construct which, in turn, determined the kinds of criterion behaviors that would be acceptable as evidence of validity. Table 2-2 outlines the requirements for the validity of a test according to each of the four strategies just discussed.

Interviews

Nearly all of you have at one time or another been interviewed for one purpose or another. Most of us have also conducted informal or unobtrusive interviews of our own. As a result, there is an easy familiarity about interviewing that is actually deceptive. Good interviewing is a complex skill that involves both science and art. Still, assessment interviews are probably the most basic and serviceable of all assessment procedures.

An assessment interview is, of course, an interaction between at least two persons. Good assessment interviews are carefully planned, deliberately and skillfully executed, and goal oriented throughout. The assessment interview is not used to achieve personal satisfaction or enhanced prestige. It is employed to elicit data and information.

Whenever interviews are conducted in a more or less freewheeling, unstructured format, severe issues of reliability and validity arise. The impact of the interviewer can be large, and the idiosyncratic mix between interviewer and interviewee can be an unpredictable one. When interviewers are free to use their own format, their biases can be overly influential in affecting their conclusions. To counteract some of these problems of bias, reliability, and validity, the structured interview is often employed. Here, the format of the interview and the role of the interviewer are much more standardized. There is much less variability from interview to interview, and the interviewer is obliged to maintain a greater degree of constancy across subjects. Of course this can result in reduced interview rapport and sometimes in a loss of information. But the advantage comes in enhanced reliability, and consequently structured interviews tend to find greater application in the research arena while unstructured interviews tend to be favored by clinicians.

TABLE 2-2   Strategies for determining the validity of a scale

Strategy	Scale Is Valid If . . .
Content validity	"Authorities" agree that the items on the scale are representative of the trait being measured
Predictive validity	Subjects respond the same way on the scale as they do on another measure taken sometime in the future
Concurrent validity	Subjects respond the same way on the scale as they do on another measure taken at about the same time
Construct validity	It measures the construct as it is theoretically defined

Interviewing remains the most widely used method of gathering data.

Self-report tests

The objective test—the psychologist's best friend or the student's worst enemy? Students are quite familiar with objective (multiple-choice and true-false) tests and often feel they have been taking them forever. Basically, **objective tests** used by personality psychologists ask the subject to provide self-reports about feelings, motives, behavior, or cognitions. Two examples will illustrate typical objective personality tests.

The **Fear Survey Schedule,** a test widely used by behaviorally oriented clinicians, was developed by Wolpe and Lang (1964) to reveal the stimuli that provoke anxiety. There are items relating to fear of death, illness, noise, planes, and so on. Subjects respond to each item on a five-point scale (from "Very much" to "Not at all"). This scale is an example of validation by content since items were selected to correspond to the authors' clinical experience; no other validity data were presented.

The **Edwards Personal Preference Schedule** (Edwards, 1959) is a little different from the preceding test. It contains 210 pairs of items, and every item is paired with every other item. The subject is asked to select the item in each pair that is more self-descriptive. It assesses fifteen needs (e.g., Achievement, Succorance, Affiliation) based upon Henry Murray's (1938) theoretical system. Each item is representative of one of the fifteen needs. To the extent that these items were chosen to be consistent with Murray's theory, one can regard this scale as illustrating the construct-validity approach described earlier.

Strengths and weaknesses of self-reports.   The prominent role of objective, self-report scales is due to a number of factors. Some of these are as follows:

■ Self-reports are economical to use. Group testing is sometimes feasible; administration and scoring by computer are possible.

■ Administration and scoring tend to be simple and objective. This, in turn, requires less interpretive skill on the part of the investigator.

■ Because of straightforward scoring, interscorer reliability tends to be high.

■ Self-report scales are often valid for specific purposes, particularly when large numbers of subjects are used. The prediction of a specific individual's behavior is less satisfactory.

There is, however, another side of the coin. The following are some of the disadvantages of these scales:

■ Because of the transparent meaning of so many of the items, it is relatively easy for subjects to manage the impressions they wish to present.

■ Since these are self-report devices, subjects are reporting on themselves. But there may be aspects of themselves of which they are unaware or about which they have distorted views.

■ Objective tests (as every student knows) prevent the subject from elaborating on or qualifying responses.

■ In some instances, the subject's limited ability to understand items, or even his or her level of literacy, may result in their misinterpretation.

■ Many self-report scales ask subjects to report mainly on various aspects of their behavior. But the same behavior can occur in different people for different reasons. This may lead to lowered validity.

■ In certain cases, scales are a mixture of items relating to behavior, needs, and cognitions. Therefore, two subjects may get the same total score for different reasons. This, too, clouds interpretation and may lower validity.

Projective tests

Because objective tests are relatively transparent, many feel they do not tap the deeper, more dynamic layers of personality. Therefore, they prefer to use **projective tests**— tests whose stimuli are relatively ambiguous.

Basic characteristics.   While the following criteria do not apply to every projective test, taken as a whole they serve to define projective devices:

■ The stimuli (e.g., inkblots, unstructured pictures) are ambiguous.

■ The method is indirect. That is, typically the subject is relatively unaware of the exact purposes of the test and thus finds it harder to slant responses.

■ There is freedom of response. Subjects do not have to respond yes or no. An inkblot can be anything.

To illustrate in a bit more detail, one of the more commonly used projective tests will be described briefly.

The Thematic Apperception Test. The **Thematic Apperception Test (TAT)** was introduced by Christiana Morgan and Henry Murray in 1935. It is designed to reveal individuals' basic personality characteristics through the interpretation of their imaginative productions in response to a set of ambiguous pictures. Originally, the test was developed to investigate personality from a psychoanalytic point of view. Later, it became a vehicle for measuring personality from Murray's (1938) theory of **needs** and **presses** (psychological and environmental forces). The interactions of these forces as they occur in subjects' stories are called **thema.**

The subject is asked to make up a story about each picture, indicating who the people are; what they are doing, thinking, and feeling; what led up to the scene; and how it will turn out. By and large, the scoring is quite subjective and intuitive even though some scoring manuals do exist, especially for research purposes. The TAT method is illustrated in Figure 2-5. A further discussion of the TAT appears in Chapter 9.

A brief evaluation of projective tests. The published reliability and validity research on projectives such as the TAT is disappointing. While their emphasis

FIGURE 2-5 TAT method.

The TAT method is important in eliciting both research and clinical data.

on the inner determinants of personality is a strength for many, others claim that the research indicates projective responses to be determined by situational, transitory influences as well. Thus, projectives tend to remain controversial. Certainly this is true clinically. In the research sphere projectives are still used but not as frequently as in the past. However, as Box 2-6 makes clear, in some respects, projectives have been misunderstood.

Behavioral assessment

In behavioral assessment the emphasis is on what subjects actually do in situations and less on what they say they do. Self-report is supplanted by performance. From the behavioral viewpoint, all behavior is determined by the conditions that prevail in any given situation. Behavior is maintained by rewarding conditions in the situation, and it drops out due to punishment or the failure of rewards to occur. Our interest as psychologists, then, is not in underlying, unobservable, hypothesized constructs (needs, self-concept, etc.) but in observable, overt behavior and the specific stimuli that maintain it. Our concern moves from underlying personality to behavior and stimuli.

What this reflects is a **sign versus sample** approach to assessment. A psychoanalyst would seek to determine the factors that underlie certain behaviors and would view responses on the Rorschach, for example, as a *sign* of an underlying problem. In contrast, the behaviorist is interested in *sampling* the behaviors that actually occur in certain situations and how they are affected by specific changes in those situations. The sign approach infers traits or motives that produce behavior while the sample approach counts behaviors and stimuli.

Naturalistic observation.
There are many examples of the systematic observation and recording of behavior in natural settings. For example, as noted earlier on, Barker and Wright (1951) followed a seven-year-old around for an entire day and recorded every move he made. And Lewinsohn and Shaffer (1971) recorded family interactions in the home in a systematic fashion.

Controlled situations.
Here, the emphasis is on observation in situations that are controlled and standardized. A rather exotic example is a clinical case reported by A. A. Lazarus (1961) in which he assessed a patient's fear of closed spaces by placing him in a closed room which was made progressively smaller by moving a screen closer and closer to the patient. Thus, degree of fear could be directly correlated with room size. In those cases where naturalistic observation is impractical or undesirable, the person may be given verbal descriptions of a specific situation and then asked to behave as he or she would in the real situation. This is a **role-playing** approach (Goldfried, 1976).

Self-report techniques.
Behavioral assessment has also borrowed heavily from traditional self-report approaches. For example, in some cases subjects are asked to monitor their own behavior and systematically record the occurrence of specific behavior or stimulus conditions. Sometimes this has involved keeping a diary. A variety

Box 2-6
RELIABILITY OR MENTAL SET?

It is often thought that test-retest reliability is a concrete attribute that a test either does or does not possess. As we have seen, self-report questionnaires often are considered to be superior to projective tests. Part of this superiority is usually attributed to the strong test-retest reliability of questionnaires and the correspondingly weak reliability of projectives. But, as David McClelland (1980) has argued, this superiority may be more apparent than real.

When subjects take tests (questionnaires or projectives), they do not do so in a vacuum, so to speak. They have an idea of what they are supposed to do. Instructions for questionnaires usually encourage honesty ("Tell us what you really feel") and consistency. Suppose the question is, "Do you get frequent headaches?" If you say "Yes" today, you are more likely to say "Yes" a month from now. Not to do so would be to imply you were not honest the first time. Therefore, even though your inclination may be to say "No" the second time, you say "Yes." The net result is more evidence of test-retest reliability than there should be.

Also, on questionnaires there is a tendency for the same question, in slightly different words, to appear over and over. In effect, you are answering the same question repeatedly. Again, high reliability is the outcome.

Many questionnaires focus on the past. "How many schools did you attend?" Did you feel anger toward your brother when you were a child?" One's answers to such questions should not vary over the time since there is only one correct answer in each case. For all the reasons above, test-retest reliability will likely be inflated for self-report questionnaires.

But what about projective tests? In most instances, the instructions encourage creativity, originality, and imagination. Therefore, if subjects are presented later with the same test stimuli (pictures in many cases), they will likely make up a different set of stories. To do otherwise would be to appear uncreative and ordinary. The pressure, then, is to be *unreliable*. The very word *imaginative* serves to spur a different response from one occasion to the next. In the final analysis, *honesty* pushes us toward reliability of responses and *originality* impels us toward unreliability.

Normally, students are taught that the validity of a test can never be greater than its reliability. However, McClelland asserts that numerous studies have shown good validity for projective tests (especially for the measurement of achievement motives). As a result, McClelland suggests, perhaps the reliability of certain projective devices has been severely underestimated because of the factors enumerated above.

of self-report inventories have also been adapted or developed to measure fears, anxieties, and the like. The emphasis, however, is on overt behaviors and the conditions under which they occur rather than on unobservable, mediating constructs.

A brief evaluation of behavioral assessment.

More than most other approaches, behavioral assessment is a loose collection of techniques. What binds them together is their emphasis on behavior and the conditions surrounding its occurrence. Many of these techniques have not yet been rigorously examined for reliability or validity. In particular, it is often unclear how much observers tend to affect what they are observing. An analogous problem exists when subjects monitor their own behavior.

Psychophysiological techniques

In some cases the investigator may wish to study how certain psychological states are reflected physiologically. Anxiety might be studied by examining its physiological reflections. For example, do subjects who receive high scores on a paper-and-pencil measure of anxiety also show rapid pulse rate, increased blood pressure, or perhaps certain biochemical changes? A specific example of this is a study with **Type A** subjects (Simpson et al., 1974). These are subjects who show an intense desire for competitiveness, aggressiveness, and a desire to do more in less time (see Chapter 15). In response to stress, Type As had high levels of norepinephrine in the blood. Norepinephrine is a hormone that raises diastolic blood pressure and when released in large amounts can lead to arterial damage.

Unobtrusive measures

Psychologists have long been concerned over the fact that testing situations almost inevitably involve an interaction between subject and assessor. Thus to some unknown extent test responses may be due to this awareness of being tested or to responsiveness to the social characteristics of the testing situation. To help counteract these factors, Webb, Campbell, Schwartz, and Sechrest (1966) have compiled and analyzed a variety of what they term **unobtrusive measures.** Subjects do not know that information is being gathered or that certain aspects of their behavior or life records will be examined. Such measures are often quite inferential and because of this and other limitations, are best employed in conjunction with additional methods. Several examples of unobtrusive measures are the following:

■ Wearing out of carpet as an indication of how popular professors are as advisers by suggesting amount of office traffic

■ Library check-out records to discover how demanding a given curriculum is

■ Suicide notes as a method of learning about causes of suicide

ETHICS OF RESEARCH AND ASSESSMENT

Thus far, the discussion of research and assessment has focused on what the investigator wishes to do and how it is done. But there is one very important missing ingredient—the person being studied or assessed. People are not lumps of clay or blobs of protoplasm that can be treated in any old fanciful way that occurs to the psychologist. People have rights, and psychologists have obligations. Somehow the legitimate needs of science must be made to fit between those two considerations. This brings us to the topic of ethics. The American Psychological Association (APA) has adopted a set of ethical principles to guide specifically investigators using human subjects (APA, 1981a). APA has also developed a general code of ethics dealing with research, teaching, therapy, testing, and assessment (APA, 1977, 1981b, 1990). It goes without saying that questions of ethics are very complex issues. Everyone agrees (in principle) that ethics are necessary and desirable. The real issue is where we draw the line between justifiable research and assessment and the rights of human participants. The ten basic APA principles outlining research ethics are presented in Table 2-3.

TABLE 2-3 APA research principles

The decision to undertake research rests upon a considered judgment by the individual psychologist about how best to contribute to psychological science and human welfare. Having made the decision to conduct research, the psychologist considers alternative directions in which research energies and resources might be invested. On the basis of this consideration, the psychologist carries out the investigation with respect and concern for the dignity and welfare of the people who participate and with cognizance of federal and state regulations and professional standards governing the conduct of research with human participants.

a. In planning a study, the investigator has the responsibility to make a careful evaluation of its ethical acceptability. To the extent that the weighing of scientific and human values suggests a compromise of any principle, the investigator incurs a correspondingly serious obligation to seek ethical advice and to observe stringent safeguards to protect the rights of human participants.

b. Considering whether a participant in a planned study will be a "subject at risk" or a "subject at minimal risk," according to recognized standards, is of primary ethical concern to the investigator.

c. The investigator always retains the responsibility for ensuring ethical practice in research. The investigator is also responsible for the ethical treatment of research participants by collaborators, assistants, students, and employees, all of whom, however, incur similar obligations.

d. Except in minimal-risk research, the investigator establishes a clear and fair agreement with research participants, prior to their participation, that clarifies the obligations and responsibilities of each. The investigator has the obligation to honor all promises and commitments included in that agreement. The investigator informs the participants of all aspects of the research that might reasonably be expected to influence willingness to participate and explains all other aspects of the research about which the participants inquire. Failure to make full disclosure prior to obtaining informed consent requires additional safeguards to protect the welfare and dignity of the research participants. Research with children or with participants who have impairments that would limit understanding and/or communication requires special safeguarding procedures.

(continued)

TABLE 2-3   (continued)

e. Methodological requirements of a study may make the use of concealment or deception necessary. Before conducting such a study, the investigator has a special responsibility to (i) determine whether the use of such techniques is justified by the study's prospective scientific, educational, or applied value; (ii) determine whether alternative procedures are available that do not use concealment or deception; and (iii) ensure that the participants are provided with sufficient explanation as soon as possible.

f. The investigator respects the individual's freedom to decline to participate in or to withdraw from the research at any time. The obligation to protect this freedom requires careful thought and consideration when the investigator is in a position of authority or influence over the participant. Such positions of authority include, but are not limited to, situations in which research participation is required as part of employment or in which the participant is a student, client, or employee of the investigator.

g. The investigator protects the participant from physical and mental discomfort, harm, and danger that may arise from research procedures. If risks or such consequences exist, the investigator informs the participant of that fact. Research procedures likely to cause serious or lasting harm to a participant are not used unless the failure to use these procedures might expose the participant to risk of greater harm, or unless the research has great potential benefit and fully informed and voluntary consent is obtained from each participant. The participant should be informed of procedures for contacting the investigator within a reasonable time period following participation should stress, potential harm, or related questions or concerns arise.

h. After the data are collected, the investigator provides the participant with information about the nature of the study and attempts to remove any misconceptions that may have arisen. Where scientific or humane values justify delaying or withholding this information, the investigator incurs a special responsibility to monitor the research and to ensure that there are no damaging consequences for the participant.

i. Where research procedures result in undesirable consequences for the individual participant, the investigator has the responsibility to detect and remove or correct these consequences, including long-term effects.

j. Information obtained about a research participant during the course of an investigation is confidential unless otherwise agreed upon in advance. When the possibility exists that others may obtain access to such information, this possibility, together with the plans for protecting confidentiality, is explained to the participant as part of the procedure for obtaining informed consent.

Source: From "Ethical Principles of Psychologists (Amended June 2, 1990)" by the American Psychological Association, *American Psychologist*, 1990, 45, 390–395. Copyright 1990 by the American Psychological Association. Reprinted by permission.

The APA principles seem straightforward enough. But when they are applied to specific situations, the answers become tougher. Is deception ever justified? What about those instances where the research is truly important or can seemingly be carried out in no other way? What if the research is on stress? If it is, how can we experimentally study stress without inducing it and thus, to some degree or other, harming our subjects? How can we inform subjects of the nature of the research if such knowledge would "spoil" them as subjects? Can we be honest with the feedback we provide subjects if their performance turns out to be poor?

These are difficult questions that have provoked heated discussion. Honorable and dedicated psychologists on either side of a specific issue sometimes disagree. Perhaps, then, the best insurance we have that the rights of subjects and the needs of science will be properly balanced lies in the continuing debate over ethical issues.

SUMMARY

- There are many theories of personality. The differing backgrounds of theorists lead them to see reality in different ways. The complexity of human beings seems to result in each theorist capturing only a part of that complexity.

- Far from being either dusty or arcane topics, personality theories are, in a real sense, used by all of us every day. Implicit personality theory is an example of this everyday use.

- Constructs used in a particular personality theory represent the ways the theorist has chosen to describe reality. They are, however, just descriptions; they are not reality itself. Their purpose is to enhance our ability to predict and understand. As a result they are judged by standards of utility. Furthermore, each theory tends to have a focus of convenience. This means that a given theory will likely work better for some purposes than for others.

- The values of personality theory are several: they assist us in communication; they provide a framework for explanation; they help us expand our knowledge; and they encourage consistency in thinking.

- Theories tend to differ in numerous ways. Several differences were discussed, including their systematic-unsystematic qualities, their operational-nonoperational nature, whether they emphasize content or process, whether they focus on experience or heredity, their general or specific application, and the degree to which they consider internal or situational factors as prime determinants of behavior. There are several dimensions that reflect the conflicting values within the field of personality.

- Typically, theories are evaluated by the extent to which they can deal with a broad range of important events. Parsimonious theories (those with an economical number of constructs) are usually preferred. Good theories were described as theories whose assumptions, propositions, and constructs are clearly and explicitly stated and which hang together in a systematic way. Finally, good theories are useful theories.

- The importance of personality research resides in its capacity to take us out of the realm of rumination and speculation and into the arena of observation and experimentation.

■ Several forms of observation were discussed. These include unsystematic observation, naturalistic observation, controlled field observation, and case study methods. Some of the chief advantages and disadvantages of each were presented as well.

■ In case study methods, qualitative studies are done on individuals, one at a time. Included are interview data, test responses, autobiographical material, and the like. Of particular value in case studies is their richness as sources of hypotheses about people.

■ Experimental methods are a major set of techniques employed in personality research. Some of their principal features were briefly outlined, particularly the use of control groups.

■ There seems to be a growing belief that the experimental-laboratory model of research has been overemphasized in the field of personality.

■ Several reasons for this presumed state of affairs were discussed, including neglect of the organization of personality, emphasis on brief experiments that do not permit sustained contact with subjects, and problems in replicating experimental findings.

■ The reasons for an overreliance on the experimental method include the inadequacies of a purely idiographic approach, a desire to emulate the physical sciences, and the "publish or perish" syndrome in universities.

■ The solution to our problems may be in combining experimental procedures with case study, idiographic ones.

■ Regarding correlation methods, it was noted that we must distinguish between practical and statistical significance, and also not confuse relationship with causality.

■ Use of the single-subject method was illustrated.

■ In approaching assessment, we must consider whether to view personality in general or specific terms. We must also keep in mind test-taking attitudes of the subject. Finally, it was noted that poorly defined concepts lead to poorly conducted assessment.

■ An important feature of test instruments is their reliability. Two forms of reliability were emphasized: test-retest reliability (similarity of scores on two occasions) and interjudge reliability (ability of multiple judges to agree among themselves).

■ Validity of assessment techniques is essential and simply means that a test must measure what it purports to measure. Several forms of validity were discussed, including content validity, criterion validity, and construct validity.

■ Some of the principal features of interviews as assessment devices were presented and described.

■ Two examples of self-report tests were briefly discussed. Also, the general strengths and weaknesses of self-reports were addressed.

■ The basic characteristics of projective tests were noted and the TAT was briefly described.

■ Behavioral assessment techniques focus less on what subjects say and more on what they actually do. The goal is to sample behaviors the subject uses rather than to seek signs of internal determinants. Several examples of behavioral assessment techniques were offered.

■ A brief description of psychophysiological methods and unobtrusive techniques was presented.

■ Closing comments focused on a discussion of the ethics of research and assessment.

2

CONCEPTIONS
OF PERSONALITY

P A R T   2

Part 2 presents the diverse theoretical conceptions and methods encountered in the field of personality. In general, one chapter is devoted to the basic concepts of a given personality theory and its implications for development, adjustment, and behavior change. Each of these chapters is followed by a chapter in which the research and assessment methods characteristic of the particular conceptions are covered, along with a critical analysis of the strengths and weaknesses of those conceptions.

Chapters 3 and 4 are devoted to the psychoanalytic perspective pioneered by Sigmund Freud. In Chapter 5 this theme is continued with a presentation of the general psychoanalytic approach to research and assessment and is closed with a summary evaluation of the psychoanalytic movement. Chapter 6 considers phenomenological theory. It focuses on the self and on personal constructs while touching upon humanism and existentialism. It also includes the information processing perspective. Chapter 7 examines the research and assessment implications of these approaches and concludes with a general evaluation of phenomenology. Chapters 8 and 9 are devoted to the theory, research, and assessment aspects of a dispositional (traits, needs, and motives) conceptualization of personality. The topic of traits versus situations is also discussed here. Chapters 10 and 11 introduce the behavioral approach, which is founded upon an experimental methodology. Finally, Chapters 12 and 13 contain social learning theory descriptions of personality. Social learning theories are outgrowths of the behavioral tradition and emphasize that the determinants of behavior are learned in the context of our interactions with others.

CHAPTER 3

PSYCHOANALYTIC THEORY I
The Freudian Revolution

Psychoanalytic theory, the creation of Sigmund Freud, has been the single most sweeping contribution to the field of personality. There is hardly an area of life today that has not been touched by Freudian thought. It is reflected in our art, our literature, and our cinema. One is as likely (perhaps even more likely) to encounter psychoanalytic discussions and analysis in English departments as in psychology offices. Historians can be heard talking about prominent figures from a Freudian perspective. Many current child-rearing dictums have distinct Freudian roots, and when we encounter anxiety in our lives, we may well wind up consulting a psychotherapist whose practice has a robust Freudian flavor. Terms such as *ego, unconscious, death wish*, and *Freudian slip* have become a part of our everyday conversation.

Nevertheless, Freud's ideas received a rough reception initially. Psychologists of the time were accustomed to the ideas of Wilhelm Wundt, the founder of scientific psychology (Leahey, 1984). Wundt made the analysis of consciousness the centerpiece of investigation. Then along came Freud with his heretical ideas about the extreme importance of unconscious forces in the mind. Nor was the community at large ready to accept Freudian doctrine. Remember that Freud wrote during the "genteel" Victorian era; straitlaced would not be an idle description of Vienna at that time (circa 1900). It takes little imagination to understand the abuse and ridicule that Freud encountered because he considered sexual and aggressive urges to be the principal motivators of human behavior. Such people perceived Freud as chaining the human mind to animal lusts. For a society that could only contemplate conscious thought and the primacy of will, this was seen as a fall from grace no less drastic than that of Adam and Eve's.

In addition, being a Jew, Freud was also subject to vehement anti-Semitic attacks. Of course, Freud's views eventually were vindicated, perhaps because good ideas have a way of enduring.

THE BEGINNINGS OF THE PSYCHOANALYTIC AGE

Oddly enough, the first stirrings of psychoanalysis began just as a bizarre interlude in Freud's life was coming to a close. (See the brief biography for additional information about Freud.) Around 1884, Freud became interested in a new drug and its stimulant properties. That drug was cocaine. He used it himself and found it not only relieved his chronic intermittent bouts of depression but also gave him a feeling of vigor. He believed his research on this new drug would provide a real boost to his career and finances. In fact a paper of Freud's extolling the virtues of cocaine treatment and its addiction-free properties resulted in widespread prescription of the drug by physicians throughout Europe. Despite this, Freud's reputation in medical circles did not appear to skyrocket. Then the reports of addiction began to surface. Freud saw cocaine's addictive properties firsthand—in a friend for whom he prescribed the drug to facilitate withdrawal from morphine. Because of all these things, Freud stopped using cocaine personally and gave up his professional identification with it.

Luckily, in 1885 Freud was awarded a grant that allowed him to get away from all this. He went to Paris to study hysteria with the famous French neurologist Jean Charcot. Hysteria was then regarded as a "female" disorder characterized most often by paralysis, blindness, deafness, and the like. Charcot had found that some hysterical patients would, while under hypnosis, relinquish their hysterical symptoms, and even at times recall the traumatic experiences that had generated them. Undoubtedly, the recall Freud observed in hypnotized patients played an important role in the development of his later ideas about the nature of the unconscious. Freud was greatly impressed by Charcot's work and lost no time in explaining it to his circle of physicians in Vienna after returning from his six-month sojourn. Although his advocacy of hypnotic techniques encountered considerable skepticism, he nevertheless began to incorporate them into his practice in the treatment of nervous disorders.

Some years earlier, Freud's curiosity had been aroused by Breuer's experiences with a young hysteric, Anna O. This young woman had many of the classical hysterical symptoms, along with a double personality. The death of her father had apparently precipitated many of her difficulties. Breuer treated Anna using hypnosis, and during one session, in the midst of a trance, she told him about the first appearance of one of her symptoms. The curious thing was that when she came out of the trance, the symptom was gone! Realizing he was on to something, Breuer repeated the procedures over a period of time, with some success. In the process, however, there developed a strong emotional relationship between patient and doctor. The intensity of Anna's attachment to Breuer and a remarkable episode in which she developed hysterical labor pains from a phantom pregnancy she believed he had produced frightened Breuer,

A brief biography of

Sigmund Freud

Sigmund Freud, born in 1856 in Austria (an area now part of Czechoslovakia), grew up in Vienna, the oldest of seven children. After completing a classical education, he decided to study medicine at the University of Vienna. He received his medical degree in 1881 and soon took a research position. Although he was not particularly interested in private practice, three things conspired to make him relinquish his research appointment. First, he recognized that as a Jew he stood little chance of achieving advancement in the academic-research environment, which was full of anti-Semitic sentiment. Second, his research work showed scant promise of ever allowing him to make much money. Third, he had fallen in love with Martha Bernays; marriage takes money, and Freud had none. As a result, he opened a practice as a neurologist. His marriage (in 1886) to Martha produced six children; one, Anna Freud, became a famous psychoanalyst in her own right.

Around the time of his marriage, Freud began a brief but highly productive collaboration with Josef Breuer, a well-known physician in Vienna. Together they followed up Breuer's discovery of the "talking cure," a method by which the patient alleviates neurotic symptoms by talking about them. In 1895, Breuer and Freud published *Studies on Hysteria*. Then, for some reason, the two men had a falling-out. Some suggest money as the problem; others believe that Breuer became alarmed over Freud's emphasis on the role of sex in hysteria.

and he abandoned the case. The jealousy of Breuer's wife undoubtedly contributed to his concern.

Freud's interest in Anna O, coupled with his experiences with Charcot, led him to expand his practice. Many of his new patients presented hysterical symptoms with no organic basis. (Although hysterical symptoms are not so common now, they were quite prevalent in the emotionally repressive environment of Victorian Vienna.) Freud treated many of these patients with hypnotic procedures. Some patients, however, were not good candidates for hypnosis. Others had the annoying tendency to awaken from a trance with no memory of what had transpired, thus canceling many of the positive features of the method. A case in point was Elisabeth, a patient Freud saw in 1892. Freud asked Elisabeth to concentrate on her ailment and remember when it began. He had her lie on a couch while he pressed her forehead with his hand. This was the beginning of what later became the method of free association, the royal road to the unconscious. It took years to perfect the technique, but in a crude form it had arrived.

But Freud's ideas did not come just from patients. Using himself as a kind of guinea

Whatever the cause, their collaboration had served its purpose: Psychoanalytic theory was on its way.

Freud's most acclaimed work, *The Interpretation of Dreams,* was published in 1900, capping a remarkably productive decade. With the dawn of the twentieth century his stature grew and his work began to attract adherents. The Vienna Psycho-Analytical Society was founded, and followers began to flock to his side. However, a few years later a number of these converts left the orthodox Freudian camp to develop their separate brands of theory. Notable among them were Alfred Adler, Carl Jung, and Otto Rank. In 1909 Freud was invited to the United States to lecture at Clark University. The whole world now knew about Sigmund Freud.

Numerous books and achievements followed. But as the 1930s began, so too did Nazi harassment. His books were burned, and he became a popular anti-Semitic target. Eventually Freud was allowed to emigrate to England. His last years were not pleasant ones. He suffered great pain from cancer of the jaw, undergoing thirty-two operations. A heavy cigar smoker, he periodically gave them up, although never completely. He died in September 1939.

An excellent biography of Freud was written by his longtime friend and fellow analyst, Ernest Jones (1953, 1955, 1957). A brief but highly readable account of the life of Freud may be found in Geiwitz and Moursund (1979).

Sigmund Freud
Brown Brothers

pig, he spent long hours in self-analysis (see Chapter 5) because he firmly believed that his theory applied not only to others but to himself as well.

Although a bit shaky and far from its ultimate shape, the basic outline of a psychoanalytic theory of personality was in hand, and a therapeutic method of dealing with neurosis was emerging. Breuer's work with Anna O had led to the discovery of the "talking cure," and this, in turn, was transformed into free association during Freud's work with Elisabeth. **Free association** meant simply that the patient was to say everything that came to mind; nothing was to be censored, no matter how silly, dull, revolting, or irrelevant it might appear. Freud also had realized that Anna had transferred to Breuer many of her feelings toward significant males in her life. This concept of **transference** would ultimately prove to be a valuable diagnostic tool in understanding the nature of the patient's problems, especially unconscious ones. By employing hypnosis, Freud learned patients could relive traumatic events associated with the onset of their hysterical symptoms. In some cases, the reliving served to release bottled-up energy. This became known as **catharsis,** a process often producing therapeutic effects.

FIGURE 3-1   **"Anna O."**

Bertha Pappenheim was identified by Ernest Jones (1953) as Breuer's patient, Anna O. She carried out a remarkable career as a pioneer in the feminist movement and as a social reformer. In 1954, eighteen years after her death, West Germany issued a stamp honoring her achievements. All of this is a reminder that problems in living need not stand in the way of personal accomplishment.

In his work with Elisabeth, Freud also observed **resistance,** a general obstinacy toward discussing, remembering, or thinking about especially troubling or threatening events. Initially, he saw this as a kind of defense, but later would analyze it as **repression,** the involuntary banishment of a thought or impulse to the unconscious. The **unconscious,** of course, was an area of the mind not accessible to conscious thought.

With his magnificent intuitive powers of observation, Freud took these crude concepts and methods and began to fashion an intricate but systematic theory that would forever change the world.

BASIC THEORY

Psychoanalytic theory (Freud, 1938) makes two important assumptions: **psychic determinism** and **unconscious motivation.** As the following pages will elaborate, these assumptions, along with his ideas about the instincts, permeate nearly every aspect of psychoanalytic theory.

Psychic determinism

Psychic determinism is Freud's assumption that everything we do, think, or feel has meaning and purpose and that all things in nature are determined. Slips of the tongue, gestures, careers—all have meaning and specific origins in the experience of the individual. Strictly speaking, of course, most behaviors have multiple determinants. Freud's early scientific training led him to seek a cause for any and all behavior. Dismissing an event as capricious or the result of free will was not in his nature. The assumption of psychic determinism allows the analyst to use an exceptionally wide array of data in the search for the roots of a patient's behavior. Often this search took Freud into the depths of the unconscious.

Unconscious motivation

Freud was convinced that a major portion of our behavior, thoughts, and feelings is determined by motives about which we are completely unaware. Although the notion of **unconscious motivation** did not originate with Freud, he made more extensive use of it than his predecessors. While the concept may seem foreign to many of you, one can easily see how Freud developed it as he struggled to explain Anna O's ability to remember certain events while hypnotized and her inability to recall them in the waking state. Box 3-1 also suggests how our motives may remain unknown to us.

Freud conceptualized the mind as a kind of psychic map (see Figure 3-2). The **conscious** area represents everything of which an individual is aware at any given moment (sensations, perceptions, experiences, memories, etc.). Freud believed the conscious mind to be only a small part of our mental life.

The **preconscious** area represents those things accessible to the person at any given time. The memories and material stored there are not immediately conscious but with some effort can be called forth. For example, I cannot at this moment recall the first psychology text I studied, but with a little concentration and a few associations I could probably dredge it up.

The **unconscious** area is a deep, inaccessible repository of urges or drives, what many refer to as the instincts. Although the individual is completely unaware of their existence, these drives or instincts are active forces that seek expression and are the major determinants of behavior as we shall see in the next paragraphs.

Instincts

Freud viewed human beings as closed energy systems. Psychic energy arises somehow from the excitation of bodily structures. Thus, in a very real sense human motivation can be traced back to tissue needs. Obviously, the bridge from the psychic side of the

Many adult activities are said by psychoanalysts to be determined by unconscious motivation.
Photograph Loren Santow.

Box 3-1
ARE WE ALWAYS AWARE OF THE MOTIVES FOR OUR BEHAVIOR?

Hypnosis played an important role in the early development of psychoanalysis. It has also been used by some to demonstrate the role of unconscious motivation. Take the following example:

> To illustrate how sincerely the subject believes in the authenticity of his posthypnotic experiences, I may cite an example of a posthypnotic negative hallucination induced in a man in the presence of one of my colleagues, Dr. S. The latter physician, skeptical about hypnosis, entered my office unexpectedly at a time when an experimental subject, known to both of us, was in a hypnotic trance. I suggested to the subject that when he woke up he would neither be able to see nor hear Dr. S. Upon awakening, the subject engaged me in a conversation regarding the pennant possibilities of the Dodgers, in the middle of which he casually asked if I had seen Dr. S. recently. I rejoined by asking him the same question. During this conversation, Dr. S. was leaning up against a window. I informed the subject that I was expecting Dr. S. and asked him to look out of the window to see whether he was in sight. The subject looked directly at Dr. S. and said, "No, he isn't." Inquiring as to what he saw, he remarked that he noticed the usual trees, grass, and buildings. At this point, Dr. S. addressed the subject directly. The latter interrupted him in the middle of a sentence with a remark pointed at myself. Dr. S. continued talking, but the subject paid absolutely no attention to him as if he were not in the room. At this point, I held an inkwell in the air and asked him if he saw it. Perplexed, he admitted that he could and wondered why I had asked him so silly a question. I then handed the inkwell to Dr. S. and asked the subject again if he could see the inkwell. He looked intently at the inkwell and exclaimed, "My God, you will think I am crazy, but the inkwell is floating around in space." He appeared to be genuinely alarmed. I took the inkwell from Dr. S. and he said, "You have the inkwell now." Even though I insisted that Dr. S. was in the room and pointed him out, the subject continued to believe that I was joking. He remarked that fortunately he had not yet lost his mind. He was certain that there was no other person in the room until I rehypnotized him and removed the suggestion.
>
> The most compulsive nature of the posthypnotic act is one of its most characteristic features. This is not to say that the suggestion cannot be resisted. Usually, however, resistance takes a tremendous effort. (Wolberg, 1948, pp. 56–57)

The exact explanation for hypnotic phenomena is still controversial. Some, such as Hilgard (1978), regard hypnosis as a state of altered consciousness in which people are more suggestible, show enhanced imagery and imagination, more uncritically accept distortions of reality, and believe firmly that they are in an altered state of consciousness. Others, such as Sarbin and Coe (1972), explain hypnosis as a state in which the person is merely enacting a role. Subjects behave in a fashion they believe to be characteristic of a hypnotized person.

Whatever the exact explanation for hypnosis turns out to be, one thing does seem clear. Hypnotized individuals have great difficulty expressing the "real" motives guiding their behavior in the trance and, indeed, even acknowledging their trance behavior in many cases. While scientific agreement here is elusive, hypnosis has, and will continue to be, an important tool for studying the nature of consciousness.

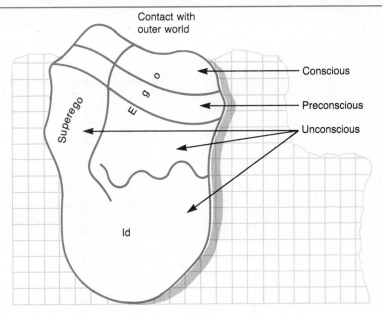

FIGURE 3-2 Freud's psychic map of the mind.
Redrawn from Healy, W., Bronner, A. F., and Bowers, A. M. (1930). *The structure and meaning of psychoanalysis.* New York: Knopf. Copyright 1930 by Alfred A. Knopf, Inc. Used with permission.

river to the physiological side is a complex riddle, and has yet to be solved satisfactorily by psychoanalytic theory. In any case, these states of excitation give rise to mental representations, or wishes. Collections of wishes are termed **instincts.** In reality, instincts merely reflect bodily sources of excitation or needs. The aim of these instincts is the reduction of tension, which is experienced as pleasure. Therefore, instincts have (1) a **source,** which is a state of excitation within the body, (2) an **aim,** which is the removal of that excitation, and (3) an **object,** which is either within the person's body or, more commonly, something in the external environment that will satisfy the aim.

Life instincts. The **life instincts (Eros)** are the bases for all positive or constructive aspects of human behavior. The instincts include bodily urges such as sex, hunger, and thirst, and also are reflected in the creative components of culture such as art, music, literature, cooperation, and love. The energy responsible for the life instincts is called **libido.** The most important parts of the body from which libido arises are the **erotogenic zones.** These are parts of the skin or mucous membranes that are extremely sensitive to irritation and which when manipulated in certain ways remove the irritation and produce pleasurable sensations (Hall and Lindzey, 1978). In a sense, the entire body is one large erogenous zone.

Death instincts.   For some time, Freud relied essentially on the life instincts as the basic human motivator. However, he found it increasingly difficult to explain the dark, destructive side of behavior; with so much cruelty, death, and destruction about, "man's inhumanity to man" created an explanatory problem. Freud was especially appalled by World War I and its crushing costs in human life and dignity.

As a result, he developed the concept of the **death instincts (Thanatos).** Incidentally, there is no term corresponding to libido here. Freud believed we are all born with the urge to return to an inanimate state. What is more, he postulated the death instincts to account for the dark side of human nature, from the compulsively self-destructive behavior of the neurotic, to the everyday minor cruelties we inflict on one another, to the holocausts that descend upon society from time to time. It should be noted, however, that modern psychoanalysts tend to pay scant practical attention to the death instincts, not finding the concept useful in their day-to-day encounters with patients.

STRUCTURE OF THE PERSONALITY

As Freud began to deal with an ever-increasing variety of patients, old concepts proved to be insufficient. The ideas of a conscious and an unconscious mind seemed to account for hysterics, but not for those patients who were paranoid or experienced an overwhelming sense of guilt. Freud's solution was to divide the mind into three components or structures that cut across the conscious-preconscious-unconscious regions: the id, the ego, and the superego (see Figure 3-2).

The id

The **id** represents the deep, inaccessible part of the personality. It is in direct contact with the somatic processes and is the repository for everything inherited and fixed in the person's constitution. The id has no connection with the external world and therefore may be said to be the true psychic reality. We learn about the id via the analysis of dreams and through various forms of neurotic behavior. Within the id reside the instinctual urges, in particular the sexual and aggressive instincts. The id is devoid of values, ethics, and logic. Its reason for existence is the immediate and unhampered gratification of the instincts.

The reigning goal of the id is achievement of an excitation-free state or, if that cannot be done, the lowest possible level of excitation. The id is said to obey the **pleasure principle,** which means that pleasure is good and nothing else matters. To reduce excitation and achieve pleasure, the id utilizes the **primary process.** This means that during early infancy, tension is discharged as quickly as it reaches the id. At first, this is done by immediately expending energy in motor activity (e.g., a swelling bladder leading to immediate urination). Later the id turns to another form of the primary process, in which it manufactures a mental image of whatever will reduce the tension. Thus, hunger results in a mental representation of food. This kind of thinking is neither logical, organized, nor mature. Failing the immediate attainment of an object that will satisfy the urge, the person may well hallucinate. Dreaming is an excellent example of primary-process thinking in which reality and logic fade and the most improbable and contradictory events go hand in hand.

Unfortunately for the id, dreams and hallucinations do not completely satisfy the needs of the organism. It is out of the failures of the id's primary-process mode of operation to provide real gratifications that the second component of the personality, the ego, arises.

The ego

The executive or manager of the personality might be the most apt description of the ego. The **ego** is the organized, rational, reality-oriented system of the personality. It operates according to the **reality principle** in that it defers gratification of instinctual urges until a suitable object and method are found. In doing this it uses the **secondary process,** which involves perception, learning, memory, reality testing, and the like. The ego is entirely pragmatic and without values; it simply does what will work. This does not, however, mean that the ego always takes the immediate, most direct route to hedonism. It is also charged with maintaining the integrity of the organism by any means possible. While its goal is to satisfy the id, it will do so only in the context of the demands of reality. This means that the ego must simultaneously juggle the often outrageous demands of the id, the constraints of the real world, and the prohibitions of the conscience.

The superego

The third structure of the personality, the **superego,** develops from the ego and out of the resolution of the Oedipus complex. The latter refers to the child's sexual attraction to the parent of the opposite sex, as we shall see in a moment. The superego represents the ideals and values of society as they are presented to the child through the words and actions of the parents or parental surrogates. These ideals and values are also fostered in the child through systematic rewards and punishments. That which is punished generally becomes incorporated into that part of the superego known as the **conscience.** Rewarded behavior becomes represented in the superego as the **ego-ideal.** Eventually the conscience comes to serve the purpose of punishing individuals by making them feel worthless or guilty. The ego-ideal rewards the individual by conveying a sense of pride and personal value. In summary, the job of the superego is to inform the ego of the value of morality rather than lust or expediency and to remind the person to strive toward perfection.

As a way of recalling the character and functions of the three components of the personality, consider the following word picture drawn by Geiwitz and Moursund (1979):

> Imagine a sex-starved hedonist, a black-frock-coated Puritan minister, and a totally humorless computer scientist chained together and turned loose in the world, and you have a good approximation of what Freud was trying to show us about the personality.
>
> Because they are chained together, the id, ego, and superego cannot decide to go their separate ways. They have no alternative but to adjust to one another. And the result, for better or for worse, is the adult human personality. (p. 27)

DEVELOPMENT OF PERSONALITY

Freud's patients had talked about their sexualized encounters with their parents— seductiveness, rivalries, and so forth. Even Freud found similar traces in his own life. Eventually, he realized that his patients were not so much recalling real history as they were remembering fantasies, and it was so with himself as well.

Sexual instincts and the unconscious joined to produce fantasies, and these fantasies are what Freud used to help formulate his theory of psychosexual development. To the generation at the turn of the century, the theory was appalling. To the modern reader, it may only seem odd or perhaps quaint, something to be memorized but hardly anything that could have personal application. But perhaps the modern reader is little accustomed to free-associating, recalling dreams, or spending hours on the analyst's couch producing long-forgotten fantasies. Box 3-2 lists some of the reasons why adults sometimes find the psychosexual stages so difficult to accept. Now let us turn to an examination of the specific developmental stages characteristic of us humans.

The oral stage

It is evident that a newborn infant is totally dependent on others. Just as evident is the fact that the infant's mouth, lips, and tongue are the center of existence and are intimately associated with survival. At this time, libido is largely distributed in the oral region, and sucking and swallowing become the chief methods of reducing tension and therefore achieving pleasure. This stage lasts from birth to roughly eight months of age and is known as the **oral sucking** period. At about eight months, weaning begins, the breast is withdrawn, and other foods are offered. This can be a traumatic time, especially if it is abrupt or uncaring or otherwise handled poorly. In such an event, vestiges of the oral sucking period may stay with the person throughout life.

From about eight to eighteen months the child is in what is called the **oral biting** period. The teeth have erupted, and the child now has a weapon with which to vent frustration. It is during this period that aggression begins to develop, and the child realizes his or her separateness from the mother.

The anal stage

With final weaning, pressure to develop cleanliness habits, and possibly the birth of a sibling, the child begins to face the intrusions of reality. The ego is beginning to differentiate itself from the id, and the reality principle begins to arise. This is the **anal stage** and lasts anywhere from about six months to four years of age. The chief mode of pleasure is in expelling feces and urine. It is during this stage that the battle of wills between parents and child occurs.

Toilet training is a major socialization period. The parents reward the child for urinating or defecating at the right time—for deferring gratification. They also punish or express disappointment at the child's accidents. All of this creates in the child the crude beginnings of the superego.

The child may also learn how to manipulate the parents by using elimination processes as aggressive weapons. Thus he or she may demand "potty" when none is

Box 3-2
WHY PSYCHOSEXUAL STAGES ARE PREPOSTEROUS

Some fifty years ago, J. F. Brown (1940) described a few of the reasons why psychosexual stages seem so unbelievable to the well-adjusted adult. One wonders whether the reactions of today's adults are all that different. In capsule form, the following are some of Brown's reasons:

1   Sexuality in children is considered scandalous. Anyone who studies it is a dirty-minded creature who is probably decadent, corrupt, or both.

2   We achieve adulthood only by overcoming our infantile sexual urges. We must be weaned; we must break the habit of infantile masturbation; we must renounce and repress all manner of infantile strivings. To read about and then accept the theory of psychosexuality is to reawaken all those old conflicts. So, we make fun of Freud and the psychosexual stages in order to protect ourselves from those old conflicts (see the ego defenses described later in this chapter).

3   There is a tendency to see the child as a miniature or incomplete adult. Thus, we say to ourselves, "If I were a child, I would certainly not react in those ways!"

4   More realistically, Freud probably erred in referring to oral and anal urges as sexual. They are not sexual in the *genital* sense of the word. Perhaps the adjective *libidinal* would have been more accurate.

All of these reasons are probably valid for some individuals. Yet, to label all failures to accept the legitimacy of the psychosexual stages as examples of resistance is at best questionable. Denial and repression are invoked as explanations here and the refusal to accept the stages becomes one more case of irrational behavior. This line of argument is, of course, maddening to those who are not psychoanalytically oriented. To the latter, it becomes one more instance of psychoanalysts insulating themselves against the necessity of providing hard, empirical evidence for the validity of their concepts.

available or sit for hours while an impatient parent waits for the ultimate present from a socialized child. This period is usually appropriately called the **anal expulsive stage** (approximately six months to three years of age). During the **anal retentive stage** (approximately twelve months to four years of age), the child learns the importance of controlling, retaining, and possessing feces. In fact, the realization of the ability to do all this can lead to a feeling of omnipotence. After all, the child can present feces to the parents almost as gifts—gifts that are greatly appreciated when they occur at the right time and in the right place. They can also serve as punishments by angering parents or disrupting their routine when presented at inappropriate times or places.

The resolution of the Oedipus complex is important in the development of the male child. Photograph Jim Whitmer.

The phallic stage

Somewhere around four years of age, the genital region becomes the object of eroge-nous interest. This marks the beginning of the **phallic stage,** which typically lasts until about the age of seven or eight. During this time the child's interest shifts to a narcissis-tic preoccupation with genitals. The child may touch, rub, and exhibit his or her own genitals and may show interest in the anatomy of brothers, sisters, and parents. Par-ents are "accidentally" intruded upon in the bathroom or even the bedroom. Little boys may engage in urinating contests with their peers, and little girls may suddenly become interested in "playing nurse." The child is beginning to formulate some ideas about sex, birth, and the like. These ideas may be naive or incorrect since they are, after all, ideas of children. But the child is becoming aware that babies are not made, say, in heaven but, rather, right there at home. The child is also learning that sex involves making choices among potential sexual objects. It is quite natural that in the limited world of the child, his or her choice for sexual interest becomes a readily available member of the oppo-site sex—mother, father, or a sibling.

This leads to the family "romance" and the inevitable triangle. The male child's burgeoning interest in his mother begins to annoy his father, and the mother, too, after awhile. Interrupting her bath, wanting to be around her all the time, climbing into bed (on the mother's side) in the middle of the night—these and other behaviors result in growing warnings from the father to lay off. The father has now become a fearsome rival. Threats of castration may be made ("If you don't quit that, we'll cut it off!"). The family is, then, in the midst of the **Oedipus complex.** To ward off conflict and the threat of castration (a real source of worry since he has already discovered that the little girl down the block has no penis, and that could happen to him!), the child begins to employ a process called **identification with the aggressor.** He resolves the Oedipus conflict by identifying with his father—adopting his values, goals, and even mannerisms. In an indirect fashion, by identifying with his father he can vicariously possess his mother. The final resolution of the Oedipus conflict brings with it, through the identification process, a more fully developed superego.

For the female child, the process is different. How different is not quite clear since the nature of the phallic-stage process for girls, called the **Electra complex,** was never as fully explicated by either Freud or subsequent analysts as it was for boys. Perhaps this is due to the fact that historically so many analysts have been men! ·

In essence, Freud's description of the Electra complex centered on the obvious fact that a girl lacks a penis. Therefore, she cannot fear castration; it has already happened. Instead, she sets about deciding who did it. She decides it was her mother and begins to hate her for what has been done. (Many analysts feel this attribution is ultimately responsible for the ambivalence many females have toward their mothers for the rest of their lives.) At the same time she starts blaming her mother, she increases her love for her father. Psychoanalysts often assert that her love for her father is heavily dependent on **penis envy.** Some believe that a woman, therefore, goes through life behaving in ways that reflect her dismay over having lost the penis: search for power, envy of the male role, or personal devaluation because of "imperfect" anatomy (even a baby becomes symbolic of regaining the lost penis). Eventually, however, the girl realizes that her loss is permanent and shifts her identification to the mother. Contemporary feminists hotly reject this notion and assert that it just illustrates psychoanalysts' lack of understanding of female psychology, or else they chalk it up to male chauvinism. What women envy about the male, they assert, is not his penis but the power and freedom society has conferred upon him. See Box 3-3 for some further ideas about this.

The latency period

Somewhere between the ages of five and six, the child enters the **latency period,** which will last until about twelve or thirteen years of age. This is a period of sexual quiet during which all things sexual are inhibited or even repressed. The resolution of the Oedipus/Electra situation has been traumatic, and the child wants to get away from it all. In the case of girls, the latency period is less sexually barren and usually shorter (perhaps boys continue to fear castration; girls have little to worry about on that score). There is little interest in the opposite sex. Boys play with boys, and any interest in girls is likely to take the form of teasing and tormenting. Above all, boys want no displays of affection. Latency is basically a period of relative sexual quiescence–a lull before the storm, as it were.

The genital stage

The biochemical-hormonal changes that usher in puberty are reflected in the **genital stage,** the final stage of psychosexual development as described by Freud. Both the aggressive and sexual instincts become active, and there is again a focus on the opposite sex. Now, however, sexuality is much less autoerotic and narcissistic. Thus, increased sexual interest and excitability are accompanied by the "ethereal" love and romance of adolescence. When the genital stage first dawns, however, the threat of castration is still present, so initial selections are often homosexual in nature. This may be seen in such a phenomenon as mutual masturbation. Gradually, however, the focus

Box 3-3
FEMININE PSYCHOLOGY—FREUDIAN STYLE

To many it has always seemed that Freud's ideas about women were focused almost exclusively on the *fact* that they lack a penis and on the *hypothesis* that this leads to penis envy. Because the woman never adequately resolved her Oedipal problems, her superego failed to develop properly, Freud claimed. It is almost as if she remains angry and unfulfilled because of her presumed castration. She becomes narcissistic, vain, and envious. If she is lucky she will later marry and have a baby (ideally a boy), which is really a penis substitute. As Bootzin and Acocella (1988) summarize the Freudian view:

> . . . (the) woman is morally feeble, culturally unproductive, and somehow "other"—a variation on the standard of masculinity, a deviation from the norm. Thus, the little girl's perception of herself as castrated, and her consequent envy, is responsible for her inferiority. (p. 45)

But as early as 1926, Karen Horney somewhat sarcastically suggested that Freud was not really in a very good position to understand little girls. Furthermore, she argued that little girls do not see their lack of a penis as being evidence of inferiority. It is little boys who react that way. And they grow up to be men who then try to force this idea of inferiority onto women (Horney, 1967).

More recently, theorists such as Nancy Chodorow (1978) and Carol Gilligan (1982) concede that the child's attachment to its mother is critical for the development of masculine or feminine outlooks. But boys and girls show differing patterns of attachment even though in the beginning they each regard the mother as the primary love object during early infancy. Later, the girl must adopt the feminine role and the boy must become masculine. For boys, an enduring value becomes a sense of being separate from others. For girls, there is not nearly so strong a need to see themselves as separate. Thus, the girl does not grow up to see herself as inferior or enmeshed in an eternal search for a penis. Rather, she becomes an adult who develops much stronger needs for close attachments to others than is true for so many men.

shifts to a concern with heterosexual relationships, courting, marriage, and raising a family. Thus, from a Freudian perspective the ultimate aim of the genital stage is mature, adult sexuality. The narcissism, autoeroticism, and continuous seeking of immediate pleasure must be exchanged for loving and caring for others, for work, for postponement of gratification, and for responsibility. In this way, the expression of the sexual instincts that begins with sucking and swallowing culminates in the maturity of adulthood, at least ideally. This may not be the outcome for those persons who have been over- or under-gratified during earlier psychosexual stages.

ANXIETY

Although the concept of **anxiety** has always played a central role in psychoanalytic theory, Freud revised his views on it several times. His final notion was that anxiety is utilized by the ego as a signal of impending danger.

Reality anxiety

Reality anxiety is a response to a threat from the real world. For example, if I become anxious as I see a car bearing down on me, this is reality anxiety. This type of anxiety is basically the same as fear and serves to warn me that I had better do something to evade the danger. Of course, in some instances the anxiety can be so strong as to actually impede the individual's ability to cope.

Neurotic anxiety

Neurotic anxiety is a response to the threatened eruption of an id impulse into consciousness. Very early we learn that expressing our sexual or aggressive instincts directly will lead to punishment or threats from our parents. Initially this is a reality kind of anxiety. But as development proceeds, we may become apprehensive whenever the ego discerns instinctual threats from the id.

Moral anxiety

Moral anxiety stems from threat of punishment from the superego. It is expressed in feelings of guilt or shame. As an id impulse threatens to gain gratification in an "immoral" fashion, the superego responds accordingly.

It should be noted that all these forms of anxiety are experienced similarly by the ego; the difference lies in the source and not in the quality of the emotion. In addition it may be obvious that reality anxiety, unless it is overwhelming, can help us deploy perception, memory, and learning in the service of avoiding the environmental threat. But what about threats from within, that is, moral and neurotic anxiety? Internal threats can be difficult to manage, all the more so when we consider that the ego's job is not just to satisfy reality threats or demands from the superego. Somehow the id must also be handled. Id impulses never go away; they leave only when the organism dies. Therefore, how does the ego handle the constant and contradictory demands of id and superego? Freud decided that id impulses can either be prevented from reaching awareness or distorted so that the superego is fooled. The particular ways this is accomplished bring us to the next topic: the **ego defenses** or, as they are sometimes called, the **defense mechanisms.**

EGO DEFENSES

All of the mechanisms described in the following paragraphs were considered by Freud to be defensive because they distort or falsify experience and utilize energy that could be put to use in more rational ways. In addition, all defense mechanisms are similar in that they are employed unconsciously. Most of us resort to one or another of these at various times. Neurotic individuals tend to use them much more frequently and sometimes focus on one, although rarely at the complete exclusion of others.

Repression

Repression is the most fundamental and at the same time the simplest of all the ego defenses. It is an active, unconscious process that results in the banishment of impulses into the unconscious, and is involuntary in the sense that the person does not consciously say, "Aha, this is threatening so I better repress it." Repression can also prevent what is in the unconscious from becoming conscious. However, it is not just the simple, selective forgetting of unpleasant experiences. To be repressed, a memory or impulse must be perceived as truly threatening to the integrity and functioning of the person. Also there are marked individual differences in what is regarded as extremely threatening. For some it may be assault or rape, for others a simple reprimand from an authority figure.

Finally, as previously noted, repressed material is never destroyed. Consequently, it may return to consciousness when resistance is lowered (e.g., during illness or sleep) or when instinctual impulses become stronger (e.g., at puberty). The repressed material may sometimes reappear as slips of the tongue, dreams, or other behaviors.

Projection

Projection allows the individual to unconsciously attribute his or her unacceptable impulses, thoughts, or actions to another person. For example, the reaction "I envy you" is transformed into "You envy me." This is a relatively common mechanism in which an internal threat becomes an external threat—one the ego feels more equipped to handle. The true emotion or thought is expressed, but the object changes. For instance, the paranoid schizophrenic who feels other men on the ward are trying to seduce him may be projecting his own unacceptable impulses onto them.

Reaction formation

In the case of **reaction formation,** "I dislike you" becomes "I admire you." The conscious feeling or cognition is the opposite of the unconscious one. Again, this is a method of handling unacceptable impulses. Often, it is assumed that strongly held or expressed attitudes are reaction formations. Thus, the fire-and-brimstone proponents of abstinence from alcohol may, in reality, be fighting off their own drinking urges. It must be remembered, however, that the uncritical tendency to label *any* strongly held opinion as a reaction formation can be a dangerous one.

Displacement

Through **displacement** an instinctual impulse is deflected from its true object to a less threatening one. Angry at his wife for the meal being served, the husband picks a fight with his son or abuses the dog.

Rationalization

Failures, inadequacies, and the like, are powerful threats to the psychic equilibrium of some individuals. Rather than accept the explicit message in failure, these persons cast about for "rational" explanations. This ego defense is called **rationalization.** Successful rationalizations are ones that have the ring of truth but are actually not correct. They are face-saving devices. An example would be, "I could have won the race today had the track not been wet." The track was wet, perhaps, but somebody else was faster on that wet track.

Regression

When a person runs into a situation fraught with potential trauma or failure, the solution can be a retreat to an earlier stage of development or mode of behavior. Such **regression** is typically to a psychosexual stage during which gratifications were more readily attainable. The executive who runs into an insoluble problem that threatens his or her status may become dependent. A child facing the trauma of the first grade may begin behaving in a much less mature fashion.

Intertwined with regression is the concept of **fixation.** If the child is overgratified or undergratified at any particular psychosexual stage, the result may be a fixation at that stage. Then, later, when the individual is frustrated in achieving gratification, there may be regression to the stage at which fixation occurred.

Sublimation

Not everyone would regard **sublimation** as a defense mechanism. However, Freud talked about it as a diversion of libido from its sexual goals to loftier, social ones. In many ways, this is a healthy mechanism since the sexual energy is not simply expended but is expended to the benefit of society. For example, anal impulses become diverted to creating sculpture. At a cultural level, law and order could be viewed as sublimations of anal eroticism. Perhaps even the violence of a football game is good since it allows the expression of hostility in socially sanctioned ways.

Some additional defensive reactions are described in Table 3-1.

NATURE OF ADJUSTMENT

Freud, like most other theorists, regarded the ability to take pleasure in love and work as the mark of the adjusted personality. This realization of one's potential depends heavily on experiences during psychosexual development. The particular stage at which difficulties are encountered will leave specific marks on the adult personality. As a general rule, the earlier the level, the more severe the effects on adjustment. For example, the child who is massively frustrated at the oral stage will likely develop much more severe problems in adapting than the individual whose problems occur at the phallic stage. In other cases, the child may regress to an earlier stage in the face of threat or become fixated at a stage during which pleasures were extensive.

TABLE 3-1   Additional defensive reactions

Mechanism	Example
Denial of reality. Protecting self from unpleasant reality by refusal to perceive or face it.	A smoker concludes that evidence linking cigarette use to health problems is scientifically worthless.
Fantasy. Gratifying frustated desires by imaginary achievements.	A socially inept and inhibited young man imagines himself chosen by a group of women to provide them with sexual satisfaction.
Emotional insulation. Reducing ego involvement by protective withdrawal and passivity.	A child separated from her parents because of illness and lengthy hospitalization becomes emotionally unresponsive and apathetic.
Intellectualization (isolation). Cutting off affective charge from hurtful situations or separating incompatible attitudes by logic-tight compartments.	A prisoner on death row awaiting execution resists appeals on his behalf and coldly insists that the letter of the law be followed.
Undoing. Atoning for or magically trying to dispel unacceptable desires or acts.	A teenager who feels guilty about masturbation ritually touches door knobs a prescribed number of times following each occurrence of the act.
Overcompensation. Covering up felt weaknesses by emphasizing some desirable characteristic or making up for frustration in one area by overgratification in another.	A dangerously overweight woman goes on eating binges when she feels neglected by her husband.
Acting out. Engaging in antisocial or excessive behavior without regard to negative consequences as a way of dealing with emotional stress.	An unhappy, frustrated sales representative has several indiscriminate affairs without regard to the negative effects of the behavior.
Splitting. Viewing oneself or others as *all* good or bad without integrating positive or negative qualities of the person into the evaluation. That is, reacting to others in an "all or none" manner rather than considering the full range of their qualities.	A conflicted manager does not recognize individual qualities or characteristics of her employees. Instead, she views them as all good or all bad; seeing most of them as all bad.

Many of the character traits of the adult are sublimations of impulses or reaction formations against them. Whether these traits represent sublimations, reaction formations, fixations, or regressions, they are predictable from the nature of the individual's psychosexual history (see Table 3-2). Remnants of the psychosexual stages exist in all of us; achievement of the total maturity that characterizes the genital stage is only an ideal.

Conflict is at the root of neurosis. The instinctual demands of the id constantly seek expression, and as the ego becomes aware of the possibility of them, neurotic anxiety is experienced. This neurotic anxiety impels the ego to take defensive measures. If the ego is strong, the threats are not serious. But a weak ego, born out of inadequate psychosexual development, will make necessary the use of one or more of the ego defenses. The extent to which these defenses are employed is a measure of the seriousness of the id impulses or the weakness of the ego (or both). Heavy or continuous dependence upon these defenses uses up energy that could better be spent on adjusted, healthy activities.

All forms of neurosis are methods the individual uses to ward off feared id impulses. The woman who fears leaving the house is said by the analyst to be avoiding situations in which sexual impulses from the id might find expression. To stay home is to avoid temptation. The severe paranoid who believes "certain" people out there are planning homosexual attacks on him is really projecting his own unconscious homosexual impulses and thereby defending against those unacceptable impulses. In addition, a demanding superego can compound the ego's problem through its insistence on perfection. Moral anxiety experienced as guilt or shame may push the individual into added defensive postures or symptoms.

As Hall (1954) has pointed out, the fear of instinctual discharges is based upon reality. That is, the individual has learned that instinctual gratification is associated with punishment. For example, if a young boy is caught masturbating and is threatened with horrible consequences (e.g., castration), is beaten, or simply notices he has thrown the whole household into turmoil, he may experience neurotic anxiety. All of this reinforces the importance of the psychosexual stages in producing a healthy or a disturbed personality, as the case may be. A calm but firm reaction by the parents to the child's awakening genital impulses sets the stage for a healthy resolution of the Oedipal situation, whereas severe punishment, wild reactions, and the like result in the child learning to fear his or her sexual instincts. The outcome, depending on the severity of the parents' reactions, may be heavy use of defense mechanisms and neurotic strategies to avoid those feared instincts.

TABLE 3-2 *Some potential relationships between the psychosexual stages and adult character traits*

Stage	Adult Extensions	Sublimations	Reaction Formations
Oral	Smoking, eating, kissing, oral hygiene, drinking, chewing gum	Seeking knowledge, humor, wit, sarcasm, being a food or wine expert	Speech purist, food faddist, prohibitionist, dislike of milk
Anal	Notable interest in one's bowel movements, love of bathroom humor, extreme messiness	Interest in painting or sculpture, being overly giving, great interest in statistics	Extreme disgust with feces, fear of dirt, prudishness, irritability
Phallic	Heavy reliance on masturbation, flirtatiousness, expressions of virility	Interest in poetry, love of love, interest in acting, striving for success	Puritanical attitude toward sex, excessive modesty

IMPLICATIONS FOR BEHAVIOR CHANGE

An unreasonable fear, an excessive character trait, a propensity for rationalization— all are signs of a deeper problem. Thus, the fear itself is not the problem, but rather a superficial manifestation of an underlying conflict. What we are interested in most of all is not the reaction formations of someone with puritanical attitudes toward sex but what the reaction formation signifies about the nature of the unconscious conflict of which it is symptomatic. The psychoanalyst will apply assessment procedures, analyses of symbolism, and interpretations of the psychopathology of everyday life in an attempt to understand the nature of the conflicts.

Goals of therapy

It would be wrong to assume that the ultimate goal of psychoanalysis is the simple removal of discrete symptoms, although that is part of it. Rather, what Freud tried to accomplish in therapy was a general strengthening of a person's ego so that instinctual impulses could be brought under control. In addition, as was noted earlier, Freud talked about enhancing the individual's capacity for love and work. The broad goal, then, became one of facilitating the sublimation of aggressive and sexual impulses. In psychoanalysis, one can learn about the nature of inner needs. But more than that, one can learn to direct those needs rather than be directed by them.

Methods of therapy

Over the years, there have been numerous variations in psychoanalytic treatment. In nearly all, however, the basic emphasis has been on the dissolution of repressions through the reanalysis of previous experience; insight remains an important tool.

The therapeutic circumstance.   Traditional psychoanalysis has always been a time-consuming, lengthy process. Typically, the patient is seen four or five times per week, and the analysis can last for two or three years. The patient often reclines on a couch and is instructed to relax while the analyst sits in a chair behind the patient (see Figure 3-3). However, modern analysts often dispense with the couch and have the patient sit in a chair beside the desk.

Free association.   The cardinal technique of psychoanalysis is free association. The patient, to remain in therapy, must say anything and everything that comes to mind, no matter how obscene, embarrassing, illogical, or seemingly trivial. Free-associating is not easy and often takes some time for the patient to learn. It is from this uncensored stream of consciousness that Freud felt insights into the nature of the patient's problems were possible.

Dream analysis.   A technique related to free association is the analysis of dreams. When the patient sleeps, the ego relaxes its control over unconscious material. As a result, dreams are often especially revealing of the unconscious. Patients are encouraged

FIGURE 3-3   Freud's office (authenticated).   News Service

to report their dreams. They will then be asked to free-associate to the dreams, and depending upon the point therapy has reached, the analyst may discuss or interpret the meaning of the dreams.

Interpretation.   Later in therapy, once the analyst feels the nature of the patient's problems is clear, the process of interpretation by the therapist will begin. Through the therapist's interpretations the patient is enabled to recognize the unconscious meaning of certain thoughts, actions, or wishes.

Interpretation is a way of facilitating the recognition of that which the patient had formerly not recognized and which was creating problems. Interpretation helps provide some connection, meaning, or reason that was not conscious but which was guiding the patient's thoughts, feelings, or behavior.

Resistance to analysis.   Insight—the realization of the relationship between one's current problems or behaviors and their unconscious origins—never comes easily. The same forces that have led to neurotic problems will also conspire to make the

CASE STUDY

The following case study of David W. is presented to flesh out some of the previously discussed concepts and methods. Although the individual described was seen for a series of therapy sessions, he would hardly be considered any more neurotic than most of us. He was seen in a university counseling center, and his stated reason for requesting the initial appointment had to do with vocational testing and career information. However, during the screening interview the counselor decided that he seemed to be seeking some sort of personal insight rather than just vocational counseling. Consequently he was referred to a clinical psychologist on staff.

It should be noted that while this case will be interpreted psychoanalytically, the actual therapy is not representative of classical psychoanalysis. It is, instead, what might be called a short-term, problem-oriented therapy. Rather than a strict Freudian form of analysis, it is what most professionals would describe as psychoanalytically oriented.

David W was a twenty-year-old chemistry major with a 3.7 grade-point average. He was vaguely discontented and had a sense of foreboding about the prospect of becoming a chemist. The field was easy for him, but he somehow did not feel right about it. The following information was elicited as the clinician and David explored the bases for David's discontent.

David was an only child. His parents were both college graduates who married when each was thirty-four. His father was a chemical engineer. His mother had been the office supervisor with the same engineering firm at the time of their marriage. She quit work immediately and set about having a family and running the home. Prior to David's birth she suffered two miscarriages. Subsequently she was advised by her physician not to have any more children.

In many respects David's childhood was typical and uneventful. He grew up in the suburbs of a large midwestern city, graduated third in his high school class, and dated frequently although never the same girl for any length of time. He was a second-string guard on the basketball team and was president of the science club. He attended the state university because, "It was just assumed that I would go to school where Dad did." Similarly, "I always knew I would major in chemistry. That's the way I grew up."

But once David was in college, things began to unravel a little. Although he did well in his chemistry and related classes, the courses that really excited him were the ones in literature and art history. He got a job on the school paper and soon began writing a column of reviews on movies and local plays. His mother was quite pleased with all this, but he sensed that his father was upset. That "sense" crystallized one weekend when David indicated he was moving out of his father's old fraternity and into an apartment with some friends on the paper. His father was furious and screamed, "If you have to work on that damned paper, at least you could be a sportswriter!"

There seemed to be a growing conflict in David's life, symbolized by his ambiva-

(continued)

CASE STUDY *(continued)*

lence about a chemistry major and reflected in his parents' differing views about his interests. But what lay behind all this? David, although obviously quite bright, was at a loss to explain his conflicting interests and his developing problems with his father.

Clearly, there must be psychic determinants of David's conflicts and discontent. His inability to come to grips with them even after a great deal of thought over the past several months suggests they are unconscious. Although a little simple encouragement enabled him to recall some animosity toward his father and a few earlier episodes of disagreement (preconscious material), it seemed fairly pedestrian in quality. As the sessions moved along, however, a clearer picture began to emerge.

During the first eighteen months or so following David's birth, his mother was extremely supportive. She devoted herself to his care and well-being. He was breastfed, and she was quite tolerant and flexible during the weaning period. She approached the beginning of his toilet training with a similar attitude. In fact David's earliest memories were of sitting on a potty while his mother read stories to him. She would also go through the comic pages or show him reproductions of paintings. All in all, David recalled these first four or five years with a real sense of warmth and security. His memories of his father during this period were quite vague. Apparently, this was a time of financial struggle for the family, and his father worked long hours and was frequently on the road troubleshooting company problems. This meant that David's primary interactions were with his mother.

It is also interesting to speculate about some of the origins of David's artistic and literary interests—interests that later figured prominently in his conflict with his father. David's mother was very interested in art, literature, and the like. These interests, along with David, occupied her life during the early years when her husband was so often gone. The warm, sympathetic relationship between David and his mother explains how David's aesthetic inclinations could have taken root. Recall that his earliest memories were of toilet training, mother, happiness, stories, and pictures. From a child's point of view, these first few years were probably very nearly idyllic.

But when David was five or six, his father assumed an executive position at the home office. This meant fewer trips, more time at home, and a generally more visible family role. David's father became someone who actively intruded into his life, not just someone who brought presents after a trip or who played with him but almost never seriously punished him. All of this took place just about the time David was beginning the phallic stage.

David recalled how his father would insist he go outside and play rather than stay indoors and thumb through books or magazines. He also remembered a few arguments his parents had over his being a "mamma's boy." His father would demand that he go to bed on time and not pester his mother to read him stories. David likewise dimly recalled a scene where he had apparently been playing with his genitals while lying in bed early in the morning. Normally his mother awakened him, but this time his father came in the room. When he saw what David was doing, he exploded with anger and threatened, "I'll cut that

(continued)

CASE STUDY *(continued)*

damn thing off if you ever do that again!"
David also remembered that he would cry
when the babysitter came over on those
few nights his parents would go to a party
or to the movies. His mother would want
to stay home, but his father always insisted
they have some time alone. A final episode
that David recalled had a clear Oedipal
theme. He and his mother were taking a
nap on her bed in the middle of the afternoon. His father came home early and
found David snuggled up against his
mother. That led to a stormy scene that ter-
rified David. His father loudly proclaimed
that his mother was turning him into a little "fairy," that he should be out playing
football or something like that.

From roughly this period on, David's
memories became rather usual, stereotyped affairs. His relationship with his father improved, and he could recall playing
on a Little League team his father coached.
He also began to show an interest in his
father's work and wanted to go with him to
the plant so he could "see what Daddy did."
It would seem, then, that David had resolved the Oedipus complex in the classic
fashion by identifying with the aggressor.

Until the therapy sessions, David had
generally repressed most of the foregoing.
Repression is a relatively simple ego defense. Because the conflicts that surfaced
mainly in the phallic stage were not over-
powering ones, his ego did not find it
necessary to resort to more complex
defenses such as projection or reaction formation. His ego was a relatively strong one.
He obviously was above average in intelligence, and his development had been
marked by security and love. It was not until

the phallic stage, with his discovery of genital urges coupled with the struggle with his
father, that unconscious id impulses began
to pose a threat. Given that strong ego and
a generally supportive family milieu, David
was able to cope for some time.

Only during his college years did the
repression begin to dissolve a bit, resulting in feelings of alienation, discontent, and
misgivings about his chemistry decision. It
was as if the reality and finality of his career choice now confronted him. The repressed longings for literary, aesthetic
experiences that had been submerged as
a way of solving the Oedipal situation began to break through. Some moderate
pangs of neurotic anxiety signaled the return of the conflict.

Blessed with a relatively strong ego,
David sought therapy, not as a debilitated
neurotic but as a coping person striving to
control his future realistically. His ego, cautious executive that it was, eased him into
therapy obliquely by first seeking vocational counseling. Parenthetically, it turned
out that his mother had sensed his conflict
and had subtly urged him to talk things
over with an "adviser."

With therapy (which lasted roughly six
months), David was able to achieve insight
into his conflicts. This, in turn, allowed him
to face his father and, through some rocky
discussions, ultimately resolve matters.
David decided to remain in chemistry. It appeared that once the unconscious determinants of his feelings had been fully aired
and understood, his commitment to
science was strengthened, and his literary
flair became the foundation for a rewarding set of secondary interests.

patient resist the therapeutic process. As the patient's unconscious is stirred and as defenses are threatened, resistance arises. Resistance is expressed in many ways. Some patients begin to miss appointments or forget to pay their bills. Others start having difficulty free-associating or dismiss interpretations as trivial or silly. Or they may spend a great deal of time discussing inflation, the oil shortage, or supply-side economics, all weighty topics but hardly what they are paying for. However, when the resistance begins to interfere, it must be analyzed by the therapist and dissolved.

Transference. Transference, an important element of nearly every successful analysis, occurs when the patient responds to the analyst as if the latter were some figure out of the patient's childhood. Both positive and negative feelings can be transferred. The therapy room, then, becomes an arena where old reactions and conflicts come alive. Transference provides important clues regarding the nature of childhood difficulties and also allows the therapist to interpret its nature to the patient. Statements of admiration, anger, or dislike are examples of transference. A patient may attack the usefulness of therapy or, conversely, express great admiration for the analyst's skill. The patient's transference reactions to the analyst or to the current situation are heavily influenced by the patient's biases. These reactions often appear unrealistic to an outside observer because they reflect emotional residues from the patient's past. The analyst's task is to search out such reactions in order to achieve a deeper understanding of the patient's problems, but not to take them personally. The latter is an error referred to as **countertransference.**

Working through. Contrary to what many laypeople think, interpretation is not a one-time thing. In example after example, the analyst must repeat interpretations and identify over and over, in one life area after another, the conflicts and motives that are fueling the patient's neurotic adjustment. Resistance and transference must be worked through repeatedly. Thus, insight comes not as a flash but as a result of laborious, repetitive working through.

SUMMARY

■ Psychoanalytic theory and practice grew out of the brilliant insights of Sigmund Freud in the late nineteenth century in Victorian Vienna. Freud's collaboration with Breuer and his clinical work treating hysterics were critical to the development of psychoanalysis.

■ Two crucial assumptions of Freudian theory are psychic determinism (the idea that everything we do, think, or feel is determined) and unconscious motivation.

■ Freud viewed the basis of all activity as residing in systems of energy. Specifically, he believed that we are motivated by two sets of instincts. The life instincts (Eros) are responsible for everything positive in our lives, whereas the death instincts (Thanatos) represent the destructive side of our personalities.

■ The structure of the personality consists of the id, the ego, and the superego. The id is the primitive, unconscious aspect that demands immediate gratification. The ego develops out of the failures of the id in realistically guiding the individual toward gratification. The ego serves an executive role in the personality by mediating between the demands of the id, the conscience, and reality. The superego is the conscience and represents the introjection of cultural values and prohibitions as conveyed by the parents.

■ The individual's personality is shaped by a series of psychosexual stages. Each stage is characterized by an emphasis on a particular erotogenic zone (oral, anal, phallic, or genital). The latency period, a stage of little apparent sexual interest, precedes the genital stage. The specific experiences the individual undergoes in each stage shape his or her personality and help determine the degree of adjustment or neurosis.

■ Anxiety was viewed by Freud as a signal to the ego of impending danger. Reality anxiety is a signal of danger from the environment. Neurotic anxiety suggests that an impulse from the id is about to erupt into consciousness. Moral anxiety is experienced as feelings of guilt or shame prompted from the superego.

■ The great sensitivity of Freud was especially apparent in his delineation of the methods the ego uses in dealing with neurotic anxiety. These are the ego defenses. Several were described, including repression, projection, reaction formation, displacement, rationalization, regression, and sublimation. All ego defenses are employed unconsciously and are ways of thwarting the impulses of the id.

■ Psychoanalytic theory has a number of implications for adjustment. For example, the particular way one negotiates the psychosexual stages leaves its mark on adjustment patterns. Both excessive gratification and excessive frustration can shape the nature of adult character traits as well as neurotic adjustments. The characteristic roles of id, ego, and superego were discussed in relation to adjustment.

■ Psychoanalysis is also a method of treatment based on the view of symptoms as signs of an unresolved internal conflict. The ultimate goal of psychoanalysis is to provide the person with insight into the nature of the unconscious conflict.

■ The methods of psychoanalytic therapy were briefly described, including free association, dream analysis, interpretation, analysis of resistance, transference, and working through.

■ A case history was presented to illustrate several features of psychoanalytic theory and therapy.

CHAPTER 4

PSYCHOANALYTIC THEORY II

Dissent and Revision

When Freud broke with Breuer in 1894, he began a period of intellectual loneliness and isolation which did not end until 1902 when a group of young doctors started meeting with him to learn the practices of psychoanalysis (E. Jones, 1955). This marked the beginning of the famous Vienna Psycho-Analytical Society.

The people Freud attracted were people of considerable intellectual power. As time went on, a number of them detected what they regarded as weaknesses, omissions, or errors in orthodox Freudian theory and practice. Freud tolerated a great deal of "discussion" from his colleagues but members who presented notions that departed "too far" from psychoanalytic doctrine were asked to leave.

Revisionists attacked Freud on many fronts. In particular, his ideas about the reigning importance of libido and sexuality were disputed. There also were attempts to reinterpret his description and explanation of the Oedipus complex. Others wished to alter his notions about the unconscious. To Freud, these were key concepts that could not be revised without seriously impairing the integrity of psychoanalysis. Three of the most famous of these early dissenters were Alfred Adler, Carl Jung, and Otto Rank.

In the following pages, some of the more important ideas and concepts of Freud's earlier critics will be presented along with more recent developments in psychoanalytic theory.

INDIVIDUAL PSYCHOLOGY

Alfred Adler had strong opinions about many things. He was greatly impressed by Freud's work, and this prompted him to become a charter member of the Vienna Psycho-Analytical Society. But in 1911 he was asked to present his views to the Society and was vehemently criticized by the other members. He subsequently resigned as the group's

Alfred Adler

Alfred Adler was born in 1870 in Penzig, Austria, a suburb of Vienna. There were six children; Adler was the second son. His father was a grain merchant, and the family was fairly comfortable financially. During his childhood, he was dogged by chronic illness and was a weak, physically inept child. His early years were also marked by hostile sibling relationships and mediocrity in school. All these elements undoubtedly played a strong role in the subsequent development of his theoretical ideas and in his conflicts with Freud.

Adler was a very independent, almost radical individual. He was a political being who loved to debate the social and governmental issues of the day. He was also a rather argumentative person and could be a formidable advocate for the weak and downtrodden. His distaste for running with the crowd was, perhaps, symbolized by his conversion from the Jewish faith to Protestantism.

Adler received his medical degree in 1895 and for a time practiced ophthalmology. He soon began to function as a psychiatrist and

president, and a few months later officially ended his affiliation with Freudian psychoanalysis.

Much evidence suggests that the break between Adler and Freud was wide and bitter. His reasons for breaking with Freud centered around what he perceived as Freud's overemphasis on the sexual instincts and underemphasis on the ego defenses. Adler saw the individual as shaped by social and familial factors. Basically, Freud accepted biological determinism as reflected in instinctual energy. In recent years there has been renewed interest in the value and utility of Adler's ideas. The following sections will present some of the more important and basic concepts of **individual psychology** (Adler, 1924).

Inferiority and compensation

Adler's earliest theoretical contributions were the notion of **organ inferiority** and resultant **compensation**. Adler became interested in the reason a person becomes afflicted with one illness rather than another and why a specific area of the body is affected rather than another. Initially, he felt that the site of illness was determined by a basic inferiority or weakness in that region, perhaps an inherited abnormality of development. Adler also noted that many individuals afflicted with an inferior characteristic eventually begin to compensate for their weakness. For example, the person with a minor speech impediment becomes a speech major or an announcer. The frail, muscularly weak person takes up weight lifting. Basically, then, an inferior organ system can lead to compensations. Although all of this may sound rather organic, Adler was more concerned with a person's attitude toward a defect than with the defect itself.

A bit later, Adler specifically embraced psychological or social inferiorities in addition to inferiorities resulting from organic or bodily defects. Thus, being born into

around 1902 joined Freud's circle. In 1911 he severed his relationship with Freud. As his professional stature grew, he was able to found his own psychoanalytic group, the Society for Individual Psychology. Subsequently, he became a leader in the child guidance movement and therefore could be regarded as one of the first community psychiatrists.

In the 1920s he spent a great deal of time lecturing in Europe and the United States. In 1934 he moved to New York City and continued to influence numerous social workers, clinical psychologists, and psychiatrists. He died in 1937 in Aberdeen, Scotland, while on a lecture tour.

An excellent source book of Adlerian concepts and methods is the edited volume by Ansbacher and Ansbacher (1956). Biographical material may be found in Bottome (1957). A succinct description of the man and his ideas has been written by Ansbacher (1977). Manaster and Corsini (1982) have written an introductory-level work.

Alfred Adler
Bettmann Archive

a family of limited financial means could set the stage for feelings of inferiority. A belief that one is not bright enough could likewise cause inferiority reactions. Adler also asserted that all of us, by our very nature are prone to develop feelings of inferiority. The human being is born weak and helpless and without a prolonged period of dependence on others would die. For a relatively long time during infancy and childhood, our world is peopled by "superior" adults who pick us up and haul us around in the most powerful of ways. Even more important, they can outthink us. Is it any wonder, then, that we learn to perceive ourselves as inferior and then set about compensating for our weaknesses? In many instances, compensation is a healthy reaction that serves to move us toward the achievement of our potential. Unfortunately, the inability to develop successful compensations can lead to an **inferiority complex.**

Striving for superiority

Eventually, Adler came to the conclusion that the basic motivation we all share is a **striving for superiority.** This is a drive that propels us toward perfection. It grows out of our need to compensate for our feelings of inferiority and represents an attempt to attain power or strength so that we can better control the environment.

It is interesting to trace Adler's thinking over the years as to what constitutes the essential human motive. Originally, he emphasized aggression. A bit later, this was replaced by the "will to power." This, in turn, evolved into a striving for superiority, which actually meant a striving for perfection, completion, or overcoming. His theorizing went from aggression to power to superiority. He considered this striving for superiority as innate. The drive is innate, but each person puts on it the individual stamp of an idiosyncratic personality.

Social interest

A later addition to Adler's theory was the concept of social interest (Adler, 1939). At times, however, it seems that his ideas here were as much products of his political views as anything. Nevertheless, Adler regarded **social interest** as a predisposition, nurtured by experience, to contribute to society. Even more, it is a feeling for others. Thus, again, we see that Adler moved from a belief that people are driven by a need for power and domination to a wish for personal superiority and finally to a desire to subordinate their own needs in favor of the greater good. We have, then, the socialization of superiority into a goal of a perfect society. Social interest develops in the context of family relationships and other formative experiences. In some cases, however, these experiences thwart the development of social interest. Indeed, the neurotic person has not yet learned to substitute interest in others for the compensatory striving for superiority.

Style of life

To overcome feelings of inferiority, a person develops a **style of life.** Adler's definition of style of life varied over the years. For example, Ansbacher and Ansbacher (1956) report such definitions as self or ego, one's own personality, the unity of personality, individuality, the method of facing problems, and the wish to contribute toward life. This principle of style of life gives uniqueness to each personality. All of us struggle to overcome our feelings of infantile helplessness. We all pursue the same basic goal, but none of us take exactly the same route.

Adler felt that by the age of five years or so, the individual's style of life has been essentially determined. Our family relationships and other important experiences have by then provided us a basic style that will characterize us throughout life. Of course, new experiences will add embellishments, but the basic structure has been molded. Whether we shall be aggressive or passive, intellectual or athletic, or whether we shall depend on a weak stomach to get us out of trouble has been determined. Our weaknesses, either real or fancied, will be crucial here.

Development of personality

In another important departure from traditional Freudian theory, Adler emphasized not only the relationship between parents and child but also such variables as family size, relationships among siblings, and the child's ordinal position in the family. Any of these factors can, in certain instances, lead to distortions of what life is really like and how goals must be pursued. Such a mistaken style of life can become the essence of neurosis.

The pampered child.   Adler saw pampering as a major determinant of maladjustment. A pampered child may learn only to make demands without ever really acquiring the ability to cope with frustration. Such a child develops a style of life of always expecting things. As almost always happens, things eventually go awry and the child (or adult by then) encounters problems and barriers and may react by retreating. Not having learned to overcome, the individual withdraws to avoid feelings of inferiority.

According to Adler, the order in which children in the family are born significantly affects their psychological development.
Photograph Jean-Claude LeJeune.

Such people do not learn to cooperate, to plan, or to become responsible. They often become egocentric and their immaturity is reflected in their neurotic style.

The rejected child. Rejected children come to perceive the world as a hostile, threatening place. Fighting for their rights becomes the preferred style of life. Such people are often antagonistic and difficult to live with. Frequently, they defeat their own purposes by being hostile and uncooperative. The basis of rejection may vary; it may be a physical defect, an unhappy marriage, financial problems in the family, and so forth. The rejection may be overt or it may be subtle; there may be physical brutality or psychological abuse. A sense of distrust may then plague the child throughout life. Often such children become delinquents or criminals.

Ordinal position. Adler believed that whether one is an only child, the eldest child, or a middle child can have profound effects on the style of life. Only children are especially vulnerable to pampering. They are likely to receive a great deal of attention and concern. There are no siblings with whom to compete, and being the central focus of parents may lead to self-centeredness. This can become a real problem later in life when one is no longer the apple of everyone's eye.

The oldest child is, in a sense, like a dethroned monarch. Once the only child, perhaps pampered and overprotected, this child must make way for a newcomer. This situation can be quite threatening. In an attempt to recoup his or her losses, the child may regress to a more childish phase or become demanding and destructive—anything to get attention. As this child gets older, however, conformity to parental dictates may become the style. Consequently, the oldest child often becomes the upholder of family law and standards. Given a place of maturity and responsibility by the parents, the individual may well develop a conforming style of life in response to authority figures.

The upbringing of the second or middle child tends to be more relaxed. The parents have been through it all before and are less concerned about being good parents this time around. The second child has never been the sole center of attention and is, therefore, not as sensitive about encroachments from younger siblings. Skills of cooperation and compromise come more easily because of the child's being around at least one other sibling. In some cases, however, a middle child may become concerned about the rights and prerogatives of that older, superior sibling. This can lead to feelings of inferiority, expressed in striving, competitive behaviors.

The youngest child may be babied, overprotected, and spoiled much like an only child. The pampering may be by older siblings as well as by the parents, especially if the youngest child is considerably younger than the other siblings. However, the youngest child has several siblings with whom to compete, and this may lead to strong feelings of competitiveness and a desire to show that he or she is just as good as the others. This child may become a real fighter. Motivation, then, is not in short supply with such a child.

All of the sibling styles just described represent possibilities. They are not meant to be inevitable or immutable. The dynamics of each family and situation are different. It was Adler's intention only to show that one's ordinal position in the family determines that certain problems rather than others are likely to be confronted.

Nature of adjustment

As we have seen, because of the inevitability of experiences that lead to feelings of inferiority, everyone attempts to compensate and strive for superiority. But the environment has a way of thrusting obstacles in the path toward achievement of the goal of superiority. According to Adler, how the individual responds to these obstacles determines whether he or she is adjusted or maladjusted.

In essence, Adler felt that the adjusted person responds to problems with courage. There is no fear of failure or unwillingness to confront the truth about oneself. Adjustment also means using common sense, that is, looking at life in realistic terms. Finally, the ultimate in adjustment is the expression of **social interest,** defined as the relinquishing of goals of personal superiority in favor of contributing to the welfare of others. These three characteristics are innately human predispositions which express themselves unless a mistaken view of life involving excessive strivings for superiority is too powerful.

Distance.   Adler used the concept of **distance** to describe the neurotic's manner of handling potential failure. People do not like to experience failure because it reinforces their feelings of inferiority. Consequently, they guard against failure situations by setting up a distance between themselves and the goal. This psychological ploy is defensive in nature since it demonstrates neither courage nor common sense. For example, the male who is fearful of being rejected by females removes himself psychologically by distancing himself. He says, in effect, "I would get involved if only I could find someone who is sensitive, pretty, and intelligent." This defensive scheme allows him to reject them before they reject him.

Masculine protest. Adler did not give sexual urges a central motivating role in his theory. To Adler, sexual problems were simply another manifestation of the striving for power and superiority. For example, he considered the Oedipus complex less a sexual matter than a struggle to achieve dominance. That is, sexual gratification from the mother is less important than having power over her.

One Adlerian concept that does have some sex-role overtones is **masculine protest.** In many societies, and specifically in certain families, masculinity is equated with power, dominance, and security. In families of male domination, both girls and boys may be impressed with the association between so-called masculinity and strength, assertiveness, and dominance. For some girls, then, the goal of superiority may become translated into a striving for strength, dominance, and the like. Men become rivals rather than being seen as superior and worthy of deference. But masculine protest can characterize males as well, as witnessed by the swagger, the macho outlook, and the chauvinist. Of course, not every family is male dominated. When the mother is obviously in control, a **feminine protest** may occur. Both boys and girls may develop such traits as femininity, nurturance, and the like. Later, Adler downplayed the concept of masculine protest in favor of a more general striving for superiority. In any event, he was certainly not arguing that men are innately superior—quite the contrary.

Three problems of life. Adler felt that, in a general way, the problems of life can be sorted into three areas. There are problems of (1) sex and marriage, (2) school and occupation, and (3) a family or social nature. As a person becomes maladjusted in one life area, there is a tendency for the difficulty to spill over into another area. In a sense, the severity of a case depends upon the degree of involvement across the three areas. In short, Adler's emphasis was not so much on type of symptom as on extent of involvement.

Implications for behavior change

Although Adler did not offer any systematic accounts of his treatment techniques, it is clear that his approach was more direct than Freud's. There was little emphasis on dream interpretation and free association. As with Freud, childhood experiences and feelings were explored. The assumption, however, was that the patient's problems stem from a mistaken style of life. Therefore, there was a focus on such things as sibling rivalry, pampering and rejection, and methods of coping with inferiority feelings.

Getting the patient to discuss such matters allows the therapist to determine the style of life. To help patients face up to their feelings of inferiority, Adlerians would be encouraging and reassuring. This helps patients find the courage and common sense

CASE STUDY

The following case study of Z excerpts (Disher, 1959) illustrates several features of an Adlerian approach to description and treatment. It is an account of a patient treated over a comparatively brief span of time, who showed decided improvement without, however, effecting any basic change in her psychic economy.

Miss Z, forty-eight years old, contacted the Alfred Adler Consultation Center and Mental Hygiene Clinic in New York City, in December 1956, having been referred by a psychotherapist with whom she had been in treatment for ten months and who dismissed her because he had to reduce his case load.

The patient was average in appearance, except for a slight limp due to polio when she was a child. She was extremely self-conscious, however, and wore long dresses to hide her "bad" leg.

Miss Z had a ten-year history of "severe" depression. She reported that she spent about nine months of every year in a depressive state. She was said to be in a "severe depression" at the time of her admission to the Clinic; however, at that time she was able to go to work every day, work which she hated, and seemed to be functioning adequately in other areas. The diagnosis was "reactive depression."

During the years of her illness, Miss Z had had nine different therapists, some of whom were well-known psychiatrists and psychotherapists. At the initial interview Miss Z complained that she had been shifted from the "best" therapist to one of lesser reputation and skill. She also complained that she had no occupation, having had a very informal education and training. She boasted that her parents were well-known people who traveled a great deal. Her spasmodic schooling was due to their frequent moving about. She was always in conflict with her mother, but was strongly attached to her father, in whose reflected glory she basked and who had assumed the role of a boyfriend until her "marriage."

Her first "husband" (this is the patient's word; she had never married) was a man of some reputation, of her father's age. In this relationship, and in all her subsequent relationships with men, she continued to be the cared-for and admired child. When the man ceased "courting" her, she lost interest. She stated that she could only be happy when she was with people of consequence. She also recognized the fact that she had to be in "control" of a situation.

The patient felt that if she had the security of a profession in which she was successful, her depression would lift. This would have to be a position in which she controlled other people, not one in which she provided menial service. (She considered being a secretary or a nurse, for example, menial and therefore not really good enough for her.) After her third interview Miss Z seemed to emerge from her depression and was able to accept her clerical job as a possible stepping stone to better opportunities. She also accepted the relationship with her current gentleman friend to a degree, although he, too, was not really suitable, being dependent, unknown, and socially inept.

However, after only two months she was again in a depressive state, having received a rebuff in her office, which she interpreted as an obstacle to her ever achieving the kind of position she wanted in life. Simultaneously, the man in her life

104

(continued)

became "completely impossible." She complained of not bathing, not eating, not sleeping, and of having to force herself to go to work each day.

During the course of her long treatment with her former therapists she had worked on her relationships with her parents and with her various men friends, and she had been made to recognize the use she was making of her depression. She had all the concepts; she knew all the words.

Rather than persist in these attempts to increase her intellectual understanding, the therapist tried to emphasize her value as a person; the therapist stressed the fact that therapy is a situation in which two people work on a problem together; that neither was superior to the other. It was also pointed out that if she conceived of her therapy as being solely the therapist's responsibility, she could prove herself superior to the therapist simply by not getting well. At this point she became impatient, said she was not satisfied with the way things were going, and suggested termination. The therapist, in turn, suggested that she work through their relationship, even though she thought she was not being helped, instead of following her old pattern of running away.

There followed five months of depression in which things were "worse than they have ever been." Three events of importance then occurred, quite by accident. First, the drug marsilid came to her attention. She made inquiries which led her to a well-known psychiatrist at a state hospital, who generously gave her some time and prescribed the drug. She took this drug for a week without side effects. Secondly, matters took a turn for the better in her office, and she moved quickly into a coveted management position, which brought her into contact with world-famous people.

Thirdly, almost simultaneously, a well-known man came into her life as a suitor. She was then "well" for six months, with the exception of two days. At the end of these two days she took another dose of marsilid and her depression lifted. At this point Miss Z terminated her therapy; she felt that "marsilid was responsible" for her cure. Actually, we are not certain to what extent this drug contributed to the patient's improvement. We are sure, however, of the role of certain other forces in her life, forces which make it possible for her to function successfully in spite of, or perhaps because of, her neurotic needs:

1 She was valued as a person at the Clinic. She was made to feel that she was important to the therapist—she was encouraged to continue with her therapy, etc.

2 One of the "greatest" psychiatrists gave her his time and thus proved that he valued her as a person.

3 She was able to achieve some status in a profession at which she had served her apprenticeship. Her present job enables her to come into contact with important people; and she plays a dominant role at her office.

4 A well-known man, very much like her father, has come into her life, is courting her, and is charmed by her little-girl ways.

Although Miss Z has not changed basically (unless marsilid has worked some change at the chemical level), she is now meeting life with greater courage because her environment has shifted. Still a child emotionally and sexually, she is doing a good job in the area of occupation, which has contributed to her self-respect. There has certainly been improvement in the patient's life-style, without, however, any real change in social feeling.

From "Improvement Without Fundamental Change" by D. R. Disher in *Essays in Individual Psychology: Contemporary Application of Alfred Adler's Theories,* edited by Kurt A. Adler and Danica Deutsch. Copyright © 1959 by Grove Press, Inc. Reprinted by permission of Grove Weidenfeld.

to confront their problems. Adler, of course, felt that lack of social interest was the ultimate defect. Therefore he would attempt to break down the patient's self-preoccupation and encourage a looking outward.

It should be emphasized again that Adler's therapy was much more directive than Freud's. The therapist was an active figure rather than one who passively listened and made occasional interpretations. Adler not only made interpretations but he also attempted to persuade the patient about various matters. Moreover, he was likely to make explicit suggestions for changes in behavior. And, although he talked about the past with patients, he also placed much emphasis on changing the present along with choosing and pursuing future behavior and goals.

Adler is perhaps best known for his treatment methods for children experiencing psychological and behavioral problems. Specifically, he is distinguished by the use of direct suggestions for changes in the behavior of significant adults (parents and teachers) in the child's life. The current revival of interest in Adler's ideas and methods may stem largely from a recognition that his work with children has much in common with contemporary behavior therapy approaches, especially those with strong cognitive overtones.

ANALYTICAL PSYCHOLOGY

Carl Jung was another follower of Freud to grow disenchanted with several aspects of classical psychoanalysis. He could not accept Freud's narrow sexual definition of libido. As Munroe (1955) points out, this objection was hardly any reflection of prudishness. Rather, for Jung, libido was a creative life force with an almost spiritual quality. This conceptualization fits with Jung's wide-ranging interests, which included archaeology, spiritualism, mythology, Eastern as well as Western philosophy, astrology, religion, and much more. This breadth of intellectual study gave his theory of personality a much wider base than could be offered merely by the dreams and free associations of patients on the couch. It gave an entirely different flavor to psychoanalysis. Jung's version of psychoanalysis is called **analytical psychology.**

Personality structure

For Jung, there were three basic components of the personality: the ego, the personal unconscious, and the collective unconscious.

The ego.   The **ego** is the conscious mind. It is composed of all those feelings, thoughts, memories, and perceptions of which we are conscious. It represents the "I" feeling and is responsible for getting us through the day. It is not unlike Freud's executive ego.

The personal unconscious.   The **personal unconscious** is roughly equivalent to Freud's preconscious since the material in it can be made conscious without much effort. The material may have been repressed, forgotten, or perhaps was not vivid enough to have registered initially.

Collective unconscious. The **collective unconscious** is what many regard as a radical innovation in psychoanalytic theory. Such a notion is pure Jungian even though Freud gave some attention to a similar concept, the "phylogenetic" origins of the id. The collective unconscious is composed of memory traces from our ancestral past. And this includes prehuman ancestry as well. As Jung (1928) himself put it, the collective unconscious is the "deposit of ancestral experience from untold millions of years, the echo of prehistoric world events to which each century adds an infinitesimally small amount of variation and differentiation" (p. 162). Because the collective unconscious arises out of the common experiences of all our ancestors, its contents are basically similar for all of us. The collective unconscious provides a guiding influence. It is, in a sense, a set of predispositions that, if ignored by the ego, can disrupt our conscious, rational processes by gaining control of them and distorting them into symptoms of various sorts.

Archetypes

Jung called the structural elements of the collective unconscious archetypes. **Archetypes** are universal, collective, primordial images. Since time began, our ancestors have seen the rising sun, experienced a mother, learned of death, admired a hero, and endured pain. These experiences predispose us to react in certain ways to similar situations. Thus, to understand fully a child's terror of the dark, we must consider the archetypal content. But at the same time, that child's fear must also be examined with a view toward his or her own life experiences.

When we fail to recognize fully our archetypes, their meaning unfolds in our dreams and fantasies. Primitive art, myths, and even the hallucinations of the psychotic can tell us much about the nature of archetypes. And these archetypes are not trivial images. They have heavy emotional components. Although Jung discussed many different archetypes, he focused extensively on four: the persona, the anima and animus, the shadow, and the self.

The persona. From the Greek word meaning "mask," **persona** is the public face presented by the individual in response to social demands. It represents our conventional role as defined by the expectations of others. This is separate from our real selves and its purpose is to impress others or to conceal ourselves from them. When we identify too closely with our persona (e.g., if I really begin to believe those academic robes represent the real me), we are in for trouble.

The anima and animus. The concepts of anima and animus reflect Jung's attempt to deal with the essential bisexuality of human nature. The feminine side of men is the **anima,** and the masculine side of women is **animus.** These archetypes have arisen over eons of time in the collective unconscious as a result of experience with the opposite sex. Men have become a bit "feminized" by living with women over the ages, and the reverse holds true for women. Again, failure to recognize the archetypal "other side" of the opposite sex can lead to difficulties in interpersonal relations.

Carl Jung

Carl Gustav Jung was born in 1875 in the village of Kesswyl, Switzerland. His father was a pastor of the Swiss Reformed Church. Jung (1961) described himself as a lonely child growing up in the midst of his parents' marital problems. His mother had a dominating personality; his father spent a great deal of time thinking about being a failure and questioning the sincerity of his religious beliefs. Some of Jung's childhood experiences played a very important role in his later theorizing. For example, he seems to have been preoccupied with dreams, visions, and fantasies. He felt he possessed secret information about the future and also had the fantasy he was two different people.

Jung's first love was archaeology, and this interest figured heavily in his later work. However, he was convinced by a dream to become a doctor and received his medical degree in psychiatry in 1900. After reading Freud's *The Interpretation of Dreams,* he became interested in psychoanalysis. In 1906 the two men began corresponding regularly, and the following year Jung visited Freud. Jung and Freud greatly admired each other and in 1909 traveled to the United States together to lecture. In fact, Freud designated Jung as his successor and even convinced the members of the International Psychoanalytic Association to elect Jung as their first president.

The shadow. The **shadow** is the dark or evil, animalistic side of our personality. It accounts in part for our aggressiveness, our cruelty and immorality, and even our passion. We find evidence for this in the monsters and devils of our dreams and in primitive art and mythology. Thus our outlook on the world and our reactions to others can be influenced by shadow images emanating from the collective unconscious.

The self. The **self** is that archetype which propels us to search for unity, harmony, and wholeness among all elements of the personality. Religion, according to Jung, can be a great facilitator of this integration. Because development of an integrated state takes time, the archetype of self is not fully achieved until perhaps middle age. When the self archetype is realized, the individual becomes a fine balance between the conscious and the unconscious.

Ego orientations

Jung described two general orientations or attitudes that individuals assume in their relationships with the world. **Introversion** refers to a subjective orientation. The introvert is more likely to be reserved, withdrawn, and interested in ideas rather than in social relations. **Extraversion** describes an attitude of interest in the outer world. The extravert is the more sociable person who is friendly and involved in things outside the self. This bipolar dimension is likely rooted in inborn temperament although

In 1912 their friendship began to cool, and in 1913 they ceased all correspondence. Jung resigned as president of the psychoanalytic group in 1914 and a few months later withdrew his membership. Freud and Jung never saw each other again. The split was probably based on both personal and theoretical grounds. However, the most obvious reason was their differing views of the libido and the nature of sexuality. The break was quite debilitating for Jung, so much so that for three years he could not bring himself to even read a scientific book. He spent the time deeply exploring his own dreams and fantasies. Some felt he was near the edge of madness.

A bizarre page in Jung's life involved accusations of pro-Nazi sentiments. He became president of Hitler's International General Medical Society for Psychotherapy. The society was based on the "truths" of *Mein Kampf* and was organized to separate the "true" Aryan psychology from "false" Jewish propaganda. Jung was condemned for giving substance to Nazi delusions, but it may well be that he accepted the position to help block the rising tide of anti-Semitism in Europe. Thus, he may have been less a Nazi sympathizer than simply very naive politically.

Jung died in 1961 in Kusnacht, Switzerland.

Carl Jung
Bettmann Archive.

experiences in life can encourage or discourage one's predisposition toward one orientation or the other.

Symbols

Jung was very much caught up in trying to understand the meaning of **symbols.** Symbols are used, he thought, to represent complex ideas that cannot be defined completely. For example, the cross in religion expresses something indescribable; it contains an almost inexpressible surplus of meaning. Symbols are especially prominent in dreams and often serve as clues to the deeper essence of our souls. Discussing the mother archetype, Jung (1970) gave the following as examples of symbols:

> Many things arousing devotion or feelings of awe, as for instance the Church, university, city or country, heaven, earth, the woods, the sea or any still waters, matter even, the underworld and the moon, can be mother-symbols. The archetype is often associated with things and places standing for fertility and fruitfulness: the cornucopia, a ploughed field, a garden. It can be attached to a rock, a cave, a tree, a spring, a deep well, or to various vessels such as the baptismal font, or to vessel-shaped flowers like the rose or the lotus. (p. 15)

Symbols, then, tell us much. They can be diagnostic of the deepest corners of our being. They can be attempts to gratify a frustrated instinctual urge. But then, they may exhibit a negative side by draining off energy that might be used in other ways. In addition, symbols can sometimes signify future lines of development of the personality as the individual strives for integration and wholeness (Hall and Lindzey, 1978).

Nature of adjustment

There is no systematic account in Jungian theory about the nature of adjustment or neurosis. Certainly when a state of integration and harmony exists among the various elements of the personality, one could be said to be adjusted. Deviant behaviors arise when there is an imbalance. When the persona dominates, or when the shadow gains control, the person will have difficulties. When archetypes are ignored, we will likely come to grief. Similarly, when there is an imbalance between the conscious and the unconscious, adjustment is not possible. As Rychlak (1981) puts it, "Insanity is thus an invasion of the unconscious of contents that are flatly incompatible with the intentions of the ego" (p. 221). But harmony and balance do not just happen; they must actively be sought with great effort.

Implications for behavior change

Jung does not seem to have had any major impact upon the psychotherapy movement. Indirectly, one can see traces of Jung in the work of Carl Rogers and Abraham Maslow, two prominent proponents of phenomenological and humanistic forms of therapy.

In achieving the aims of therapy, the patient typically passes through four stages. The first stage is a period of **confession,** or catharsis as Freud would term it. The patient then moves into the **elucidation** stage, during which he or she attempts to explain or account for the problems being experienced. Much of this stage is taken up in transference phenomena. Later, the stage of **education** is reached as the therapist promotes new learning to enable the patient to cope with the challenges of the present. In the case of a few patients with a great deal of potential, merely getting them to return to normalcy would be a waste. Such patients begin a stage of **transformation,** which enables them ultimately to achieve self-realization. Self-realization is accomplished through a process called **individuation,** which culminates in the attainment of selfhood, that is, the full development of all components of the personality.

Ultimately, the role of the therapist is to help the individual learn to differentiate the various aspects of the psyche. This will, in turn, facilitate the person's ability to achieve harmony among them and to realize his or her potential.

Concluding notes

Jung's is hardly a scientific theory. His affinity for the occult, religion, and mythology tends to insulate his ideas from many. Therefore, Jung's ideas have not had the impact they might otherwise have enjoyed. Jung's emphasis on the future and on the importance of meaning in life have had important influences on contemporary personality theory. Jung also was never one to construe humans as helpless hostages of their psychosexual history. Rather, self-actualization was a magnet that pulled the individual forward.

Jung's ideas about the collective unconscious continue to fascinate many people. He saw the unconscious as a rich lode of wisdom and experience. If we could but turn the key to its symbolism, it could become a guiding force in our lives. Finally, Jung's emphasis on the spiritual element of life coupled with his stress on "listening" to our unconscious through the vehicle of symbols has renewed interest in Jungian theory. For example, Jung felt that much of the variety in personality and interpersonal behavior was due to the differences in people's cognitive-affective style.

THE NEO-FREUDIANS

Several psychoanalysts began to argue for the essential social nature of the human being and thereby revised the orthodox Freudian doctrine of instinctual, sexual motives in human nature. The principal members of this revisionist group are usually considered to be Alfred Adler, Karen Horney, Erich Fromm, and Harry Stack Sullivan. We have already examined how Adler "socialized" traditional psychoanalytic theory. The other three pushed psychoanalytic theory even farther in this direction and probably, therefore, ought to be referred to as neo-Adlerian rather than neo-Freudian.

Many present students, perhaps, would be especially interested in Karen Horney's work because of their interest in feminist issues. Horney, for example, rejected penis envy as a dominant motive in women along with notions that "anatomy is destiny." Instead, as noted in Chapter 3, she argued that many of the feelings of inferiority and inadequacy experienced by some women are a function of the way our culture regards women in general. Both Quinn (1987) and Westcott (1986) have provided biographical material on Horney and also a look at her ideas about the psychology of women.

Even more than Adler, Horney adopted a sociocultural view. To understand the individual's conflicts, we must understand how personality is shaped by the texture of society. It is within this broader context that she placed one of her primary concepts, **basic anxiety** (Horney, 1937). For example, in a highly competitive culture like ours, the child feels helpless, alone, and menaced by others due to, if nothing else, the smallness of the child relative to the adult. To meet such a threat, the child must develop ways of coping with this basic anxiety. Horney (1945) discussed several strategies that are commonly employed:

- *Moving toward people* — Protecting oneself by overtures of affection, dependency, and submission to others

- *Moving against people* — Protecting oneself through aggression, hostility, and attack

- *Moving away from people* — Protecting oneself by isolation and withdrawal

Everyone normally uses all three of these strategies. Neuroticism arises when we rigidly adopt a reaction pattern that dominates our personality and takes over our life.

The social theme continues with Fromm's views. Our compelling need, according to Fromm (1941), is the need to belong. A basic terror wells up out of feelings of being alone and insignificant. Methods of escaping this terror arise out of fears of our emerging freedom. Thus, the basic conflict is between the self and the agony of being separate. The human being is defined by a search for significance and relationship to others. However, in our attempts to develop methods of relatedness and ways of escaping from freedom, we more often than not find that the methods themselves cause conflict and anxiety.

The Neo-Freudians

Karen Horney
Bettmann Archive.

Karen Horney was born in 1885 in Hamburg, Germany. After medical training at the University of Berlin, she spent fourteen years as a psychoanalyst at the Berlin Psychoanalytic Institute. She moved to New York and affiliated with the New York Psychoanalytic Institute, where she remained until her death in 1952.

Erich Fromm
Rene Burri/Magnum

Erich Fromm was born in 1900 in Frankfurt, Germany. After a Ph.D. he took psychoanalytic training at the Berlin Psychoanalytic Institute. In 1933 he emigrated to the United States. After lecturing at the Chicago Psychoanalytic Institute and being in private practice, he accepted a professorship in Mexico City in 1949. In 1976 he moved to Switzerland, where he died in 1980.

Harry Stack Sullivan
Historical Pictures Service, Inc., Chicago.

Harry Stack Sullivan was born in Norwich, New York, in 1892. His medical degree was from the Chicago College of Medicine and Surgery. After military service during World War I he was associated for a number of years with hospitals in the Washington, D.C. area. He built an outstanding reputation there for his therapeutic work with schizophrenics. He died in 1949 in Paris while returning home from international meetings.

Fromm outlined several orientations that individuals use to cope with their loneliness. The first four are distinctly nonproductive ones in contrast to the fifth one:

■ *Receptive* — The individual expects and requires support from the environment — from parents, friends, authorities, God, etc.

■ *Exploitative* — The person takes from others by force or cleverness. Everything becomes an object of exploitation, and the prevailing attitude is one of hostility and manipulation coupled with feelings of envy, jealousy, and cynicism.

■ *Hoarding* — Security is defined by acquisitions. Spending is a threat to society. Love becomes nothing more than possessiveness. There is no faith in the future.

■ *Marketing* — Personal qualities have no intrinsic value; they are commodities of exchange. Personality is something to sell, and the "right" personality is whatever is in vogue. Such people are basically empty, anxious individuals.

■ *Productive* — This is the healthy type whose productiveness represents the ability to employ one's powers and to achieve everything possible in one's nature.

Sullivan's basic emphasis was on the interaction between individual and environment. For Sullivan (1953, 1964), every situation was an *interpersonal* one; even when alone, the individual is in tune with past experiences with others.

He also made great use of the concept of **self.** This is not an inborn self but one that grows out of the "reflected appraisals" of others. This means that the manner in which we are evaluated by others comes to be the manner in which we evaluate ourselves. Positive interactions with significant adults as the child is developing will lead to a positive view of the self; negative interactions will produce negative self-esteem. The major aspects of the self are therefore firmly established in the early years of childhood.

Sullivan emphasized stages of development, but the emphasis was interpersonal rather than psychosexual:

■ *Infancy* — This period lasts from birth to the development of articulate speech. Self-esteem begins as the child very early reacts to the moods and feelings of the parents through empathy.

■ *Childhood* — From about two to six years of age, the child is shaped by the parents into their vision of the socialized human being. Language develops, and the child learns ways of manipulating people in the service of the overriding goal of security.

■ *Juvenile* — This period lasts throughout the elementary school years and consists of experiences that widen the scope of living and socialization beyond the home. The child learns about competition, cooperation, and rejection.

■ *Preadolescence* — This is marked by the stirrings of the capacity for love. The first object may be a same-sexed peer who affords the individual the initial opportunity to express very personal feelings. The child is now beginning to discard a purely egocentric orientation.

■ *Adolescence* — Here we have the development of genital interests and the maturation of heterosexuality. As Hall and Lindzey (1978) describe it, "When the individual has ascended all these steps and reached the final stage of adulthood, he or she has been transformed largely by means of interpersonal relations from an animal into a human person" (p. 192).

THE ELABORATION OF THE EGO

In the pages that follow, it will become apparent that classical Freudian notions about the importance of the instincts, the psychosexual stages, and even traditional ideas about the id, ego, and superego are giving way. Now on the ascendance are new conceptions about the ego, object relations, and the self. This signals much that is new and exciting in psychoanalytic theory. It is sometimes fashionable in academic psychological circles to pronounce psychoanalysis dead. But virtually every issue of *Contemporary Psychology,* a journal of book reviews, contains one or more new books dealing with some aspect of psychoanalytic theory. If anything, there seems to be a real revival of interest in psychoanalysis.

Part of the need to rejuvenate psychoanalytic theory arose from Freud's insistence on the critical importance of the id. The id was master, the ego slave. Granted, as in most master-slave scenarios, the ego often secretly outwitted the id and was extremely adept in balancing all kinds of outrageous and conflicting demands. More often than not, it could even save the id from itself. Still, the id was the straw that stirred the drink. Every function the ego performed — thinking, sublimating, rationalizing, or whatever — was done to ward off the demands of the id. And Freud never relinquished his views about the supremacy of the id.

Rise of the ego

Not everyone agreed with Freud. Some wanted a theory that would grant a greater role to the ego. Foremost among these revisionists were Erik Erikson (1963), Heinz Hartmann (1958, 1964), David Rapaport (1959), and Ernst Kris (1952). These theorists emphasized the need to account for behaviors such as thinking, perceiving, and learning, not just ego defenses. They did not regard such activities as being necessarily to conflicts within the personality. Nor did they see how psychoanalysis could continue to develop as a major theoretical force if it focused exclusively on unhealthy personalities. They felt that it must contribute to our understanding of the healthy individual as well.

These ego psychologists, then, began to develop the idea of a **conflict-free sphere** of the ego — a part of the ego whose processes of thinking, perceiving, and learning are not in conflict with the id, the superego, or the real world. Hartmann (1958) went on to describe an **autonomous ego.** This was an ego that grew not out of the id but arrived with its own predispositions and continued to develop independently. In a sense, this means that we do not have to account for every human achievement as the result of conflict between id and ego or as a compromise designed to solve some intrapsychic problem. These ego psychologists wanted a theory that would explain why we think, compose music, or remember anniversaries, not one that explains everything healthy as the result of a compromise born out of some internal conflict.

Ego psychology also has important implications for development. The internal focus on oral, anal, and genital stages begins to shift to external, environmental questions. For example, what has been the quality of the mothering experienced by the infant? What can we say about the infant's attachment to the mother? How has the infant's environment affected cognitive and social development? In short, to understand later development, we need to look at not just the frustration of instinctual drives but also at the unique characteristics of early attachment and environmental stimulation (Bowlby, 1969).

Psychosocial theory

Psychosocial theory is the product of another member of the ego psychology movement, Erik Erikson. Erikson maintains the emphasis on ego functions that is the hallmark of the ego psychologists. He also stresses the optimistic view that human trauma and crisis offer the opportunity for us to triumph over adversity and master our world. With Freud we always seem to be dealing with adult psychopathology fostered by unsuccessful resolutions of psychosexual disasters. This will become clearer as we describe Erikson's stages of development in the next section.

Erikson's eight stages of psychosocial development

Erikson's first book, *Childhood and Society,* was published in 1950 and revised in 1963. It was in this book that he described the eight stages of human development.

According to Erikson, the eight stages unfold in a genetically determined sequence. This sequence is guided by an **epigenetic principle,** which means that the growing personality follows a "ground plan" that guides it toward broader and broader social interactions. Furthermore, the very organization of society tends to encourage the unfolding of development. This is an innately planned development that occurs in an orderly fashion and at an appropriate rate. Although the details vary from one culture to another, the basic elements of the psychosocial stages are universal.

Each stage presents the individual with a **crisis**—a point at which personality development can go one way or another. In essence, the person's level of physiological development, combined with society's expectations for a person of that age, brings about a crisis characteristic of each stage. If the crisis is resolved negatively, adaptation and the likelihood of a successful resolution of the crisis in the next stage will be diminished. A positive resolution has the opposite effect (see Table 4-1). Of course, rarely is a resolution completely positive or negative. It is, rather, the balance of the positive to the negative in each stage that is important.

Although Erikson, like Freud, emphasizes the concept of stages, there are important differences. For example, it is no accident that Erikson chose *psychosocial* rather than *psychosexual* as a descriptor. In addition, Erikson's stages span the entire life of the individual, with special emphasis on adolescence and adulthood. His willingness to address the crises of adulthood has made his work useful in the field of gerontology.

TABLE 4-1   *Erikson's eight stages or crises and associated emerging traits*

Stage	Age	Successful Resolution Leads to:	Unsuccessful Resolution Leads to:
I. Trust vs. Mistrust (Oral)*	Birth–1 yr.	Hope	Fear
II. Autonomy vs. Shame and Doubt (Anal)*	1–3 yrs.	Will power	Self-doubt
III. Initiative vs. Guilt (Phallic)*	4–5 yrs.	Purpose	Unworthiness
IV. Industry vs. Inferiority (Latency)*	6–11 yrs.	Competency	Incompetency
V. Ego Identity vs. Role Confusion	12–20 yrs.	Fidelity	Uncertainty
VI. Intimacy vs. Isolation	20–24 yrs.	Love	Promiscuity
VII. Generativity vs. Stagnation	25–65 yrs.	Care	Selfishness
VIII. Ego Integrity vs. Despair	65 yrs.–death	Wisdom	Meaninglessness and despair

*Roughly corresponding Freudian stage.

Finally, whereas Freud's preoccupation seemed to be with the id, Erikson looked toward the ego and the personal and social attitudes that arose out of the resolution of each crisis.

1   Trust vs. mistrust.   Corresponding roughly to Freud's oral stage, this stage lasts from birth to about one year. When the mother's care is sensitive, confident, and consistent, the child is more apt to develop a basic trust of others and a sense of confidence and trust in self. The child will tend to see the world as safe and supportive and a place where he or she can rely on others. What is important in promoting basic trust is the quality of the mother-child relationship. Without such a quality relationship, basic mistrust will develop, along with feelings of anxiety and estrangement.

2   Autonomy vs. shame and doubt.   This stage lasts from about the close of the first year until around the end of the third year. It is analogous to Freud's anal stage. This period serves as an arena for the developing battle of wills between parents and child. It is often described as the crisis of deciding to "hold on" or "let go." The child must decide whether to hold on to feces and urine or to let them go. He or she must choose whether to run, walk, spit, eat, or obey. The main battleground is in the bathroom, of course, but it is everywhere else as well. The stake is autonomy. The parents' failure to exercise firmness in an overall context of tolerance may lead the child to regress to Stage 1. Hostility or stubbornness may result.

3 Initiative vs. guilt. Between the fourth and sixth years (Freud's phallic stage), the child learns through testing his or her environment what is permitted and what is not. There is growing language ability and physical skills that enable the child to think, imagine, and do things. A sense of what is possible is beginning to emerge. When the parents guide these initiatives with sensitivity and encouragement, all the while unobtrusively protecting the child from serious harm, an attitude of initiative and self-sufficiency will arise. Excessive punishment or ridicule can foster feelings of guilt, as can the parents' unwillingness to allow the child to complete self-initiated activities. Although some of the conflicts of this stage are sexual, Erikson's conceptualization is a broader, more psychosocially encompassing one.

4 Industry vs. inferiority. From about six through eleven years of age, the child is occupied with school. This corresponds to the Freudian stage of latency. However, Erikson attributes much greater importance to it than did Freud. This is a period of activity during which children learn the fundamental behaviors that will enable them to compete in the world. Play, imagination, and fantasy must be curbed. But at the same time, the industry that will translate into becoming a productive member of society should be encouraged. Failure to learn and the inability to take pleasure in work or to persevere with a task can only serve to blight the individual's confidence and feelings of personal value.

5 Ego identity vs. role confusion. This stage, lasting from approximately the age of twelve to about twenty, marks the close of childhood and the beginning of adulthood. Erikson attached particular importance to this period of adolescence, as indicated in the following description:

> Like a trapeze artist, the young person in the middle of vigorous motion must let go of his safe hold on childhood and reach out for a firm grasp on adulthood, depending for a breathless interval on a relatedness between the past and the future, and on the reliability of those he must let go of, and those who will "receive him." (Erikson, 1964, p. 90)

In fact, Erikson attached so much importance to this stage that he invented the term **identity crisis** to help explain it.

In this stage the child moves from childhood into the role of an adult. The child must consolidate the information and skills acquired in previous stages and finally establish a personal identity. Children in this period become very concerned about the image others have of them and how they match up with that image. At the same time, they must fit all this into a plan for their place in the world. Establishing an **ego identity** is the work of this stage. It involves a confidence that one's self corresponds with how others perceive one, and that this can form the foundation for one's niche in life.

Erik
Erikson

Erik Erikson was born in 1902 close to Frankfurt, Germany. His parents, who were Danish, separated prior to his birth, and when he was three years old his mother married Dr. Theodor Homburger, the pediatrician who had treated Erik for a childhood disease. It was a number of years before Erik was told Homburger was not his real father. In fact, Erikson used the name of his stepfather for quite a few years, even on his first published papers. It was not until he became a United States citizen in 1939 that he used the name Erikson. Even though his mother and stepfather were Jewish, he was sometimes taunted by his Jewish peers for being gentile, perhaps because of his Scandinavian blond hair and blue eyes. These kinds of experiences probably contributed to a feeling of not belonging, which is reflected in his later writings about identity crises, confusions, and the like (Coles, 1970).

Erikson finished high school, but that was all. Although interested in art and history, his was a generally mediocre school career. Thus, he decided, after a brief stint of studying art, to travel. In fact, he wandered about Italy until, at age twenty-five, he accepted the offer of a friend from his high school days to become a teacher at a small American day nursery in Vienna. One thing led to another, and Erikson be-

This, of course, is a very stressful period. "Finding" oneself can be hard work and often involves trying on for size a variety of roles and aspirations. Things can run the gamut from idealism, to vandalism, to falling in love, studying, or having anxiety attacks. Role confusion, a major pitfall during this stage, happens when the individual is unable to make a firm choice about an occupational identity. Often, this results because of insecurity over skills, sexual identity, or personal value. The turbulence of this period, with its accompanying role confusion and identity crisis, may explain the attraction of rock groups, movie stars, and other charismatic figures. Such figures provide a starlike quality to which the individual can relate and thereby achieve some sense of personal identity. To fall in love, as adolescents are so prone to do, is another method of attaining identity by projecting one's own ego qualities onto the other person and then seeing them clarified as they are reflected by that other person.

6 Intimacy vs. isolation. This period is a relatively brief one that spans the ages of twenty to twenty-four or so. It is a period when one's newly found identity can be committed to another person. With personal identity comes the capacity for love, affiliation, intimacy, and stable commitment. The person who has failed thus far in the task of building ego identity cannot establish such a relationship and often withdraws into personal isolation or creates a false form of intimacy through promiscuity or transitory relationships that fail the true test of commitment. Keeping others at an emotional arm's length prevents any real intimacy and leads to shallow, unrewarding experiences.

came acquainted with the Freud family. This culminated in an invitation to undergo psychoanalytic training under the tutelage of Anna Freud and August Aichhorn. This training lasted from 1927 to 1933.

Erikson married in 1929 and with his wife and two sons moved to Copenhagen in 1933. Shortly thereafter, the family moved again, this time to Boston, where Erikson became a practicing children's analyst and also held an appointment at Harvard Medical School. From 1936 to 1939, he occupied a position at the Yale Medical School. In 1939 he resumed his psychoanalytic work with children after a move to San Francisco. He became a professor of psychology in 1942 at Berkeley, but was discharged in 1950 along with other faculty who refused to sign the infamous loyalty oath. Later, he was asked to return but refused on ethical grounds.

From 1951 to 1960, Erikson served as a senior consultant to the Austen Riggs Center in Massachusetts, a residential treatment center for disturbed adolescents. He was also a part-time faculty member of the University of Pittsburgh Medical School, as well as being affiliated with several other institutions. In 1960, he returned to Harvard. He is now retired.

Erik Erikson
Jon Erikson.

7   *Generativity vs. stagnation.* These are the middle years of life (twenty-five to sixty-five), when the dominant motive becomes contributing to the next generation. Whether this motive is fulfilled by raising a family or by being a productive, creative person in other ways, the specific activity is directed toward concern for those who will come next. The important quality here is a wish to be needed—a wish that achieves fruition by different means depending on the person. There can be many selfish and immature reasons for having a family or embarking upon a career. It is not the act itself but the quality of its motivation that defines generativity. To fail to be guided by aspirations of generativity ultimately leads to stagnation and boredom.

8   *Ego integrity vs. despair.* From the age of sixty-five or so until death, the individual has the opportunity to consolidate the experiences of the previous seven stages into a final period of ego integrity. Ideally, it represents a period of contentment, resulting from the acceptance of the worth of one's brief tenure on earth. One cherishes the experiences, people, or events of life without wishing they could have been different. The person can review life and find much that has been good. Of course, when ego integrity fails, despair will take its place. Fear of death, disappointment, resentment, and the like are common coin that make reviewing one's life painful and examination of the present unrewarding. However, the circle is complete, as Erikson remarks, when mature adults who exude ego integrity provide models that will convince the young that life can be trusted.

After the age of sixty-five, a major task is the maintenance of ego integrity. Photograph
Paul Fusco/Magnum.

THE THEORY OF OBJECT RELATIONS

Earlier, it was observed that infantile attachments are very important in shaping development. Object relations theory is an outgrowth of ego psychology. It emphasizes
that the way in which the individual relates to other people is of more interest than
internal conflicts among the id, ego, and superego. The attachments of the infant to
the mother and to other environmental figures shape the development of the ego and
enable the individual to move from intense maternal attachment to a separate, autonomous state. In this developmental process we have the foundation for the style of later
interpersonal relationships.

An example of the foregoing ideas comes from the work of Melanie Klein (1937).
Although some of her notions are rather extreme, her emphasis on early, pre-Oedipal
experiences (e.g., attachment to mother) provide a nice contrast to traditional Freudian dogma. She asserts that the infant experiences two stages during the first twelve
months of life. Initially, the infant does not see "whole" objects such as the mother.
Instead, the infant attaches itself to "part" objects such as the mother's breast. Klein
emphasizes the importance of aggression here as well. She feels that the child desires
the maternal object but is also hostile toward it. This leads to a situation where the

child divides the world into good and bad objects. Later, in the second stage, the infant starts integrating the parts. The mother, for example, is now seen as a whole; the whole replaces what was formerly a collection of parts. It is realized that the good and bad aspects are part of the same whole. This leads the child into feelings of ambivalence toward the mother. Recognition ensues that one's self is separate and, at the same time, that one is also dependent on that separate mother. All this is normally resolved by the child. But in a climate of neglect or lack of love, a fertile basis for hostility, envy, and anger is laid.

Fortunately, perhaps, the child begins to form cognitive images or representations of important environmental objects such as bottle, mother, father, and the like. These representations are considered to be **internalizations** of object relations. In the beginning, the child is attached to the mother and does not differentiate between the self and the mother. This primitive period is referred to as **symbiosis** (Mahler, 1968).

Later, as the sense of separateness develops, the child comes to depend on **object representations.** These are the individual's internalized images of an important object (e.g., the mother). Through such representations the child becomes able to handle the absence of the mother and to delay gratification. As the child matures it is these abilities that foster the growth of thinking and the related element of symbolism. So, regardless of the absence of an object or despite its varying appearance as a result of being seen under differing conditions, the child learns to develop a constant image of that object. The father who plays with the child is the same person who becomes angry or impatient with the child. The mother who stands before the stove is the same object that sits before the computer and balances the checkbook. For ego psychologists, it is disturbances in object relations and the inability to develop adequate images of consistency that contribute to maladjustment. Indeed, extreme disturbances in object relations can even lead to psychosis. But in Box 4-1 we can see how environmental objects can help foster adjustment.

THE SELF-PSYCHOLOGY OF KOHUT

Heinz Kohut
A leader in the field of self-psychology

For Heinz Kohut (1971, 1977), the critical task is not the successful negotiation of the psychosexual stages, but rather, the development of an integrated self. Such a self will allow the individual to appreciate who and what one is so that life will have direction and meaning. In a sense, Kohut's work represents a kind of integration between psychoanalysis and the self theory of Carl Rogers (see Chapter 6). Children have the desire for their expressions and achievements to be recognized, approved, and admired;

most notably by the mother. There is also the child's need to admire and identify with more powerful figures such as the father. When these needs for recognition and identification are not fulfilled, the child's development will be at risk.

Ideally, the person will develop an **autonomous self.** This is a type characterized by self-esteem and self-confidence and by ambition. One's talents and skills become developed in the service of ambition and the establishment of goals (Maddi, 1989).

Much of Kohut's insights arose out of his therapeutic work with narcissistic patients. More and more, Kohut believes, such patients have replaced the traditional ones who were burdened with specific, crisp symptoms. Today's narcissistic patients express vague dissatisfactions with life. They see themselves as futile with no aims in life. They experience feelings of emptiness and depression or else lament a loss of "selfness." While they often function quite well, there is no sense of happiness, accomplishment, or meaning. Table 4-2 presents some of the common disorders associated with narcissism. Traditional psychoanalytic approaches were not effective. Therefore, Kohut set about using techniques that conveyed the therapist's positive regard for and acceptance of the patient. Again, we see the influence of Rogers (see Chapter 6).

TABLE 4-2 Personality disorders associated with narcissism

Narcissistic Personality Disorders
Involve thought processes more than action.

The *understimulated self* (resulting from lack of parental response) will do anything (e.g., promiscuity, perversion, gambling, drug and alcohol abuse, hypersociability) to create excitement and ward off feelings of deadness.

The *fragmented self* (resulting from lack of parental response) is extremely vulnerable to setbacks, responding with sharp decrease in self-esteem and disorganization.

The *overstimulated self* (resulting from excessive parental response) shies away from creative and leadership activities for fear of being flooded by unrealistic fantasies of greatness.

The *overburdened self* (resulting primarily from frustrated idealizing need) perceives others as hostile, reacting with irritability and suspicion to hardly noticeable events as frustrations or attacks.

Narcissistic Behavior Disorders
Expressed primarily in action rather than in thought.

The *mirror-hungry personality* (resulting from failure to mirror parental response) is famished for admiration, leading to incessant displays in an insatiable attempt to get attention.

The *ideal-hungry personality* (resulting from lack of parental response) can experience self as real only when related to others who conform slavishly to the person, though full satiation of the hunger is never really achieved.

From *Personality Theories: A Comparative Analysis*, Fifth Edition by Salvatore R. Maddi (The Dorsey Press, 1989). Reprinted by permission of Brooks/Cole Publishing Company.

SUMMARY

■ The revolutionary and brilliant ideas of Freud attracted adherents who did much to further the psychoanalytic cause. Several of these followers developed theoretical conceptions that differed from those of Freud and ultimately led to their alienation from him. In general, their ideas revised the role of sexuality and the ego.

■ Adler, the first to depart, emphasized the part played by inferiority feelings and the resulting tendency to compensate for them. Eventually, he concluded that the basic human motivation is a striving for superiority. Still later, he developed the concept of social interest and defined it as a predisposition to contribute to society.

■ A prominent Adlerian concept is style of life. This refers to the specific means the person employs to overcome his or her sense of helplessness.

■ Adler wrote extensively on the role of the family in shaping the person's style of life. For example, he discussed both pampering and rejection as parental reactions that can lead to a mistaken style. He also considered ordinal position in the family to be a potent determinant of different styles of life.

■ For Adler, adjustment meant facing problems with courage. An example of a maladjusted response is the tendency to put distance (either psychological or physical) defensively between oneself and other people or goals. The compulsive search for power (masculine protest) is another example of a maladjusted style.

■ Adlerian therapy was described as a more straightforward, commonsensical approach as compared with Freudian methods.

■ Jung also broke with Freud over issues of sexuality and libido. In the process, he gave psychoanalysis a much different cast by drawing upon archaeology, mythology, religion, and the like.

■ The structure of the personality, Jung asserted, contains the ego, the personal unconscious, and the collective unconscious. Jung gave special emphasis to the last as a repository of the cumulative experiences of our ancestors. The structural elements of the collective unconscious are called archetypes.

■ Four archetypes — persona, anima and animus, shadow, and self — were discussed as especially important ones that exert a powerful influence on behavior.

■ Jung is noted for his descriptions of the ego orientations of introversion and extraversion, that is, interests that are, respectively, oriented subjectively and directed toward the outer world.

■ Symbols, Jung thought, are crucial in pointing the way toward the future and also in revealing the nature of the deepest corners of our minds.

■ Jung did not write extensively about adjustment as such. However, it would appear that he saw it as a kind of balance among the various elements of the personality. Jung's major contribution to psychotherapy probably resides in his influence on subsequent therapists.

■ The neo-Freudians — including Horney, Fromm, and Sullivan — continued the Adlerian trend in emphasizing the role of the social context. Several of their principal concepts were noted, including ways of coping with basic anxiety (Horney), mechanisms for dealing with basic loneliness (Fromm), and stages of development from an interpersonal vantage point (Sullivan).

■ Ego psychology was discussed as a further elaboration of the Freudian concept of ego. The ego psychologists gave a greater role to the ego and saw it as more autonomous as well.

■ The psychosocial theory of Erikson was described as a prime example of the ego psychology movement. Erikson is particularly noted for his eight stages of psychosocial development. He saw these stages as genetic predispositions that unfold according to a ground plan. Each stage presents the individual with a crisis, and how each crisis is resolved, for good or ill, markedly affects the person's capacity to cope successfully with the next stage.

■ In contrast to Freud's stages, Erikson's stretch across the entire lifespan, with an emphasis on adolescence and adulthood.

■ Another outgrowth of ego psychology has been object relations theory as exemplified by Klein. Here, the process of the infant's attachment to the mother is seen as critical for subsequent development and for the growth of thinking and cognition.

■ The self-psychology of Kohut was described as an integration of self theory and psychoanalysis and has developed out of therapeutic work with narcissistic patients.

CHAPTER 5

PSYCHOANALYSIS
Research, Assessment, and Summary Evaluation

Freud exerted a lasting effect on personality theory because he was able to make sense out of his patients' behavior in a way no one else had ever been able to do. He was able to alleviate the phobic's fear of heights or the hysteric's physical symptoms because he had invented a new set of concepts to apply through therapy. Suddenly, the irrational symptom became rational.

But even today, many dismiss psychoanalytic concepts and observations. Like an irrational fear of heights, they make no sense at all. Some of you may have had this feeling when you first encountered descriptions of the id or the psychosexual stages in Chapter 3. As was noted then, there could be several reasons for this confusion—some of them defensive in nature. But another possibility is that the concepts were not presented in the wider context of psychoanalytic research and methods of observation. To help remedy this situation, the first goal of this chapter is the description of some of the chief methods by which observations have been made and research conducted from the psychoanalytic perspective. The second goal is an examination of some of the more prominent psychoanalytic assessment procedures. Finally, an overall evaluation of psychoanalytic theory and method will be offered.

METHODS OF INVESTIGATION

Let us begin our exploration of psychoanalytic methods with an examination of the case study method.

Intensive study of the single case

Freud did not pursue his subject matter with the methods and paraphernalia characteristic of objective science. There were no test tubes or tachistoscopes, no experimental or control groups, and certainly no statistics or computer printouts. What he did was listen carefully to his patients. It was not that he was unfamiliar with the scientific methods of the day. In fact, he was widely recognized for his achievements in medical science. But when he came face to face with patients suffering from agonizing neuroses, it became clear to him that the normal scientific routes to understanding were not going to be very fruitful.

Instead, he began listening intently to these patients, one by one. His laboratory became the consulting room. His instruments were his own sensitivity – the ability to detect consistency in apparent incoherence and to abstract the similarities from the superficial differences among patients. The test of significance for his conclusions became the frequency with which his patients relinquished their debilitating behaviors or fears. What is more, Freud's most enduring case study was himself. Let us briefly examine a case that reveals some of the ways in which Freud proceeded.

The case of Little Hans

Freud's (1955) analysis of a phobia in a five-year-old boy has long been respected in psychoanalytic circles. It has become a milestone in the psychoanalytic method of case investigations. Actually, the analysis was based on letters the boy's father wrote to Freud; Freud saw the child only once. Nevertheless, the case illustrates the kind of data upon which Freud built his notions of infantile sexuality, the Oedipus complex, castration anxiety, and the like.

At the age of three, Hans showed a noticeable interest in his penis, which he called a "widdler." He like to touch it, wondered about the widdlers of others, and asked whether his mother had one. He noted the very large size of a horse's widdler and then remarked to his mother that he expected she had one as large as that. He observed that animals have widdlers but that tables and chairs do not. When Hans was three-and-a-half, a sister was born, and he remarked on how small her widdler was but that he expected it would grow as she did. Eventually, his mother warned him about touching his widdler and even threatened to have it cut off. When Hans was about four-and-a-half, his mother was powdering the area around his penis after a bath when he asked why she did not touch his penis. His mother explained that it was not proper, whereupon Hans exclaimed, "But it's great fun."

One day, about six months later, Hans was out for a walk with his nursemaid. When a horse-drawn van turned over, he began to cry and wanted to go home to be fondled by his mother. Shortly thereafter, he developed strong anxiety over leaving the house, fearing that a horse would bite him if he did. Even before, he was having bad dreams, and as a result his mother often took him to bed with her. He began to fear that a horse would enter his room. Soon his dread of horses escalated into a rather typical horse phobia. An additional aspect of this fear was his preoccupation with the "black things around horses' mouths and the things in front of their eyes." In addition, prior to the onset of the phobia he was with his mother when the father of one of his friends remarked to her that there was a white horse nearby that bit and that she should not hold her fingers up to it.

The foregoing are some of the obvious features of the situation of Little Hans. You will find many additional details in Freud's (1955) lengthy case description. By minutely observing all these details, Freud put together an explanation of Han's phobia

An overly strong attachment to the mother can sometimes precipitate neurotic symptoms. Photograph Jean-Claude LeJeune.

of horses. Briefly, there was Hans's enormous interest in his (and everybody else's) penis. There was his apparent sexual attachment to his mother—his wanting her to touch his penis and their frequent sleeping together. There was the biting horse and its relationship to castration. And there was the likelihood that horses' black blinders and muzzles were representations of his father's glasses and mustache. From these elements and many others, Freud concluded that Hans was in the midst of a severe Oedipus complex. His sexual attraction for his mother was very strong, and his fear of punishment for these desires equally so. While he loved his father, he also feared him, and this fear was then converted into a fear of horses. Even though it was his mother who threatened him with castration, Hans was trying unconsciously to avoid his fear of castration by his father by staying away from horses (which also made it more likely that he could spend time with his mother).

There are, of course, many problems with Freud's analyses of such cases as Little Hans. We shall deal with some of them later in this chapter. But for the moment, it is enough to point out that this case illustrates the way psychoanalytic investigation proceeds.

Criterion of internal consistency

Without question, Freud's patients provided the material from which he built his theory. As Hall and Lindzey (1978) observe, "Inferences made from one part of the material were checked against evidence appearing in other parts, so that the final conclusions drawn from a case were based upon an interlocking network of facts and inferences" (p. 59). He sought verification of his hypotheses by repeatedly looking for consistency in his patients' verbalizations or reports. Much like the anthropologist or folklorist, he continually searched for the underlying thematic structure or recurrences in what his patients told him. Only when he found strong evidence for consistent, recurrent themes did he feel satisfied that he had discovered the correct key to a patient's problems. He would apply the same strategy to the data from many subjects when hypothesizing about a general principle. He would pursue evidence in case after case until he was convinced the principle held. A particularly revealing example of this procedure involves Freud's original belief that many of his patients had been seduced as children by their parents. Later, he became painfully aware (through careful analysis of the case data) that these patients were really reporting their fantasies, not reality. He had built so much of his theory on what turned out to be a fantasy! Yet, scientist that he was, he set about revising his theory to fit the data.*

Before some of you dismiss all of this as terribly subjective, it would be well to remember that Freud spent hour upon hour with patients gathering a wealth of rich data. Likewise, in looking for themes across patients that would enable him to verify a general principle, he examined the cases of many different individuals. There certainly are flaws in the method of internal consistency and in the single-case approach employed by psychoanalysts, as we shall see later in this chapter. At the same time, there probably are equally serious flaws in experimental methods. So when one opts for one investigative approach rather than another, what really happens is the exchange of one set of problems for another. The question, then, is which set of problems is the more serious.

Associations, dreams, fantasy, and behavior

Free association. As we have seen throughout the past several chapters, free association was Freud's major investigative tool. It continues to be a prime psychoanalytic method of inquiry, both clinically with the individual client and as a broader research approach. It is assumed that as one association leads to another, the person gets closer and closer to unconscious thoughts and urges. In one sense, free associations are hardly "free" at all. They are the outgrowth of unconscious forces that determine the direction associations take. Frequently, these associations lead to early childhood

---

*It might be noted, however, that some revisionist scholars of Freudian thought now proclaim that Freud relinquished his seduction theory of neurosis prematurely. They suggest that the childhood seductions reported by his patients were often real and not fantasies after all (see Masson, 1985). Others assert that Freud never completely gave up his original ideas. Still others dismiss the whole question as trivial or feel the issue is being blown out of proportion because of the current furor over incest in our society.

Make believe and fantasy are important components in a child's development.
Photograph The Hennepin Reporter

memories, as was the case with Freud's self-analysis. Such memories of long-forgotten experiences provide the analytic investigator with clues to the structure of personality and its development. Since it is rare to have detailed, objective accounts of development, free association can help the psychoanalyst reconstruct the vital elements of the patient's past. Box 5-1 provides an example of where free associations can lead.

Dream analysis.   Dreams are seen as highly revealing of the unconscious since they are assumed to be heavily laden with unconscious wishes albeit in symbolic form. Typically, dreams are construed as symbolic wish fulfillments that, like free associations, often provide important clues to childhood desires and feelings. Patients are encouraged to give free associations to their dreams. Thus, the techniques of dream interpretation and free association are highly related.

   Of course, not all psychoanalysts have viewed the role of dreams exactly the way Freud did. Adler, for example, regarded dreams as more than elements or residues from the day combined with infantile wishes. He saw them as purposeful attempts to solve problems in a way that corresponds to the person's style of life. Jung also took a somewhat different view of dreams. As noted earlier, he placed great emphasis on the role of archetypes. He felt that these archetypes become known principally through

Box 5-1
AN EXAMPLE OF FREE ASSOCIATION

In the following description, Munroe (1955) offers an excellent example of how free association works. What is especially interesting is the contrast between the rather pedestrian opening and the emotionally tinged closing. Such is the value of free associations.

> The patient begins with a brief report on the previous day—a sort of routine in his analytic sessions. Nothing special: he had a conference with his boss about a project. He didn't quite like the boss's policy, but it was not too bad and who was he, in the hierarchy of his institution, to contradict the boss? By now this was an old issue in the analysis: did he habitually give in too easily, or did he evaluate correctly the major contours of his job? In any event, the conference was just a conference like any others. He'd had a dream—something about an ironing board, but that was as far as he could go. Associations to ironing board? Well, we have one. "Matter of fact, my wife said our maid irons badly. She could iron my shirts better herself, but I don't think she could and I'm sure she wouldn't. Anyhow, my shirts look alright to me. I wish she wouldn't worry so much. I hope she doesn't fire that maid." The patient suddenly hums a bit from *Lohengrin* and has to hunt for the words on the request of the analyst. It is the passage where Lohengrin reveals his glorious origin. ("My father, Parsifal, wears his crown and I am his knight, Lohengrin.") Patient: "Now I think of that last report X (his boss) turned in. That was *my* work—only I can't say so. That ironing board—my mother was ironing. I jumped off the cupboard, wonderful jump, but I sort of used her behind as support—she was leaning over. She told father I had been disrespectful and he gave me a licking. I was awfully hurt. I hadn't even thought about her old behind—it was just a wonderful jump. Father would never let me explain. My sister says he was proud of me. He never acted that way. He was awfully strict. I wish he hadn't died when I was so young—we might have worked things out." (p. 39)

(It should be noted that Munroe telescoped the reconstruction of these associations somewhat.)

dreams and their interpretation. For example, according to Jung, a dream has specific personal associations for the dreamer. But beyond that is a meaning that stems from the collective unconscious.

Fantasy. Fantasies and daydreams are close relatives to free associations and dreams and can, therefore, tell us much about the unconscious. In particular, psychoanalytically oriented therapists have contended that the fantasies, play, and make-believe of children can reveal much about child development. In addition to its diagnostic value, play has been employed for many years as a therapeutic device with children who are experiencing psychological difficulties. Some investigators believe that fairy tales have been employed by cultures throughout history not only to teach children but to help them confront their own developing emotions (Bettelheim, 1976). Box 5-2 expands on this latter point.

Psychopathology of everyday life.   A further source of data for the psychoanalyst is the everyday slips of the tongue, memory distortions, and other mistakes of various kinds (Freud, 1938). Such mistakes are often regarded by the analyst as having dynamic significance: They have their origin in the unconscious.

For example, there is the man who persists in calling an old girlfriend by her maiden name or who cannot remember her married name. This would indicate that the attraction still lives. And there is the egotistical person who rises at a scientific meeting to comment on the paper of a friend and says, "May I offer a few brilliant remarks on this very modest paper?" Leaving objects such as umbrellas, hats, briefcases, or books in someone's office or home provides a very nice opportunity to return. Likewise, was it *really* an accident when you broke that horrible ashtray given to you by your father-in-law? These and other examples of everyday psychopathology may be found in J. F. Brown (1940). More recently, Heckhausen and Beckmann (1990) have analyzed such behaviors as "action slips".

The comparative-anthropological approach

Although the case study has served as a major tool for the psychoanalytic investigator, some attention has been paid to more indirect sources. The work of Jung is a notable example. Jung was not adverse to seeking support or additional evidence for the nature of archetypes in a variety of places, including religion, mythology, and the occult. And, like Freud, he did not shrink from analyzing his own dreams and visions. Needless to say, many regard Jung's methods as highly unorthodox and controversial. On the other hand, there is always some utility in testing the limits of one's ideas, and Jung certainly did that—from Kenya to Arizona, from theology to alchemy, from literature to mythology. In these scholarly wanderings he found what he regarded as evidence for the universality of archetypes.

Fromm was another who moved outside the consulting room in the search for evidence. In a study more empirical than anthropological, he went to a Mexican village seeking verification of his ideas about the nature of personality. He used interviews, questionnaires, and a projective test (the Rorschach) to show how personality is affected by social structure and change (Fromm and Maccoby, 1970). And Erikson (1945) studied several North American Indian tribes in the hope of shedding additional light on the relationship between adult personality and childhood experiences.

Psychobiography and psychohistory

Freud, on a number of occasions, delved into the lives of historical figures such as Leonardo da Vinci, Dostoevsky, and Moses (Freud, 1957, 1961, 1964). These were basically psychobiographical studies that served both to validate his theory and also to clarify the psychodynamics of these figures. This tradition continues with, for example, Liebert's (1983) psychoanalytic study of Michelangelo. These are essentially

Box 5-2
CHILDREN AND FAIRY TALES

Critics often decry the terror and violence that is so much a part of fairy tales. Yet Bettelheim (1976) wrote persuasively that there are great benefits to be had from those frightening symbols in fairy tales. After all, even if that horrible old witch threatens to eat children alive, it is that same witch who winds up burning in the oven. Within the framework of fairy tales, children can come face to face with their greatest fears and get rid of them in the end.

The fairy godmother is simply fantasy's way of telling the children that their real and loving mother will always be there to help when needed. Or else it could be that the fairy godmother symbolizes in a reassuring way the child's own inner strength. Even the "littlest" brother or sister can deal with or overcome an older, smarter sibling. Also, kindness can become a magical tool with which to confront impossible odds. And in the end, the child achieves the impossible.

What is more, Bettelheim believed that fairy tales personify the good versus evil theme that lives everywhere in reality. Fairy tales can, then, help the child find a moral meaning to life. Whereas teaching and preaching will often fail to sway a child, a good fairy tale can successfully convey the moral message that not only should goodness triumph over evil, it will. Although children know intuitively that such stories are not real, they learn constructive lessons from them (Crain, 1980):

1 In "Hansel and Gretel," the children are abandoned, but they learn to overcome that calamity and to be independent and intelligent.

2 Although Cinderella's mother died at her birth and she was given a menial place in her stepmother's home, the prince and happiness eventually arrived.

3 In "Jack and the Beanstalk," Jack learns to be strong and daring. In the process he overcomes the giant and brings comfort and help to his mother.

case history approaches that may be returning to favor in the field of personality (Runyan, 1982). In a sense, **psychobiography** refers to the study of individuals. The related field of **psychohistory** refers to the study of individuals but places these individuals in the larger context of historical movements and contexts.

Erikson's essays on Hitler's childhood and Gorky's youth and his books on Luther and Gandhi were psychobiographical, but they provided a powerful impetus to the growth of psychohistory as a field (Erikson, 1958, 1963, 1969). In Box 5-3 some of the flavor of Erikson's psychohistorical treatment of Gandhi is presented.

Psychohistory is an active field (Lifton, 1974) and, depending upon the point of view, "a substantive new area of social science" (Kren and Rappoport, 1976) or a "murky

Box 5-3
ERIKSON ON GANDHI

Identity, as we have seen, has been a key concept in Erikson's writings. Nowhere did Erikson more clearly use this concept than in his book, *Gandhi's Truth,* published in 1969. Identity became Erikson's key concept in understanding Gandhi, but also Gandhi's life became a way for Erikson to better understand the concept of identity.

In an analysis of Erikson's description of ideology and identity in Gandhi's life, Scroggs (1985) makes several points. Among them is the description of how clothing came to symbolize Gandhi's struggle to achieve an identity. The little brown man in the cotton loincloth became universally associated with Gandhi and his cause, the freedom of colonial people. In the beginning, he tried to find his own identity by identifying with his oppressors, the British. Thus, as a young man in England he wore clothing (silk hat, black coat) that would proclaim his "English" identity. He even took dancing lessons to solidify his image. Later, in South Africa, it would be his clothing that would lead a South African judge to refuse to allow Gandhi to remain in his courtroom.

If the foregoing signified a definite identity crisis on the part of Gandhi, it was South African racism that pushed him toward a resolution of that crisis. Scarcely a week after being tossed out of the courtroom, he was thrown off a train when he refused to give up his compartment to a white man. It was this experience that led him to resolve that he would lead a movement to eradicate such discrimination. In a real sense, his identity crisis was now over.

Photograph India
Information Service

Twenty years later, he returned to India to be met by dignitaries all decked out in their finest formal attire. Gandhi, in contrast, stepped off the gangplank dressed in his customary shawl and loincloth. As Scroggs (1985) puts it, "Gandhi learned the hard way that you are what you wear; but once he had learned this lesson, he applied it with great effectiveness" (p. 104).

In searching for and establishing his own identity, Gandhi really restored India's identity. To understand India, we must, then, understand Gandhi and his struggle for a personal identity. To understand Gandhi, we must, in turn, learn about India. The influences are reciprocal ones.

quagmire, unredeemed even by its more comical extravagances" (Barraclough, 1973). For Erikson, however, the in-depth study of great figures in history permits an understanding of the people they led, along with the events that flowed from their decisions and actions. The psychohistorical analysis of important men and women can lead to insights into the causes of notable historical events. Thus, psychohistory is more than an account of how great people have worked out their private psychopathology. It is the study of how the person manages his or her problems and, in so doing, changes the course of world events.

There is a clear analogy between the analysis of a patient and the retrospective analysis of a historical figure, but there are clear differences as well. In psychotherapy, the patient's history is minutely examined to understand how the pathology developed. The neurosis is seen as an unsuccessful attempt to solve a problem of unresolved infantile sexuality. In a psychohistorical analysis, the search is for the adult reenactments of childhood traumas. Here, the focus is on the adult behaviors that unfolded in such a way as to transform society.

By focusing on "great man" themes the hope is that a deeper understanding of the forces of history will follow. There is, of course, the ever-present danger that the "psychoanalyzing" of famous figures will disintegrate into shallow, self-serving interpretations bordering on mudslinging (something that crops up from time to time in heated political campaigns).

However, sensitive analyses made by those knowledgeable both about the dynamics of the individual and about the complexities of the world can lead to a deeper understanding of events than could be achieved by considering either set of data alone. If it is true that we cannot really understand individuals apart from their sociohistorical context, it must be equally true that our grasp of historical events will never be complete without considering the case histories of the great individuals so intimately connected with those events.

A recent issue of the *Journal of Personality* was devoted entirely to psychobiography and life narratives (although not entirely from a Freudian perspective). In introducing that issue, McAdams (1988) felt compelled to comment, "Today, personality psychologists seem less ashamed than they did twenty years ago to admit that the subject of their study is human lives" (p. 1). While it is sad to observe that personologists have taken so long to return to psychobiography and case studies, it is clear that the legacy of Freud is once more beginning to bear fruit.

Experimental studies

Empirical research has never been the strong suit of psychoanalytic practitioners. The training of psychoanalytic practitioners rarely provides them with either the skills or the inclination to pursue empirical research. Nor is private practice a setting that offers much opportunity for research. The attitude of Freud himself seems to have reinforced this state of affairs. In an often-cited exchange, Rosenzweig (1941) wrote to Freud about his experimental research on repression. Freud responded by observing that psychoanalytic concepts had developed out of a host of clinical cases and thus did not require experimental proof. This succinctly states the prevailing attitude that verification of psychoanalytic concepts is best accomplished by intensive study of individual cases, by self-analysis, and by events that transpire during the therapy session (free association, dream analysis, etc.).

Psychoanalysts who are in training must themselves undergo lengthy personal analyses. Some critics have contended that being placed in the vulnerable role of a patient in these training sessions makes the budding analyst so susceptible that it becomes too easy to see the beauty and accuracy of psychoanalysis and thereby to lose one's scientific objectivity. But it is likely that struggling, dependent graduate students in, say, experimental psychology are equally vulnerable and susceptible to a powerful or charismatic major professor.

There is a growing number of experimental studies of psychoanalytic phenomena. Many suggest that the empirical testing of psychoanalytic hypotheses is not only possible but promising (Masling, 1983, 1986). In the next few pages, we shall briefly sample some of this work.

Research on Freudian concepts.   Ernest Hilgard (1952) commented many years ago that even though laboratory studies of psychoanalytic concepts often are supportive, they turn out to be rather trivial demonstrations that do little to advance understanding. Furthermore, the research often addresses itself to the more superficial aspects of the theory. When these things happen, experimentally oriented critics are left unimpressed and the psychoanalysts themselves dismiss the research as silly demonstrations of what is already known from clinical experience. Moreover, most such studies are laboratory analogs. That is, simulated events are created in the laboratory so that greater experimental control can be exerted. However, there is always the danger that in the process, the events become so artificial that we are no longer studying what we think we are studying.

Because repression is a concept so basic to psychoanalytic theory, it has been the subject of widespread investigation. After years of such study, Holmes (1974) concluded, following an extensive review, that little evidence exists to support the predictions that follow from the concept of repression. Although much of this research does suggest that material associated with threat is not recalled very well or is relearned poorly, these findings can often be explained more parsimoniously by other hypotheses. And in other cases, it is not clear that Freud would have agreed that repressive mechanisms were operative.

An example of such work on repression is a study by Zeller (1950). He asked subjects to study a list of nonsense syllables until they were recalled perfectly. Three days later, subjects were asked to relearn the list to one correct trial. They also performed a psychomotor task that was manipulated by the experimenter so that half the subjects were led to believe they were succeeding and half that they were failing. Both groups had done equally well in their initial recall of the nonsense syllables. According to the theory of repression, it was expected that the effects of ego threat would spread to recall of the nonsense syllables. Thus, the group that believed it did poorly on the psychomotor task was expected to forget (repress) the syllables to a greater extent than the group that believed it succeeded. This did happen. In fact, the difference in recall for the two groups carried over to three days later. After this, all subjects were again administered the psychomotor task and allowed to succeed. This latter step presumably eliminated the ego threat. Under this condition, the differences in recall of the nonsense syllables between the two groups evaporated; the same recall results occurred three days later. Thus, Zeller seems to have demonstrated that ego threat leads to repression and that the lifting of that threat erases the repression. However, some people have argued that this experimental analog of repression is trivial compared to what happens in real life. Still others have contended that it was not repression that produced lowered recall. Rather, failure may have led subjects to become preoccupied with that failure so that they no longer concentrated on the syllable task. So what do we have? Repression or an attentional deficit? Such have been the vicissitudes of research on repression.

Recently, Klein (1987) has proposed that there are three ways of studying repression and the unconscious. First, there is the **precept-genetics method.** In this method, pictures or other stimuli that are threatening to the subject are presented through a tachistoscope. There is a series of exposures under gradually increasing illumination levels. The subject must describe or draw the stimulus and the longer it takes to do so accurately, the more it is assumed that repression is operative. The classical study by McGinnies (1949) exemplifies this approach. He flashed neutral or "taboo" words (e.g., *house, flower* versus *whore, bitch*) on the tachistoscope. He found that a longer flash interval was necessary for subjects to perceive the taboo words and that galvanic skin responses were heightened when the subject did not correctly report a taboo word. But how could a subject defend against a taboo word without first perceiving it? That is, how can we perceive the stimulus well enough to provoke anxiety (heightened skin response) and yet block the stimulus (by not reporting it) to avoid anxiety? Others argued that it was not repression that blocked recognition of the taboo words; rather, it was relative unfamiliarity with them (Howes and Solomon, 1951). Such criticisms are reminiscent of those brought against Zeller above and were enough for many to reject such studies as proof of the operation of repression.

Klein's second method is referred to as the **drive-activation method.** Here, the idea is to activate repressed, unacceptable drives that, according to psychoanalytic theory, would be said to create pathology. The activation occurs through the subliminal presentation of relevant stimuli (subliminal so the activation is unconscious). If the material becomes conscious it no longer functions as a drive.

The work of Silverman (1976) illustrates this drive activation method. He has described two independent programs involving the laboratory study of psychoanalytic theory. The programs have stimulated numerous doctoral dissertations and have sparked a great deal of interest despite several serious failures in replication by other investigators. The research has involved the relationship between psychopathology and unconscious libidinal and aggressive wishes. Box 5-4 presents a description of this approach with the use of hypnosis.

In another approach, Silverman has employed subliminal methods (Silverman and Weinberger, 1985). He assumes that there are powerful unconscious wishes for a state of oneness with the "good mother of early childhood." He further assumes that, if these wishes are gratified, an enhanced level of adjustment will be achieved. A variety of populations have been studied ranging from schizophrenics to psychotherapy candi-

Box 5-4
EFFECTS OF UNCONSCIOUS MOTIVES

Silverman (1976) describes an example of the research carried out by Reyher and his coworkers at Michigan State University. The basic approach is to hypnotize normal subjects, implant a memory that will activate unacceptable impulses, and then give a posthypnotic suggestion that after awakening, sexual or aggressive feelings will become aroused in response to certain stimuli. The question is, will subjects develop symptoms as they try to cope with this conflict-laden situation?

In one procedure, male subjects under hypnosis were told a story with Oedipal connotations and instructed not to remember it. The story was as follows:

> One evening while you were out for a leisurely walk, your attention was drawn to an attractive, older woman who seemed quite upset. She had lost her purse and did not have money for bus fare. Wishing to help the woman you took out your wallet, but discovered that you only had a $10 bill. Still wanting to help, you offered to accompany her to the bus stop and pay her fare. She, however, insisted that you accompany her to her apartment in order that she might repay you. You agreed, although somewhat reluctantly. Once within her apartment, she suggested that you might find some money. There were pieces of brass, gold, lead, steel, tin, platinum, bronze, iron, copper, silver, chromium, and other kinds of metal. If you saw all these as I mention them, raise your right hand. You also remember seeing some coins. There was a penny, a dollar, a nickel, a peso, a pound, one cent, a mill, a quarter, a dime, a shilling, a farthing, a franc, assorted coins, cash, and other kinds of money. If you saw all of these as I mentioned them, raise your right hand. When she returned, she seemed very friendly and was reluctant to have you leave. After talking about the collection, she offered you a drink and snack. She then turned on the record player and invited you to dance. Gradually, you became aware of some stimulating, but disquieting,thoughts and feelings. She was very good looking, and it seemed like such a pity to have all her beautiful softness and curves go to waste. She seemed to be silently inviting you by her physical closeness, glances, and words. Her heavy breathing indicated that she was becoming extremely aroused sexually. You were just starting to make love to her when it occurred to you that she was old, respectable, perhaps married, and undoubtedly, very experienced. You wondered if you would

(continued)

dates, smokers who wish to quit, and adolescents with personality disorders. The typical procedure is to expose the stimulus (MOMMY AND I ARE ONE) for four milliseconds. Pre-experimental and postexperimental assessments of pathology are taken. For males the typical finding is a reduction in pathology following the exposure. For females the message (DADDY AND I ARE ONE) produces comparable results. Silverman concludes that therapy owes its effectiveness, in part, to activation of symbiotic-like fantasies through the patient-therapist relationship. Others (e.g., Vitiello, Carlin, Becker, Barris, and Dutton, 1989) suggest that the subliminal approach does not confirm psychoanalytic predictions.

Box 5-4 *(continued)*

be able to satisfy her, and thought of how traumatic it would be if she laughed at your advances. In spite of these thoughts, you found yourself becoming increasingly excited and aroused. You wanted to make love to her right there, but the telephone rang. While you waited, you became so aroused and excited that you could hardly speak. You made a hurried excuse for leaving, promised to call her back and left the apartment. Later you learned the only way you could attain peace of mind was to completely push the whole experience into the back of your mind. (p. 631)

The posthypnotic suggestion was as follows:

Now listen carefully, the woman I have told you about actually works in this laboratory. In fact, you will meet her briefly later on. [That did not actually happen.] After you are awakened, you will not be able to remember anything about this session. However, sexual feelings will well up inside of you, whenever words associated with money or metal are mentioned. You will realize that the sexual feelings are directed toward the woman you will see shortly and you will want to tell me how you would like to express these feelings toward her. (p. 631)

After awakening, subjects were shown cards with words printed on them, words associated with the repressed memory, such as *peso, dollar, bronze, steel,* and so on. After each word was presented, the subject was asked how he felt. Many subjects responded to the initial words by developing headaches, muscle tremors, guilt, nausea, and the like. No such responses occurred to the control words. Subjects had no idea why they felt as they did. (It should be noted that subjects were debriefed to make sure these symptoms did not recur.)

These results appear to support Freudian theories of how repression works and how symptoms develop in response to stimuli that activate the repressed memories. Questions remain, however, about this kind of research. After all, subjects were hypnotized, and considerable evidence suggests that hypnotized individuals are motivated by a desire to please the hypnotist. Furthermore subjects were not individuals presenting naturally occurring symptoms. This was a laboratory analog. Therefore, although the results are consistent with psychoanalytic theory, they do not, in themselves, confirm it.

A final method discussed by Klein is what he calls the **G analysis of projective data.** In effect, this involves the development of reliable scoring schemes for projective tests (see projectives later in this chapter). This allows the experimenter to count and thus statistically deal with the specific test responses. Projectives are used since it is assumed that they are more disguised than questionnaires and thus allow the experimenter to probe more deeply into the subject's unconscious. Cramer (1987) used this general approach in her study of defense mechanisms. She employed the TAT and developed and validated a method for categorizing the stories produced by four age groups: preschool, elementary school, early adolescent, and late adolescent. She found that denial was used most frequently by preschool children who decreased their usage as they grew older. Identification was very little used by preschoolers but increased steadily through adolescence. The use of projection was most frequent in the two middle age groups (see Figure 5-1). Presumably, these results are consistent with the hypothesized development of defenses in psychoanalytic theory.

The unconscious, repression, and the defense mechanisms. These have long been regarded as critical elements of psychoanalytic theory (Ihilevich and Gleser, 1986). In Box 5-5, a final example of work in this area is provided.

Another area of research crucial to psychoanalytic theory involves dreams and related matters of psychosexual development. As an example, Hall and Van de Castle (1965) attempted to provide evidence relevant to Freud's notions about castration anxiety and penis envy. They predicted that male dreamers would report dreams expressing castration anxiety rather than penis envy. For female dreamers the reverse was expected to occur. Males and females were asked to keep a log of their dreams. A

FIGURE 5-1   Relative defense scores of primary, intermediate, early adolescent, and late adolescent groups.

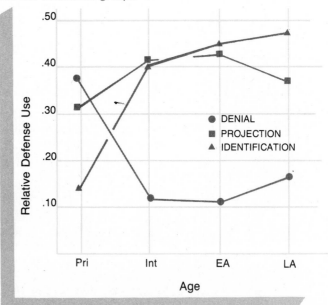

From Phebe Cramer, "The Development of Defense Mechanisms," *Journal of Personality* 55:4, December 1987. Copyright © 1987 by Duke University Press. Reprinted by permission.

Box 5-5
REPRESSION AND THE INACCESSIBILITY OF PAINFUL MEMORIES

One of the basic tents of psychoanalysis is the idea that repression serves to keep painful, unpleasant memories out of consciousness. Davis (1987) hypothesized that if this is true, then people who characteristically utilize repression as a defensive technique should have less access to emotional memories that involve negative or unpleasant events. Davis carried out three studies to investigate her hypothesis. To identify those who were typically repressors and those who were more characteristically likely to experience anxiety, she used a combination of scores from a short form of the Manifest Anxiety Scale (Bendig, 1956) and the Marlowe-Crowne Social Desirability Scale (Crowne and Marlowe, 1964).

In the first experiment, she asked the repressors and nonrepressors to recall (a) personal real-life childhood experiences in which they had felt the emotions involved (e.g., happy, sad, angry, fearful), and (b) similar instances in which the various emotions were experienced by another person. The basic result was that repressors, compared to the other subjects, recalled fewer childhood experiences in which *they* felt happy, sad, angry, and fearful.

In the second experiment, subjects were asked to recall and describe real-life events that were fairly neutral, emotionally speaking. It was found that, here, repressors responded no differently than the other subjects. This means that the results of the previous experiment cannot be attributed merely to some sort of general memory deficit for real-life events.

The third experiment was basically an extension and replication of the first one. Now, the emotions tapped were extended to include guilt and self-consciousness. This time, the length of time taken to retrieve memories associated with happiness, sadness, and guilt was similar for repressors and nonrepressors alike. But this was not the case for memories associated with anger, fear, and self-consciousness.

What all this research seems to tell us is that difficulty in recalling emotion-producing events does not simply reveal high levels of defensiveness. Rather, it is specific to individuals who characteristically employ the defense mechanism of repression accompanied by low levels of anxiety.

manual was developed so that dreams could be reliably scored for castration anxiety and penis envy. For example, a dream in which a part of the body was injured or removed was counted as an instance of castration anxiety. The investigators trained judges to score the dreams of the subjects. The results of the study supported Freud's speculations. Male dreamers did, in fact, report a greater frequency of dreams expressing castration anxiety, whereas females' dreams contained penis envy imagery.

Despite a checkered history, attempts continue to validate or explore a variety of psychoanalytic concepts. Research is conducted on dreams, defensiveness, psychosexual phenomena, and anxiety. Some of it is confirmatory, some is negative, and much is equivocal. Whatever the case, some investigators remain convinced that there is scientific vitality to psychoanalytic theory. For example, Kline (1981) and Fisher and Greenberg (1977) have reviewed nearly two thousand papers and they conclude that psychoanalytic theory has been confirmed. Although not every Freudian idea has been validated, they contend that, as a whole, the weight of scientific evidence favors Freud.

Research on Jungian concepts.

Meier (1984) has provided a historical overview of a great many of Jung's early studies. In his research, Jung (1910) made use of a word-association technique to uncover complexes, that is, areas of emotional conflict, in patients. A list of one hundred words was presented to patients. Following the presentation of each stimulus word, patients were instructed to respond with the first word that came to mind. Time to respond was recorded by a stopwatch. Mechanical measures were sometimes used, for example, a pneumograph to record breathing changes. Other indicants of emotional reactions included flushing and long reaction times. Although such work did attract the attention of experimental psychologists, it had little impact on psychoanalytic thought.

Carlson and Levy (1973) have contended that Jungian theory has been misunderstood and neglected by academic investigators. They reported on four empirical studies to help validate the theory. In the areas of memory, judgment, and volunteer service, they found predictable differences between introverts and extraverts. Carlson (1980) has also noted that introverts and extraverts differ—in this case with respect to their affective memories, the nature of their personal constructs, and their self-descriptions.

Although typologies have not found much favor in past psychological research, there does seem to be renewed interest in Jung's typology. Consider that Jung felt that neurotics were out of touch with their collective unconscious and hence developed numerous symptoms. In studying this idea, Cann and Donderi (1986) believed that archetypal dreams would be a good vehicle. It was noted in the previous chapter that Jung believed that neurotic individuals tend not to be in touch with their unconscious. Therefore, the investigators predicted that subjects scoring high on a neuroticism scale would report relatively few archetypal dreams. More intuitively oriented subjects, being in closer contact with their unconscious, would likely report more archetypal dreams. And this is exactly what happened.

Research on Adlerian concepts.

The effects of birth order have long fascinated researchers (Vockell, Felker, and Miley, 1973). An excellent example of research in this area is a study by Schachter (1959). Female college students who volunteered for the research were brought to a very "medical-appearing" suite of rooms. They were told they were participating in a study of the effects of electric shock on blood pressure and pulse rate. There were two conditions: instructions designed to generate high anxiety and instructions designed to generate low anxiety. Subsequent to the instructions, subjects were told they could wait for their turn alone or they could wait with other participants. As expected, high-anxious subjects were more likely to choose to wait with others than were low-anxious subjects. Interestingly, first-born and only children reported being more anxious than later-born children. Also, a larger percentage of first-born and only children chose to wait in the company of other participants. Schachter's explanation for these latter results suggests that parents create greater affiliative tendencies in firstborn and only children because they are more solicitous and insecure about them. They give them more attention, and consequently, these children learn to expect that the presence of others will help them better deal with stress-producing situations.

Falbo (1981) found that firstborn and only children have higher levels of educational aspiration than later-born children. This may be due to the fact that they receive more positive parental attention and are also the objects of higher parental expectations. Furthermore, last-born children show lower self-esteem than firstborn children. Perhaps this is because last-born children have always had older and therefore more competent siblings against which to compare themselves.

Social interest has also come under extensive study. J. E. Crandall (1980) reviewed the meaning of the concept and also reported on the development of an objective scale to measure it. Indications are that a concern for others contributes to one's adjustment. Furthermore, such variables as sex, age, and stress affect the relationship between social interest and adjustment. In addition, Crandall (1982) has investigated the connection between social interest and what Adler regarded as the tendency of neurotics to think in terms of hard and fast dichotomies. He found that subjects low in social interest are more likely to make extreme judgments about themselves, others, and a wide variety of issues.

Research on ego psychology.   Like orthodox psychoanalysis, ego psychology has not been the subject of extensive experimental research. One exception, however, is the work of Wagner, Lorion, and Shipley (1983). They designed questionnaires to measure resolutions of the psychosocial crisis of ego integrity versus despair. Using an elderly population, they discovered that high levels of despair in these individuals were related to insomnia. Thus, an ineffective resolution of the crisis of old age led to symptoms. With a college-age population they again found a greater incidence of insomnia in those students who had failed to resolve the crisis of identity versus role confusion.

Erikson felt that the ages of thirty-five to forty-five were critical ones in adulthood. In an ambitious study of this age period, Levinson, Darrow, Klein, Levinson, and McKee (1978) studied a group of forty male novelists, biologists, hourly industrial workers, and business executives who belonged to a variety of ethnic, racial, educational, and social class categories. Interviews and, in some cases, later follow-up interviews, were conducted. Material on leisure-time activities, religious involvement, reactions to the death of a spouse, and the like was covered in order to draw an in-depth picture. A research team then integrated all this information with Erikson's theoretical concepts. This procedure is not unlike what a psychoanalyst might do with a single case. However, in this instance there were multiple observers and forty different subjects so that comparisons and contrasts could be made. Analysis led Levinson and his colleagues to conclude that there are age-linked periods in adult development and that our lives can be viewed in terms of the choices we make and the coping strategies we employ. The major choices involved are concerned with occupation; marriage and family; friends; leisure; activities in the political, religious, and community spheres; and immediate and long-range goals. All these conclusions are consistent with Erikson's theorizing. However, it is well to consider the possibility that pre-existing Eriksonian ideas may have influenced the interpretations made by the investigators.

More recently, Van De Water and McAdams (1989) have suggested that to be generative in adulthood, people must have a fundamental "belief in the species" or a faith that human progress is possible and worth working for. Using a variety of self-report and open-ended measures, they were able to garner modest support for their hypothesis.

PSYCHOANALYSIS AND ASSESSMENT

The general posture of psychoanalytic theories is that human behavior, normal or abnormal, is determined by relatively stable internal characteristics. In the assessment of these internal determinants, it is important to minimize the influence of the situation. In this way, the operation of internal characteristics can be observed uncontaminated by situational stimuli. This is why psychoanalysts traditionally reveal so little of themselves to their patients. For example, an analyst's talking about his or her interest in football to a patient who detests the sport might account in part for that patient's aversion to the therapist. That is, such antipathy could not automatically be interpreted as evidence of negative transference ultimately stemming from problems in parent-child relationships; it might be more simply understood as a function of the therapist's characteristics.

The same principle holds in the development of specific testing procedures. Emphasis has always been placed on tests that are inherently ambiguous and thus require the person to draw upon internal resources to interpret them. In the process the individual reveals something of those internal characteristics. In psychoanalytic assessment and other orientations that emphasize the part played by core personality determinants, the role of clinical intuition is readily apparent. The approach is subjective and intuitive rather than objective or normative. The clinician's skill and sensitivity are the means by which insight into the results of testing is achieved.

Therapy processes as assessment

The process of psychoanalytic assessment takes place throughout the course of therapy. This assessment is not a formal, predetermined procedure but rather an outgrowth of the ongoing therapy processes themselves.

We have already examined such matters as dreams, free associations, resistance, transference, and the like. Free associations give important clues about the contents of the unconscious. These clues permit the reconstruction of the dynamics motivating the individual's behavior and feelings. Dreams, too, with their wish-fulfillment qualities, suggest to the analyst some of the unconscious determinants of behavior. Over the course of therapy, the analyst uses these processes to identify the forces driving the patient and the themes constantly recurring in his or her life. And, in a real sense, the extent to which a patient displays therapeutic change serves to validate the assessment that has been going on during the therapy process.

Projective techniques as assessment

For assessment questions couched in a psychoanalytic framework, psychologists have generally turned to projective techniques. For example, their ambiguous nature, the reduced ability of subjects to present themselves in a favorable light or create the impression they wish, and the freedom of the subject to respond in a multitude of ways make projectives ideally suited for psychoanalytic assessment. It is more likely that the person's responses will reflect unconscious processes that are the core determinants of personality. The ambiguity of the test material prevents the individual from relying on specific cues in the test in selecting a response. Instead he or she must structure the stimulus material and in so doing reveals something of that inner core.

The Thematic Apperception Test (TAT).   The **TAT** was originally designed as a method of eliciting material analogous to that usually obtained through dreams and free associations (Morgan and Murray, 1935). Thus, it has always been an attractive assessment tool for those interested in learning about unconscious personality trends or hypothesizing about central personality characteristics. As was seen in Chapter 2, the individual is asked to make up stories to a series of pictures (about what is happening, who the people in the picture are, what led up to the scene, how it will turn out, and so on) (Phares, 1988). This is a subjective technique that depends on the skill of the examiner. A variety of interpretations are possible for any story, depending upon the nature of the client and the characteristics of the other stories. One cannot just look at a story and then casually thumb through a TAT manual until the correct interpretation pops out. Interpretation is a skilled process best thought of as a means of generating hypotheses that can later be checked against other data. Several examples of TAT interpretations are presented in Table 5-1. Again, the likelihood that these are useful for a specific person depends on other information. In both Chapters 2 and 9, additional discussion of the TAT may be found.

Other tests.   The **Blacky Pictures,** although not widely used, is an interesting test because it was specifically developed to elicit data relevant to a psychoanalytic perspective (Blum, 1968). The test consists of a series of cartoon pictures showing the adventures of a dog named Blacky. Each of the cards is designed to provoke responses relevant to a specific psychosexual stage. The test has been used chiefly with children. A Blacky card is shown in Figure 5-2. The Children's Apperception Test (CAT) (Bellak, 1954) is another example of a TAT-like test appropriate for children that has a definite psychoanalytic origin. It is composed of cards showing animals engaged in

---

TABLE 5-1　Examples of interpretations of TAT responses

Type of Response(s)	Possible Interpretation
Omitting reference to a gun shown in the picture	Repression of aggressive impulses
Plots emphasizing sudden physical accidents, emotional trauma, loss, etc.	Anxiety
Stories describing loss of parts of the body; themes of sexual inadequacy	Castration anxiety
Male gives evidence of repeatedly identifying with female characters in stories	Latent homosexual impulses
Tendency to introduce figures not depicted on the cards	Potential use of projection
Hero of stories typically adequately deals with problems	Ego strength

---

a variety of human activities. Presumably, children can more easily identify with animals and thus provide richer stories for analysis.

Concluding comment.　Without question, projective techniques are not as popular as they formerly were. In part, this is due to the rise of behavioral approaches to therapy, which downplay the importance of assessment in general and psychodynamic assessment in particular. Another reason is the equivocal research evidence regarding the validity of projective tests. Yet, in spite of this, projective tests continue to be used widely by clinical psychologists. Wade and Baker (1977) surveyed 500 clinicians. They discovered that clinicians of many theoretical persuasions (not just psychoanalytically oriented ones) used projective tests with substantial number of patients. These clinicians felt that their own experience with tests such as the TAT was more important in their decision to use a particular test than the research evidence. Thus, in the real world of assessment and patients, projective testing is still quite alive.

Myers-Briggs Test

Increasingly, the **Myers-Briggs Type Indicator Test** (Myers, 1980) is being used to measure Jung's four functions of the mind: thinking, feeling, sensing, and intuiting. It has become a very popular instrument among counselors and industrial and organizational psychologists because it purports to explain the person's personality characteristics simply and easily. It is often held out as a more psychometrically elegant example of the possibilities of Jungian assessment. Unfortunately, recent research provides little support for the utility of the Myers-Briggs test (McCrae and Costa, 1989).

SUMMARY EVALUATION

Before proceeding with this discussion, several points should be mentioned. The term *psychoanalysis* covers a lot of territory. It refers to early speculations by Freud during the Breuer era, but it also covers his later views (changes in the nature of the role played

FIGURE 5-2 **A Blacky card.** Reproduced by permission of Gerald Blum.

by anxiety, role of the death instincts, etc.). Furthermore, psychoanalysis is a large umbrella that shelters everyone from Jung to Erikson—from the orthodox Freudians to the neo-Freudians and the ego psychologists. In addition, psychoanalytic theory, as with most things in life, is a mixed bag. However, even though several features are real liabilities, this does not mean that the theory as a whole should be discarded. Finally, there is a distinction between psychoanalysis as a theory and psychoanalysis as a form of treatment. Acceptance of the former does not automatically require that one accept all of the latter or vice versa. It is far from obvious that traditional psychoanalytic therapy procedures are the only ones that can be deduced from psychoanalytic theory.

Strengths

The following are some of the more salient positive features of psychoanalysis.

Breadth. Psychoanalysis, especially the orthodox Freudian variety, has a sweep unmatched by any other personality theory. It has been applied in almost all areas of human endeavor. Plays have been written with Freudian themes (e.g., those by Tennessee Williams and Lillian Hellman). The CIA has commissioned what are essentially psychoanalytic studies of world leaders. Historical figures have been analyzed psychohistorically. Recently, the relevance of psychoanalysis for political theorists has been examined (Frosh, 1987). Even industrial firms are not above buying advice about the unconscious reactions of potential consumers to their products. In fact, psychoanalytic themes are so ubiquitous in our lives that we scarcely notice them.

Although scientists may scorn the respectability of the theory, there is no denying the attraction psychoanalysis has always held for many people. For some, there is a strong intuitive appeal. Thus, Freud changed the way we think about ourselves.

Systematic nature.

As a theory, psychoanalysis is complex yet systematic. There are many concepts, more than in most theories. At the same time, the concepts all tie together. Knowing something about a person's ego very likely implies something about his or her tendencies to repress. Characterizing the nature of someone's Oedipus complex conveys information about the nature and extent of that person's adjustment status. Choice of defense mechanism is linked to psychosexual development. In short, Freud wove an intricate theoretical pattern whose colors and shapes are balanced and interlocked.

Obviously, however, what is true in Freudian theory is not always true for revisions of that theory. Adler's theoretical constructs are few and his theory is not nearly as systematic as Freud's. Jung's emphasis on the introvert-extravert concept foisted upon us a simplistic notion that cannot adequately deal with the complexity of human behavior. In general, neither the neo-Freudians nor the ego analysts were the theory builders Freud was. They generally used fewer concepts and their work was often an extrapolation from Freudian ideas. Moreover, it is not always completely clear which aspects of Freudian theory they reject and which they accept. For example, Adler admitted to no formal concept of the unconscious yet seemed to proceed as if he did.

Psychic determinism and unconscious motivation.

Until the systematic observations of Freud, whole areas of human behavior seemed closed to rational analysis. People did weird things. Therefore, they were weird. Or perhaps they were invaded by devils or influenced by forces not entirely of this world. However, with the use of the idea of unconscious motives and desires, things began to make sense in a way they had never done before. The paralysis of an arm where no structural injury existed, the compulsive rush to destroy oneself by one stupid decision after another, the hatred of a surly son for a doting father—all these things began to have meaning. Freud's brilliant insight led him to create a tool of unparalleled explanatory potential.

Role of sexuality.

Here, again, Freud's insights bore tremendous fruit. The pervasive role of sexuality, from infancy to old age, from culture to culture, had not been realized before. With that realization, much human behavior came into sharper focus. Now we understand that sex sells everything from soap to automobiles. But when Freud saw sexual impulses in children, the door opened to a fresh understanding of another major determinant of human behavior. The abuse heaped upon Freud for all this was probably a clear signal that a nerve in society had been exposed.

Many, including those neo-Freudians who broke with Freud, felt he emphasized the role of sexuality much too much. However, although this emphasis may have served to blind him to the role of other important familial-cultural determinants, he had identified a pervasive factor in our lives.

Freud the observer.   From all that has been said, it seems obvious that Freud was an unusual and intrepid observer. For us, given the benefit of Freud's insights, it is no great feat to conclude that reaction formation may lurk behind the vehement outbursts of someone every time the topic of alcohol, for example, arises in conversation. But for Freud to locate the concept itself out of the rambling, incoherent mutterings of patients was, indeed, an accomplishment of enormous proportions. To find the common threads of infantile sexuality (especially in an era of Victorian repression) among the accounts of different patients is truly remarkable. Thus, Freud was an observer of the most notable kind. That he was not always right does not detract from his overall achievements.

Clinical utility.   Students sometimes get the impression that psychoanalysis, both as a theory and as a form of treatment, has been discarded. Such an impression is easy to get in an academic environment, not typically a bastion of psychoanalysis. Yet every year, new books propounding the theory are published and psychoanalytic forms of treatment continue, especially on the east and west coasts of the United States and in all its largest cities.

The general practice of psychoanalysis has been, and continues to be, a major therapeutic force. There are now numerous different brands of therapy, and psychoanalysis as a treatment surely has its limitations (as we shall see in later discussions). Nonetheless many continue to feel that it has significant clinical utility. The psychoanalytic movement gave birth to techniques such as dream analysis, free association, and analysis of transference and resistance, all of which have become important both as assessment devices and as therapeutic instruments. And tests such as the TAT and other projectives are outgrowths of the psychoanalytic way of looking at things.

Psychoanalytic treatment methods have percolated so far through the layers of clinical practice that we hardly notice their influence these days. But it is there. Whether as pure, orthodox psychoanalysis or as its less obtrusive descendants, the technique is influential and still widely practiced.

Revisions.   Freud, of course, continued to modify his ideas up to the moment of his death. But, as we have seen, both the neo-Freudian and ego movements made important changes in and additions to orthodox psychoanalytic theory. The influx of these ideas has given the whole analytic movement a more contemporary flavor, particularly with respect to the influence of environmental variables and the role of the ego. In addition, modern psychoanalysis continues to attempt to update and revise itself, especially as regards the ego.

At the treatment level, the influence of these revisions has been less visible. Adler did advocate a rather different approach to therapy. But others, such as Horney and Fromm, continued to conduct therapy pretty much in the Freudian style. That is, they continued to use such methods as free association, resistance, and transference. However, the specific content of their interpretations (e.g., moving against others, escaping from feelings of loneliness) departed from Freudian doctrine. Still, changes in modern psychoanalysis are growing by leaps and bounds (Stolorow, Bandcraft, and Atwood, 1987).

Weaknesses

Psychoanalytic theory does have its share of problems that detract from its overall usefulness. Some of the more prominent of these are as follows.

Problems of measurement.

Perhaps nothing has created so many difficulties in establishing the utility of psychoanalytic theory and adding to our knowledge than the problems in measuring psychoanalytic concepts. The theory, then, is deficient on what was referred to in Chapter 2 as the operational dimension. The theory proclaims that unconscious processes guide much of our significant behavior. In addition, these unconscious processes, by their very nature and through ego pressures, rarely express themselves directly. How, then, do we measure them? Surely without reliable, valid measurement both clinical prediction and research efforts are severely hampered. For example, how do we determine the strength of one's instincts? Is altruism evidence for strong life instincts? Is the sexual athlete driven by surges of libido? Or are both, through the operation of unconscious processes, examples of reaction formation? Is the altruist really covering up aggressive urges, and could it be that our sexual athlete is fighting off feelings of sexual inadequacy? Not much in the theory provides us with objective clues as to which is which. There is little specification of precise antecedent conditions for a given behavior, and there are so many potential outcomes for a given antecedent that it is very difficult to decide on exact measurement operations.

As a result, psychoanalytic theory is excellent at explaining things after they occur but very poor in predicting events. Suppose someone commits suicide by jumping off a bridge. To say that Thanatos made the person do it may be correct, but being able to measure, in advance, and thus ascertain the growing strength of the death instinct, is certainly the preferable alternative. But the behavioral signals specified by the theory are difficult to identify with any assuredness.

Picturesque language.

Part of the problem in measuring psychoanalytic concepts stems from facile descriptions couched in literary, picturesque language. To some extent, this relates to the reification of concepts such as the id, ego, and superego. Actually, such concepts are just that—concepts. They imply no reality or specific location in the brain (where would you go in the brain to remove someone's ego?). They are simply constructs that have been erected to help us explain things (see Chapter 2). Unfortunately, the ego too often conjures up such images as a person running about frantically plugging holes in the dike to ward off the waves of the id. And the id may be described as a region "down below," and the superego as "up there"—almost like heaven and hell.

While such vivid language and rich descriptions serve a real purpose in making the theory attractive there arise extensive problems in restraining the language long enough to get independent observers to agree among themselves so that measurement can proceed.

Potential for interpretational excess. Because of these measurement and language defects, there is a strong potential for interpretational excesses within the theory. For example, an analyst or two have been known to discuss the psychic life of a spermatozoon. Moreover, with concepts like reaction formation and the unconscious, it becomes nearly impossible to disprove a hypothesis. Any strongly held opinion can become subject to a charge of reaction formation. If it is said that a patient is pessimistic yet on the TAT reports happy stories, this may be taken as confirmatory evidence. After all, these must be the products of reaction formation.

Theory of psychosexuality. For many years, critics have argued that Freud's notions about psychosexuality have not been supported. Not every culture is like Western society. The universality of the Oedipus complex has been questioned by crosscultural research. Nor is it clear that Freud was right about the implacable march of the child through the psychosexual stages, driven by the beat of the instincts.

But, then, it is hard to know how literal we should be in our understanding of psychoanalytic pronouncements. Does every little boy literally fear that his penis will be cut off, or is this again just a case of picturesque language rife with symbolism? There is always as tendency, too, for those who follow the "master" to wring every ounce of meaning from his statements.

Overemphasis on childhood. Scarcely anyone would deny the importance of childhood in establishing predispositions for adult behavior. Yet the Freudians place such store in childhood determinants that they sometimes seem to ignore the role of current determinants or situational factors. The individual is construed as being driven by internal forces established in childhood. Every adult event then seems to represent merely a reinstatement of some childhood occurrence. There is an analog in psychoanalytic therapy in which patients' criticisms of their therapists are so often interpreted as evidence of negative transference rather than as being determined by real characteristics of the therapists themselves.

In short, there seems to be no systematic way in psychoanalytic theory to incorporate the role of situational variables in the explanation of human behavior. To some extent, however, this criticism is tempered by the cultural emphasis of the neo-Freudians and the work of the ego psychologists.

Observational bias. From the very beginning, charges of bias were leveled at Freud's observations. For one thing, Freud never checked his observations and inferences with other observers. Indeed, if anything, he became the standard against which others judged themselves. Thus, there is a massive lack of interjudge reliability in the Freudian camp. Also, psychoanalysts rarely quantify their data, so we are forced to rely on their subjective reports. And, more recently, Mahony (1986) has examined Freud's process notes written while he was treating the famous case of the "Rat Man." What Mahony found were marked discrepancies between those notes and the published case history.

The single-case approach also raises the question of sampling. How representative were Freud's cases, or, indeed, the cases of most psychoanalysts? Perhaps Freud was generalizing from the restricted perspective of one who saw too many hysterical, middle-class Viennese female patients. Likewise, how representative today are patients of psychoanalysts whose fees are rather large and who have exclusive offices in New York or Los Angeles? Thus, the cases from which analysts generalize may be so atypical that the concepts developed have little applicability to the larger universe of patients. Many argue that psychoanalysis as both a theory and a method of treatment has no utility for those members of minority groups who may have problems in living. Indeed, their problems seem more often attributable to their reduced access to power and material benefits than to such factors as Oedipal complexes or unconscious defenses.

Another problem with relying on single cases is the analyst's tendency to concentrate entirely on reports from patients. There is rarely any contract with relatives, spouses, friends, or employers. With no opportunity to check one's impressions of a patient against those of others, the way is opened for biases and self-serving errors.

Psychoanalysis as science.   Clearly, psychoanalysis is a failure when judged against the rigorous standards of exact science. There is little or no quantification. It is virtually impossible to develop operational definitions of its constructs. Hypotheses are difficult to test, and it is just as hard to get two psychoanalysts to agree on what the proper hypotheses are. What experimental efforts have been made too often turn out to be trivial demonstrations of the theory; little or no insights have been added to the theory as a result of such research.

The feminist critique.   There has always been a question as to how valid certain aspects of psychoanalytic thought are when applied to women. For years, it was common to hear the remark, "We, of course, do not understand the Oedipal (Electra) conflict in women as well as we do for men." It is quite possible that this was due to the fact that so many analysts were men. As men, they were handicapped by a lack of firsthand knowledge of the female experience, and probably also by their share of male myths and stereotypes.

There has long been a tendency for analysts to view women as more vain, sensitive, and dependent than men. These attributes have been seen as part of being female. Women have often cried out in anger and frustration that Freud was wrong about penis envy as a basic motivator of women. They have also taken exception to the psychoanalytic implications that anatomy is destiny, arguing that this is just another instance of Freud's failure to appreciate the role of learning and culture. However, as we observed earlier, some analysts, notably Karen Horney, early on declared their disagreement with Freud on these issues. Similarly, many psychoanalysts have long contended that women display a "natural" masochism. Caplan (1984) asserts that not only is such a view unnecessary, it also does women a profound disservice. Finally, it appears that Freud's misconceptions are being rectified (see Alpert, 1986).

The psychoanalytic cult.   For some, psychoanalysis is viewed as a kind of cult mentality. Many psychoanalysts have emerged from a medical background, characterized by an "appeal to authority" approach to evidence. The usual modes of experimental inquiry are foreign to them. Indeed, the very process of becoming a psychoanalyst contributes to this dogmatic, cultish climate. Before a person can become a psychoanalyst, he or she must undergo a training analysis. But at the same time, the analysis may serve as a powerful tool of indoctrination that will later alienate the individual from other modes of inquiry. As further evidence of the fact that there has long been a very strong psychoanalytic in-group, it was necessary a few years ago for psychologists to file legal action in order to gain admission to psychoanalytic institutes so that they could undergo training in psychoanalysis.

SUMMARY

- The chief method of investigation in psychoanalysis has always been the study of single cases. The case of Little Hans was offered as an example of Freud's approach.

- Freud used internal consistency as the criterion for verifying his hypotheses about these cases. Evidence from numerous separate elements of one case, or from numerous separate cases, were examined before he considered a hypothesis confirmed.

- Specific methods that were typically used included free association, dream analysis, and evidence from the psychopathology of everyday life.

- Other psychoanalysts, such as Jung, Fromm, and Erikson, sought evidence from comparative-anthropological sources.

- A more recent development has been the psychohistorical approach pioneered by Erikson in which historical figures are analyzed from the perspective of both history and psychoanalysis.

- Experimental research has never been a principal method of investigation in psychoanalysis. Although some studies have been undertaken, critics usually describe them as trivial demonstrations rather than harbingers of new knowledge. Several examples of psychoanalytically oriented experimental studies were given.

- Psychoanalytic assessment has typically involved the assumption that stable internal characteristics determine behavior. This being the case, assessment techniques used usually attempt to minimize the influence of situational factors in determining responses in the assessment situation.

- Much assessment is carried out during the therapy process itself. Thus free associations, dreams, transference, and the like become assessment methods.

- Projective tests have long been favored assessment devices. Tests such as the TAT are often used in the search for internal determinants. The Blacky Pictures was described as a specific tool developed to measure psychoanalytic variables.

- The Myers-Briggs tests has been used to measure Jungian concepts.

■ Any evaluation of psychoanalysis must take care to acknowledge the tremendous impact this approach has had on how we view ourselves. It has indeed altered the texture of Western society.

■ Specific strengths of psychoanalysis discussed included: its breadth of description and application, its stature as a systematic statement of a point of view, its emphasis on psychic determinism and the role of the unconscious, its recognition of the importance of human sexuality, and its clinical utility. Above all, psychoanalysis as both theory and practice reveals the remarkable observational power of Freud. It was also pointed out that both the neo-Freudians and the ego psychologists made important revisions that have added to the utility of the theory.

■ All theories of personality have shortcomings, and psychoanalysis is no exception. Problems with psychoanalysis include difficulties in measuring psychoanalytic variables, the use of vague or picturesque language, the potential for interpretational excesses, overemphasis on psychosexual development, failure to recognize the importance of situational or currently impinging events, the inherent potential for observational bias, the status of psychoanalysis as science, the feminist critique, and alleged cultish aspects of the movement.

CHAPTER 6

PHENOMENOLOGY
The Self and Personal Constructs

Thus far, our survey of personality theory has described the human being as one who is motivated, directed, or driven. Whether it is caused by instincts, archetypes, or something else, there is nearly always an urge (usually unconscious) lurking in the depths that impels us to action. If we consult the dictionary* and define the language being used, we can better grasp the image of the human organism:

- *Motive*—An inner urge that prompts a person to action with a sense of purpose

- *Urge*—A strong impulse

- *Instinct*—An inborn tendency to action

Such is the psychoanalytic theory of personality. The Adlerians, the neo-Freudians, and the ego psychologists began to move us away from this view of psychoanalysis with their emphasis on a thinking, planning ego. However, their ideas remained ensnared in the larger psychoanalytic framework.

Is this the complete explanation of personality theory? Has psychoanalysis presented the essence, or is it just an alternative? Once again, let us consult the dictionary:

- *Know*—To have information; to perceive or understand

- *Experience*—The encountering or undergoing of things as they occur in the course of time

- *Cognition*—The act of knowing or perceiving

- *Existential*—Relating to the belief that people have freedom of choice

- *Humanism*—Beliefs that human interests and values are of primary importance

*The Random House Dictionary (1978) (Jess Stein, editor in chief), N.Y.: Ballantine Books.

These words suggest a very different approach to the investigation of personality. They steer us away from the study of motives and toward an analysis of the way the human being experiences, knows, chooses, and becomes aware. Personality ceases to be a system in which structures in the mind grapple for supremacy or stake their claims for gratification. Instead, the focus shifts to an experiencing organism whose perceptions and cognitions are grounded on encounters with an environment that provides alternatives.

NATURE OF PHENOMENOLOGY

The basic assumption of most phenomenological perspectives is that our behavior is largely determined by the way we perceive and understand events. Events do not cause behavior, but people's perceptions of those events do. For example, I do not shrink from snarling dogs just because they are there, but because I perceive them as a threat.

Another way of saying this is that all behavior is determined by the **phenomenal field.** The phenomenal field is everything experienced by the person at a given moment. It follows, then, that to predict or understand behavior, we must somehow discover the individual's perceptions. Indeed, carried to its extreme, this means that I cannot ever fully understand you until I can get behind your eyeballs and see the world exactly as you do.

By the same token, changes in behavior result from changes in perception. People who avoid social situations because those situations provoke anxiety reactions will no longer be anxious once their perceptions of those situations change. Changes in the phenomenal field will be followed by changes in behavior.

The phenomenological movement is complex and quite diverse. To simplify matters a bit while still offering a sense of the contrasts inherent in the field, the emphasis will be on two major theorists: Carl Rogers and George Kelly. In addition, some related contributions from existential and humanistic psychology will be covered briefly. Furthermore, some ideas from a cognitive, information processing viewpoint will be introduced.

THE SELF

One of the key elements in many brands of phenomenology is the self; even though there is certainly less than total agreement about the nature of that self (Epstein, 1980). Indeed, the concept of self cuts across several versions of phenomenology, humanism, existentialism, and, as we shall see later in this chapter, the recent information processing approach to personality.

COMPONENTS

Quite often the **self** is regarded as the "I" or the "me." Everything that people see as theirs will be incorporated into the self. Thus, William James (1890), considered by many to be the father of psychology in North America, set the tone for many of our present ideas about the self when he described it in part as the:

. . . total of all he can call his, not only his body and his psychic powers, but his clothes and his house, his spouse and his children, his ancestors and friends, reputation and works, and his land and horses, and yacht and bank account. (p. 291)

Although written in the late 1800s and a bit sexist in its language, James's description is not so very different from those of today. It also suggests that questions like "Who am I?" are not the exclusive inventions of modern people wrapped up in themselves. Deciding who and what we are is an activity with a very, very long history.

Ruth Wylie (1984) contends that the self really has three major aspects. The first is called the **personal self-concept** and refers to that part of the self that includes the physical, behavioral, and psychological characteristics that help establish one's uniqueness. For example, my eyes are green, my favorite color is purple, and I am an inveterate jogger. It includes racial or ethnic identity and age as well. While the personal self is basically stable over time, there are occasional fluctuations (e.g., though generally calm, John sometimes becomes anxious prior to an exam). These aspects of the self are very similar to James's definition noted earlier.

Social self-concepts refer to how you believe others see you. These concepts will often vary with the person or group with which you find yourself. For example, when Sally is with her mother she can sense that the latter views her as selfish and materialistic. Yet when she is with her friends she knows that they regard her as generous and giving. Obviously, personal self-concepts may, at times, be at odds with one's social self-concepts.

Idealized images of what you would like to be are termed **self-ideals.** Few of us ever really attain our ideal selves and often the latter clash with our personal selves.

Development

Many years ago, Cooley (1902) wrote that our attitudes about ourselves are not really objective self-appraisals but rather, to a large extent, products of our worry over how others feel about us. In fact, he felt that our self-concepts are basically anticipations of the reactions of others (see Box 6-1). George Herbert Mead (1934) saw individuals as attending to their own reactions so as to understand better how others will react. But like Cooley, Mead regarded the self as an object whose character was shaped by our estimation of how others view us.

Whereas Cooley and Mead tended to focus on societal determinants of the self, Harry Stack Sullivan (1953) zeroed in on more immediate influences. In particular, he described the extensive role played by family members in shaping the child's self. The mother, father, and significant others influence the self of the child by their overt and subtle reactions. As a result of their interpersonal relationships, the child develops a three-component self-system: the **good-me,** the **bad-me,** and the **not-me** (Sullivan, 1953). The "good-me" is made up of the positive vibrations the child receives from the mother and others. High self-esteem results when the appraisals of significant others are largely positive. The "bad-me" stems from negative evaluations and helps the child build a conscience. The "not-me" component arises out of strong disapproval from others—a disapproval so strong that anxiety is the result. To avoid the anxiety, dissociation of certain thoughts, feelings, or actions may occur. When this happens, the basis for psychopathology is laid.

Functions

Lecky (1969) has long considered a major aspect of self-systems to be their organizing properties. Personality then, is an integrated, consistent scheme of experience. With it we make sense of the world. Without it everything becomes chaotic and experience is little more than a collage of unconnected elements. Therefore, individuals will guard the consistency and coherence of their systems with enormous care. Experiences will be assimilated into the self-system only if they do not threaten the stability of that system. If the system will not allow for the incorporation of new experiences, the road is opened for maladjustment. Experiences that overwhelm the system likewise can precipitate psychopathology.

With this brief introduction to the world of phenomenology and the self, let us turn to the work of Carl Rogers, the most influential exponent of this general point of view.

ROGERS: A PERSON-CENTERED APPROACH

Although the phenomenological theory of Carl Rogers is about as different from psychoanalysis as night is from day, the two approaches do have several things in common. As theories of personality, they arose from therapeutic encounters with troubled people. To some extent, each also developed as a way of accounting for what took place in those therapeutic encounters. In addition, as with psychoanalytic theory, the person-centered orientation probably cannot be fully grasped without some understanding of what transpires during therapy situations.

The full import of Rogers's contribution is best understood by recalling the personality-therapy world of the late 1930s. Psychoanalytic theory and practice were riding very high in the saddle. Of course, there were debates in academic circles about Allport's ideas; the contributions of Lewin and others were getting attention. But the high-stakes action revolved around those theories associated with specific forms of therapy. These were the theories that captured the public's eye, and for all intents and purposes, this meant psychoanalysis or some derivative of it. If anything, this attention increased as the clouds of war began to sweep over Europe. Prominent psychoanalysts, many of them Jewish, were forced to emigrate from western Europe to escape Nazi oppression. A number of them, as noted in previous chapters, came to the United States (most often to New York City). The effect of all this was to increase the visibility of psychoanalysis.

Against this backdrop, we have an obscure clinical psychologist laboring in Rochester, New York, attempting to solve the problems of disturbed children. Like most therapists of those days, Rogers was thoroughly familiar with psychoanalytic thought. But in the pragmatic environment of a bustling clinic grappling with real problems, one learns to pay attention to anything that offers hope of improving one's effectiveness. While in this eclectic setting, Rogers came in touch with the will therapy of Otto Rank and the relationship therapy of Jessie Taft. According to Rank, patients should be given the opportunity to exert their wills. Taft, a social worker, had brought Rank's ideas to the United States and emphasized the relationship between therapist and patient.

Box 6-1
THE LOOKING-GLASS SELF

Cooley (1902), in describing his concept of the looking-glass self, had this to say:

The kind of self-feeling one has is determined by the attitude . . . attributed to that other [person's] mind. A social self of this sort might be called the reflected or looking-glass self:

> Each to each a looking glass
> Reflects the other that doth pass

As we see our face, figure, and dress in the glass, and are interested in them because they are ours, and pleased or otherwise with them according as they do or do not answer to what we should like them to be; so in imagination we perceive in another's mind some thought of our appearance, manners, aims, deeds, character, friends, and so on, and are variously affected by it.

A self-idea of this sort seems to have three principal elements: the imagination of our appearance to the other person; the imagination of his judgment of that appearance; and some sort of self-feeling such as pride or mortification. The comparison with a looking-glass hardly suggests the second element, the imagined judgment, which is quite essential. The thing that moves us to pride or shame is not the mere mechanical reflection of ourselves, but an imputed sentiment, the imagined effect of this reflection upon another's mind. This is evident from the fact that the character and weight of the other, in whose mind we see ourselves, makes all the difference with our feelings. We are ashamed to seem evasive in the presence of a straightforward man, cowardly in the presence of a brave one, gross in the eyes of a refined one, and so on. We always imagine, and in imagining share, the judgments of the other mind. A man will boast to one person of an action—say some sharp transaction in trade—which he would be ashamed to own to another. (pp. 152-153)

Rogers, although having broken away from his strict, fundamentalist beliefs, nonetheless continued to have a religious outlook, albeit a more liberal one. He found the ideas of Rank and Taft particularly congenial since they resonated well against both his religious beliefs and his democratic convictions about the nature of human relationships in society. The belief that no one has the right to run another person's life found subsequent expression in his therapeutic practices of permissiveness, acceptance, and unwillingness to give advice. Later, as he sought to build a theoretical structure to account for his therapeutic techniques, he naturally found theoretical and philosophical notions from phenomenology comfortable ones. Now let us turn to an examination of Rogers' theory and his views on personality development, adjustment, and behavior change.

Carl Rogers

Carl Ransom Rogers was born in Oak Park, Illinois, in 1902. The fourth of six children, he grew up in a financially secure family. His father, a civil engineer and contractor, moved the family to a farm outside Chicago when Rogers was twelve. The family was devoutly, almost dogmatically, religious. The parents' strict beliefs may have been responsible for the family's being a tight little unit. As a result, Rogers had few friends and spent most of his time alone or reading. Although an outstanding student in high school, he was not much a part of the social scene.

In 1919 he began college at the University of Wisconsin, majoring in agriculture. For the first two years, he was very active in church affairs. During this period, he attended the World Student Christian Federation Conference in Beijing, China. For the first time, he came face to face with cultural and religious diversity. This prompted him to discard his traditionalist familial and religious views and adopt a less fundamentalist approach to God and family. In 1924 he received a degree in history.

Following this, he married Helen Elliott, with whom he had two children. The newlyweds moved to New York City, where Rogers attended Union Theological Seminary for two years. A growing skepticism of religious doctrine coupled with a desire to help others prompted him to pursue a degree in clinical psychology at Teachers College, Columbia University. He received his Ph.D. in 1931.

At this point, he became a staff psychologist in a child guidance clinic in Rochester, New York. It was during this period that he encountered the ideas of Otto Rank, which had a profound effect on his developing views of therapy. He remained at the clinic for ten years, and in 1939 published a successful book, *Clinical Treatment of the Prob-*

Basic theory and concepts

The basic elements of Rogers's view of personality were set forth as a series of propositions in what is still often regarded as his major work, *Client-centered Therapy: Its Current Practice Implications, and Theory,* published in 1951. A shorter, revised version appeared in 1959.

World of the person. The person's world is a world of experience. This experience is a flowing, continually changing process with the individual at the center. But what is meant by experience? For Rogers, experience was the **phenomenal field** which, in turn, is the entire panorama of the person's consciousness at a given moment. Although some unconscious elements may be included in the phenomenal field, Rogers's definition of unconscious probably is closer to what Freud called the precon-

lem Child. Partly as a result of this success, he was invited to become a member of the Psychology Department at Ohio State University. This appointment gave Rogers added recognition and also provided him the opportunity of refining and polishing his theoretical ideas with the help of graduate students and faculty colleagues.

In 1945 he moved to the University of Chicago as professor of psychology and director of the Counseling Center. It was here that his point of view really became a major force in the world of theory and practice. In 1957 he took a position at the University of Wisconsin, where he hoped to apply his ideas to the problems of schizophrenia. This did not work out well. Furthermore, he did not find the academic-research establishment receptive to his humanistic views about graduate education.

Carl Rogers

As a result, Rogers moved to California, where he became a fellow in residence at the Western Behavioral Sciences Institute in La Jolla. In 1968 he left that position to join the Center for Studies of the Person, also in La Jolla. In more recent years, he worked toward the application of his person-centered approaches to school systems, industrial organizations, and the encounter movement. Rogers died in February 1987.

Rogers was the author of numerous books. His autobiography, written in 1967, is included in *A History of Psychology in Autobiography* (Vol. 5). He also published a paper in 1974 entitled "In Retrospect: Forty-Six Years," which appeared in the *American Psychologist.* A recent book, *A Way of Being,* was published in 1980 and provides some insight into the changes in his thinking over the years. A particularly sensitive and revealing portrait of Rogers—both psychologist and person—has been provided by Gendlin (1988).

scious. In the final analysis, it is the phenomenal field that determines behavior. Consequently, the ultimate source of information about a person is that person. As we shall see, it is this assumption that led Rogers to rely heavily on self-reports.

For the individual, the phenomenal field is reality. All reactions of that individual, then, are based on the phenomenal field as it is experienced and perceived. To grasp the full meaning of someone's behavior requires that we be aware in some measure of that person's experience regarding the stimuli being confronted. Just knowing that Stimuli X, Y, and Z are present is not sufficient; it is the person's interpretation of those stimuli that is crucial. Something of these views, and more, is conveyed in the following:

> The only reality I can possibly know is the world as I perceive and experience it at the moment. The only reality you can possibly know is the world as *you* perceive and

experience it at this moment. And the only certainty is that those perceived realities are different. There are as many "real worlds" as there are people! (C. R. Rogers, 1980, p. 102)

In many respects, Roger's views about the importance of the phenomenal field led him to adopt an **ahistorical** stance. That is to say, events are explained as products of one's current perceptions and not as outcomes resulting from the past. Understand people's perceptions of reality and you explain their behavior. It is not that Rogers did not believe there is a train of events culminating in a given behavior. It is simply not necessary to study the past in order to understand the present. For example, if we understand the current perceptions of the conforming person, we will also understand why the conformity occurs: it is a response by the person to the world as it is perceived now.

The basic human striving.   The ultimate human motivation is a single tendency that subsumes all other motives, including hunger and sex. An inborn quality that serves to move all living things forward, it is embedded in the very genetic fiber. One can observe this striving everywhere—in the plant as well as in the human; in the adjusted, achieving person as well as in the regressed psychotic. The striving to enhance and maintain oneself is a potent force upon which the therapist relies for the individual's self-cure. Within each person, there is a potential for growth that constantly seeks expression. Of course, many people have lived lives so barren, so fraught with fear and threat, that they cannot readily perceive the choices open to them. But even in these cases, that inner potential is seeking release and awaits only the proper conditions to express itself. Thus, we all contain within us the living germ of actualization—the force that energizes us all.

Rogers (1980) described this actualizing tendency with a boyhood memory:

> I remember that in my boyhood, the bin in which we stored our winter's supply of potatoes was in the basement, several feet below a small window. The conditions were unfavorable, but the potatoes would begin to sprout—pale white sprouts, so unlike the healthy green shoots they sent up when planted in the soil in the spring. But these sad, spindly sprouts would grow 2 or 3 feet in length as they reached toward the distant light of the window. These sprouts were, in their bizarre, futile growth, a sort of desperate expression of the directional tendency I have been describing. They would never become plants, never mature, never fulfill their real potential. But under the most adverse circumstances, they were striving to become. Life would not give up, even if it could not flourish. (p. 118)

The self.   Out of the individual's ongoing experience, there gradually emerges an awareness of the **self.** This is the "I" or the "me." The process is a fluid one that encompasses what one is and does. Although all aspects of the self are not always conscious, they are available to consciousness.

Rogers came to accept the necessity for the concept of the self as he began to realize the extent to which his therapy clients were committed to the notion. They tenaciously expressed their problems in self-like terms. They spoke of their "real" selves and seemed always to include the self as a vital part of their experience. Or they sought relief from debilitating anxieties but did not want their real selves altered, demonstrating the vital

Every human endeavor, even dangerous ones such as firefighting, is an expression of the striving for self-actualization. Photograph E. Herwig/The Picture Cube.

reality and importance of the self through their fear. This self (or self-concept) has another feature. It contains the **ideal-self,** that is, what the person would like to feel, be, or experience. The ideal-self is roughly analogous to Freud's superego.

Some feel, however, that our preoccupation with the self and its actualization has led to problems, as Box 6-2 illustrates.

Development of personality

Rogers had little to say about so-called stages of development. Unlike psychoanalytic writers, he did not see the person as passing through a discrete series of stages. Rather, he construed development as dependent upon the way one is evaluated by others. In this regard, we see the influence of Sullivan.

Positive regard.   Development can be considered largely in "self" terms. How the self-concept develops depends heavily on several factors that involve interactions

Box 6-2
THE SELF VERSUS SELFISM

For some, the past twenty years or so have been years of self-indulgence. In fact, in the 1970s we often heard about the "me-generation". Cultural observers such as Peter Marin (1975) and Christopher Lasch (1979) have suggested that the search for self-identity and self-fulfillment has crossed over into self-indulgence.

The roots of this self-indulgence or selfism are undoubtedly highly complex. But some observers contend that psychology itself has unwittingly contributed in some measure to this development (Wallach and Wallach, 1983). Certainly, the Freudian movement has preached that neurosis results from insufficient satisfaction of instinctual drives (sexual and aggressive). Psychoanalytic therapy sometimes involves an emphasis on weakening the superego so that instinctual gratification can be more easily pursued.

In particular, Carl Rogers and Abraham Maslow are often cited to support the idea that individuals should be free of the restraints and demands of others and thereby permitted greater spontaneity. Both Rogers and Maslow seemed to encourage people to act in accord with their true feelings. The goal became the achievement of some inner potential (often tantalizingly elusive) or the self-actualization of one's life even if, at times, this meant going rudely against the grain of society. They felt that only by being good to yourself could you be good to others!

But all this can become an invitation to selfishness. As the Wallachs (1983) put it:

> Far as it was from [Maslow's and Rogers's] intention, these psychologists inevitably promote selfishness by asking us to realize ourselves, to love ourselves, to view the environment as a means for our own self-actualizing ends, and to consider whether something will contribute to our own development as the only real criterion for what we should do. (p. 196)

So, is the promotion of understanding and loving oneself the key to personal happiness or the first step down the road toward selfishness? You be the judge.

with the environment. First, there is the need for **positive regard.** This is such an urgent need that the child will sacrifice nearly everything for its satisfaction. Naturally, the road to positive regard lies through approval from others. In addition, the child develops a need for **positive self-regard.** One comes, then, to require from the self what one has all along required from others.

This need for positive regard is an insistent, encompassing urge for love, acceptance, warmth, and respect from significant other people. Indeed, the individual may reach the point where the positive regard of others is as important as, or more important than, being true to one's self. This is not a conscious choice but rather the result of early experience. Furthermore, true psychological maturity can come only from a resolution of conflicts between the need for positive regard and the integrity of self-enhancement processes. Independence and maturity also require that the person possess positive self-regard. One must gain approval not only from others but also from the self.

Conditions of worth.   Increasingly, the child depends upon others for positive regard. But, as most of us soon learn, positive regard has strings attached; it requires that we fulfill certain conditions. In one family, the child receives positive regard by getting an A in English, but not by hitting a home run. What we learn to deal with is **conditions of worth,** which are the bases upon which approval, attention, and rewards are forthcoming. When we meet these conditions, we increase the likelihood that our self-esteem will be enhanced.

Although these conditions of worth serve the important function of providing the framework in which we are all socialized, they also present a danger. Our need for positive regard almost compels us to pay attention to them. In so doing we run a real risk that whole segments of experience will be closed off to us, and our potential for growth and actualization will be reduced accordingly.

Unconditional positive regard.   Rogers felt that everyone should be loved and valued. When parents say (or imply by word or deed) that their love is conditional on the child doing this or that, or on becoming this rather than that, then the child cannot attain total actualization. What is required is **unconditional positive regard,** that is, total and genuine love and respect regardless. This does not imply that parents must cater to the child's every whim. Nor does it mean that standards and discipline cannot be maintained. However, it does suggest that the individual's worth and respect as a human being must be upheld above all else.

Consistency and threat.   A person strives to maintain consistency between the phenomenal self and experience. Experiences that are consistent with the structure of the self are perceived and incorporated into that structure. Some experiences are simply ignored because there is no perceived relationship to the self. But experiences that are inconsistent with the self or with conditions of worth pose a threat. To counter the threat, the individual will often refuse to accept them into the self or else distort their meaning. For example, a person who perceives herself as intelligent may refuse to admit a grade of D in a psychology class to her self-structure. Instead, she distorts its meaning by claiming the test was unfair or the instructor was a terrible lecturer. All of this may occur without awareness. The real danger, however, is that distortion and denial prevent the person from the full experiencing of events.

The self is quite conservative and self-protective. It affects our perceptions and filters our experiences and memories. This screening function of the self is important in Rogers's theory because it explains why personality change is so difficult. Change involves threat, and this threat can be resolved by screening out that which is threatening. Thus, the need for change dissolves. Many conditions of worth will likewise lead to a narrow, constricted self-concept. Such narrowness ensures that many experiences, perceptions, and memories inconsistent with the self will not be permitted into our conscious thoughts and imagery.

Nature of adjustment

Most of the elements of Rogers's conceptualization of adjustment have already been mentioned. To the extent that there is incongruence between self and experience, there will be less than perfect adjustment. The more threat is perceived, the greater will be the tendency to deny and distort. Relatively moderate incongruence would likely lead to behavior that most would call neurotic. Extreme incongruence would end in psychosis. In the latter situation, the person's defenses disintegrate and behavior becomes irrational. Often, this means that the psychotic person's behavior is more in tune with those aspects of reality that have been denied than it is with the self-concept. The psychotic who reports wild fantasies of destroying the world may have once been a very overcontrolled person who could not admit to his or her feelings of hostility toward others. The essence, then, of maladjustment is a denial of experience into the self-structure (C. R. Rogers, 1951).

In his 1961 book, Rogers described the **fully functioning person.** Fully functioning persons live up to their potential, use completely their talents and capacities, and are in tune with their experience. Such people are open to experience, are able to live every moment to its fullest, can rely on the self rather than on others, feel a sense of freedom to live any way they choose, and can respond with creativity. As Rogers stated: "It involves the stretching and growing of becoming more and more of one's potentialities. It involves the courage to be. It means launching oneself into the stream of life" (1961, p. 196). Whether many people ever achieve this level of existence is questionable.

Implications for behavior change

It is debatable whether Rogers's theory of personality would ever have gained prominence without its association with a form of therapy. Over the years, the name of his therapy has changed from **nondirective** to **client-centered** (and now to **person-centered**) (C. R. Rogers, 1977). However, the basic message in Rogers's view of therapy remains unchanged. A proposition from Rogers's 1951 book clearly presents this rationale for client-centered approaches:

> Under certain conditions, involving primarily complete absence of any threat to the self-structure, experiences which are inconsistent with it may be perceived, and examined, and the structure of self revised to assimilate and include such experiences. (p. 517)

Techniques.   Client-centered approaches are distinguished as much by what the therapist does not do as by what he or she does do. Neither advice nor information is given, and reassurance and persuasion are considered inappropriate. Asking questions, making interpretations, and offering criticisms are likewise avoided. The major activities of the therapist are recognizing and clarifying clients' feelings so that they

The epitome of adjustment is the ability to use fully one's talents and capabilities.
Photograph Robert Amft.

can discover the distorted self-images with which they have been shackled. For Rogers (1959), psychotherapy involved the "releasing of an already existing capacity in a potentially competent individual, not the expert manipulation of a more or less passive personality" (p. 221). Thus, therapy is not a set of techniques. If anything, the essence of therapy resides in the core of values and attitudes of the therapist. A sense of what Rogers was trying to do is contained in the following quote:

> Rogers eliminated all interpretation. Instead, he checked his understanding out loud, trying to grasp exactly what the patient wished to convey. When he did that, he discovered something: The patient would usually correct the first attempt. The second would be closer, but even so, the patient might refine it. Rogers would take in each correction until the patient indicated, "Yes, that's how it is. That's what I feel." Then there would be a characteristic silence. During such a silence, after something is fully received, the next thing comes in the client. Very often it is—*something deeper.* (Gendlin, 1988, p. 127)

In Box 6-3 some of Rogers's therapy techniques are briefly illustrated.

Box 6-3
THERAPY, ROGERIAN STYLE

The following is a brief set of excerpts from the therapy sessions of a depressed young woman. It contains several of the typical Rogerian tactics.

CLIENT: I cannot be the kind of person I want to be. I guess maybe I haven't the guts—or the strength—to kill myself—and if someone else would relieve me of the responsibility—or I would be in an accident—I—I—just don't want to live.

THERAPIST: At the present time, things look so black to you that you can't see much point in living.

CLIENT: Yes—I wish I'd never started this therapy. I was happy when I was living in my dream world. There I could be the kind of person I wanted to be—But now there is such a wide, wide gap—between my ideal—and what I am. . . .

THERAPIST: It's really a tough struggle—digging into this like you are—and at times the shelter of your dream world looks more attractive and comfortable.

CLIENT: My dream world or suicide. . . . So I don't see why I should waste your time—coming in twice a week—I'm not worth it. What do you think?

THERAPIST: It's up to you . . . It isn't wasting my time—I'd be glad to see you whenever you come—but it's how you feel about it—if you don't want to come twice a week—or if you do want to come twice a week—once a week?—it's up to you.

CLIENT: You're not going to suggest that I come in often? You're not alarmed and think I ought to come in—every day—until I get out of this?

THERAPIST: I believe you are able to make your own decision. I'll see you whenever you want to come.

CLIENT: (note of awe in her voice) I don't believe you are alarmed about—I see—I may be afraid for myself—but you aren't afraid for me.

THERAPIST: You say you may be afraid of yourself—and are wondering why I don't seem to be afraid for you?

CLIENT: You have more confidence in me than I have. I'll see you next week—maybe. (Rogers, 1951, pp. 46–47)

The client-therapist relationship.   In recent years, Rogers had focused even more intensely on the nature of the relationship between therapist and client as the essential ingredient for successful therapy. It is this relationship that can remove threat from the therapy situation. When threat is absent, clients will feel free to examine the experiences they have been denying or distorting. The way is then open for the person's growth potential to promote movement toward self-actualization.

Three therapist characteristics are critical in this relationship. They are (1) accurate emphatic understanding, (2) unconditional positive regard, and (3) genuineness (also called congruence). When these three elements are operative in the therapeutic situation, the client can achieve a feeling of personal worth and growth. The empathic therapist is one who can communicate to the client the feeling of being understood. A sensitivity to the client's needs, feelings, and situation is transmitted. Unconditional positive regard refers to a respect and liking for the client as a human being. Finally, by genuineness is meant a capacity to rise above mere technique or skill and participate in an emotional and involved fashion in the client's problems. A therapist who can convey all this will provide a climate in therapy that will enable the client to change. However, as Truax (1966) has tried to show, not even Rogers himself could, in every instance, respond in uniformly empathic ways throughout a therapy session.

Other applications.   The client-centered approach has long been popular in the therapy world. This is, in part, probably due to the fact that it is not very technique-centered and thus appears easy to learn. It also does not seem to require extensive knowledge of personality theory or diagnosis. Furthermore, it promises improvement in a much shorter time than more traditional, psychoanalytically derived techniques. As a result, the client-centered movement has become a magnet for a variety of people and purposes. Counseling and therapy remain its chief applications. But elements of it appear in everything from human relations training to encounter movements. With the emphasis on relationships, empathy, and the like, it has become a part of the education of those who work in crisis centers, paraprofessionals involved in counseling relationships, and volunteers in charitable organizations. The approach has made heavy inroads in small therapy groups, encounter groups, and personal growth groups. It is often used in institutional settings where one of the major goals is to foster improved human relations (e.g., churches, businesses, schools, racial confrontations).

THE HUMANISTIC-EXISTENTIAL APPROACH

The theory of Carl Rogers was described as phenomenological because the grist for its mill is subjective experience. But others might call it an existential theory because it emphasizes or strongly implies that people are freely choosing beings who exercise control over their own destinies. Still others would label Rogers's theory as humanistic because there is an aura of optimism about his views of the human being. The emphasis is on people's creativity and assets rather than on their failings. There is, then, a common conceptual thread running through phenomenology, existentialism, and humanism.

Maslow and humanism

Maslow, unlike Rogers, was not a therapist. He studied people who were, relatively speaking, normal and healthy. Perhaps because of this, Maslow's view of us all was even more optimistic than Rogers's. Abraham Maslow was an advocate of **humanism.** To him, this meant a focus on our positive characteristics. Although he acknowledged the dark side of human nature, he believed the way to prevent psychopathology was by studying the good side. By understanding our capacity for **self-actualization** – the potential to be all that we can become – we can eventually realize our potential. We will not grasp the meaning of the human experience by concentrating on our baser instincts as do the psychoanalysts. Nor is the way to enlightened understanding through a conceptualization of ourselves as mechanical robots activated by conditioned stimuli or reinforcers – the view of behaviorists. What Maslow was advocating has come to be described as the **third force** in psychology, the first force being psychoanalysis and the second force behaviorism (see Chapter 10). The key concepts in this force are experience, choice, creativity, and self-actualization. The key goals are the dignity and enhancement of people.

Hierarchy of needs.
According to Maslow (1970, 1987), humans are motivated by a series of innate needs that lend meaning and satisfaction to life. Moreover, these needs continually place the individual in a deficit state. That is, no one is ever satisfied for very long. One need clamors for satisfaction just as another is gratified. These needs are arranged in a hierarchy, as shown in Figure 6-1. Those needs lowest in the hierarchy are physiological (hunger, thirst, etc.) and must be satisfied before the next layer of needs, involving safety (pain avoidance, security, etc.), can be pursued. For example, the members of a primitive society cannot be terribly concerned about their needs for self-actualization since they are usually preoccupied with their physiological and safety needs. But in a society such as ours, needs for esteem and actualization become all-important.

Maslow's needs can be described as follows:

■ *Physiological Needs* – These include needs for food, water, sex, sleep, and elimination. These needs are not unlike those that drive other animals. They must be generally satisfied before we can contemplate the next level. Of course, we occasionally can be hungry or thirsty, but persistent nonsatisfaction of these needs will prevent our graduation to the next higher level.

■ *Safety Needs* – Here we have needs for structure, security, order, avoidance of pain, and protection. The importance of these needs is especially apparent in children and in neurotics who constantly sense impending danger.

■ *Belongingness and Love Needs* – Once physiological and safety needs have been secured, needs for affiliation and affection become prominent. These are powerful motives. Unfortunately, certain characteristics of modern society (urbanization, bureaucracy, decline of family ties, etc.) have led to massive failures in their satisfaction. The result has been alienation which, among other things, has led to the popularity of encounter groups, psychotherapy, etc.

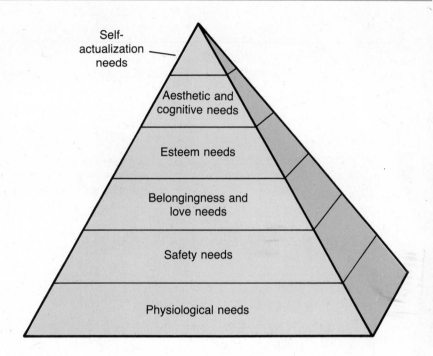

FIGURE 6-1   Maslow's need hierarchy represented as a pyramid.

- *Esteem Needs* — These are the needs of self-respect and esteem from others. We need to feel competent and worthy. At the same time, we require that others recognize our value and competence. Failure to be accepted by the self or others leads to feelings of inferiority and discouragement.

- *Aesthetic and Cognitive Needs* — These are growth needs whose satisfaction moves us closer to the ultimate goal of self-actualization. They involve an awareness of knowledge, understanding, goodness, justice, beauty, order, and symmetry.

- *Self-Actualization Needs* — That unusual person who has, on the whole, satisfied all the previous needs is in a position to seek self-actualization. This person can pursue the attainment of his or her full potential. The goal is to become all that person can become.

Self-actualization and being.   With the satisfaction of our basic needs comes the opportunity for self-actualization. Self-actualizers are significantly different from nonactualizers. The latter are motivated primarily by deficiencies (e.g., lack of food)

Abraham Maslow

Abraham Maslow was born in Brooklyn, New York, in 1908. He was the son of Jewish parents who had emigrated from Russia. He described his childhood as a terrible one. Because he was the only Jewish boy in the neighborhood, he had few friends and was alone most of the time.

His parents insisted that he study law, but after only two weeks he dropped it. He first went to Cornell but later transferred to the University of Wisconsin, from which he received the B.A. in 1930, the M.A. in 1931, and the Ph.D. in psychology in 1934. At the age of twenty, he married Bertha Goodman; they had two children.

At first, Maslow was strongly attracted to behaviorism. Then, his first child came along and behaviorism seemed a faint hope to account for the miracle of a baby's experience. Then, too, the atrocities of World War II were something he could not put out of his mind. All of this served to push him toward the study of factors that would improve the human experience.

whereas the former are ruled by **being values,** or metamotives. Being values are growth motives whose purpose is to extend our experience and enrich our lives. This kind of motivation does not compensate for deficits; rather, it pulls us toward enlarged vistas. Some of the chief characteristics of self-actualizers are shown in Table 6-1.

Self-actualizers are not, however, perfect. They show human vanities and foibles like all of us. They can, at times, be victims of temper outbursts, and be ruthless, boring, or stubborn. They are strong individuals, and this very strength sometimes leads them to behave in a cold, detached manner.

Not all of us are self-actualizers. But why not, if indeed self-actualization is innate as Maslow claimed? A look at Figure 6-1 will provide the answer. As you can see, the need for self-actualization is at the top of the pyramid. It occupies the least amount of space, which symbolizes the fact that it is the weakest of all the human motives and thus can be dominated by other motives and environmental forces. In addition, pursuing self-actualization is a tenuous course that requires that we know ourselves. Most people find such knowledge threatening and therefore resist it. It is also true that most of us cannot stand up to society. We become prisoners of social demands and fear the risks of escape. Finally, only the most courageous among us can choose actualization over safety. Again, the risks are too great.

Nevertheless, self-actualization is possible—but only in an environment that has satisfied all our lower needs. In addition, that environment must have afforded the opportunity for free speech, freedom of action (assuming those actions do not harm others), freedom of inquiry, and freedom to defend oneself. The qualities of fairness, justice, and honesty must also be present. Most of us, then, are only able to slip, struggle, and climb *toward* the top of the pyramid. But for those select few who make it to the top, the view is breathtaking (Jourard and Landsman, 1980).

After receiving his Ph.D., Maslow accepted a position as a Carnegie Fellow at Columbia University. He moved on to Brooklyn College, where he remained until 1951. That year, he went to Brandeis University as chairman of the psychology department. In 1961, he stepped down from that position but remained as professor of psychology. He became a resident fellow of the Laughlin Foundation in Menlo Park, California, in 1969. He died in June 1970.

Maslow was the author of a number of books. Three of them are: *Toward a Psychology of Being* (1962), *Religions, Values, and Peak Experiences* (1964), and *Motivation and Personality* (1970). His wife helped compile a posthumous volume entitled *Abraham H. Maslow: A Memorial Volume*. It was published in 1972. A summary of his approach is contained in Hjelle and Ziegler (1981). An interesting biography of Maslow has appeared recently (Hoffman, 1988). A review of that same book also contains some poignant insights into Maslow the man (Bugental, 1989).

Abraham Maslow

TABLE 6-1   *Some characteristics of self-actualizers*

- *Perceive reality accurately and fully*
- *Show greater acceptance of themselves, others, and things generally*
- *Are spontaneous and natural*
- *Tend to focus on problems rather than on themselves*
- *Prefer detachment and privacy*
- *Are autonomous and thus tend to be independent of the physical and social environment*
- *Have a fresh outlook; appreciate much of life*
- *Have mystical or peak experiences*
- *Enjoy a spirit of identify and unity with all people*
- *Have deep interpersonal relations with only a few people, usually self-actualizers like themselves*
- *Possess a character structure that emphasizes democratic ideals*
- *Are quite ethical*
- *Are creative*
- *Have an excellent sense of humor that is philosophical rather than hostile*
- *Resist enculturation; are not easily seduced by society*

Box 6-4
EXISTENTIALISM

In **existentialism,** the present does not flow from the past nor does it determine the future. The individual exhibits freedom of choice. If there is stability and predictability to personality, it is only because the person chooses in a manner that makes it appear so.

Existentialists look upon Kierkegaard, the troubled Danish writer, as the fountainhead of the movement. But the writings of Heidegger and Sartre have been heavily studied by recent psychologists and psychiatrists. Inherent in the works of all three writers are six themes (Rychlak, 1981). First, there is **alienation**. Alienated people are those who have become separated or detached from their experience. They describe themselves or explain their actions in the language of yesterday or in terms with shopworn meanings. Another prominent theme is **authenticity.** People who are not authentic allow others (culture, church, family, etc.) to define who they are and what they feel. Alienation arises out of the inability to be oneself. It ends in failure to achieve one's potential. **Anxiety and dread and despair** are the three horsemen of the inauthentic experience. These are the emotions that sweep over those who cannot define their being. They are clues to the basic emptiness of the alienated individual. The last theme is **absurdity.** That is, many of our beliefs are essentially absurd. Yet, their very absurdity seems to lend credence to them. Being born only to die is absurd. Teaching our children to become carbon copies of ourselves is absurd. Maybe even textbooks that seek to instruct are absurd!

Two prominent existentialists are Ludwig Binswanger (1963) and Medard Boss (1963, 1977). They reject traditional notions of causality in favor of *Dasein,* a German word translated as "being there." The focus becomes a **Daseinsanalysis,** that is, the analysis of immediate experience. They see motivation not in terms of past events but in the sense of Dasein offering future possibilities that draw us to them. For example, a student works hard not because her superego tells her to. Rather, it is because there is a part of her Dasein that contains a potential for achievement toward which she is striving.

The neurotic person is inauthentic and dominated by the wishes and plans of others. In extreme cases (e.g., psychosis), the experienced delusions and hallucinations reveal a new form of Dasein which is truly threatening to the individual. Boss and Binswanger were trained in psychoanalysis. Consequently, their therapy has a distinct psychoanalytic flavor. Their interpretations, however, differ significantly from Freudian ones. The emphasis is on the clarification of the person's phenomenal world and on the necessity for taking charge of one's life and exercising free choice. Thus, like psychoanalysis, the goal is insight—but it is an existential insight.

Existentialism is another approach to self-actualization which also rejects the idea that our current status is totally determined by the past. It is, in many respects, similar to both humanism and phenomenology (see Box 6-4).

KELLY: A PERSONAL CONSTRUCTS APPROACH

If phenomenology requires that we understand the subjective experience of the person before we try to predict behavior, then the personality theory of George Kelly surely qualifies as a phenomenological one. Yet, his theory contrasts sharply with that of Rogers. Both are phenomenological, but each seems to focus on a different aspect of the phenomenal world. With Rogers, one comes away with the impression of the individual as a feeling, experiencing organism. With Kelly, we seem to have more of a knowing, thinking being. Again, we are reminded that theories deal not with reality but with the theorist's construction of that reality.

The psychologist forms hypotheses and makes predictions. To test these hypotheses, the psychologist performs experiments. But why, Kelly asked, must scientists consider this mode of operation their own private preserve? Might not everyone, scientist and layperson alike, be doing the same thing? He put it this way:

> It is customary to say that the *scientist's ultimate aim is to predict and control*. . . . Yet curiously enough, psychologists rarely credit the human subjects in their experiments with having similar aspirations. It is as though the psychologist were saying to himself, "I, being a *psychologist,* and therefore a *scientist,* am performing this experiment in order to improve the prediction and control of certain human phenomena; but my subject, being merely a human organism, is obviously propelled by inexorable drives welling up within him, or else he is in gluttonous pursuit of sustenance and shelter." (1955, p. 5)

Thus, according to Kelly, all of us attempt to *construe* our world. We interpret, try to understand, and explain. To do this, we employ **personal constructs.** These are our conclusions, interpretations, or deductions about life; a kind of cognition or private logic (Sechrest, 1977). In the following pages we shall examine Kelly's theory and its implications for development, assessment, and behavior change to see the role of personal constructs in action.

Basic theory and concepts

Kelly's theory is formally stated in a fundamental postulate and eleven corollary assumptions. This fundamental postulate states: "A person's processes are psychologically channelized by the ways in which he anticipates events" (Kelly, 1955, p. 46). It tells us that the focus of the theory is a psychological one. The theory does not handle biochemical events nor does it pretend to deal with occurrences better left to a sociologist or economist. What it does assert is that human thought and action are geared toward the enhanced ability to predict (anticipate) events. Each of us strives to improve our understanding of our world. To do this, we make predictions. Some are cor-

George Kelly

George Alexander Kelly was born in 1905 in Kansas. His parents were quite religious; his father, at one time a Presbyterian minister, turned to farming out of health considerations. At the age of thirteen, Kelly was sent away to school; he never really lived at home after that. He attended Friends University, a Quaker school in Wichita, and received his B.A. in physics and mathematics from Park College in 1926. Deciding against a career in engineering, he became interested in education and sociology and received his M.A. in 1928 from Kansas University. At this time, he began a series of teaching jobs, including positions at a junior college (where he met his wife), at a labor college, and as a speech instructor for the American Bankers Association. A scholarship enabled him to study under Sir Godfrey Thomson at the University of Edinburgh. In 1930 he returned from Scotland with an education degree and an interest in psychology. In 1931 he received a Ph.D. from the State University of Iowa; his dissertation dealt with common factors in speech and reading disabilities. This closed the book on Kelly's formal education, a period during which he studied at five different schools.

There then began a highly formative time in Kelly's life. With the onset of the Great Depression, he returned to Kansas to teach at Fort Hays State College, where he remained until the beginning of World War II. It was here that Kelly developed a traveling clinic. Kelly and his students covered nearly the whole state, providing consultation services to help teachers better deal with problems with their students. This immersion in the world of psychological problems and how to deal

rect; others show us how wrong we were. But right or wrong, we should be better able to predict next time around.

How do we go about this prediction? Well, we interpret our experiences. We note how events are similar and different from one another. By recognizing these similarities and contrasts, our ability to predict grows. Furthermore, since no two of us have exactly the same experiences, we will show individual differences in our interpretations and subsequent predictions. But, as always, our constructions of events are only constructions; they are not reality itself. Sechrest (1977) recounts Kelly's fondness for illustrating this point by telling an audience that the shoes of someone sitting in the front row are "neurotic." Everyone strains to look at those neurotic shoes as if neurosis really were a part of them. Kelly would then admonish his listeners for looking at the shoes rather than at him (Kelly). After all, it was he who called them neurotic!

The nature of constructs.   People also develop construct systems in such a way that some constructs are more general than others. For example, one construct may subsume another. That is, the construct *beautiful-ugly* may apply to nearly every-

with them undoubtedly exerted a marked effect on Kelly's thinking. His pioneer efforts here are still remembered by some in Kansas.

Kelly emerged from the plains of Kansas to serve in the Navy when World War II began. He became an aviation psychologist. During this time, he also came into contact with many other psychologists as the role of psychology in the armed forces was being defined. These contacts no doubt helped him secure a position at the University of Maryland in 1945. A year later, he moved to Ohio State University, where he established a training program in clinical psychology. This program, with the cooperation of Julian Rotter, developed into an outstanding model of the scientist-practitioner approach to Ph.D. training in clinical psychology.

It was at Ohio State that Kelly published his major work, *The Psychology of Personal Constructs: A Theory of Personality* (1955). With the acclaim that followed this publication, Kelly began globetrotting, receiving invitations to lecture all over the United States, as well as in Europe, the Soviet Union, South America, the Caribbean, and Asia. In 1965, he accepted an endowed chair at Brandeis University. He died in March 1967.

Kelly was not a prolific writer. Aside from his two-volume work, he wrote very little. Maher (1969) has collected some of his more important papers. Sechrest (1977) has an excellent chapter on Kelly's theory. Interestingly, since the 1960s, Kelly's work has attracted much attention in England. This has been reflected in several books over the years (e.g., Adams-Webber, 1979; Bannister, 1985; Button, 1985).

George Kelly
Photograph by Ralph Norman
Courtesy of Brendan Maher.

thing in the world while the construct *intelligent-stupid* may fit only humans or mammals. And each construct system will be organized differently from the next. Box 6-5 will give you some idea of the hierarchical nature of such a system.

In Kelly's theory, constructs are considered as being **dichotomous**—a view that is quite distinctive. People define constructs in an either-or fashion. For example, my assertion that Tom is short implies a contrast. The only way I could have developed such a construct is by observing contrasting events. To have abstracted the idea of shortness, I must have seen several "short" people but also at least one "tall" person. Thus, at one moment in time my construct is tall versus short. At another time I may observe several people, some of whom are well above 6 feet, others around 5 feet 10 inches, and still others only 5 feet 5 inches. If I am choosing people for a basketball team, I may regard those well above 6 feet as tall and everyone else as short (a dichotomous construct). If I am choosing them for a baseball team, I may regard those well above 6 feet as giants and those below as of reasonable height (again, a dichotomous construct). At each moment of decision, I make a dichotomous judgment. But over a series of decisions, it would appear that I am aware of gradations in height.

Box 6-5
CONSTRUCT HIERARCHY

Bannister (1970) illustrates how constructs have hierarchical relationships to one another:

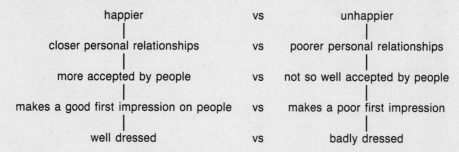

The person was asked whether he would prefer to see himself as *well dressed* or *badly dressed* and replied that he would like to see himself as *well dressed.* He was asked "why" and he replied that it was in order to make a *good first impression on people.* . . . When asked "why" he said that once you have made a good first impression on people then you are *more accepted by them* and in response to "why" he said that in that way you could go on to form *better personal relationships with them.* When asked "why" he wanted to form better personal relationships he said that in that way he would be *happier.* When asked why he wanted to be *happier* he gave no direct answer but argued that it wasn't in aid of anyting—it was what life was about. Thus he appeared to have reached his personal ceiling for this particular hierarchy—the overarching principle which, for the time being, was at the top of this particular ladder and which had no verbally accessible "why" to it. (p. 56)

Normally, people revise their constructs with experience. Suppose I make a prediction based on my construct system and that prediction is wrong. After several such errors, I will conclude that I had better start construing things somewhat differently. Otherwise, I run the risk of making more predictive errors. Construct systems, then, may change over time. However, change is possible only when there are **permeable** constructs within the system. A permeable construct is one that can be applied to new events not yet incorporated into the system. For example, a person may have the construct *good music-bad music,* but that construct is impermeable—for instance, good music includes everything up to and including Glenn Miller but no good music has been played since. Such an impermeable construct closes off to change a portion of

Many people in our society are both physically and psychologically alienated.
Photograph Fournier/Contact Press.

my construct system. But if I regard rock music as an interesting sociocultural event, then I can construe it within my framework and enjoy it.

Some constructs may also be **preemptive**. Such constructs do not permit their elements to belong to any other category. For example, the religious fanatic may label all who drink as children of evil. These people are not thought of as intelligent, dependent, or skilled; they are just evil!

For most of us, perhaps, constructs become something like labels. We label people as handsome or unattractive, intelligent or stupid. But labels are not always attached to our constructs, nor are they always verbal. In addition, the fact that two individuals use the same label does not imply that their constructs are identical.

The dynamics of constructs. From time to time, all of us are faced with the possibility of change in our constructs. Sometimes the changes are trivial. For example, I may discover that my favorite writer has churned out a few bad books. This forces me to reconstrue my former conception of him as the all-time greatest writer of mysteries. But this is not likely to be an earth-shattering reconstruction, nor does it imply neurosis on my part. In other cases, however, things may become a bit more serious. Perhaps I construe myself as the leading researcher in the country. However, after several years of failed research programs, an inability to get studies published, and the like, I am compelled to reconstrue myself. This situation produces **threat**, that is, an awareness of an imminent major change in my construct system.

Kelly also discussed the role of **guilt**. We all have a core construct system. Certain aspects of this core structure relate to the predictions of our interactions with other persons or groups. Suppose, for example, that an employee construes herself as prompt, responsible, and hard-working. Yet, for some reason, she finds that recently she has been coming to work late, leaving early, and not finishing all her work. She will respond by experiencing guilt.

Anxiety is an experience we all have to one degree or another. Kelly viewed anxiety as an awareness that perceived events cannot be construed within one's construct system. A student who cannot figure out how to write a term paper often experiences anxiety. This suggests that the individual cannot, with the constructs at hand, construe how to go about the task. When important events in life repeatedly fall outside the range of convenience of the person's construct system, an anxiety reaction will result.

Another response that is possible when constructs are not working is **aggression**. Aggression is an attempt to extend or elaborate the perceptual field and thereby incorporate a greater range of events into the system. Aggression involves initiative more than attack. Kelly would use the term in the sense that a salesperson is aggressive. An aggressive sales plan, then, allows one to extend one's ability to anticipate and thus control the outcome of the sales contact.

Kelly also dealt extensively with **hostility,** which he described as a person's attempt to extort validating evidence for a prediction that is failing (or has failed). In short, rather than change our constructs, we try to change the characteristics of what we are predicting. For example, a mother may insist on construing her little daughter as a budding homebody who loves to "help Mommy." But her little girl repeatedly forsakes helping for the lure of outdoor games. The hostile mother does not change her view of the girl. Instead, she starts offering her daughter money to help with the dishes and housework. Some mothers would simply have altered their constructs relating to their daughters. The hostile mother alters her daughter and thereby validates her constructs. This is not unlike the mythical robber Procrustes who would stretch or cut off the legs of his victims to adapt them to the length of his bed!

Development of personality

It is probably clear by now that Kelly saw people as oriented toward the future. They seek to anticipate, predict, and extend the range of their constructs. To understand people, we must understand their constructs now—not yesterday, not last year, and certainly not when they were three years old. The explanation for behavior lies in today's constructs and the likelihood of their changing in the future. Kelly's approach, then, is ahistorical; it is not necessary to dig up the past to explain the present. For this reason, Kelly had practically nothing to say about development of the person. He paid scant attention to how the individual comes to construe events.

Nature of adjustment

According to Hjelle and Ziegler (1981), Kelly's perspective contains four characteristics associated with the healthy personality. Psychologically adjusted individuals exhibit:

■ A willingness to evaluate their constructs and test the validity of their perceptions of others

■ The ability to discard constructs and alter their core systems when they appear to be invalid

■ A wish to extend the range or coverage of their construct systems

■ A well-developed repertoire of roles

Implications for behavior change

In recent years, there seems to have been a renewal of interest in Kelly's approach to therapy (Epting, 1984). Kelly, a clinical psychologist by trade, used a variety of therapeutic devices to induce change in his clients. All of them served the ultimate purpose of effecting changes in the client's construct system. After all, the fact that clients sought help meant to Kelly that their ways of construing events were not working well.

Kelly was fond of describing the therapy room as a laboratory where the client could safely carry out experiments in cognitive change that would be risky in a real-life setting. Like most therapists, Kelly advocated permissiveness. He thought such a technique encouraged the client's experimentation. New ideas, plans, or behaviors could be contemplated without embarrassment or fear. Naturally, Kelly would respond (by gesture, facial expression, comment) to his client's attempts at experimentation. It was only from such reactions that the client could achieve a sense of the effect of the attempt. Kelly also emphasized the need to create novel situations for the client (in therapy and in other places in the client's life). He saw this as a creative activity that promoted a change in the client's constructs by showing the client how ineffectual those constructs had been. It was a way of highlighting their lack of utility. For example, Kelly might encourage a client to date a woman the client thought he did not like just to prove to him that his ways of construing her were faulty. Another technique Kelly used was to encourage the client to make specific predictions. He thought that many clients would be unable to resist trying an experiment if they had actually made a prediction about its outcome.

Kelly attached considerable theoretical prominence to procedures of **fixed-role therapy** even though his own use of them was modest. As a technique, fixed-role therapy is especially notable because it is so consistent with his theory. Kelly would sometimes provide clients with a role sketch, or *prescription,* which they would be asked to play in a variety of situations and for various lengths of time. A particular role was selected to provide contrasts with the client's customary behavior. This procedure was not meant to imply that the client should permanently take on the characteristics of the role. Rather, it was a technique used to alter constructs by showing the client that his or her predictions about what would happen to the person in the role were not necessarily correct.

INFORMATION PROCESSING

It was not long before the development of high speed digital computers that George Kelly was putting the finishing touches on his theory of personality. He helped usher in a new, more cognitive approach to the study of personality. With his work, it became possible to construe the self cognitively and not just as an inaccessible subjective experience. Also, with computers came the idea that humans could be construed in information processing terms. Does the human brain function like the artificial computer? At first, this cognitive, information processing approach was largely confined to the study of learning and memory phenomena in psychology. But in recent years, it has spilled over into the field of personality. In particular, information processing has been applied to the study of the self; an application that bears some definite similarities to Kelly's approach.

The computer metaphor

The basic premise of the information processing perspective is an emphasis on how we attend to information, store it, think about it, and retrieve it. Like the computer, we **encode** information, then **recode** it by actively processing the information, and then **decoding** it as we interpret its meaning by comparing it to and combining it with other stored information. The completion of all this activity results in some sort of **output** in the form of an action or solution to a problem (Siegler, 1983). Some people take this computer metaphor almost literally and try to reduce thinking to the computer model. Others, however, use the computer as a figure of speech or analogy. In doing so, they hope that new hypotheses and models of action will be suggested. However, their intent is not to assert that computers and people are programmed alike as far as solving problems are concerned. A well-known model of information processing is shown in Figure 6-2.

Some basic concepts

Information processing as applied to personality has three major premises. First, individuals organize their experiences according to the repetitive themes of those experiences. Second, this organization involves **schemas**, which are structures of knowledge that reside in memory. Finally, these schemas can be used later to recognize and comprehend new stimuli and events.

Obviously, memory is critical in information processing models. Memory involving information about concepts and meaning is called **semantic memory** while memory for events is referred to as **episodic memory.** In addition, there is also information about behavior that is stored in our memories. Some of this information describes simple acts. But there are also **scripts.** These are organized representations of familiar daily activities. They can be used to perceive, understand, and influence events such as paying a bill, buying gasoline, or doing the wash (Schank and Abelson, 1977).

Once behavioral information is stored in memory, the process of **self-regulation** becomes possible. This refers to a continuous and conscious evaluation and monitoring of progress toward some goal. It may involve monitoring outcomes and the redirection

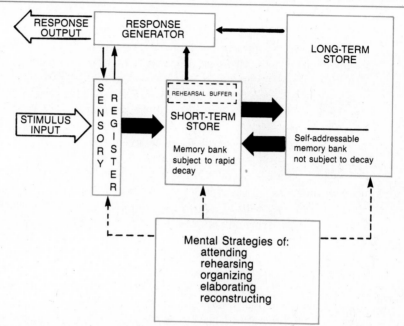

FIGURE 6-2 Flow chart illustrating a model of information processing.
From R. M. Shiffrin and R. C. Atkinson, "Storage and Retrieval Processes in Long-Term Memory," *Psychological Review*, Vol. 76, No. 2, March 1969. Reprinted by permission of Richard M. Shiffrin.

of unsuccessful behaviors. What occurs here are processes not unlike those built into a thermostat or a computer (Powers, 1973). This is accomplished through feedback control, which really involves a kind of perception of one's present behavior. By monitoring current behavior one can evaluate progress toward some goal or intention. If that monitoring fails to show any discrepancy between what you intend and what you are doing, the behavior will continue. Thus, if the thermostat fails to sense a difference between actual room temperature and that for which it is set, then the thermostat will not signal the furnace to come on. This overall view suggests that behavior is purposive and that one's life is basically a matter of establishing goals and intentions and then, through feedback of information, adjusting present behavior so that proper progress occurs (Carver and Scheier, 1981).

Emotions may be incorporated into information processing perspectives by regarding them as events that interrupt behavior thereby providing information that leads to a reordering of one's goals. Emotions may also provide information that allows for easier access to certain memories associated with that emotion.

With this brief introduction to the world of information processing, let us now turn to an examination of the self from that perspective.

The self and self-schemata

For years, the self had been regarded as a very broad and stable structure. This "I" or "me" was crude, almost undifferentiated but was, nevertheless, called upon to mediate and regulate behavior in an extremely fine-grained fashion. But how could such a simple structure successfully accomplish such a herculean task? One solution has been to regard the self-concept as a collection of images, schemas, conceptions, prototypes, and the like (Markus and Wurf, 1987). The history of such a strategy touches upon the work of Bartlett (1932), Kelly (1955), and Piaget (1951). But a good place for us to begin our examination is with the more recent conceptualizations of Hazel Markus (1977).

Individuals are active, constructive processors of information. In doing this, it is necessary for them to organize, summarize, and account for their behavior. This will result, eventually, in the formation of cognitive structures about the self or what are referred to as **self-schemata** or **self-schemas**: ". . . cognitive generalizations about the self, derived from past experience, that organize and guide the processing of self-related information contained in the individual's social experiences" (Markus, 1977, p. 64).

The self-schemata become cognitive representations based upon specific events in our lives. For example, "That funeral I attended yesterday was grim but I could have been a little less nervous." But the representations may also become generalizations constructed out of repeated categorizations and evaluations both by the individual and by those with whom the person interacts in some way. Thus, "I am generous; after all, I just gave a hundred dollars to that charity." Or, "I am clumsy; my father always told me I couldn't walk and chew gum at the same time."

These schemata are derived from information the individual processes and they influence input and output of information relative to the self. Self-schemata are, of course, stored in memory. But they are more than mere repositories of the cognitive representations of past experience that passively reside in our memories. They can become selective mechanisms that determine whether information is attended to, how important it is thought to be, and what happens to it later. Once established and once there are repeated experiences accumulated that are relevant to them, self-schemata become increasingly resistant to change; even in the face of inconsistent information.

Not unlike Kelly's (1955) personal constructs, self-schemata arise out of the invariant themes of our experience. And like personal constructs, they are helpful in understanding events and in guiding our behavior. They even allow us to look beyond present information and make educated guesses about the future.

These self-schemata affect the manner in which information is processed. For example, Markus and Wurf (1987) have identified several consequences or effects: (1) heightened sensitivity to self-relevant stimuli; (2) more efficient processing of self-congruent stimuli; (3) enhanced recall and recognition of self-relevant stimuli; (4) more confident behavioral predictions, attributions, and inferences in areas relevant to the self; (5) resistance to the acceptance of information that is not congruent with one's self-structure. In summary, after reviewing their own research on self-schemata as well as other recent work on the self, Markus and her colleagues have described what they refer to as the **dynamic self-concept** (Markus and Wurf, 1987). It is an active, force-

Box 6-6
A GENDER SCHEMA ILLUSTRATING THE ENCODING AND REGULATION OF SEX-TYPED PREFERENCES AND BEHAVIOR

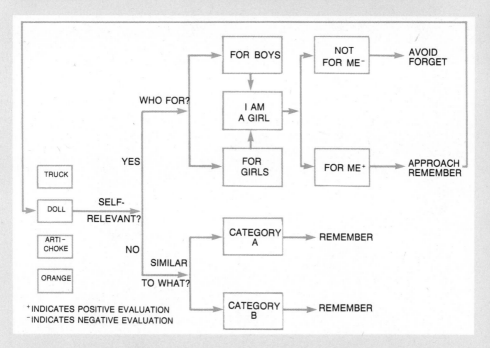

+INDICATES POSITIVE EVALUATION
−INDICATES NEGATIVE EVALUATION

According to the gender schema or flow chart above, a little girl finds herself in a situation in which she is presented with a doll. Based upon her gender schema she will make several decisions that will, in turn, determine the manner in which she interacts with that doll. First, she will decide that dolls are self-relevant. Next, she will conclude that since she is a girl and that dolls are for girls, she should approach the doll, examine it, perhaps ask questions about it, and then play with it. In the process of playing with it she gains further information about it, which is then elaborated and stored in memory. Should she be confronted with a toy truck, her responses will be quite different. Trucks are for boys; she is a girl. The decision, in most cases, will be to avoid the truck since it is not self-relevant. As a result of all this, information about it will be largely ignored and poorly remembered. Thus, her cognition and her behavior will be consistent with her schema.

Adapted from "A Schematic Processing Model of Sex Typing and Stereotyping in Children" by Carol Lynn Martin and Charles F. Halverson, Jr., *Child Development,* December 1981. Copyright © 1981 The Society for Research in Child Development, Inc. Reprinted by permission.

ful, and changing structure. In this sense, it replaces older views of the self-concept as a passive reflection of on-going behavior. It now becomes an active regulator of our behavior in which our thoughts shape our behavior. In Box 6-6 a self-schema involving gender identity is shown.

SUMMARY

■ The emphasis in phenomenology is on the experiencing organism. This implies a focus on cognition, subjective experience, freedom of choice, and human values. Phenomenology contrasts sharply with traditional psychoanalytic views.

■ In phenomenology, behavior is seen as an outgrowth of the phenomenal field, which is everything experienced by the person at a given moment.

■ The self (the "I" or "me") is a prominent construct in most phenomenological approaches. Several components of the self and its development and functions were briefly outlined.

■ Carl Rogers, a prime example of a phenomenologist, especially stressed the importance of knowledge of the subjective world of the person as a prerequisite for understanding and prediction. He also felt the basic human striving to be the quest for self-actualization.

■ In Rogers's theory, the growth of the self and the realization of one's potential are achieved when several conditions are present: the experiencing of positive regard, the presence of factors that lead to a feeling of worth, the presence of unconditional positive regard from significant others, and the absence of threat to the phenomenal self.

■ According to Rogers, perceived threat leads to maladjustment. The ideal state of adjustment is the fully functioning person—the individual who lives up to his or her potential and experiences every moment fully.

■ One of Rogers's major accomplishments was the introduction of client-centered therapy. This clinical approach is characterized by complete acceptance of the person by the therapist, and by a heavy emphasis on the client-therapist relationship. The client-centered approach has now come out of the therapy room and has been widely applied to encounter groups, personal growth groups, and the like.

■ Closely related to phenomenology is a set of approaches referred to as humanistic. Abraham Maslow, like all humanists, focused on the positive aspects of human experience (e.g., creativity, self-actualization).

■ Maslow is especially noted for his concept of a hierarchy of needs. These needs range from physiological needs to self-actualization needs. A person cannot move on to the satisfaction of a higher need until the lower ones have generally been satisfied.

■ Existentialism is still another offshoot of phenomenology. It emphasizes freedom of choice as an inherent human quality.

■ George Kelly represents a contrasting approach to phenomenology. His theory is based on the premise that all of us seek to anticipate and predict our world much as scientists do.

■ Kelly argued that we develop construct systems to enable us to anticipate events. These individual constructs are dichotomous (e.g., tall-short), and some are more pervasive than others. Still others are permeable. That is, they can be applied readily to new events. Others are preemptive in that they will permit an event to be described in only one fashion.

■ As examples of the dynamics of Kelly's system, concepts of threat, guilt, anxiety, aggression, and hostility were described.

■ Kelly paid little attention to how constructs develop and, in that sense, his is an ahistorical system.

■ In Kelly's terms, adjustment may be said to exist when the person is willing to evaluate his or her constructs and alter them when they seem to be failing in prediction. Adjusted individuals try to extend their construct systems and to develop reasonably extensive repertoires of roles.

■ Several techniques for altering the person's construct system were discussed. The approach of fixed-role therapy was cited as a particularly good example.

■ Information processing, usually based on the computer metaphor, has recently become an alternative approach in personality.

■ An information processing approach relies on schemas, memory, and scripts, and also involves self-regulation.

■ Self-schemata were described as a current specific application of information processing in personality.

CHAPTER 7

PHENOMENOLOGY AND THE SELF

Research, Assessment, and Summary Evaluation

The previous chapter described a set of theoretical views variously describing the human being as someone who (1) behaves according to the ways reality is perceived, (2) should be cherished and construed optimistically, and (3) is a freely choosing organism. This is the classic phenomenological-humanistic-existential axis. But we also examined related yet distinct approaches that construe people in more cognitive, information processing terms. This is a diverse collection of perspectives, to be sure. In the present chapter, we shall review and illustrate some of the chief research and assessment implications of these perspectives and close with a summary evaluation of each approach.

METHODS OF INVESTIGATION

Phenomenological research methods run the gamut from the experimental to the correlational to the case study. They span the continuum between qualitative and heavily quantitative studies. Because so many of the leading figures of the movement have been clinicians of one sort or another, much of the research has taken place in the context of psychotherapy and has involved clients or patients as subjects. But through it all, the constant emphasis has been on the way people perceive events and themselves. In short, the basic content has been subjective experience. Specifically, this has most often involved the self and its actualization, enhancement, consistency, or esteem. However, with the advent of personal constructs theory and information processing metaphors, more objective, experimental methods have often been employed.

The Rogerian research legacy

For many people, the name Carl Rogers springs immediately to mind when the subject of phenomenology arises. Yet these same people often are taken aback when informed that Rogers was a pioneer in a variety of research methods. They think of him in terms of encounter groups, the world of experience, or therapeutic techniques whose major focus is on when to emit a calculated "M-hm."

But Rogers did, indeed, place heavy emphasis on research. He certainly depended on it in developing his major theoretical statement (C. R. Rogers, 1951). He also carried out what was probably the first sustained program of psychotherapy research. It was he who pioneered the use of recordings of therapy sessions to study both process and effectiveness. Recorded interviews are now a staple ingredient in both research and training. But it was not always so, and we who live in a world awash with records, tapes, and disks sometimes forget this. Prior to Rogers, the therapy room was very nearly a holy place the sanctity of which was guarded with a vengeance. However, Rogers opened up therapy and the personality processes within it and made them objects of study rather than subjects of mystery. He also made available recordings and transcripts of therapy sessions that he conducted. In so doing, he exhibited a measure of courage unusual for his time.

Qualitative-idiographic research

To gain an understanding of people, phenomenologists like Rogers, existentialists such as Binswanger, and humanists like Maslow have always tried to stay close to the experience of their subjects or clients. This means listening to them and searching their words for keys to the phenomena in question. In particular, there has been a heavy reliance on case studies and excerpts from therapy sessions.

The following excerpt from a therapy session reported by Rogers (1951) is illustrative here. But the problem with it and others like it is deciding whether it is only illustrative or is, somehow, proof of the validity of the experiential approach.

> CLIENT: It all comes pretty vague. But you know I keep, keep having the thought occur to me that this whole process for me is kind of like examining pieces of a jigsaw puzzle. It seems to me I, I'm in the process now of examining the individual pieces which really don't have too much meaning. Probably handling them, not even beginning to think of a pattern. That keeps coming to me. And it's interesting to me because I, I really don't like jigsaw puzzles. They've always irritated me. But that's my feeling. And I mean I pick up little pieces *(she gestures throughout this conversation to illustrate her statements)* with absolutely no meaning except, I mean, the, the feeling that you get from simply handling them without seeing them as a pattern, but just from the touch, I probably feel, well, it is going to fit someplace here.
>
> THERAPIST: And that at the moment that that's the process, just getting the feel and the shape and the configuration of the different pieces with a little bit of background feeling of, yeah, they'll probably fit somewhere, but most of the attention's focused right on, "What does this feel like? And what's its texture?"

CLIENT: That's right. There's almost something physical in it. A, a . . .

THERAPIST: You can't quite describe it without using your hands. A real, almost a sensuous sense in . . .

CLIENT: That's right. Again it's, it's a feeling of being very objective, and yet I've never been quite so close to myself.

THERAPIST: Almost at one and the same time standing off and looking at yourself and yet somehow being closer to yourself that way than . . .

CLIENT: Um-hum. And yet for the first time in months I am not thinking about my problems. I'm not actually, I'm not working on them.

THERAPIST: I get the impression you don't sort of sit down to work on "my problems." It isn't that feeling at all.

CLIENT: That's right. That's right. I suppose what I, I mean actually is that I'm not sitting down to put this puzzle together as, as something I've got to see the picture. It, it may be that, it may be that I am actually enjoying this feeling process. Or I'm certainly learning something.

THERAPIST: At least there's a sense of the immediate goal of getting that feel as being the thing, not that you're doing this in order to see a picture, but that it's a, a satisfaction of really getting acquainted with each piece. Is that . . .

CLIENT: That's it. That's it. And it still becomes that sort of sensuousness, that touching. It's quite interesting. Sometimes not entirely pleasant, I'm sure, but . . .

THERAPIST: A rather different sort of experience.

CLIENT: Yes. Quite.

(p. 505)

Content analysis

At first, the Rogerian use of interviews was a rather simple extension of the qualitative methods just discussed. But it was soon recognized that to determine the effectiveness of therapy and to chart the change in verbalizations of the self, a more rigorous and objective set of methods was necessary. What gradually evolved was the content analysis of interview data.

A good example of this early research is a study by Raimy (1948). Raimy was interested in the way references to self change over the course of therapy. Therefore, he constructed six self-reference categories (positive or approving self-references, negative or disapproving ones, ambivalent ones, etc.) to study fourteen clients who had undergone from two to twenty-one interviews. Transcriptions of each session were examined, and each client's self-references were sorted into the six content categories. Raimy discovered that clients generally made negative or ambivalent self-references at the beginning of therapy. By the end of therapy, clients whom judges determined to be improved were referring to themselves in largely positive terms. Those who had showed no improvement were still making ambivalent and disapproving self-references. These results have turned out to be common ones. Another example of content analysis is a study by Stoler (1963). Stoler's interest was in client likability and its relationship to success in psychotherapy. He provided ten raters with twenty, two-minute taped segments of client-therapist interactions drawn from ten recorded cases. In advance of this, five of the cases had been determined to be relatively successful, five unsuccessful.

The judges rated each segment on a scale of liking to disliking the client. The results suggested that client likability is related to successful outcomes in therapy and that ratings of client likability can be reliably made from content segments of therapy exchanges.

Marsden (1971) has remarked that "content analysis has proved itself a tool particularly well suited to the study of psychotherapy" (p. 392). But the content analysis of therapy sessions has other implications as well. For example, Rogers (1951) asserted in the presentation of his theoretical propositions that people who are accepting of themselves are necessarily more accepting of others. Several studies (e.g., J. Seeman, 1949; Stock, 1949) have analyzed the content of therapy interviews to determine whether clients who make positive self-references make similar references to others. Although the results of this series of studies are inconclusive, they do explicate a method of investigation.

Certainly one of the most direct routes to people's subjective experience is through listening to what they say. But judgments of different observers often do not agree. Furthermore, predictions of future behavior based upon interview data are seldom as accurate as we would like (Phares, 1988). On the other hand, Rogers and his colleagues have shown that when care and patience are applied to the analysis of interview data, reliable ratings can be made. This work involves the use of objective, standardized steps for the analysis of content. Of course, the ability to render reliable judgments of interview content still does not answer the question as to whether observers perceive a given set of events in exactly the same way as does the interviewee.

Rating scales

As time went on, Rogerian investigators gradually shifted to the use of rating scales. These scales were typically applied to the rating of typescripts or taped interview data. A good example is a validation study of the Process Scale undertaken by Tomlinson and Hart (1962). The Process Scale is a seven-stage scale for rating therapy interviews. It is divided into seven strands or vertical subcategories:

- Feelings and Personal Meanings

- Experiencing

- Incongruence

- Communications of Self

- Construing of Experience

- Relationship to Problems

- Manner of Relating

Raters keep in mind each strand and then arrive at a global rating of the client's process level, which can range from 1 to 7. Tomlinson and Hart had two experienced raters examine nine two-minute excerpts from each of ten therapy cases. For each case, there was an interview late in the therapy series, and an early one as well. Each judge rated a total of twenty tapes. Several results were obtained. First, interjudge reliability was satisfactory (correlation = .60). Second, the Process Scale distinguished between more successful and less successful cases and indicated that the more successful ones begin and end at a higher level of process. Third, some evidence suggested that there was greater process change in the more successful cases.

The Q-sort technique

In 1953, Stephenson described a research method that he called the Q-technique. It did not take Rogers and his colleagues long to realize that here was a method uniquely appropriate to the study of the self-concept. They quickly developed a Q-sort adaptation of the Stephenson technique.

The **Q-sort** is a procedure in which the subject is asked to sort into a series of piles a number of statements about the self (e.g., "I am generally a happy person"; "I usually think of myself first"; "I am upset much of the time"; "I concentrate well"). Normally, the statements are printed on cards. The subject is instructed to read each statement and then place it along a continuum ranging from "Very characteristic of me" to "Not at all characteristic of me." The subject is also asked to place the cards along the continuum according to a prearranged scheme—usually a normal distribution. To achieve a normal distribution, the largest number of cards must be placed at the middle of the distribution, the fewest at each extreme. A forced distribution is used to facilitate statistical treatment of the data and also to prevent the possible operation of response sets (e.g., subjects giving only extreme ratings or else placing every statement in the neutral range). Figure 7-1 illustrates the Q-sort technique.

The most common use of Q-sorts has involved the comparison between self and ideal-self. The oft-cited Butler and Haigh (1954) research provides an excellent example. These investigators hypothesized that clients would be relatively dissatisfied with themselves prior to therapy but that following successful therapy this level of dissatisfaction would decline. They selected twenty-four clients in therapy and a control group of sixteen adults comparable in characteristics of sex, age, socioeconomic status, and so forth. The experimental group did Q-sorts prior to therapy, at the conclusion of therapy, and again at a point between six months and a year after therapy had been concluded. Control subjects, who were not in therapy, did the comparable sorts at similar points in time. This was to determine whether factors other than therapy (e.g., sheer passage of time, other life experiences) might affect changes in the sortings.

At each point, subjects sorted 100 statements such as "I am an impulsive person" or "I am likable." Subjects made two sorts on each occasion. The first was a self-sort (how they saw themselves at that time) and the second an ideal-sort (how they would most like themselves to be). This was done by assigning each sort two numbers. The first was the pile number for the self-sort and the other the pile number for the ideal-sort. These numbers were then correlated. A high positive correlation would indicate a close relationship between the ideal-sort and self-sort; a low correlation would indicate little relationship. Improvement in therapy was determined by judges and by the results of psychological tests. The basic findings of this research are shown in Table 7-1.

The control group failed to show any change in their self—ideal-self correlation whereas the mean correlations for the therapy group showed a significant change toward a greater relationship between self and idea-self. The improved relationship was

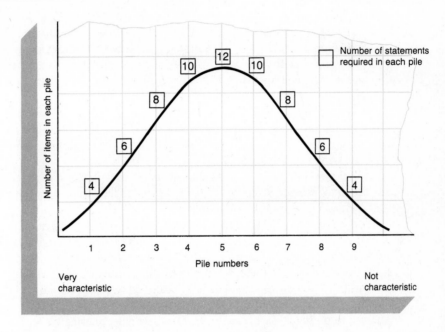

FIGURE 7-1 Illustration of self-statements in a forced-distribution Q-sort.

TABLE 7-1 Mean self-ideal self correlations for therapy and control groups

Group	Before Therapy	After Therapy	Follow-Up
Therapy	– .01	.34	.31
Control	.58	Not reported	.59

After "Changes in the Relation between Self-Concepts and Ideal Concepts Consequent upon Client-centered Counseling" by J. M. Butler and G. V. Haigh, in *Psychotherapy and Personality Change: Coordinated Studies in the Client-Centered Approach* by C. R. Rogers and R. F. Dymond (eds.). Copyright 1954 by University of Chicago Press. Adapted by permission.

maintained during the follow-up period. As expected, the control group showed a higher level of initial correlation, and that level did not change over time. It was also found that improved clients, as compared to nonimproved clients, showed somewhat stronger self—ideal-self congruence at the follow-up point but not at the therapy termination point. The reasons for this latter finding were not clear although butler and Haigh thought it had something to do with defensiveness or the desire to place themselves in a positive light.

Although there are many uses for the Q-sort technique, its strongest association remains with the study of the self-concept. There are, of course, difficulties with its use in this area. Even though it is a relatively sophisticated technique for tapping into a person's subjective experience, how close is the match? As was noted, the Butler and Haigh (1954) research raised the issue of defensiveness. They suggested that some subjects may provide defensive sortings that make the discrepancy between self and ideal-self seem less than it really is. If this is so, it raises critical questions about how much faith we can put in the validity of self-reports—the key Rogerian data for understanding the subject's experience. Many sorting tasks require subjects to examine 100 or more cards. This can place a real strain on subjects' powers of concentration as well as on their cooperative spirit. Also, if a forced-distribution format is used, some subjects may have to make judgments they really do not want to make. For example, a subject who wishes to place twelve cards in the "Very characteristic" pile may not be allowed to do so. In such a case, the Q-sort is not capturing subjective experience; rather, it is distorting it. In addition, we cannot forget that it is the investigator who determines what cards will be used. As a result, the self-descriptions chosen by an investigator may not reflect a given subject's experience at all but instead the investigator's approximation of it. Still, the Q-sort method has been useful. As much as anything, it represents a serious attempt to deal with the world of subjective experience within the framework of a nomothetic strategy.

The semantic differential

A method related to the Q-sort is the **semantic differential** (Osgood, Suci, and Tannenbaum, 1957). Originally developed as a means of assessing the meaning people attach to events, this technique has an obvious potential in phenomenological research.

With the semantic differential, a subject rates a concept (e.g., ideal-self, father, narcissism) on a series of seven-point scales. Each scale is defined by polar adjectives, such as *strong-weak, hard-soft, active-passive, good-bad,* and so forth. The subject would rate, for example, the concept of ideal-self on each of the seven-point scales. That subject's rating of the concept on a given scale would represent the degree to which that descriptive dimension is applicable to the concept in question. In effect, the semantic differential is a way of measuring the personal meanings the individual attaches to concepts, events, or objects. Like the Q-sort, it is an attempt to combine phenomenological experience with an objective approach to measurement. And as with the Q-sort, subjects can distort their ratings if they choose. Furthermore, it is the experimenter who selects the polar dimensions along which subjects make their ratings. Table 7-2

TABLE 7-2 Use of the semantic differential

BELOW IS A SERIES OF ADJECTIVES WHICH MIGHT BE USED TO DESCRIBE SOMEONE. USE THESE ADJECTIVES TO DESCRIBE HOW YOU PERSONALLY PERCEIVE THE PERSON WE HAVE JUST BEEN TALKING ABOUT.

Example: If you perceive this person as slightly positive you would place your checkmark like this:

POSITIVE: ___ : ___ : X : ___ : ___ : ___ : ___ : NEGATIVE
(Note that the checkmark is placed *between* the dotted lines.)

SINCERE: ___ : ___ : ___ : ___ : ___ : ___ : ___ : INSINCERE
INTELLIGENT: ___ : ___ : ___ : ___ : ___ : ___ : ___ : UNINTELLIGENT
ALTRUISTIC: ___ : ___ : ___ : ___ : ___ : ___ : ___ : OPPORTUNISTIC
WORTHY: ___ : ___ : ___ : ___ : ___ : ___ : ___ : UNWORTHY
HONEST: ___ : ___ : ___ : ___ : ___ : ___ : ___ : DISHONEST
AMBITIOUS: ___ : ___ : ___ : ___ : ___ : ___ : ___ : UNAMBITIOUS

Source: From *An Investigation into the Construct Validity of the Selfism Scale* by N. J. Erskine, 1981, Unpublished master's thesis, Kansas State University.

---

illustrates how a semantic differential approach can be used to study reactions of subjects to a woman described as victimized by a drinking, abusive husband.

As the brief survey provided thus far has shown, much of the Rogerian research effort has had to do with the therapy situation. How the self changes over the course of therapy has been a prominent research theme. In addition, the emphasis on self-reports has tended to encourage a correlational approach to investigation. The proliferation of various scales to measure self-concept, self-actualization, self-awareness, and the like has led to a multitude of correlations among these various instruments and among other variables as well. An example is a study by D. M. Zuckerman (1980). In addition to numerous other relationships, she found that for white women eighteen to twenty-five years old, intelligent, unconventional, and nonreligious self-concepts are related to nontraditional goals and feminist attitudes.

Other correlational and experimental research

One of the cornerstones of several approaches to the development of the self has been the reflected appraisal process (e.g., see Cooley, Meade, and Sullivan in Chapter 6). Basically, the idea is that the actual appraisals of important figures such as parents or siblings affect reflected appraisals (i.e., the individual's perceptions of the appraisals of others). These reflected appraisals, in turn, affect one's self-appraisal and thus the development of the self. To test this conceptualization, Felson (1989) tested twenty-two children from Grades 4 through 7. He also interviewed their parents and the children themselves and also got ratings of the children from teachers. Applying a series of regression equations to the resultant data was the next step. Data were based on questions such as, "How smart do you think you are?" or "How well do you do in sports?" The evidence suggested that children are, indeed, affected by reflected appraisals. However, these reflected appraisals involved the influence of "generalized" others rather than the evaluations of specific significant others.

Phenomenologically derived concepts can be studied in the laboratory as well. Conditions can be manipulated and their effects on, for example, self-esteem observed. A case in point is a study by McFarlin and Blascovich (1981). These researchers reasoned that a person's chronic level of self-esteem is based upon a large number of experiences involving success and failure. These experiences accumulate so that one isolated instance of success or failure in a laboratory setting should do little to change that chronic level of self-esteem. Accordingly, they selected three groups of female subjects based upon level of self-esteem: high, moderate, and low. One third of each group was failed on an anagrams task; another third of each group succeeded; the remaining third in each group was not told how well or poorly it did. While there were several interesting results in this study, it was particularly notable that when subjects were given performance feedback inconsistent with their chronic level of self-esteem, that level did not change. For example, subjects high in self-esteem did not lower their self-esteem just because they failed on the task.

Another example is research on the widely held view that people who regard themselves favorably will regard others in a similar light. Certainly this was Rogers's (1961) sentiment. To test this notion, Epstein and Feist (1988) compared the self-ratings on seven personality variables (e.g., kind, friendly, nonbossy, etc.) of 129 preadolescent boys and girls to their ratings of others on the same variables. The results showed that, true to expectations, favorable self-ratings are positively associated with favorable ratings of others. In the case of boys, however, the relationship was much stronger when they were rating other boys rather than girls. Girls, in contrast, did not show this discrepancy. The investigators concluded that the positive relationship between views of the self and others is quite robust even though the strength of the relationship is affected by how closely one identifies with those others who are rated.

Other research has indicated that, depending on the specific circumstances at hand, there is both stability and malleability to the self-concept (Markus and Kunda, 1986). For example, Wells (1988) used an ingenious technique to show how mothers' self-esteem will change in daily life. She selected forty-nine middle-class, white working mothers who were employed either full-time, half-time, or part-time. These mothers carried pagers and a series of one-page questionnaires about with them over the course of the day from 8:00 A.M. to 10:00 P.M. Whenever a signal sounded (activated on a random schedule by the investigator), they were to stop and report their present activity and experience. This happened four to five times each day for two weeks. Analysis of these mothers' reports indicated, as shown in Figure 7-2, that mothers' ongoing self-esteem fluctuated according to whom they were with at any given time. It was lower when they were with children than when they were with adults. The results clearly showed these daily variations in self-esteem. However, overall levels of self-esteem calculated over the two-week period did show stability as well.

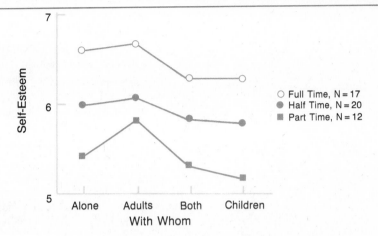

FIGURE 7-2 Mothers' self-esteem as determined by the people with whom they are interacting.

Adapted from "Variations in Mothers' Self-Esteem in Daily Life" by Anne J. Wells, *Journal of Personality and Social Psychology,* Vol. 55, No. 4, October 1988. Copyright © 1988 by the American Psychological Association. Reprinted by permission of the author.

Humanistic research

As was noted in the preceding chapter, Maslow began his career with a strong bent toward behaviorism. Indeed, his doctoral dissertation was an observational study of monkeys. But his enthusiasm for the experimental paradigm quickly waned. Later he was to state that animal research is not only irrelevant for our understanding of humans but can also promote a dehumanizing view of human behavior. Such research, he felt, simply cannot come to grips with human activities such as poetry and music; nor can it shed light upon human characteristics such as love, courage, and grief. Nevertheless he understood experimental research and had experience with it. It was not that he felt that experimental investigation should be abandoned. Rather he wanted it to divest itself of the obsession with brass instruments and sterile methodology and focus on methods that would highlight the meaningfulness, vitality, and significance of human existence. Aronoff (1985) has described a great deal of supportive research on Maslow's ideas.

Need hierarchy.   It will be recalled that according to Maslow's need hierarchy scheme, physiological and safety needs take precedence over needs higher in the pyramid. This almost commonsensical notion has been supported empirically. Research on the other needs, however, is not so supportive. For example, Leith (1972) placed subjects under stress that probably constituted a threat to their needs at the lower levels of the hierarchy. They were administered several tests of creativity immediately afterward. Contrary to what might have been expected, subjects increased both the number and originality of their responses in the face of threat to their basic needs. In addition, Graham and Balloun (1973) predicted that when any two needs in Maslow's hierarchy are paired, the one at the lower level will show greater evidence of having been satisfied. Interviews were used to classify need strength. The results were a bit equivocal, and methodological shortcomings make it difficult to determine just how much support this study provides for Maslow's theory. Recently, Williams and Page (1989) have developed a self-report measure of the hierarchy of needs. So far, it manifests good reliability and validity.

Self-actualization.

As was observed earlier, Maslow's self-actualized individuals have escaped from the straightjacket of society and have achieved their true inner potential. The vagueness of such a proposition makes its validation difficult. In fact, there is little evidence for it save some work by Maslow (1950) himself. Maslow selected forty-nine prominent individuals who fitted his definition of psychological health. Some of these people were alive, others were dead, but all seemed characterized by achievement, adjustment, and maturity. This selection procedure was, of course, a rather loose, unreliable one. He divided these people into three categories: (1) definite actualizers such as Jefferson and Lincoln, (2) possible actualizers such as Renoir and Adlai Stevenson, and (3) partial actualizers who fell short of self-actualization. Based on a variety of informational sources, Maslow compiled a list of fifteen traits (see Table 6-1) or qualities he felt characterized the self-actualizer. This work is replete with methodological shortcomings and does not rise much above sheer speculation; yet it is widely quoted, and Maslow himself regarded it as a cornerstone of his theorizing about self-actualization.

Peak experience.

Generally, **peak experience** refers to intense joy and **peak performance** to superior functioning; they are models of optimal human experiencing (Privette, 1983). Maslow (1962), in searching for the meaning of peak experiences, turned to a group of 190 college students for help. He asked them for their written responses to the following instructions:

> I would like you to think of the most wonderful experiences of your life; happiest moments, ecstatic moments, moments of rapture, perhaps from being in love, or from listening to music or suddenly "being hit" by a book or a painting, or from some great creative moment. First, list these. And then try to tell me how you feel in such acute moments, how you feel *differently* from the way you feel at other times, how you are at the moment a different person in some ways. (With other subjects the questioning asked rather about the ways in which the world looked different.) (p. 67)

From these responses, Maslow was able to describe nineteen characteristics of the "peak-experience cognition." An example is:

> The emotional reaction in the peak experience has a special flavor of wonder, of awe, of reverence, of humility and surrender before the experience as before something great. (p. 82)

In concluding his discussion, however, Maslow warns that regardless of how fruitful or penetrating cognitive experiences may appear to be, there can be no substitute for the routine and cautious procedures of science.

Existential research

Existentialists are not oriented toward experimental research. Indeed, one looks in vain in the index of Binswanger's 1963 book for an entry such as *Research, Experiments,* or *Investigation.* The emphasis is not on research or experimentation in any conventional sense. It is, instead, on the description of experience—the phenomenological analysis of immediate experience. The focus is one of describing what is immediately presented in experience through the analysis of verbal reports and behavior. One does not start with universal truths or psychological laws and then deduce hypotheses that will later be tested in the laboratory. W. F. Fischer (1978) illustrates this version of research from the existential perspective when he says:

> I understand being empirical to mean that the researcher is open to all perceivable dimensions and profiles of the phenomenon that is being researched. Hence, the experiences of the subjects, as well as those of the researcher, are immediately acknowledged as potentially informative. (p. 168)

Fischer went on to describe how one may investigate being anxious. It involved a clinical-like analysis of descriptions provided by students of situations in which they experienced anxiety. A similar example is a study carried out by van Kaam (1966). High school and college students were asked to recall situations in which they experienced "being understood" and also how they felt in those situations. The descriptions were collected and the investigator examined them with the following questions in mind:

■ Does this concrete, colorful formulation by the subject contain a moment of experience that might be a necessary and sufficient constituent of the experience of really feeling understood?

■ If so, is it possible to abstract this moment of experience and to label the abstraction briefly and precisely without violating the formulation presented by the subject? (van Kaam, 1966, p. 323)

Descriptions not meeting these criteria were eliminated. By this procedure, nine constituents were identified as elements of the experience of really feeling understood. They are shown in Table 7-3.

There are, of course, monumental problems in this kind of research. Chiefly, they involve the extent to which independent judges can agree in their understanding and classification of a subject's experience.

Research on personal constructs

Research on Kelly's personal construct theory hinges greatly on the ability to define and measure a person's constructs. Because the study of personal constructs has become virtually synonymous with the instrument Kelly devised to measure them, it is important to describe this assessment device.

TABLE 7-3　Constituents of being understood

Constituent	Percentage of Subjects Expressing Constituent
1 Perceiving signs of understanding from a person	87
2 Perceiving that a person coexperiences what things mean to the subject	91
3 Perceiving that the person accepts the subject	86
4 Feeling satisfaction	99
5 Initially feeling relief	93
6 Initially feeling relief from experiential loneliness	89
7 Feeling safe in the relationship with the person understanding	91
8 Feeling safe experiential communion with the person understanding	86
9 Feeling safe experiential communion with that which the person understanding is perceived to represent	64

SOURCE: *Existential Foundations of Psychology* by A. van Kaam (Pittsburgh, Pa.: Duquesne University Press), 1966. Copyright 1966 by Duquesne University Press. Reprinted by permission.

In his 1955 volumes, Kelly described the **Role Construct Repertory Test (Rep Test).** In a sense, this test is a triumph of elegant deduction from theory. It is one of the truly novel assessment devices of recent decades. This test is based on the premise that a construct can be measured by first noting the similarities and contrasts among events. Typically, a subject is asked to list a series of people or events he or she regards as important (e.g., relatives, teachers, friends; or graduation, marriage, purchase of a house). Once a list is generated, the individual items in the list are presented in groups of three, called triads. For each triad, the subject must indicate how two of the members of that group are alike and yet different from the third. By going successively through the list with these triads, the subject's construct system is elicited.

An informal example of this procedure is shown in the following case illustration. The person in question is a male college student who was being seen for individual counseling in a campus counseling center.

COUNSELOR: List three people you most admire.
CLIENT: My brother, my uncle, and my girlfriend.
COUNSELOR: How are any two of these alike and yet different from the third?
CLIENT: My brother and my uncle are calm. They don't get flustered, and they are usually very patient. My girlfriend flies off the handle—never stops to think.
COUNSELOR: How are your reactions to two of these individuals alike but different from your reactions to the third?
CLIENT: I suppose I respect my brother and my uncle but I react to my girlfriend as if she's not as bright as me.

The Rep Test is highly adaptable for a wide variety of purposes. It also does not force the experimenter's constructs onto the subject as much as does the Q-sort or the semantic differential. Box 7-1 presents a more formal example of the Rep Test.

Several studies indicate that Rep Test data are reliable over various intervals of time (Bonarius, 1965; Landfield, Stern, and Fjeld, 1961; Pederson, 1958). However, under some conditions constructs will change. For example, Poch (1952) asked subjects to make predictions about friends. These predictions were based on subjects' personal constructs. It was "arranged" so that some of their predictions were correct while others were incorrect. Interestingly, validated constructs (those that led to correct predictions) did not change during an intervening period; invalidated ones did show some change. Of even more interest was the fact that invalidated constructs were less frequently used for a second set of predictions. In a related study, Levy (1954) observed that *strongly* invalidated constructs precipitated more changes in the construct system than *weakly* invalidated ones. Furthermore, **constellatory constructs** (constructs with pervasive connections throughout the construct system) were especially potent in leading to changes. In a related study, Hinkle (1965) found that **superordinate constructs** which undergo change lead to widespread changes in other constructs.

A more recent study bridges personal construct theory and self-theory. Hayden (1979) used the Self-Identification Form of the Rep Test. He determined that people seek to maintain or enhance the meaningfulness of their view of self. They do so either by moving toward more implications or by resisting a change that would reduce meaningfulness. In short, a person will maintain a given view of the self until something better comes along. However, change will occur if the possibility of extending the meaningfulness of one's self-view is offered.

Self-schemata research

A great deal of current research on the self is being carried out in the language of self-schemata or schemas. The idea of self-schemata is their function in guiding the processing of self-relevant information (Markus, 1983). Continuing research on the construct validity and utility of self-schemata is vital, however. An example of this kind of research is a study by Bruch, Kaflowitz, and Berger (1988). They divided a group of undergraduate subjects into "schematics" and "aschematics." The former were those who tended to endorse a series of assertive self-rating items while the latter did not. They performed a laboratory recall task. Later, they were asked to recall material from the task that they had not expected to be of interest to the investigators. Interestingly, schematic subjects recalled more "assertive" adjectives during the recall period than did the aschematic subjects. In a second portion of the study, schematics and aschematics were asked to determine, as regards a conflict situation, how reasonable certain requests from another person really were. It had been established in advance by the investigators that these requests were of high, low, or moderate legitimacy. Results indicated that in the high and low legitimacy conditions, schematics and aschematics did not differ in their judgments of reasonableness. But in the case of requests of moderate legitimacy, the assertive schematics judged the requests as less reasonable than did the aschematics. In short, in relatively ambiguous (moderate) circumstances, one's assertive self-schemata will operate. In very structured (high or low) situations, however, individual differ-

Box 7-1
ROLE CONSTRUCT REPERTORY TEST

Sechrest (1977) has provided the following example of Rep Test instructions and analysis.

NAME Sue B.

SEX M Ⓕ AGE 19

	CONSTRUCT	CONTRAST
1	easy-going	tense
2	artistic	not artistic
3	female	males
4	outgoing	introverted
5	nervous	calm
6	tense	easy-going
7	my family	not my family
8	down to earth	sort of pretentious
9	fun loving	serious
10	females	males

Modified instructions

Step 1. The three persons to be compared on each line have a circle under them. For example, on the first line, think of an important word that describes two of the persons *(self, mother, father).* Write that word on Row 1 under *construct* and also place an *X* in those two circles under the two people to whom the word applies. On Row 1 under *contrast,* write the opposite of that word.

(For Sue B, *X*'s in the circles under *self* and *father* mean that she sees herself and her father as easy-going in contrast to her mother, who is seen as tense.)

Step 2. Follow this same procedure for each of the succeeding nine lines.

(continued)

ences in assertiveness will be overwhelmed by the situation. These latter results are shown in Figure 7-3.

A study in a similar vein required clinically depressed and nondepressed subjects to provide a series of ratings of a list of depressed and nondepressed content adjectives

Box 7-1 *(continued)*

Analysis of Rep Test protocol for Sue B

The first construct elicited *(easy-going—tense,* in this case) often is of special importance and tends to represent a fundamental dichotomy for the subject. Sue B chooses to view people in her life space in terms of how they approach the world. Some in her thinking are "loose," "relaxed," "free flowing," and some are "up tight," "constricted," or "wound up." Since the circles on Row 1 have been put in for *self, mother,* and *father,* this construct of easy-going versus tense may be of special significance, perhaps even a core construct.

Note that in Sort 6 *(tense—easy-going)* this construct is repeated, and that Row 5 *(nervous—calm)* is semantically about the same, thus indicating that for Sue this whole area of tension versus calm in people is crucially important. Everyone categorized as easy-going on Sort 1 is calm on Sort 5, and those tense on Sort 1 are nervous on Sort 5. Sort 9 *(fun-loving—serious)* appears to be simply a relabeling of *easy-going—tense.*

We can now conclude that for Sue B there are easy-going, calm, fun-loving people and nervous, tense, serious people. One can be down to earth without being easy-going, and one need not be tense to be artistic.

Most of Sue B's constructs are fairly abstract and "psychological" in nature, but when faced with certain sorts, e.g., self-boyfriend-girlfriend and self-brother-cousin, she comes up only with rather concrete and evaluatively neutral constructs such as *female—male* and *my family—not my family.*

(Derry and Kuiper, 1981). It was hypothesized that the negative self-schemata of depressed subjects would lead them to better recall the self-referent depressed adjectives relative to nondepressed subjects. This is exactly what happened when subjects were unexpectedly asked later to recall all the adjectives that they had rated earlier. A similar result was reported by Moser and Dyck (1989) using subjects with hostile self-schemata. The idea was that subjects, after being exposed to uncontrollable failure, would show better recall for hostile adjectives than a comparable group of subjects who lacked such hostile schemata. The hypothesis was confirmed, thus extending once more the construct validity of the schemata approach to the self.

Finally, Klotz and Alicke (1989) investigated the effectiveness of a person-schema as an information processing structure when the schema is either appropriate or inappropriate. Subjects were asked to evaluate another person (either a positive or a negative individual) while comparing her either to themselves, to someone they liked, or to someone they disliked. It was predicted that the self and the liked-other would be appropriate schemas for the positive person, while the disliked-other would be appropriate for the negative person. Subsequent recall of target information about the positive

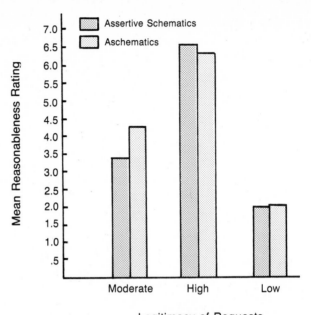

FIGURE 7-3   Degree of legitimacy and ratings of reasonableness.
Adapted from "Self-Schema for Assertiveness: Extending the Validity of the Self-Schema Construct" by Monroe A. Bruch, Nadine G. Kaflowitz, and Pat Berger, *Journal of Research in Personality*, Vol. 22, No. 4, December 1988. Copyright © 1988 by Academic Press, Inc. Reprinted by permission.

and negative persons supported the hypothesis. This, again, suggests that one's schemata affect the ways in which information is received, stored, and retrieved.

PHENOMENOLOGY, THE SELF, AND ASSESSMENT

In the preceding sections of this chapter, we examined some of the principal methods of investigation. Since research in personality is intimately associated with assessment, several major approaches to assessment have already been covered, including interviews, Q-sorts, the semantic differential, the Rep Test, and others. In this section, we shall take a further look at specific assessment issues and techniques.

Measurement of the private world

To play what must seem like an old tune by now, the phenomenologist believes that the best source of information about a person is that person. This is not unreasonable given the assumption that behavior results from the way people perceive events and the meaning they attach to things that happen around them. But what are some of the implications of this belief for assessment?

Behavior. Most of us learn that psychology is the study of behavior. We become accustomed to searching for the keys to personality by observing what people do. But for the strict phenomenologist or existentialist, this is not the case. Assessing behavior by simply noting what people do or how often they do it leaves out the crucial assessment ingredient—the meaning of the behavior to the individual. For example, suppose there is an item on a test "How often do you date?" Three different subjects answer the question by saying "Seven times a month." How do we treat those pieces of data? It could be risky treating them all alike. For example, one subject may date frequently to escape the monotony of classes or studying. The second may have doubts about his personal acceptability and is seeking reassurance. The third may just be a friendly soul who, in the natural course of events, finds himself frequently in the company of women. What we have is the same behavior, but the meaning of the behavior is vastly different for each subject. The phenomenologist, then, would not rest with a simple analysis of behavior. It would be necessary to assess the meaning ascribed to it by the subject.

Inferences. Assessment is often a method by which we infer the underlying determinants of behavior. Responses on a test or in an interview are analyzed for their significance. Thus, the basic interest lies not in the responses themselves but in what the responses signify (the sign approach discussed in Chapter 2). For the phenomenologist the danger here is that we are dealing with the *assessor's* inferences. Kelly often commented that the analyses of projective test data tell you more about the clinician than they do about the patient. There is more than a little truth in this quip. In phenomenology, we are concerned with the meaning of a response or experience to the *person;* the clinician's personal projections or inferences can do nothing more than confuse the situation. Meaning is filtered through the assessor's experience when, in fact, the person should serve as the filter.

The major problem with the phenomenological posture is determining the means whereby one person can become aware of another's experience and meaning. It is one thing to say "I understand where you are coming from," and another to be sure that it is so. And this is no more true for the layperson than it is for the trained phenomenologist. In the latter case, the research literature is full of instances where phenomenological analyses have no supporting evidence of interjudge reliability. A great deal seems to be accepted on faith.

Today. Phenomenological assessment is concerned with the present. Whether the goal is eliciting the subject's personal constructs, determining evaluative judgments, or asking for a Q-sort, the focus is on today, for it is today's meaning and not yesterday's refrain that powers behavior. Just as phenomenological theories are ahistorical, so, too, are their assessment procedures.

The unconscious.   As noted before, phenomenologists differ somewhat in their attitudes toward unconscious processes. However, the predominant assessment strategies tend to emphasize conscious processes through self-reports. When one is sorting among cards, reporting how two events are alike and yet different from a third, or simply responding "true" or "false" to an objective test, the tacit assumption is that the word of the subject can be trusted. This, of course, is a large assumption. Can people be relied upon to report their experience correctly? Do they ever distort in order to create a calculated impression? Can they free themselves from the unconscious long enough to provide valid reports? For the phenomenologist, the answers seem to be yes. In a sense, the phenomenologist seems to adopt the strategy of sampling the subject's verbal responses rather than looking for unconscious determinants. The issue is not whether phenomenologists are gullible but whether the sampling strategy is powerful enough.

Conditions of assessment.   As we learned in Chapter 6, Rogers emphasized the need for warmth, empathy, and unconditional positive regard in the therapy room. It was his conviction that such conditions will promote a nondefensive client who can then get in touch with the potential self. The same philosophy can be applied to the testing situation. When a situation is free of threat, this should encourage the client or subject to be open and thus provide self-reports that are more meaningful and closer to real experience. Again, it is questionable whether such testing conditions can routinely obliterate needs to distort or deny certain aspects of experience or, what is even more probable, whether the assessor can reliably distinguish when subjects are distorting and when they are not.

Accuracy of personal assessment

Because so much in phenomenological assessment hinges upon self-reports, the question naturally arises as to just how accurate these reports are. In a sense, the issue comes down to a comparison between predictions based on self-reports and those based on the results of psychometric tests or on impressions of experienced judges dealing with interview data. When a college student tells you he can pass statistics without having taken college algebra, do you accept this or do you turn to his performance on standardized tests or to his high school transcript before laying your bets? When a patient extolls the virtues of her mother and tells you how close they have been, do you accept the remarks or do you look to a clinician's inferences of hostility based on her Rorschach and TAT performance?

Both Mischel (1972) and Scott and Johnson (1972) seem to place much of their faith in direct measures such as self-reports. Their reviews of a number of studies led them to conclude that direct self-reports about aggression, hostility, achievement, opinions of others' reactions to subjects, and personal feelings of distress often outstrip the predictions developed by experts from sophisticated testing devices. On the other hand, McClelland (1972) argues that self-reports are largely opinions about oneself. What they predict is the opinions of others who are exposed to their verbalizations. He feels they do not predict behavior in laboratory or real-life settings. McClelland also asserts that considerable evidence exists for the ability of indirect measures (e.g., projective tests) to predict overt behavior.

There is much evidence that self-reported items of information during interviews are often erroneous. And if we consider clinical interviews, which are so often laced with threat and by their very nature are frequently complex and convoluted, the problems multiply. Thus, Janis (1958) found that hospitalized medical patients could not adequately report their preoperative fears and anxieties even a few days after their operations. Kanfer and Phillips (1970) quite properly note that self-reports, like anything else, are determined by one's learning history and by present stimulus conditions. Errors in prediction are likely if we automatically assume that self-reports are correct. Such a conclusion is underscored by a voluminous set of studies dealing with **response style** (Jackson and Messick, 1958). This refers to the tendency of subjects to respond to questions in a particular way regardless of the content of the item. For example, one subject may repeatedly give extreme responses while another may always settle for responses in the neutral range. **Acquiescence,** the propensity to respond "true" to every true-false item, is another example. Still another predisposition involves **social desirability,** the tendency to give what the subject believes are socially acceptable responses rather than true ones (Lanyon and Goodstein, 1971).

What does all this suggest? Well, it probably indicates that self-reports are both reliable and unreliable! The real question is whether the psychologist can detect when self-reports are faithful reflections of real feelings and when they are distortions, either calculated or unknowing. Perhaps the basic message here is that a strategy that unfailingly regards all self-reports as under suspicion is as likely to come to grief as one that inevitably views self-reports as the epitome of truth. Given the present state of our knowledge, this means that sensitive clinical judgments must be brought to bear on the task of deciding in each case how much faith to put in a self-report. For the phenomenologist who is totally committed to the uncritical acceptance of the self-report, the waters appear to be troubled here.

Assessment in therapy

Many Rogerians adopt the position that diagnosis and assessment of therapy clients should be severely curtailed. They seem to feel that assessment via psychological tests is not only unnecessary but in many cases actually detrimental. Assessment puts the psychologist in a superior, authoritative role that can impede the development of the client's sense of autonomy and self-actualization. What is required, they believe, is an aura of genuineness, empathy, and unconditional positive regard that will strip the therapy situation of any threat and thereby promote self-actualization. For those Rogerians who do use tests, there is a heavy emphasis on their administration in a climate of acceptance and warmth.

When Rogerians abandon or heavily deemphasize psychological evaluation through testing, they seem to be assuming that their therapy method is so potent or effective that it will work regardless of the specific strengths or weaknesses in a given client. This, in turn, suggests the invariant application of a therapy method in spite of any individual differences among clients that might be revealed by testing. All clients are treated alike in the orthodox Rogerian approach.

As for personal construct theory, Kelly used testing as a way of charting a plan to help change the client's constructs. A favored tool, quite naturally, was the Rep Test, described earlier. In fact, Kelly felt that a variety of tests, from objective ones to projective techniques, could be employed to elicit the client's construct system. The most important consideration was a sensitive therapist who could, with the help of assessment devices (1) define the client's problem, (2) identify the pathways along which the client is free to move, (3) generate clinical hypotheses, (4) identify usable resources in the client, and (5) identify any problems that might otherwise be missed by the therapist.

Some additional self-report techniques

Because of their highly inferential, indirect nature, projective techniques have never been widely employed by phenomenological-existential investigators. Occasionally the Rorschach (e.g., Carr, 1949) and the TAT (e.g., C. R. Rogers, 1967b) have been used by Rogerians, but this has been the exception rather than the rule. Objective tests that have distinct psychiatric overtones are not likely to find favor with phenomenologists.

The Personal Orientation Inventory (POI).   As noted earlier, self-actualization is a difficult concept to measure objectively. In recent years, however, there has been an increasing use of the **Personal Orientation Inventory (POI).** Starting from Maslow's theory, Shostrom (1965, 1966) constructed a 150-item questionnaire consisting of paired opposites. Subjects are required to select the one from each pair that is most characteristic of them (e.g., "I will continue to grow only by setting my sights on a high-level, socially approved goal" or "I will continue to grow best by being myself"). The test is scored several ways. Two major scores—inner-directedness and time competence (present orientation)—are derived. In addition, ten complementary subscores are possible. These include self-actualization values, existentiality, feeling reactivity, spontaneity, self-regard, self-acceptance, nature of man, synergy, acceptance of aggression, and capacity for intimate contact. A number of studies dealing with the psychometric properties and construct validity of the POI have now been completed (Maddi, 1989). Many of these are promising. At the same time, one must wonder about the measurement of self-actualization (said to reflect the uniqueness of each individual) by means of a standardized test based upon average profiles. Such a contradiction is a general one that must be addressed by those who wish to apply psychometric or nomothetic research methods to phenomenologically construed events.

Tennessee Self Concept Scale.   Fitts (1965) developed the **Tennessee Self Concept Scale (TSCS).** The scale consists of 100 self-report items that emphasize the multidimensionality of the self. It has been widely employed and is considered to have been a very heuristic instrument. Despite its popularity, however, Marsh and Richards (1988) conclude that research support for many of the scales the TSCS contains is scant.

Measures of meaninglessness.   From the existential perspective, a pervading sense of the meaninglessness of life, alienation, and normlessness are prominent aspects of the contemporary scene. Consequently, several scales have been devised to measure these concepts. Most such tests have not progressed far enough in their development to allow for definitive conclusions. There are, for example, the Purpose in Life Test (Crumbaugh and Maholic, 1964), a measure of Frankl's notion of the existential vacuum; the Existential Study (Thorne, 1973); and the Alienation Test (Maddi, Kobasa, and Hoover, 1979).

Information processing and assessment

It has been noted that the information processing perspective is still quite new. By and large, it has, thus far, drawn on existing assessment techniques and has yet to develop truly distinctive methods and devices. However, Carver and Scheier (1988) have made some suggestions as to how assessment might take place. For example, asking people to respond with the first thing that comes to mind might be inappropriate since some information (e.g., about the self) might not be easily retrieved from memory; perhaps because it is not encoded in a form that meshes easily with the form of the question. In short, recognizing the various forms in which information is stored should alert us to the importance of framing questions in the right fashion.

As to what should be assessed, this is still an emerging issue. Again, Carver and Scheier (1988) emphasize the importance of assessing the self-regulatory aspects of the personality. For example, Fenigstein, Scheier, and Buss (1975) distinguish between the public aspects of the self and its private aspects. As the person evolves and adopts either a predominantly personal or social orientation, the ways in which behavior is regulated will vary accordingly. Thus, it becomes important to understand the person's private and public self-domains in order to correctly predict behavior.

An example of the way in which the concept of public self-consciousness can aid in prediction involves the behavior of self-handicapping (Shepperd and Arkin, 1989). **Self-handicapping** is a defensive strategy (perhaps a close relative of rationalization) in which the individual acquires an impediment to a successful performance which, in turn, provides an excuse for potential failure. Shepperd and Arkin discovered that people who are concerned about the public aspects of the self (high in public self-consciousness) are more likely to handicap their performance on a task than are individuals who are less concerned about issues of public self-consciousness. These results suggest that people who are sensitive about social approval, loss of face, and the evaluations of others will be more likely to adopt defensive strategies. However, it should be noted that some investigators question the validity of the public-private self-consciousness distinction altogether (Wicklund and Gollwitzer, 1987).

SUMMARY EVALUATION

In the preceding sections, a number of evaluative comments were made. This section will summarize these and other comments.

Strengths

The world of phenomenology brings with it some decided advantages. The following are some of them.

Phenomenology as an alternative.

Phenomenology and its existential and humanistic offshoots serve to remind us that humans are not just mosaics of instincts, urges, or habits. They are more than simple robots that respond mindlessly to drives or external stimuli. Humans interpret their experience, make choices, and change themselves. The essential human qualities of inner experience and self-awareness are not shunted aside in the interests of a slavish adherence to what psychology understands to be the scientific method. It is recognized that humans are more than objects of study; they are initiators of study as well. The humanists and existentialists, particularly, remind us that a headlong dash down the research paths cleared by physicists and biologists may, in the process, ignore the basic human data—experience and awareness. There exist, then, alternatives to psychoanalysis as well as to mechanistic behavior theories and to quantification-happy researchers.

Emphasis on the positive.

Theorists such as Maslow and Rogers would not allow us to forget that we possess the capacity for positive growth. For many in psychoanalysis and psychology, the emphasis always seems to be on psychopathology, sickness, behavior deficits, and the like. We end up wondering by what miracle any of us ever achieve even a semblance of mental health. However, the phenomenological-humanistic-existential axis expands our subject matter by including love, creativity, health, competence, and the actualizing potential. The seeds of such a focus have begun to encourage those in the assessment field to examine not just human deficits but human competencies as well (Sundberg, Snowden, and Reynolds, 1978).

The goals of personologists and their clinical brethren have begun to shift as a result of all this, from the simple containment of pathology to the liberation of awareness and the enhancement of feeling and freedom. Therapy has become not just a province inhabited by neurotics and the more promising psychotics but a place where one can grow, actualize, and encounter the self. We talk not just about therapy for the sick but about the possibility of further growth for those with self-awareness. All of this is not without its dangers, however, as we shall see a bit later. But as a counterbalance to the traditional ways of doing business, it certainly merits our attention, particularly if we consider this general approach to be an antidote to an earlier overemphasis rather than a total replacement of more traditional ideas and practices.

Emphasis on the present and future.

Whether it be Kelly, Rogers, Maslow, or Boss, the pitch is toward the present. The argument is that the "now" is the determinant of our behavior. The past is gone forever and only exists insofar as it is construed in our current awareness. By clutching firmly to a deterministic view of behavior, more conventional theories direct us toward a relentless search of our past. We become products of childhood conflicts and can never really change ourselves until we achieve insight into them, or else we are prisoners of our previous conditionings. When we make a choice, it is preordained by earlier experience. We are, in essence, captives of the past.

But phenomenologists say otherwise. They assert that we exercise free will. They tell us that we are not pushed by the past but pulled by the future. Our potential pulls us toward actualization and we anticipate events by construing their repetitive occurrences. In a sense, they are saying that the future is a magnet pulling us while others have implied that the past is a set of chains that binds us. Again, all of this is controversial. And if the argument comes down simply to choosing up sides over free will versus determinism, who can say which is correct? In any case, it is true that blind allegiance to a deterministic model of science has not solved all of the problems of the psychology of personality. Perhaps, then, by reopening the debate, by challenging some comfortable assumptions, phenomenological approaches have served an important function.

Rogers: Some specific strengths.   When we turn to Rogers specifically, a number of strengths are apparent. From a historical standpoint, it is important to note that his development of a theory led to a great deal of research. Much of this research dealt with therapy processes and demonstrated that such investigation could be done. Furthermore, the results of this research were important in modifying Rogers's ideas about client-centered therapy as well as about self-theory.

Rogers developed a comprehensive and systematic theory of personality, which he stated in a propositional form that enhanced its clarity. As we shall see, there is inherent ambiguity in many of his concepts; yet the utility of the theory was undoubtedly heightened by its propositional format.

As much as anything, Rogers will be remembered for his introduction of client-centered therapy—the first major alternative to psychoanalysis. His emphasis on the therapy relationship and his deemphasis of the necessity for an elaborate reconstruction of the past produced a set of therapy procedures that both shortened the process and required less training on the part of the therapist. This, in turn, has led to the development of encounter groups, self-help groups, and so on, making available to more people the possibility for personal growth and enhancement. To some extent, however, this is a double-edged sword. Some claim that this client-centered, humanistic movement has produced a generation of pseudotherapists whose lack of training can never be fully offset by their enthusiasm and "authenticity."

Kelly: Some specific strengths.   Kelly's theory was also stated formally in propositional form. It is likewise a comprehensive and systematic formulation. With its emphasis on how people construe events, it demonstrates just how far one can go with a cognitive theory. What is more, Kelly's application of a cognitive approach to clinical events was an achievement of major proportions. His introduction of the Rep Test was an equally important contribution. Similarly, fixed-role therapy, a method logically derived from his theory, is a significant addition to therapeutic practice.

Information processing.   At the present time, it is really too early to evaluate the efficacy of the information processing approach. It certainly does seem to have definite heuristic merit. It capitalizes on the computer metaphor to suggest an entirely new way of construing people. It also promises a more rigorous, objective research approach to the phenomena of the self. It certainly has energized many investigators who are generating a great deal of current research.

As Carson (1989) has observed, the cognitive revolution has had real effects in the personality domain. Although some, notably Neisser (1980), have warned of the dangers of overextension of the information processing model, Carson (1989) seems more hopeful when he comments "that the situation has improved appreciably—for example, by the increased incorporation of motivational and other dynamic variables into the conception and design of cognitively oriented studies" (p. 229).

Weaknesses

Given the foregoing catalog of the strengths of phenomenology, it is now time to examine the other side of the ledger—a task all critics worth their salt find quite attractive.

Subjective experience and self-reports.
By extolling the virtues of subjective experience as the prime mover of behavior, phenomenologists avoid the pitfalls of exclusive reliance on the objective properties of stimuli as predictors. But by putting all of their eggs in the experience basket, they encounter equally serious problems. How are we to see the world as the subject does? How do we enter the phenomenal world of that subject, carrying with us (as we surely must) the baggage of our own idiosyncratic biases and the filters of our own phenomenal field? Perhaps it is not necessary to perceive the world *exactly* as does a client (indeed, if we did we would have the same problems as that person) but only enough to gain *some* understanding and empathy. But how much is enough, and how can we ever be sure our phenomenal field overlaps that of the subject or client enough to permit understanding? These are serious problems whose ultimate resolution may lie in philosophy rather than in psychology. In any case, the mere feeling that I understand the experience of someone else is more glibness than proof.

This search for the understanding of the meaning of another's experience has led most phenomenologists to an almost exclusive reliance on self-reports. Now, many psychologists deal in self-reports, but these reports are examined and weighed, and *inferences* about their significance and meaning are made. However, phenomenologists sometimes seem to ignore the operation of unconscious processes. Their set to be accepting may lead them to overlook distortions and the purposeful withholding of material. At best this approach is inefficient. Then, too, some people have a very limited capacity to express themselves. They have never learned or else do not have the resources to report extensively on their feelings and experiences. A warm, nonthreatening atmosphere will probably facilitate communication, but it will not likely overcome everything.

Research subjects.
The last point takes on added significance when we consider the targets of many phenomenological interventions. Both Kelly and Rogers dealt primarily with college students and developed their theories out of data provided by them. Indeed, the client-centered movement grew up on college campuses. As a group,

college students are brighter and more verbal than the average population. They are better equipped to deal with their problems. In a sense, they are the ideal population with which to employ personal construct theory or for probing verbalizations in an attempt to understand phenomenal fields. When one moves off-campus to a less verbal population or one not so in tune with a romantic view of the person, things become more difficult (as Rogers discovered with a schizophrenic population). One wonders how effective the Rep Test would be with less educated individuals who have difficulties in self-expression.

Just as psychoanalysis may have its greatest application with neurotic individuals, so may phenomenological approaches work best with bright, verbal individuals who can express themselves. The popularity of such methods as encounter groups may be due largely to the fact that people attracted to them have a strong need for self-expression and confrontation with their own emotions. This is not to say that such methods are wrong. The alienated, constricted person searching for the meaning of life may benefit greatly from an existential approach. And the Rep Test may be just the assessment device for the verbal client. However, it may be true that with the present state of knowledge, no single theory or therapy technique works equally well for every individual. As Kelly believed, we must consider the focus of convenience of the theory or technique we are using.

Predictive potency of the phenomenal field.
Some have raised the question of whether we can afford to use the phenomenal field (or personal constructs or experienced meaning) as the only predictor of behavior. The argument that the phenomenal field is information enough runs the risk that more is being left out than included. Yet the phenomenologist proclaims that an objective description of the environment is unnecessary. While it may be true that we must, to some extent, go beyond mere physical descriptions of stimuli, can we afford to ignore those physical properties completely? Similarly, this point of view gives short shrift to biological factors. Again, the argument appears to be that biology is important only as it is represented by conscious awareness in the person. Few would argue that biological descriptions must be included to predict and understand a person on every occasion. But by closing off data sources outside the phenomenal field—and these include situational determinants, biological considerations, and unconscious material—it seems that phenomenologists are ensuring that they remain less aware of the individual's world than they need be.

The master motive.
Much of phenomenology is tied to a view that explains all aspects of behavior as an enhancement of the self, an extension of one's construct system, or the attainment of the meaning of life. At times, this appears to be a rather simplistic set of ideas. For example, there is the risk that by explaining everything in terms of the need for self-enhancement, nothing is really explained. If marrying, going to school, eating pizza, and collecting baseball cards are all due to the need to enhance the self or extend the range of a construct system, can we explain in the same way the person who remains single, drops out of school, eats lasagna, and collects stamps? This is not unlike the dubious tendency of psychoanalysts to explain everything by recourse to the life instincts (or death instincts). The concept of self is a highly complex

one. Somehow, this complexity gets lost in the simplified treatment accorded it by many phenomenologists.

Development.   For some critics of phenomenology, the most disappointing feature of self-theory, personal construct theory, and existentialism is the lack of emphasis on development. The ahistorical position, although theoretically consistent, seems to result in serious practical omissions. While logically it may be true that all we need to know is the person's phenomenal field today, practically it would seem that a more complete picture would include information about the antecedents of that field. In terms of child-rearing issues or methods of changing behavior, knowledge of how individuals have acquired their construct system or their particular phenomenal field would seem highly important. However, Rogers and especially Kelly had very little to say about such matters. In practice, however, many phenomenologically oriented clinicians do attend to developmental matters.

A romanticized view.   As previously noted, the phenomenological orientation (not including Kelly) seems to present us with an overly romanticized, almost naive, view of the human being. It may be true that other conceptions overemphasize the negative, pathological side of human nature. But phenomenology seems to go just as far in the opposite direction. There are frequent statements that self-actualization is an innate tendency. But there is no research to support such a contention. Views such as this seem to be largely philosophical, or almost religious, pronouncements rather than scientific statements. There does not seem to be a recognition of the dark potential residing in all of us. It is assumed that if we simply accept and warmly regard others, their innate tendency to self-actualize will emerge. Although there is considerable merit to this position, a total commitment to it can result in a failure to identify our destructive and self-centered side. There often seems to be an unreasoning faith that if we will get in touch with ourselves—be ourselves—then all manner of good outcomes will occur. Others might argue that the outcomes can just as easily be narcissistic ones that are destructive to the individual's long-term adjustment or to society.

Potential for circularity.   Since we cannot directly observe the phenomenal field of another, we must infer it from that person's behavior and verbalizations. There is some danger that this process will become circular. For example, suppose one of my patients appears quite anxious and uncomfortable following a question about his relationship with his father. Based upon this observation, I make the inference that the question is threatening. I then turn around and explain his discomfort as being due to the threat. This really amounts to little more than saying he acted in a threatened manner because he acted in a threatened manner. I inferred the explanation from the very behavior I was trying to explain!

Nature of the language.   There is a vague, subjective quality to much phenomenological language, making it difficult to operationalize concepts. Definitions of the self as the "I" or "me" are hardly more than restatements. And the term *self-actualization* seems to have a surplus of meaning that is almost mystical. Methods such as the Q-sort do lessen this criticism somewhat. However, the language of self-theory, immersed as it is in the world of experience, leads us into thickets of imprecision from which it is difficult to escape. All of this increases the problem in arriving at agreed-upon methods of measurement and in achieving reliability among observers looking at the same event.

In existentialism, the situation is even worse. There is an undisciplined, almost wild quality to the writing that ensures that independent observers will make different inferences from the same data. It is almost as if the language has assumed a life of its own. Terms such as *internal silence, from here-to-there rhythmic awareness exercises, peak experience, Dasein, authenticity, being-in-the-world, sick point,* or *whatness* are hardly calculated to facilitate communication. Every theoretical framework in psychology tends to lead to its share of word salads, but the humanistic-existential branch of the psychology family seems particularly well endowed.

To some extent, self-theory also tends to reify its concepts. This is especially true in the case of the self. Descriptions of the self often make it seem like a little person in the head. This situation is similar to the tendency of psychoanalysis to make things out of the id, ego, and superego.

The foregoing criticisms are not meant to apply to Kelly. Although his use of the English language is at times a bit unusual, the problem is not vagueness or subjectivity. Rather, it is a matter of our paying careful attention to his definitions and not just assuming that a word such as *hostility* means what it is commonly thought to mean.

Personal constructs.   If Rogers has been criticized as having been immersed in the world of feelings, Kelly has been attacked for having taken an overly rational view of the person. Before the ink was scarcely dry in Kelly's books, both Bruner (1956) and Rogers (1956) expressed their criticism of his emphasis on a thinking organism, which ignored the emotional side. Kelly's view of the organism, they suggested, was one of all brains and no guts. Sechrest (1977) dismisses this critique and notes that few theorists give affect any systematic treatment; they regard it as a given. He goes on to argue that Kelly's construct approach provides ample room for emotions and non-verbal construction of events. At the same time, he expresses concern over the difficulty the theory has in directly linking a person's constructs to the choices he or she makes and to ensuing behavior.

Therapy.   Another language criticism is directly applicable to Rogers's brand of therapy. Rogerians have described their therapy variously as *nondirective, client-centered,* and *person-centered.* These terms do not just describe a philosophy of therapy. They also serve a propaganda function by implying that other therapies or therapists are directive or therapist-centered. A language replete with terms such as *genuine, warm, authentic,* and *democratic* seems to suggest that therapists of other persuasions are insincere, cold, phony, and authoritarian. Actually, most therapists—whatever their theoretical commitments—are warm, caring persons.

Two other points might be made regarding strict Rogerian therapy. First, this clinical approach is as much technique-centered as it is person-centered. This is so because all clients, regardless of presenting problems, are treated alike. Thus, there is little need for diagnosis; it would be superfluous since everyone receives the same therapeutic treatment. One could argue that the kind of treatment provided should be determined by the specific nature of the client's problem—especially for a theory that emphasizes uniqueness in individuals!

The second point is that most outcome studies of Rogerian therapy use criteria that are internal in nature. That is, behavior within therapy determines whether the case is regarded as successful or unsuccessful. Others argue that behavior outside therapy should be the ultimate criterion since it is adjustment to life settings, not therapy settings, that is critical.

Information processing.

Some feel that the computer metaphor has been stretched too far already. Although human cognitive activity is, they contend, similar in some ways to computers, it is far from identical. The danger is that some enthusiastic souls will take the metaphor literally.

Others have commented about the "homunculus" problem. For example, the self has sometimes been regarded as a little executive "in the mind" who issues orders or processes information. Such views really beg the question, however, of how the mind works. As Epstein (1980) has said, "It is then no easier to account for the behavior of the little person than to account for the behavior of the big one" (p. 88). The same point applies to the computer issue. Computers function because they are programmed. That being so, who has programmed the computers in our heads?

Also, like the criticism leveled at Kelly, some feel there is too much emphasis on thinking and not enough on the affective aspects of human beings. Carver and Scheier (1988), however, contend that emotions are, indeed, included as an important part of the information processing perspective.

Finally, it may be argued that although research thus far has supported the construct validity of the schemata approach, little that is really new has been uncovered about human behavior. For example, to show that schemata affect how information is "processed and remembered" demonstrates the validity of the schemata strategy in research. But it is also true that we have known for decades at least that perspectives, biases, needs, and the like strongly affect learning and memory.

SUMMARY

■ Phenomenological research owes much to Carl Rogers, the person who pioneered the use of tapes, recordings, and transcripts in his extensive program of research into therapy processes and outcomes.

■ The basic content of phenomenological research is subjective experience. Consequently, phenomenological research is often qualitative and idiographic in nature. Several case illustrations of this kind of research were provided.

■ Content analysis of interview data is another important research strategy. Typically, this involves having trained judges classify interview content into various categories (e.g., positive versus negative self-references). A similar approach involves the use of rating scales to assign values to various aspects of client-therapist interactions.

▪ Rogers and his colleagues made extensive use of the Q-sort method. In this technique, subjects are asked to sort statements about the self into various piles according to whether the statements are characteristic or uncharacteristic of the self or of the ideal-self.

▪ A technique related to Q-sorts is the semantic differential. The semantic differential is designed to ascertain the meaning people attach to events.

▪ While Rogerian research efforts are most frequently applied to the therapy situation, a number of investigators have conducted experimental research into a number of processes associated with the self. Several examples were provided.

▪ As an example of humanistic research, work by Maslow on the need hierarchy and self-actualization was noted.

▪ Several principles characterizing the existential research approach were briefly described.

▪ The Rep Test, an instrument devised by Kelly, was described as a method of eliciting the personal constructs used by the individual.

▪ A currently popular utilization of the information processing approach to research has to do with self-schemata. Several examples of such research were offered.

▪ Turning specifically to phenomenological assessment, several implications of the measurement of the person's private world were discussed. First, the meaning rather than sheer presence of behavior is stressed. Second, the focus on meaning tends to downplay the making of inferences from behavior. We search for meaning rather than look for signs of underlying processes. Third, most assessment methods emphasize the present rather than the past. Fourth, the conscious aspects of experience, rather than unconscious elements, are considered. Finally, the assessment situation should be characterized by lack of threat.

▪ The question of the accuracy of people's self-reports was raised. In view of evidence that subjects frequently make errors and that response styles such as acquiescence and social desirability may be operative, it was concluded that an attitude of caution in accepting self-reports should be adopted.

▪ It was noted that in the clinical setting, Rogerians have historically discouraged assessment activities.

▪ Several other self-report assessment devices, including the POI and the TSCS, were briefly covered.

■ Although assessment from an information processing perspective is still quite new, several methodological suggestions were made along with a recommendation as to what should be assessed (e.g., private versus public self-consciousness).

■ In a summary evaluation, several positive features of phenomenology were described. First, phenomenology holds that humans are not mindless—they interpret their experience, make choices, and change themselves. Second, this approach encourages a positive view of human beings and does not focus exclusively on pathology or incompetencies. Third, there is recognition that the past is less important than our awareness of the present and our anticipation of the future.

■ Several specific strengths associated with Rogers, Kelly, and information processing were observed.

■ There are, of course, numerous weaknesses of phenomenology. First, there is an almost exclusive emphasis on self-reports. The problem here is whether one person can really ever totally understand another by listening to self-reports.

■ A criticism leveled at both Kelly and Rogers has to do with their heavy reliance on college students as a population for study.

■ Other critics of phenomenology are bothered by its rejection of all data not stemming from the phenomenological field (situational determinants, biological data, etc.).

■ A question was raised as to whether one master motive (e.g., self-enhancement or anticipation of the future) can adequately account for the differences among individuals.

■ Other criticisms included a lack of interest in developmental issues, an overly romanticized view of people, the potential for circularity in phenomenological explanations, and the excessive use of imprecise language.

■ Kelly's view of people has been attacked as an overly rational one.

■ The language Rogers used to describe his therapy can be seen as serving a propaganda function. His theory could also be depicted as a technique-centered approach in which criteria for improvement are principally internal ones.

■ In the case of information processing, several weaknesses regarding the computer metaphor were noted along with the homunculus problem and the question of how many new insights the approach has really produced with respect to human behavior.

CHAPTER 8

THE DISPOSITIONAL PERSPECTIVE

What happens when you ask someone about the personalities of people they presumably know well? Most likely they will respond with rather similar strategies. They will begin to enumerate the personal characteristics they feel are associated with that person. A friend is attractive or driven by a need for power. Mother is selfless or nurturing. Nixon was not very trustworthy. What this suggests is that the enduring ways in which people differ from one another are regarded by most of us as the essence of personality. This was discussed in Chapter 1, in which personality was defined in terms of those characteristics. By this definition, the study of personality should provide us with comprehensive schemes for the classification and description of the characteristic and enduring ways individuals differ from each other. This is exactly the goal of the dispositional perspective.

Unfortunately, most of the major personality theories have not fared well when it comes to describing or classifying people's traits or dispositions in a systematic fashion. Of course, Freud had his anal and oral characters. Horney divided the world into those who moved against, toward, or away from people. And Maslow described those self-actualizers while Rogers outlined the fully functioning person. But these were neither systematic classificatory efforts nor were they major conceptual thrusts.

The major purpose of this chapter will be to sketch briefly some of the better known dispositional approaches in personality. The kinds of **dispositions**—those so-called inclinations or tendencies that help direct and energize our behavior—that we shall focus upon are traits along with needs and motives.

ALLPORT: A TRAIT THEORY

Before beginning a description of Allport's approach to trait theory, let us digress a moment to provide some brief background comments about the dispositional perspective.

Some background notes

The early Greeks often used **characterology** to classify a variety of human types. In characterology, categories of various kinds are constructed and then people are described as fitting a particular category, or **type.** For example, Aristotle is said to have described the "Magnanimous Man" and Theophrastus the "Penurious Man." The mark of a really good type is that it is described so vividly and concisely that everyone immediately recognizes the kind of person being depicted. It was Hippocrates who contended that there are four basic types of temperament and that each can be accounted for by a coexisting and predominant body fluid, or "humor," as shown in Table 8-1.

Another historically popular approach to personality characterization has been **physiognomy.** This is a method by which personality is inferred from appearance, especially from the shape and expression of the face. The person who has close-set eyes or looks like a fox must be crafty and sly! This general method can be traced at least as far back as Aristotle. Evidence for its utility is rather sparse. Nevertheless, it persists and nearly everyone from time to time makes personality judgments on such a basis. The modern legacy of all this has been the search for correlations between physique and temperament (see Chapter 1).

In some instances, classification systems have dealt with types; in other cases a classification of traits has been developed. The classical distinction between these two concepts hinges on the differences between discrete categories and dimensions. A typology most often is viewed as a set of discrete categories into which people can be sorted. Thus, you are classified either as an introvert, an extravert, or an ambivert. In contrast, traits represent continuous dimensions. You can, for example, possess the trait of aggressiveness to a marked degree, moderately, or almost not at all. In illustrating this distinction, Allport (1937) remarked: "A man can be said to *have* a trait; but he cannot be said to *have* a type. Rather he *fits* a type" (p. 295).

In practice, however, this distinction becomes blurred. Sheldon, as an example, developed a typology of physique (with corresponding temperaments) which allowed people to be classified on a seven-point scale. Similarly, as we shall see, Eysenck (1970) has tried to discover the basic personality types; yet he views them not as discrete categories but as dimensions on which people differ.

Also, typologies most often deal with a small number of concepts — usually from two to seven categories. But in the case of traits, their number can be extremely large depending upon the methodological approach used by the investigator. As a result, typologies are especially vulnerable to the criticism that they seek to explain behavior by recourse to a very small number of simple variables.

Introduction to Allport

Exactly where Gordon Allport fits into the personality scheme of things is unclear. He was briefly encountered in an earlier discussion about the nature of the self. Therefore, some would regard him as a phenomenologist. But for others, his unflagging belief in the uniqueness of every individual and his penchant for looking at the whole organism with all its potential for growth and actualization would stamp him unequivo-

TABLE 8-1 The "humoral psychology" of Hippocrates

Humor	Corresponding Temperament
Blood	Sanguine (optimistic)
Black bile	Melancholic (depressed)
Yellow bile	Choleric (irritable)
Phlegm	Phlegmatic (listless, calm)

cally as a humanist. At the same time, he was a staunch advocate of the utility of traits, and this seems to warrant our labeling him as a prominent trait theorist as well.

There is, then, an elusive quality to Allport's work. He fits nowhere but belongs everywhere. In part, this reflects his eclectic theoretical stance. He certainly was not a dogmatic, one-track theorist. The building blocks of his brand of personality came from a variety of sources, including literature, philosophy, sociology, religion, and psychology. Yet the mortar holding everything together was an unwavering commitment to the uniqueness of the individual.

Perhaps because of his eclecticism, Allport's influence has been subtle yet persistent. Although few psychologists describe themselves as "Allportian," there is a timeless and fundamental quality to his work. He certainly was a pioneer in the personality field. His 1937 text helped define an area of psychology that had scarcely existed before. It was *the* personality text for quite a few years and was undoubtedly responsible for the sharp increase in the number of personality courses offered after 1937.

Basic theory and concepts

Allport defined personality as "the dynamic organization within the individual of those psychophysical systems that determine his unique adjustments to his environment" (1937, p. 48). The word *dynamic* indicates that personality constantly changes and evolves; yet there is a persistent *organization* which exists to lend structure and coherence to personality. In a sense, one's personality never changes but it is always different! By *psychophysical*, Allport meant to emphasize both the mind and the body aspects of personality. The personality is everything a person is—flesh as well as self. Finally, personality tendencies *determine* characteristic behavior and thought.

Nature of traits. Allport defined a **trait** as *a neuropsychic structure having the capacity to render many stimuli functionally equivalent, and to initiate and guide equivalent (meaningfully consistent) forms of adaptive and expressive behavior* (1961, p. 347). A trait, then, is almost like a readiness to think or act in a similar fashion in response to a variety of different stimuli or situations. As shown in Figure 8-1, a trait has the

A brief biography of

Gordon Allport

Gordon W. Allport was born in 1897 in Indiana and grew up in Cleveland. He was the youngest of four brothers. One of these, Floyd, became a renowned social psychologist. Allport's father was a doctor who, because of inadequate local hospital facilities, often brought his patients home. He was also a believer in hard work. As a result, young Gordon learned very early about the world of work—from washing bottles to tending patients. His relationship with his father was also marked by trust and affection.

Allport was academically inclined almost from the beginning. After graduating second in his high school class, he followed his brother Floyd to Harvard. He majored in economics and philosophy, receiving his B.A. in 1919. During a brief teaching stint in Turkey, he was awarded a fellowship for graduate study in psychology at Harvard. On his way home, he wangled an interview with Freud in Vienna (Allport, 1968). When they met, Freud had little to say and Allport grew increasingly uneasy over the lengthening silence. In desperation, Allport recounted an incident that occurred on a streetcar while he was en route

capacity to smooth out the differences among situations and to prompt responses to them that are basically alike.

Aggressiveness, dishonesty, and all other traits are not just hypothetical dispositions (see Chapter 2) that prime us to respond one way rather than another. They really exist within the person. They also actively cause or impel behavior that will result in our being loving, aggressive, or dishonest, as the case may be. However, some traits or dispositions (e.g., politeness) are not so much motivational as they are stylistic. In a sense, such traits steer or stylize behavior more than they initiate it.

It is also important to differentiate traits from other concepts such as habits. **Habits** are rather limited or narrow dispositions that tend to be confined to certain situations. The executive who characteristically cleans off and arranges her desk carefully before leaving the office at the end of the day is manifesting a habit. In all likelihood, that habit is part of a larger trait system that integrates several habits. It is even probable that this executive has other habits that do not seem consistent with a trait of orderliness. Allport recognized such inconsistencies but did not view them as invalidating his notion of traits. Perhaps our executive's orderliness trait is not as well integrated or important as it is for someone else. It is even possible that two traits are involved. The executive may have an orderliness trait related to her professional life but not to her private life, where behavior may be guided by a different trait, say, comfort. In still other instances, a behavior may be determined by a particularly compelling situational stimulus. In sum, we must be wary of assuming that simply because a trait exists, every tiny corner of a person's life will, on every occasion, be guided by it. In a real sense, Allport was an interactionist who saw both traits and situations combining to produce behavior (Zuroff, 1986).

to Freud's home. It involved a young boy who was quite fearful about getting dirty and the boy's mother, who appeared obsessed with cleanliness. To Allport's surprise and chagrin, Freud responded with only a slightly veiled suggestion that perhaps this incident had aroused some unconscious conflict in Allport. This encounter with Freud may have reinforced Allport's growing suspicion of theories such as psychoanalysis, which heavily emphasized unconscious motives at the expense of conscious ones.

In 1922, Allport was awarded the Ph.D. After some additional postdoctoral work and two years of teaching at Harvard, he accepted a teaching post at Dartmouth. But in 1930, he returned to Harvard, where he remained on the faculty until his death in 1967.

Allport's best known book is his personality text published in 1937 and revised in 1961 as *Pattern and Growth in Personality.* Another widely read book is *Becoming: Basic Considerations for a Psychology of Personality,* published in 1955. His autobiography appears in the 1967 *A History of Psychology in Autobiography* (Vol. 5).

Gordon Allport

Classification of traits. Allport elaborated on the foregoing discussion in his description of three kinds of traits which differ in the pervasiveness of their influence on behavior. First, there are **cardinal traits.** These might be called master motives or ruling passions; they invade every segment of our lives. A person ruled by such a trait would be consumed by it; perhaps obsessed would be a more appropriate description. Such a person would spend every waking hour seeking to become more attractive, build a fortune, or expand power, as the case may be.

More often, we are directed by a relatively small number of **central traits** which together influence much of our behavior. When someone writes a letter of recommendation and characterizes another person as reliable, punctual, self-starting, and trustworthy, a set of central traits is probably being described. Central traits are relatively pervasive and are usually apparent to other people.

Beyond this intermediate level are the **secondary traits.** Such traits, although influential, are less consistent and generalized than cardinal or central traits. A preference for certain kinds of clothes or automobiles or a dislike of specific types of movies are examples of secondary traits. Being aware of a person's secondary traits presumes quite a bit of knowledge about that individual. So it is that many acquaintances might agree that Joe Smith is industrious, neat, and charming, whereas his wife knows that he is also slovenly when it comes to household repairs, never shaves on the weekend, and barks at the children when they interfere with his TV football binges.

What Allport was describing with these three classes of traits was a kind of trait hierarchy of influence on behavior. Cardinal traits have the most pervasive influence, with central and secondary traits following, in that order.

Allport also emphasized, as has been noted repeatedly, the uniqueness of each in-

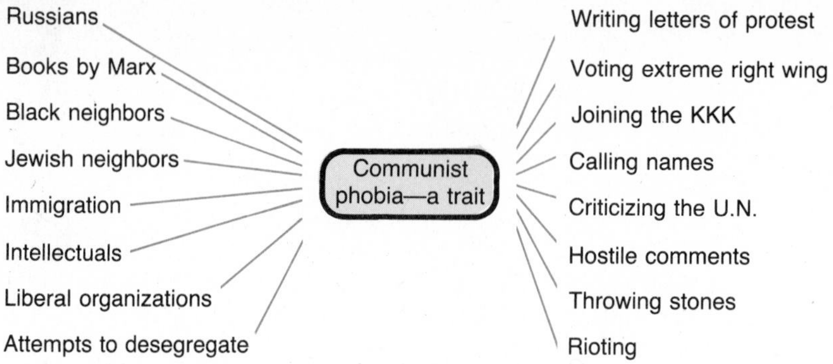

Russians
Books by Marx
Black neighbors
Jewish neighbors
Immigration
Intellectuals
Liberal organizations
Attempts to desegregate

Communist phobia—a trait

Writing letters of protest
Voting extreme right wing
Joining the KKK
Calling names
Criticizing the U.N.
Hostile comments
Throwing stones
Rioting

FIGURE 8-1   "The operation of a Communist phobia trait." A trait operates something like a filter by rendering a variety of stimuli more alike than they otherwise would be. The result is a set of behaviors which, although not identical, are still clearly related.   Adapted from Allport, 1961.

dividual. This emphasis is apparent in another trait classification elaborated by him. He described **personal traits,** which are unique to each person and which serve to define the differences among us all. Allport accorded these traits or personal dispositions the highest status in understanding an individual's personality. In contrast, **common traits** are those traits related to our similarities and permit comparisons across individuals. Aggressiveness viewed as a common trait could be studied by comparing the scores subjects receive on an inventory designed to measure that trait.

Intentions.   Allport viewed behavior as guided less by the past than by the future. The riddle of behavior can be solved by examining **intentions,** that is, a person's hopes, plans, wishes, and aspirations. Like Adler, Allport saw individuals as not so much pushed by the past as pulled by their expectations about the future.

Functional autonomy.   Also symbolic of Allport's rejection of the past as the ultimate mover of all behavior was his concept of **functional autonomy.** Allport could accept the idea that a particular behavior or activity may have originated as a way of achieving a certain goal. But he contended that some of those behaviors will persist for no other reason than the person likes the activity in question. Although a child may have developed a passion for reading because it led to recognition by an esteemed teacher or a loving parent, reading may continue as goal or end in itself. Nor do we need to assume that reading persists because it has become linked to some new set of motives. Some might argue that although reading once depended on reinforcement from a teacher, now the person reads as a way of gaining knowledge and thus power. But Allport would demur. No, the person just likes to read. However, not even Allport believed that all adult behavior is functionally autonomous from the past.

Allport felt that personal traits are unique to each person. They are keys to the understanding of individual personalities.

Proprium. Allport (1961) used the term **proprium** to describe his views on the essential features of the self. The proprium is composed of everything important in the personality that a person regards as his or her own. It includes bodily sense, self-identity, self-esteem, self-extension, rational thinking, self-image, knowing, and propriate striving. This proprium develops as the person grows and experiences; it is not innate.

Development of personality

Nowhere is the gulf between Freud and Allport wider than in their views about human development. At the very moment of the infant's arrival from the womb, psychoanalysts assert, the shaping of the personality begins. In these earliest moments of commerce with the environment, the first fledgling directions of personality development are laid down. According to Allport, the early months of life are spent in the pursuit of pleasure and the avoidance of pain. The only reality for the child is a biological one. It is only in the second six months that the infant begins to show signs of being anything more than a bundle of hereditary characteristics motivated by primitive needs. Then, gradually, some elemental emotional characteristics begin to emerge that stamp the organism as human after all.

225

Allport provides little that is truly distinctive in describing the developments lead-ing to the adult personality. He makes use of principles of learning and conditioning and he even occasionally resorts to employing psychoanalytic defense mechanisms. He also talks about the individual's progressive differentiation and integration. However, one comes away from all this with little tangible understanding of the developmental process.

A somewhat clearer picture of development emerges as we consider Allport's description of the evolving sense of self. He described seven aspects of selfhood, or the proprium (Allport, 1961):

■ *Sense of Bodily Self*—The sense of bodily "me" which emerges around the age of fifteen months.

■ *Sense of Self-Identity*—The recognition of oneself as separate and distinctive; lan-guage is vital in enhancing this identity, and one's own name further helps solidify this sense as it develops in the second year and onward.

■ *Sense of Self-Esteem*—Self-enhancement is important around the age of two years. Often this appears as negativism. But by the age of four or five, the desire to enhance the self turns negativism into competitiveness.

■ *Extension of Self*—This is a very egocentric period. It is also marked by extreme possessiveness. The focus is on things and events as they relate to "me." This period lasts from about the age of four to about six.

■ *The Self-Image*—Another aspect of the four to six period is the manner in which others evaluate the child. Starting to school triggers an incorporation of the perceptions of others. These expectations of others become quite important.

■ *The Self as Rational Coper*—From six to twelve, the awareness of self as one who can cope, solve problems, and think rationally emerges. The capacity to "think about thought" begins. This is also a period of close alliance with family, peer group, reli-gious institutions, and so on—the age of conformity.

■ *Propriate Striving*—This refers to the tendency to seek self-enhancement through the choosing of a life goal. We move toward self-enhancement by following our star. The mature stage of propriate striving is realized when we have a well-conceived and highly articulated sense of purpose.

Nature of adjustment

When Allport discusses the nature of adjustment, he begins to sound very much like the humanist we examined in an earlier chapter. Unlike so many personality theorists, he had little experience with psychotherapy or psychopathology. Many clinical psy-chologists and psychiatrists view neurotic or even psychotic behavior as continuous with normal behavior. This means that the differences between the normal and abnor-mal person are not in kind but in degree. But Allport saw normals and neurotics or psychotics as quite different from one another. Perhaps his immersion in traits, charac-

Sometimes we seek self-esteem by trying too much to be like everyone else.
Photograph Jay King.

terology, and typologies led him to concentrate on the differences among people or categories rather than on their similarities. Or perhaps his humanistic bent predisposed him to focus on competencies and growth rather than on sickness and deficits. Whatever the reasons, he gave a wide berth to any notions that even faintly suggested an illness model. For him, psychological health was an outgrowth of self-esteem and competence and not just the absence of neurotic problems. Hjelle and Ziegler (1981) have summarized Allport's criteria for psychological maturity as follows:

- An extended sense of self

- An ability to relate warmly to self and others

- Emotional security or self-acceptance

- Realistic perceptions, skills, and assignments

- Capacity for self-objectification and of insight in humor

- A unifying philosophy of life

Implications for behavior change

Two themes permeating Allport's writings have important implications for behavioral change. In one sense they are contradictory. The first theme is expressed in Allport's commitment to a trait orientation. This means that, by definition, there will be a great deal of stability throughout a person's life. The second theme is embodied in Allport's concept of functional autonomy. Here, the emphasis is on the transformation of motives over time. So within the same system Allport describes significant opportunities for both stability and change. Unfortunately, there is little in the theory that allows us to predict when functional autonomy will prevail and when the enduring aspects of traits will dominate. This is a critical omission which seriously curtails the utility of Allport's theory.

Since Allport was not a psychotherapist, his discussion of psychotherapy as a means of promoting personality change is a bit superficial. He seems to accept psychotherapy as a procedure for change, but there is no detailed attempt to integrate it with his theory of personality.

CATTELL: A FACTOR THEORY OF TRAITS

It would be hard to find someone who offers a sharper contrast to Allport than Raymond Cattell. This is doubly interesting since both are trait theorists. Their differences arise more out of the methods they employ to identify traits than out of the actual traits used to account for human behavior. In a sense, it is a matter of the humanist-idiographer versus the statistician-mathematician.

If achievement in the field of personality were measured by the sheer volume of publications, then Cattell would be far and away the foremost personologist of our time. The number of research papers, chapters, books, and tests published by Cattell is staggering. To illustrate this enormous output, Wiggins (1968) observed that in a three-year period in the mid-1960s, Cattell published four books, twelve chapters, and forty articles, adding up to a total of nearly 4,000 pages. In addition, he began a new journal and edited a lengthy handbook. As Wiggins implies, such a prodigious output intimidates some who would try to absorb Cattell's point of view. Thus, in a paradoxical fashion, by publishing so much Cattell may have actually reduced his impact on personality theory.

Another reason for the less than wholehearted acceptance of Cattell's work is its heavy reliance on the statistical method of factor analysis. Although the basic rationale for factor analysis is not especially complicated, the techniques used can be rather forbidding. For students of personality put off by approaches that seem to focus more on statistical applications than on people, papers cluttered with formulas and equations do more to confuse than enlighten.

Basic theory and concepts

Cattell does not offer much in the way of a formal definition of personality. In effect, he defines personality as whatever it is that allows us to predict what a person will do in a specific situation (Cattell, 1950). His real definition of personality resides in his descriptions of the various kinds of traits he has indentified. **Traits** are the elements out of which the structure of personality is formed. More specifically, they are mental structures inferred from behavior and which predispose the individual to behave with consistency from one situation to another and from one time to another. Cattell describes several classes of traits.

Surface vs. source traits.   A **surface trait** is represented by a series of behaviors that all seem to belong together. Even the casual observer would identify a trait of friendliness by noting that behaviors such as saying hello on the street, smiling, and responding to a greeting all generally occur together and, indeed, belong together. A surface trait is not an explanatory concept; it is simply an observation that a group of behaviors or characteristics tend to be correlated. On the other hand, **source traits** have an explanatory role. They are the basic, underlying structures which Cattell regards as constituting the core of personality. They are what cause behavior and, in that sense, determine the consistencies in each person's behavior. Since one source trait will influence several surface traits, it follows that source traits are fewer in number.

Cattell also believes that everyone possesses the same source traits, but not to the same degree. Thus, everybody has a source trait that we might call guilt. One individual may be predisposed by this trait of guilt to such an extent that he or she becomes very depressed, moody, or self-reproachful. Another person, at the opposite extreme, would be cheerful, self-confident, and the like. Most of us would likely occupy a place midway between these two extremes. In addition, a strong source trait will influence a wide variety of behavior, thoughts, and feelings while a weak source trait will have correspondingly little influence.

Hereditary vs. environmental traits.

Most personologists regard behavior as an outcome of the joint operation of genetic and environmental factors. Cattell is no exception. He feels that surface traits are clearly the product of such joint influences. However, in the case of the basic determinants—the source traits—he contends that some have a constitutional origin whereas others develop out of experience. The former class of source traits are called **constitutional traits,** and the latter are termed **environmental-mold traits.** At the present time, Cattell believes the evidence suggests that a given source trait must spring from either hereditary *or* environmental influences, but not from both.

For Cattell, one behavior relates to another. We do one thing in order to do another. Riding a roller coaster can be a way of achieving a more remote goal.
Photograph courtesy Marriott's Great America.

Raymond Cattell

Raymond B. Cattell was born in England in 1905. He was sixteen years old when he enrolled at the University of London. Majoring in chemistry, he received his B.Sc. degree in 1924. His growing awareness of social problems led him to an increasing interest in psychology. He finally decided to pursue graduate work in psychology and ultimately was granted the Ph.D. in 1929 from the University of London. During his graduate study, he worked closely with Charles Spearman, a noted psychologist and statistician who pioneered the method of factor analysis. Cattell obviously was deeply impressed with this technique, as it has played a major role in his research throughout his career.

Following the award of the Ph.D., Cattell knocked about for a few years in what he regarded as a minor teaching post and subsequently in a clinical position in Leicester, England. In 1937, the famous American psychologist Edward Thorndike invited him to become his research associate at Columbia University. The same year he was awarded a D.Sc. degree by the University of London for his outstanding contributions to personality.

Adjusting to the United States was a bit difficult at first for Cattell. But he plunged into his work and soon was offered the post of G. Stanley Hall Professor of Psychology at Clark University. He remained at Clark until 1941, when he moved to Harvard University.

Ability traits. Some traits determine how effective we are in our pursuit of goals. These are **ability traits.** Perhaps the most important of these is intelligence. Cattell (1971) differentiates between crystallized and fluid intelligence. **Crystallized ability** is a broad, general kind of intelligence which reflects experience in school and in related activities in a given culture. **Fluid ability,** in contrast, represents a person's biological capacity and manifests itself regardless of exposure to any formal learning opportunities.

Temperament traits. A **temperament trait** is a constitutional source trait responsible for a person's level of emotionality. Such a trait determines how reactive an individual will be. The speed, energy, and emotion with which the person responds to environmental stimulation are determined by these temperament traits.

Dynamic traits. What motivates the individual? Cattell states that **dynamic traits** do. Whereas temperament traits may determine the style of the individual's response and ability traits the effectiveness of the response, dynamic traits set the response in motion to begin with. Cattell describes several kinds of dynamic traits, each of which serves a motivational function. For example:

The year 1945 saw him move once more, this time to the University of Illinois, where he remained for thirty years. He was Distinguished Research Professor of Psychology and Director of the Laboratory of Personality Assessment at Illinois until his retirement in 1973. Since then, he has been a visiting professor at the University of Hawaii and has also established an institute in Boulder, Colorado. In 1953, he was awarded the Wenner-Gren prize by the New York Academy of Science for his work on the psychology of the researcher.

Only a few representatives of the nearly mind-boggling output of Cattell will be mentioned here. A series of three books provides a fairly comprehensive statement of his views on personality: *Description and Measurement of Personality* (1946); *Personality: A Systematic, Theoretical, and Factual Study* (1950); and *Personality and Motivation Structure and Measurement* (1957). He wrote a much less technical introduction to his ideas, *The Scientific Analysis of Personality,* which was published in 1965. A good summary of his work is presented in Hall and Lindzey (1978). A more recent book (Cattell, 1980) deals with personality and learning theory.

Raymond Cattell

Erg A dynamic constitutional source trait that motivates the individual. It is innate and determines a number of surface traits. Examples of ergs are pugnacity, self-assertion, gregariousness, and so on.

Sentiment An environmental-mold trait that arises out of experience with various sociocultural institutions and customs.

Attitudes Overt expressions of interest marked by a particular level of intensity (e.g., the fanatic golf fan or the old-movie junkie). There are virtually endless numbers of attitudes.

The dynamic lattice. Cattell believes that behaviors are very much related to one another. We engage in one behavior in order to do something else. What this means is that dynamic traits are interrelated in such a way that one is subsidiary to another. As a general rule, ergs are superior to sentiments which, in turn, are superior to attitudes. These relationships represent the **dynamic lattice.** An example is illustrated in Figure 8-2. The right portion of the figure presents this individual's ergs—the basic innate motivational elements that direct his life. Closer to the middle of the figure are several sentiments toward wife, country, God, and so on. It can be seen that each of

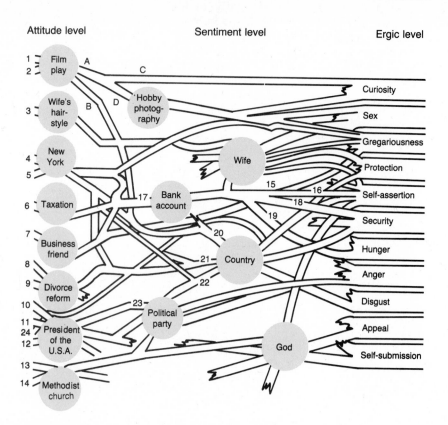

FIGURE 8-2   One segment of a dynamic lattice.

From *Personality: A systematic, theoretical, and factual study* by R. B. Cattell (New York: McGraw-Hill Book Co.), 1950. Copyright 1950 by R. B. Cattell. Reprinted with permission.

these sentiments is determined by or subsidiary to several ergs. Sentiment toward wife, for example, is connected to the ergs of sex, gregariousness, protection, and self-assertion. The left side of the figure depicts the individual's attitudes toward several events or behaviors. Each of these attitudes is subsidiary to several sentiments, and some are directly subsumed by an erg. Thus, traveling to New York is subsidiary to both bank account and country but also to gregariousness. Although trait theorists are often accused of having an overly simplistic view of human motivation, the dynamic lattice makes it abundantly clear that Cattell's vision is a complex one.

Unique vs. common traits.   Like Allport, Cattell feels that some traits are possessed, in varying degrees, by all members of the same culture. These are **common traits**. In addition, an individual will have **unique traits**. Furthermore the strength of both unique and common traits will vary over time within the same person.

The specification equation. The next question is how we combine all of our information about traits in order to predict behavior in a specific situation. This brings us back to the statement in the beginning of this section to the effect that personality for Cattell is whatever allows us to predict what a person will do in a specific situation. In large measure, this "whatever" turns out to be the traits relevant for a given situation, but not exclusively so, as we shall see in a moment.

The method Cattell uses to make predictions is called the **specification equation.** He states it in the following form (1965, p. 265):

$$P_j = s_{j_A}A \ldots + s_{j_T}T \ldots + s_{j_E}E \ldots + s_{j_M}M \ldots + s_{j_R}R \ldots + s_{j_S}S$$

where

P_j = Performance in Situation j
A = Ability source traits—how well the performance is executed
T = Temperament traits—the style of behavior
E = Ergic drives—the first class of dynamic traits
M = Sentiments—the second class of dynamic traits
R = Roles demanded by the situation
S = Temporary moods and bodily states (e.g., anxiety, illness)
s = Weighting factor to indicate the importance of Situation j

What this formula signifies is that the nature and quality of a person's response (P) in a given situation (s_j) can be predicted from that person's trait characteristics (A, T, E, M, R, S), with each of the latter weighted by its relevance for the situation. This equation includes several traits previously discussed, but it also introduces two so-called **transient variables:** states and roles. **States** refer to temporary conditions such as fatigue, illness, anxiety, and so on. **Roles** suggest that a person may perceive things in various ways depending upon the circumstances. For example, as a politician I might respond to a question one way, but as a close friend I might respond in quite a different fashion. The specification equation again indicates that Cattell appreciates the complexity of human behavior.

Development of personality

Cattell, like most personality theorists, looks to both heredity and environment as determinants of personality. Through complex statistical methods, he has attempted to analyze the data from personality measures to determine the exact ratio of hereditary and environmental influences on each trait. He also asserts that one's genetic background will indirectly influence personality development by determining, in part, the reactions of other people. For example, height is strongly influenced by genetic factors. However, other people may exacerbate the shyness of an especially tall person by making frequent references to his or her height. Similarly, how one learns or the degree to which certain reactions are modifiable by the environment is dependent upon genetic background.

Learning. Cattell depends heavily on two old standbys, classical conditioning and instrumental conditioning, to account for learning and personality development. In **classical conditioning,** a new stimulus becomes capable of eliciting a response previously produced by a different stimulus. In the case of **instrumental conditioning,** the person learns to perform a response to achieve a particular reward. These are tried and true learning principles, heavily emphasized in every introductory psychology course. Cattell's views here, then, are very conventional ones.

However, Cattell goes on to describe classical conditioning as especially important because through it we come to respond emotionally to specific environmental stimuli. For example, I learn to take little joy in sitting down to a meal because in the past this was followed by a fight between my parents. The sight of a dinner table becomes a signal that something bad is about to happen. And in the case of instrumental conditioning, we learn to satisfy our ergs via particular behaviors. Going back to Figure 8-2, the male in question learns that going to New York will satisfy his gregarious urges or that joining a church will satisfy his needs for submission. This is a form of instrumental conditioning.

Cattell also writes about **integration learning.** By this, he is referring to our tendency to repress, suppress, or even sublimate some ergs for a time even while permitting the satisfaction of other ergs. This is a kind of maturity that, in the long run, allows the individual to achieve a higher level of satisfaction.

Syntality.   The ways in which individuals develop are also greatly influenced by the groups to which they belong. Therefore personality development, as well as behavior in general, can be understood more fully by examining the churches, families, schools, and other groups with which the individual is associated. In the same way that people may be said to have traits, groups also have traits. The dimensions along which groups can be described are called their **syntality.**

Nature of adjustment

By and large, Cattell views maladjustment in terms of conflict. Ergs are often stimulated by a variety of events. But their satisfaction is sometimes thwarted. When this occurs there is a failure to achieve gratification, which leads to conflict, anxiety, and ultimately neurosis. Although much of Cattell's discussion here has distinct psychoanalytic overtones, it lacks the richness and clinical sophistication of psychoanalysis.

Using his specification equation, Cattell has also attempted to express the degree of conflict inherent in a proposed behavior by assigning positive or negative weights to each entry in the equation. Negative weights, for example, are assigned to those ergs, sentiments, or other traits that portend negative outcomes, whereas positive weights are attached to those that signal the potential for reward. The amount of conflict associated with a given course of action then becomes the ratio of the sum of negative weights to the sum of positive weights for those source traits involved. In analogous fashion, the degree of conflict throughout the entire personality could be computed by considering all the person's generalized traits.

Implications for behavior change

Just as Cattell recognizes the inherent complexity of the human personality, so too does he recognize our capacity for change. Nevertheless his absorption with traits which, by definition, imply considerable stability over time and situations, seems to have impaired the ability of his theory to come to grips with issues of change. He does, of course, discuss various forms of learning, and this obviously implies change. Likewise, he recognizes maturation as an important factor in the orderly change of traits across age levels. Similarly, he has made a distinction between states and traits. For example, Cattell and Scheier (1961) observe that in the case of anxiety, some individuals are chronically anxious while others fluctuate depending on the nature of the situation. But overall, the focus of his theory seems to be on the structure of personality rather than on the processes by which it changes and the specific conditions responsible for those changes.

EYSENCK: A THEORY OF TYPES

Hans Eysenck, like Cattell, is committed to factor analysis as a method of discovering the basic dimensions of personality. But factor analysis, as will be shown in the next chapter, can be an ambiguous and fickle statistical method that sometimes produces as much disagreement as it does clarity. A prime example of this is the work of Eysenck and Cattell. For example, whereas factor analysis has led Cattell to compile a lengthy list of source traits, Eysenck's research convinces him that there are just a very few basic personality dimensions. This is a further example of the old adage that there is no truth separate from the means of discovering it.

Another characteristic of Eysenck's views is his focus on a small number of personality **types.** Eysenck defines a type differently than most. For him, types are not categories that people fit, as Allport contended they are. Instead, they are dimensions along which people differ. One need not be either an introvert or an extravert; instead, one can fall anywhere along a dimension ranging from extreme introversion at one end to extreme extraversion at the other. Most people would fall somewhere near the middle.

Eysenck also employs his statistical methods with a philosophy different from that adopted by Cattell. It is Cattell's contention that by administering large batteries of tests and then subjecting the resultant data to factor analysis, the basic dimensions of personality will emerge. In contrast, Eysenck begins with hypotheses about how things should be and then checks the fit between hypothesis and data with factor analysis. This is called **criterion analysis** (Eysenck, 1950) and will be more fully considered in the next chapter. Some have described Cattell's method as a shotgun approach. In contrast, Eysenck seems to have adopted a rifle approach.

Major types

Eysenck states that the structure of the personality is dominated by a few **types.** These basic personality dimensions exert a powerful influence over behavior. Types are composed of **traits** which, in turn, are comprised of numerous **habitual responses.** Finally, there are a multitude of **specific responses,** which are the elements of habits. This hierarchical model of personality is schematically shown in Figure 8-3 as it relates to introversion.

Hans Eysenck

Hans J. Eysenck was born in 1916 in Berlin, Germany. When Hitler rose to power, Eysenck emigrated to England. At the age of eighteen he began the study of psychology at the University of London. During his career Eysenck has been especially influenced by the statistical work of Spearman, by early typologists such as Jung and Kretschmer, and by Burt's work on the heritability of intelligence. He also admires Hull's systematic learning theory.

During World War II, Eysenck worked at an emergency hospital in England where military patients suffering from stress reactions were treated. This led to his interest in the factors that predispose certain people to this kind of response to stress. Given Eysenck's prior interests, it is not surprising that he approached this task armed with the tools of statistics, learning theory, typology, and heritability indices.

Eysenck has been an extremely prolific author (over 30 books and 600 articles) and investigator who is well known throughout Europe and in the United States. But he has been a highly controversial figure as well. In part this has been due to his rather polemical attacks

Basic types.   The two principal types discussed by Eysenck are **introversion-extraversion** and **stability-instability.** Together, these two dimensions are ultimately responsible for a major portion of human behavior. Eysenck had been impressed for years with the fact that writers and philosophers had preached for centuries about the four "humors" of the body being responsible for the four basic human temperaments: sanguine, melancholic, choleric, and phlegmatic (see Table 8-1). To support these ideas, Eysenck began to gather data based on ratings of subjects and the questionnaires they completed. In the end, information from thousands of subjects was examined, and the results convinced him of the existence and usefulness of the introversion-extraversion and stability-instability dimensions. What is more, Eysenck feels that these dimensions have confirmed some of the wisdom of those ancient humoral conceptions of personality, as illustrated in Figure 8-4. Not only are the older temperament types shown in relation to the two major type dimensions, but a series of traitlike adjectives further define the characteristics associated with each type.

More recently, Eysenck (1975) has emphasized the importance of a third type, which he calls **psychoticism.** An individual at the extreme end of this dimension would be solitary, without loyalties, uncaring of others, and insensitive. In the language of abnormal psychology, this describes a person with psychotic and psychopathic tendencies. Eysenck regards psychoticism as being largely genetic and also more common in men than in women. But psychoticism is different from the other two types. It is not a dimension on which one can be either high or low. Rather, it is a characteristic present in different amounts in particular personalities.

on psychoanalysis and the conventional methods of psychotherapy. Although his critiques have not always been entirely on the mark, they have frequently catalyzed people to produce better arguments and more data to support their positions. Others feel that prejudice against Europeans may have stimulated some of his critics. Most recently, Eysenck has been embroiled in a heated debate with Leon Kamin over the heritability of the IQ.

He has written several books, including: *Dimensions of Personality* (1947); *The Scientific Study of Personality* (1952); and *The Structure of Human Personality,* which was revised in 1970. *Sense and Nonsense in Psychology* appeared in 1957 and is an entertaining introduction to several of his stronger interests. He is co-author with Kamin of *The Intelligence Controversy: H. J. Eysenck vs. Leon Kamin,* published in 1981. A more recent book, *Personality and Individual Differences: A Natural Science Approach,* was published in 1985 with his son as co-author.

Hans Eysenck

Nature of introversion-extraversion.

The introversion-extraversion concept was long associated with Jung. Eysenck (1947), however, constructed the Maudsley Personality Inventory in an attempt to put the concept on a more solid psychometric and empirical footing. In a general way, introverts as compared to extraverts are more oriented toward internal stimuli — they are concerned with their own thoughts, reactions, and moods. As a result, they tend to be more shy, self-controlled, and preoccupied. There is an introspective, reserved, and almost inhibited quality to their behavior. In sharp contrast are extraverts, who are more likely to be exuberant, sociable people who crave activity, like parties and excitement, and are frequently impulsive. To the question "Are you always ready for adventure?" the extravert would respond yes and the introvert no. To the question "Are you put off by loud and rowdy parties?" the introvert would likely say yes and the extravert no.

Other differences can be traced to the brain and central nervous system. For example, introverts and extraverts differ in their arousal level, as shown by electroencephalographic measures. Introverts seem to avoid stimulation from external sources while extraverts constantly seek it. This effect is traceable to a differential capacity for cortical arousal. It is almost as if extraverts were always trying to avoid boredom by seeking stimulation whereas introverts long for a quiet, contemplative state (Geen, 1984). The famous lemon juice demonstration illustrates this arousal phenomenon (see Box 8-1).

Throughout his writings, Eysenck emphasizes the important role of heredity. This is true whether he is discussing intelligence, psychoticism, or introversion-extraversion.

Eysenck believes that introverts are more likely to be attracted to quiet, solitary pursuits. They tend to be preoccupied with their own thoughts and to be reserved.
Photograph Jean-Claude LeJeune.

Box 8-1
THE LEMON JUICE DEMONSTRATION

It has been reported that introverts produce more saliva than do extraverts (Corcoran, 1964). The following test has been used as a simple method of determining one's introversion-extraversion status.

A length of thread is tied to the center of a double-tipped cotton swab. It should be tied so that when the swab is held by the thread, it hangs in a perfectly horizontal plane.

Next, the person swallows three times and then immediately puts one end of the swab on the tongue, holding it there for thirty seconds. Then, four drops of lemon juice are placed on the tongue. After swallowing, the person places the other end of the swab on the same portion of the tongue. After the swab is held there for thirty seconds, it is removed and allowed to hang by the thread.

If all goes according to the hypothesis, the swab will remain virtually horizontal for extraverts. But for introverts the swab should hang down on the lemon juice end. This indicates that a relatively large amount of saliva has been produced in response to the lemon juice.

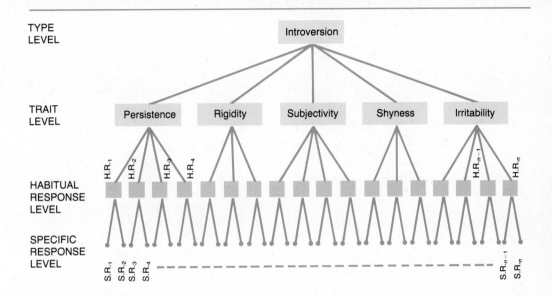

FIGURE 8-3   Eysenck's structural model of the personality as illustrated by introversion.
From *The structure of human personality* by H. J. Eysenck (London, Methuen), 1953.
Copyright 1953 by Methuen & Co. Reprinted by permission.

Like it or not, says Eysenck, the roots of personality are in neurophysiology and the hereditary forces that give it form. To a significant extent, differences in the personalities of individuals reflect differences in their neurophysiological makeup.

TRAITS OR SITUATIONS?

For Allport, Cattell, Eysenck, or virtually any trait theorist, a key characteristic of basic traits is their stability over time and situations. The intelligent woman is intelligent not just today, but yesterday and tomorrow as well. The hostile man is one who is hostile in many settings and for long periods of time. At the very least, people's traits interact with the nature of situations so that one's predispositions combined with situational cues produce behaviors that are predictable (given knowledge of both the person's traits and the situational characteristics).

Situational specificity

But in 1968 Walter Mischel published *Personality and Assessment.* This book catalyzed a debate that lasted the better part of twenty years. After an intensive review of the evidence, Mischel concluded that, "with the possible exception of intelligence, highly generalized behavioral consistencies have not been demonstrated, and the con-

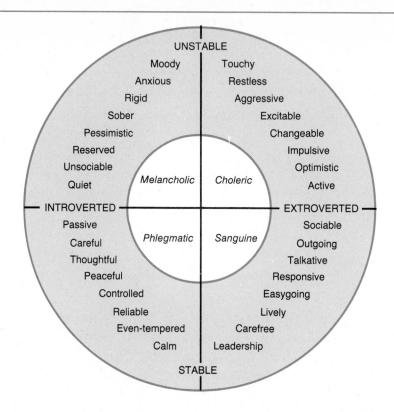

FIGURE 8-4   Eysenck's dimensions of personality and their relationship to Greek temperamental types.

From *The causes and cures of neurosis* by H. J. Eysenck and S. Rachman (San Diego, CA, EdITS), 1965. Copyright 1965 by EdITS. Reprinted by permission.

cept of personality traits as broad predispositions is thus untenable" (p. 146). In short, a person's behavior is controlled not by stable traits but by the special characteristics of each situation in which he or she functions. This early attack of Mischel's might be considered a radical position, because, carried to its logical extreme, it denied the existence of personality.

Stated simply, the position of situational specificity asserts that in the main there is little stability to human behavior. We as individuals do not exhibit cross-situational consistencies in our behavior. Furthermore our behavior is determined almost entirely by the cues in a given situation, not by internal predispositions that we carry about with us from situation to situation (see Box 8-2). Such an argument gains considerable credence when we consider Mischel's 1968 review. He noted that in the vast majority of studies, correlations between individuals' behavior in one situation and their behavior in another situation were typically quite modest.

Traits and stability

Actually, Mischel abandoned his "radical" position long ago (Mischel, 1973). But the "great debate" has only now neared its conclusion (Carson, 1989). Some have characterized this debate as having been fruitless (e.g., Kihlstrom, 1987). In contrast, Kenrick and Funder (1988) feel we have learned some valuable information from the debate but still argue that seven of the more basic tenets of the debate have *failed* to gain support. In short, none of the following statements are true:

■ Personality traits are merely in the eye of the beholder; they are mainly the by-product of faulty information processing.

■ When people agree about a given person's traits, the agreement is due to shared delusions based on common linguistic usage.

■ Agreement among observers of trait behavior is just an artifact of the base rates for the trait in the general population.

■ Interrater agreements are often due to stereotypes based on obvious but erroneous cues (e.g., fat people are jolly).

■ Agreement on traits and behavior is due to discussions among observers.

■ The reason behavior seems consistent over situations is because we see others in the same setting repeatedly (e.g., my student seems consistent in her behavior only because I never see her anywhere but at school).

■ Relationships between traits and behavior are too small to be of any importance.

Even in earlier years, when the evidence seemed to overwhelmingly support the situationist position, there were always several possible defenses for the trait position. For example:

■ **Phenotypic vs. genotypic analysis.** Although a person may appear to be reacting differently in two situations, in reality the behaviors may be quite similar (Alker, 1972; Bowers, 1973). For example, suppose Joe has a strong need to be accepted. Therefore, in a bar he laughs at dirty jokes; with his girlfriend he does not even smile when someone tells an off-color joke. On the surface (phenotypically), his behaviors are different. But underneath the surface (genotypically), they serve the same dynamic purpose.

■ **Are there individual differences in stability?** Some evidence exists that some people are generally more variable in their behavior than others. Thus, while an entire group of persons may appear to show instability, this is due to a subgroup whose members are highly variable. In this vein, it has been discovered that when a given trait or set of behaviors is not especially relevant for an individual, there will be little consistency in behavior (Bem and Allen, 1974).

■ **Laboratory vs. real life.** By its very nature, laboratory research is highly controlled. Subjects are assigned on a prearranged basis to specific experimental conditions. Freedom of choice is usually nil. However, in everyday life we choose the situations in

Box 8-2
WHO IS RESPONSIBLE, THE PERSON OR THE SITUATION?

About two days before Christmas several years ago a fourteen-year-old boy entered a large downtown department store in Chicago. At first he wandered around aimlessly. But he had a furtive look about him that attracted the attention of a store detective. The boy finally stopped at a perfume counter and began examining the various bottles. At the same time he surreptitiously glanced around to see whether anyone was watching him. Finally, with a casual yet swift movement he dropped a very expensive bottle into his jacket pocket. As soon as he stepped outside the store, the store detective caught up with him and arrested him for shoplifting.

This is a common scenario today, one that is acted out over and over throughout the nation. But how do we explain this boy's act? Was he basically just a thief? Did an urge to give his mother a Christmas gift account for the behavior? Was this the inevitable response of someone with criminal tendencies? Or was the boy perhaps unstable, a victim of his own internal psychopathology? These are some of the possible *personality* explanations.

But, then again, maybe he was simply caught up in the Christmas spirit reflected in thousands of stimuli around him. Perhaps such behavior is routine for his peer group. Or possibly he would never have stolen the perfume had it not been displayed so temptingly or openly. All of these explanations suggest that the boy's behavior was determined by the overall *situation* in which he found himself. Change the situation (e.g., make the merchandise less accessible), and you change the behavior.

Also possible is an interpretation that would explain his behavior as some complex *interaction* between *personality* (love for his mother, criminal tendencies) and the *situation* (Christmas season, accessible merchandise).

which we behave (Snyder and Kendzierski, 1982). As Wachtel (1973) points out, it is misleading to ignore this fact. Such freedom of choice will inevitably lead to greater consistency in our behavior, a consistency that will just as inevitably be underestimated by research carried out in highly restrictive laboratory settings that deny choice.

■ **Aggregation research.** For a long time, no one seemed to be able to generate hard evidence for the stability of behavior across situations. But all too often what had been correlated were single pieces of behavior in two situations. It does not, however, make sense to argue that because I am aggressive in a softball game but not at a political meeting, I am not showing stability in aggressive behavior. A belief in stable traits should not force us to argue that an aggressive person must be aggressive in every situation, or that in one, specific class of situations aggression must occur every time. All that is required is that over a range of situations, an aggressive person will behave more frequently in an aggressive manner than will a nonaggressive person. Indeed, when behavior is aggregated over a variety of situations, the demonstration of stability in behavior is possible. Epstein (1979a) has attacked this problem by averaging behavior over a number of instances. In several separate studies, he showed that stability coefficients for several kinds of data (objective behavior, self-ratings, ratings by others) can be increased to acceptable levels when the data are averaged over an increasing number of events. In a historical review of the person-situation debate, Epstein and O'Brien (1985) examined a variety of studies. In every instance they found that the aggregation approach provides strong evidence for the stability of behavior over time and situations.

■ Buss and Craik (1983) contend that traits or dispositions are nothing more than the names given to the cumulative acts of a person. For example, the label *deference* might include the following behaviors: apologizing profusely, letting others talk first, asking your friend where she wants to eat, and so on. This approach, the so-called **act frequency approach,** measures the relative frequency of acts that we can agree are characteristic of a broad dispositional category. It is a *descriptive* approach rather than an *explanatory* one. Block (1989), however, is quite critical of this approach.

The case for interaction

Which is more important, the situation or the person? For the interactionist this is a pseudoquestion because, after all, behavior is always determined by both variables. It is akin to asking a freezing man whether he would like a shirt or a pair of pants. "If it's all the same to you, I'd like both." The interactionist position is an old one, appearing in several forms (Brunswik, 1943; Kantor, 1924; Lewin, 1935; Murray, 1938; Rotter, 1954). However, as Rotter (1981) points out, none of these theorists found it easy to use the presumed person-situation interaction predictively. To a large extent, this was due to the emphasis on the subjective or learned nature of the environment. Let us expand on this point.

Obviously, situations can be cataloged in many ways. They can be described in terms of their physical characteristics (size of the room, temperature of the environment, number of people present, etc.), the behaviors they typically elicit (aggression, dependency, sexuality, etc.), or the needs they satisfy (love and affection, achievement, etc.). They can likewise be organized according to the way they are perceived by the person. All of these approaches have been employed. The merits of each approach are heavily dependent upon what each investigator is trying to accomplish.

The prediction of complex human behavior in the social context must rely on more than mere physical descriptions of situations. One must know what the situation means to the individual. For example, what kinds of situations does the person see as threatening? The answer will lie less in the physical properties of situations than in the cues they offer. As Rotter (1981) describes it, these cues (subtle as well as obvious) will trigger in the individual expectancies that certain behaviors will be rewarded or that achievement of these rewards will lead, in turn, to still other rewards. Situations that contain similar cues (even though the situations are rather different physically) will be construed as similar or functionally equivalent. For example, if classroom settings, one-to-one conversations with females, and confrontations with college presidents all contain cues that I am going to make a fool of myself, I may well clam up and thereby avoid such a negative outcome. All these situations, then, are similar because they contain cues that lead to expectancies for a particular outcome.

The interaction between personality and situation in this last example arises in the following fashion. To predict my behavior in a given situation, one needs to know about certain general personality characteristics (e.g., fear of failure), and also about the subjective meaning of that situation for me. Prediction will be superior when information from both situation and person is available. Unfortunately, determining the subjective meaning of situations for an individual is rarely easy. Nor is it easy to tease out of situations the cues that lead an individual to attach a particular meaning to a particular situation.

When situational factors are intense or when the reactions to them are greatly over-learned by the vast majority of people, personality variables will exert little influence. For example, if a snarling lion is suddenly let into my personality class, nearly everybody (including me) is going to get out, given half a chance. Likewise, a red traffic light will cause nearly everyone to stop, and a ringing telephone will prompt most people to answer it. Of course, in all these examples a small number of individuals will behave differently. On the other hand, when situational stimuli are very weak or quite ambiguous, behavior is more likely to be predicted accurately from personality information. Indeed, the whole field of projective testing is predicated on the notion that ambiguous stimuli (e.g., inkblots) will produce interpretations heavily influenced by personality characteristics. Thus my response to a vague, indeterminant stimulus will tell you more about me than it will about the stimulus.

A conclusion

The foregoing discussion suggests several things. First it is not fruitful to consider all human behavior as being propelled solely by broad internal dispositions. Knowing only that a person is cerebrotonic or has received high scores on a dependency scale or is "suffering" from anxiety is little knowledge indeed. Perhaps if people were *perfectly* stable in their behavior, such a strategy would work. But such is not the case.

Conversely, human beings are not automatons at the mercy of simple conditionings. Situations alone do not determine behavior. People bring with them to every situation something of themselves. This "something" is what makes each person different from all others. Therefore, every situation is interpreted, analyzed, filtered, and perceived based on the unique set of past experiences, learnings, and biological qualities of each individual. In this sense there is an interaction between personality traits and situations in the determination of behavior (Ekehammer, 1974; Magnusson and Endler, 1977; Pervin, 1985). Indeed, traits are every bit as important as situations (Buss, 1989).

To paraphrase David McClelland (1981) and a country song at the same time, perhaps we have been looking for consistency in all the wrong places. Evidence of consistency lies less in the symbolic marks subjects make on questionnaires than it does in the lives of real people studied over *lengthy* periods of time. Both consistency and interaction will be discovered in the complexities of human behavior, not in its simplicities.

NEEDS AND MOTIVES

A number of the trait concepts discussed earlier had motivational overtones. Certainly, many of us, in trying to explain someone's behavior, resort to underlying motives or needs. Freud, of course, drew heavily on motivational concepts in his attempts to understand human behavior.

Motivation refers to the forces within us that activate our behavior and direct it toward one goal rather than another. The related concept, **motive,** is the goal or outcome that a given behavior seeks to attain. For example, my reigning motivation may be achievement and the related motive toward which I direct my actions is, perhaps, a vice-presidency or maybe a salary increment.

Innate motives are rooted in the physiology and neural structures of the body. All humans share them and they relate directly to the survival of individuals and the species. We all need food and drink to live. And even though one can survive without sex, the species cannot. For people in modern industrialized societies, the innate motives can be readily achieved. Food, water, and protection from the cold are all easily attained. Therefore, they do not become major motivators. But for the poor, the homeless, or many in deprived Third World countries, much of one's energies is wrapped up in getting enough to eat and drink and in finding adequate shelter. As Maslow observed, however, once these motives can be satisfied readily, the learned or acquired motives become prominent in directing our lives.

Acquired motives are learned both in the sense of the motive's value and the behaviors necessary to satisfy it. Not everyone places the same value on a given motive nor does everyone so motivated attempt to satisfy it in the same fashion.

It is these learned or psychological motives and needs that are especially relevant to the study of personality. Therefore, let us turn now to a brief examination of several approaches that hinge on such concepts.

Murray: A system of needs

To many, Henry A. Murray was the first person to be entitled to the label "personality psychologist." Born in 1893, his career spanned the middle half of the twentieth century. He died in 1988—an Olympian figure to those who knew him (Smith, 1989). What also makes his career so extraordinary was his educational background—a bachelor's degree in history, an M.D. degree from Columbia, and a Ph.D. in biochemistry from Cambridge University. But his seminal work in personality was carried out at the Harvard Psychological Clinic in collaboration with a group of dedicated colleagues whose ideas culminated in the classic, *Explorations in Personality* (Murray, 1938).

Needs.   Murray attempted to develop a theory of personality based upon people's needs. In a sense, human behavior may be understood in terms of the processes of satisfying those needs. For Murray (1938), **needs** were construed as forces that organize and give direction to feelings, thoughts, and behavior so that an unsatisfying state of affairs can be remedied. Needs help determine the ways in which a person responds to or seeks out environmental stimulation.

There are the **primary** (viscerogenic) **needs** which are physiological (e.g., needs for air, water, food, etc.). The **secondary** (psychogenic) **needs** arise out of primary needs but are not specifically connected with organic processes (e.g., achievement, affiliation, nurturance, etc.). As noted earlier, it is such needs that account for most of the truly salient human behavior (although under conditions of physical deprivation, the primary needs may become prepotent). Personality is largely describable in terms of these needs and the ways they interact with environmental forces. In effect, though needs may be intense or weak, enduring or momentary, they most often persist and prompt courses of action which will bring about satisfaction. Table 8-2 lists twenty such needs.

Sometimes, needs are inhibited or repressed because they are regarded as threatening or unacceptable. Needs may be very broad and diffuse or highly focused and thereby capable of satisfaction by only a narrow range of goals. Then, too, needs often operate in concert. One need may become subordinate to another or may even assist in the satisfaction of another need. Thus, my need for domination may become secondary to my need for affiliation as I become lonely. But at times, needs may conflict with each other and lead to great turmoil. My need to be liked may conflict with my need for affiliation and thereby cause all manner of difficulties for me. In any case, identifying and organizing needs in a given person is often a very difficult task; but one which, in a real sense, only reflects the enormous complexity of the human being.

Press.   Needs are the internal determinants of behavior. But there are external determinants as well. A **press** is a characteristic of the environment that either facilitates or interferes with the efforts of the individual to achieve a given goal. A few examples would be:

lack of family support	religious training
absence of a parent	physical inferiority
poverty	birth of a sibling
inclement weather	praise
fire	nurturance
accident	betrayal

Murray also noted that some environmental forces are significant only because they are perceived as so (**beta press**). Other environmental characteristics are real in their effects on the individual (**alpha press**).

Thema.   One specific unit of interaction between need and press is referred to as a **thema.** This helps Murray view behavior in a more global, less segmented fashion.

TABLE 8-2 An example of Murray's taxonomy of needs

Need	Definition	Sample Test Item to Measure It
n Abasement	To submit, surrender, admit inferiority	My friends think I am too humble.
n Achievement	To accomplish tasks, surpass others	I set difficult goals for myself which I attempt to reach.
n Affiliation	To approach liked others, win their affection	I become very attached to my friends.
n Aggression	To fight opposition, attack, seek revenge	I treat a domineering person as rudely as he treats me.
n Autonomy	To seek freedom, independence, resist coercion	I go my own way regardless of the opinions of others.
n Counteraction	To overcome past failure, repress fear, master weakness	To me a difficulty is just a spur to greater effort.
n Defendance	To defend oneself against attack, criticism, blame	I can usually find plenty of reasons to explain my failures.
n Deference	To admire, praise, imitate, and support another person	I often find myself imitating or agreeing with somebody I consider superior.
n Dominance	To control others, to influence, persuade, command	I usually influence others more than they influence me.
n Exhibition	To impress, excite, amaze, fascinate, or shock others	I am apt to show off in some way if I get a chance.
n Harmavoidance	To avoid pain, injury, illness, danger, death	I am afraid of physical pain.
n Infavoidance	To avoid humiliation, embarrassment, failure	I often shrink from a situation because of my sensitiveness to criticism and ridicule.
n Nurturance	To give sympathy, support, and to console others	I am easily moved by the misfortunes of other people.
n Order	To put things in order, be neat, organized, clean	I organize my daily activities so that there is little confusion.
n Play	To seek fun, jokes, laughter	I cultivate an easy-going, humorous attitude toward life.
n Rejection	To avoid, exclude, snub disliked others	I get annoyed when some fool takes up my time.
n Sentience	To seek and enjoy sensuous experiences	I search for sensations which shall at once be new and delightful.
n Sex	To form erotic relationships, have sex	I spend a great deal of time thinking about sexual matters.
n Succorance	To have others give sympathy, support, and consolation	I feel lonely and homesick when I am in a strange place.
n Understanding	To seek answers, to enjoy analysis, theory, logic, reason	I think that *reason* is the best guide in solving the problems of life.

For example, an experience of rejection might engage a person's need for abasement which, in turn, leads to passive behavior or the wish to blame oneself. The concept of thema, although a loose one, clearly places Murray in the interactionist camp described earlier in this chapter.

Unconscious.   Although in some ways Murray's theory bears some resemblance to Allport's, this is certainly not the case when it comes to **unconscious** processes. Murray saw unconscious processes as very important. To some extent, his ideas here were quite neo-Freudian. Indeed, he has even recommended that serious personologists undergo psychoanalysis so that they will better understand their own psyches.

There are other aspects of Murray's system that involve the id, ego, and superego. Likewise, he discusses many aspects of development (although he does tend to neglect psychopathological processes). Still, his most extensive and prominent contributions rest with his taxonomies of need, press, and thema.

Achievement motivation

We have seen that there is more to motivation than simple biological needs. For example, White (1959) talked about **competence motivation.** This is the need to deal effectively with our environment, to be competent, and to do well, process information efficiently, and to improve our world. This is an intensive desire to interact effectively with our environment.

But the need most studied in Murray's list of twenty psychogenic needs (see Table 8-2) has been achievement (often referred to as *n* Achievement). Although *n* Achievement is but one of many personality dimensions it is important for several reasons (Weiner, 1978). For example, it provides a model for ways to study psychogenic motivation. But it also is important simply because achievement itself is so prominent in Western society both behaviorally and in terms of values. It is almost an article of faith that "good" people are high achievers. They are competitive and if they are not, then we try to devise ways to make them so!

The central figure in this field has long been David McClelland. He and his colleagues (McClelland, Atkinson, Clark and Lowell, 1953) published *The Achievement Motive* and thereby launched a tide of research that has made *n* Achievement one of the most heavily studied variables in the history of personality. McClelland chose to study achievement largely because it was possible to rather easily arouse the need in laboratory situations and because a fantasy device, the TAT (see Chapter 2), existed to measure it. Both these elements will be discussed more fully in the next chapter as we more carefully address research and assessment issues. For now, however, let us examine the nature of achievement motivation.

The nature of n Achievement.   Over the years, a great deal of research has been done on *n* Achievement. Although not all this research has been consistent, some general features do seem to stand out (McClelland, 1985). The need seems to be a stable disposition that is manifested in many corners of an individual's life. People high in n Achievement tend to show several differences from those low in n Achievement. For example, they are more likely to be competitive and they are also more likely to take responsibility for their own successes. What is more, they expect that if they exert the proper effort, they will succeed. They have a penchant for setting challenging goals that are, nevertheless, realistic. As a result, they perform better than individuals low in n Achievement in a variety of situations. They prefer tasks of intermediate difficulty where neither success nor failure is guaranteed. Low n Achievement individuals, in contrast, seem to prefer very easy tasks (where success is virtually inevitable) or else very difficult tasks (where failure is sure and where, therefore, no one can blame them for failing). High n Achievement people select tasks in which performance provides information about their ability. Terribly difficult and terribly easy tasks are the same in that they do not offer the opportunity for feedback about one's abilities.

Other characteristics of those high in n Achievement include a tendency to go into sales or into entrepreneurial work that involves some risk but also work that is realistically congruent with their abilities. They avoid jobs that are routine in nature. They take pride in their accomplishments and are able to delay gratification of smaller, immediate rewards in favor of later, larger rewards. They have a positive self-concept and in school they are likely to get good grades when those grades are related to subsequent success.

Development of n Achievement. It is difficult to point definitely to a specific set of determinants of n Achievement that are inevitable in their consequences. For example, although experiences in the home would certainly seem to indirectly affect achievement, the fact is that the same family that encourages independence may also be very permissive so the ultimate personality product will vary depending on the interactions among family child-rearing characteristics. In this connection, some have commented on gender differences in n Achievement. We will, however, postpone this discussion until Chapter 19. In the meantime, three examples of antecedents of n Achievement may be noted. First, there is the degree of stress the parents and the culture place on high achievement (McClelland, 1961). Second, children taught to be self-reliant and confident and urged to establish their own goals seem more likely to become high achievers (Rosen and D'Andrade, 1959). However, because the research here is not always consistent, McClelland (1961) has suggested an "optimal level" hypothesis: independence training instituted too early may actually inhibit the development of the achievement motive. Third, the father's or mother's occupation may play a role. More specifically, a father whose job involves decision making and initiative may lead the child toward the development of achievement motivation (Turner, 1970).

McClelland (1961) has attempted to extend his ideas about the influence of parents, culture, and social class to economic growth. He says that as a society's children become more achievement oriented, the general level of productivity will rise in the decades to follow when those same children become adults. For example, he argues that the n Achievement themes in children's readers in the second, third, and fourth grades from 1925 and 1950 for twenty-three countries were correlated with an index of economic growth rate and industrialization between 1929 and 1950 (see Figure 8-5).

A model for achievement behavior.   Atkinson (1957, 1964) has developed a theory or model of achievement behavior. He sees achievement-related behavior as the result of a conflict between approach and avoidance tendencies. Thus, when one succeeds, there is pride and a sense of satisfaction. When one fails there is the feeling of shame and unhappiness. The relative strengths of these expected emotions determine when the person will approach or avoid a given set of achievement-oriented activities or tasks. When a person's need for achievement is strong, when that person expects that a given behavior will achieve the goal, and when there is "excitement" generated by the achievement-oriented behavior, the chances are good that achievement-oriented behavior will occur. In contrast, when the foregoing three variables are relatively low in strength, the person will likely back off.

Need for power

The **need for power** (*n* Power) bears some similarities to *n* Achievement and has been investigated in much the same way. It is the desire to exert control over the events that affect our lives (McClelland, 1975). If anything characterizes the history of human beings it is their incessant struggle for power. This motive has triggered wars, fueled political turmoil, and stimulated innumerable interpersonal conflicts.

Winter and Stewart (1978) have identified several features that characterize those who are high in *n* Power. For example, there is the tendency to select careers that allow one to affect others through the selective use of rewards and punishments. Such careers might include public office, teaching, business, journalism, religion, and many others. Basically, those high in *n* Power desire to influence events, to make things happen.

Many who seek power are individuals who want to achieve visibility. They have the tendency to build loyal groups of supporters who will help them attain their desired goals. Sometimes, power comes about merely by getting things done (or getting others to do the work). As Winter and Stewart (1978) put it, "For wielding power, the rules seem to be: speak up, define the problem (but encourage others to offer solutions), participate, and do not neglect evaluations of others in an attempt to be liked" (p. 404).

People high in *n* Power tend to prefer prestigious possessions and they like to suggest their own importance by doing such things as putting their names on their doors or by placing their term papers in expensive binders (Winter, 1973).

Need for affiliation

Another widely studied need has been affiliation. **Need for affiliation** (*n* Affiliation) typifies those who are motivated to seek out others, to value being with them, and to care about them. They have learned that others can offer aid and comfort or that others can provide information helpful in achieving goals. People high in *n* Affiliation are more likely than others to conform to the wishes of others. They need to be liked and accepted and to seek out the friendship of others. They tend to be more active socially. It often seems, too, that caring for others as well as being cared for by others can counteract some of the potential harm stemming from a high-powered life-style (McClelland, 1982).

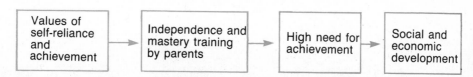

FIGURE 8-5 Achievement motivation and economic growth. After McClelland (1961)

In conclusion, achievement, power, and affiliation are just a few of the more important examples of the universe of needs that stimulate and guide our behavior. Their effects are complex, profound, and ubiquitous.

SUMMARY

- Trait psychology involves the development of comprehensive systems for classifying and describing the characteristic and enduring ways people differ from one another.

- The study of traits has a very long history that includes characterology, typology, and physiognomy. Sheldon's search for the relationships between physique and temperament is but a more recent example of this ancient approach. Others, such as Freud, Jung, Rogers, and Maslow, also have described traits or types, although with limited success.

- Traits most often refer to the personality dimensions along which people differ, whereas types tend to represent discrete categories. However, not all theorists accept this distinction. In addition, types are usually thought to be few in number while traits are potentially very numerous.

- For Gordon Allport, traits lead the person to respond to differing situations in a generally similar fashion, producing the consistency so characteristic of individuals. Traits are broad concepts whereas habits are more narrow, situationally specific tendencies.

- According to Allport, there are cardinal traits, central traits, and secondary traits. These kinds of traits differ in the pervasiveness of their influence in guiding behavior.

- Allport also emphasized personal traits, which are unique to the individual, and common traits, which are relevant to everyone. Intentions also play an important role in shaping our lives by orienting us to the future rather than to the past.

■ Allport claimed that some behavior loses its connections to the past and becomes self-motivating. This is called functional autonomy. He also described the proprium, a concept which refers to the self and integrates the various elements of the personality.

■ Allport did not accord infantile or childhood experiences nearly so important a role as did Freud. Although his description of human development was a bit vague, he thought of development largely in terms of the self. Similarly, his notions of psychological health involved the growth of self-esteem and competence. His views on behavior change were likewise not very explicit.

■ Raymond Cattell, the second major trait theorist described, has his theoretical rationale strongly anchored in statistical-mathematical procedures.

■ Cattell distinguishes between surface traits and source traits. Surface traits refer to behaviors that all seem to relate to a common theme. Source traits are the basic elements that explain behavior. Source traits developed out of experience or learning are called environmental-mold traits, while constitutional source traits reflect hereditary influences.

■ Cattell also describes temperament traits, which involve emotionality and are constitutional, as well as ability traits, which may stem from either hereditary influences (fluid ability) or experience (crystallized ability).

■ Motivational traits are referred to by Cattell as dynamic source traits and are subdivided into ergs (constitutional) and sentiments (environmental-mold). Attitudes are the overt expressions of interest from which we infer ergs and sentiments. The interplay of all these concepts can be depicted by the dynamic lattice.

■ Cattell believes that some traits are unique to the individual while others are common to all of us.

■ The specification equation is the means by which Cattell combines a variety of trait information to predict behavior in a specific situation.

■ Cattell views personality development as a function of both hereditary and environmental factors. For this reason, he regards classical conditioning and instrumental conditioning as important. He also discusses integration learning as it relates to ergs, as well as syntality, which refers to the influence exerted by groups and social institutions.

■ For Cattell, adjustment is related to conflict and, while he recognizes the human potential for change, his emphasis seems to be primarily on the stability of personality.

▪ Hans Eysenck was another theorist discussed in this chapter. Using statistical methods, he focuses on types but regards them as dimensions rather than discrete categories.

▪ Eysenck's two principal personality dimensions are introversion-extraversion and stability-instability. More recently, he has emphasized a third type, which he calls psychoticism.

▪ Trait theorists have always argued that traits are stable over time and situations but in 1968, Mischel asserted that, on the contrary, there is little consistency and that situational factors are more important than traits as determinants of behavior.

▪ Subsequent research has revealed, however, that the radical view of the importance of situations is probably invalid. Several possible defenses for the trait position are: phenotypic versus genotypic analysis, individual differences in stability, laboratory research versus research in real-life settings, and aggregation research.

▪ The most serviceable position is that of interaction; that is, broad personality factors combine with specific situational factors to produce behavior in any given setting.

▪ Other dispositional approaches emphasize needs and motives (both innate and acquired). An early example of such an approach is Murray's system. He developed a lengthy list of needs and suggested that behavior is an outcome of needs that combine with an environmental press.

▪ Other examples of needs that have been investigated heavily are achievement, affiliation, and power.

CHAPTER 9

DISPOSITIONS
Research, Assessment, And Summary Evaluation

Many investigators have worked long and hard to discover how personality characteristics are arranged and how they function. They believe that until this is successfully accomplished, the orderly study of personality cannot properly proceed. But how do we identify and classify traits and how do we study or analyze dispositions? What tests and procedures have been used to discover the traits and dispositions described in the previous chapter? The aim of this chapter is the examination of the principal research and assessment methods that have been employed in the study of dispositions. As usual, we will close with a summary evaluation of the strengths and weaknesses of the dispositional perspective.

ALLPORT: THE SEARCH FOR INDIVIDUALITY

As we have seen, the theme running throughout Allport's work is the emphasis on individuality. Despite his identification with the idiographic camp, however, the bulk of his research was nomothetic. Nonetheless, his heart always seemed to beat in harmony with research that focused on the uniqueness of the individual.

Any description of Allport's trait research must be limited to what amounts to a few examples, however. The fact is, Allport mounted no systematic program of trait research, nor have there been any concerted efforts by others to validate empirically his theoretical concepts. His ideas have been influential, but the research void has severely limited their potential for even greater application.

Letters from Jenny

As previously noted, Allport advocated the use of personal documents such as diaries, letters, autobiographies, and interviews to understand the individual personality. This is exemplified by his collection of 301 letters written by Jenny Masterson (not her real name) over a period of eleven years — the famous *Letters from Jenny* published in 1965.

Jenny was widowed shortly before the birth of her son, Ross, in 1897. Jenny and Ross were very close up to the time Ross left home to attend Princeton University. He later enlisted in the Army and served in France during World War I. He was a changed person when he returned, and he and his mother quarreled frequently. He was also beset by a series of personal failures. Jenny's letters were written to two friends of Ross. The following are excerpts from those letters (Allport, 1965):

> Well, that's the way—there is nothing in this life worth living for except money, and one must find that while they are young. If one is so ridiculous as to slip into old age without money one must put up with being crowded into insanity, or "take arms against a sea of troubles, and by opposing, end them." (p. 133)

> You have all my best love. I am going out to the Sea now to blow the horror of Ross's women out of my brain and to try to believe that there is indeed a God somewhere. (p. 54)

> Have you read "The Magnificent Ambersons" by Tarkington? If not get it, it's about an only son, and how his *mother* ruined him. (p. 99)

Allport asked thirty-six judges to read Jenny's letters. Based pretty much on common sense, they listed 198 trait names to describe her. A number of these trait names proved to be synonyms or overlapped significantly, so Allport was able to reduce the list to eight traits which he felt were highly descriptive of Jenny's personality. These traits are shown in Table 9-1. Subsequently, Baldwin (1942) analyzed Allport's data statistically and essentially confirmed those eight central traits. Then, in 1966, Paige published a computer analysis of the letters. Using the statistical technique of factor analysis, he identified several trait factors which turned out to be quite close to Allport's list. In fact, there was so much overlap that Allport concluded that while the statistical analysis was nice, it added little to his own work.

TABLE 9-1 Jenny's central traits as revealed by two methods

Commonsense Traits (Allport)	Factorial Traits (Paige)
1 Quarrelsome-suspicious; aggressive	1 Aggression
2 Self-centered (possessive)	2 Possessiveness
3 Sentimental	3 Need for affiliation; need for family acceptance
4 Independent-autonomous	4 Need for autonomy
5 Esthetic-artistic	5 Sentience
6 Self-centered (self-pitying)	6 Martyrdom
7 (no parallel)	7 Sexuality
8 Cynical-morbid	8 (no parallel)
9 Dramatic-intense	9 ("Overstate")

SOURCE: From ''Traits Revisited'' by G. W. Allport, *American Psychologist*, 1966, *21*, 1–10. Copyright 1966 by the American Psychological Association. Reprinted by permission.

Even though Allport was much taken with idiographic studies, he realized that they do not unlock all the secrets of personality. He did feel, however, that they keep us close to material produced by the subject and also take us a bit behind that material by helping us to make inferences about individual personality structure. Wrightsman (1981) has made a plea that we return to the use of personal documents.

Expressive behaviors

True to his theme of uniqueness, Allport regarded all behavior as having two components. There is an adaptive function, which refers to the effects created by behavior. But there is also an expressive element, which involves the style that characterizes behavior. His special interest was in the expressive component because he felt that if we analyze the unique style of a person's behavior, we will find clues to the underlying structure of that individual's personality. In this respect he was not unlike Freud. Both men felt that even trivial behaviors can be diagnostic of the central, underlying features of personality. Whereas one's reasons for doing something may only reflect fleeting demands of the moment, the way the act is carried out reaches into the heart of one's lasting dispositions.

Allport's best known work in this vein was carried out with his collaborator, P. E. Vernon (Allport and Vernon, 1933). They tested twenty-five subjects on three different occasions; all sessions were separated by an interval of about four weeks. The tests included such things as estimation of weights, speed of walking, and strength of handshake. In other instances, raters observed such things as speech fluency, neatness, and voice intensity. Allport and Vernon quickly determined that both the consistency (reliability) of the various acts and the ratings of them over time were acceptably high. They also found that there was consistency in the same act performed by different muscle groups or, for example, by the left arm versus the right arm or by arms versus legs. This meant, Allport decided, that some central structure must mediate behavior, lending it a characteristic style regardless of which part of the body is involved. Additional evidence for this mediating notion was found by intercorrelating all thirty-eight measures used. These correlations were predominantly positive and led to the impression that there were three general factors behind the separate measures. From their overall analysis, Allport and Vernon (1933) decided the following:

> From our results it appears that a man's gesture and handwriting both reflect an essentially stable and constant individual style. His expressive activities seem not to be dissociated and unrelated to one another, but rather to be organized and well-patterned. Furthermore, the evidence indicates that there is a congruence between expressive movement and the attitudes, traits, values, and other dispositions of the "inner" personality. (p. 248)

Although identifying the specific cues that enable us to infer personality from expressive movement is difficult, our ability to make correct inferences seems certain (Riggio, Lippa, and Salinas, 1990).

Allport on assessment

Allport felt strongly that normal individuals are motivated by conscious, easily accessible needs even though it may be true that neurotics are dominated by unconscious ones. Consequently, he argued that projective techniques are appropriate for disturbed individuals but are not necessary for normals. Therefore, in the realm of assessment, Allport is most closely identified with self-report inventories.

True to his stress on central dispositions, Allport emphasized that we all require a unifying philosophy of life or a system of values that will direct and give meaning to our lives. Therefore, he set about the task of identifying these basic values. The **Study of Values,** a test designed for this purpose, was first published with Vernon in 1931; it is now in its third edition (Allport, Vernon, and Lindzey, 1960). The scale assesses the degree to which an individual emphasizes the following values in life:

■ *The Theoretical*—This person emphasizes the search for truth.

■ *The Economic*—Whatever is useful is valued. This is a pragmatic person.

■ *The Aesthetic*—Artistic experiences are sought. The value is on form and harmony.

■ *The Social*—Love of people characterizes this person. Warm human relationships are vital.

■ *The Political*—This person is motivated by the search for power and influence.

■ *The Religious*—An almost mystical belief in the essential unity in the universe describes this person.

On the whole, the reliability of the scale is quite good, and several construct-validity studies support its utility. For example, physicians scored high on the theoretical and social values and men in business scored high on the economic and political values. These value measures were obtained while the respondents were still undergraduates (Huntley and Davis, 1983). The scale is a simple, straightforward instrument that in many ways reflects Allport's faith in the importance of conscious determinants. Some sample items from the scale are shown in Table 9-2.

TABLE 9-2   Sample items from the Study of Values

From Part I (30 questions)

1. The main objective of scientific research should be the discovery of truth rather than its pratical application.
   (a) Yes   (b) No

4. Assuming that you have sufficient ability, would you prefer to be:
   (a) a banker?
   (b) a politician?

15. At an exposition, do you chiefly like to go to the buildings where you can see:
   (a) new manufacturing products?
   (b) scientific (e.g., chemical) apparatus?

SOURCE: From *A Study of Values* by G. W. Allport, P. E. Vernon, and G. Lindzey (Boston: Houghton Mifflin), 1960. Copyright 1960 by Houghton Mifflin Co. Reprinted by permission.

FACTOR-ANALYTIC APPROACH TO TRAIT RESEARCH

The leading figure in the factor-analytic approach to trait theory is Cattell; therefore, the present discussion will pivot on his methods and philosophy of research. Before plunging into the specifics of Cattell's methods of research and assessment, however, let us take a look at his view of the scientific enterprise.

Bivariate-multivariate-clinical axis

Cattell is very critical of the **bivariate** research strategy. This is a time-honored approach going back to Wundt and Pavlov in which only two variables are considered at one time. The *independent variable* is manipulated by the experimenter, who then observes its effects on the *dependent variable* (see Chapter 2 for a discussion of these variables). For example, success or failure on a task (independent variable) might be varied to learn what happens to the subject's anxiety level (dependent variable) following the experience. Thousands of bivariate experiments, each dealing with a different independent variable, may be carried out just to determine how humans become anxious. But because each is a separate study varying only one condition at a time, we are left with a piecemeal view of the human being. Not only is the holistic picture of the organism shattered but we are left with no idea about how all these separate studies fit together. Furthermore, by considering anxiety in isolation from other variables such as competency, adjustment, and confidence, we get no notion of how the presence of these other variables affects anxiety or how they relate to the failure-success variable noted earlier. There is an artificial, laboratory quality to bivariate research which Cattell believes diminishes its contribution to our knowledge.

In contrast, there is the **multivariate** strategy. This approach utilizes a variety of measurements on the same person instead of just looking at one variable at a time. There is no experimental manipulation of variables, and so the artificiality of the situation is reduced. By taking multiple measures at the same time, the wholeness of the organism is preserved and we are not left with the impossible task of putting "Humpty-Dumpty together again."

The third strategy is the **clinical** method, which Cattell asserts is basically akin to the multivariate method. Perhaps Cattell's own words will best convey matters here:

> In this respect, the emphasis on "wholeness" in the multivariate method is actually the same as in the clinical method, but it is quantitative and follows explicit calculations of laws and general conclusions. For the clinician appraises the total pattern "by eye," and tries to make generalizations from a good memory, whereas the multivariate experimenter actually *measures* all the variables and may then set an electronic computer to abstract the regularities which exist, instead of depending on human powers of memory and generalization. The clinical approach to personality is thus really that of a multivariate experimenter without benefit of apparatus—and has had the additional drawback that it produces its personality theories from data gathered from abnormal, diseased processes rather than normal ranges. (1965, pp. 21–22)

For all the foregoing reasons, Cattell is a staunch advocate of the multivariate approach. But what, exactly, is this multivariate method? For an answer we must begin with a more detailed examination of factor analysis.

Nature of factor analysis

Many years ago, Allport and Odbert (1936) looked through a dictionary and came up with over 3,000 traitlike words to describe various aspects of personality. Even allowing for a certain amount of overlap and redundancy, using so many words presents a real problem. But according to Cattell, the problem is mainly for those who would use a bivariate research strategy. Can you imagine, for example, how an investigator looking to study authoritarianism could ever begin to get a handle on the myriad relationships possible? Authoritarianism would have to be related separately to perhaps 3,000 other traits, to say nothing of combinations of these other traits. And this assumes there is only one established scale to measure authoritarianism!

The sheer magnitude of the task of dealing with such a mass of variables has led some investigators to myopically concentrate on one trait while ignoring how other, simultaneously acting traits might affect matters. Others have chosen a clinical strategy and simply argue that in their experience, people fall into two or three categories or else are motivated by a few basic traits. There is no quantification or measurement but only an appeal to clinical experience. But Cattell's is an appeal to research! The next problem, of course, is how to execute this research. Cattell (1965) stated the problem this way:

> The problem which baffled psychologists for many years was to find a method which would tease out these functionally unitary influences in the chaotic jungle of human behavior. But let us ask how, in the literal tropical jungle, the hunter decides whether the dark blobs which he sees are two or three rotting logs or a single alligator? He watches for movement. If they move together—come and disappear together—he infers a single structure. (p. 56)

Here we have the prescription for the identification and classification of the unitary structures of the human personality. What Cattell is suggesting by his metaphor about moving alligators is that we resort to correlational methods to determine the degree of covariation among different measures. In essence, a correlation states the degree of relationship between *two* sets of scores in quantitative terms. Cattell, however, is asking us to use **factor analysis,** a statistical method that utilizes *many* separate correlations in order to determine which variables increase or decrease in concert and therefore can be considered to be functionally related. The technique of factor analysis is based on the principle that when variables (behaviors, test responses, emotional reactions, etc.) change together, they must have some basic element in common that is responsible for their relationship. By examining large arrays of correlations, one can, through factor analysis, determine the basic unities in personality. A detailed example should make all of this clear.

Hypothetical example of factor analysis

Problem.   An investigator is attempting to determine the basic elements of what might be termed *clinical skill*. In this hypothetical example, the identification through factor analysis of the underlying attributes of skilled clinicians might help us better select candidates for training in clinical psychology.

Initial steps.   In collecting the necessary data, we first select 100 clinical psychologists who have been judged by a panel of three experts to have an exceptional record of skilled service. Each clinician is then administered a large number of tests that assess a wide variety of skills and achievements.

The correlation matrix.   The next step is to correlate each of those tests with every other test. This will provide us with a **correlation matrix** in which the correlations between all possible pairs of tests are arrayed. An example of such a matrix with hypothetical correlations entered is shown in Table 9-3. In this case, seven tests were used. Suppose these tests were as follows:

A = Measure of Clinical Sensitivity

B = Measure of Interpersonal Trust

C = Measure of Nonjudgmental Attitudes

D = Measure of Empathy

E = Measure of Amount of Research Completed

F = Number of Professional Societies Joined

G = Number of Professional Journals Subscribed To

As we examine the correlation matrix, an interesting pattern emerges. Measures A, B, C, and D all show a strong positive relationship (i.e., the correlation between any two measures in this group of four is between .70 and .80). At the same time, measures E, F, and G also correlate highly with one another (i.e., from .75 to .85). However, there is virtually no relationship between the group E, F, G and the group A, B, C, D (e.g., A and E = .15, B and F = .10, D and G = .12). What these patterns suggest is that A, B, C, and D all hang together. This indicates that they constitute a functional unity. By the same token, E, F, and G also go together, suggesting another functional unity.

The example at hand is a simplified one. The task becomes much more difficult when, say, 100 or more measures are used. In these more complex cases, we depend upon the technology of the computer to process the data. But the key is the reduction of these data by means of factor analysis to a small number of dimensions, or **factors** (sometimes called **unities**). Factor-analytic formulas are complex, and their exact nature is beyond the scope of this discussion. If you are interested in a more detailed presentation, consult Comrey (1973) or Harman (1960). Basically, factor analysis does statistically with large correlation matrices what we did by inspection with Table 9-3 and its correlations from only seven measures.

Factor loading.   In the preceding example, we decided that two factors are involved. Factor X, let us call it, was derived from the correlations among A, B, C, and D. Factor Y stems from the interrelationships among E, F, and G. Taken together, these two factors account for all the relationships in the matrix. Factor X **loads** on A, B, C, and D, and Factor Y loads on E, F, and G. Conversely, an individual measure

TABLE 9-3 *Hypothetical correlation matrix for seven tests*

Test	A	B	C	D	E	F	G
A		.70	.80	.75	.15	.20	.10
B			.75	.70	.12	.10	.10
C				.70	.18	.15	.11
D					.12	.14	.12
E						.80	.85
F							.75
G							

loads on a factor to the degree that it correlates with that factor. To go back to our example, two factors, X and Y, seem responsible for the performance of our successful clinicians on the seven measures used.

Factor names. Most investigators do not rest with the extraction of factors from a matrix. For communication purposes, they find it desirable to name their factors. This is a highly inferential phase and can lead to problems and disagreements. It often happens that the name chosen for a given factor suggests things that were not intended by the factor analyst. For example, I may extract a factor that loads on measures of self-interest, selfishness, and greediness. Suppose I then name the factor *narcissism,* which is a psychoanalytic term. Actually, none of my measures contained psychoanalytic items or data. Therefore, choosing narcissism as a label may suggest something about the factor that goes far beyond the measures used. In short, one must exercise extreme care in naming. Some theorists, such as Cattell, often seem purposely to use factor or trait names that do not conjure up images from other theories. For example, Cattell has dubbed one particular source trait *parmia versus threctia.* This almost forces one to go back to the original measures in order to interpret its meaning exactly.

Since Factor X loads on A, B, C, and D, the name we choose should reflect the essence of those measures. Perhaps *interpersonal sensitivity* would be appropriate since those measures deal with sensitivity, trust, nonjudgmental attitudes, and empathy. Our Factor Y might be termed *research-professional activity.* Again, however, we must not get carried away with names; we must always keep a wary eye on the test items themselves.

Sources of data

In the previous chapter, the various classes of traits (ergs, sentiments, etc.) that Cattell employs were described at some length. The factor-analytic method he uses to identify those traits out of a multitude of intercorrelations among various measures was briefly outlined a moment ago. But just as important as the method are the data to which the method is applied. Indeed, some would argue that no matter how sophisticated the factor analysis may be, no investigation is any better than the information on which it depends. Stated another way, if data are drawn from stimuli or assessment procedures that are trivial, superficial, or otherwise suspect, no amount of statistical analysis is going to salvage the research.

Cattell draws his measures from three basic sources: life records, or L-data; self-rating questionnaires, or Q-data; and objective tests, or T-data. **L-data** can consist of a wide range of sources, including school grades, health records, court records, and so on. More often, however, the L-data used by Cattell have come from ratings of the person on such things as friendliness, emotionality, patience, thoughtfulness, and the like. These are ratings provided by individuals who know the person well in real-life settings. **Q-data** tend to come largely from self-ratings or from the person's own statements about his or her behavior, feelings, or thoughts. Such data reflect the individual's introspections and self-observations. The essential characteristics of L-data and Q-data sources are shown in Table 9-4. Based on both ratings by observers and

---

TABLE 9-4   *Tender-minded–tough-minded source trait as identified through L- and Q-data*

L-Data (Observer Ratings)

Loads Positively:		Loads Negatively:
Demanding, impatient	vs.	Emotionally mature
Dependent, immature	vs.	Independent-minded
Gentle, sentimental	vs.	Hard, realistic
Expresses fastidious feelings	vs.	Overrules feelings
Enjoys imaginative fancies	vs.	Not fanciful
Easily anxious	vs.	Does not show anxiety
Likes to be with people	vs.	Self-sufficient

Q-Data (Subject's Questionnaire Responses)

Are you brought to tears by discouraging circumstances?
  (a) *yes*   (b) no

Would you rather be:
  (a) *a bishop*   (b) a colonel

Do you have good physical endurance?
  (a) yes   (b) *no*

Would you rather work:
  (a) *as a guidance worker for young* (b) as a manager in a technical manufacturing
     people seeking careers   concern

Do your friends regard you as:
  (a) practical   (b) *soft-hearted*

SOURCE: From *The Scientific Analysis of Personality* by R. B. Cattell (Baltimore, Md.: Penguin), 1965. Copyright 1965 by R. B. Cattell. Reprinted by permission.
NOTE: Italicized response indicates tender-mindedness.

responses by subjects themselves, Cattell has identified a source trait of *tender-mindedness–tough-mindedness*. The upper portion of Table 9-4 shows observer or L-data items and the lower portion illustrates Q-data items.

Finally, there are **T-data,** which come from objective tests (objective in the sense that independent scorers will arrive at the same conclusions when the subject's responses are scored). T-data can come from a variety of situations: paper-and-pencil tasks as well as laboratorylike behavioral settings involving certain tasks or apparatus. The defining characteristic here, according to Cattell, is that subjects are placed in contrived situations without knowing exactly in what respects their behavior is being evaluated. This provides a different kind of data as compared to Q-data sources if for no other reason than self-reports can easily allow the subject to fake or otherwise try to deceive the examiner. Figure 9-1 provides an example of one of these sources. This item presumably measures one's capacity to integrate. Cattell has found that this kind of task loads significantly on a source trait called *regression*, a contributor to neuroticism.

Empirical derivation of traits

In deriving source traits, Cattell has proceeded in the following fashion. Initially, he reduced the Allport and Odbert (1936) list of trait names to 171 by combining names

Where Do the Lines Cross?

Instructions:
    Your job in this test is to decide just where two lines cross. The lines are not drawn for you; you are just given end points of the line. Let us try an example. In the following example, where do lines AB and CD cross?

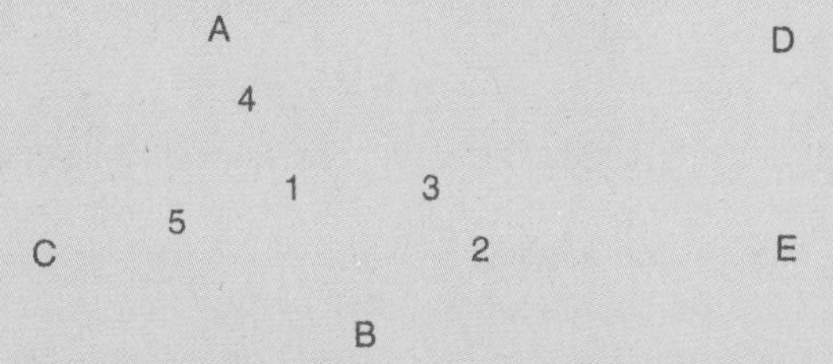

    The lines cross at point 1, not at point 2. Therefore, writing down 1 gives you a correct answer. To the question CE-DB, 2 would be the correct answer.

FIGURE 9-1   Spatial judgment: A T-data task.
From *The Scientific Analysis of Personality* by R. B. Cattell (Baltimore, MD: Penguin), 1965. Copyright 1965 by R. B. Cattell. Reprinted by permission.

that overlapped. Next, a heterogeneous group of 100 adults was assembled. People who were well acquainted with them then were asked to rate them on the 171 traits. Through factor analysis, these ratings were further reduced, and an additional group of over 200 men was rated on this shortened list of trait variables. A few of the traits on which these subjects were rated were *emotional, conscientious, tender,* and *self-effacing.*

Armed with these L-data, Cattell and his colleagues set about building a personality questionnaire. This is a Q-data approach that requires the individual to provide self-ratings. The instrument that emerged is the **Sixteen Personality Factor Questionnaire (16 P-F Questionnaire).** The sixteen personality factors included are shown in Table 9-5. The first twelve are factors found in both Q-data and L-data. The last four factors are from Q-data that could not be matched to L-data. Three sample items from the 16 P-F Questionnaire that happen to load highly on what Cattell calls Factor A *(sizothymia-affectothymia)* will illustrate the general format of the test:

■ I could stand being a hermit: True or False

■ I trust strangers: Sometimes or Practically always

■ I would rather work as: An engineer or A social science teacher

Profiles can easily be derived from the 16 P-F Questionnaire. While the test is most often regarded as a research instrument, profiles can be used in individual personality assessment. This assessment can include basic personality characteristics, vocational recommendations, and predictions of occupational fitness.

A moment ago it was mentioned that some factors may appear in Q-data that do not emerge from L-data. Cattell was aware of this, and therefore he began to use objective tests so that subjects' behavior in specifically contrived settings could be observed by trained raters—the so-called T-data source. The problem, however, was that just as before, T-data did not always match with data derived from the other two sources.

Analysis of heredity and environment

Cattell (1965) has said that "one can conclude that roughly four fifths of the differences we obtain on intelligence tests would disappear if people were all of identical heredity, whereas two thirds of the variance on extraversion-introversion would vanish if all people were brought up identically" (p.33). In making such a statement, Cattell is drawing on the results of research based on the statistical tool of **multiple abstract variance analysis (MAVA).** According to Cattell, this method is superior to conventional approaches to the study of heredity-environment differences, which rely exclusively on comparisons between identical and fraternal twins.

In practice, a number of personality trait tests are administered to the members of many different families. Data area gathered on twins and siblings raised together and on those adopted by other families. The data are then plugged into a series of simultaneous equations and analyzed in terms of four types of influence: within-family environmental differences, between-family environmental differences, within-family

TABLE 9-5 The sixteen major factors represented on the 16 P-F Questionnaire

Factor Label	High Score	vs.	Low Score
A	Reserved (Sizothymia)		Outgoing (Affectothymia)
B	Less intelligent (Low *g*)		More intelligent (High *g*)
C	Emotional (Low ego strength)		Stable (High ego strength)
E	Humble (Submissiveness)		Assertive (Dominance)
F	Sober (Desurgency)		Happy-go-lucky (Surgency)
G	Expedient (Low super-ego)		Conscientious (High super-ego)
H	Shy (Threctia)		Venturesome (Parmia)
I	Tough-minded (Harria)		Tender-minded (Premsia)
L	Trusting (Alaxia)		Suspicious (Protension)
M	Practical (Praxemia)		Imaginative (Autia)
N	Forthright (Artlessness)		Shrewd (Shrewdness)
O	Placid (Assurance)		Apprehensive (Guilt-proneness)
Q_1	Conservative (Conservativism)		Experimenting (Radicalism)
Q_2	Group-tied (Group adherence)		Self-sufficient (Self-sufficiency)
Q_3	Casual (Low integration)		Controlled (High self-concept)
Q_4	Relaxed (Low ergic tension)		Tense (Ergic tension)

SOURCE: From *The Scientific Analysis of Personality* by R. B. Cattell (Baltimore, Md.: Penguin), 1965. Copyright 1965 by R. B. Cattell. Reprinted by permission.

hereditary differences, and between-family hereditary differences. The use of MAVA so far suggests that for intelligence, the contribution of heredity is 80 percent, and the environmental contribution 20 percent. For the temperament trait of tough-mindedness–tender-mindedness, the hereditary contribution is about the same. However, for neuroticism the hereditary component is said to be only about 30 percent to 40 percent. Not everyone agrees with these ratios, however.

Measurement of similarity and change

There is no question that trait theory conjures up an image of people as collections of relatively unchanging characteristics. It is equally true that Cattell has contributed to that picture. But at the same time, he seems aware of the instability that can be so much a part of the human personality. In tune with that awareness, he has made some creative uses of correlational techniques.

The traditional correlational approach — the **R-technique** — involves administering a large number of tests to a large number of subjects and then observing which tests are related to each other. But Cattell has also used the **P-technique.** In this case, a single individual's scores on a number of measures are compared from one time to another. The resultant index can tell us how stable over time that person's behavior is and which aspects of behavior vary together. This technique could be used in clinical settings. A third technique, really a variant of the first, is called the **differential R-technique.** In this case, measures are given on two occasions and the changes between them are correlated. These change correlations are then subjected to factor analysis. The P-technique and the differential R-technique are regarded by Cattell as especially useful in the study of transient mood states. He views states such as anxiety and depression as more than mere noise obscuring the operation of more stable personality traits. Rather, he sees them as fascinating problems which can, like anything else, be described and classified through factor analysis. This is also further evidence of his recognition of the importance of the less stable elements in human behavior.

Finally, there is the **Q-technique** (no relation to Q-data). This is a method for defining types, but Cattell has also described it as a means of identifying roles such as father, business executive, banker, and so on. In effect, people's scores on a number of measures are correlated, and the resultant index tells us how similar those individuals are. When certain persons cluster together on the measures, they can be said to constitute a type or to define a role, as the case may be.

Eysenck's search for types

As noted earlier, Eysenck views the elements of personality as being arranged in a hierarchy. But unlike Cattell, he focuses on a relatively small number of basic dimensions or types. This results in a very broad level of personality description that would probably subsume Cattell's source traits at the next lower level. He feels that this type level (introversion-extraversion, stability-instability, and psychoticism) offers the greatest potential for prediction and understanding.

Eysenck prefers large-scale research efforts to small, bivariate investigations of isolated traits. He also believes that factor-analytic studies too often emphasize self-ratings, questionnaires, and subjective data. He likes to include behavioral observations whenever possible. The important thing, however, is to engage the total personality, which means that many different data sources must be used.

A good example of Eysenck's approach is his use of **criterion analysis**, which is basically hypothesis testing through factor analysis. This means that Eysenck starts out with a hypothesis or conviction about some basic trait or type. He then selects a series of measures that appears to be relevant to this underlying dimension. Next, he chooses two criterion groups known to differ along the dimension in question. Each measure is then correlated with the difference between these two criterion groups. These correlations will then indicate the degree of association between such measures and the underlying dimension. To illustrate this method, let us consider the dimension of neuroticism.

Eysenck (1952) and his colleagues selected two groups, each containing slightly more than 200 subjects. The normal group included male soldiers of at least average intelligence who had served in the Army for at least six months. The neurotic group contained soldiers being discharged because of psychiatric problems. Although otherwise well matched with the neurotic group, the normal group did appear to be somewhat more intelligent. The subjects were administered a large number of personality measures over a two-day period. All measures were selected because they appeared to relate in some way to the underlying dimension of neuroticism. In analyzing the capacity of each measure to distinguish between the neurotic and normal groups, a number of conclusions were reached. First, several questionnaires and objective behavioral tests distinguished between the two groups. Second, measures derived from expressive movements were not effective. Third, two Rorschach measures differentiated between the normal and neurotic individuals. On the basis of these analyses, twenty-eight measures were selected and intercorrelated. This correlation matrix was then factor analyzed. From these and other calculations, Eysenck (1952) concluded that "in neuroticism we are dealing with a personality factor which can be measured as reliably and as validly as intelligence" (p. 155).

Recent evidence (e.g., Pedersen, Plomin, McClearn, and Friberg, 1988), based on statistical analyses of several of Eysenck's personality variables such as neuroticism and extraversion, suggests a strong genetic component.

Critique of factor analysis

In the last few pages, several remarks have been made to the effect that the specific results of a factor analysis are a function of the particular technique chosen. Since so much of trait theory is heavily dependent upon factor analysis, it is time to take a critical look at this methodology.

Data sources. A popular battle cry against computers has always been "garbage in–garbage out!" What this suggests is that no technique—no matter how sophisticated—can rise above the quality of the data upon which it depends. Factor-analyzing data from unreliable tests or poorly conceived and invalid observations will not produce much of substance. The warning is, in effect, to avoid being so dazzled by the statistical analysis that we fail to examine closely the data sources used.

A related point is that different data sources sometimes produce different factors (e.g., L-data, Q-data, T-data). In addition, there seems to be little guarantee that subjecting data from different populations and age groups to analysis will always produce the same factor structure (Peterson, 1965). This brings up the question as to whether a universal set of personality factors independent of group membership can ever be developed (see Box 9-1).

Technique. Some have argued that factor analysis is less objective than it would appear at first glance. They are referring to the fact that during a factor analysis, certain points are reached that require the investigator to make decisions. All too often, goes the criticism, the choices made represent value judgments rather than objective mathematical decisions. A good example is the decision whether to use an **orthogonal** system or an **oblique** system. The former system specifies that obtained factors must

Box 9-1
THE BIG FIVE OF PERSONALITY

For many years, psychologists have argued about the nature of the truly basic components of personality. In short, to what elements can personality be reduced? For some, the answer would even reveal the biological bases of personality, no less (Zuckerman, Kuhlman, and Camac, 1988). Factor analysis has been applied energetically to the search in recent years (e.g., Noller, Law, and Comrey, 1987). The five resulting personality dimensions to emerge are often called the *Big Five* and, roughly speaking, include the following (Carson, 1989: Digman, 1990):

Introversion-Extraversion
Friendly Compliance-Hostile Noncompliance
Will (or conscientiousness)
Neuroticism (or emotionality)
Openness to Experience

So convinced are some of the robustness of the Big Five, that they urge that tests measuring the five factors be included in routine clinical assessment (McCrae and Costa, 1986). Others are equally confident when they report that in seven different data analyses, evidence for the existence of the Big Five was always found (Peabody and Goldberg, 1989). And Costa and McCrae (1988) not only believe in the efficacy of the five-factor model, they also assert that these factors exist among the needs listed by Murray (1938)—a fact which, they say, is a tribute to Murray's thoroughness.

However, others are less sure about the Big Five. For example, Waller and Ben-Porath (1987) suggest that the robustness of the five-factor model is less due to its validity than to the reliability of the tests designed to measure the factors involved. Likewise, Botwin and Buss (1989), although generally supportive of the model, also note that the basic structure of personality uncovered is very much determined by the nature of one's assumptions when starting an investigation.

Two considerations would seem to lead us to be cautious about the universality of the five-factor model. The first has to do with the nature of factor analysis and its weaknesses, as described in the surrounding pages. These points are salient because of the almost total reliance of the model on factor analytic evidence. The second point involves the nature of theory as described earlier in Chapter 2. Theories, like factor analysis, are grounded on assumptions—assumptions on which not everyone agrees. Theories are not reality; they are only descriptions of it! And descriptions are very much influenced by the past experience of those who construct them.

be uncorrelated, whereas the latter allows for correlated factors. Cattell chooses the oblique strategy but others advocate the orthogonal procedure. Because of Cattell's preference, his factor analyses permit second-order factors to emerge. In short, the number of factors one comes up with can be directly traced to one's preferences for specific factor-analytic procedures.

Meaningfulness.   Clinicians have long contended that the factors derived from factor analysis seldom seem to correspond very well to the traits derived from clinical studies. Clinical investigations of subjects seem to produce a different structure of personality. This is not to say that factor analysis cannot deal with the individual. What is really being stated is that derived factors are not particularly psychologically meaningful—that they fail to capture the essence of human nature in the same way that other methods do. The derivation of mathematically pure factors is not the same as psychological meaningfulness. Of course, no personality theory ever corresponds exactly with everyone's subjective experience. Some find Freud's ideas to be counterintuitive and others can make little sense of Maslow. The ultimate criterion is that the theory (or factors) be useful. Hall and Lindzey (1978) also note that were Cattell's or Eysenck's traits to correspond exactly with other people's observations, then their work would likely be dismissed as trivial or a mere repetition of what we already know.

Complexity of behaviors.   Identification of factors depends on the idea that two behaviors which vary (increase or decrease) together are related. But this is a fairly simple definition of a relationship. Some behaviors covary under certain circumstances but not under others. Love and hate may have one relationship in a situation where one individual is dependent on another. But in a different circumstance, there may be a different relationship or none at all. Whether factor theories that emphasize traits (which so often seem static in nature) can ultimately deal with this complexity is still an open question.

Classification vs. explanation.   Factor analysis is unquestionably a powerful tool for reducing complex data to their simpler elements. It helps immensely in the classification and categorization of data. To illustrate, a jumble of 1,000 letters scattered over the floor defies description by its very disorganization. But if someone comes along and puts the letters into neat piles according to their destination, we immediately feel better able to deal with the situation. However, although we have classified these letters, we have not explained them or even necessarily defined their basic characteristics. And so it is with factor analysis. For all the reasons discussed thus far, we should be wary of assuming that factor analysis can reveal underlying structure.

The humanist critique.   Many humanistically oriented observers object to the factor-analytic strategy. To them, it defiles the essential human qualities of a person. What emerges is hardly human at all, but rather an uninterpretable mosaic of sterile factors that have no human meaning. Again, however, the real issue would appear to be one of utility rather than any lack of humanistic underpinnings.

RESEARCH ON NEEDS

In this section we shall focus on research and assessment involving several psychogenic needs. As in the last chapter, the names of Murray, McClelland, and Atkinson will figure prominently in our discussion as will needs for achievement, affiliation, and power.

Murray's research legacy

A growing number of personality psychologists have expressed impatience with the currently fashionable style of personality research methods. For example, White (1981) has pointed out that investigators ignore the complexity of personality and too often seem to exhibit little curiosity about personality as it appears in their friends, in themselves, or in everyday life. They correlate, they conjure up complicated experimental situations, and they analyze with great statistical sophistication. Yet they rarely have sustained contact with their subjects. White (1981) referred to this as *"studying personality without looking at it"* (p. 15)!

There are, then, at least two reasons for studying Murray. First, his efforts had a great influence on the development of the field of personality. Second, as noted in Chapter 2 earlier, Murray's methods can provide us with a model so that we can escape the pitfalls of those shallow experimental or correlational methods that take snapshots of people but fail to capture them as lives in progress (Phares and Lamiell, 1977).

Three features of Murray's research and assessment approaches stand out (Hall and Lindzey, 1978). Let us examine them in turn.

Intensive study of individuals.   Murray was a passionate believer in the intensive study of small numbers of normal subjects—an approach that yields large amounts of data on those subjects. Studies of 300 subjects whose responses are tabulated and then averaged are of limited use, he felt. For example, knowing that 75 percent of our subjects respond a given way does not tell us why the other 25 percent responded differently nor is it of much help in predicting and understanding the behavior of any one subject. This is not unlike the criticism leveled by Lamiell (1987) at the experimental method noted earlier in Chapter 2. Essentially, then, Murray sees the road to understanding as being paved with the intensive scrutiny of a few individuals. Of course, this limits the number of subjects that can be studied by a given investigator over a period of time. But the payoff is in terms of greater understanding. Such a strategy, however, is difficult for many to follow since they see their professional advancement as hinging on the production of a large number of publications—the so-called "publish or perish" syndrome.

Murray also contended that our emphasis should be on the intensive study of *normal* subjects. He felt that case analyses of pathological subjects are traditional in psychiatry and clinical psychology. Therefore, similar study of normal populations should prove complementary.

Since we ultimately wish to predict the behavior of individuals in real-life settings, Murray believed that it was illogical to focus our studies exclusively on contrived or laboratory situations. We should include the systematic study of individuals in their "natural habitats."

Finally, he was a pioneer in assembling an interdisciplinary staff to study people. The staff at the Harvard Psychological Clinic, for example, included psychiatrists, psychologists, anthropologists, and others (Hall and Lindzey, 1978).

An application of Murray's general philosophy of research is shown in Box 9-2.

The diagnostic council.   To understand people, we must observe them. Tests and rating scales are important, but the ultimate instrument must be the observer. However, observers are imperfect. They are sometimes biased and at other times not sensitive enough. We must, therefore, do what we can to improve the reliability, precision, and efficiency of human observations. One way of helping us to accomplish this is through a **diagnostic council.** Having several observers study the same individual is a means of overcoming the limitations of any one observer. A council involves several observers who meet for a discussion of their separate views, interpretations, and conclusions about a given subject. The group puts together all their interpretations and comes to a consensus about the final product or conclusion. This approach is similar to that used in clinical settings where decisions about a patient's diagnosis or course of treatment are arrived at.

The TAT.   In both Chapters 2 and 5, the **Thematic Apperception Test (TAT)** was briefly described. As noted earlier, this test, a so-called projective device, was published by Christiana Morgan and Murray in 1935. The test was developed at the Harvard Psychological Clinic as part of a long-term study of fifty-one college-age men. It was used along with other tests, interviews, and autobiographies to formulate hypotheses about the nature of subjects' personalities. Murray (1951) described several propositions that should guide interpretations of the imaginative fantasies or stories produced by subjects in response to the TAT pictures. Siipola (1984) has summarized them as follows:

■ The TAT reveals drives, emotions, complexes, and conflicts of the personality.

■ The subject will identify with the main character in the TAT story and project his or her own perceptions, motives, feelings, and thoughts onto that character.

■ In describing other figures in the stories, the subject may well reveal attitudes toward significant others (e.g., parents, siblings, spouse, etc.)

■ Not all material produced is very significant. However, significance tends to be suggested by the following elements:

> Repetition
> Uniqueness
> Self-involvement
> Symbolic significance
> Interrelatedness (one theme relates to or is consistent with another)

Box 9-2
ASSESSMENT IN WAR

Murray's chief message was the intensive, multidimensional study of people as the best way to understand them. Test them, observe them, put them in controlled experimental settings, and then analyze their behavior, using an interdisciplinary group of experts. Would it also work in pressure-packed settings where the purposes involved national defense?

Murray was an integral part of the assessment program operated by the Office of Strategic Services (OSS) in the early 1940s. This was the World War II forerunner of the present CIA. The purpose of the program was to evaluate candidates for espionage and intelligence missions overseas (often behind enemy lines).

The strategy was to put the candidates through an intensive, three-day series of screening activities. The goal was the identification of intelligent, resourceful individuals who could cope with enormously stressful situations and thereby successfully carry out a variety of dangerous missions.

The candidates were from all walks of life. Some were civilians; some were military (both officers and enlisted men). Their identities were complete secrets. Everyone wore the same clothing without any external markings or insignia that could reveal a person's status or rank. Nor were any personal belongings permitted that might suggest something about the candidate (no letters, no pictures, no newspapers, etc.). All of this was carried out in a large estate outside Washington, D.C.

Many traditional psychological tests (ability, intelligence, personality) were administered along with many interviews. Life histories and medical dossiers were likewise available. The candidates were intensively observed in groups and individually. Although they were admonished not to reveal their true identities, OSS staff often attempted to trick or fool them into doing so. Sometimes informants or "stooges" were used to mislead them. But remember: this was wartime and it was vital that clever, stress-resistant personnel be discovered. A variety of situational tests were also employed to evaluate candidates' reactions to stressful demands, to gauge their spontaneous problem-solving aptitudes, and to observe their leadership potential. Here is Anastasi's (1976) description of just such an OSS task:

> [In] the Construction Test . . . a 5-foot cube had to be assembled from wooden poles, blocks, and pegs. The examinee was informed that, since it was impossible for one man to complete the task within the 10 minutes allotted for it, he would be given two helpers. Actually, the helpers were psychologists who played prearranged roles. One followed a policy of inertia and passive resistance; the other obstructed the work by making impractical suggestions, asking irrelevant and often embarrassing questions, and needling the candidate with ridicule and criticism. So well did the helpers succeed in frustrating the candidates that the construction was never completed in the history of the assessment program. (p. 596)

Although the demands of war did not permit many good opportunities for the strict validation of the OSS assessment program, it did illustrate what is possible with an intensive, multi-pronged approach like Murray's (OSS Assessment Staff, 1948).

Murray also felt that, while TAT stories can predict the subject's overt behavior on occasion, they do not always do so by any means. The relationship depends on the degree of conflict over the behavior. For example, sexual themes might not be indicative of the subject's actual behavior unless no conflict or guilt over sexuality is exhibited by that same subject.

The n Achievement tradition

The same basic procedures are used for measuring *n* Achievement, *n* Affiliation, and *n* Power. Furthermore, those procedures have hardly changed at all since the first studies were done nearly forty years ago (McClelland et al., 1953). A TAT-like method is utilized. Why the TAT approach? It was McClelland's contention that while other measures such as questionnaires, ratings, and behavioral observations often show good reliability, they fail to satisfy other criteria of a good measure. For example, they do not really reflect the motive in question or else they sometimes reflect other motives (such as acquiescence). The use of a fantasy measure like the TAT continued the psychodynamic tradition. Such a tradition views our deeper, more pervasive motives as best able to find expression in response to ambiguous stimuli that prompt them but fail to alert our more consciously directed motives and purposes.

Procedure. Some four to six TAT-like pictures (see Figure 9-2 for an *n* Achievement picture) are administered (often in a group setting). Subjects are given about four

FIGURE 9-2 Typical picture for eliciting achievement themes.
(After McClelland et al., 1953)

mınutes to write a story in response to each picture. They are instructed to answer the following questions in their stories: What is happening? What led up to this situation? What is being thought? What will happen? Each story is then judged for the presence of achievement imagery. For example, stories that describe unique accomplishments, the desire to be successful, competition with a standard of excellence, or the like would qualify (see Table 9-6). Take, for example, the following story:

> Here is a student preparing for an upcoming exam. He is studying hard because on the last exam he got a B but wants to do better this time. He is thinking about what questions will be on the exam. He looks like he will do well and eventually after graduation will get a good job somewhere.

All stories are examined and then scored according to a complex scoring manual that contains a variety of subcategories such as affect ("He feels depressed"), instrumental activity ("He will study carefully"), and obstacles to achievement ("His father hasn't the money to send him to school"). With only modest training, judges can readily learn to produce reliable scores.

The major criticism of the foregoing TAT methods has always revolved around issues of test-retest reliability (Entwisle, 1972). As noted earlier in Chapter 2, McClelland (1980) counters with the argument that because fantasy measures encourage creativity they inevitably promote a degree of unreliability. Self-reports, although very reliable, sacrifice validity, he says, on the altar of that very reliability.

Other measures.

Despite the presumed limitations of the traditional fantasy measures of *n* Achievement, few serious alternatives have arisen. Two attempts to develop self-report measures are illustrated by the work of Mehrabian (1968) and Helmreich and Spence (1978). Typical items are:

- I look more to the future than to the past or present (T or F)
- I enjoy situations that allow me to use my skills (T or F)

The problem, of course, is that fantasy measures and self-report measures rarely correlate. McClelland, Koestner, and Weinberger (1989) suggest that this is because the two kinds of measures are tapping into different processes. They hypothesize that fantasy measures tap motives that have been built on early affective experiences, before the development of language. Self-report measures reflect motives that developed later, after concepts of self, others, and what is valuable have been learned.

Validating the TAT procedure.

Any *n* Achievement research that employs the traditional fantasy measures addresses issues of validity to some extent or other. But early efforts focused *specifically* on the validity of the TAT approach. For example, McClelland, Clark, Roby, and Atkinson (1949) asked 200 male college students to write five-minute stories in response to several slides. However, prior to writing the stories, the subjects were administered preliminary tests under one of two conditions. The first was a relaxed condition in which the tests were described casually as new ones being tried out. There was *no* emphasis on achievement whatsoever. The

TABLE 9-6 Typical stories produced in response to achievement, affiliation, and power cues

Achievement Arousal	Affiliation Arousal	Power Arousal
George is an engineer who *(need, +1)* wants to win a competition in which the man with *(achievement imagery: standard of excellence, +1)* the most practicable drawing will be awarded the contract to build a bridge. He is taking a moment to think *(goal anticipation, +1)* how happy he will be if he wins. He has been *(block, world, +1)* baffled by how to make such a long span strong, but remembers *(instrumental act, +1)* to specify a new steel alloy of great strength, submits his entry, but does not win and *(goal state, negative, +1)* is very unhappy.	George is an engineer who is working late. He is *(affiliation imgery, +1)* worried that his wife will be annoyed with him for neglecting her. *(block, world, +1)* She has been *objecting* that he cares more about his work than his wife and family. *(block, personal, +1)* He seems *unable to satisfy* both his boss and his wife, *(need, +1)* but he *loves her* very much, and *(instrumental act, +1)* will do his best to *finish up fast* and get home to her.	This is Georgiadis, a *(prestige of actor, +1)* famous architect, who *(need, +1)* wants to win a competition which will establish who is *(power imagery, +1)* the best architect in the world. His chief *rival*, Bulakovsky, *(block, world, +1)* has *stolen* his best ideas, and he is dreadfully afraid of the *(goal anticipation, negative, +1)* disgrace of losing. But he comes up with *(instrumental act, +1)* a great new idea, which absolutely *(powerful effect, +1)* bowls the judges over, and he wins!
Thema +1, Total *n* Achievement score = +7.	Thema +1, Total *n* Affiliation score = +6.	Total *n* Power score = +7.

From *Human Motivation* by David McClelland (Glenview, IL: Scott, Foresman and Company). Copyright © 1985 by David McClelland. Reprinted by permission.

other condition involved failure—an outcome designed to arouse achievement motivation. Here, the preliminary test was introduced as an IQ-type test and the levels of performance required for success were set so high that all subjects did poorly. Following all of this, the fantasy measures of *n* Achievement were administered.

When a single *n* Achievement score was computed for each subject, a clear effect of motivation was evident. Thus, when *n* Achievement was aroused through failure, the ensuing TAT performance yielded higher achievement scores as compared to scores following the relaxed condition. Results from these and other studies support the notion that TAT-like pictures can be used successfully to measure individual differences in *n* Achievement.

Enhancing achievement striving. Many relationships between *n* Achievement and behavior have been observed over the years (McClelland, 1985). Several of them are noted in Box 9-3. Our society tends to value and encourage such behaviors. Once the measurement technology and correlates of *n* Achievement were settled, attention turned to ways of enhancing achievement striving in those who were, relatively

Box 9-3
THE CASE OF RICHARD NIXON

It is one thing to study achievement in college sophomores. But what about the lives of famous people? Can our methods be applied to the lives of known achievers and can we learn anything about achievement from them? Winter and Carlson (1988) tried to answer these questions by combining the methods of content analysis and a psychobiographical approach to the study of *n* Achievement in Richard Nixon. They scored his 1969 first inaugural address for *n* Achievement themes. The resulting picture revealed him to be high in *n* Achievement. A subsequent analysis of his 1973 inaugural address was also replete with achievement elements thus indicating a certain degree of stability in the motive.

Can we be sure, however, that speeches really are valid indicators of Nixon's *n* Achievement strivings? The authors reviewed a variety of studies that collectively outlined the major behavioral correlates and features of the achievement motive (e.g., McClelland, 1985). A few of these features are:

High aspirations
Persistence
Feedback to modify performance
Innovativeness
Entrepreneurial activity
Parental high standards
Mother warmer than father
Occupational success
Success in school
Ability to delay gratification
Taking responsibility for one's performance

Photograph UPI/Bettmann Newsphotos.

speaking, unmotivated. They also looked for ways of counteracting others' fear of failure. Several research programs have been mounted to do this and we can take a look at two examples.

Kolb (1965) was interested in raising the level of academic achievement in a group of underachieving high school boys. In a six-week summer school session, boys with IQs above 120 but grades below C participated in a program designed to teach them the characteristics of people high in *n* Achievement. The training program included: the use of positive role models; development of positive expectancies about the outcome of participating in the program; learning and practicing the *n* Achievement scoring system; participation in games that simulated achievement-related situations. The

Next, Winter and Carlson analyzed Nixon's everyday behavior as reported in his memoirs and in the memoirs of six former aides. By this process, they were able to identify twenty-eight separate behavioral correlates of the achievement motive. The investigators found positive or confirming evidence for twenty-three correlates, negative or nonconfirming evidence for three correlates, and inconclusive evidence for two. Here are a few examples of those correlates:

Feedback: Nixon's tendency to critique everything; even to the point of analyzing the previous night's state dinner.

Mother warmer than father: Nixon's description of his mother as radiating warmth and love coupled with his description of his father as having a temper.

Parental high standards: Again, Nixon's description of how his father constantly impressed upon him his son's good fortune in being able to go to school.

Persistence: His political record of losing, then winning, then losing again, and sticking it out until he absolutely had to quit.

High aspirations: Others who knew him well saw him as possessed of overwhelming ambition.

The relationships uncovered in this study, then, would seem to confirm the utility of using methods of psychobiography and content analysis to study n Achievement.

boys also received ordinary summer school classroom training. A matched control group, however, received only the ordinary classroom training without the achievement training.

The basic results indicated a rise in n Achievement scores for the experimental group over the six weeks as compared to the control group. The critical outcome, however, was subsequent grades. Interestingly, after six months there were no differences between experimental and control groups as regards improvement in school grades. But after a year and a half, the grade point average of the experimental group had improved significantly over that of the control group.

A second example is work by Dweck (1975). She studied twelve students (ages eight to thirteen) who had been identified by school officials as highly failure-oriented. The goal of this research was to determine whether alterations in the way the students looked at failure would improve their reactions to failure in problem-solving situations. She taught them in a series of training sessions that failure in these situations was due to lack of effort. In contrast, the more popular method has always been a behavior modification approach that entails providing success only. Therefore, a control group was included in this study—a group that experienced just the customary success that had been thought effective in overcoming failure expectations. Sure enough, as Dweck hypothesized, teaching children to take responsibility for failure and to attribute it to poor effort resulted in smaller decrements in performance following failure (see Figure 9-3). Thus, it would appear that part of the "achievement syndrome" is taking responsibility for our behavior and teaching people to do this enables them to better resist the effects of failure.

SUMMARY EVALUATION

The dispositional approach, whether it emphasizes traits or needs, has exerted a broad and profound influence on all aspects of the field of personality. Indeed, as observed earlier, for many, dispositions are *the* essence of personality. In Part III of this book, topics such as intelligence, anxiety, and perceived control will be discussed. These, and many other personality characteristics, have strong ties to the dispositional tradition in research and measurement. In the next few pages we will examine, in turn, the strengths and weaknesses of the dispositional perspective.

Strengths

Since the dispositional perspective is so different depending upon whether Allport or Cattell, Murray or McClelland is the subject of discussion, it will be simpler to evaluate these theorists separately. Let us begin with Allport.

The unique organism.   Without doubt, those who find uniqueness and individuality the supreme human attributes will point to Allport's theory with pride. They see in it recognition and confirmation of the human essence. Other theorists often seem to make all humans prisoners of the normal curve. But Allport did not. Indeed, to describe adequately the unique individual, he advocated a whole series of idiographic methods. This philosophy of research attracted admirers many years ago and, with recent charges about the sterility of nomothetic methods, it may be resurrected and rehabilitated. Allport's studies of expressive behavior also demonstrated methods of investigating an important facet of human behavior that was in tune with his focus on the individual. Finally, the humanistic theme also emerged in his belief that human beings are oriented toward the future and that no simple deterministic analysis of the past will suffice. Although the concept of functional autonomy has many critics, it, too, proclaims Allport's faith that the key to understanding does not always reside in the past.

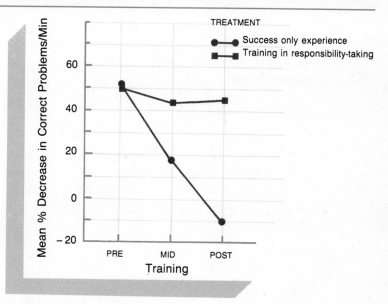

FIGURE 9-3   Mean percentage of decrement in correct problems following failure.

Adapted from "The Role of Expectation and Attribution in the Alleviation of Learned Helplessness" by Carol Dweck, *Journal of Personality and Social Psychology*, Vol. 31, No. 4, April 1975. Copyright © 1975 by the American Psychological Association. Reprinted by permission of the author.

The rational person.   Allport repeatedly asserted that human personality cannot be understood by the exclusive study of neurotics. As a result, the view he offered is one of the rational person. This emphasis had at least two important consequences. First, it gave further support and encouragement to the ego analysts, who were trying to develop and define a role for the ego that encompassed more than the struggle to reconcile warring factions of the mind. Allport's views helped define an ego that reasoned, solved problems, and thought ahead. Second, if people are essentially rational beings who are not overwhelmed by unconscious processes, can they not be assessed by reasonably direct methods? Allport's answer was yes, and he developed a strong preference for self-report questionnaires, the analysis of personal documents, and other surface measures. Indeed his Study of Values is an important device still widely used today.

As we turn to Cattell, a wholly different set of strengths emerges. Some of them would not, of course, be regarded by Allport as strengths at all.

The tough-minded approach.   If there is any message at all in Cattell's work, it must be that the riddle of personality will be solved through hard work and the empirical analysis of objective data. The magnitude of Cattell's work is awe-inspiring. The hundreds of publications and thousands of separate factor analyses attest to his convictions. If nothing else, the sheer amount of data collection and analysis, and the accompanying theoretical structure to support the results, are achievements of the first magnitude (Wiggins, 1984).

Factor analysis.   It is evident that with Cattell, everything stands or falls on his factor-analytic methods. Indeed, the relationship here between data and method is so intimate that one can scarcely be separated from the other. Many criticisms can be lodged against factor analysis, as we saw a bit earlier. Nevertheless, this methodology stands as an extremely important technique for refining and ordering data. In fact, one need not be an ordained trait theorist to make use of the technique. As a method of multivariate analysis, it lends itself to the complex study of many simultaneously interacting variables.

The very complexity of personality almost ensures that factor-analytic procedures will be enormously useful in reducing data to understandable proportions. Whether factor analysis can tell us all we need to know about personality is another question. For those who prefer an intuitive approach that reaches into the clinical arena for its evidence, factor analysis seems more like a curse than a technique. However, this response seems to signify a lack of understanding or a phobia not unlike a fear of arithmetic or statistics. Empirical vigor and faith in quantitative methods should hardly be regarded as vices. Of course, by the same token, they do not in themselves guarantee that useful products will emerge.

Cattell has been instrumental in developing and elaborating factor-analytic techniques for studying the relative contributions and hereditary influences. Again, although not everyone agrees with his conclusions in this sphere, he has demonstrated a set of methods that can be very helpful.

The central core.   Without doubt, both Cattell and Allport have taken aim at what many consider to be the central core of personality study—the identification and classification of the stable, enduring dispositions that make the organism run. Each has sought to do it in a different way but, in one sense, their efforts come closer to the heart of personality than do those of other personality theorists. For this, they are to be applauded. Whether those efforts are sufficient can better be gauged as we turn to some of the weaknesses inherent in their work.

As we switch next to Murray and McClelland, however, the focus shifts from traits to needs.

The Murray tradition.   As we turn to Murray, it is altogether appropriate to use such words as *tradition* or *legacy*. Few active personality investigators would think of themselves as belonging to a "Murray school of personality." Yet almost all of them have been the beneficiaries of his work. Anyone who uses projective devices, who thinks of unconscious motivation or psychodynamic factors as important determinants of behavior, or who believes that a classification or taxonomy of personality characteristics is useful should be grateful to Murray. He was a staunch advocate of needs as the great motivators of human behavior. But his use of the concept of press lent an interactionist flavor to his views that is entirely in step with current philosophies.

Finally, all who feel that the heavy experimental or laboratory emphasis that has characterized personality research of the past thirty-five years or so has now reached the limits of its utility will find solace in Murray's orientation. His insistence on sustained contacts with subjects and his interdisciplinary posture provide a style that most of us would do well to emulate.

n *Achievement*.   This approach has profited greatly from the Murray legacy. McClelland and his colleagues have shown that the projective methodology can be applied fruitfully to the measurement of needs. A host of clever studies involving achievement, affiliation, and power have been the result. With the help of Atkinson's work, a theory of *n* Achievement has emerged and been widely examined. Innovative applications of the *n* Achievement theory and measurement technology have occurred in such diverse areas as understanding economic growth and enhancing *n* Achievement.

Weaknesses

A number of fairly specific weaknesses are also evident in the dispositional perspectives.

Conceptual ambiguity.   The most obvious criticism that can be made about Allport is his conceptual imprecision and ambiguity. For example, it is hard to know exactly what is encompassed by the proprium. In other instances, concepts are defined but exactly how they operate is quite unclear. A case in point is functional autonomy. Exactly how does it take place and why? Is every motive functionally autonomous? If not, which are and which are not, and why?

One outgrowth of this ambiguity may well be the paucity of research directly stemming from Allport's theory. Although the aura of Allport has pervaded the field of personality for some time, little specific research can be said to have been stimulated by the theory or to have demonstrated its utility. Quite simply, it is difficult to do empirical research within the framework of Allport's theory. The formal adequacy of the theory, then, leaves much to be desired.

Similar statements can be made about Murray. His theory is not stated in a form that readily encourages research. It is, in fact, hard to generate testable hypotheses from it. Sometimes it seems that his system's breadth and complexity gives it an unfocused aura. In this vein, Hall and Lindzey (1978) have suggested also that some critics feel there "is too much of the poet and too little of the positivist in his make-up" (p. 238).

Although *n* Achievement theory has been articulated in a relatively precise manner, how widely the need operates across individuals' lives is still unclear. This is true in part, perhaps, because the Atkinson-McClelland theory is not a comprehensive behavioral theory. Therefore, the limits of its applicability are uncertain.

The nomothetic critique.   From one point of view, Allport's idiographic thrust is a crowning virtue. But some believe that what is unique cannot be accounted for by conventional scientific principles. What is more, the study of so-called unique individuals can never produce results that will generate principles by which we can under-stand behavior in general. Thus, it is said, Allport's plea for the study of individuality can lead at best to pointless ruminations about individual cases that have no generalizability to others. Interestingly, as noted earlier, Allport produced little idiographic research himself aside from the Jenny case. What he asked others to do, he did not much do himself.

Development.   Although staunchly advocating the role of traits, Allport was vague about their development. The same is true about his speculations on the growth of the self. We are left with a cross section of time—a picture of traits without antecedents. This seems to limit the potential for understanding traits as well as our ability to change them.

Cattell, Murray, and McClelland all are likewise uneven in their treatment of developmental issues. While there is some work in the Murray-McClelland frameworks that suggests some specific developmental correlates of needs, this is hardly a systematic body of work. Murray, for example, seems much more interested in classifying motives than in articulating the conditions under which they develop.

A similar point arises in Allport's treatment of abnormal behavior. Mostly, he seemed to avoid dealing with abnormal phenomena by asserting that abnormal behavior is fundamentally different from normal behavior. Yet most clinical psychologists regard neurotic behavior as only quantitatively different from normal behavior—not qualitatively different. Allport seemed to say that neurotic behavior is of little importance. This gives the theory an appearance of narrowness.

At this juncture, a few specific weaknesses relevant to Cattell's work will be enumerated. Following that will be a discussion of some points that apply to trait theory in general.

Data sources.   Cattell has often been criticized for the indiscriminate inclusion of sources that produce either trivial or unrepresentative data. He sometimes uses tests that have little demonstrable validity. Unless the tests and observations employed are valid and representative, no amount of sophisticated factor analysis is going to rectify matters. Some have even accused Cattell of using a shotgun approach—of employing numerous measures with the hope that a few will hit their mark. As a result, there is a lot of noise in Cattell's research; factors emerge that have little psychological meaning. Rather than carefully selecting tests beforehand on the basis of their presumed connection with some set of factors, Cattell sometimes seems to pull the trigger and only later tries to decipher the holes in the target.

Like Allport, Cattell relies heavily on self-report questionnaires. This can lead to a situation where the effects of subjects' needs to present a positive image or respond in a socially desirable fashion take precedence over reality.

As for Murray and McClelland, their heavy reliance on the TAT method has led to sharp criticism from some quarters. The method, they say, is unreliable and, therefore, it becomes virtually impossible to determine how needs present themselves over the lifespan of a person.

Fact vs. theory. Although it is true that Cattell has collected an enormous amount of data, his speculations sometimes seem to outrun it. Because his interests have been so widespread, he has investigated many diverse areas. He sometimes seems to leave a research area before he has nailed down all the relationships necessary to support his theoretical generalizations. This can give his writings a dogmatic ring, particularly in those cases where the data are sparse or the measures rather superficial.

Factor analysis. The sharpest criticisms of Cattell's theory and research are usually reserved for his factor-analytic methods. Since a fairly lengthy critique of factor analysis was presented earlier, there is no need to repeat it here.

A general critique

Despite what appears to be a complex list of traits or motives identified by Allport, Cattell, or Murray, trait theory is at root a rather simple approach. This simplicity reveals itself in several ways and leads to a number of problems.

Borrowing tendency. As if in tacit recognition of this simplicity, both Allport and Cattell have frequently borrowed concepts from other disciplines and theories. An obvious example is when Allport turns to biology to describe and elaborate his theory. Cattell seems equally unable to handle the complexity of human behavior without turning to psychoanalysis. Like raisins in a pudding, his traits often seem suspended in a psychoanalytic context. A similar comment could be made about Murray. Also, the theory of achievement motivation is similar in several respects to Miller's conflict theory (see Chapter 10) as well as having elements in common with decision theory and social learning theory (see Chapter 12).

Lack of theory. While the term *theory* has been used repeatedly throughout these past two chapters, many would claim that as regards traits and dispositions there is actually very little theory at all. At most, they contend, it appears to be a series of traits arranged in hierarchical order. But there is no larger theoretical framework to account for the acquisition and change of traits or dispositions. Nor is there any solid basis on which to predict the behavior of a single individual in a specific situation. Likewise, it is unclear when a given disposition will prompt a response in tune with that trait and when a situational stimulus will lead the person to respond differently from what we would expect from the trait.

Situations vs. traits. Trait theory traditionally relies so much on generalized traits that it has difficulty incorporating the situational pressures so often implicated in behavior. While Cattell does propose in his specification equation that traits be weighted for their relevance to the specific situation, and that situational roles and temporary states of the organism be considered, this is not a carefully worked out blueprint. He seems to have devoted his energies more toward the identification of traits than toward the exact manner in which traits interact with situational variables to produce a response.

Static nature.   A dispositional approach, whether by design or not, often paints a static picture of the organism. It is almost like stepping on the scales, inserting a coin, and then receiving a card on which is printed, "You are the kind of person who is . . . ." Similar to a movie frame frozen in time, there is no indication of how the person got there or where he or she is going. Dispositional approaches do not really suggest that individuals never change or that behavior never varies from situation to situation. Still, the approach is nearly mute when it comes to questions about development, change, and therapeutic intervention.

Description vs. classification.   It has been noted before that trait theories often seem to come perilously close to explaining by classifying or naming. This is true whether we are considering the idiography of Allport or the factor analysis of Cattell. To say that a man behaves intelligently because he is intelligent or that a woman trusts others because she is trusting seems to be more descriptive than explanatory. This is especially true when our inferences about the existence of a trait are based essentially on the same behaviors we are trying to predict. Suppose we observe someone who often attends art exhibits, subscribes to several art magazines, seeks out friends who have aesthetic preferences, and takes night courses on art appreciation. If from this we infer the presence of an aesthetic trait and then use that trait to account for the foregoing behavior, we are engaging in circular reasoning. This is not unlike the circularity observed earlier that can arise out of phenomenological inferences about someone's inner experiences.

The dangers of explaining by naming, confusing description with classification, and circular reasoning are not exclusive to trait approaches by any means. Their potential is inherent in every theoretical approach. They do, however, seem to pose a specific problem in trait theory.

SUMMARY

■   The idiographic approach advocated by Allport is illustrated by his *Letters from Jenny.* The commonsense analysis of these letters allowed him to infer eight traits that described her personality.

■   Another illustration of Allport's concern with uniqueness is shown by his studies of expressive behavior, which he saw as a clue to central dispositions. This was, however, a nomothetic series of studies.

■   Allport's best known assessment device is the Study of Values, which measures value orientations along six dimensions.

■   Cattell's research exemplifies the multivariate strategy, that is, using many measures on the same person. He prefers this to the bivariate approach, which focuses on one variable at a time.

▪ Because of Cattell's heavy reliance on factor analysis, this method was presented in some detail. The procedure was described in terms of a specific problem entailing the administration of a large number of tests. The ensuing steps involved generating a table of intercorrelations among the tests (the correlation matrix), determining the factor loadings, and naming the factors that emerged.

▪ Cattell uses three data sources: life records (L-data), self-rating questionnaires (Q-data), and objective tests (T-data).

▪ Cattell has empirically derived sixteen source traits through factor analysis. The 16 P-F Questionnaire was devised as a means of eliciting self-ratings from subjects relevant to these sixteen source traits.

▪ Cattell has developed a statistical tool, called multiple abstract variance analysis, which purports to assess the relative contributions of heredity and environment to a given trait.

▪ In an attempt to come to grips with the change and instability that are part of the human behavioral scene, Cattell has described several statistical techniques. The P-technique analyzes the stability and instability of one person's behavior over time. The differential R-technique is a method for factoring changes in measures over time. The Q-technique is a means of identifying people's roles in various situations.

▪ The research of another noted trait theorist, Eysenck, was briefly described, and his method of criterion analysis illustrated. This is a method which dictates that we start with a hypothesis about the nature of personality structure. Measures are then selected in accordance with this hypothesis.

▪ Since factor analysis is so much a part of many trait approaches, a special critique of this method was offered. The following aspects were examined: the adequacy of data sources, the internal debate among factor analysts as to which specific procedures are appropriate, questions about the psychological meaningfulness of factors, whether factor analysis can deal with the complexity of human behavior, the issue of whether factor analysis leads to anything more than classification or description, and the humanist critique.

▪ Relying heavily on needs as his dispositional focus, Murray's legacy may largely be his intensive study of individuals, the use of a diagnostic council, and the development of the TAT method.

▪ The *n* Achievement tradition is epitomized by the work of McClelland and Atkinson. McClelland developed a standardized TAT method for identifying *n* Achievement that has been validated in a variety of ways. As a specific example of research, several studies of techniques of enhancing achievement strivings were noted.

■ Allport's particular contributions seem to be his emphasis on the unique organism and his view of the individual as a rational being.

■ Cattell brings to personality theory and research a method that is tough-minded, objective, and based on research. His use and development of factor-analytic techniques to identify and describe trait structure are notable achievements.

■ Murray's greatest contribution has been his legacy noted just above.

■ The *n* Achievement tradition benefited from Murray's work and provided a model projective method of measuring motives. It also has produced a theory of achievement along with a series of innovative applications.

■ All conceptual approaches suffer from weaknesses, and trait theory is no exception. In the case of Allport, there is a great deal of conceptual ambiguity in his writings. For some, his advocacy of idiographic methods means that he abandoned the scientific method. Murray's approach also suffers from conceptual vagueness. The *n* Achievement tradition has difficulty showing the generality of the needs studied. Allport, Cattell, Murray, and McClelland all have relatively little to say about development.

■ In the case of Cattell, questions have been raised about the legitimacy of his data sources, his tendency to sometimes go beyond his data in developing theoretical notions, and his reliance on factor analysis. Similarly, McClelland has been criticized for his heavy reliance on the TAT.

■ The chapter closed with a general critique of trait and dispositional theories. Several points were made. These included theorists' tendencies to borrow concepts from other theoretical frameworks, questions as to whether these dispositional or trait theories are really theories at all, the inability of these theories to adequately accommodate situational factors in the prediction of behavior, a picture of the human being that is essentially static, and a tendency to describe and classify without really explaining.

CHAPTER 10

THE BEHAVIORAL TRADITION

For many people, the last two chapters epitomize personality study: the identification and elaboration of the internal characteristics that guide human behavior. Indeed, up to this point in the book the focus has been mainly on what goes on inside the organism. Whether it be the instincts and mental apparatus described by Freud, the growth potential postulated by Rogers, or the traits churned out by Cattell, personality has taken on a decidedly "within the organism" look. Of course, people like Adler discussed family organization, Rogers enumerated some of the conditions under which self-esteem arises, and Cattell noted that traits must be weighted in terms of their situational relevance. Yet one can hardly escape the impression that for all these theorists, the real action was taking place underneath the skin.

It is almost as if the structure of personality was so much on everyone's mind that in their rush to describe that structure they too often looked past the organism's overt behavior and the situational conditions with which it was associated. Of course, when we do look closely at behavior, we cannot fail to find evidence for its stability over both time and situations. But equally impressive is the way it can change and grow over time and the manner in which it can vary across situations. In fact, as we focus increasingly on what the person does, we seem to be considering personality less and less. We are suddenly in the realm of learning and the conditions that facilitate or retard its development. If we arrange conditions so that a child learns to be anxious, we can, by applying the same principles, rearrange conditions so that they will promote relaxation instead. What has happened here is that our interest begins to shift from the internal elements of personality that mark each person as different to the processes by which learning occurs. And the principles by which these processes operate are the same for everyone.

The implications of this shift in focus are profound. In the present chapter, some of these behavioral learning developments will be traced and their implications for a psychology of personality elaborated.

THE BEGINNINGS

The study of learning began in the laboratory. If we date the start of the saga with Ivan Pavlov, we find that not only was learning investigated in a laboratory setting but also that animals were the chief subjects. Pavlov, a Russian physiologist, was studying the digestive process. He observed, almost casually, that dogs would begin to salivate even before food was placed in their mouths. This observation led eventually to the enunciation of classical conditioning. **Classical conditioning** is the process whereby a previously neutral stimulus (e.g., a bell) becomes conditioned or associated with an unconditioned stimulus (one that naturally evokes a response such as salivation, e.g., food). Of course, the conditioned stimulus (bell, in this case) must be associated repeatedly with the unconditioned stimulus (food), and the interval between pairings of the stimuli must not be excessive. If, in the example used here, the bell fails over a series of trials to be followed by the food, the association may be broken and salivation in response to the bell will cease. Recently, however, Rescorla (1988) has argued that such descriptions of conditioning are inadequate. Instead, he says, classical conditioning should refer to the learning of relations among events so as to allow the organism to represent its environment.

A second major figure in the rise of learning theory was John B. Watson. In fact Watson is usually regarded as the founder of behaviorism. He contended that the only appropriate subject for psychology was behavior. After all, it is readily observable— open for all to see. In contrast, events transpiring inside the head are not. Thoughts, wishes, or expectancies are private; they can only be inferred from behavior. Therefore, if we are going to build a science of psychology, we must commit ourselves to the study of behavior rather than inferred states of consciousness (J. B. Watson, 1919).

For Watson, the great shaper of behavior was the environment. Our behavior, he asserted, is determined by the associations we learn to make between stimuli and outcomes. To emphasize this point, he made the following oft-quoted and rather exuberant remarks (which even he regarded as a bit of an exaggeration):

> Give me a dozen healthy infants, well-formed, and my own specified world to bring them up in, and I'll guarantee to take any one at random and train him to become any type of specialist I might select—doctor, lawyer, artist, merchant-chief, and, yes, even beggar-man and thief, regardless of his talents, penchants, tendencies, activities, vocations, and race of his ancestors. (J. B. Watson, 1930, p. 65)

Perhaps the best-known study conducted by Watson is the laboratory research on Little Albert and the white rat (Watson and Rayner, 1920). The study was an illustration of the conditioning of an emotional reaction, and it purported to demonstrate how a neurosis can develop in a child. In the Pavlovian tradition of conditioning, Little Albert was given a white rat to play with. But each time the rat was present, a loud noise was simultaneously introduced. After several such trials, the white rat (previously a neutral stimulus) brought forth in Albert a very strong fear response that generalized to similar furry objects. This experiment is, upon closer examination, not as convincing as it might first appear (B. Harris, 1979). But it seems to get better with the retelling. As a result, it has become to be *the* classic example of the behaviorist position rather than a tentative conclusion based on a pilot study, as it should be (Samelson, 1980).

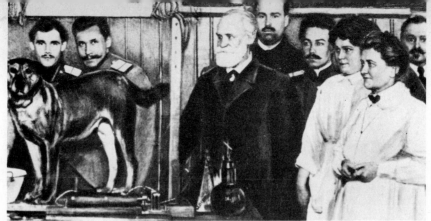

Ivan Pavlov, a pioneer in the study of learning, investigated classical conditioning in dogs. Photograph Bettmann Archive.

It might be added that Mary Cover Jones (1924) demonstrated that learned fears such as the foregoing can be removed. Peter, a three-year-old boy, was afraid of rabbits, rats, and the like. To erase the fear, Jones moved a caged rabbit closer and closer as Peter was eating. The previously feared object thus became associated with the pleasant experiences of eating, and after a few months Peter's fear of rabbits disappeared. Of course, one must make sure that conditioning does not flow in the opposite direction. That is, if Peter's fear of the rabbit had been very intense, he might have developed negative responses to the food. In any event, Jones's work was an early precursor of systematic desensitization, a widely used therapeutic technique which will be described in the next chapter.

The next developments on the behavioral learning scene arrived with the work of Edward L. Thorndike. While Pavlov and Watson were busy in their laboratories, Thorndike was doing the research that resulted in his formulation of the "law of effect" (Thorndike, 1905). In essence, this law stated that when a specific stimulus precedes a specific response and that response is, in turn, followed by a positive outcome, the bond between that stimulus and that response will be strengthened. When the response is followed by a negative outcome, the bond will be weakened. A simple notion, yes, but one that has far-reaching consequences. Thorndike's work solidified the status of learning in psychology and increased the emphasis on objective definitions and procedures. After all, rewards and punishments and the internal states they produce are defined solely in operational terms. For example, a satisfying goal is one that induces movement in the organism toward it; an unpleasant goal is one that causes movement away from it. The prediction of behavior is possible through an understanding of the laws of learning, and the role of mediating traits or egos is superfluous.

The final figure in this brief historical sketch is that of Clark L. Hull. By and large, his approach is now mainly of historical interest. But beginning in 1930 and for the next thirty years or so, his learning theory was a major force in psychology—perhaps the most important one. His *Principles of Behavior,* published in 1943, stated what became the foremost example of a mathematical-deductive theory in psychology. It was a rigorous, systematic presentation of the conditions leading to the formation of habits. **Habits** are stimulus-response associations that occur as the result of rewards. This was an **instrumental conditioning** theory. That is, the events (rewards and punishments) following a response were the critical elements affecting the subsequent likeli-

John Dollard

Because of their collaborative work on learning and imitation, John Dollard and Neal Miller have become inextricably linked. Dollard was born in 1900 in Menasha, Wisconsin, and died in 1980. His undergraduate work was done at the University of Wisconsin, and he received his Ph.D. in sociology from the University of Chicago in 1931. Neal Miller was born in 1909 in Milwaukee, Wisconsin. He attended the University of Washington and was awarded the Ph.D. in psychology in 1935 from Yale University.

Dollard became an assistant professor of anthropology at Yale University in 1931. A year later he joined the Institute of Human Relations at Yale as an assistant professor of sociology. He maintained his affiliation with Yale and the Institute until his retirement in 1969. Miller was appointed to the same Institute at Yale in 1936. During World War II, Miller directed an Army Air Force research project. He rejoined Yale in 1946 and in 1952 became the James Rowland Angell Professor of Psychology. In 1966 he moved from Yale to Rockefeller University as professor of psychology and head of the Laboratory of Physiological Psychology. Neal Miller has received numerous honors for his work. For example, he was elected to the National Academy of Sciences (an extremely prestigious honor), served as president of

hood of the response occurring again. His was a grand theory—an elegant conceptual presentation that captured the imagination of many theorists and elevated the role of learning to a commanding position in American psychology. Eventually, the theory faded as psychology began to be absorbed with very specific topics. But its influence had been felt even by those who had definite sympathy for the psychoanalytic perspective. The next section will illustrate this point.

THE STIMULUS-RESPONSE THEORY OF DOLLARD AND MILLER

There is no doubt that Freud created a monumental theory of personality. But for many psychologists (especially experimental ones), psychoanalysis contained two fatal flaws. First, it was couched in such vague, picturesque language that research with it was well-nigh impossible. Second, exact predictions of behavior were extremely hard to come by. Yet John Dollard and Neal Miller (see brief biography) understood psychoanalysis and knew that for all its flaws, it was based on a rich store of astute observations of human behavior. If only these observations of such great value could be placed in an objective framework—what a powerful tool it would become. The framework they chose was the learning theory of Clark Hull, the theoretical godfather of the Yale Institute of Human Relations, where Dollard and Miller and their colleagues flourished for so long.

Drawing upon Hullian learning theory, psychoanalytic theory, and social anthropology, Dollard and Miller developed a theory about the ways habits develop in hu-the American Psychological Association, was a recipient of the Warren Medal from the Society of Experimental Psychologists, and was awarded the President's Medal of Science.

While at Yale, Dollard and Miller began their collaboration which has so influenced psychology. Dollard brought to this joint effort an anthropological-sociological perspective. Miller contributed an approach from experimental psychology. Beyond that, they shared a psychoanalytic viewpoint. Dollard had been trained in psychoanalysis at the Berlin Psychoanalytic Institute, and Miller underwent a training analysis at the Vienna Institute of Psychoanalysis. So it was that in the stimulating environment of the Institute of Human Relations, they were able to fuse their interests in psychoanalysis, Hullian learning theory, and social interactions into a provocative new analysis of personality development.

Although both Dollard and Miller have published numerous things separately, they are best known for their collaborative efforts. They, along with several other members of the Institute of Human Relations, published a 1939 monograph called *Frustration and Aggression*. In 1941, Miller and Dollard's *Social Learning and Imitation* appeared, and in 1950 it was Dollard and Miller's *Personality and Psychotherapy*.

Neal Miller

man beings. These *habits* are stable connections between stimulus and response, and Dollard and Miller used them to account for or describe unconscious processes, motives, conflicts, defenses, and the like. With great adroitness, they blended the findings from laboratory research on animals with the skilled clinical observations of Freud. Some have dismissed their work as a mere translation of Freudian concepts into more palatable learning terms. But from this "translation" emerged a bridge from the psychodynamics of Freud to learning theory and, ultimately, to social learning, which is so popular in personality today. This work stimulated the thinking of a whole new generation of personality psychologists and retains even today a striking measure of vitality.

Basic theory and concepts

The research from which many of Dollard and Miller's ideas were derived was carried out with animals. Many critics have argued that we can hardly gain insight into human learning and personality by spending our time observing rats. Maybe so. But rats do have a few attractive characteristics. They are, relatively speaking, rather simple organisms. Therefore, it is possible to note things about their behavior that may get lost in the enormous complexity of human behavior. Then, too, rats are easier to manipulate and experiment on than humans. In the final analysis, this animal research can be viewed as providing data and interpretations whose validity can later be checked with humans.

An experiment.   Suppose we place a rat in a white compartment whose floor contains an electrified grid that allows us to deliver a painful shock to the rat (Miller, 1948). Adjacent to the white compartment is a black one. The compartments are separated by an open door. Placed in the white compartment, our rat shows no fear. But now we begin to shock him. Very quickly he learns to flee through the door and escape into the black compartment. In a short time, he learns to escape from the white area as soon as he is placed in it. Later, we note that the rat will show all the signs of fear when placed in the white compartment even though we have stopped administering shock. Despite the lack of shock, our rat continues to run to the black area. What can we learn from observing this rat? Well, for one thing it illustrates what Dollard and Miller (1950) referred to as the "four fundamentals of learning."

The four fundamentals.   Miller and Dollard (1941) proposed that "in order to learn one must want something, notice something, do something, and get something" (p. 2). This progression becomes clear as we contemplate our rat's behavior. He certainly wanted something—escape from the pain he was experiencing. Among other things, he noticed the adjoining black compartment. He did something, too. He ran through the open door and into the black compartment. By doing this, he got something, namely, relief from a painful shock. This little scenario, then, illustrates four basic aspects of learning: drive, cue, response, and reward.

Drives are strong internal stimuli that impel the organism to action. They may be innate (primary drives, e.g., hunger, thirst, pain) or they may be learned (secondary drives, e.g., fear, guilt, need for approval). But whether a drive is primary or secondary, it has the same effect—it energizes the organism.

Cues are stimuli that determine what response the organism will make, when it will be made, and where it will be made. Cues may be external events or stimuli or they may be internal stimuli. As a matter of fact, drives not only energize but they can also serve as cues. Any stimulus either internal or external that the organism can distinguish from another stimulus is capable of acting as a cue.

For a **response** to be reinforced, it must first occur. But if learning can take place only if a response is reinforced, how is it that responses occur initially? It must be that certain responses will occur prior to any reinforcement. Dollard and Miller suggest that an organism's responses can be ranked into an **initial hierarchy.** In terms of innate factors or earlier learning, responses vary in their probability of occurrence. What learning does is alter the rank order of response hierarchies. For example, a response rather weak in its initial potential for occurrence now becomes stronger in its potential.

Reward is the fourth basic factor of learning and is defined as anything that increases the probability of a given response being elicited by a particular stimulus or cue. Responses that reduce the strength of a drive will gain in their potential for occurrence next time when the circumstances are similar.

Let us now return to the rat described earlier to reiterate how all this operates. The rat experienced pain in the white compartment. This ultimately resulted in a fear of the white compartment. The fear was a learned fear since that compartment was previously a neutral stimulus. Fear, then, served as a learned drive that impelled the rat to action. In this case the rat, in the process of running around, fled to safety into the black area. His reward was a reduction of fear. But even when the shock no longer occurred, the rat continued to exhibit fear in the white compartment. That fear acted as a cue to direct behavior toward the haven of the black compartment. What followed was the very reinforcing reduction of fear. Thus, all the conditions for the establishment of a habit were met.

Interestingly, an observer dropping by *after* the rat's habit had been established might have found the animal's behavior totally irrational. After all, why run pell-mell from an innocuous compartment? Had that observer been present from the beginning, however, the behavior would have appeared perfectly reasonable—a logical outcome of the rat's experience. There may be a lesson here for those who find so much of a neurotic's behavior to be silly or unreasonable. You have to be there from the beginning to appreciate the full meaning of what appears to be unreasonable behavior. An example of this at the human level is shown in Box 10-1.

Liberalization of stimulus-response. Applying Dollard and Miller's concepts of drive, cue, response, and reward to the rat's predicament seems like pretty standard learning fare. But as we move to an analysis of the pilot's case, things have actually become less objective and precise. Stimuli are not just explosions; they are also thoughts about planes and memories of a distant terror. Likewise, responses are not ones of merely avoiding airplanes; they also refer to subtly changing a conversation or to thinking of other things. By their broadening of the definition of what constitutes a stimulus and a response, Dollard and Miller transformed learning theory from a dusty set of concepts that seemed to explain only the trivial behaviors of simple organisms to one that suddenly had meaning and application to complex personality questions. Naturally, the traditionalists claimed that the ensuing loss in objectivity of the definitions of stimulus and response put learning theory in the same predicament as psychoanalytic theory—it became very imprecise and slippery. Perhaps. But it probably also saved traditional learning theory from the sterility of its own objectivity.

When reinforcement fails. If a certain behavior is going to occur, it must continue to be reinforced when it is expressed. If reinforcement fails to occur, then eventually the behavior will drop out. A child who is reinforced for showing off will stop doing so when the attention of others fails to follow. This is called **extinction.** But assuming that attention from others is a strong drive, that child is now faced with a problem—how to satisfy the attention drive. It is out of such problems that new learning arises. The child will cast about and eventually hit upon a response that leads to attention. Of course, it may be a desirable form of new learning (e.g., studying and doing well in school) or an undesirable one (e.g., tormenting other children until someone pays attention). In any event, changes in behavior occur in the face of our failures to achieve drive reduction by using an old response.

Sometimes a behavior seems peculiarly resistant to extinction. It just goes on and on. Many conditions may account for such a strong habit, including the strength of the drive, how often the response has been rewarded in the past, how satisfying the rewards have been, and the availability of alternative responses. Also important is the notion of **partial reinforcement**. Many behaviors are made especially impervious to

Box 10-1
A PILOT'S PHOBIA

Dollard and Miller (1950) describe how a phobia can be learned in a manner that in principle is no different from how many other behaviors are learned. During World War II, a pilot flew an extremely dangerous mission. While on the way to attack an oil refinery, his squadron came under heavy enemy antiaircraft fire. In addition, they had to fly at rooftop level over their targets. The oil tanks exploded, bombs were bursting everywhere, and many planes simply disappeared in a wall of flame. Managing somehow to get through all this, the pilot had to return at reduced speed because of aircraft damage. He was subjected to repeated enemy fighter attacks and several of his crew members were killed. Eventually they had to ditch the plane in the Mediterranean. After drifting in an open life raft, the survivors eventually were rescued. Prior to this mission, the pilot had shown no evidence of any fear of airplanes. Yet shortly after returning to his base, he began to exhibit all the classic signs of a full-blown phobia. He was now frightened to death of airplanes. Why?

Dollard and Miller's analysis went something like this. Over and over during the flight, the pilot was exposed to terrifying and fear-provoking stimuli (explosions, fire, death of comrades, etc.). Cues present in the situation at the time became associated with the intense fear. The plane itself, the sound of engines, and even images of or thoughts about the plane and the mission came to evoke fear. A drive of intense fear, then, had been learned in response to all these cues. But unfortunately, such a fear does not remain confined to one specific set of cues. It generalizes to other, similar cues and situations. And so it was with the pilot. Being near other planes, thinking of planes, being asked about flying, and so on, were all cues that served to stimulate fear and panic.

But we learn that as we move away from a feared event, the fear tends to diminish. Therefore, our pilot quickly discovered that he felt better when he avoided planes. When he talked about flying, the old anxiety returned; when he changed the topic of conversation, the anxiety lessened. These and other avoidance responses became learned as habits. Whatever reduced his fear became a learned avoidance response.

Dollard and Miller's analysis takes us a long way toward understanding how the process of learning shapes personality functions. However, some might argue that something is still missing in this case of the pilot. Why, for instance, did not every pilot react to such experiences with a phobia? Were there ingredients in the specific flight experiences that were different for those who became phobic as compared to those who did not? Or are we back to the familiar personality theme? That is, can we ignore preexisting personality differences in our learning explanations?

From Dollard and Miller, *Personality and Psychotherapy* (New York: McGraw-Hill, 1950).

extinction because they are partially reinforced. This means, to continue our previous example, that a father may decide to stop rewarding his son with attention every time the boy does something "cute." Unfortunately, the father often does not stick to his resolve. Most of the time he does, but occasionally he shows subtle breakdowns or else the child becomes so resourceful that his father cannot avoid paying attention. This partial reinforcement is enough to keep the old responses going. Because the child is never sure that the reinforcement for this behavior has ceased once and for all, extinction does not happen.

Importance of learned drives.   Another important contribution of Dollard and Miller was showing how learned drives (secondary drives) develop. In complex societies such as our own, behavior is not pervasively regulated (except under dire circumstances) by primary reinforcements such as food and water. Our lives are shaped through the pursuit of prestige, happiness, wealth, and the like. How this comes about is, in principle, no different from the experience of the rat in the shock compartment. In the rat's case, fear was learned as a response to a previously neutral set of cues, and escape from these cues was a learned response calculated to lead to a reduction in fear. The fundamental argument that Dollard and Miller made is that the acquisition of our most civilized and sophisticated drives arises out of the early satisfaction of primary drives.

How is it, for example, that children come to love their mothers, seek approval from them, or strive to be near them? Dollar and Miller would claim that any stimulus or cue associated frequently with the satisfaction of a primary drive will eventually itself become a secondary reinforcement. For a child, the sight, feel, smell, and touch of the mother are discernible cues that occur repeatedly in direct connection with the satisfaction of hunger and the relief from various physical discomforts. The association is learned. And once learned, the sight of the mother and her presence close by will become powerful reinforcements to be sought now in their own right. According to this analysis, then, there is no reason why other learned drives or motives (e.g., status, money, dependency) cannot be traced ultimately to an early association with primary-drive reduction. Of course, the chain of events and associations is surely a complex one that offers challenging problems for those who would trace the origins of secondary drives. But in principle it is possible.

There are two especially interesting facets of secondary drives. First, when secondary drives repeatedly fail to be reinforced, they will become weaker. This is in contrast to primary drives. For example, frequent nonreinforcement of the thirst drive would hardly keep us from looking for water. But repeatedly finding that our achievements fail to impress our parents will often teach us to reduce our efforts in this direction. At the same time, it is true that such behaviors in pursuit of secondary reinforcements are sometimes persistent and do not always die out easily. This brings us to the second point, which is an observation about the strength of certain secondary drives. It is paradoxical that some secondary drives, even though they were born out of an early association with the satisfaction of hunger, thirst, and needs for physical comfort, may later persist even in the face of the threat of starvation or excruciating pain. For example, the value of truth and integrity may become so strong that even the prospect of death will not deter some individuals from maintaining them. Thus, out of what once were fragile learned associations are forged secondary drives that can assume the strength of iron.

Stimulus generalization.

Long before Dollard and Miller, psychologists recognized that responses learned in connection with one stimulus will also occur in relation to other, physically similar stimuli. This is called **stimulus generalization.** In addition, the more the second stimulus is like the first one, the more probable it is that generalization will take place. So it is that behaviors, emotions, thoughts, or attitudes learned in one situation will occur in other situations that are similar.

There is another kind of generalization particularly important to humans. It is called **mediated stimulus generalization** and refers to those instances where a response learned in one setting generalizes to another setting because the latter is classified or labeled as similar to the first. The similarity is not, however, of a physical nature. Take the example of a person who is taught that all Russians are untrustworthy. Upon meeting someone who is introduced as being from Russia, the person immediately responds with distrust. Generalization here is not based upon any physical similarity among Russians. Rather, the generalization is mediated by the label *Russian.*

Language, then, produces cues that can facilitate generalization across physically dissimilar situations. Such **cue-producing responses** can also facilitate discrimination among situations that may otherwise appear physically similar. This cue-producing role of language is also important in arousing drives. Thus, a male may become more easily sexually aroused in the presence of a female labeled as "responsive" than in the case of one who is physically similar but thought to be "cold." Language can likewise influence our behavior in the present by allowing us to think of its future consequences. I can decide that studying is a good thing to do because it will pay off three years in the future but that reading novels every night is unwise since it will produce negative consequences down the road.

Labeling, imagining, planning, and reasoning are all important cue-producing responses that enable us to think our way through life rather than having to deal with every problem on a separate trial-and-error basis. Such cue-producing responses are also what separate the human from the beast. The less able we are to employ these mediating processes, the more likely it is that we will have adjustment problems, suffer disappointments, or become the captives of events rather than their masters. All in all, what Miller and Dollard were trying to do here was to make learning theory a viable tool in accounting for human cognitive behavior. Many had previously thought that learning theory was helpful in explaining the viscerally dominated behavior of laboratory animals but almost irrelevant to the complex behavior of humans who depend so much on higher mental processes. Miller and Dollard helped shatter this conception.

Structure of personality.

Dollard and Miller never had any intention of trying to describe personality structure, identify traits, or otherwise catalog enduring personality characteristics. Rather, they were concerned with the *process* of learning. They tried to spell out the process whereby human behavior was acquired and changed. The closest they came to a basic structural element was habit. The conditions that facilitate the acquisition of these associations or that subsequently extinguish them provide the focus of Dollard and Miller's theory.

Development of personality

Dollard and Miller have a variety of things to say about the development of personality.

The basic characteristics.   Dollard and Miller began their explanation of development by postulating three basic characteristics of the infant. First, each infant is endowed with a set of **specific reflexes** that make it responsive to a very narrow range of stimuli in any given situation. Second, there are **innate response hierarchies.** That is, on an innate basis certain responses are more likely to occur in a specific situation than are other responses. Third, there is the usual set of **primary drives.** The question is, How does an infant with these three rather limited features move from such a primitive state to what we all recognize as a superbly complex adult? Not surprisingly, the answer lies in the learning process. Through the ever-present mechanism of drive reduction, existing responses become attached to new stimuli, new responses are reinforced, secondary motives arise out of primary ones, and higher mental processes flourish through mediated stimulus generalization. It is through these processes multiplied by a million occasions that the human organism slowly and almost imperceptibly becomes an adult.

But any learning process occurs in a context. Without knowing the cultural environment and the family milieu, it is not possible to predict the outcome or content of one person's learning. Whether a child learns to be aggressive or passive is not inherent in the learning process. Rather it is determined by what reinforcements the environment provides. Germans, Australians, and Japanese each learn quite different things. My child learns things that are different from those learned by a child down the block. Nevertheless everyone learns what they learn according to the same rules.

Four critical training situations.   Not unlike Freud, Dollard and Miller discuss four sets of early social conditions important for the learning of conflicts that shape adult personality. The child's vulnerability to such situations stems from helplessness. Children are, in a very real sense, at the mercy of adults, so what the child learns depends heavily upon the nature of the training situations provided by those adults.

First, there is the **feeding situation,** and it is here that so many things are first learned. For example, if children are not fed when they cry but are left to "cry themselves out," the groundwork may be laid for the creation of apathy or apprehensiveness. On the other hand, a pleasant feeding situation can lay the basis for subsequent feelings of sociability and love. At the same time, an infant who is fed when not hungry may never truly learn to appreciate the full value of food rewards, and thus little association between gratification and the presence of the mother will develop. This may retard the growth of social feeling. The child who often experiences hunger while alone will learn to fear being alone and may come to desire obsessively the presence of others. Weaning can also be fraught with difficulties and pain. The important thing to remember here is that no matter how it may appear to others, the young child is learning many things in the course of hunger and feeding cycles. The nature of those things helps determine the degree of conflicts that may arise later. This is what Dollard and Miller call the "secret learning of the early years."

Next, there is **cleanliness training**. Learning to control the processes of urination and defecation is a complex and difficult task. But this learning is regarded as terribly important by many parents. When the child has accidents and is punished, there may develop a learned association between parents and punishment. Avoiding the parents can then become an anxiety-reducing response. In other cases, children may get the feeling that they are pursued by all-seeing parents who can literally read their minds. In the face of such superior odds, the child may become excessively conforming. All of this is an example of how Dollard and Miller reworked the observations of Freud into a learning framework.

Early sex training is another potential source of conflicts. Taboos on masturbation can result in the parents inculcating in the child severe anxiety over sexuality. Sex-typing begins at an early age and provides a context in which to learn the taboo on homosexuality. These and many other Freudian-like learnings take place.

Another set of conditions can provoke **anger-anxiety** conflicts. Parents often get very upset when they see their children being angry. They punish such behavior in various ways, and the child may, as a consequence, learn to suppress anger. As Dollard and Miller (1950) put it, "Robbing a person of his anger completely may be a dangerous thing since some capacity for anger seems to be needed in the affirmative personality" (p. 149).

The foregoing is but a very abbreviated sketch of some conditions that can foster the learning of conflicts. Nevertheless, it does suggest the extreme importance that Dollard and Miller place on the social context. Theirs is indeed a social learning approach — the forerunner of more formal social learning theories.

Nature of adjustment

It is clear from what has been said thus far that Dollard and Miller have developed a point of view that contains many implications for adjustment.

Conflict.   As viewed from the psychoanalytic perspective, conflict is an essential feature of maladjusted behavior. It is no less so with Dollard and Miller. For example, they used clues from animal research to describe three kinds of conflict situations. When two positive motives are in conflict (e.g., watch an exciting TV program or go to an equally exciting movie), they classified it as an **approach-approach conflict.** **Avoidance-avoidance conflicts** confront the person with two equally negative possibilities (e.g., mow the grass or wash the car). A third conflict situation is that of **approach-avoidance** (e.g., a student is very angry over having received a D on a term paper; should that anger be expressed, thereby satisfying a motive, or will doing so result in retaliation from the instructor and thus prevent the satisfaction of another motive — getting a decent grade for the course?). Dollard and Miller proposed five principles by which one can predict the outcome of these conflict situations:

■ One's tendency to approach a positive goal becomes stronger the closer one is to that goal.

■ One's tendency to avoid a negative goal becomes stronger the closer one is to that goal.

■ The tendency to avoid a negative goal becomes stronger with nearness than does the corresponding tendency to approach a positive goal.

■ An increase in drive strength will increase the tendency to approach or avoid a particular goal.

■ Whenever there are two competing responses, the stronger will win out.

In Figure 10-1 a conflict is shown graphically.

The unconscious. Neurotic behavior entails the individual's search for ways to resolve or minimize conflict. But much of that conflict is unconscious. For example, an individual does not know that an obsessive preoccupation about orderliness is an unconscious way of masking hostile thoughts that would provoke considerable anxiety were they conscious. But for Dollard and Miller, the unconscious is not a mysterious region of the mind inhabited by dastardly urges. Rather, as Levy (1970) puts it, "They conceive of the unconscious as the equivalent of the unlabelled" (p. 400). As noted earlier, labels are cue-producing responses, and an absence of labels cuts down the degree to which our own thought processes can monitor and control unconscious events. This is one reason why neurotics are so often unable to understand the nature of their own behavior—why it fails to make sense to them.

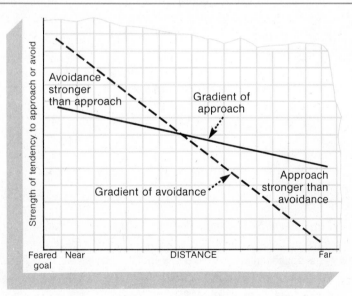

FIGURE 10-1   Representation of an approach-avoidance conflict.
From Dollard, J., and Miller, N.: *Personality and psychotherapy: An analysis in terms of learning, thinking, and culture,* New York, McGraw-Hill Book Co., 1950. p. 356.

Box 10-2
DOLLARD AND MILLER ON DEFENSE MECHANISMS

1 The Explanation for Rationalizations

According to our analysis a rationalization involves the following steps: Social training of the type described [previously] produces a need to have a logical explanation for obvious features of one's behavior and plans; the person tends to feel uneasy in the presence of any behavior that is illogical or unexplained. In some instances, however, the true explanation would provoke anxiety, guilt, or some other drive. Thus the person is motivated to find *some* explanation but to avoid the true one. When he happens to hit upon a rationalization that meets cultural standards of sensibleness, it is reinforced by a reduction in anxiety about unexplained behavior. Furthermore, if some of the sentences that would constitute a true explanation have been tending to come into the subject's mind and elicit anxiety or guilt, the alternative sentences in the rationalization tend to block them out and hence remove the anxiety or guilt that they elicit. When this occurs, it serves as an additional reinforcement. (1950, pp. 177–178)

2 An Example of Projection

The subject was homosexually excited by this particular associate. The incipient homosexual responses and thoughts aroused intense anxiety and were repressed. Because of the conflict, the subject felt miserable whenever he was in the presence of the other man and better whenever he avoided him. He reacted to this state of affairs with thoughts such as "I don't know why but I don't like him!" But as long as there was no rational explanation for this behavior, he felt uneasy. In previous situations the dislike had often been mutual and involved aggressive and discriminatory acts on the part of the other person. The thought that the other person disliked him and was persecuting him occurred and was reinforced by the reduction in anxiety it produced through providing a logical explanation. (1950, p. 183)

3 An Example of Reaction Formation

For example, as a little girl Mrs. A hated her mother but was severely punished whenever she expressed her anger in any way. When she apologized by saying that she really loved her mother and by acting like it, the punishment was terminated. In this way, she learned to substitute statements of love for statements of hate. Years later, when she started to hate her mother-in-law, this aroused intense anxiety that could only be reduced by protestations of love. The mechanism was discovered through the fact that Mrs. A most protested her love just at the time her mother-in-law was treating her in a very nasty way. (1950, p. 184)

In a related vein, Dollard and Miller regard **repression** as an example of "stopping thinking" even though most of us are not accustomed to regard "not thinking" as a response. But it can be viewed that way. When it is, repression becomes a learned inhibition about thinking of events that stimulate strong anxiety or guilt. The "not thinking" response is reinforced because it leads to anxiety reduction. See Box 10-2 for some behavioral analyses of other defense mechanisms.

How a neurosis is learned: A case example

Dollard and Miller (1950) strongly believed that neuroses are learned. They described a case in which this learning is illustrated. That case also shows how directly removing a symptom without attacking its root cause will increase drive which, in turn, produces a severe learning dilemma for the patient. Current behavior therapists might, however, disagree. They tend to argue that the symptom is the problem and its removal will not necessitate resolving some presumed unconscious conflict. In any event, the case in question involved Mrs. C and her fear of sex. Mrs. C had not really wanted to marry but did so only to escape her mother. After marriage her aversion to sexual intercourse became extreme and she hated being "touched" by her husband. Eventually, she developed a paralysis of the legs. In the words of Dollard and Miller (1950):

. . . she was shortly brought to the hospital with her legs in an acute spastic condition. She was unable to flex her knees, to walk, or to stand. According to our analysis, this symptom must have been reinforced by the reduction in anxiety that the condition produced by making intercourse impossible. At the time she was brought in, her anxiety level was low; she accepted the symptom and displayed that *belle indifférence* of which Charcot spoke.

The doctors proved that the symptom was not organic. The signs of organic paralysis were not present, and the limbs were freely movable when the patient was under the influence of pentothal. The patient, however, was highly resistant to any explanation of her symptom on the basis of emotional factors. She said it is something "organic, inwardly, not emotional."

The fact that the symptom had been producing the kind of reduction in anxiety and conflict that would be expected is demonstrated by the increase in drive that occurred after its removal. Mrs. C was angry at her doctors and suffered an attack of rage at one of the nurses on the very night that she was first convinced she could walk.

The increase in drive motivated the kind of trial and error that almost certainly had occurred and failed to solve her problem before the symptom was learned. When she was released from the hospital and returned to her home, she tried a series of new escape responses. She first considered divorce, but this measure threatened to produce still new conflicts—moral scruples and fears of loss of financial support for herself and children. She went to live with her sister, using the rationalization that she was not yet strong enough to run her own house. This means of escape kept her out of contact with her husband but created problems with her sister's husband and family, so she eventually had to come home. After she came home, Mrs. C refused intercourse with her husband and avoided all occasions when it might occur. Of course, this created problems with him but not sufficiently severe ones to make her willing to risk sex relations. Finally she sought and received contraceptive advice but then did not actually make use of it. Evidently her fears were attached to the sex act as well as to pregnancy, since she was not willing to use contraception to avoid pregnancy while accepting sex relations.

In this case the motivation for the symptom is clear. The fact that it allowed the patient to escape an anxiety-provoking dilemma is clear, but the details of the reinforcement and learning were not observed. After the symptom was removed, it is clear that the patient was put back into a high state of motivation and a severe learning dilemma. (passages excerpted from pp. 169–170)

SKINNER'S OPERANT CONDITIONING

A second major influence on contemporary behavioral learning approaches to personality has been the work of B. F. Skinner. In the strictest sense of the word, this statement contains a strange bit of irony. Skinner remained true to his operant philosophy which, simply put, is that behavior is maintained by its consequences, that is, by rewards and punishments. We do not control our behavior through any ephemeral free-will choices, nor does the control reside in any mind entities or traits. Rather, our behavior is determined by events in the environment. When these environmental events are identified, we have the key to the understanding and control of human behavior. The system of rewards that keeps a troupe of trained dogs performing to the delight of screaming audiences is no different in principle from that which impels the sophisticated performance of a troupe of Shakespearean actors.

To confer upon Skinner a place of honor among personality theorists is a little like inviting a wolf to a party of lambs. Quite simply, Skinner rejected personality theory—or any theory for that matter. So here we have the contradiction. For someone who was so completely suspicious of theory and, indeed, regarded his own work as being guided entirely by the results of empirical research rather than by theory, he had an enormous impact on the field of personality.

Skinner believed that all behavior is determined. What is more, the determination occurs in a lawful, orderly way. Nothing is capricious; nothing arises out of free will. This leads inevitably to the corollary belief that behavior can be controlled. This promise of control can, Skinner said, be fulfilled through a **functional analysis** of behavior. This means that by analyzing the way in which responses follow stimuli or specific conditions, the cause-and-effect relationships can be discovered. Therein lies the essence of the ability to control.

Skinner was not interested in variables inside the organism that might be said to mediate these relationships. Some have even said that Skinner regarded the human organism as an "empty box." A more precise way of saying this is that he saw no necessity for opening the box. A stimulus impinges on the box and a response emerges from that box. For him, this was the essence of a science of psychology—the discovery of the lawful relationship between inputs and outputs.

Take the example of a student who reads every assigned article on the course syllabus and who takes to heart every casual suggestion by the instructor that students might find a recent book by so and so of great interest. Some would attribute to this student a thirst for knowledge. Others might be less charitable and explain it as an obsequious subservience to authority. But Skinner would have shrugged and said that there is no way of knowing and, indeed, no need to know. What is clear is the systematic relationship between stimulus (syllabus or suggestion) and response (reading). And we can control the response by manipulating the stimulus. If all this sounds simple, it is—in a way. But it is not necessarily very easy. The functional analysis of complex behaviors can be very difficult, time-consuming, and intricate.

Skinner was not completely unmindful of genetics. He did admit that we are evolutionary products and that we have certain species-specific capabilities and characteristics. Our individual repertoires of responses do give us identities that have arisen out of the learning situations to which we have been exposed over the course of our lives. What I do today says something about the stimuli that are controlling my behavior. But the fact that I have been able to acquire this repertoire of behavior through conditioning reflects my genetic endowment as well. In practice, however, Skinner seemed much less interested in genetics than in conditioning processes.

Basic concepts

The concepts that Skinner employed have a distinct learning emphasis that seems to come from the research laboratory.

Respondents.   Classical conditioning was mentioned earlier in this chapter. Skinner called this **respondent behavior**—behavior that is a response to some identifiable stimulus. A low-flying aircraft causes us to duck; an instructor asks you a question in class and you become nervous; someone compliments you and you smile shyly.

Operants.   Respondent behavior is important, and its conditioning has been used to account for the acquisition of a wide array of behavior including fears as well as attraction responses. Skinner, however, was always more interested in what he terms **operant behavior.** This refers to behavior acquired on the basis of instrumental conditioning. Such behavior is *emitted,* and the frequency of its occurrence depends upon the effects it has on the environment or the consequences that follow from it. People continue to flip light switches because doing so results in a consequence—the light comes on. When being friendly to another person is repeatedly met by icy aloofness, one stops being friendly.

Since the appearance of Skinner, it has become abundantly clear that operant conditioning need not apply strictly to laboratory settings or involve only the behaviors of pigeons pecking at colored disks to receive a pellet of food or of rats doing strange things to obtain a treasured drop of water. The husband who continues reading the paper while his wife tries to tell him about a personal problem may well be decreasing the likelihood that she will confide in him in the future.

Discriminative stimuli.   Some stimuli serve a discriminative function. They come to act as cues or signals that a given response is likely to be rewarded and are called **discriminative stimuli.** A mother's frown becomes a signal that one kind of response rather than another is more likely to win her approval. A highway patrol car is a cue that I had better reduce my speed or else risk a citation. This does not mean that a discriminative stimulus completely controls our behavior. There is still the out-

A brief biography of

B. F. Skinner

Born in 1904 in Susquehanna, Pennsylvania, B. F. Skinner grew up rather uneventfully in a home marked by stability and warmth. His father was a lawyer, and his mother has been described as ensuring that he learned the difference between right and wrong. During his childhood, he was constantly building things, from wagons and slingshots to gliders and kites. He even tried his hand at creating a perpetual-motion machine. Interestingly, in his subsequent professional career he often made use of novel laboratory equipment. The continuity between childhood and adulthood seems clear.

He attended Hamilton College as an English major and hoped to become a writer. He even sent several short stories to Robert Frost, from whom he received encouragement. Trying his hand full-time at writing, he lived for a while at home, in Europe, and even spent six months or so in Greenwich Village. Finally, he concluded that a writing career was not likely to bear fruit.

Even though Skinner had no background in psychology, he began to read about the work of Pavlov and Watson. He applied to and was accepted for graduate work in psychology at Harvard. It was during this period that his interest in animal behavior developed. Receiving his Ph.D., he moved to the University of Minnesota in 1936 to assume his first academic post. He remained at Minnesota for nine years. After a brief stint at Indiana University, he went back to Harvard in 1948 and has remained there ever since.

If his work at Minnesota established him as an experimental psychologist of national repute, his later years at Harvard witnessed his becoming a major scientist with a worldwide constituency. It is hardly an overstatement to say that many regarded B. F. Skinner as the

come itself—such as receiving a $50 fine. But a discriminative stimulus does suggest to us which behavior should be selected so as to achieve a desirable (or less punitive) consequence. It is through such stimuli that our world is rendered more predictable and therefore more manageable.

Reinforcers. Any event or stimulus that follows a response and is then determined to have increased the likelihood of that response occurring again is called a **reinforcer.** This concept is very nontheoretical. That is, what is reinforcing is determined by its effects on the behavior in question. A lot of trial and error can go into determining what will serve as a reinforcer for the response one is trying to produce in a particular person. Sometimes we know on the basis of the general culture in which we operate what will likely be reinforcing. In our culture, money, approval, and the like will probably work. In a rat's culture, food pellets would undoubtedly work better. But remember, in dealing with one specific individual we must sometimes go beyond the culture and examine the individual's life history for clues about what will be especially reinforcing. But once we find the reinforcer, we can begin to exert the control necessary to regulate the individual's behavior. As they say in the executive suite, every person

world's foremost psychologist. Certainly he received many honors, including the Distinguished Scientific Award of the American Psychological Association, membership in the National Academy of Sciences, the position of William James Lecturer at Harvard, and the President's Medal of Science.

While Skinner may have failed in his early literacy aspirations, he seemed never to completely forsaken them, In 1948 he published *Walden Two*, a novel depicting how an experimental society can be built on a foundation of psychological principles. His single most important scientific work is probably *The Behavior of Organisms,* which appeared in 1938. Many other significant works followed, including *Science and Human Behavior* (1953), *Verbal Behavior* (1957), and *About Behaviorism* (1974). A brief autobiography has appeared in Boring and Lindzey's (1967) *A History of Psychology in Autobiography* (Vol. 5). Skinner also completed the first volume of a two-volume autobiography, *Particulars of My Life,* which appeared in 1976. Far and away his most controversial book, however, was his 1971 national bestseller, *Beyond Freedom and Dignity.* In it, he argued that notions such as freedom and dignity should be set aside and that we should look to the manipulation of environmental conditions and rewards in building a better society. Needless to say, this prescription touched off a firestorm of criticism, shock, and outrage. But Skinner was not one to be dissuaded easily from his beliefs. He and his behaviorism remain potent forces.

His most recent book, *Upon Further Reflection*, published in 1987, is a collection of essays covering many topics from international relations to self-management. He died in August, 1990.

B. F. Skinner
Christopher S. Johnson

has a price. An example of how this can operate in a concrete setting is shown in Box 10-3.

Schedules of reinforcement.

Life, unhappily, is not a perfect dispenser of rewards. Sometimes when children look to their parents for approval everyone is so busy that they are hardly noticed let alone reinforced. At times, we pull the slot machine lever and quarters cascade around us. Other times, nothing. Even with pigeons it happens. Sometimes the apparatus jams or is faulty and food pellets do not arrive on schedule after the appropriate peck. As a matter of fact, Skinner began to think about **schedules of reinforcement** when he discovered that it was either spend all day manufacturing food pellets (when he could be doing something more interesting) or start reinforcing his rats less frequently for the desired response. This initiated a series of studies that culminated in a book on schedules of reinforcement (Ferster and Skinner, 1957).

The world is not organized so that it can reinforce every response. This being the case, what are the effects of various schedules of reinforcement on behavior? Which schedule is better and when? What will happen when the organism is under **continu-**

Box 10-3
THE REINFORCEMENT OF NEW BEHAVIOR

Allen, Hart, Buell, Harris, and Wolf (1964) described the case of a four-year old girl, Ann, who was enrolled in a preschool class. It was not long before Ann started paying less and less attention to the other children and increasingly wanted to be near the teachers. She began to just stand about, stare, pick her lower lip, pull on her hair, or rub her cheek. All her behavior seemed geared toward obtaining attention from adult teachers. At the same time, this behavior directly interfered with playing with the other children.

A program was initiated so that Ann was rewarded by attention from a teacher whenever she played with another child. This was done so it did not interrupt her play with that other child. When she was alone, no attention was provided. There was an immediate and obvious increase in her play with other children and a corresponding drop in her behavior directed toward adults, as can be seen in the figure on the next page.

But can we be sure it was the teachers' reinforcement that was responsible for the change in Ann's behavior? After five days, the teachers reversed their reinforcement patterns. They went back to reinforcing Ann for her withdrawn, shy behavior. As the figure shows, her behavior quickly returned to its baseline level. After five more days, Ann was once more reinforced only for playing with other children, and her behavior changed again. Toward the end of this latter period, the teachers began reinforcing her intermittently in order to build up her resistance to extinction. After twenty-five days, no particular effort was made to sustain Ann's new behavior. But postexperimental checks coming on Days 31, 38, 40, and 51 indicated that her interactional behavior with other children was holding up well. In all likelihood, Ann was now receiving reinforcements from her play with the other children so that the interactional behavior was maintained.

ous reinforcement (i.e., is reinforced 100 percent of the time) as compared to various forms of **intermittent** or **partial reinforcement**? It was discovered fairly quickly that partial reinforcement schedules of learning make it less likely that a given response will be extinguished even after a fairly lengthy period of nonreinforcement. For example, if I learn that smiling at people on the street is frequently but not always followed by a smile in return (partial reinforcement), I will continue to smile at strangers for a long time, even after I move to another part of the country where smiles hardly ever

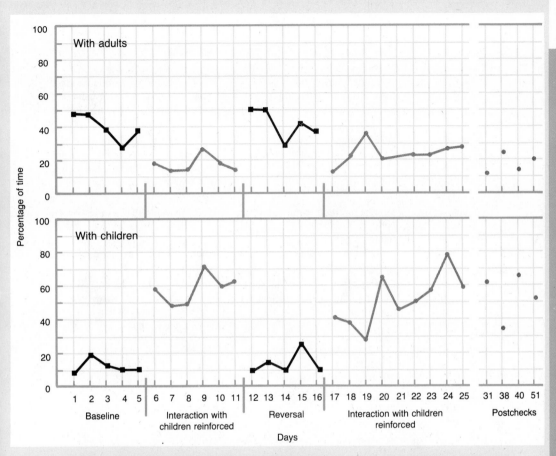

A graphic presentation of Ann's behavior. The percent of time Ann spent interacting with adults is shown in the upper panel; the lower panel depicts her interaction with other children.
From "Effects of Social Reinforcement on Isolate Behavior of a Nursery School Child" by K. E. Allen, B. Hart, J. S. Buell, F. R. Harris, and M. M. Wolf, *Child Development,* 1964, *35,* 511–518. Copyright the Society for Research in Child Development, Inc. Reprinted by permission.

bring a response. In Table 10-1, several of the more common reinforcement schedules are shown along with some real-life examples.

Schedules of reinforcement at first glance appear to be esoteric descriptions of sterile laboratory exercises which, with some effort, can be stretched to cover a few simple human behaviors. But, as Table 10-1 suggests, Skinner has provided a descriptive scheme that can apply to nearly all our activities. "Personality" behaviors are fair game as well. The father who will pay attention to his child only before the football game starts and

TABLE 10-1 *Schedules of partial reinforcement*

Schedule	Description	Illustration
1 Fixed-interval	Reinforcement is given for responses made after a specified time interval has passed.	Paid once a week, the worker continues working throughout the work week but the pace usually accelerates on payday and then slacks off afterward.
2 Fixed-ratio	Reinforcement is given after a specified number of responses are made.	In industry, workers are paid on a piecework basis. Theoretically, the workers will produce numerous pieces in order to increase their wages.
3 Variable-interval	Interval between reinforced trials varies but, on the average, reinforcement occurs after an identifiable interval (e.g., every 2 minutes).	The fisherman is rewarded, on the average, with a catch every 45 minutes. But sometimes the interval is 5 minutes, and other times 2 days.
4 Variable-ratio	Reinforcement is given, on the average, after some specified number of responses.	The slot machine, let us say, pays off, on the average, every tenth time. But sometimes it may take only 5 plays, and others 15 plays.

Source: After *Abnormal Psychology,* by M. Duke and S. Nowicki, Jr. Copyright © 1979 by Wadsworth Publishing Company, Inc. Reprinted by permission of the publisher. Brooks/Cole Publishing Company, Monterey, California.

after it is over is placing the child on a schedule that fits the fixed-interval mold. But if the child is active, demanding, and persistent, then a ratio schedule of some sort may actually come about. The child's demanding behavior may be rewarded, setting the stage for learning that perhaps several emotional outbursts are enough to achieve the reward of the father's attention. In any case, behavioral patterns are being fixed by a schedule of reward. In like manner, an increase in the number of temper tantrums can be understood through an analysis of the schedules of reinforcement in force. Whether it is temper tantrums, sexual behavior in a relationship, or gambling—all can be understood in terms of schedules.

Secondary reinforcement. **Primary reinforcers** are things such as food, water, and the like. Neutral stimuli consistently paired with a primary reinforcer will become reinforcers in their own right. Such **secondary reinforcers** eventually come to play a dominant role in human behavior. As we saw earlier with Dollard and Miller, the mother takes on secondary reinforcing properties because of her association with primary care. A host of secondary reinforcers thus arise and include such things as smiles, compliments, money, awards, grades, recognition, and so on.

The presence of this policeman should have been a cue for the driver to slow down.

Some secondary reinforcers are associated with more than one kind of primary reinforcement. For example, a mother's presence becomes associated with the satisfaction of hunger, reduction in physical discomfort, and others. This is an example of a **generalized reinforcer**—a reinforcer that does not depend solely on one drive state. Money is another example since it is associated with nearly everything—physical comfort, food, drink, and so on. There is even a **chaining** process that goes on here. That is, secondary reinforcers can produce additional secondary reinforcers through pairing. Mother is associated with hunger reduction, then perhaps mother becomes associated with music, and so music is now a secondary reinforcer. Music, in turn, becomes associated with a certain restaurant, which then takes on reinforcing properties—and on and on. This chaining notion presumably accounts for the complex system of reinforcers in every person's life.

Shaping.   Based upon the discussion thus far, it is probably not too difficult to see how fairly simple responses (ones the organism naturally makes) could be reinforced and thus made to occur more often. But what about a complicated behavior that consists of many separate acts and thus, in total, has never occurred before? Can that which does not exist be reinforced? Skinner discovered what every good animal trainer now knows—you **shape** the behavior. You do this by reinforcing some responses and not others and by reinforcing those responses that progressively bring the animal closer and closer to the desired behavior **(successive approximation).** Suppose you wish to train a rat to dance—hardly a normal part of an everyday rat's repertoire. You might begin by pairing food and a "click" so that the latter becomes a secondary reinforcer. Clicks are easier to administer than food as the rat moves about. Now, when the rat

309

looks up, you reward him with the clicking noise. Next, you reward him with the click only when he really stretches his head upward and, eventually, only when he rears up on his hind legs. Then, you reward him for taking steps to the right; then to the left. When you are done, you have a dancing rat!

The same principle works for humans. In this case, however, it is more than an entertaining demonstration. It is, in reality, a description of how we learn complex skills and behaviors. Sometimes it happens haphazardly and inefficiently. But when the technology of shaping is carefully harnessed, it can become a potent method for producing desired behaviors. Hergenhahn (1972) suggests in the following example how reading can be shaped in a young child:

1 Have a number of children's books available and leave them where the child is likely to come across them.

2 If a child avoids books, reward activities related to reading such as noticing signs, naming and/or labeling things, and so on.

3 As the activities in number 2 above are rewarded, the child will tend to do them more often, and when he does, one must become more rigorous in what is expected before giving additional rewards, for example, reading longer signs and attending to more detailed labels.

4 A next step could be to ask the child to get you certain books, such as the red one, the one with the duck on the cover, the one with the A, B, C's on it. When he does, he is rewarded.

5 The next step involves getting the child still more involved with the book, for example, asking him to find certain things like the red barn, the dog, and so on. Again, the child is rewarded in some way for doing this.

6 The above process is continued and refined until the child is reading on his own.

7 To maintain this interest in reading once it has been brought about through these procedures, it is important to go on rewarding the child even when he starts reading on his own, at least to begin with. Eventually, the content of the stories will begin to be enough of a reward to maintain the child's interest in reading. (pp. 40–41)

Structure of personality.   At this point, it will hardly come as great news to learn that Skinner did not much believe in personality structures. For him, they were merely excess baggage and tend to confuse more than enlighten. Once you understand how to modify behavior, the game is over. Skinner's interest was mainly in modifiable behavior and the environmental events that control it. His contention was that ego, trait, and need are unnecessary concepts and that he could, with his operant methods alone, do an acceptable job of prediction and control.

The ideographic method.   For Skinner, personality was little more than a collection of behavior patterns. Of course, these behavior patterns are distinctive and allow us to recognize easily one person from another. Strangely enough, B. F. Skinner and Gordon Allport, who were in so many ways antithetical to each other, had one thing in common. They both believed in an idiographic approach. But with Skinner, this referred to the intensive analysis of the individual's history of reinforcement, not trait relationships. Personality, then, is the distinct pattern of relationships between an individual's behavior and its reinforcement consequences. For each person, the pattern will be different even though the principles of learning by which the pattern was acquired apply to all. These patterns are revealed not by projective tests and the like but by an intensive behavioral analysis. An individual's unique genetic background combines with an equally distinctive set of environmental conditions to produce a personality (pattern of behavior).

Development of personality

To the extent that personality development involves change, Skinnerian approaches are entirely relevant since their real strength lies in the process of behavioral change. But as far as introducing any special concepts to account for the development of social behavior in humans, Skinner felt no need. Social behaviors are acquired the same way as any other behaviors. Of course, it may be more difficult to identify exactly what the social stimuli are in a given situation or even what may be serving as secondary reinforcers. It is easier with rats—we can use food pellets, clicks that have been linked with food, and so on. Furthermore, because we have done the training ourselves, we know exactly what the chain of learning events has been. But though all of this is more difficult and complicated with humans, the process is the same.

Development of cooperation.
To illustrate how the development of behaviors normally thought of as belonging to the domain of personality can be explained, let us consider an experiment by Azrin and Lindsley (1956). They took twenty children (ages seven to twelve) and split them into ten teams. The two children in each team were, in turn, seated on opposite sides of a table. Confronting each child were three holes and a stylus. If both children placed their styluses in the holes directly opposite each other (cooperative response), a red light flashed and a single jelly bean was delivered to the table. When they put their styluses in holes not directly opposite (uncooperative response), no reward was forthcoming. All ten teams learned very quickly to be cooperative, and, almost as quickly, eight of the teams divided the candy. In the other two cases, one child took all the candy until the other child refused to cooperate. At that point, they came to an understanding and began to divide the candy. This simple laboratory example can provide insight into how a host of responses during childhood can be developed through simple conditioning.

The making of a worrier.
Suppose a child's parents are rather anxious people who worry a lot. They worry about the doors being locked, whether the food is possibly tainted, whether their feet will get wet in the rain, whether their bowel movements are regular, and on and on. The child notices this. But even more important, that child is probably reinforced for worrying about the same things. The child's request for guidance about wearing galoshes brings a cluck of approval from the mother.

Returning to see if the garage door is locked prompts a nod of subtle approval from the father. Over time and instances, the child has become a worrier through operant principles. Later, of course, when the child is less supervised by the parents, reinforcement will not be so inevitable. Rather it will be intermittent. If anything, however, this only serves to retard the extinction of worrying. Perhaps another child with a similar reinforcement history has, for certain reasons, developed the ability to discriminate among cues. Such a child may be free from worry when outside the home only to once more become a worrier when interacting with the parents at home.

Nature of adjustment

For the behaviorist, maladjusted behavior is not the product of an underlying disease nor is it some bizarre outgrowth of warfare among id, ego, and superego. Maladjusted behavior is simply a failure to make an appropriate set of responses (Ullmann and Krasner, 1975). Inappropriate responses are learned in the same manner as appropriate ones. This view moves us away from the idea that maladjustment is a series of symptoms brought about by some underlying disease process. Instead, certain individuals among us learn to make responses that are inappropriate in specific situations or else they do not learn to make the desirable response at all. What we have here is a faulty conditioning history. Sometimes this history is only mildly faulty, resulting in neurotic behavior. In other cases, there have been gross distortions in learning and psychosis is the result.

According to Davison and Neale (1990), this general behavioral philosophy has several important implications. First, the influence of physiological factors is seen as minimal and the focus shifts to the learning process. Second, the gap between normal and the abnormal is viewed as narrow since both are explained in the same fashion. Third, adjustment becomes a relative concept. What is normal depends on the cultural milieu and its values. Shoplifting on the part of a wealthy executive is maladjusted; that same shoplifting by a fifteen-year-old gang member is probably reflective of the learned values shared by the gang.

A good example of the foregoing point of view would be certain school phobias. A child, for a variety of reasons, may not want to go to school. Perhaps it is fear of other children at school; perhaps it is a younger sibling at home who is seen as a rival for the mother's attention. For operant theorists, however, the causes mediating such fears are largely irrelevant. What happens, they assert, is that certain behaviors, such as reporting an upset stomach or a headache, expressing anxiety over a long bus ride, and the like, bring about certain outcomes. The mother rewards such responses by allowing the child to remain at home, and a learned connection is formed. The phobic reactions are learned because of the consequences of their expression. While this is, of course, a neat explanation, many psychopathologists regard it as simplistic and feel that it fails to account for the whole picture.

In general, the operant approach emphasizes several factors in the production of maladjusted behavior. There can be **behavioral deficits** brought about by poor reinforcement histories. This often translates into inadequate socialization, which then prevents the individual from coping adequately with environmental demands. In other cases, it seems that the **schedule of reinforcement** is the real culprit, as in the case of some depressions. The person possesses the correct or desirable responses but the environment does not reinforce them properly. In still other instances, there seems to be a failure in the **discrimination of cues.** This is sometimes said to occur with schizophrenics and other psychotics. They do not pay attention to the same environmental cues as do you and I. Perhaps this is due to the fact the proper cues have become associated with punishment while the improper ones lead to reward. For example, a schizophrenic may have learned long ago that paying attention to people leads to rejection and heartache. But paying attention to inanimate objects avoids this pain or rejection and is, therefore, rewarding. What at first glance seems to be terribly bizarre behavior would become clear if only we understood the person's complete reinforcement history. Finally, some individuals have acquired an **inappropriate set of responses.** The neurotic who compulsively counts heartbeats does so because the act is rewarded by preventing unpleasant thoughts. After all, one cannot count and think of other things at the same time. Thus, absorption in counting is reinforcing even though to us it may appear completely inappropriate.

SUMMARY

- The origins of the behavioral tradition in personality can be traced to the early conditioning research of Pavlov. However, the real founder of behaviorism is generally regarded to be John Watson. Other important milestones were Edward Thorndike's formulation of the law of effect and Clark Hull's elegant elaboration of a mathematical-deductive theory.

- John Dollard and Neal Miller translated the insights of Freudian theory into a Hullian learning framework and thereby stimulated a whole new generation of personality psychologists.

- For Dollard and Miller, the four fundamentals of the learning situation were drive, cue, response, and reward. These elements can be used to account for the simple behavior of a rat as well as for complex human behavior.

- Through the work of Dollard and Miller, definitions of what constitutes a stimulus and a response were liberalized to encompass complex human behavior. Basic learning notions such as extinction and partial reinforcement were also expanded to apply to the personality domain.

- Dollard and Miller explained the growth of secondary drives, such as those that result in the pursuit of happiness or wealth, through early associations with primary drives.

- Dollard and Miller used principles such as mediated stimulus generalization and the concept of cue-producing responses to account for such behaviors as thinking, reasoning, and planning.

■ Since Dollard and Miller were mainly concerned with the process of learning, they focused little on personality structures except for habit, the learned association between stimulus and response.

■ Dollard and Miller did discuss four critical training situations in their analysis of how personality develops. They are the feeding situation, cleanliness training, early sex training, and situations involving anger-anxiety conflicts. These definitely have Freudian overtones, but the analysis is in learning terms.

■ Dollard and Miller's analysis of conflict relates to the individual's attempts to cope with three types of conflict situations: approach-approach, avoidance-avoidance, and approach-avoidance.

■ Another noteworthy accomplishment of Dollard and Miller was their description of repression as a form of "stopping thinking."

■ The discussion of Dollard and Miller's theory ended with a presentation of a case illustrating how a neurosis is learned.

■ The second major figure of this chapter was B. F. Skinner, whose operant approach made him one of the foremost psychologists of this century. Through a functional analysis of the manner in which responses follow stimuli, he believed we can understand and control human behavior.

■ Skinner's prime focus was always on operants, that is, behaviors whose frequency of occurrence depends upon the effects they have on the environment. Other major concepts are discriminative stimuli (stimuli that signal that a given response will likely be rewarded) and reinforcers (events that follow a response and increase the likelihood that the response will occur again).

■ Schedules of reinforcement received much attention from Skinner, and his work on intermittent versus continuous reinforcement helped considerably in accounting for how a variety of human behaviors are maintained in real-life settings.

■ Skinner described a chaining process whereby secondary reinforcements arise out of associations with primary reinforcements, ultimately creating networks of reinforcers.

■ Skinner used the notion of shaping to account for the way complex acts are built out of a series of smaller, separate ones. Through reinforcement for successive approximations of the desired behavior, the organism learns complicated skills.

■ While Skinner disdained the personality structures that so many theorists have discussed, he did employ an ideographic method involving the intensive analysis of the reinforcement history of the individual. Personality for the individual thus is the distinct pattern of relationships between behavior and its reinforcement consequences.

■ Skinner did not discuss personality development. But in the sense that development involves behavioral change, his principles could be said to apply. For example, the development of cooperative behavior is the result of rewards that follow from such cooperation.

■ In the Skinnerian system, maladjustment is regarded as a failure of the individual to make appropriate responses in a given situation. This may mean either that appropriate responses have not been learned or that inappropriate ones have been reinforced. In any case, the focus is on behavior and not on some hypothetical set of underlying symptoms.

■ Although Skinner clearly rejected the mediating concepts and personality structures that fascinate so many personologists, his work has had a major impact upon the field.

CHAPTER 11

BEHAVIORISM

Therapy, Assessment, and Summary Evaluation

If theories or conceptualizations in personality are judged on the basis of how influential they have been in generating new methods of therapy or behavior change, then behaviorism has surely been a resounding success. For many years, therapists had grown accustomed to viewing therapy as a series of verbal transactions between therapist and client. Through talk, one's growth potential was released, or perhaps through insight one finally came to realize that id impulses were not really so bad after all. Personality characteristics of various sorts were thought to play critical roles in the development of symptoms or problems. It followed, then, that to bring about change, it was necessary to alter those personality characteristics. The real problem, for example, was not an individual's obsessions or compulsions but the underlying forces that impelled the person to resort to such protective symptoms. To rid the person of these symptoms, the factors that lay behind them must first be discovered. Then, after insight into their nature, the symptoms would take care of themselves since the individual would no longer have any need to resort to defenses.

As we shall see, the behavioral tradition has changed all that. This approach tells us to forget about underlying factors and to begin work directly on the undesirable behavior. Such behavior becomes the target of a variety of methods of conditioning and relearning. We do not *talk* our way out of problems; we *learn* our way out of them. To illustrate how this is done, the next few pages will focus on several stimulus-response and operant approaches to behavioral change.

BEHAVIOR THERAPY

Before beginning a description of several of the many different modern forms of behavior therapy, it is fitting that the contributions of Dollard and Miller be acknowledged.

The legacy of Dollard and Miller

For Dollard and Miller, there is no great mystery about how to rid neurotics of their problems. If neurotic behavior is learned, it can be unlearned—according to the same principles by which it was acquired. Just as bad tennis habits can be broken by a good coach, they argue, so too can bad mental or emotional habits be corrected by a good therapist.

The contribution of these two men lies not in any therapeutic innovations but in their describing traditional psychotherapy procedures in learning terms. For example, the expression of neurotic anxiety, emotions, and guilt in the therapy room is not followed by punishment. Consequently, the extinction of these neurotic symptoms will often eventually result. The sympathetic, understanding therapist helps patients label their unlabeled thoughts and feelings. In this nonpunitive environment, patients gain greater control over previously unconscious material and become better able to deal with it. More reasonable solutions to their difficulties begin to occur to them and are reinforced by positive outcomes. None of this is necessarily easy, automatic, or quick. But learned solutions to learned problems are possible.

Even though Dollard and Miller failed to produce any startling new therapeutic techniques, others have used classical conditioning and general stimulus-response theory to do just that. Following are several examples of those techniques.

Counterconditioning

A distressed mother once remarked: "I don't understand it. Most kids see a puppy and they want to pick him up. But my son only wants to run away!" In the language of learning, what she really wanted was for her son to make a desirable response to a particular stimulus instead of an undesirable one. This is what **counterconditioning** is all about: the conditioning of a desirable response incompatible with the undesirable one that now occurs to a given stimulus. Somehow this mother must get her son to approach rather than avoid puppies. If she can get him to approach, the problem is solved since approach and avoidance are incompatible responses; one cannot run toward and away from the puppy at the same time.

Many years ago, Mary Cover Jones (1924) provided an excellent clinical example of counterconditioning, as noted in the previous chapter. A three-year-old boy, Peter, was afraid of rats, rabbits, and related objects. To eliminate the fear, Jones instituted a program of bringing a caged rabbit closer and closer to the boy as he was eating. The feared rabbit thus became associated with food, and after a few months Peter's fear of the rabbit disappeared. Of course, we must recall Jones's warning that the fear of the rabbit must not be so intense that the child develops an aversion to food.

Jones, who was almost ninety-one when she died in 1987, was active professionally until just before her death. Although widely known as a developmental psychologist early in her career, she came to be known later as "the mother of behavior therapy" (Mussen and Eichorn, 1988).

Systematic desensitization.

Some years later, Joseph Wolpe (1958) used a very similar technique with phobic patients. The idea, very simply, is that an individual cannot be simultaneously anxious and relaxed. Therefore, if we can get the individual to relax in the face of a previously anxiety-producing stimulus, we will have solved the phobic problem. In effect, the person is **systematically desensitized** to the fearful stimulus by virtue of having experienced or confronted it in a relaxed state.

To employ systematic desensitization, the clinician usually begins by examining the patient's complaints and background data to identify the problem. Next, the nature of the problem, how it developed, and how it can be changed are all carefully laid out in commonsense learning terms the patient can easily understand. Following this, the rationale of systematic desensitization is explained. The actual desensitization procedures are illustrated in Box 11-1.

Aversion therapy.

In **aversion therapy,** the idea is to induce negative feelings or reactions to a stimulus that is regarded as attractive by the individual but is viewed as undesirable by the larger culture. As Wolpe (1973) says, "Aversion therapy consists, operationally, of administering an aversive stimulus to inhibit an unwanted emotional response, thereby diminishing its habit strength" (p. 216). Over the years, many forms of aversion therapy have been used. For example, to reduce the attractiveness of alcohol, patients are given a drug that produces nausea or vomiting. Then they are given a drink. Soon these patients become quite ill. The combination of drug and alcohol is given for seven to ten days and eventually the sight or smell of alcohol is enough to induce vomiting or nausea—a simple example of classical conditioning. Male homosexuality has even been treated by pairing the sight of a nude male with painful electric shock delivered to the penis.

Aversion therapy has become controversial for several reasons. First, there are issues of human dignity and whether people can ethically be punished for what amounts to undesirable behavior as defined by someone else. Second, there is real doubt as to whether improvements brought about by aversion techniques really produce lasting behavioral changes. After all, most alcoholics are smart enough to realize that by stopping the ingestion of the nausea-producing drug, the nausea will not follow drinking. In short, human beings are thinking organisms not automatically at the mercy of simple classical conditioning procedures.

The operant approach

True to the operant code, one does not conduct therapy to remove the symptoms of some inner turmoil. Instead, one engages in behavior modification. In short, there are no "cures" for behavioral "diseases"; there is only the modification of behavior. From the Skinnerian viewpoint, the therapist is really an engineer of behavior—one who carefully examines the undesirable behavior, analyzes the reinforcements inherent in the situation, and then comes up with a plan to produce the desired behavior. Consider the following examples.

Conditioning in the cafeteria.

In institutions for the severely disturbed, patients often fail to pick up the proper eating utensils before entering the cafeteria

Box 11-1
SYSTEMATIC DESENSITIZATION PROCEDURES

The following case example of systematic desensitization procedures was provided by Davison and Neale (1990):

> The thirty-five-year-old substitute mail carrier who consulted us had dropped out of college sixteen years ago because of crippling fears of being criticized. Earlier, his disability had taken the form of extreme tension when faced with tests and speaking up in class. When we saw him, he was debilitated by fears of criticism in general and by evaluation of his mail-sorting performance in particular. As a consequence, his everyday activities were severely constricted and, though highly intelligent, he had apparently settled for an occupation that did not promise self-fulfillment.
>
> After agreeing that a reduction in his unrealistic fears would be beneficial, the client was taught over several sessions to relax all the muscles of his body while in a reclining chair. A list of anxiety-provoking scenes was also drawn up in consultation with the client.
>
> You are saying "Good morning" to your boss.
> You are standing in front of your sorting bin in the post office, and your supervisor asks why you are so slow.
> You are only halfway through your route, and it is already 2:00 P.M.
> As you are delivering Mrs. McKenzie's mail, she opens her screen door and complains how late you are.
> Your wife criticizes you for bringing home the wrong kind of bread.
> The officer at the bridge toll gate appears impatient as you fumble in your pocket for the correct change.
>
> These and other scenes were arranged in an anxiety hierarchy, from least to most fear-evoking. Desensitization proper began with the client being instructed first to relax deeply as he had been taught. Then he was to imagine the easiest item, remaining as relaxed as possible. When he had learned to confront this image without becoming anxious, he went on to the next scene, and so on. After ten sessions the man was able to imagine the most distressing scene in the hierarchy without feeling anxious, and gradually his tension in real life became markedly less. (pp. 48–49)

line. As a result, they wind up eating with their fingers, perhaps use only a knife, or simply do not eat. Furthermore, many of these patients are so withdrawn that they do not react to verbal or written instructions. To attack this problem (modify behavior), Ayllon and Azrin (1964) selected a group of patients who fit the pattern described. The plan was that whenever any of these patients picked up all three utensils, immediate access to the food line would be permitted. But any patients who failed to pick up all three would be forced to return to the end of the line (or, if already last, to wait five minutes). For the first ten meals, no instructions were provided to the patients, nor were consequences introduced (baseline period). During the next ten meals, instructions to take all three utensils were given but, again, no consequences ensued for either following or not following the instructions. For the next ten meals, the instructions continued to be given and definite consequences resulted. Doing as instructed led to immediate access to the food counter; not following instructions meant going to the end of the line. The results were quite interesting. In the initial period, there was rarely an instance of the correct behavior. The addition of instructions in the second period resulted in 40 percent of the patients selecting the proper utensils, but the behavior was quite erratic from day to day. In the third phase, during which proper selections led to immediate entry to the cafeteria counter and improper selection meant the end of the line, correct responses increased to 80 percent over the first four meals. For the fifth meal, the rate was up to 90 percent.

Thus, a simple system of reinforcement led to dramatic improvement of behavior in the cafeteria. Hardly a breakthrough in the field of mental health, you say. True, but through such measures, patients can become more accessible to treatment, and a series of such operant programs can have a real impact on institutional management.

Time-out.   Another example of an operant intervention has been reported by Wolf, Risley, and Mees (1964). They describe a case study of an autistic child (one who becomes absorbed in the self, communicates very poorly, shows little interest in others, and may appear mentally defective). The child was subject to severe temper tantrums. The investigators assumed that the tantrums continued because they led to attention from others. As a result, they would isolate the child for brief intervals whenever a tantrum began. It took very little time for the behavior to be eliminated. This procedure is called **time-out** since the individual is briefly removed from situations where positive reinforcement from the unwanted behavior is possible.

Token economies.   One of the most dramatic implementations of the operant philosophy is the **token economy.** As a method of improving the quality of life of chronic patients in mental hospitals, it has enjoyed notable success. The most widely quoted examples come from the work of Ayllon and Azrin (1968), whose experiments were grounded on earlier research by Staats and Staats (1963). In effect, the idea is to provide explicit rewards whenever patients behave in desirable ways (as determined by the staff). For example, behaviors such as making one's bed, washing, combing, and the like are reinforced. Undesirable behavior, for example, screaming, being uncooperative, and so on, is not reinforced. Typically, plastic tokens are awarded whenever the right behavior occurs. These tokens can be exchanged later for a variety of special privileges (going to a movie, visiting the canteen, etc.). The program is organized carefully so that it plays a major role in patients' lives. The rules for the token economy are carefully explained to the patients, and great pains are taken to ensure that they understand. There is little doubt that the token economy can have a marked effect on institutional life. It is, of course, important to emphasize again that such operant programs have not "cured" patients. They have, however, made institutions more livable and the patients more accessible to rehabilitative programs.

There are, of course, critics of the token-economy approach. Some argue that what people learn in the system is simply that everything reduces to monetary value. How much is a smile worth? Two tokens. What will I get if I learn to read faster? Perhaps twenty-five tokens. Everything becomes a medium of exchange, which can lead to a cheapening of relationships. Gagnon and Davison (1976) also suggest that what token economies teach is that the right behavior is inevitably followed by a reward. But in real life, reinforcement is not so predictable. The art of successful living, so some argue, is learning to accept the fact that life is not only sometimes unpredictable but also downright unfair.

Conditioning in the classroom. The following scenario often takes place in large classrooms in colleges and universities. The lecturer has been talking for nearly forty-five minutes. Four or five minutes before the bell is to go off, the students, almost as one, begin to shuffle about in their seats, move their feet restlessly, and pick up their books and notes. The lecturer hesitates for a moment and then rapidly brings the day's topic to a conclusion. The students rise and begin leaving. As the last one goes out the door, the bell rings. From an operant point of view, the students' restless behavior has been reinforced by the reward of having class terminate a few minutes early. Over a series of trials (classes), the behavior of the students has been reinforced in true operant style. Of course, if our focus is on the lecturer's behavior, then it would appear that the lecturer is the one being conditioned. This also illustrates the interactive nature of learning encounters between people.

Biofeedback

Biofeedback is a process whereby the person is given information regarding his or her muscle activity, skin temperature, heart rate, blood pressure, or even brain waves. Normally, individuals would not be aware of these activities. But through complex apparatus, they can be given quick read-outs of data on these internal activities. The use of these techniques is growing rapidly and has clearly outstripped the supporting research evidence. Clinical use has involved the treatment of essential hypertension, headache, epilepsy, and many other conditions.

Many regard biofeedback as an example of operant conditioning. Thus, for example, a reduction in heart rate is followed by a signal from the apparatus that a specific degree of change has occurred. This information is construed as a secondary reinforcer that will enhance the strength of this response. But not everyone is sure things work this way. Perhaps what is involved is not a signal that is rewarding; maybe the signal merely provides increased information. If so, the response of lowered heart rate will be strengthened because of what the person has learned rather than as a function of some secondary reward. In any event, biofeedback techniques are controversial. The harsh judgment is that "there is absolutely no convincing evidence that biofeedback is an essential or specific technique for the treatment of any condition" (Roberts, 1985, p. 940). In any case, biofeedback appears most useful when used as part of a larger treatment package.

The engineered society

From Watson to Skinner, learning theorists have focused on the conditions in the environment that can be manipulated to produce a desired outcome. Watson could (or so he remarked) turn children into beggars or thieves if they would just be given over to him. While his statements contain a great deal of hyperbole, they do have a kernel of seriousness. The implicit threat was enough to make many people nervous. This nervousness is reflected in contemporary concerns over the possibilities of brainwashing or the programming of minds attributed to religious cults.

To some it seems that in the rush to identify the conditions that can shape people and their minds, we have lost sight of the inner person. The learning approach professes not to be interested in what people are made of. Instead, it concentrates on the processes by which behavior can be altered. For many people, the very preoccupation with such a cold and sterile word as *behavior* increases the chance that the importance of the person will get lost in the shuffle.

Skinner did little to calm such fears. If you can manipulate a rat's environment so as to make him dance, who is to say that by manipulating the human environment you cannot make us all dance? In *Walden Two,* his 1948 novel, Skinner described how a society could be built and could function on the principles of reinforcement. And in 1971 he published *Beyond Freedom and Dignity,* in which he explicitly stated how reinforcement contingencies could be applied to religion, politics, government, business, and indeed every corner of modern society.

Central to Skinner's prescriptions for an engineered society is a good behavioral technology. However, we can never accomplish this if we continue to hold our archaic beliefs about autonomy and free will. All of our behavior is determined by genetic predispositions and chains of environmental influences. We do not choose to behave in a particular fashion. The environment acts, and the person reacts. Free will and autonomy are illusory inner qualities that we attribute to ourselves to make us eligible for praise from others and for a dignified place in the world. But once we truly understand all the forces acting on a person, our admiration or our contempt (as the case may be) vanishes. Neither the altruistic nor the rapacious choose to do what they do. They are impelled by the sum total of a lifetime of environmental influences.

Depending on your interpretation, all this is a prescription for horror or a design for a utopian existence. Images of dictatorlike technocrats compete with dreams of the Good Life. As Skinner (1948) put it:

> The one fact that I would cry from every housetop is this: the Good Life is waiting for us. . . . It does not depend on a change in government or on the machinations of world politics. It does not wait upon an improvement in human nature. At this very moment we have the necessary techniques, both material and psychological, to create a full and satisfying life for everyone. (p. 193)

The gathering cognitive emphasis

The behavioral tradition as represented by the work of Dollard and Miller, Skinner, Wolpe, and others has shown a lusty growth over the past twenty years or so. In the last few pages, a variety of behavior-therapy approaches have been described, ranging from systematic desensitization to token economies. But in recent years, a new language has begun to intrude into the world of behaviorism. Such terms as *cognitive behavior modification, cognitive relabeling, stress inoculation,* and *rational restructuring* have started to infiltrate the language. What this signals is a growing cognitive emphasis in the field of behaviorism.

For ardent Skinnerians, these are evil code words for a return to the dismal morass of psychodynamics. In fact, things have "gotten so bad" that even some humanists feel there is a fusion developing between the behavioral and humanistic orientations. Could it be, then, Skinner and Maslow are on the same team?

What has happened is that behavior therapists have begun to develop methods of manipulating not just overt behavior but thinking, reasoning, and other so-called private events as well. As behavior therapists started to deal with a wider range of human problems, they began to realize that there was more out there than just phobias and simple behavioral deficits. Some patients were alienated; others felt inferior; some just seemed unfulfilled. To develop a credible approach that would apply to the entire range of human problems, a way had to be found to deal with cognitions. The following are two examples of this emerging cognitive behavior therapy.

Cognitive restructuring.
Based upon earlier work by Albert Ellis (1962), Goldfried and Davison (1976) suggest that a lot of human misery stems from inappropriate ways of construing the world. Methods must, therefore, be found to get these maladjusted people to label situations more realistically. Patients need to be taught that when they begin to feel upset in a given situation, they must pause and reflect on what it is they are telling themselves about the situation. **Cognitive restructuring** is an eclectic set of techniques, all designed to manipulate patients' thoughts just as formerly in the strict behavioral tradition certain stimuli were introduced to manipulate overt behavior. In some ways, the following example is not far removed from Dollard and Miller's approach, since it is an attempt to induce the client to label situations more rationally and thereby perceive environmental cues more appropriately:

> This is an excerpt from a therapeutic encounter with a thirty-year-old woman who was experiencing episodes of anxiety, guilt, and depression.
>
> CLIENT: I feel so unattractive.
> THERAPIST: God, here you go again with that same old logic of yours.
> CLIENT: I know.
> THERAPIST: Tell me again. We went over it last time. You get depressed because of what you say to yourself about yourself.
> CLIENT: But I can't understand why I am so down all the time. (Starts sobbing quietly)
> THERAPIST: How can you say that? I am sure you were listening when a moment ago I said you tell yourself things.
> CLIENT: OK, OK!
> THERAPIST: Why are you crying? Can you explain it?
> CLIENT: I, I (smiling now) tell myself I am no good. But if I act unattractive, then people will accept me.

THERAPIST: No, no! What other people think doesn't matter. It's what you think that's crucial. As long as you feel good about yourself, that's all. To hell with anybody else. Got it?

CLIENT: Yes . . .

The session continues with the client giving further examples of her concern over what others think about her.

Stress inoculation.

Meichenbaum (1977) has described **stress inoculation,** and Novaco (1977) has provided an example of its application to the anger problems of depressed patients. With this technique, patients are cognitively prepared and then taught to acquire, rehearse, and practice the skills necessary to deal with their problem. For example, they are given instructional manuals that describe the nature of anger and how it functions. Illustrations of situations in which anger can be a problem are provided, along with examples of what causes anger and how it can be regulated. Patients are taught how to view provocative situations in alternative ways and how to put themselves in the shoes of the anger-producing person. Even methods of relaxation are taught, as well as ways of cultivating a sense of humor. Finally, anger-producing situations are induced by imagination and role playing. Hierarchies of anger situations are generated. By gradually working up the hierarchy (first by imagination and then by role playing), patients learn to hone anger-management skills rehearsed earlier with the therapist.

The hidden goal of understanding.

Behavior therapists have long claimed that their target is behavioral change rather than the patient's achievement of understanding or insight. But it has always seemed that people have a strong need to know. If we are depressed, we go to a therapist to become happy, or at least to have our depression lifted. Some of us, however, are not content with just this outcome. We also want to know *why* we were depressed in the first place. As patients, we have not only behavioral goals but cognitive ones as well. Interestingly, it would appear that this cognitive urge for understanding is not confined to laypeople. In a revealing paper, Arnold Lazarus (1971) describes his discovery that twenty-three clinical psychologists who described themselves as "behavior therapists" were undergoing psychoanalysis or a related form of nonbehavioral psychotherapy. As has been noted, behavior therapists typically steer clear of such mentalistic phenomena as insight, transference, and resistance when dealing with their own patients. They prefer to change behaviors or build up behavior repertoires without the dreaded encumbrances of insight. Yet here we have more than a few behavioral therapists seeking the very thing they condemn as superfluous. Why? In Lazarus's (1971) own words:

> From what I know of the behavioral clinicians who have elected to undergo nonbehavioral therapies themselves, they are all relatively assertive individuals without debilitating phobias, compulsions, or sexual aberrations, who wish to be in better touch with their own feelings and who desire a better appreciation and understanding of the antecedents of their current actions. (p. 350)

Lazarus seems to be suggesting that behavioral therapies are suitable when the problem is a kind of behavioral deficit (sexual dysfunction, lack of assertiveness, etc.) but that more cognitively oriented therapies are preferable when understanding is sought or the need to recapture the meaning of life is involved.

The cognitive emphasis means that we can alter our behavior by altering the way we think about events. Photograph Ken R. Buck/The Picture Cube.

BEHAVIORAL ASSESSMENT

As we have seen in previous chapters, the traditional role of assessment has been the identification of the underlying personality variables that mediate behavior. Assessment from this vantage point revolves around the measurement of stable internal characteristics (traits, growth potential, inferiority complex, etc.). But as we move into the framework of classical and operant conditioning, our conceptualization of personality is dramatically altered. Table 11-1 summarizes the major differences between traditional personality assessment approaches we have seen in previous chapters and the behavioral approach.

Sign versus sample

A major implication of this general philosophy involves the distinction between sign and sample (Goodenough, 1949). The traditional approach to personality assessment views test data as **signs** of some underlying state or condition. Unhappy TAT stories are signs of an underlying depression. Macho talk may be interpreted as symptomatic of insecurity. But the behaviorist does not look at things this way. Observed behaviors such as the foregoing are merely **samples** of a larger pool of possible observations that could be made in other situations. When a patient talks little, appears tired, and does not respond to humor, this would be seen by the behavior therapist as a sample of the patient's demeanor outside the consulting room. Avoiding the threatening portions of a Rorschach card would be viewed not as a symptom of some malignant underlying problem but as a sample of a more general avoidance tendency at home, on the job, or elsewhere.

SORC

Behaviorally oriented clinical psychologists are often said to be interested in the identification and measurement of four kinds of variables. First, there is S — the stimuli or environmental settings that seem to trigger the behavior in question. Second, there is O — the organismic (both physiological and psychological) factors that are associated.

TABLE 11-1   Differences between behavioral and traditional approaches to assessment

	Behavioral	Traditional
I. Assumptions		
1. Conception of personality	Personality constructs mainly employed to summarize specific behavior patterns, if at all	Personality as a reflection of enduring underlying states or traits
2. Causes of behavior	Maintaining conditions sought in current environment	Intrapsychic or within the individual
II. Implications		
1. Role of behavior	Important as a sample of person's repertoire in specific situation	Behavior assumes importance only insofar as it indexes underlying causes
2. Role of history	Relatively unimportant, except, for example, to provide a retrospective baseline	Crucial in that present conditions seen as a product of the past
3. Consistency of behavior	Behavior thought to be specific to the situation	Behavior expected to be consistent across time and settings
III. Uses of data	To describe target behaviors and maintaining conditions	To describe personality functioning and etiology
	To select the appropriate treatment	To diagnose or classify
	To evaluate and revise treatment	To make prognosis; to predict
IV. Other characteristics		
1. Level of inferences	Low	Medium to high
2. Comparisons	More emphasis on intraindividual or idiographic	More emphasis on interindividual or nomothetic
3. Methods of assessment	More emphasis on direct methods (e.g., observations of behavior in natural environment)	More emphasis on indirect methods (e.g., interviews and self-report)
4. Timing of assessment	More ongoing; prior, during, and after treatment	Pre- and perhaps posttreatment, or strictly to diagnose
5. Scope of assessment	Specific measures and of more variables (e.g., of target behaviors in various situations, of side effects, context, strengths as well as deficiencies)	More global measures (e.g., of cure, or improvement) but only of the individual

Adapted from "Some Relationships Between Behavioral and Traditional Assessment" by D. P. Hartmann, B. I. Roper, and D. C. Bradford, *Journal of Behavioral Assessment, 1, 4,* 1979. Reprinted by permission of Plenum Publishing Corporation and Donald P. Hartmann.

For example, an individual's depressed outlook might be related to the use of certain drugs or perhaps to negative internal self-statements. It might be noted parenthetically that the introduction of *O* factors here has the distinct aroma of cognitive behaviorism. The third variable, *R,* refers to overt, observable responses which represent the problem. The identification of these *R* variables is the heart of the behaviorist's task. The fourth variable, *C,* signifies the consequences of the individual's behavior. These are the reinforcements which presumably maintain the behavior the clinician wishes to change. For example, does a child's disruptive classroom behavior *(R)* lead to the positive consequences *(C)* of attention from the teacher, which are reinforcing? Let us now review some of the principal behavioral assessment techniques currently in vogue.

Interviews

It is hard to imagine a more common technique than the interview. The behavioral clinician, no less than a psychodynamically oriented investigator, is likely to use it. Goldfried and Davison (1976) have offered a pragmatic description of interview procedures calculated to elicit behavioral information. Naturally one begins by establishing rapport with the individual so that a climate likely to produce the desired information will be established. The information sought essentially revolves around the **SORC** data noted a moment ago. That is, the clinician needs to know about the stimuli that seem to be associated with the problem behavior, any factors within the person that are involved, the nature of the problem behavior itself, and events following the behavior that may be playing a role in maintaining it. Very often, relevant case history data are sought and an assessment made of the client's current strengths and past attempts to cope with the problem. Many clinicians also find it important to solicit the individual's expectations regarding therapy. Again we see the growing influence of the cognitive point of view.

Inventories and checklists

A variety of self-report techniques have been used to identify behaviors, emotional reactions, and perceptions of the environment. A good example is the **Fear Survey Schedule** (Geer, 1965). This instrument describes fifty-one potentially fear-arousing situations and asks the individual to rate the degree of fear or the extent of unpleasant reactions produced by each. Examples of these situations include anticipating having an operation, being in a high place, hearing thunder, and speaking before an audience. Another inventory sometimes used is the **State-Trait Anxiety Inventory (STAI)** Spielberger, Gorsuch, and Lushene, 1970), which measures anxiety both as a chronically experienced emotion and as a more transitory reaction to specific situations. Insel and Moos (1974) have utilized an inventory that assesses the person's perception of the social environment. The important thing to note about all these devices is that they try to pinpoint specific behaviors and reactions in relation to specific situations.

Direct observation

With people like John Watson and B.F. Skinner serving as heroes of the behavioral movement, it is not surprising that direct observation of behavior is a prominent assessment method. There have been examples of naturalistic observations that involved meticulous recordings of a person's every move. One such instance is the research of Barker and Wright (1951), in which the detailed activities of a seven-year-old were minutely noted over an entire day. In most instances, however, such extensive observations are impractical and too time-consuming. More common are the limited observations of a subject in a more confined environment. For example, Ayllon and Michael (1959) had nurses systematically observe and record the behavior of patients in an institutional setting. In this case, a given patient was watched for one to three minutes every thirty minutes. Another example is provided by O'Leary and Becker (1967), who developed an objective method for observing the presence, duration, and frequency of behaviors such as raising one's hand, pushing, and so on. This was in connection with assessing the effectiveness of a token reinforcement program in a class of disruptive children. Patterson (1977) and his colleagues have used the **Behavioral Coding System (BCS)** to record observations in the homes of predelinquent boys exhibiting problems in aggressiveness and noncompliance. (See Figure 11-1)

Controlled settings.   Obviously, naturalistic observations are not always possible or practical. Then, too, there are always questions of ethics. Observing people without their permission raises a variety of professional issues. Furthermore, friends and associates of the person being observed can be drawn into the observational net, and without their approval a host of problems can arise. Beyond these important problems, however, naturalistic observation means that we are at the mercy of free-flowing events which can sometimes interfere with what we are trying to observe. Besides, there is always a great deal of observational chaff that goes along with the wheat. For such reasons, controlled observations are sometimes used. They enable the observer to make more finely calibrated observations and ratings.

A rather exotic example of this is a case in which Arnold Lazarus (1961) observed and assessed a patient's claustrophobic behavior by placing him in a closed room made progressively smaller by moving a screen closer and closer to him. The direct observation of his fear reactions by the clinician could thus produce information unfiltered by the subjective reports of the patient or third persons. Such assessment procedures are also illustrated by the following example from the Bandura, Adams, and Beyer (1977) study of chronic snake phobias:

> *Behavioral avoidance.*   The test of avoidance behavior consisted of a series of 29 performance tasks requiring increasingly more threatening interactions with a red-tailed boa constrictor. Subjects were instructed to approach a glass cage containing the snake, to look down at it, to touch and hold the snake with gloved and then bare hands, to let it loose in the room and then return it to the cage, to hold it within 12 cm of their faces, and finally to tolerate the snake crawling in their laps while they held their hands passively at their sides. . . .
>
> . . . Those who could not enter the room containing the snake received a score of 0; subjects who did enter were asked to perform the various tasks in the graded series. To control for any possible influence of expressive cues from the tester, she stood behind the subject and read aloud the tasks to be performed. . . .
>
> The avoidance score was the number of snake-interaction tasks the subject performed successfully.

```
Blank Sample Coding Sheet for the BCS

                        Family number _____

                         ID number _____

              BEHAVIOR CODING SHEET

                     Phase _____

Subject _____  Observer _____ Date _____ No. _____

AP  Approval          HU  Humiliate          PP  Positive physical
AT  Attention         IG  Ignore                   contact
CM  Command           LA  Laugh              RC  Receive
CN  Command           NC  Noncompliance      SS  Self-stimulation
     (negative)       NE  Negativism         TA  Talk
CO  Compliance        NO  Normative          TE  Tease
CR  Cry               NR  No response        TH  Touching,
DI  Disapproval       PL  Play                    handling
DP  Dependency        PN  Negative physical  WH  Whine
DS  Destructiveness         contact          WK  Work
HR  High rate                                YE  Yell
```

1				
2				
•				
•				
•				
10				

Description _____

FIGURE 11-1   A blank sample coding sheet.

From Jones, R. R., Reid, J. B., and Patterson, G. R., " Naturalistic observation in clinical assessment" in P. McReynolds, ed., *Advances in Psychological Assessment,* Vol. 3, 1975. Reprinted by permission of Jossey-Bass, Inc., Publishers.

Fear arousal accompanying approach responses.   In addition to the measurement of performance capabilities, the degree of fear aroused by each approach response was assessed. During the behavioral test, subjects rated orally, on a 10-interval scale, the intensity of fear they experienced when each snake approach task was described to them and again while they were performing the corresponding behavior. (pp. 127–128)

Role playing.   Many years ago, Rotter and Wickens (1948) suggested **role playing** as a technique of behavioral assessment. This technique capitalizes on the fact that not every problem can be systematically observed. Role playing involves the acting out of a problem or situation with the resulting opportunity to observe how the patient reacts. Although role playing obviously does not deal with behavior in a real-life setting, it is a practical compromise in many instances (Goldfried, 1976).

Self-monitoring.   Individuals are sometimes asked to maintain daily records of their behavior, with particular attention to the problem behaviors and the specific situations or conditions that seem to be involved (Wolpe and Lazarus, 1966). Use of such **self-monitoring** procedures is a recognition, again, that one usually cannot efficiently or economically follow individuals about to record their every move. The procedure of self-monitoring is one in which individuals maintain their own diaries or records according to the behavioral clinician's instructions. Self-monitoring has often been used with specific target behaviors such as smoking or eating. As might be expected, there can be problems in the reliability of the data when individuals record their own behavior. On the other hand, specifically training individuals in exactly how to observe and record their own behavior can reduce this unreliability, particularly when they are also given motivating instructions to be accurate.

An interesting sidelight to self-monitoring is that people often react to their own observations by reducing the frequency of the problem behavior. This means that there can be a therapeutic potential in the very act of self-monitoring. Take the example of smoking behavior reported by Lipinski, Black, Nelson, and Ciminero (1975). In this study, two groups of college students were the subjects. One group was solicited through advertisements for "individuals who want to stop smoking." The other group responded to an advertisement which asked only for "individuals who are cigarette smokers." Initial instructions were provided in separate meetings for each group. The instructions required all subjects to keep a daily count of the number of cigarettes they smoked. All subjects were told that the self-monitoring might tend to reduce their smoking. Each subject was then given a card on which to record the daily cigarette consumption for one week. Subjects turned in their weekly records for a four week period. The results shown in Figure 11-2 clearly indicate that motivated subjects reduced their smoking during the course of the experiment. At least with motivated subjects, then, the very act of self-monitoring can produce important reactive effects.

SUMMARY EVALUATION

Psychology in the United States has always been highly receptive to learning theories and to research strategies that emphasize the quantification and careful control of variables. When behavior-therapy methods finally crystallized out of the earlier work of Watson, Dollard and Miller, and Skinner, it was not surprising to find that they were warmly embraced. Academic psychologists in particular had never found psychoanalysis to be an especially congenial companion. As the behavioral tradition began to gain visibility, the psychoanalytically oriented and behaviorally oriented camps took turns hurling caustic remarks at each other. This scenario has never really disappeared. For example, Wogan and Norcross (1982) comment that the psychodynamic school typically regards behavior therapists as "naive, unanalyzed symptom treaters who are acting out their impulses to control" (p. 100). Wolpe (1981), in turn, fires a typical salvo

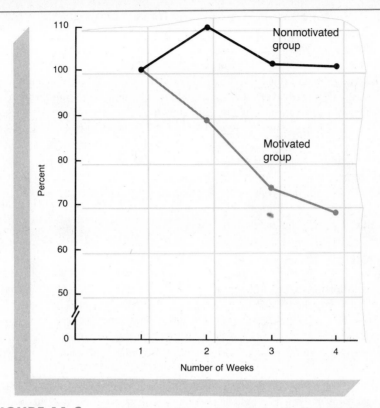

FIGURE 11-2 Motivation and the reactive effects of self-monitoring.
Adapted from "Influence of Motivational Variables on the Reactivity and
Reliability of Self-Recording" by D. P. Lipinski, J. L. Black, R. O. Nelson,
and A. R. Ciminero, *Journal of Consulting and Clinical Psychology,* 1975,
43, 637–646. Copyright 1975 by the American Psychological Association.
Used with permission.

from the behaviorist camp when he says, "In actuality, not a single one of the [psycho-analytic] theory's main propositions has ever been supported" (p. 160).

The move toward cognitive behaviorism has begun to lessen this warfare some-what; nevertheless, a lively debate continues. It is out of such debates that we can be-gin to gain a clearer picture of the strengths and weaknesses of the behavioral learning point of view.

Now, let us take a critical look at the behavioral learning tradition as typified by Dollard and Miller and Skinner.

Strengths

The following are several of the chief strengths of this general approach.

Synthesis of laboratory and clinic.   Until Dollard and Miller arrived on the scene, the chasm between the animal learning laboratory and the therapeutic consulting room was wide and deep. Dollard and Miller were able to bridge that chasm by the brilliant translation of psychodynamic processes into the language of learning. To a large extent, they did this by liberalizing the definition of both stimulus and response. They also added sociocultural variables and drew upon the data of cultural anthropology to create a blend that ultimately transformed the nature of personality theory. While it is popular now to regard their work as little more than of historical interest, many of their analyses of the manner in which neurotic problems are acquired and the functions they serve still seem remarkably vital. They did not just say that personality is learned; they provided extensive descriptions of just what the process involves. Needless to say, not everyone in the learning establishment has agreed with their analyses. Eysenck, Wolpe, Skinner, and Bandura have all decried what they perceive as an overreliance on psychoanalysis.

Skinner's work has also found extensive applications to therapeutic situations. Although Skinner himself never seemed all that interested in finding clinical applications, his followers, nonetheless, have been especially active and ingenious in their search for the therapeutic application of operant principles. Dollard and Miller stuck essentially to the traditional verbal psychotherapy model and translated it into learning terms. But the Skinnerians have created an entirely new collection of therapeutic methods that have found application everywhere from prisons and institutions for the retarded to day-care centers and family therapy. We shall come back to these points a bit later.

A scientific approach.   Dollard and Miller were among the first to show that personality and science could be compatible enterprises. They did this by carefully defining their concepts in operational terms. Their approach had been polished in the laboratory and they did not find it necessary to appeal to either intuition or authority. Hall and Lindzey (1978) describe their perspective as both hardheaded and positivistic. Theirs was a scientifically objective approach steeped in a deterministic philosophy.

They found no need to turn their concepts into things that existed inside the head somewhere. Thus, whereas Freudian theory became entangled in rampant reification, Dollard and Miller sought refuge in objectivity and operational definitions. Concepts were not defined in terms of metaphors but in terms of the operations necessary to measure them. Indeed, their concepts resist being transformed into things inside the mind. Freud made it very easy to describe the id as a seething cauldron of impulses or as a sex-starved hedonist. Can you imagine trying to do this with a concept like avoidance gradient? This concept is easily defined in terms of the way we measure it—moving away from an object, speed of withdrawal, and the like. It is clearly a concept and not a thing. All of this illustrates that Dollard and Miller had a grasp of theory. They knew theory to be merely a set of concepts that aids us in making predictions rather than a map of reality.

Skinner would hardly have described himself as a theorist. He felt that theory was both unnecessary and pretentious. But he certainly epitomized the objective, scientific approach to psychology. No one did it better when it came to basing conclusions on meticulously controlled and replicated laboratory experiments rather than argument.

For him, issues were settled in the arena of experimentation and not on the debating floor. Each set of facts he discovered in the laboratory became a launching pad for the discovery of a further set of facts. By this process he was able to specify in great detail just what was involved in the learning process. Skinner, of course, was an enormously prolific experimenter. This in no small measure accounts for his eminent position in psychology today. He was also an innovative experimenter with a real flair for coming up with novel techniques and apparatus to study behavior. Had this been his only contribution, he still would have had a significant impact on experimental psychology.

Broadening the application. It has been noted that both Dollard and Miller's and Skinner's work helped blur the distinction between laboratory and clinic. But Skinner's operant methods have spilled out far beyond that point. Educational institutions now use self-paced instructional procedures that rely on operant principles. Programmed learning and teaching machines are commonplace these days. And, of course, Skinner promoted the ultimate application—a society run on operant principles. By creating a society where one's acts are carefully regulated by the consequences they engender, he hoped a more nearly perfect life would result for all of us. A society engineered and directed by operant principles is certainly a remarkable aspiration and a testimonial to Skinner's confidence in his own research. Whether it provides a blueprint for the future or a threat for everyone is still uncertain. What is certain is that Skinnerian principles have been successfully employed by animal trainers, teachers, and therapists alike.

An idiographic approach. One of the reasons Skinner's work has had so many successful applications is that it is idiographic. The focus has always been on individual organisms whether they be pigeons or persons. Other investigators have often been busy formulating general principles based on data averaged over many subjects. Consequently, the results never seem to apply to the single individual—who somehow never quite fits the average. But Skinner averaged data over trials for each separate individual. As a result there emerged a psychology of the individual. Skinner combined laboratory precision, control, and rigor with a focus on the single person. This stands out in bold relief from other idiographic approaches which too often have been conceptually elastic and methodologically soft.

Schedules of reinforcement. The previously noted precision and rigor are nowhere more apparent than in Skinner's research on schedules of reinforcement. Both in the animal realm and in the case of the discrete responses of humans, Skinnerians are now able to predict both the acquisition and the extinction of responses with great accuracy. This, too, is one of the reasons why operant methods have found such widespread application in a variety of learning situations from the classroom to the institution to the therapy room.

Behavioral assessment. It is important to recognize that, at best, behavioral assessment is a loosely joined confederation of techniques running the gamut from interviewing, inventories, and observation to role playing, behavioral avoidance techniques, and self-monitoring. What these techniques have in common are their goals and not their formal structure. They are all geared to the accumulation of information about the person's behavior, the environmental conditions that produce and maintain that behavior, and the positive and negative consequences that flow from it. The emphasis is on obtaining an accurate sample of the individual's behavior rather than on rooting out hidden conflicts or mind entities. All of this is a direct outgrowth of the behavioral philosophy.

Behavioral therapy.   What has really changed the landscape of therapy, however, has been the introduction of methods such as systematic desensitization, aversion techniques, token economies, and the like. In the words of London (1964), these newer behavior therapies were sounding an "epitaph for insight." What this means is that the long-term psychotherapy approach was being replaced by a series of shorter, more behaviorally targeted methods that focused on the person's specific complaints. The quest for insight, the search for an underlying pathology, and the endless hours of working through gave way to an emphasis on present behavior and a pragmatism inherent in the use of specific techniques for specific problems. The passivity of the listening psychoanalyst disappeared in a whirl of activity by the behavior therapist—the construction of anxiety hierarchies, the dispensing of specific rewards, and the offering of specific recommendations and interventions.

These newer, more direct techniques have demonstrated that therapy need not be reserved for the affluent, the very intelligent, or the middle and upper classes—those persons who have the money, time, and psychological inclination for traditional therapy. Behavior therapy works for these populations just as it does for the lower-class individual with modest verbal skills. And because less time is required, the methods are more available to those of limited financial resources. Even the poorly endowed retardate or the regressed schizophrenic can profit to some extent from these techniques.

Most of all, perhaps, the success of these behavioral methods has challenged many of the assumptions and myths that had so long surrounded the psychotherapy enterprise. Is insight really necessary for lasting changes in behavior to occur? Will one undesirable behavior resurface in the guise of some other undesirable behavior unless insight is provided? Is the resolution of childhood conflicts the only answer to adult problem behavior? In pursuing the answers to such questions, the whole face of the therapy enterprise has been altered.

Weaknesses

While the behavioral movement has brought with it a distinct set of assets, it is not without its share of problems, as the following paragraphs will illustrate.

The wrong emphasis.   Many have argued that any approach tied so strongly to the laboratory and to animal populations can never claim to be in harmony with the reality of human existence. No matter how much Dollard and Miller argue to the contrary, so the claim goes, rats scurrying into safe compartments are less an analog of the human condition than they are a travesty of it. To build a science of human behavior out of the data from Skinner's pigeons pecking at colored disks is worse than a bad joke. The behavior studied is so molecular and superficial that it cannot possibly relate to human behavior except in its most simplistic aspects. Somehow, the emphasis on primary drives will have to give way to a realization that humans are guided less by their guts than they are by a sense of self. To see us like animals is to deny the existence of choice and free will. Are we simple mechanisms impelled by primary needs, or rational individuals as much pulled by our aspirations and expectations as pushed by our visceral needs?

Too much environment and too little cognition.   The behavioral tradition depicts the human being as a creature at the mercy of environmental forces. In its extreme form, Skinnerian doctrine has it that we are like "empty boxes." There is environmental input in the way of stimulation and there is output by way of our responses. But what transpires within the box? Surely we do not all respond to the same stimulus in the same fashion. Is it enough to say only that this reflects different reinforcement histories? If that is true, then we are totally dependent in predicting a person's response in a given situation on an examination of past responses in similar situations. But what happens when a person is in a situation never before encountered? Under these circumstances, we cannot look to the past because no such situation has ever arisen. How, for example, are we to predict suicide on the part of someone who has never attempted it? Because of Skinnerian unwillingness to consider any mediating variables or to infer any personality characteristics, it would seem that our ability to predict many kinds of behavior is severely curtailed. Although this may be no great handicap with rats or pigeons and their simple behavior in laboratory settings, it may well be a fatal shortcoming in dealing with the tremendous complexity of human behavior in social situations.

The whole arena of cognitive behavior seems to be overlooked by the Skinnerians. In many ways, the most human of all characteristics is our ability to think, plan, aspire, and reflect. Yet these are the very elements missing in the more radical versions of behaviorism. Little attention is devoted to how individuals perceive objectively similar stimuli in different ways, or to how stimuli may be defined. There is a lack of interest in how we humans cognitively process information in ways different from one another. In their rush to develop an objective science, some behaviorists seem to have so restricted the kinds of behavior they will study that a question arises as to how valid their sample of human behavior really is. So much of human behavior is covert that, somehow, the behavioral approach will have to come to grips with it. Not to do so is, as Hall and Lindzey (1978) put it, tantamount to dealing with a "decorticate" organism. As noted earlier, however, several cognitive behavioral approaches are beginning to grapple with these problems.

Lack of predispositions.   While Dollard and Miller do discuss initial hierarchies of responses and Skinner did admit the importance of genetics, in practice neither predispositions nor genetics gets much attention. The focus is largely on learned behavior, which is regulated by environmental input. Much less emphasis is placed on predispositions that affect the behavioral output.

Definition of stimuli and reinforcements.   A moment ago it was noted that individuals define stimuli in different ways. Indeed, what is a stimulus for one is not for another. Dollard and Miller have often been criticized (sometimes by behaviorists) for their inability to identify specifically what is a stimulus for a given person. As they broadened the definition of a stimulus and moved outside the laboratory, much of the rigor and definitional clarity of the learning approach began to fade. Thus, their liberalization of what can constitute a stimulus has turned out to be a double-edged sword.

By the same token, some learning theorists have difficulty in identifying in advance of a given situation what will turn out to be reinforcing for the person. If an event has been reinforcing in the past, it will likely be so again. But there is a circularity to this definition of a reinforcement. A reinforcement is whatever exerts an effect on behavior. Sometimes it is difficult to specify a reinforcer in advance, particularly in the case of maladjusted people who do not view either stimuli or rewards in the same way as most people in the culture. For example, some individuals actually regard pain as positively reinforcing and make every effort to subject themselves to it. While a behavioral analysis of masochism is possible (Brown, 1965), such an example does illustrate the problems these learning approaches can have in defining reinforcements before the fact.

Lack of theory.   Whereas Dollard and Miller had a real understanding of and appreciation for the role of theory, Skinner was entirely opposed to the use of theory. While Skinner (1969) did to some extent accept the role of theory when it is defined in his own terms, he has been widely criticized on this score. In the view of many scientists, no one can approach a field of study without some assumptions and presuppositions. This being the case, it is better to make them explicit and understand how they guide our work. Furthermore, a systematic theory can be a powerful deductive tool which stimulates research.

Behavioral assessment.   Behaviorally oriented diagnosticians often assert their pride over the fact that behavioral assessment springs from a heritage of scientific rigor. Actually, however, behavioral assessment itself comprises a heterogeneous collection of techniques that are often far from rigorous, objective, or psychometrically adequate. Many of these diagnosticians have barely dealt with such issues as the extent to which subjects or patients are really responding to specific characteristics of the assessment situation. Many techniques have not even begun to meet modest standardization criteria. Interestingly, we know considerably less about many of these methods than we do about projective techniques. Projective testers have often been criticized for using unreliable, invalid instruments. Yet in the realm of behavioral assessment, the situation is often equally bad. One should not assume that any technique described as "behavioral" is automatically an elegant psychometric achievement.

There are real questions about the reliability of many behavioral assessment procedures. Not all raters or coders of a given set of behaviors use similar methods, and this can lead to unreliability. In addition, assessment procedures are often "customized" for a specific problem or setting, with the result that we have little assurance that raters from other clinics will produce comparable ratings.

For a long time, everyone was so excited about the rigor and objectivity of the behavioral approach that not many questioned the validity of their assessment. But do these assessment procedures measure accurately what they set out to measure? Is the frequency of aggressive remarks made in a role-playing situation a valid indicator of one's general level of hostility? Does the observer's ratings of an individual's dependency behavior exhibited in the family accurately reflect dependency shown when the rater is not present? Most certainly, we have to be concerned about the effects of the observer on what is being observed. From our own experience, we all realize that sometimes we put on "fronts." As someone was once overheard to say, "It is so hard being charming all day; now I can go home and be myself!" Behavioral assessors must constantly be on guard lest they fail to note such effects. The point is not that these problems cannot be overcome, only that we must be aware of them and work on them.

It is somewhat ironic that projective testers and inventory users were long criticized for generalizing too far from very small samples of behavior. Yet sometimes behavioral assessment seems to fall into the same trap. One must constantly ask questions about the **ecological validity** of one's methods. That is, are the samples of behaviors, situations, and consequences being derived actually representative?

Of course one of the hardest things for observers of human behavior to do is to dissociate themselves from the phenomena they are observing and rating. Too often one finds evidence for what one expects to find. Even the carefully trained person has to guard against this tendency. One's own needs and expectations often have an insidious way of intruding.

Behavior therapy.   Before proceeding with a critique of behavior therapy, it would be wise to heed the admonition of Lazarus and Wilson (1976), who remarked that behavior therapy has

> no universally accepted definition, no consensus as to goals, concepts or underlying philosophy, no agreement as to its purview, no monolithic point of view, no overriding strategy or core techniques, no single founding father, no general agreement about matters of training, and there is no single profession to which primary allegiance is declared. (p. 153)

Despite the frequent claims that behavior therapy is steeped in an experimental-learning tradition, others have observed that it can lay no more claim to scientific respectability than other forms of therapy (Breger and McGaugh, 1965). Locke (1971) has even asserted that behavior therapy methods contradict every major premise of behaviorism. What, for example, is objective or observable about an image conjured up by a patient in the middle of an anxiety hierarchy?

Of course, the truly important questions are those directed toward the effectiveness of behavior therapy techniques. Some have suggested that while such techniques do relieve anxiety or lessen symptoms, they do not promote inner growth or help us reach our potential. Such criticisms do not, however, appear so telling in view of the more recent cognitive emphasis in behavior therapy. Also, pleas for inner growth seem to come primarily from those identified with a phenomenological-humanistic perspective.

Calvin and Hobbes

by Bill Watterson

A more critical point arises in connection with the ability of behavioral techniques to deal with problems that are vague or existential in character. Fear of snakes or elevators is more easily dealt with than feelings of depression, an enveloping sense of life's basic meaninglessness, or some moral dilemma. Behavioral approaches seem at their best when applied to the correction of specific behavioral deficits or the reduction of specific anxieties. Again, as behavior therapy becomes more cognitively oriented, it may yet be able to merge the psychodynamic perspective with behaviorism and thus have the best of both worlds.

Another question involves the issue of whether the effects of behavior therapy generalize to other situations. Such a question really applies to all forms of therapy. But in the case of token economies, for example, the issue can become a compelling one. Token economies are often quite effective in sheltered institutions where it is easy to exert a great deal of control over a person. But when that person leaves the controlled setting, the positive effects of the therapy frequently do not generalize to the new environment. Similar questions have arisen about aversion techniques. Whether such behavior modification techniques are truly useful in natural, uncontrolled settings is still an issue. Such problems have led some to characterize these methods as superficial, simplistic techniques that produce little of lasting value. Furthermore, Condrey (1977) has observed that when we use external incentives to induce behavioral changes, we are undermining any intrinsic motivation to change that the person may have. Once the external incentives are removed, the desired behavior drops out. For instance, can you ever teach a sloppy child the value of orderliness by *paying* her to clean her room each week?

A volatile issue has been whether behavior therapies are improper attempts to control and manipulate people. Are they really insidious efforts to undermine the person's capacity to make decisions, assume responsibility, or maintain dignity? It is not hard to see behavior therapy in that light when we are talking about electric shocks to the penis, drugs to make you ill when you drink, or tokens to induce you to behave in a manner desired by institutional authorities. However, as Goldfried and Davison (1976) assert, such criticisms lose much of their force when applied to adults who voluntarily seek such treatment. But in the case of children, incompetent adults, prisoners, and others who do not have control over their lives, such questions are nagging ones. Of course, it must be pointed out that there may be an inherent contradiction here. One can hardly describe behavioral techniques as superficial and simplistic on the one hand and insidious and mind-altering on the other.

Regardless of whether behavioral techniques are effective, simplistic, dehumanizing, or marvelous, one thing is quite clear: they are a heterogeneous amalgam. Some are from the operant tradition, others are offshoots of classical conditioning, and still others are quite cognitive in nature. There is theoretical chaos here, which in the long run makes it difficult for the practitioner to understand what is really transpiring in behavior therapy. For example, is it conditioning or is it the relationship between therapist and patient that is crucial in improvement? What is needed is an integrating theoretical framework.

SUMMARY

- The major contribution of Dollard and Miller to the practice of psychotherapy lies in their translation of traditional methods into learning terms.

- Counterconditioning methods of behavior change arose out of the classical conditioning paradigm. The idea is to condition the individual to make responses incompatible with the undesirable ones (e.g., relaxation rather than anxiety). Wolpe's method of systematic desensitization is a popular example of this general approach.

- A variety of aversion techniques have also been developed. In aversion therapy, the habit strength of an undesirable response is reduced by associating the response with an unpleasant stimulus.

- Skinnerian approaches are based on operant principles, wherein behavior is modified by making the achievement of reinforcements contingent upon the person's emitting the desired behavior. The time-out procedure briefly removes the individual from the situation in which positive reinforcement for an undesirable behavior occurs until more desirable responses begin.

- Token economies are dramatic examples of the operant technology. Tokens are given to the individual whenever the desirable behavior occurs. These tokens can be exchanged at a later time for reinforcements of value to the individual.

- Biofeedback is a process whereby the individual is given information regarding such things as skin temperature, heart rate, and the like. Presumably, such information serves as a secondary reinforcer that can enhance the strength of the response (e.g., lowered heart rate). The technique has been used to treat a variety of conditions ranging from headache to hypertension. However, the exact nature of biofeedback and its effectiveness is still controversial.

■ The operant philosophy has been strongly pushed by Skinner as a means of engineering a better society. Needless to say, Skinner's prescriptions here have been hotly debated. Some describe them as the way to a utopian society; others see them as the road to tyranny.

■ In recent years, the behavioral tradition has begun to incorporate a cognitive emphasis. The focus remains on behavior, but now a variety of covert behaviors are included. For example, the cognitive restructuring technique teaches individuals to reflect on how they construe certain situations so as to become emotionally upset. With stress inoculation, patients are cognitively prepared so that they can acquire the skills necessary to cope with threatening situations. Clearly, the role of understanding and insight has begun to infiltrate the behavioral camp.

■ In behavioral assessment, the major goals are the identification of the specific behavior that requires change, the most practical means of changing that behavior, and the determination of the factors in the environment that maintain it and have led to its acquisition. Such assessment is not oriented toward discovering some underlying pathology (signs) but toward eliciting representative samples of behavior. Specifically, four kinds of data are sought: the stimuli that elicit the undesirable behavior, the organismic factors associated, the responses that ensue, and the consequences that result from these responses.

■ A variety of behavioral assessment techniques were briefly described, including interviews, inventories and checklists, direct observation, the use of controlled settings, role playing, and self-monitoring.

■ Several strengths of the behavioral perspective were elaborated. They are its ability to integrate data from the laboratory with clinical information and practice; its basis in scientific methodology; its broad set of applications with relevance for therapeutic, educational, and even social and institutional practices; its idiographic focus; and its concern with precise methods of administering reinforcement.

■ Behavioral assessment techniques have also taught us to focus on specific behavioral and situational variables and not just on internal determinants.

■ Behavior therapy methods have turned us away from the exclusive reliance on insight as the way to mental health and taught us to look at the individual's specific complaints rather than underlying pathology. As a result, therapy has now become available to a wider clientele and has been applied to a greater range of problems.

■ The behavioral movement also has its share of problems. They include an emphasis on superficial behavior derived from a laboratory model of animal behavior; a disregard of the most human of all data—cognitions (although the gathering cognitive emphasis is beginning to blunt this criticism); a very narrow focus on environmental contributors to behavior at the expense of the ways in which we process information about that environment; the failure to incorporate systematically predispositions such as genetic endowment; problems in defining exactly what constitutes a stimulus or a response; and (especially as regards Skinner) the lack of an overall, explicitly stated theory of behavior.

■ Behavioral assessment encompasses a very heterogeneous set of techniques that often fail to meet standardization criteria and whose reliability and validity are frequently suspect.

■ Behavior therapy, too, represents a loosely defined series of methods that are often not so nearly derived from good science as their proponents claim. Questions have arisen regarding their success rate with those vague, almost existential complaints patients so often present. Once we step outside the realm of specific anxieties or behavioral deficits, their efficacy is much less certain. Also at issue is the ability or willingness of patients to generalize what they have learned in controlled settings to natural situations. Ethical questions have sometimes been raised (especially regarding aversion therapies) and behavioral methods have been characterized by some as dehumanizing. Finally, it was noted that there is no integrating theoretical framework by which we can order and classify these techniques.

CHAPTER 12

SOCIAL LEARNING THEORY

The relationship between learning and personality had clearly impressed many psychologists, as the preceding two chapters have shown. But the role models were often people like Pavlov, Watson, Hull, and Skinner, and the only game in town seemed to be reinforcement. Reinforcement is a powerful determinant of behavior, particularly when we are dealing with the behavior of animals in highly controlled laboratory settings. Tightly scheduled reinforcement is also highly effective in shaping human behavior, especially so when we are dealing with individuals who are in carefully controlled environments such as mental hospitals, prisons, and the like.

In the eyes of many personality psychologists and clinicians, however, this general model suffered from several crucial defects. First, it ignored the role of cognitive factors. We think, we plan, we believe, and we imagine. Reinforcement does not just occur; it is interpreted, evaluated, and weighed. Second, the whole learning superstructure seemed to depend on experiments with animals. This is probably why reinforcement came to be emphasized at the expense of cognitions. Third, the research tended to ignore the fact that human learning and behavior occur in a largely interpersonal environment. The lonely pigeon in the operant box or the human subject sitting before a complex reaction-time apparatus is not a good research model for human social behavior. Fourth, the model portrayed us as passive recipients of environmental input and influence. In fact, however, we affect our environment just as we are affected by it, and we often choose the environments in which we will behave.

Out of these shortcomings arose what has come to be called *social learning theory* by some and *cognitive social learning theory* by others. Although the origins of **social learning theory** and the disputes over who deserves to be called a social learning theorist are not easily resolved (Woodward, 1982), John Dollard and Neal Miller were among the first to use the term *social learning*. Julian Rotter (1954) is usually credited with the development of the first social learning *theory*. But others played a significant role in the development of this perspective. Gabriel Tarde, George Herbert Mead, and

O. Hobart Mowrer are just a few who made early contributions. Also, someone once remarked that had Harry Stack Sullivan studied psychology instead of psychiatry, he would have become the world's first social learning theorist. Currently, however, the major theorists are usually considered to be Julian Rotter, Albert Bandura, and Walter Mischel, and it is upon them that we shall focus in the following pages.

ROTTER'S SOCIAL LEARNING THEORY

Like so many of the theorists encountered thus far, Julian Rotter has been a psychotherapist. His experience in clinical psychology, learning theory, and experimental research has enabled him to bring to bear on personality a particularly well-rounded view.

Rotter's social learning began to take formal shape in the late 1940s and early 1950s. Rotter's personal associations with Alfred Adler, Kurt Lewin, and J.R. Kantor helped shape his theory. Ideas from Clark Hull, Edward Thorndike, Prescott Lecky, Sigmund Freud, B.F. Skinner, and Edward Tolman are also apparent. These individuals reflect a heterogeneous intellectual heritage ranging from the importance of family relationships, environmental influences, and the self-concept to conditioning, repression, and cognitions. Such a variety of influences is not surprising when we consider what Rotter set out to do. He wanted to construct a learning theory that would be broad yet systematic. His theory was to be both motivational and cognitive and one that would emphasize not only the importance of individual differences but also the role of environmental influences. Furthermore, Rotter fully intended to build a theory that would be useful for the practicing clinician as well as for the research-oriented personality psychologist.

Some major issues

As Rotter proceeded with the construction of his theory, he made several important assumptions and decisions (Rotter, 1954). He has stated them formally in a series of seven postulates and twelve corollaries. To place his theory in the proper perspective, we need to take a brief look at these propositions.

A construct point of view. Rotter consciously sought to build a theory that would help us predict and understand human behavior in a social setting. However, he recognized that there is no "true" reality but only our personal construction of it. His social learning theory is, then, one person's attempt to describe the significant variables that determine human behavior. We live in a world of multiple personality theories. As Chapter 2 made clear, in the final analysis, which theory is judged best will be decided by how well it predicts and not by how true it is.

A language of description. At the time Rotter began to formulate his theory, the most prominent personality theories were either psychoanalytic or phenomenological. Both of these approaches contained terms and concepts that often seemed quite ambiguous or vaguely defined (as we have seen in earlier chapters). Therefore, Rotter resolved to develop a terminology that would be clear and precise. In doing this, he

A brief biography of

Julian Rotter

Julian B. Rotter was born in 1916 in Brooklyn, New York. He was the third son of immigrant parents. His father emigrated from Austria at the age of thirteen, and his mother from Lithuania when she was a one-year-old. Rotter remarked once how rough it was growing up in Brooklyn and how quickly one learned the world of the streets. As a student, his academic marks were generally good, and better than his grades for conduct. He often checked books out of the public library; ones by Adler, Freud, and Menninger seem to have sparked his interest in psychology. Nevertheless, he majored in chemistry at Brooklyn College.

The 1930s was an era of social injustice and economic deprivation in the United States. Rotter was very concerned and spent his share of time on the picket line. He also undoubtedly understood discrimination from firsthand experience. All of this probably conspired to fan a flame of idealism and a desire to help others. Perhaps because of this, he decided to pursue a career in clinical psychology.

He attended graduate school at both the University of Iowa and Indiana University, receiving his Ph.D. in 1941 from the latter institution. Shortly thereafter, he entered Officer Candidate School in the U.S. Army and served his tour of duty doing work involving military psychology, officer candidate selection, and so on.

In 1946 he joined the faculty of Ohio State University where, in collaboration with George Kelly, he helped build a clinical psychology training program of national renown—one that became a model of the scientist-practitioner tradition. It was here that he completed

tried to provide objective definitions so that different observers using his concepts while viewing an event would agree among themselves in their judgments of that event. He also attempted to use terms that did not overlap and thus cause confusion. For example, it is not uncommon today to hear a psychologist use the term *anxiety* one moment and five minutes later begin discussing *stress*. The two terms overlap so much that confusion results.

A social learning perspective. Why the term *social learning?* Well, it is not an accidental choice of words. In Rotter's own words, "It is a *social* learning theory because it stresses the fact that the major or basic modes of behaving are learned in social situations and are inextricably fused with needs requiring for their satisfaction the mediation of other persons" (1954, p. 84).

Motives and cognitions. One of the most distinctive assumptions that Rotter makes is that human behavior is determined not just by the rewards that follow it but also by our expectations that the behavior chosen will, in fact, bring about reinforce-

his major theoretical work. In 1963 Rotter moved to the University of Connecticut, where he continued to teach, supervise students, and contribute to national professional committees. Despite a rich and prolific scientific career, Rotter has always maintained his identity as a practicing clinician. In 1987 Rotter retired from his post at the University of Connecticut. Even so, he continues to teach and supervise the research of graduate students there.

Rotter has been the author of numerous papers, chapters, monographs, books, and test manuals published over the years. His best-known work, *Social Learning and Clinical Psychology,* was published in 1954 and is the major statement of his theory. In 1972, with the collaboration of June Chance and Jerry Phares, *Applications of a Social Learning Theory of Personality* appeared. A monograph on the topic of internal versus external control of reinforcement was published in 1966 and was to have a major influence on research concerning this personality dimension. In recent years, Rotter has turned his attention to the study of interpersonal trust. A chapter providing an overview of social learning theory and its background, concepts, research, and implications may be found in Phares (1980). A collection of Rotter's important papers has appeared more recently (Rotter, 1982).

In 1989 Rotter was the recipient of the American Psychological Association's Distinguished Scientist Award for his pioneering efforts in establishing a social learning framework that transformed behavioral approaches to personality and clinical psychology.

Julian Rotter
The University of Connecticut

ment. Although he realized that human beings, like the animals in experimental research, are motivated by needs, he also believed that an essential human quality is our pervasive tendency to think and to anticipate. We are not mechanical beings that respond blindly to reinforcement. There has been a long history in psychology of theorizing about the relationship between expectancy and behavior (Zuroff and Rotter, 1985). Rotter has been especially adroit in combining expectancy and reinforcement within the same theory.

At the time Rotter's theory was first published, no one thought of it as especially cognitive since *cognitive* was not an "in" term at that time. Clearly, however, Rotter's thinking here anticipated by a good many years developments in the field of personality (Sechrest, 1984).

Performance vs. learning. Rotter is less concerned with how discrete bits of behavior are acquired than he is with how people choose to behave one way rather than another. He simply assumes that the individual builds up a large repertoire of behaviors through conditioning and learning. His main concern is our ability to predict which behavior (once acquired) will occur in a specific situation. In this sense, his theory might better be labeled a theory of choices or performance.

Basic theory and concepts

Rotter's basic concepts can be introduced by an example. Imagine a college senior who is beginning to make plans for the future. She schedules an appointment at the university placement center and subsequently manages to locate two job opportunities that match her training and interests exactly. The first job pays $18,000 per year, and the second $25,000. Common sense tells us that the second job is considerably more reinforcing and, other things being equal, we ought to predict that she will apply for it in preference to the $18,000 job. The key phrase here is "other things being equal." But for Rotter, there are two variables which we must consider in deciding upon a prediction. First, there is the reinforcement value of the goal toward which the behavior is directed. This refers to the degree of our student's preference for one goal over the other. Undoubtedly, she would prefer to make $25,000 rather than $18,000, and so we could be confident that the former is more reinforcing than the latter. Will she, then, automatically apply for the $25,000 position? The answer may well be no, since we have failed to consider the role of expectancy—the second key variable. Consequently, this student may not apply for the higher-paying job if her expectancy is very low that by going through the rigors of application she will actually get it. Therefore, Rotter's contention is simply that in predicting human behavior in complex social situations, we must consider both the value of the goal involved and the person's expectancy that the behavior in question will actually achieve that goal. We can now more carefully examine the basic concepts that Rotter finds useful.

Behavior potential.   In any particular situation, individuals have at their disposal a myriad of possible behaviors with which to attempt to achieve their goals. For example, when I meet a person for the first time, I want to make a good impression. Which behavior should I use to achieve this goal? Shall I remark about all the good things I have heard about him? Will I make a little joke to put him at ease? Or will I work into the conversation a reference to my latest personal accomplishment? Each of these behaviors has a potential for occurrence. In Rotter's conceptual framework, **behavior potential (BP)** is the potential for a behavior to occur in a specific situation as a way of achieving a particular goal. Each behavior possible in a given situation has a potential. The higher the potential, the more likely the behavior will occur in the case of that individual. Obviously, the potential for a behavior to occur may be strong in one setting and weak in another. Telling jokes may be high in potential at a party but very weak at a funeral.

Rotter's concept of behavior is a broad one. Anything that a person does in response to a stimulus is included, assuming it can somehow be detected and measured. Writing a letter, flipping a coin, and tying your shoelaces all qualify. But, then, so do having an erotic fantasy, feeling guilty, or being uneasy. Rationalizations, studying, and talking too much fit as well. Behavior, in brief, "may thus consist of actual motor acts, cognitions, verbal behavior, nonverbal expressive behavior, emotional reactions, and so on" (Rotter and Hochreich, 1975, p. 96).

According to social learning theory, all behavior, including applying for a specific job, is determined by expectancy and reinforcement value. Photograph Stacy Pick/Uniphoto.

Expectancy. Rotter's second major variable is **expectancy (E)**. By the use of this concept, he is stating that behavior potential is determined not just by how badly we want a certain goal but also by the extent to which we believe that a specific behavior will do the job. Expectancy refers to the probability that a certain reinforcement will occur if a specific behavior is selected in the situation in question. In one situation, my expectancy that hard work will pay off may be high; in another situation, my expectancy regarding the utility of hard work may be equally low.

When Rotter talks about expectancy, he is referring to a subjective probability. As a result, one's expectancies do not always correspond to reality. Some people are often overconfident or have unrealistically high expectancies for their success in a given situation. In other cases, individuals consistently underestimate the likelihood of their own success. But if we are to predict a behavior accurately, we must consider the subjective probabilities of the person and not those that someone else feels are realistic.

This cognitive variable of expectancy is quite important in Rotter's system. Accordingly, he distinguishes between expectancies that are specific to one situation—**specific expectancies (E′)**—and those that are more general or that apply to several situations. The latter are called **generalized expectancies (GE)**. A good example of this distinction is the case of a student who has a low specific expectancy for doing well in an algebra class yet has a rather high generalized expectancy for academic success in other classes. A generalized expectancy reflects experiences accumulated over a variety of related situations (in this example, academic ones). A specific expectancy, in contrast, is based upon experience in one specific situation (an algebra class, for example).

347

The foregoing distinction helps account, in part, for the difference between a person's subjectively held probability for the success of a given behavior and what others feel should be a realistic expectancy. The individual may see similarities between a certain situation and other, previously encountered ones and generalize accordingly. Observers may not perceive this similarity and fail to make the generalization. Take basketball, for example. A team has won ten games in a row and tonight is playing a relatively weak rival. By every right, Jones, the starting center, should be confident of victory. Yet he appears strangely tentative in his pregame statements. Other people, figuring he should be generalizing from the past ten victories, are puzzled. What they fail to realize, however, is that his parents will be attending the game. He knows from past experience that he rarely plays well in front of them and is generalizing his expectancy for victory from that experience in addition to the previous ten games and tonight's weak opponent.

One final point about the nature of generalized and specific expectancies is illustrated by our basketball example. An expectancy for success is the product of the joint influence of both specific and generalized expectancies. Jones's expectancy resulted from the interaction of his expectancies based upon prior experience with his opponents and those generalized from what he perceived as related experience. It is also true, however, that when we face a situation for the first time, expectancies generalized from past related situations will weigh heavily. As we gain more experience in the situation, specific expectancies will begin to take over. For example, when students first enroll in a class, their expectancies for passing the course will be based almost entirely on their overall experience generalized from related classes. However, after they are two-thirds through the term and have taken four examinations, their expectancies will then be determined almost exclusively by that latter specific experience; generalized expectancies will play a minor role.

Reinforcement value.   Suppose you could have a new wardrobe, an A in this class, or somebody to really confide in? Which would you choose? This illustrates the essence of **reinforcement value (RV)** — the degree of your preference for any of the foregoing reinforcements to occur if the possibilities of all of them occurring were equal. This, then, is Rotter's motivational concept, just as we saw previously that expectancy is his cognitive variable. Similarly, just as people differ among themselves regarding their expectancies, they also differ in the value they place on various reinforcements. I prefer steak over seafood; you do not. You order salad; I order soup. And so it goes.

It should be emphasized that reinforcement value is a relative term. That is, the value of a reinforcement is always relative to the other reinforcements available. If I must choose among a Chevrolet, a Ford, and a Plymouth, I may pick the Ford, in which case the Ford can be said to have more reinforcement value for me than the Chevrolet. But if you add a Buick to the list, I may choose it. In short, a given reinforcement has no absolute value, only value relative to a finite list of other possibilities.

What determines the value of a reinforcement? Value is determined by the expectancy that the reinforcement will lead to other reinforcements of value. Money has value not in and of itself but because it buys things of value — food, clothes, prestige, and so on. Of course, in a sense what Rotter is implying here is that no reinforcement has value in and of itself. It achieves value only through the individual's expectancy that it will, in turn, lead to something else. The idea that goals have no intrinsic value obviously will provoke a lively debate in some quarters.

The psychological situation. By now, you have read the words *specific* and *situation* numerous times in reference to Rotter's theoretical constructs. But it is very hard not to use such qualifiers because Rotter insists on emphasizing the explicit role of the psychological situation as a determinant of behavior. He recognizes the importance of enduring predispositions that we all carry about with us. But he feels that personality psychologists for too long ignored the role of situational contexts and their effects on human behavior (Rotter, 1981). His contention is that in every case, we must calculate the value of a reinforcement or the magnitude of an expectancy in relation to a specific situation. We learn through experience that a goal is more likely to be attainable in one situation than in another. We also learn that attainment of a goal in one setting is more valuable than it is in another. For example, a child may learn that a kiss from mother is very reinforcing at home but that in the park it may lead to mocking taunts from other children that considerably reduce its value.

The predictive formulas. To pull together the four preceding variables and to illustrate their relationships, the following formula is used to predict goal-directed behavior:

$$BP_{x,s1,Ra} = f(E_{x,\,Ra,\,s1} \text{ and } RV_{a,s1})$$

This may be read as follows: "The potential for behavior x to occur in situation 1 in relation to reinforcement a is a function of the expectancy of the occurrence of reinforcement a following behavior x in situation 1 and the value of reinforcement a, in situation 1" (Rotter, 1967b, p. 490). This sounds a bit formidable perhaps, but it really is not. For example, imagine you are faced with a choice between going to the football game on Saturday afternoon or going to the library to work on a term paper. The behavior with the higher potential will occur. If I knew the value of the reinforcements associated with each behavior and the corresponding expectancies that each behavior would lead to the reinforcements involved, I could readily predict which of the two behaviors would occur.

There is a problem, however, in using this formula. It deals with very specific behaviors in relation to single reinforcements. Although a highly useful equation for testing specific hypotheses in controlled laboratory settings, it has a limited application in broader situations. For example, an academic counselor may be less interested in predicting the occurrence of the very specific behavior of a student's cutting a chemistry class than in predicting that student's overall academic avoidance behavior in all classes — skipping class, being late with assignments, failing to study, and so on. To do this, we must consider multiple behaviors, expectancies, and reinforcement values. In doing so, Rotter (1954) uses the following formula:

$$NP = f(FM \text{ and } NV)$$

This equation tells us that the potential for the occurrence of a set of behaviors (**need potential,** or **NP**) that leads to the satisfaction of a certain need is determined by (1) the expectancies (**freedom of movement,** or **FM**) that these behaviors will lead to those goals and (2) the value of those separate goals constituting the need (**need value,** or **NV**).

To continue the previous example, our academic counselor is initially puzzled as to why the student behaves in so many different ways that, together, result in a poor academic performance. In short, she wonders why his need potential for academic recognition is so low. Through interviews, she discovers several things. First, the average value he attaches to reinforcements such as A's in class, praise from teachers, and recognition from peers is reasonably high. That is, these reinforcements, which taken together compose need value for academic recognition, are fairly high in value. However, he has a low expectancy that studying will pay off, he is not at all confident that his teachers will really respect him if he does well, and he doubts his peers will recognize him for his achievements. In sum, his overall expectancy (freedom of movement) that academically oriented behaviors will really bring him academic recognition is quite low. given all this, he fails to study, cuts class, daydreams, and so on. This contrast between the *BP* and *NP* formulas is shown in Table 12-1.

Problem-solving generalized expectancies.

In their pursuit of goals, people develop generalized expectancies or attitudes as to how best to construe situations. Situations may be thought of as presenting problems that need to be overcome in order to achieve reinforcement. Individuals will differ in these **problem-solving generalized expectancies** based upon their unique prior experiences. One such prominent attitude or generalized expectancy is **interpersonal trust**—the extent to which one can rely on the word of others (Rotter, 1971a). We know from research that a person high

TABLE 12-1   *Specific versus general prediction*

BP		E		RV
1. Potential for: Attending chemistry class	*is determined by*	Expectancy that attending class will lead to a passing grade	&	Value of achieving a passing grade in chemistry
NP		**FM**		**NV**
2. Potential for the following *set* of behaviors: studying, reading assignments, attending class regularly, writing optional papers	*is determined by*	Average expectancy that the set of behaviors will satisfy the need for academic recognition	&	Average value of the following goals, which together comprise the need for academic recognition: good grades, making the honor roll, praise from teachers and peers

in interpersonal trust is likely to trust others when confronted with a problem situation involving statements by other people. **Internal versus external control of reinforcement (I-E),** or as some refer to it, **locus of control** is another generalized expectancy which has been the subject of widespread research (Phares, 1976; Rotter, 1966). People who are internally oriented tend to attribute the outcomes of their behavior to their own efforts or to personal characteristics. More externally oriented persons are likely to view outcomes as the result of luck, fate, and other powerful forces. The importance of the distinction can be illustrated by the fact that when "internals" are faced with a problem, they tend to confront it actively; after all, one's own efforts can make a difference. "Externals" are more likely to respond with resignation since outcomes are really in the hands of forces over which we have little control. These problem-solving generalized expectancies will be discussed further in the next chapter.

Development of personality

Rotter does not devote much attention to questions of development. This does not mean that social learning has no implications for personality development. Indeed, a variety of studies relating to children's behavior, role of parental attitudes, development of achievement motivation, and the like, have been carried out (e.g., see Rotter, Chance, and Phares, 1972).

Like Dollard and Miller, Rotter believes that psychological needs arise out of the satisfaction of physiological ones. Because the mother is associated with the satisfaction of the infant's hunger, thirst, and physical comfort needs, she takes on value in that infant's eyes. And because the satisfaction of our tissue needs depends upon the intervention of parents, nurses, or other adults, the child's earliest psychological needs come to involve strivings for love, attention, protection, and recognition.

Rotter (1954) has described six broad needs:

- *Recognition-Status*—Need to excel; be viewed as competent, good, or better than others in school, occupation, athletics, social standing, good looks, etc.

- *Dominance*—Need to control others; exercise power and influence over others

- *Independence*—Need to make own decisions; rely on oneself; achieve goals without help from others

- *Protection-Dependency*—Need to have others prevent frustrations, provide protection and security, and help one achieve valued goals

- *Love and Affection*—Need to be accepted and liked by others; have the devoted interest, concern, and affection of others

- *Physical Comfort*—Need to enjoy physical satisfactions associated with security and a feeling of well-being; avoid pain; experience bodily pleasures

Nature of adjustment

Social learning theory provides no ready catalog of maladjusted behaviors. Ultimately, the question of maladjustment is an ethical one and the definition of maladjusted behavior resides in cultural norms or in personal attitudes. Consequently, there are no social learning principles that apply to maladjustment separate from behavior generally. However, social learning has some definite implications for the nature of maladjustment (Katkovsky, 1976; Phares, 1972), as we shall see in the following paragraphs.

Low freedom of movement—high need value.
In general, maladjustment may be said to exist when the individual places a high value on the satisfaction of a particular need yet has very low freedom of movement (expectancies) for the success of behaviors that could lead to the satisfaction of that need. For example, take the male who very much wants love and affection but does not believe he possesses the behaviors likely to achieve those goals. There is a strong possibility that he will avoid females, fail to show up for a blind date, or engage in excessive fantasy behavior, which only serve to further remove him from situations where heterosexual satisfactions are likely. Of course, were this individual not to place much value on love and affection, his low expectancies would not be a problem. By and large, most neurotic symptoms represent a set of avoidant behaviors calculated to handle this discrepancy between need value and freedom of movement. These behaviors are used because the person expects that they will avoid punishment or discomfort. Thus, repeatedly missing parties avoids the punishment that would occur because of not knowing how to dance or how to carry on a conversation.

Conflict.
In some cases, the individual places a high value on needs that are incompatible. For example, the homosexual who also wants acceptance from his parents may find himself in a no-win situation. The result may be a variety of avoidant behaviors. Or the woman who has strong needs for both professional recognition and dependency satisfactions may find herself enmeshed in a conflict that may lead to a variety of maladjusted behaviors.

Lack of competency.
Repeatedly avoiding certain situations prevents the individual from learning the behaviors that would result in competency. Not attending parties precludes the development of both dancing and conversational skills. In some cases, the very absence of certain skills represents the heart of the problem. For example, a child with a chronic, severe physical ailment may not have been able to interact with other children in such a way as to develop good social skills. Subsequently, the lack of those skills may lead to a variety of adjustment problems.

Minimal goal level.
In social learning theory, **minimal goal level** refers to the lowest goal in a hierarchy of reinforcements that is perceived by the individual as reinforcing. Thus, for some students a grade point average of C is viewed as reinforcing—their minimal goals are low in the academic need area. For other students only A's are reinforcing. In the absence of competency, extremely high minimal goal levels will increase the possibilities of experiencing failure and disappointment. In other instances, people have very low minimal goals and thus appear so unmotivated that others in the culture may regard them as deviant individuals with many problems.

Failure to discriminate. Sometimes the value of a need may become so high that it dominates the person's life. This may result in a variety of distortions of reality or in a failure to discriminate among situations. For example, an individual may have such a strong need to be liked that he or she indiscriminately gives expensive gifts to casual acquaintances. Very likely, such behavior will come to be regarded as rather bizarre by others.

The case study on p. 354, which deals with a social learning theory analysis of anxiety reactions in an executive, illustrates several of the foregoing concepts.

Enhancement behaviors. Rotter (1982) has also discussed "enhancement behaviors." Such behaviors may allow the person to behave in a way that allows the effects of positive reinforcement to be prolonged or the effects of punishment or discomfort to be diminished. For example, some people are generally happy, content, optimistic, or in a good mood most of the time. But their objective life circumstances may not be all that different from others who are just as often unhappy, discontented, pessimistic, or depressed. Perhaps there are specific cognitive behaviors that some people use to maintain a good feeling. These behaviors might include: imaginative rehearsal of good outcomes, conscious resistance to raising one's minimal goals, a tendency to focus on positive features of situations rather than their negative aspects, and the like. Although some would generally regard such cognitions as distortions of reality that are unhealthy, Rotter thinks otherwise. He believes that they may sometimes function like an inoculation against stress. This view is not unlike his contention that in certain clinical testing situations, individuals who can respond with some humor are showing reactions that may well signal a tendency toward adjustment rather than defensiveness.

Implications for behavior change

In the most general sense, behavior changes come about due to changes in the values of various needs, the expectancies the individual has about satisfying those needs, or both. Therefore, to change behavior, freedom of movement or need value must first be altered.

As a clinical psychologist, Rotter has an intimate knowledge of psychotherapy. But unlike traditional psychotherapists who always seemed totally committed to verbal approaches that focus solely on the goal of insight, he has also emphasized the need to work directly on ways of changing behavior and to examine the role of situational or environmental contributors to the patient's problems. In a very real sense, the way Rotter has conducted therapy over the years anticipated behavior therapy (especially cognitive behavior therapy). However, Rotter never developed any unique or startling techniques. He simply used a wide array of unlabeled procedures to alter patients' freedom of movement and need values. Sometimes this included the goal of insight, and at other times it involved environmental manipulation.

Rotter's social learning theory has been especially useful in providing ways of analyzing patients' problems and aiding in the setting of therapeutic goals. In this sense, it has been a good friend to the therapist. For example, using the theory as a framework, the patient's needs can be identified along with the corresponding expectations for their fulfillment. Once this is done, therapeutic goals often become apparent. A patient ex-

CASE STUDY

A social learning theory case study.

A thirty-five-year-old insurance executive reports that for the past two months he has been experiencing intermittent panic reactions, nausea, insomnia, and a variety of other rather vague physical complaints. A complete medical workup fails to reveal any somatic basis for these complaints. The patient himself is quite alarmed and despite the negative medical report feels that he has some dread and yet subtle disease. He can provide no psychological explanation and reports that everything in his life is going quite well. With a great deal of reluctance, he finally accepts his physician's recommendation and visits a psychiatrist. With the material elicited during his therapy contacts it was possible to construe his problem in the following terms.

For many years the patient had been motivated by strong needs for achievement and recognition. His father had been quite prominent in the community and his mother had made it clear in abundant ways during his childhood that great things were expected of the patient.

Nonetheless, the patient always harbored strong doubts about his capabilities. In short, his expectancies for the achievement of success and recognition were not commensurate with the strength of these needs. In most instances, however, during childhood, high school, and college he operated in fairly structured situations and was able to perform quite well. Prior to examinations in both high school and college he would become quite anxious. In other words, the cues in the examination situations were so overwhelming that the dis-crepancy between expectancy for success and the strength of his recognition needs generated a great deal of subjectively felt distress. By virtue of diligent preparation, however, he was able to do well. Indeed, at the time this anxiety did not alarm him, since he "explained" it to himself as purely situationally determined and something that everybody experienced.

After college he joined the insurance firm and through hard work, following orders, and just doing his job, he was steadily promoted. During this period he acquired a wife and two children and all the usual responsibilities inherent in middle-class America.

It was only after his promotion to the executive position that massive anxiety reactions occurred. Suddenly he was placed in an unstructured position—he was no longer following orders, he had to establish policy, develop original ideas, and so on. His expectancies were quite low that he could achieve success in such a situation. Through generalization, he construed the present situation where both his employers and family expected great things from him as being very similar to those situations early in life where his parents expected him to achieve in the image of his father. Now he was expected to achieve in the image of an executive.

Placed in this situation he clearly expected to encounter failure. Added to this situation was the fact that failure would now disrupt the lives of his wife and children also. Such, then, was the onset of his anxiety attacks. (Phares, 1972, pp. 458–459)

pressing severe anxiety might turn out to have very strong needs for dependency. Yet, his wife is not very supportive, with the result that his expectations for satisfying these needs have declined to the point where a variety of symptoms have arisen. Likewise, thinking within a social learning framework will help clarify and separate a variety of focal areas. For one patient, the problem is a behavioral deficit. For another, it is low expectancies for success or perhaps needs that are too high. In still another case, the individual's minimal goals may be too high (or too low). In short, the theory offers a way of conceptualizing problems in adjustment that goes considerably beyond the sheer attachment of labels such as *depressed, anxious,* or *neurotic.*

Social learning theory has a variety of other implications for therapeutic practice (Rotter, 1970), a few of which are listed here:

■ Therapy is basically a learning process through which the therapist helps the patient achieve planned changes in behavior and thinking.

■ A patient's difficulties are best viewed as efforts to solve problems.

■ Very often the therapist guides the learning process so that inappropriate behaviors and attitudes are weakened and more appropriate ones strengthened.

■ Particular attention should be devoted to the manner in which inappropriate behavior and expectancies arise and also to the ways in which patients overgeneralize from their previous experience.

■ New experiences in real life are often quite effective in bringing about behavior changes and, in that sense, are more important than what transpires during the therapy session.

■ Therapy can be viewed as a form of social interaction.

The foregoing implications specifically suggest flexibility of techniques from one patient to another, the desirability of enhancing patients' problem-solving skills, an active role for the therapist ranging from interpretations to direct reinforcement, the importance of guiding patients into real-life settings that will help promote change, and the idea that those laws which apply to behavior generally also apply to the therapy process.

In tune with his interest in problem-solving generalized expectancies, Rotter (1978) has provided a number of examples of how certain cognitive strategies can be promoted in patients so as to enhance their problem-solving capabilities. These cognitive strategies include the development of an internal locus of control, looking for alternative behavioral solutions, interpersonal trust, understanding the motives of others, long-term planning, and discriminating differences among situations.

BANDURA AND SOCIAL LEARNING THEORY

Albert Bandura's approach to social learning (or what he has recently been referring to as *social cognitive theory*) is decidedly complementary to that of Rotter. It is hardly a theory at all in the sense of presenting a well-integrated set of concepts that will ac-

Albert Bandura

Albert Bandura was born in 1925 in a small town in Alberta, Canada. He spent his childhood surrounded by wheat farms but very few people. He received a B.A. degree in 1949 from the University of British Columbia. His M.A. (1951) and Ph.D. (1952) degrees were from the University of Iowa. Although he was interested in clinical psychology, one could not in those days attend Iowa without feeling the strong presence and scholarly influence of Kenneth Spence. This general Hullian ambience coupled with an atmosphere of vigorous conceptual analysis and experimental rigor undoubtedly had a marked effect on Bandura. After a clinical internship at the Wichita Guidance Center, he accepted a faculty position at Stanford University, where he remains today.

His career at Stanford has been a prolific one. In his early years there, his research was focused on psychotherapy processes and the role of family patterns in producing aggression in children. Since then, his interests have included behavior modification, modeling, observational learning, self-regulatory processes, and self-efficacy.

Many professional honors have come Bandura's way. For exam-

count for the behavioral choices people make. But it does exactly what Rotter's theory does not do—it helps explain how people acquire a variety of complex behaviors in social settings. For Rotter the emphasis is on choice; for Bandura it is on acquisition.

To Bandura's way of thinking, psychodynamic theories such as psychoanalysis always seemed to explain behavior as the product of some devilish set of inner forces, needs, or conflicts (often unconscious ones). Then along came learning, and it was now environmental stimulation that carried all the predictive freight. For Bandura, both of these extreme positions were unfortunate ones, since he felt behavior could best be understood by considering it as a joint product of personal variables and environmental ones.

Bandura has demonstrated a remarkably successful facility for integrating ideas from the past with newer research emphases and turning the resulting mix into a rich and stimulating product. For example, like Rotter, he believes that behavior is determined by both reinforcement and expectancies. Unlike many earlier learning theorists, however, he contends that behavior can be learned in the absence of reinforcement. That is, one can learn how to do something without ever actually having been reinforced for doing it. By observing others, we can learn many things. But whether or not we then do those things that we have learned may very well depend on our expectations for reinforcement. More recently, Bandura has investigated the role of **self-efficacy** (belief that one can successfully perform a given behavior) in human behavior. He regards one's personal sense of self-efficacy to be a powerful influence on thought patterns, behavior, and emotional arousal (Bandura, 1982). But whether we are talking about observational learning, expectancies, or self-efficacy, Bandura has demonstrated a remarkable commitment, both by word and deed, to the role of empirical research

ple, in 1980 he received the Distinguished Scientist Award from the American Psychological Association for being a leader in the application of the social, symbolic, and self-regulatory determinants of meaningful learning and behavior change. Following that he was elected president of the American Psychological Association. At Stanford he continues teaching both undergraduate and graduate courses.

Because Bandura has been such a prolific contributor to the literature over the years, it is difficult to single out just a few works. Two early well-known books, *Adolescent Aggression* (1959) and *Social Learning and Personality Development* (1963), were written in collaboration with the late Richard Walters. *Principles of Behavior Modification* appeared in 1969, followed by *Aggression: A Social Learning Analysis* in 1973. In *Social Learning Theory,* published in 1977, he attempts to integrate theoretical and experimental work in the field of social learning. His most recent book, *Social Foundations of Thought and Action: A Social Cognitive Theory,* appeared in 1986. He is also the author of many articles and chapters.

Albert Bandura
Photograph C. Painter/
Stanford University

in personality study. He has produced a very large volume of careful research which has helped establish the credibility of his theoretical ideas both within and without the laboratory.

Basic theory and concepts

Bandura's approach sets forth several ways in which events must be construed. Let us begin by reviewing several of them.

Reciprocal determinism.

A moment ago it was stated that for Bandura behavior is the result of an interaction between personal variables and environmental ones. Actually, Bandura feels this is an incomplete statement. In personality, there traditionally have been three major views of this interaction. First, there is the idea that persons and situations can be treated as independent variables that combine somehow to produce behavior. Thus, to explain why someone gets involved in a fight in a bar, you would consider his characteristic trait of aggression and the situational fact that there was an especially obnoxious person standing next to him.

A second view of this interaction would take account of the notion that personal characteristics bring the individual in contact with certain situations which, in turn, serve to stimulate those very characteristics. A person with aggressive needs may seek out situations which present opportunities that stimulate those very same needs. So it is that an aggressive person repeatedly patronizes a bar that caters to the kind of people who pick fights with other customers, including our aggressive friend.

But Bandura asserts that this is not all there is. To complete the picture, he offers

357

a third view—the notion of **reciprocal determinism.** This means that all three variables—behavior, person, and situation—influence each other. Getting into the fight stimulates aggressive needs, which in turn impel the person later to seek out the bar again, which will provide the opportunity to satisfy the aggressive needs, and on and on. Behavior influences needs which influence behavior which influences needs which influence the environment which. . . . All of the foregoing interactions are shown schematically in Figure 12-1.

For Bandura (1986), people are neither autonomous nor mechanical responders to environmental influence. They are, instead, active contributors to their own motivation and action. Behavior, thought, emotion, other personal factors, and environmental events all combine to determine behavior.

Beyond reinforcement.   Many personologists had never found the reinforcement ideas of Hull or Skinner very congenial ones. Too much depended on reinforcement. If every single response unit in complicated social acts had to occur separately and then be reinforced, it would take us forever to learn anything. While Bandura accepts the importance of reinforcement, he does not regard it as the only way behaviors are acquired. People can learn merely by observing others and can then repeat what they have seen. The customary reinforcements on which classical and operant conditioning depend are not always necessary. So it is that children born in the United States have grown up in an automobile-oriented country. Most have ridden in cars for longer than they can recall. Therefore, when they finally begin to learn to drive, they have already acquired many of the needed techniques by simple observation. In contrast, young adults who come to the United States from Third World countries sometimes have great difficulty with driving, largely because they have had much less opportunity to observe this activity as youngsters.

On the other hand, Bandura does not claim that reinforcement is irrelevant for complex behavior. Quite the contrary. Once a behavior is learned, reinforcement is important in determining whether that behavior will occur. Therefore, while I may learn much about driving by observing others, whether I climb behind the wheel and turn the ignition switch depends upon the goals toward which the behavior is directed.

FIGURE 12-1   Diagram of interactional patterns. B = behavior; P = person; E = environment.

After "The Self-system in reciprocal determination" by A. Bandura, *American Psychologist*, 1978, *33*, 344–358, copyright 1978 by American Psychological Assoc. Used with permission.

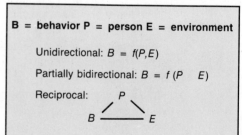

B = behavior P = person E = environment

Unidirectional: $B = f(P,E)$

Partially bidirectional: $B = f(P\quad E)$

Reciprocal:

Cognition. Behavior is determined not just by actual reinforcement but also by anticipated reinforcement. This suggests the importance Bandura attaches to cognition. Traditional learning theorists were often hampered by their inability (or unwillingness) to come to grips with cognitive processes. Bandura sees the human organism not merely as a machine guided by the judicious application of reinforcements by others. He views us as thinking, knowing creatures who use images, thoughts, and plans. We plan for the future, we regulate our behavior through internal standards, and we foresee the consequences of our behavior. This is hardly the animal model of behavior that developed out of the old experimental laboratories.

Observational learning

The keystone of Bandura's social learning is the process of observational learning. Of course, observational learning is hardly a new concept. Many years ago, George Herbert Mead (1934) wrote on the subject of imitation, and the later analysis of imitation by Miller and Dollard (1941) provided an important springboard for Bandura. He was able to see in this and other work the opportunity for novel paths of research on learning.

Observational learning is, very simply, learning through observing the behavior of others. A simple notion, surely, and one that we can all validate by a thousand examples from our own experience. Teenagers sometimes learn the newest dances by watching them on TV. Children may learn how to smoke by watching their parents. A new way of robbing a bank is learned while munching popcorn at the latest movie.

But there is more to it than this. We do not just imitate the actions of others by rote. We pick and choose from different models and instances and combine them into novel behavioral products (Bandura 1974). Again, we are not mere parrots but thinking consumers of the examples of others. The struggling young singer may begin by slavishly imitating the style of her pop heroine. But gradually she takes a bit from this singer, copies a little of the style of another, and imitates some of the gestures of still another. Ultimately, this melánge is fashioned into a single, unique style scarcely recognizable as an imitation at all. What this singer has done is to develop images of other singers working. She processes, codes, and stores this information in memory so that it will be available on subsequent occasions should the need arise. Thus she has learned without being reinforced. But the use of this information will depend upon situations that prompt her to anticipate that a certain kind of performance will lead to reinforcement. Furthermore she will not have to go entirely through the heartache and time involved in making every possible mistake or laboriously build up complex behaviors out of simple elements.

Certainly, then, observation provides us with information. But what exactly are the processes that make up observational learning? For Bandura (1977), observational learning is a four-stage process.

Attentional processes. The first stage comprises **attentional processes.** We learn through observation only if we attend to the model's behavior, recognize its important aspects, and differentiate among its distinctive features. And what leads us to pay attention? Certainly important is the opportunity for observation. I cannot imitate

All of us learn a great deal about how to do things by observing others.

the behavior of those with whom I seldom interact or rarely see. The child who never sees anyone at home read a newspaper has little opportunity to attend to such behavior. Models who have little status or are viewed by others as unimportant or lacking in value will not likely be attended to. Models who are interpersonally attractive, glamorous, or magnetic are much more likely to influence us. Then, too, able, competent people more frequently get our attention.

Retention processes.   Often we see a model only infrequently. Therefore, in order to reproduce the model's behavior, we must remember it. Our capacity to recall the critical elements of the model's behavior is crucial. Bandura proposes that our **retention processes** (second stage) are facilitated in two principal ways. We form mental images that provide us with long-lasting and readily retrievable sources of information about the model. We also verbally code the model's actions. For example, I may say to myself, "The pitcher steps on the rubber, looks at the runner on first, takes a deep breath, and looks to the catcher for the sign." These verbal cues provide me with a very helpful code that I can invoke later when the need arises.

Motor reproduction processes.   In the third stage, the previously coded mental images and verbal cues are translated into **motor reproduction**—I do what those images and cues tell me that my model did previously. This may take time, effort, and practice depending upon the level of complexity and skill involved. Although executing a dance step may appear simple, no matter how well I have attended to and retained the actions of my dancer-model, I will likely be something less than a gazelle the first few turns around the floor.

Motivational processes. As was stated previously, observational learning can occur in the absence of reinforcement. But this is not to say that **motivational processes** (fourth stage) are unimportant. The manner in which we attend to models has already been identified as being influenced by motivation. Whether we do what we have observed is also affected by motivation. In one sense, these motivational processes provide the spark that impels the cognitive-behavioral sequence. Without motivation, the processes of attention, retention, and reproduction will suffer. But in combination with motivation, they are powerful determinants of the acquisition and performance of complex social behaviors. Together with conditioning, they explain much of what becomes human social behavior.

Vicarious learning and conditioning

By observing models, we learn to do things we have not done before. But in some instances, the behavior is already in our repertoire and the effect of the model is to encourage us to do what we have already learned. Here the role of the model is a facilitative one.

Also important is **vicarious reinforcement.** Watching a model being reinforced for a given behavior serves as a reinforcement for the observer, albeit somewhat less intensely so. If I watch someone tip a headwaiter and then be rewarded with an excellent table, I can vicariously experience the reward. The result is that I am more likely to tip (assuming I have the money and wish to have a good table). Things work the same way for punishment. Observing a police officer writing a ticket for a speeder leads me to reduce my speed since I can vicariously experience the other driver's punishment. Naturally, I will imitate only those behaviors that lead to outcomes which are, for me, reinforcing and avoid those behaviors which result in consequences that are, to me, negative.

Vicarious conditioning also occurs. We all know that through classical conditioning a person can be taught to react fearfully to a buzzer if it is consistently followed by a painful electric shock. What is also interesting, however, is that someone merely observing this model will often become vicariously conditioned and likewise react to the buzzer with fear (Bandura and Rosenthal, 1966). This strongly suggests that a variety of human fears are learned not so much through direct personal experience but by watching the experience of others.

Self-regulation

The more radical views of reinforcement (e.g., that of Skinner) would depict us as buffeted about by the capricious winds of external rewards and punishments. They would suggest that we constantly look to the environment to check the consequences of our latest behavior. If the behavior was rewarded, we will do it again; if not, we try something else. This is not Bandura's view. His is a more complex perspective that takes into account the possibility of self-reinforcement. In addition to being governed by external rewards and punishments, our behavior is also governed by **internal standards.** Our thoughts, behaviors, and emotions are heavily influenced by the reinforcements we dispense to ourselves. I feel pride when my performance exceeds my expectations. I push myself to greater effort when I fail to achieve the goal I have set for myself. People constantly monitor their own behavior. Consequently, our actions are regulated not just by environmental rewards and punishments but by self-regulated standards. This gives a consistency and coherence to our behavior and cognitions that would not exist were we totally at the mercy of external events.

We learn our standards through the rewards and punishments administered by significant others in response to our behavior. When a child brings home a C in arithmetic, her mother may frown and demand that she work harder. Another mother might have been pleased with a C, in which case the daughter would have learned to be satisfied with such a grade. These standards acquired from others form the basis of one's self-regulatory system. This concept is rather similar to Rotter's notion of minimal goal levels. There is also evidence to suggest that these standards can be acquired from others on a vicarious basis. For example, children who observe the behavior of a model with low standards may impose lower standards for their own behavior when they are later called upon to perform (Bandura and Kupers, 1964).

Self-efficacy

In recent years, Bandura (1982) has increasingly emphasized the role of self-efficacy. **Self-efficacy** is simply the belief that one can successfully execute a given behavior. No belief is more central or pervasive in its effects on behavior, emotions, and motives (Bandura, 1989). We all repeatedly decide on courses of action for ourselves based upon our estimate of our own self-efficacy. It is important that we gauge it correctly; otherwise, we will have embarked on a course likely to bring failure. But right or wrong, we act on the basis of an assessment of our capabilities. Our judgments not only determine whether we will act but also how long we will persist and how much punishment we will absorb in carrying out the action. Our beliefs about self-efficacy also determine how extensively we will prepare ourselves for tasks and which ones we will select. Beyond that, self-efficacy influences our thought patterns and emotions. A person lacking in confidence often dwells upon personal inadequacies and typically judges tasks as more difficult than they really are. This increases the likelihood of failure through misplaced concentration.

Kirsch (1985) has observed that Bandura's concept of self-efficacy is little different from Rotter's expectancy concept. Indeed, in the next chapter, it will become apparent that the ways of measuring self-efficacy and expectancy are virtually identical. Even when one attempts to measure the two concepts differently, it is not clear that one is a superior predictor over the other (Maddux, Norton, and Stoltenberg, 1986).

Development of personality

Bandura does not find stage theories useful in understanding the development of personality. He prefers to emphasize the differences among individuals of a similar age and sees in them proof of the role of biological, socioeconomic, ethnic, and cultural factors. He does not regard people as passing through well-defined stages and, indeed, asserts that stage theorists rarely agree among themselves as to the characteristics of the stages or even their number (Bandura and Walters, 1963). For Bandura, issues of development center around changes in individuals' goals, plans, self-efficacy, and the like. These changes may be understood through the principles of observational learning, vicarious reinforcement, self-regulation, and so on.

Similarly, Bandura is not optimistic about any help in understanding the process of personality development likely to come soon from biology. As he says:

> It is probable that, until further advances in biochemistry and psychopharmacology have been made, there is more to be gained by studying the role of undoubtedly important social-learning variables in personality development than by seeking to establish relationships between constitutional factors and personality characteristics. (Bandura and Walters, 1963, p. 29)

Nature of adjustment

Bandura's social learning approach to issues of adjustment and maladjustment bears a strong resemblance to the behavioral outlook discussed in earlier chapters. It includes a focus on environmental factors that currently serve to maintain undesirable behavior and an analysis of maladjustment as a series of overt behaviors rather than as the product of some underlying pathology. Maladjustment arises out of the learning process either as the result of direct experience or through vicarious learning. Once acquired, deviant behavior is maintained by the direct and vicarious reinforcement it brings.

With his strong cognitive emphasis, however, Bandura goes beyond the simplicity of Skinnerian notions of maladjustment. Also important are expectancies and beliefs about oneself. Expecting that certain behaviors or situations will lead to negative reinforcement often causes the person to use a variety of defensive behaviors. If the individual expects to be rejected by others or is low in perceived self-efficacy, the result may be to avoid them. This, in turn, may lead others to regard the person as a bit strange and someone to avoid. Ultimately, then, the environment reinforces those maladaptive expectancies and beliefs. Similarly, if the person imposes exceptionally high standards for himself or herself, the result may be frequent failure, which may force the individual to resort to a variety of defenses.

But what is so bad about defensive behaviors? Well, for one thing they tend to remove the individual from situations in which new learning is possible. If a person never ventures into new settings, the old maladaptive expectancies and beliefs about self continue. Furthermore, the individual does not get the opportunity to come into contact with new models. For example, suppose my parents have consistently told me how unimportant or stupid I am. They repeatedly play upon my negative self-image. These, then, are my models. Because they have taught me to be unsure and to lack confidence, I am fearful of meeting new people, engaging new ideas, or trying new behaviors. As a result, I avoid the very things that might rescue me from inadequate parental models and provide me the opportunity for changing my expectancies and beliefs about self-efficacy.

Implications for behavior change

Like so many from the behavioral movement, Bandura's best-known work having direct relevance to therapy involves rather specific behavior problems such as phobias. Whether this work will have direct implications for the entire panorama of human complaints (psychoses, alienation, identity crises, malaise, etc.) remains to be seen.

Snake phobias.   We have already encountered the idea of observational learning. In the case of **guided participation,** the patient or subject is helped by assistants to perform the desired behavior. The best illustration of this procedure comes from a widely quoted study by Bandura, Blanchard, and Ritter (1969). These researchers were interested in the relative efficiency of several methods of treating snake phobias in adults. Their subjects, all intensely afraid of snakes, answered a newspaper advertisement that promised help for their fears.

The subjects were randomly divided into four groups. The first of the three experimental groups received Wolpe's systematic desensitization treatment; the second, a form of symbolic modeling via watching a film; and the third, access to a live model with guided participation. The fourth group consisted of control subjects who received no treatment. Subjects in the symbolic modeling condition viewed a film depicting children, adolescents, and adults who gradually became involved in more and more "frightening" contact with a snake. This contact ranged from handling plastic snakes to allowing a large and very real snake to crawl all over them (see Figure 12-2). These subjects also learned how to relax during the course of the film, and they could stop the film when they felt anxious or rewind it to an earlier, less threatening segment. This procedure obviously bears a marked similarity to what normally goes on with anxiety hierarchies in systematic desensitization. Subjects in the live modeling group observed a model (behind a window) handling a snake in a rather carefree manner. Then the model came out from behind the window and continued handling the snake in the presence of the subject. Gradually, the model induced the subject to participate by touching, rubbing, and eventually, holding the snake. At first the subject used gloves, then bare hands. The whole procedure was very much a self-paced one keyed to the subject's level of anxiety at each stage.

The results indicated several things. First, control subjects showed no changes in their fear of snakes over the course of the study. Second, subjects in both the systematic desensitization and symbolic modeling groups showed significant reductions in fear. However, the live modeling-guided participation group demonstrated an even more substantial reduction in fear. In fact, their improvement was so great that all of them eventually could sit for thirty seconds with a live snake crawling about their laps. These results are shown in Figure 12-3.

Role of self-efficacy.   How are we to account for the loss of fear in the foregoing subjects and their increased willingness to confront their previous fear of snakes? In former years, Bandura would have been prone to invoke the behaviorist's usual explanations: counterconditioning, extinction, and the like. But no longer. In line with his accelerating cognitive emphasis, he has turned to the concept of self-efficacy. The perception of oneself as competent and in control can exert a mighty effect on one's

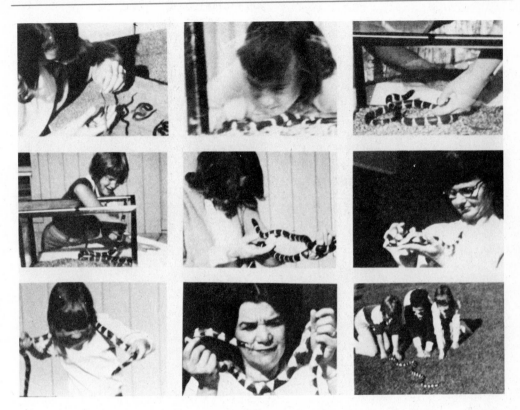

FIGURE 12-2 Models handling a snake.

From "Relative Efficacy of Desensitization and Modeling Approaches for Inducing Behavioral, Affective, and Attitudinal Changes" by A. Bandura, E. B. Blanchard, and B. Ritter, *Journal of Personality and Social Psychology*, 1969, *13*, 173–199. Copyright 1969 by the American Psychological Association. Reprinted by permission.

anxieties and defensive symptoms. Through the previously described methods of observation and guided participation, an expectancy of self-efficacy arises from four principal sources. The most influential source is **enactive attainments** (one's own performance in the dreaded situation). But information can also come from **vicarious experience** (watching the performance of others), verbal persuasion from others, and one's own physiological state.

MISCHEL: A COGNITIVE SOCIAL LEARNING RECONCEPTUALIZATION

The third major figure on the contemporary social learning scene is Walter Mischel. He was born in 1930 in Vienna, but his family emigrated to the United States when

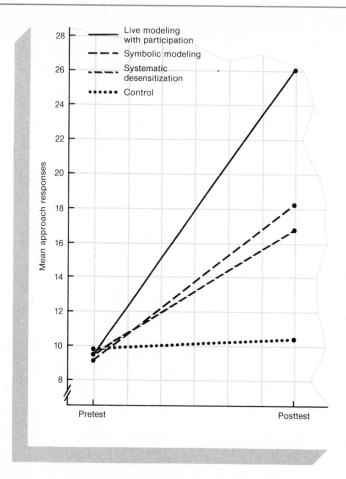

FIGURE 12-3 Mean number of approach responses performed by subjects before and after receiving their respective treatments.

Adapted from Bandura, A., Blanchard, E. B., and Ritter, B.: "Relative Efficacy of Desensitization and Modeling Approaches for Inducing Behavioral, Affective, and Attitudinal Changes." *Journal of Personality and Social Psychology*, 1969, *13*, 173–199. Copyright 1969 by the American Psychological Association. Reprinted by permission.

he was about nine years old. He grew up in New York City and attended City College there. As a graduate student in clinical psychology at Ohio State University, he worked closely with Julian Rotter and was also influenced by the personal construct theory of George Kelly. After several faculty posts, he settled in at Stanford University in 1962. Returning to New York City in 1983, he joined the faculty at Columbia University.

Clearly, Mischel's social learning ideas have been strongly influenced by Rotter's theory and by his close contact with Bandura at Stanford. The impact of Kelly can be noted in some of his cognitive ideas. While he has described himself as fascinated early in his career by Freudian doctrine, it is clear that his relationship with Rotter, Kelly, and Bandura served to cool his ardor for psychodynamic theory. This change is nowhere more obvious than in his 1968 attack on the supremacy of traits and related psychodynamic variables as reliable predictors of behavior. This attack (noted in Chapter 8) was, in effect, an argument for the role of situational variables and was in tune with the behavioral orientation of the day. At the experimental level, much of Mischel's early work dealt with the social learning variables that influence our capacity to delay personal gratification (Mischel, 1966). This is a topic that will be explored in some detail in the next chapter.

In recent years, Mischel has become increasingly involved in the cognitive movement within social learning theory (Mischel, 1973). He has become convinced that in addition to situational factors, observational learning, and the like, we must begin to focus on *personal variables* (individual differences) that influence the meanings attached by the person to stimuli and reinforcements. These meanings are usually called *strategies* or *styles* and grow out of the individual's previous experience with both situations and rewards. It would appear that Mischel's (1979) emphasis on these cognitive person variables marks a deemphasis of his previous "situationist" position and a return to a more explicitly "interactionist" approach where the influence of both personal and situational factors is stressed. The person variables that he discusses are as follows:

■ *Competencies* — These variables refer to what a person knows and can do. They are not so much static accumulations as they are abilities to generate, transform, and use information to create thought and to solve problems. They refer to competency, intelligence, ego development, social-intellectual achievements and skills, and social and cognitive maturity.

■ *Encoding Strategies and Personal Constructs* — Here we are dealing with the manner in which people represent and symbolize information. We categorize, code, and select information, thereby giving it a meaning beyond its raw stimulation properties. The information "We are going to have a test next week" is coded by some students as an opportunity to demonstrate their abilities and by others as a threat to their very existence. People, then, differ in the way they process the same information.

■ *Expectancies* — We also show differences in our expectations. In general, three types of expectancies are important. First, there are *expectancies for the outcomes of the behavior* we select. For example, there is little likelihood that I have the skills to pass a calculus course. Therefore, I had best make a choice that offers a higher probability of success. Second, there are *expectancies for stimulus outcomes*. A smile leads me to expect friendliness from another person. A haze around the moon may mean to me that it is going to rain tomorrow. Finally, there are *self-efficacy expectations*. These reflect a person's confidence in being able to perform an act success-

The subjective values that people place on specific activities will play a major role in what they choose to do. Photograph Eppridge/Sports Illustrated, Time, Inc.

fully. I can find a job or I can impress other people. While similar to behavior-outcomes expectancies, these expectancies seem to refer to a kind of generalized self-confidence or belief about one's competency.

■ *Subjective Values* — Another important determinant of behavior is the value attached to the outcomes of that behavior. Money is important to me but less so for you. I like candy; you prefer ice cream. Values refer to our preferences and aversions, our likes and dislikes.

■ *Self-regulatory Systems and Plans* — These refer to the ways we regulate our own behavior by self-imposed goals and standards. They also refer to self-produced consequences like self-criticism or self-praise. We also adopt plans or rules that will guide our behavior even in the absence of environmental restraints or pressures.

At present, the foregoing list of person variables represents a blueprint for research rather than a finished scheme. it is an outline that incorporates a number of concepts from the Rotter-Bandura axis as well as ideas from Kelly.

SUMMARY

- Contemporary social learning theory developed because of what many perceived to be inadequacies of traditional learning theory; underemphasis of cognitive variables, a model based on animal experimentation, failure to recognize the importance of social and interpersonal factors, and a view of the human being as a passive recipient of environmental stimulation.

- Rotter developed what might be called the first comprehensive social learning theory designed to be useful to clinician and personality psychologist alike.

- Rotter's theory is characterized by several features. It emphasizes a construct point of view and uses a careful, concise language of description. It adopts a social perspective that stresses the importance of both cognitive and motivational variables. Finally, it attempts to explain why individuals select one behavior instead of another rather than to deal with the manner in which behavior is acquired.

- Rotter's theory includes four major variables: behavior potential, expectancy, reinforcement value, and the psychological situation. Behavior potential in a given situation is determined by the strength of one's expectancy for the success of the behavior in question and the value of the goal toward which that behavior is directed.

- Rotter holds that expectancies in a given situation are determined by specific experience in that situation and by experience generalized from related situations. Reinforcement value is determined by the value of the reinforcements to which the reinforcement in question leads. Value, then, is not absolute but relative to the subsequent reinforcements involved.

- Often we wish to predict not a specific behavior but a class of related behaviors all oriented to achieve similar goals. In such instances, the constructs of need potential, freedom of movement, and need value are employed. These are broader analogs of Rotter's previously noted basic constructs.

- More recently, Rotter has emphasized the importance of problem-solving generalized expectancies. These represent beliefs as to how best to construe situations so as to solve the problems they present. Two prominent generalized problem-solving expectancies are interpersonal trust and internal versus external control of reinforcement.

- Rotter has little to say regarding formal stages of development. However, he does accept the notions of Dollard and Miller in which psychological needs are seen as growing out of the satisfaction of physiological needs. He has described six psychological needs: recognition-status, dominance, independence, protection-dependency, love and affection, and physical comfort.

■ The maladjusted person in Rotter's system is seen as possessed of low expectancies (freedom of movement) for the satisfaction of important needs. Conflict, lack of competency, deviant minimal goal levels, and inability to discriminate among situations that do or do not offer the possibility of need satisfaction are also often involved in maladjustment. In contrast, enhancement behaviors may facilitate adjustment.

■ Although Rotter has never developed any distinctive methods of therapy, his theory does have several therapeutic implications. These include flexibility in techniques, the enhancement of patients' problem-solving skills, an active role for the therapist, and an emphasis on behavior.

■ The second major social learning theorist to be discussed was Bandura. Like Rotter, Bandura has emphasized the role of both cognitive and motivational factors. He also contends that while reinforcement may be necessary for the performance of a behavior, it is not necessary for the acquisition of behavior. More recently, he has emphasized the role of self-efficacy in both learning and behavior.

■ In addition, Bandura stresses the notion of reciprocal determinism. This means that all three critical variables—the behavior, the person, and the situation—affect one another.

■ Bandura contends that people can learn not just by experiencing reinforcement themselves but also by the process of vicarious reinforcement, that is, by observing others being reinforced. This emphasizes Bandura's commitment to cognitive variables. Indeed, he believes that our behavior is guided not just by reinforcement but by our expectations of being reinforced.

■ Much learning, Bandura states, occurs through our observation of models who are attended to on a selective basis. He describes a four-stage process of observational learning which involves attention, retention, motor reproduction, and motivation.

■ According to Bandura, by observing models we learn to do things we have not done before. Observation often involves both vicarious reinforcement and vicarious conditioning.

■ Bandura also holds that much of our behavior is self-regulated through internal standards which are acquired through the rewards and punishments administered to us by significant others early in life.

■ Self-efficacy, the belief that we can successfully execute a given behavior, is also a potent determinant of behavior in Bandura's theoretical framework.

■ Like Rotter, Bandura does not describe stages of development as such. Issues of development devolve into questions about changes in goals, plans, self-efficacy, and the like.

■ Similarly, Bandura invokes no special processes to account for deviant behavior. Maladjusted behavior is learned in the same manner as adjusted behavior. One especially malignant feature of defensive behavior, however, is that it often removes the individual from settings in which more adjusted behavior could be learned.

■ In discussing behavior change and therapy, Bandura especially focuses on modeling procedures. For example, phobias have been shown to yield to techniques that enable the person to watch others who are not fearful. Phobic individuals can be guided into previously feared situations by models who demonstrate the desired behavior. Bandura suggests that successfully performing the previously feared behavior enhances the person's feelings of self-efficacy.

■ The third major contributor to social learning theory has been Mischel. Blending concepts from Rotter, Bandura, and Kelly, he has fashioned a cognitive social learning reconceptualization.

■ Mischel's reconceptualization incorporates a number of person variables which emphasize individual differences in cognitive styles. These variables are competencies, encoding strategies and personal constructs, expectancies, subjective values, and self-regulatory systems and plans.

CHAPTER 13

SOCIAL LEARNING
Research, Assessment, and Summary Evaluation

In the preceding chapter, we encountered a set of personality approaches firmly committed to the experimental research strategy. Although the experimental method is hardly foreign to the other perspectives we have discussed, it has not been the chief strategy either. The psychoanalytic theorists looked primarily to the case study. Phenomenologists have been interested in qualitative-idiographic methods or else immersed in content analysis or self-reports as they try to capture the subjective experience of their subjects. The trait theorists have stressed methods ranging from the idiography of Allport to the multivariate statistical tools of Cattell and Eysenck. Of course, the behavioral tradition was rooted in the experimental method. However, this perspective never made a really smooth transition from animal experimentation to human research. And, indeed, the radical behaviorists seemed loath to talk about personality at all.

But with the likes of Rotter, Bandura, and Mischel, we discover a comfortable marriage of the traditional content and process of personality to the experimental method. As we shall see in the following pages, these investigators have found ways of applying rigorous scientific research methods to a subject matter that others before them often found too elusive or soft for empirical study. In so doing, they have placed the field of personality on a more solid scientific footing. Along the way, they have also demonstrated that the precision of objective research methods need not be reserved for the study of laboratory phenomena.

The range of phenomena studied by social learning theorists has been so extensive that we cannot hope to cover it all. Therefore, in this chapter we shall focus on a few examples that seem to typify the larger body of investigation. We will also examine some of the more common assessment methods and then finish the chapter with the customary summary evaluation.

METHODS OF INVESTIGATION

Social learning, as a full-fledged theory of personality, took center stage in 1954 with the publication of Rotter's theory. At that time, Rotter's focus was on research that would give its basic concepts a solid empirical foundation. To illustrate, we will sample from research on three basic concepts: expectancy, reinforcement value, and the psychological situation.

Generalization of expectancies

Chance (1959) wondered whether expectancies will generalize from one situation to another that is physically dissimilar when both situations are involved with the satisfaction of similar needs. She used two personality tests with her undergraduate subjects. One group was told that both tests measured the same thing (e.g., leadership potential) while another group was told they measured different things (e.g., heterosexual adjustment versus leadership). All subjects indicated what scores they expected to receive on both tests prior to taking either. After the first test, subjects received scores that were either seven or fourteen points higher than their stated expectancy. Next, all subjects estimated their probable score for the second test, but before actually taking it. Generalization was measured by taking the difference between the first and second estimates for the second test. Subjects who generalized were those who were influenced by their scores on the first test and thus raised their estimates for the second task over what they had initially stated. Chance confirmed her hypothesis since there was more evidence of generalization when the tests were described as measuring the same thing even though they were physically different.

V. J. Crandall (1955) approached the question of generalization differently. He developed two equivalent sets of nine pictures each so that he could measure freedom of movement in three need areas. There were three pictures for each area. The need areas were recognition for physical skill, recognition for academic skill, and love and affection. One group of male subjects made up stories to the physical skills pictures. Subjects were then asked to perform next to impossible coordination tasks at which they all failed. To measure any changes in freedom of movement in the three need areas, the equivalent set of pictures was administered following the subjects' experiences of failure and frustration. Judges rated all stories for freedom of movement on a scale of zero to ten. A control group of males was administered both sets of pictures but instead of the intervening failure, they spent the same amount of time in a neutral activity. The results of the study are shown in Figure 13-1, which depicts the degree of lowering of freedom of movement in the three need areas for the frustrated subjects as compared to the control group. Failure had the effect of disproportionately reducing subjects' expectancies for success (freedom of movement) in the physical skills need area. Crandall's study shows how failure can influence freedom of movement through the process of generalization and also how the amount of generalization is related to the degree of similarity among need areas.

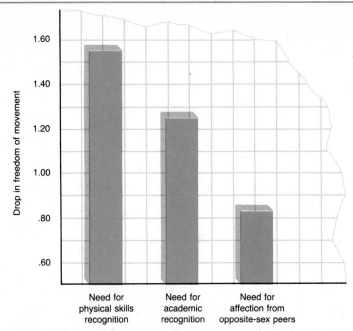

FIGURE 13-1 Effects of failure on reductions in freedom of movement.
From data reported by Vaughn J. Crandall, "An Investigation of the Specificity of Reinforcement of Induced Frustration," *Journal of Social Psychology 41* [1955]: 311–18, in Julian B. Rotter, *Clinical Psychology,* 2nd Ed., © 1971b, p. 91. Reprinted by permission of Prentice-Hall, Inc., and The Journal Press.

Reinforcement value

In the last chapter, it was noted that the value of a reinforcement depends on the expectancy that by achieving it, we will, in turn, attain subsequent reinforcement. Is this really a useful way of viewing things? Dunlap (1953) decided to investigate the issue experimentally. He did this by studying the preferences for toys of eight- to ten-year-old boys. In a pretest phase, he determined the relative value of a group of toys by having boys rank them in the order of their preferences—a common measure of reinforcement value. In the experiment proper, a new group of boys ranked a set of nine toys. The crucial toy was a plastic brick set. Any subject who failed to rank the bricks fourth to seventh was discarded since it was important for the design of the study that this toy be free to move either up or down in value (ranking). Subjects were assigned to one of four conditions: (1) play with the toy did not bring any comments from the experimenter (control group); (2) play was followed by mild criticism; (3) play was followed by strong praise; (4) play was followed by strong praise along with the direct suggestion that people other than the experimenter would also approve. Following this experimental manipulation, subjects were asked to rank the nine toys again. Dunlap discovered that the changes in rankings took place in predicted ways. The greatest increase in ranking occurred for the group that was praised and also given the suggestion of approval from others. The next greatest increase was for the simple praise group, followed by the control group, which showed a slight increase. A small decrement in the ranking of the plastic bricks occurred in the mild criticism group. Dunlap's work, then, suggests that the value ascribed to a reinforcement in a given situation is dependent upon the subsequent reinforcements to which it is expected to lead. If playing with plastic bricks is expected to result in criticism, the value of such play will decline.

The situation

Hardly anyone disputes the fact that specific situations play a crucial role in determining behavior. But social learning theory more than most approaches to personality (e.g., psychoanalysis, trait theory) emphasizes this role. Several early demonstrations of the ubiquitous part played by situations were couched in the framework of social learning theory constructs. For example, Phares and Rotter (1956) devised a list of eighteen reinforcements. Of these, six were athletic reinforcements (e.g., win a wrestling match with a friend), six were related to manual skills (e.g., win a prize for building the best lamp in woodworking class), and six were academic in nature (e.g., receive an A in English). All were designed for the junior high school age range, and each set of six had approximately the same mean reinforcement value. The eighteen reinforcements were rank-ordered under three conditions by seventh- and eighth-grade male students. The three conditions were (1) a gym class, (2) an English class, (3) a woodworking shop class. It was found that reinforcements changed their rank (value) depending upon the class in which the ranking took place. For example, academic reinforcements moved up in value when they were ranked in the English class as compared to the gym class. Thus, cues in each specific situation influenced the value of specific reinforcements occurring in that situation.

The foregoing studies of expectancy, reinforcement value, and the situation have perhaps more historical than contemporary significance. However, they illustrate that by using operational definitions, objective methods, and controlled designs, the utility of the basic concepts in Rotter's social learning theory can be shown. This gives us increased confidence that we can move on to the study of broader personality processes.

Broader personality processes

In the 1960s Rotter's theory was increasingly used to investigate a variety of personality processes. To provide something of the flavor of these efforts, several studies will be described.

Conformity.   Crowne and Liverant (1963) were interested in identifying some of the reasons that people conform. If individuals are placed in a public situation and are faced with a conflict between their perceptions of an event and those of their peers, what determines whether they come down on the side of their peers' judgments (conformity) or uphold the validity of their own perceptions (independence)? Crowne and Liverant decided that one factor contributing to conformity might be a low expectancy for success in a public evaluative setting.

They contrived an experimental situation so that subjects would have to make perceptual judgments after having listened to several confederates of the experimenter make their judgments. Of course, the subjects thought the confederates were subjects just like themselves. There were three conditions. In the first condition, subjects were required to announce publicly their judgment of how many dots had appeared on a screen. The slide containing the dots was exposed for one second. In the second condition, subjects not only expressed their judgment but also indicated on a ten-point scale how confident they were. The third group made their judgments but instead of expressing expectancy statements, made bets of zero, twenty-five cents, or fifty cents on each trial. In a sense, then, the three groups differed in terms of the commitment required of them.

Conformers were defined as subjects who frequently yielded to their peers' judgments, and independents were those who showed a below-average tendency to yield. The results indicated that conformers tended to express a lesser degree of confidence in their judgments than did independents. Therefore, the conformer—at least in this situation—has a low expectancy for success in evaluative situations. This leads such a person to behave in an avoidant fashion to resolve the conflict between self and others. In addition, the more the person is required to make a personal commitment (bet money), the greater is the defensiveness or conformity.

Expectancies and drinking patterns.   No one needs to be reminded that alcohol is a major national problem. It is a problem with myriad aspects and dimensions. From a social learning perspective, one of those aspects may be the likelihood that drinking serves as a way of attaining goals that the person sees as otherwise unattainable. It was in this vein that Jessor, Carman, and Grossman (1968) studied a group of undergraduates. Questionnaires measuring needs for achievement and affection as well as expectancies for the attainment of such goals (freedom of movement) were given to thirty-eight males and fifty females. In addition, a questionnaire about frequency of drinking, amount consumed, and frequency of drunkenness was administered. In essence, it was discovered that the lower one's expectations of achieving need satisfaction in the two areas studied, the more likely one was to resort to alcohol. This relationship was particularly noticeable in females. Other results suggested that drinking served as an escape or relief from problems and shortcomings or as a way of achieving goals that could not be reached otherwise. Again, this interpretation came through most clearly in the case of females. Whether the stronger results for women were due to the frequently observed tendency of women to be more truthful in answering questionnaires is unclear at this point. It may be, alternatively, that drinking on the part of males is more determined by social norms and expectations whereas for females it is more directly linked to personality factors.

Eye contact and expectancies for approval.   Maintaining eye contact is one of those everyday behaviors that ranges from the barely noticeable to the ex-

Low expectancies for success can sometimes lead to a reliance on alcohol as a compensation. Photograph Barbara Pfeffer/Peter Arnold, Inc.

cruciatingly embarrassing. Eye contact sometimes comes easily and naturally but at other times is psychologically painful to maintain. If we reach into Rotter's bag of constructs for an explanation of such behavior, one distinct possibility might be expectancies for social approval. That is, we more frequently maintain eye contact with those from whom we have come to expect relatively greater approval. To test this hypothesis, Efran and Broughton (1966) constructed a situation in which a subject was required to talk about himself for five minutes in front of two undergraduates who were really confederates of the experimenters. Prior to this situation, the subject had been given an opportunity to engage in friendly conversation with one of the two confederates. Eye contact in the experimental situation was measured by recording equipment operated by an observer seated in an adjoining room behind a one-way mirror. Using a total of thirty-three male college students as subjects, the investigators found that subjects spent significantly more time looking at the confederate with whom they had previously interacted than at the unknown confederate. Furthermore, subjects who had scored highest on a scale measuring need for social approval tended to spend more time looking at the preferred confederate than did subjects who were low in need for approval. Once again, the pervasive importance of expectancies and needs in determining our behavior comes through loud and clear.

Quitting therapy. Therapy is a serious enterprise by which we try to reduce human misery and increase both life satisfactions and contributions to society. Yet patients sometimes terminate their therapy prematurely. There are surely many reasons for this. To the extent we can identify some of the factors involved, we will be in a better position to stop this attrition. Given the central role of expectancies and reinforcement values in human behavior, Piper, Wogan, and Getter (1972) turned to them in their search for some answers to this problem.

The subjects for their study were ninety-seven male and female patients at a campus mental health clinic. Subjects were administered a questionnaire listing a variety of problems and instructed to check those that were of concern to them. Also, for each item checked, they indicated on a five-point scale whether they expected therapy to make the problem better or worse. They also rated each problem, this time on a four-point scale, as to how important it was to them. These two ratings served as measures of expectancies and reinforcement value, respectively. Finally, *terminators* were defined as patients who completed three or fewer sessions and then left therapy prematurely. As predicted, terminators had lower combined scores of expectancy and reinforcement value than did patients who remained in therapy. While such findings may not be startling, the study does suggest a set of concepts that may be used to attack this attrition problem systematically. Once having identified the role of expectancies and reinforcement values, we can begin to look for ways of increasing patients' expectancies that therapy will help them and also of enhancing the value of that help in their eyes.

Generalized problem-solving expectancies

In 1966, Rotter published his monograph on internal versus external generalized problem-solving expectancies (a subject to be covered in detail in Chapter 16). This ushered in what was to become nearly two decades of furious research activity. Such generalized expectancies are important because they help determine the behaviors an individual will select in meeting the problems posed by both the social and physical environments. Individuals differ in the strength with which they hold these various expectancies. Since Rotter's theory was designed to help predict the behavior of individuals, these differences in magnitude will, in part, account for the reasons different persons select different behaviors in response to what are objectively similar situations. To better illustrate what is involved here, let us examine some research concerning two kinds of generalized problem-solving expectancies: interpersonal trust and selfism.

Interpersonal trust.   Each of us must constantly make decisions about whether and how much to trust other people and institutions. Should I trust the filling station attendant who gives me directions? Can I rely on the word of students who tell me their term papers will be turned in on time? Can I believe the government when it tells me tax policies are being applied evenly to rich and poor alike? How trusting I am will surely help determine the way I approach the problems inherent in each of these questions.

Rotter (1967a) developed a questionnaire to measure people's generalized trust expectancies. Since then, he has mounted a research effort to determine both the nature of unwarranted distrust and the personal costs of being too trusting (Rotter, 1971a, 1980). In general, it has been discovered that people who are more trusting are less likely to lie and probably less likely to cheat or steal. They are prone to give other people a second chance and to respect the rights of others. Also, they are less likely to be unhappy, full of conflict, or maladjusted. They tend to be sought as friends more often than are distrustful persons. Interestingly, too, more trusting individuals cannot be easily characterized as gullible or naive. It has also been found that interpersonal trust, over the years 1964 to 1967, declined—at least in college students (Hochreich and Rotter, 1970). Not only that, but the drop in trust was rather generalized and particularly apparent in the realm of national and international politics, the communications media, and in terms of the ability of nations to keep peace in the world.

It might be expected that low trusters would be suspicious of strangers. But are they? Wright, Maggied, and Palmer (1975) decided to find out. They asked a group of college students to fill out the Interpersonal Trust Scale and also to write their telephone numbers on the answer sheets so they could be contacted later to participate in some experiments. Later, groups of high and low trusters were called to take part in a study. Carefully standardized methods of categorizing subjects' questions about the nature of the experiment produced several findings. In particular, it was noted that high trusters asked significantly fewer questions indicating suspicion (e.g., "How did you get my name?" "What is the experiment about?"; "Why me?"). They also asked fewer ordinary questions (e.g., "Where is the experiment?"; "Could you repeat the instructions?"; "Could I participate at a different time?").

Another behavior likely to be characteristic of low-trusting individuals is a sensitivity to stimuli suggesting the negative aspects of trustworthiness. In their desire to see the world as they believe it to be, low-trusting persons should be on the alert for such evidence. Gurtman and Lion (1982), using a tachistoscope that flashed words on a white background at very rapid exposure rates, asked subjects to identify the word exposed each time. Words were either positive (e.g., *loyal, sincere, truthful*), neutral (e.g., *healthy, slender, barefoot*), or negative (e.g., *reckless, deceitful, malicious*). As expected, low trusters showed better recognition of the negative words than they did of the positive or neutral ones. High trusters showed no differences across the three categories of words.

Selfism.   If some see this as the age of suspicion, others have been impressed by the rise of self-interest. Earlier, in Chapter 6 (see Box 6-2) we observed that some feel we are in the midst of the me-generation. From a psychoanalytic perspective, we can view narcissism, love of self, or self-interest as a driving force within us. But from a social learning viewpoint, it seems possible to regard selfism as a generalized problem-solving strategy. When faced with problems requiring solutions, some people may have developed the generalized expectancy that they will be most successful if they think of themselves first.

Phares and Erskine (1984) completed the preliminary scale development of the Selfism Scale—a questionnaire designed to measure this generalized expectancy. It might be noted that the correlation between the Selfism Scale and a more traditional measure of narcissism is .45 (Emmons, 1987). To investigate the construct validity of the Selfism Scale, Erskine (1981) hypothesized that subjects receiving high selfism scores would tend to view persons who behave altruistically as really engaging in cynical or opportunistic acts. In addition, they would see such people as less sincere, intelligent, and worthy than would subjects low in selfism. This hypothesis was based on the idea that subjects whose generalized expectancies were highly self-oriented would project these attitudes onto others. Erskine tested her hypotheses by first selecting groups of high and low scorers on the Selfism Scale. Each subject was then given a series of brief vignettes to read. These vignettes contained a variety of situations in which the main character was depicted as helping another person. Following each vignette was a series of potential explanations for the main character's behavior. Three explanations were self-serving ones, and the fourth was altruistic in nature. High scorers on the scale more strongly endorsed the self-serving motives than did low scorers. Such a finding supports the validity of the scale and further underscores the utility of generalized problem-solving expectancies in understanding behavior in the interpersonal context.

Observational learning

If there is a single concept most identified with Bandura's point of view, it is surely observational learning. A key factor here has been his distinction between acquisition and performance, as outlined in the previous chapter. One study in particular has come to symbolize this distinction. It is a study that graphically illustrates Bandura's general empirical approach—in this case, in the area of aggression.

To study the acquisition of aggressive responses, Bandura (1965) used thirty-three boys and thirty-three girls who were enrolled in the Stanford University Nursery School. Two adult males served as models while a female experimenter conducted the actual procedures. The behavior for the children to imitate was contained in a five-minute film. Bandura described this film as follows:

> The film began with a scene in which the model walked up to an adult-size plastic Bobo doll and ordered him to clear the way. After glaring for a moment at the non-compliant antagonist the model exhibited four novel aggressive responses, each accompanied by a distinct verbalization.
>
> First, the model laid the Bobo doll on its side, sat on it, and punched it in the nose while remarking, "Pow, right in the nose, boom, boom." The model then raised the doll and pummeled it on the head with a mallet. Each response was accompanied by the verbalization, "Sockeroo . . . stay down." Following the mallet aggression, the model kicked the doll about the room, and these responses were interspersed with the comment, "Fly away." Finally, the model threw rubber balls at the Bobo doll, each strike punctuated with "Bang." This sequence of physically and verbally aggressive behavior was repeated twice. (pp. 590–591)

But what happened to the model after he aggressed against the Bobo doll? Was he rewarded or punished? Bandura felt such outcomes would have a distinct effect on the child's tendency to imitate and acquire the model's behavior. To determine this, one group of children observed the film without seeing any consequences following the model's behavior (the control condition). A second group—the model-rewarded condition—observed the following scene, which was appended to the previous film:

> A second adult appeared with an abundant supply of candies and soft drinks. He informed the model that he was a "strong champion" and that his superb aggressive performance clearly deserved a generous treat. He then poured him a large glass of 7-Up,

and readily supplied additional energy-building nourishment including chocolate bars, Cracker Jack popcorn, and an assortment of candies. While the model was rapidly consuming the delectable treats, his admirer symbolically reinstated the modeled aggressive responses and engaged in considerable positive social reinforcement. (p. 591)

The third group of children—the model-punished condition—observed the earlier five-minute film plus the following final scene:

> The reinforcing agent appeared on the scene shaking his finger menacingly and commenting reprovingly, "Hey there, you bully. You quit picking on that clown. I won't tolerate it." As the model drew back he tripped and fell, the other adult sat on the model and spanked him with a rolled-up magazine while reminding him of his aggressive behavior. As the model ran off cowering, the agent forewarned him, "If I catch you doing that again, you big bully, I'll give you a hard spanking. You quit acting that way." (p. 591)

To determine the extent to which the aggression would be spontaneously imitated, each child was taken to a room after viewing the film. The room contained numerous toys (balls, mallet, dollhouse, plastic animals, Bobo doll, etc.) Behind a one-way mirror, observers recorded the extent of spontaneous play, both aggressive and nonaggressive. After this phase, the experimenter entered the room and offered rewards of fruit juice and sticker pictures for every response of the model's the child could imitate. These two procedures then, constituted the measures of performance and acquisition, respectively.

In Figure 13-2, we can see that acquisition and performance are not the same thing. In particular, children *acquire* (learn) more responses than they actually *perform* in a free-play situation. Not only that, watching a model who is punished versus one who is rewarded leads to somewhat different outcomes.

Self-efficacy

Bandura feels that we need to know "how people judge their capabilities and how, through their self-percepts of efficacy, they affect their motivation" (Bandura, 1982, p. 122). To understand why self-efficacy is regarded as so important, let us briefly examine several examples of research on the concept.

Clinical examples. Bandura, Adams, and Beyer (1977) studied the manner in which self-efficacy can affect fears of snakes. A group of subjects, all of whom said that they experienced nightmares about snakes, could not concentrate, and so on, were split into three groups. Each group experienced a different set of conditions. In the participant modeling condition, the therapist briefly showed subjects how to handle snakes. Then the therapist joined with the subject and together they engaged in an increasingly difficult series of snake-handling behaviors—from touching the snake all the way up to releasing the snake in the room and then recapturing it. In the modeling condition, subjects watched the therapist engage in the preceding set of graduated behaviors but did not actually perform the acts themselves. Finally, in the control condition, subjects were tested both before and after the experiment to check the extent of their avoidance of snakes, but no intervening modeling experience was provided.

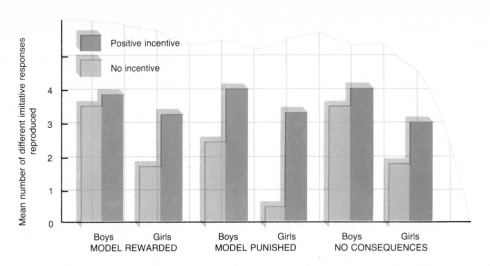

FIGURE 13-2   Imitative responses under reward and free-play conditions as influenced by three modeling experiences.

After "Influence of Models' Reinforcement Contingencies on the Acquisition of Imitative Responses," by A. Bandura, *Journal of Personality and Social Psychology,* 1965, *1,* 589–595. Copyright 1965 by the American Psychological Association. Used with permission.

Analysis of their avoidance behavior showed a variety of encouraging results. As might be anticipated, participant modeling was most effective at increasing feelings of self-efficacy, followed by the modeling condition, which was, in turn, superior to the control condition. In addition, ratings of self-efficacy were excellent indicators of the behavioral tasks that could be completed. For example, high ratings were associated with subjects' ability to carry out the more difficult and frightening tasks. Both modeling treatments and the corresponding increases in self-efficacy produced generalization so that subjects reported increased confidence in dealing with their fears in other, related situations.

Another study also provides data indicating that as coping performance improves so, too, does the sense of self-efficacy. Bandura, Adams, Hardy, and Howells (1980) studied several agoraphobics (individuals who show unreasoning fears of leaving the confines of their homes). After these subjects were trained in a variety of coping skills (e.g., relaxation techniques), therapists accompanied them into community settings involving such activities as shopping, walking alone, climbing high stairs, and entering restaurants. All of these situations were previously much dreaded by subjects. Interestingly, as their behavior in these settings improved, their expressed feelings of self-efficacy also increased.

There has been an increasing volume of research on the role of self-efficacy in a variety of special populations. For example, Baer, Holt, and Lichtenstein (1986) studied subjects who were in a program to help them quit smoking. Those subjects who, at the end of the program, were confident that they could resist smoking for at least six months were, indeed, better able to do so than subjects who had been less confident. In a similar vein, overweight clients of Weight Watchers who reported relatively low self-efficacy were much more likely to drop out of the program than were clients with stronger feelings of efficacy (Mitchell and Stuart, 1984).

Self-efficacy and pain.   Pain is a complex experience that is affected by numerous factors including intensity of stimuli, the way one's attention is focused, how the experience is appraised, and many others. Two studies (Bandura, Cioffi, Taylor, and Brouillard, 1988; Bandura, O'Leary, Taylor, Gauthier, and Gossard, 1987) strongly implicate the role of one of these "other" factors — self-efficacy. For example, Bandura et al. (1988) had students perform mathematical operations under conditions in which they could exercise full control over the demands of the task (self-efficacy) or in which the demands of the task exceeded their capabilities (inefficacy). The self-efficacious subjects subsequently showed very little stress while the inefficacious subjects experienced both stress and high levels of autonomic arousal. In Figure 13-3 the differential stress experienced by subjects along with the mental strain from time pressure and perceived stress-induced impairment in problem-solving is shown.

Self-efficacy and self-regulation.   Bandura and Wood (1989) contrived a simulated managerial situation. When subjects who managed the organization believed that such organizations are not easily controlled, their feeling of self-efficacy was low. And this was true even when organizational goals were easily attainable. In contrast, subjects who acted with a strong sense of self-efficacy set increasingly challenging goals and were quite effective in their analytic thinking. Likewise, extent of subsequent attainments were directly linked to the level of one's self-efficacy. These general findings are illustrated in Figure 13-4.

Immediacy of reward.   People need standards against which they can evaluate their performance. But if the rewards for doing well come long after that performance, their effectiveness may be severely hampered. It is also true that when we attain subgoals along the way toward achieving major ones, this will help bolster and verify our growing sense of self-efficacy. The increase in self-efficacy then serves to motivate our performance further. These ideas gained some support from a study by Bandura and Schunk (1981). In this research, children of about eight and a half years who showed gross deficits and disinterest in mathematical tasks were selected as subjects. They were put into either of two self-directed programs of learning. The first was a learning condition involving the use of *proximal goals*. Here, the experimenter suggested that the children set for themselves the goal of completing at least six pages of instructional items each session. The entire set of items covered forty-two pages. The second group was given a *distal goal* treatment in which the experimenter suggested that they might set for themselves the goal of completing the entire forty-two

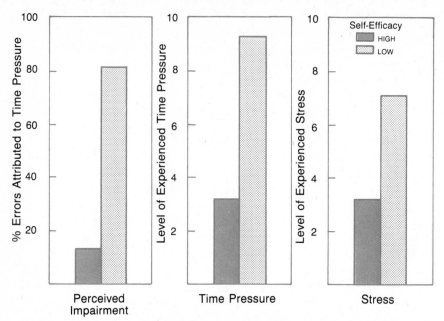

FIGURE 13-3   Performance, mental strain from time pressure, and level of experienced stress in high and low self-efficacy subjects.

Adapted from Albert Bandura, et al., "Perceived Self-Efficacy in Coping With Cognitive Stressors and Opioid Activation," *Journal of Personality and Social Psychology,* September 1988. Copyright © 1988 by the American Psychological Association. Reprinted by permission of the author.

pages by the end of the seventh session. Self-efficacy was measured by very briefly showing the children sets of mathematical problems and then asking them to rate their ability to solve those kinds of problems. The results indicated that with proximal sub-goals, children progressed rapidly in their self-directed learning. They also substantially mastered the mathematical operations involved and developed a strong sense of self-efficacy. In contrast, the use of distal goals produced no demonstrable effects in any of these areas.

Delay of gratification

For a number of years, social learning investigators have been particularly interested in the topic of **delay of gratification**—the ability to defer immediate, smaller rewards in favor of larger but delayed ones. The capacity to endure such self-imposed postponements is a fascinating topic that has been described by some as willpower and by others as ego strength. Let us focus on a few examples of the cognitive and motivational variables that contribute to this capacity.

Role of expectancy.   In one of the early studies, Mahrer (1956) assumed that over time, people accumulate experiences with delayed and immediate gratifications. Some children learn, for example, that when their fathers tell them that if they will forget riding their bicycles today and help clean up the yard they can go to a movie next Saturday, somehow next Saturday never comes. Mahrer's contention was that our ability to tolerate self-imposed delay of reward is determined, in part, by our expectancies that the delayed reward will really occur.

Mahrer used three groups of second- and third-grade boys. Each group was given a series of training trials in which they were promised that the experimenter would return the next day with a free balloon if only they would help him with selecting some pictures. This was done for five consecutive days. In the case of one group, the experimenter fulfilled his promise four out of the five days in order to create a high

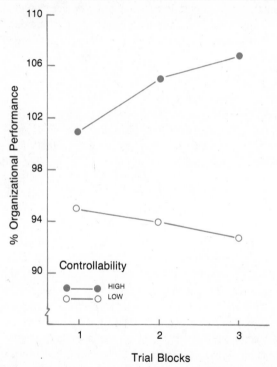

FIGURE 13-4   Level of organizational performance in a simulated managerial setting.

Adapted from Bandura and Wood, "Effect of Perceived Controlability and Performance Standards on Self-Regulation of Complex Decision Making," *Journal of Personality and Social Psychology,* May 1989. Copyright © 1989 by the American Psychological Association. Reprinted by permission of Albert Bandura.

expectancy for delayed reinforcement. A second group was given the balloon on two of the promised days (moderate expectancy), and a third group was never given the balloon (low expectancy). Three days after this training sequence, the experimenter returned and offered to give each of the boys a small toy airplane immediately or a flying saucer toy the next day. On the basis of earlier work, it had been determined that most boys valued the flying saucer more than the airplane. Also, to determine whether experience with one experimenter would generalize to a different experimenter, half of the subjects were given their choice by the first examiner, who was a male, and the other half by a female.

The results showed that boys who had been trained to strongly expect the occurrence of delayed rewards more often chose the flying saucer (delayed reward) over the toy airplane (immediate reward). Their tendency to do this was significantly greater than it was for either the moderate- or low-expectancy groups. Furthermore, these effects were confined to subjects offered choices by the male experimenter. In the case of the female experimenter, there were no differences among the three expectancy groups in their choice of delayed versus immediate gratification. Thus, whether generalization occurs from one set of experiences to another may depend heavily upon the similarity of the social agents involved in the two situations.

Effects on reward value.

Mischel (1966) has long been a central figure in research on the antecedents of the ability to delay gratification and has carried out an extended program of research in this area. Much of his work has highlighted the critical role of expectancies. He also has speculated that having to endure a delay might enhance the perceived value of the reward involved. The following study demonstrates how this might work (Mischel and Masters, 1966). Sixth-grade boys and girls were viewing an exciting film when just at the climactic point (a spaceship was being launched), the projector broke down. The children were told it was due to a damaged fuse. Under one condition, the children were told there was a 100 percent chance the film would resume. For two other groups, the probabilities were 50 percent and zero, respectively. A control group viewed the film without interruption. The children were asked to assign a value to the film both before and after the imposed delay. After the film ended, the children once more rated it for its attractiveness. The major finding was that subjects who were led to believe there was no chance of the film being resumed increased their evaluation of it significantly more than did subjects in the other groups. In addition, this difference was maintained even after the entire film was shown. These results, shown in Figure 13-5, indicate that a blocked or delayed reward can rise in value simply by virtue of the expectancy that it is unlikely to occur. Controlled experimental research, then, confirms our folk wisdom that telling people they cannot have something only makes them want it more.

Imitating delay behavior.

Bandura and Mischel (1965) joined forces to provide an illustration of how willingness to delay gratification can be affected by observational learning. They chose to study fourth- and fifth-grade boys and girls who characteristically chose either a small, immediate reward or a larger, delayed one.

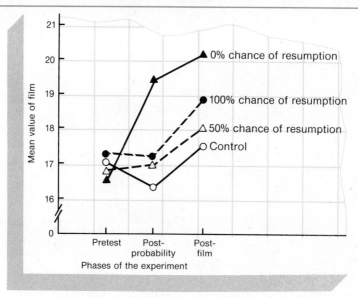

FIGURE 13-5   Mean value of the film at each phase of the experiment. From Mischel, W. and Masters, J. C.: Effects of probability of reward attainment on responses to frustration. *Journal of Personality and Social Psychology, 3,* 1966, 390–396.

There were three experimental conditions. In the first, children were exposed to live adult models whose choice behavior was the opposite of their own. For example, a child who characteristically chose immediate rewards observed a model who chose delayed rewards. The children not only observed these choices being made but also listened to accompanying comments for the models, such as: "The wooden chess figures are of much better quality, more attractive and will last longer. I'll wait two weeks for the better ones" (Bandura and Mischel, 1965, p. 701). In the second condition, the children did not observe live models but instead were exposed to a written record of the model's choices. This constituted the symbolic condition. In the control condition, children were not exposed to any models. Children's own choices for immediate versus delayed rewards were tested immediately after they were exposed to the models. To determine whether the children's choice behavior was stable over time, the initial set of choices was readministered four to five weeks after the experiment. The results of this study showed clearly that children's subsequent choices were markedly affected by their experience with both live and symbolic models. What is more, this effect persisted over time, showing that effects need not be confined to the immediate learning situation.

Personality correlates.   Do children who are able to delay gratification show particular personality characteristics? Funder, Block, and Block (1983) presented four-

---

TABLE 13-1   *Personality characteristics associated with delay of gratification*

Children Who Delayed Gratification	Children Who Did Not Delay Gratification
Boys	
Deliberative	Irritable
Attentive	Restless and fidgety
Able to concentrate	Aggressive
Reasonable	Generally not self-controlled
Reserved	
Cooperative	
Able to modulate impulses	
Girls	
Intelligent	Go to pieces under stress
Resourceful	Victimized by other children
Competent	Easily offended
	Sulky
	Whiny

SOURCE: Adapted from "Delay of Gratification: Some Longitudinal Personality Correlates" by D. C. Funder, J. H. Block, and J. Block, 1983, *Journal of Personality and Social Psychology, 44,* pp. 1198–1213. Copyright 1982 by the American Psychological Association. Reprinted by permission.

---

year-old children with laboratory tasks measuring delay of gratification. Personality test data and ratings by teachers and examiners were available on these children when they were at the ages of three, four, seven, and eleven years. Table 13-1 shows the personality characteristics that tended to be associated with the ability to delay gratification in a laboratory setting.

Will children who were able to delay gratification when they were preschoolers show distinguishable personality characteristics a decade later? Mischel, Shoda, and Peake (1988) were able to secure personality ratings by parents for ninety-five children who ten years earlier had been studied for their delay abilities. Specifically, children of both sexes who had been able to wait longer at ages four or five grew into adolescents whose parents rated them as more academically and socially competent, verbally fluent, rational, attentive, playful, and resistant to stress and frustration.

It might also be noted in conclusion that many of the studies on self-imposed delay of gratification have been carried out with normal, low-risk young children. Recent work strongly suggests that the results of such studies also apply to older children (six to twelve years) who show adjustment problems (Rodriguez, Mischel, and Shoda, 1989).

SOCIAL LEARNING THEORY AND ASSESSMENT

Social learning theory, regardless of whether it bears the stamp of Rotter, Bandura, or Mischel, has always focused on behavior. In his 1954 book, Rotter devoted considerable space to a description of what he called "controlled behavioral tests." However, it has been Bandura's work that has helped elevate behavioral assessment to its current prominence. An integral part of social learning research, then, has been devising specific ways of measuring behavior (see Chapter 11). You may wish to review those procedures since they apply equally here. In addition, social learning theorists have devised a variety of techniques to measure expectancies and reinforcement values. Finally, it has been necessary to assess the broader aspects of personality, including Rotter's traitlike concepts such as need value and internal versus external control. Furthermore, as Bandura increasingly expands his emphasis on self-efficacy and as Mischel turns to person variables such as competencies and encoding strategies, we will probably witness still more attempts to measure these broader concepts.

Measuring expectancies

Rotter (1954) has defined an expectancy as a subjectively held probability that a particular behavior will lead to a particular reinforcement. But how do we measure such a thing? Actually, there are several ways. For example, we might simply ask subjects to rate, on a scale from zero to ten, how confident they are that their upcoming responses will achieve a certain outcome. Of course, sometimes the things people say are contaminated by what they want to happen (wishful thinking), and in some instances they feel the need to appear especially confident. To circumvent such factors, betting techniques can be used. The assumption here is that when I bet two dollars, I am more confident than when I bet only one dollar. Furthermore, if my expectancy statement does not match my subsequent task performance, I lose the money. This places a premium on accuracy and discourages both defensiveness and wishful thinking. Another method is to ask subjects which score, in a series of possible scores, they are most confident of achieving.

Turning to the concept of self-efficacy, Bandura (1982) has defined it as a kind of self-confidence that one can accomplish what a given situation demands. This is quite similar to Rotter's definition of expectancy. Consequently, the measurement techniques are also quite similar. Often the method used requires subjects to specify their degree of confidence that a given task can be successfully executed. The measure can be made as broad or narrow as one wishes (e.g., "How confident are you that you will solve this arithmetic problem on the next trial?" or "At a social gathering, how likely is it that you will make a good impression on the other guests?").

Ryckman, Robbins, Thornton, and Cantrell (1982) have developed a physical self-efficacy scale. This is a twenty-two-item instrument in which subjects express the extent of their agreement or disagreement with each item. Three examples of these items are

1. I have excellent reflexes.
11. I am not hesitant about disagreeing with people bigger than me.
20. I find I am not accident prone. (p. 893)

The scale shows relationships with self-esteem and self-consciousness. It also discriminates between subjects who perform well or poorly on a physical skills task as well as identifying those who report an active involvement in sports activities.

Reinforcement value

Reinforcement value is defined as the degree of preference for a given reward to occur if the chances of its occurrence were perfect (Rotter, Chance, and Phares, 1972). The typical measurement procedure is to provide subjects with a list of potential rewards and simply ask that they be rank-ordered in terms of decreasing preference. Subjects would also be instructed to assume that they could, in fact, have any of the rewards involved. The Phares and Rotter (1956) study cited earlier in this chapter provides an example of this general technique.

Broader personality assessment

While retaining a strong behavioral emphasis, Rotter has always shown interest in procedures designed to assess broad individual differences. The focus of his theory has been on predicting the behavioral choices people will make in specific situations or in classes of situations. Since he assumes that these choices are in part determined by generalized personality characteristics (e.g., freedom of movement, need value) that they bring with them to the situation, it is necessary to devise methods of measuring those characteristics. This has led him to use a variety of the more traditional personality measures such as projective techniques and objective questionnaires. Bandura, on the other hand, has been more interested in identifying the methods by which people learn in social contexts. This has resulted in his concentrating on the situational determinants of observational learning, aggression, and self-control. In the process, he has developed the various behavioral assessment methods noted earlier but has shown relatively little interest in measuring enduring personality characteristics or traits.

Projective techniques.   Rotter and his colleagues have made considerable use of the TAT as a measure of generalized expectancies and needs (see Chapter 2 for a brief description of the TAT). This projective device requires the subject to construct stories in response to a series of pictures that portray people engaged in a variety of activities. Sometimes conventional TAT cards are used; in other cases specially constructed pictures have been employed. Rotter (1954) justifies the use of such assessment techniques as follows:

> Since social learning theory deals primarily with a subject's interaction with his meaningful environment, we are concerned with his reactions to stimuli such as the mother, the father, and cues relating to vocational or academic goals. The TAT stories are responses that provide information about these reactions; it would seem, therefore, that this would be an ideal instrument for obtaining information useful in a social learning approach. (p. 295)

Rotter is not unmindful of the reliability and validity problems involved with such instruments. Therefore, in most cases very careful and explicit manuals have been constructed so that reliable inferences can be made from the stories. Interpretation of the meaning of stories is, then, not as intuitive a process as it is in most clinical settings. For example, to infer the presence of low generalized expectancies for success, one might look for the following kinds of cues in a series of stories:

- Environment is described as threatening, hostile, or unpredictable

- Central character shows withdrawal, guilt, suspiciousness, denial, etc.

- Central character expresses feelings of self-doubt or inadequacy

- Stories show unrealistic endings

And as an example of how stories can suggest a strong need for academic recognition, the following cues in relation to the central character's behavior might be considered:

- Attends college despite family objections

- Reduces extracurricular activities to concentrate on studies

- Feels college is essential to get the right job

- Expresses unhappiness over an average grade

Incomplete sentences.   The **Rotter Incomplete Sentences Blank (ISB)** (Rotter and Rafferty, 1950) is a widely used personality test. Because its stimuli are less ambiguous than the typical projective test, it might better be regarded as a semiprojective test. The ISB consists of forty sentence stems, for example, I like . . .; What annoys me . . .; I wish. . . . The subject's task is to complete each stem. Each completion can then be scored along a seven-point scale for adjustment. From a social learning standpoint, the resulting overall score for adjustment can be thought of as reflecting the relationship between freedom of movement and need value. Maladjustment suggests, overall, low freedom of movement coupled with strong need value whereas adjustment implies a balance between the two.

Questionnaires.   The two most widely used questionnaires within the context of Rotter's social learning theory are the I-E Scale and the Interpersonal Trust Scale. The **Internal-External Control Scale (I-E Scale)** was published by Rotter in 1966. It is a twenty-three-item scale that locates people along a dimension of personal control. The internal end of this dimension describes a person who believes that the outcomes of behavior are due to one's own behavior, efforts, or relatively permanent characteristics. The other extreme reflects external beliefs—perceptions that reinforcements occur as the result of luck, chance, fate, or the interventions of powerful others. The following is an item similar to ones on the I-E Scale:

> Select *a* or *b*.
> a. It is silly to think one can really change another's basic attitudes.
> b. When I am right I can convince others.

Internal versus external control (or **locus of control,** as it is sometimes called) has been one of the most heavily investigated personality variables in the history of personality psychology. It has shown a host of relationships to such things as mastery of the environment, achievement, personal health care, competence, exercise of interpersonal influence, social activism, helping behavior, and adjustment (Lefcourt, 1982;

Phares, 1976; Strickland, 1977, 1989). In recent years, a variety of more specific I-E scales designed to measure narrower aspects of I-E beliefs have been developed (Lefcourt, 1981).

Interpersonal trust was illustrated earlier in this chapter. The **Interpersonal Trust Scale** (Rotter, 1967a) consists of twenty-five items on which people can express their opinions along a five-point scale ranging from "Strongly agree" to "Strongly disagree." Some items similar to those on the scale are

■ Given the opportunity, most people would steal if there were no way of being caught.

■ By and large, people who repair appliances like washing machines and TV sets are honest.

SUMMARY EVALUATION

Each of the contrasting social learning orientations presented in the past two chapters has its characteristic strengths and weaknesses. And, as was stated earlier, the approaches of Rotter and Bandura are less antithetical than they are complementary. For Bandura, the focus is on explaining how social behaviors not presently in the person's repertoire can be learned. For Rotter, the problem is accounting for the choices among behaviors that are available—those already learned and in one's repertoire. Of course, highlighting this contrast may well have served to stereotype each focus. Certainly Bandura, for example, would agree that with a concept such as self-efficacy one can predict whether a person will attempt to perform or to avoid a certain act. Likewise, Rotter will try very hard to arrange environmental conditions so that a patient learns one thing rather than another. But each of these social learning theorists has developed a set of concepts whose focus of convenience lies more in one direction than in the other. In the following sections, we shall consider the several strengths and weaknesses that characterize each social learning orientation.

Strengths

As for social learning theory's strengths, at least eight points can be noted.

Research emphasis.   As has been pointed out repeatedly, social learning theorists do not resort to idle speculation or endless debates in answering questions or resolving controversies. Issues are settled by marshalling evidence derived from carefully controlled experimental research. This is especially notable in the case of Bandura. While Rotter is hardly a stranger to the world of experimentation, his impact has been equally attributable to his skill at theory building. Bandura has wielded his influence primarily through a steady flow of high-quality research on a wide variety of specific content areas.

Heuristic issues.   Rotter, Bandura, and Mischel have each articulated ideas and issues that have captured the attention of those in the field and have influenced the course of research. Many of these notions are, at heart, relatively simple. But then watershed ideas, emphases, or critiques often seem obvious or simple in hindsight. Three examples should suffice to illustrate this point. First, there was Rotter's insistence that human behavior should be regarded as being determined both by reinforcement and by expectancies. His ability to integrate two major themes in psychology—motivation and cognition—into one broad theoretical schema has had an enormous impact on personality psychology. Then there was Bandura's elevation of the role of observational learning in humans. Not a new idea, of course, but his treatment of it, supported by numerous ingenious studies, gave it a scientific luster it had not enjoyed before. In the process, he was able to illustrate the fact that learning does occur in the absence of any apparent reinforcement. In the case of Mischel, his critique of the role of traits as determinants of behavior served to correct an imbalance in emphasis that had long plagued the field. In retrospect, his critique was probably an overstatement, but it did get everyone thinking and investigating. Some may regard the controversy over the role of traits versus situational influences as an aberration in the history of personality research. However, the net effect has been to force us to reexamine the nature of the interaction between personality and situation.

Content of research.   For some years, the behavioral approach seemed to be bogged down in research based on an animal model and confined to narrow laboratory settings. But social learning research has attended to important human content. Bandura has filled the literature with studies of modeling, observational learning, self-efficacy, delay of gratification, and aggression. These are hardly trivial content areas. They involve vital human activities that illustrate the study of personality in a most representative manner. Likewise, Rotter's work on internal versus external control of reinforcement and interpersonal trust deals with truly important human concerns. For the past fifteen years or so, one could hardly pick up a major journal in personality without encountering some facet of Bandura's work. By the same token, Cox (1978) determined that in the *Journal of Consulting and Clinical Psychology* during the years 1970 through 1974, two of Rotter's contributions were the second (Rotter, 1966) and tenth (Rotter, 1954) most frequently cited works, and Rotter the most frequently cited author. In summary, the contributions of Bandura and Rotter have played a seminal role in contemporary personality research, and this is due in no small way to their attention to important human activities.

Also, Rotter's system makes use of traitlike terms (e.g., need potential). But these terms are embedded in a theory that describes them as determined by expectancies and reinforcement values. This means that for Rotter, traits are not required to bear all the predictive freight since their role is molded by other aspects of the theory. This is in marked contrast to, for example, Allport's use of traits (Zuroff, 1986).

Open-ended theory.   Neither Rotter's nor Bandura's version of social learning theory has remained static. For example, over the years Bandura's emphases have gradually changed and evolved. From observational learning, aggression, and the like, the stress has shifted to cognitive processes, self-regulation, and self-efficacy. Partly, this evolution has been possible because Bandura operates from a very loosely structured theory (as we shall see later). Because of his ability to gradually shift his emphasis, social learning has been able to maintain its contemporary, relevant posture.

Much the same may be said for Rotter. While his is a much more structured theory, its concepts are open-ended and allow for the addition of variables. In a sense, it is a content-free theory. That is, it specifies certain variables (needs, expectancies, etc.) but does not dictate their exact content. His 1954 statement of the theory did not refer to such generalized expectancies as interpersonal trust or internal versus external control of reinforcement. But it did include generalized expectancy as a construct. Thus, within the existing framework, specific content can be added as the culture changes and our preoccupations are modified.

Cognitive emphasis.

Social learning theory has always had a cognitive bent. This became apparent as Rotter first articulated that behavior is determined by both reinforcement and expectancies. This cognitive emphasis has become even more obvious in recent years as research on problem-solving generalized expectancies has burgeoned. Indeed, Levy (1970) chose to describe Rotter's social learning theory under the label of "cognitive learning." And then there is Bandura's research on self-efficacy expectations and his labeling of his theory as social *cognitive* theory. As was stated earlier, the cognitive theme is also growing within behaviorism. The effect of all this is to present a nonmechanical view of the human being. For many psychologists, this view is entirely appropriate. We do not become mere accumulations of conditioned responses. Our capacity for thinking, planning, expecting, and reflecting seems better represented by the current cognitively based social learning theories than by the older, more mechanistic and animal-based learning models. In no small measure, this cognitive flavor has enabled social learning theory to engage matters of social concern—ones that are so typically human in character.

Behavior change.

In Chapter 11, several methods of behavior change or modification were discussed. Bandura's research on observational learning and modeling has played a major role in these developments. His focus on the means by which behaviors are acquired and changed in the social context has helped to increase the use of various behavior therapy techniques.

Role of the situation.

Social learning theory has long emphasized the role of situational factors in the determination of human behavior. Rotter, Bandura, and Mischel have all worked to redress the balance in personality research which for so long was tilted in favor of traits. Their work has shown how situational factors are also important. Rotter, of course, has always stressed the interaction between situational variables and more enduring personality characteristics. Bandura and Mischel have been less emphatic in their discussion of traitlike variables. The recent upsurge in interest in self-efficacy and Mischel's outline of five cognitive social learning person variables make it appear likely that individual differences will increase their visibility in the Bandura-Mischel wing of the party.

Theoretical structure.   Rotter's theory could be regarded as one of the few grand attempts in the last thirty years to articulate a broad theory of personality. It is a classical approach to theory construction, with its formal statement of assumptions, postulates, and corollaries. In an age of minitheories, Rotter's theory stands out even more. Because of its formal characteristics, along with its utilization of cognitive, motivational, behavioral, and situational variables, it has been able to serve an integrating theoretical role in personality research. As Sechrest (1984) has commented, "History will not need to be generous to Rotter, just fair" (p. 230).

Weaknesses

As is true with any approach, social learning theory has its share of drawbacks. Let us look at a few of them.

Narrowness.   It seems as if all behavioral learning approaches suffer at least from the appearance of narrowness. For a long time, the behavioral focus was exclusively on overt behavior. Progressively, social learning theories have come to deal with covert events, especially as the cognitive orientation has grown. Still, social learning approaches do not seem to compare with the sweep, of, say, psychoanalysis. The cultural impact of psychoanalysis cannot be explained solely in terms of Freud's use of picturesque language. It also has stemmed from his construction of a system that could delve into so many facets of human life—emotion, childhood, aggression, sexuality, defensiveness, and on and on. Somehow, when pitted against such a panorama of application, social learning theory seems much less broad.

What many find especially lacking is any systematic attention to the development of the organism. Of course, many of Bandura's studies involve children, and Rotter's concepts have been applied to the development of achievement behavior in children (e.g., Crandall, Good, and Crandall, 1964). Yet there is no description of stages of development. For many, this is a critical omission that prevents us from grasping the full import of human behavior. There are biological, hormonal, and physical aspects of development that no amount of learning will ever explain. By choosing to focus only on certain aspects and phases of the life cycle, social learning theory seems to limit its potential effectiveness.

The preceding point can be expanded to note that not all of personality can be explained by learning principles. Certainly Rotter and Bandura recognize this explicitly. However, without a way of integrating biological and hereditary contributions to individual differences in learning and personality, we often seem to be dealing with a truncated point of view. The bottom line here is simply that certain aspects of personality are ignored or inadequately explained.

Theoretical integration.   A few paragraphs ago, it was noted that Rotter's theory is both formally elegant and systematic. However, the same cannot be said for Bandura's approach. It is neither systematic nor unified. At best, it is a collection of concepts (e.g., observational learning, self-regulation, self-efficacy) which have, of course, been heavily investigated. But there is no comprehensive statement of exactly how each part fits to make the whole. In Rotter's system, the relationships among concepts are carefully stated, even to the point of being presented in a series of formulas. By quantifying each variable in the formula, specific predictions can be made about the behavior of a given person in a specific situation. No such possibility is readily available in Bandura's scheme. Indeed, it is really not appropriate to describe Bandura's approach as a theory at all.

A similar situation exists in Mischel's recent presentation of the five person variables that constitute his reconceptualization of social learning. Although intriguing and potentially of great utility, these variables are simply listed and briefly described. There is no statement about how they relate to each other. In the case of both Mischel and Bandura, it is not unlike having a list of the descriptions of all the parts that go to make up an automobile. But, unfortunately, there are no diagrams to show how those parts go together.

Another aspect of this integration problem has been Bandura's tendency to switch his focus over the years. Again, some may regard this not as a criticism but as the very thing which keeps him current in the field. But by moving from observational learning to self-regulation and on to self-efficacy, there develops an unsettled quality to his work which, in turn, gives it the appearance of a patchwork quilt.

Observational learning.
Over the years, Bandura has been criticized for not really explaining the nature of observational learning. Some have said that although he describes it, he does not explain it! Skinnerians have argued that learning by observation is actually a generalized tendency that is indeed reinforced from time to time. They suggest that what really happens is that imitation occurs and this imitation is sometimes reinforced. In fact, one may learn something today without reinforcement; observation is enough. But this does not exclude the possibility that somewhere in the past the person was rewarded for observation, thus leading to a generalized tendency to observe and learn in the presence of certain cues. If so, there is no "learning without reinforcement" after all. At any rate, by not explaining in detail the exact process of observational learning, Bandura leaves himself open to such attacks. Furthermore he has broadened the concept of a model to include very nearly everything—from actual persons to written instructions and on to "symbolic" models. In summary, Bandura often paints with a very broad brush. By so doing, he leaves the door ajar for others to rush in and readily explain things with concepts from alternative points of view.

Anything new or special?
We have already observed that Rotter drew heavily from the diverse contributions of Hull, Tolman, Adler, Skinner, Thorndike, and others. Some may see in this a lack of virtue. However, from such diversity he was able to fashion a blend of reinforcement, cognition, behavior, and situationism unlike anything before.

Similar charges have been leveled at Bandura. It has been said that his is a recycled amalgam of Miller and Dollard's work on imitation, Rotter's cognitive concepts, Tolman's latent learning, and Staats's (1975) social behaviorism. Undoubtedly, Bandura has been influenced by all these sources. Indeed, one of his strengths may be the capacity to integrate new developments in psychology into his framework and then to set off upon a vigorous program of careful research. The final product, while hardly unique, usually contains a fresh outlook that takes us farther along the road to understanding personality processes.

Finally, it does not appear that social learning theory contains any distinctive or special principles of learning. Social learning refers not to a separate set of principles but to the context in which one gathers data (Levy, 1970). Its uniqueness resides not in its concepts but in its functional qualities. That is, it provides a framework by which new information can be gathered and better research executed.

SUMMARY

■ The chief research strategy used by social learning theorists has been an experimental one.

■ Early research by Rotter and his colleagues focused on the goal of providing a solid scientific foundation for the basic concepts of expectancy, reinforcement value, and the psychological situation. Two studies were presented to illustrate how expectancies generalize across situations and need areas. Another study was described to show how the value of a reinforcement is affected by the value of subsequent reinforcements which are associated with it. Finally, it was shown how the situation can differentially affect the value of reinforcements.

■ In the 1960s and 1970s, research on Rotter's theory shifted to the study of broader personality processes. Experiments linking expectancies and reinforcement value to conformity, drinking patterns, eye contact, and termination in psychotherapy were described.

■ Research on problem-solving generalized expectancies has been prominent in recent years. Internal versus external control of reinforcement and interpersonal trust have been the focus of much of the attention. In this chapter, emphasis was placed on interpersonal trust. High trust has been shown to correlate with a reduced tendency to lie, cheat, and steal. High trusters tend to be better adjusted, more sought after as friends, and not especially naive or gullible. Low trusters are more alert to negative stimuli and more suspicious of strangers. Evidence also suggests that distrust increased during the 1960s. More recently, work has begun to determine the correlates of selfism—another problem-solving generalized expectancy.

■ In Bandura's work, observational learning has been the object of considerable investigation. In a now classic study of the modeling of aggression, Bandura was able to show that children can acquire more responses than they actually perform and that a punished model is responded to differently than one who is rewarded.

■ Self-efficacy has been an increasing subject of research. Several studies indicate the importance of this concept. For example, modeling can enhance feelings of self-efficacy which, in turn, are good predictors of mastery or competency with specific tasks. Research indicates that as self-efficacy increases, so, too, does one's ability to cope with previously threatening stimuli or activities, deal effectively with pain, and better regulate one's behavior. The growth of self-efficacy feelings can be facilitated by ensuring that rewards for doing well occur soon after a successful performance.

■   The ability to delay gratification has been the center of much social learning research. Early studies implicated the role of expectancies by showing that subjects who expected a delayed reward of greater value to occur were more likely to choose it over an immediate but lesser reward.

■   Over the years, Mischel has been a leading figure in research on delay of gratification. He has, for example, shown that a delayed reward will increase in value because of the expectancy that it will not occur. He and Bandura have also been able to demonstrate that choices of delayed versus immediate rewards can be influenced through modeling. Finally, there are personality correlates of the ability to delay gratification and these may well last at least through childhood.

■   A variety of assessment techniques have been employed by social learning theorists. To measure expectancies, Rotter has used two chief methods: subjects' ratings of their confidence in being successful and betting techniques. Similarly, Bandura has used self-confidence ratings as indicators of self-efficacy.

■   Reinforcement value has typically been measured by asking subjects to rank-order a list of reinforcements while assuming that they could, in fact, have any of the reinforcements listed.

■   Broader concepts such as freedom of movement and need value have frequently been assessed via responses to projective techniques. Typically, manuals are developed to facilitate objective scoring. Rotter has also used incomplete-sentences methods to measure discrepancies between need value and freedom of movement—in short, maladjustment.

■   Objective questionnaires have been developed to measure problem-solving generalized expectancies such as internal versus external control of reinforcement and interpersonal trust.

■   The strengths of social learning theory are several. First, there is its decided research emphasis. Also important has been the ability of social learning theorists to focus on truly important issues, including the critical role of both expectancies and reinforcement value, the tremendous part played by observational learning, and the contribution of situational factors in the determination of behavior.

■   Another strength has been the ability of social learning theorists to come to grips with vital human activities such as aggression, self-efficacy, modeling, interpersonal trust, delay of gratification, and control of reinforcement, to mention just a few.

■ Other strengths include the open-endedness of social learning theoretical systems, their cognitive emphases, Bandura's focus on methods of behavioral change, and the role of the situation.

■ Also noteworthy is Rotter's achievement in constructing a systematic, integrated theoretical framework whose breadth contrasts sharply with the minitheories so in vogue these days.

■ However, social learning theory contains its share of weaknesses. For example, despite Rotter's attempt to construct a broad theory, there is an element of narrowness in both his and Bandura's approaches. Especially lacking is a systematic focus on human development. Their overriding emphasis on learning phenomena results in a relative inattention to behavioral and personality features that are linked to biological and hereditary factors.

■ Bandura's approach is rather poorly integrated theoretically and lacks systematization. It is probably fair to say that Bandura does not have a theory at all in the formal sense of the word. Similarly, Mischel's reconceptualization, which involves several person variables, shows little evidence of any integration among the proposed variables.

■ Some critics have also noted that Bandura's work on observational learning is more descriptive than explanatory and thus fails to explicate the exact mechanisms involved in the process.

■ While it may be said that social learning theory has drawn ideas from many diverse sources, much the same might be said of most other approaches. However, it does not appear that social learning theory has, in fact, developed any truly distinctive principles of learning.

3

PERSONALITY PROCESSES

P A R T 3

Part 2 dealt with the various ways personality psychologists have viewed personality. Also covered were the characteristic methods of research and assessment associated with each viewpoint. The focus was on the ways personality has been conceptualized.

Part 3 deals with specific personality processes. Specific aspects and topics in personality are described and analyzed. The topics chosen, though hardly exhaustive, are representative of some of the major areas occupying the attention of personality investigators today. Subjects discussed include intelligence (Chapter 14), anxiety, stress, and health (Chapter 15), perceived control (Chapter 16), aggression (Chapter 17), altruism, empathy, and moral judgment (Chapter 18), and sex roles and gender differences (Chapter 19). These are areas of behavior that are so vital in modern society.

You will note as we go along that the previously discussed theoretical conceptualizations have played important roles in shaping the research in each area. While the major goal is the presentation of what is known about the particular personality process in question, it will be interesting to note how the various theoretical conceptions have influenced the research in each area.

CHAPTER 14

INTELLIGENCE

Intelligence is the single topic that best illustrates the trait approach in personality. In fact, it is very hard to imagine any comprehensive account of the determinants of human behavior without the inclusion of some trait-like notion of intelligence. Intelligence, ability, competence, or whatever term we choose is as important to personality as are wings to a bird. All of our enduring predispositions to think, act, or feel in characteristic ways are affected by intelligence. Even our tendencies *not* to think, act, or feel in certain ways can be linked to intellectual factors in many instances. Concerns about intelligence in children helped launch the entire field of clinical psychology—a field that now boasts more members than any other single branch of psychology. Indeed, whatever respect psychology now enjoys in the eyes of the public is attributable in no small measure to the identification of psychology with "mental testing."

Yet personality psychologists, curiously enough, often appear uninterested in this most basic disposition. A quick check of this author's bookshelves turned up five prominent introductory personality textbooks. Two of them did not mention intelligence at all, one dealt with the topic in two lines, one devoted eight pages to it, and the last covered it in ten pages.

But make no mistake—people take intelligence very seriously indeed. Controversy has swirled around intelligence and intelligence testing over the past fifteen years that has sometimes culminated in violent attacks. These attacks have most often centered around issues of fairness and discrimination. Take the following, for example:

In 1986 Judge Robert Peckham upholds his judgment that California schools may not use IQ tests to assess black children for placement in special education classes.

In a 1977 editorial, a college newspaper proclaims, "The only fair IQ test is no test at all."

At the 1976 meetings of the American Psychological Association in Washington, D.C., Ralph Nader assails the influence of educational testing on the lives of students.

The state of New York passes a "truth-in-testing" law in 1979.

In this chapter, we shall try to foster some understanding of the concept of intelligence, correct some common misconceptions about it, and illustrate its role as a personality trait. There is real potential for abuse in intelligence testing although the difficulties seem to lie more in some of the specific uses to which testing has been put (Elliott, 1987; Lerner, 1988) than in the nature of the concept itself.

NATURE OF INTELLIGENCE

All cultures recognize individual differences in intelligence but there is much less agreement about its nature (Weinberg, 1989). Most often it is considered to be a trait—a trait that Mischel (1968) regards as more consistent and generalized than any other personality variable. As he remarks, "Results indicate that correlations across situations tend to be highest for cognitive and intellectual functions" (p. 36). There are many views about the nature of intelligence, how it should be measured, and where we should be heading in our research efforts (Sternberg and Detterman, 1986). In the succeeding pages we shall look at these questions.

Definitions

There is still no universally accepted definition of **intelligence.** However, most definitions usually fall into one of the following broad definitional classes: (1) the ability to adjust to the environment, adapt to new situations, or deal with a broad range of situations; (2) the ability to learn or the capacity for education (broadly defined); (3) the ability to employ abstract concepts and to use a wide range of symbols and concepts. To illustrate some of the long-standing diversity of definitions, consider the following sample:

> [Intelligence is] the aggregate or global capacity of the individual to act purposefully, to think rationally, and to deal effectively with his environment. (Wechsler, 1939, p. 3)

> Intelligence is defined as the entire repertoire of acquired skills, knowledge, learning sets, and generalization tendencies considered intellectual in nature that are available at any one period in time. (Cleary, Humphreys, Kendrick, and Wesman, 1975, p. 19)

> The word [*intelligence*] might be expressly reserved to denote without prejudice whatever these tests may some day, after full investigation, show themselves to measure. (Spearman, 1923, p. 22)

> . . . intelligence is expressed in terms of adaptive, goal-directed behavior. The subset of such behavior that is labeled "intelligent" seems to be determined in large part by cultural or societal norms. (Sternberg and Salter, 1982, p. 24)

Prototype approach

Some have given up trying to develop a simple, crisp definition. Instead, they have resorted to the use of "prototype" definitions. As Neisser (1979) argues:

> Our confidence that a person deserves to be called "intelligent" depends on that person's overall similarity to an imagined prototype, just as our confidence that some object is to be called "chair" depends on its similarity to prototypical chairs. There are no definitive criteria of intelligence, just as there are none for chairness; it is a fuzzy-edged concept to which many features are relevant. Two people may both be quite intelligent and yet have very few traits in common—they resemble the prototype along

different dimensions. Thus, there is no such thing as *chairness*—resemblance is an external fact and not an internal essence. There can be no process-based definition of intelligence, because it is not a unitary quality. It is a resemblance between two individuals, one real and the other prototypical (p. 185).

However difficult it has been to articulate functional definitions of intelligence, there is some evidence that laypeople and experts do agree on their conceptions of it. For example, Sternberg, Conway, Ketron, and Bernstein (1981) carried out three experiments. First, they approached people studying in a college library, entering a supermarket, and waiting in a train station and asked them to list behaviors characteristic of either intelligence, academic intelligence, everyday intelligence, or "unintelligence." Second, experts and laypersons (including students) were asked to rate how important or characteristic of intelligence the behaviors listed in the first experiment really were. Third, laypersons were given written descriptions of behaviors characterizing fictitious people and asked to rate the intelligence of those people. The investigators found that people do have rather well-formed prototypes for intelligence and that these prototypes are similar for layperson and expert alike. Furthermore, intelligence seemed to be comprised of several behaviors, including problem solving, verbal facility, social competence, and possibly motivation.

Clearly, precise definitions of intelligence are difficult to come by. Yet there seems to be an implicit core of meaning struggling to emerge. Let us now turn to an examination of several theories of intelligence that have been offered over the years.

Theories

A theory of intelligence should take us beyond a mere definition and elaborate its components, origins, and manner of operation. Many theories have been proposed. Some have emphasized neurological and biological aspects and others have focused on learning and developmental features (Maloney and Ward, 1976). However, psychometric approaches involving factor analysis have had the greatest impact (Brody and Brody, 1976).

Charles Spearman (1927) decided on the basis of elaborate analyses of test scores that all intellectual activity was dependent on a broad, **general factor (g).** Subsequently, he contended that a number of **specific factors (s factors)** also were important. He suggested that the element which tests have in common could be represented by *g*, whereas those elements unique to a given test would be *s* factors. However, his factor analyses led him to conclude that, basically, intelligence is a broad, generalized entity. In contrast, Louis Thurstone's (1938) factor analyses persuaded him of the importance of **group factors**—factors neither as broad as *g* nor as specific as *s* factors. He described seven group factors: number, word fluency, verbal meaning, perceptual speed, space, reasoning, and memory. Yet a different view was presented by Edward Thorndike and his colleagues (Thorndike, Bregman, Cobb, and Woodyard, 1926), who denied the presence of a broad *g* factor and claimed instead that intelligence could be reduced to numerous specific factors. The disagreements among Spearman, Thurston, and Thorndike serve to remind us again of the points made in Chapters 8 and 9 regarding factor analysis. Because of the different methods of factor analysis used and the varieties of assumptions made by the various investigators, several interpretations of the same set of correlations are often possible. Despite this, Anastasi (1976) has stated that "the prevalent contemporary American view of trait organization recognizes a number of moderately broad group factors, each of which may enter with different weights into different tests" (p. 371).

Hierarchical models. Cattell (1963) and Horn (1968) have proposed their versions of a **hierarchical model of intelligence.** Their models emphasize the central role of a *g* factor. Subsumed under the *g* factor are somewhat narrower group factors, and at the lowest level are the specific factors. And Cattell has partitioned Spearman's *g* into two components: **fluid ability** (biological capacity) and **crystallized ability** (capacities attributable to culture-based learning). An example of a hierarchical model of intelligence is shown in Figure 14-1.

The SOI model. In contrast to other theorists who often seem to try to infer a model of intelligence from the results of their factor analyses, J. Paul Guilford (1967) proposed a model and then set about generating data to test its utility. His model is called the **structure of the intellect (SOI) model.** It classifies intelligence along three dimensions: **Operations** (what the subject does), **Contents** (the material or information on which the operations are performed), and **Products** (the form in which information is processed). If we sort out all the possible combinations among Operations, Contents, and Products, we arrive at 120 separate intellectual abilities. The main reservation about Guilford's model is that it appears to be a taxonomy or classification rather than an explanation of intellectual activity.

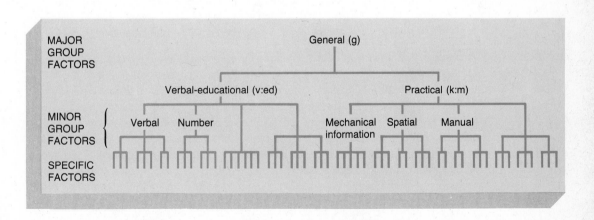

FIGURE 14-1   Hierarchical model of the organization of abilities.
From *The Structure of Human Abilities* by P. E. Vernon [London: Methuen], 1960.
Copyright 1960 by Methuen and Co. Reprinted by permission.

Current developments. Most intelligence tests (as we shall see in a moment) assess *what* we know. In contrast, Jean Piaget's approach focused on developmental changes in how children perceive, understand, and operate on their environments (Ginsburg and Opper, 1988). Currently, research on intelligence has taken on an even more cognitive or information-processing look. Now, researchers try to describe a person's moment-by-moment attempts to solve a problem—from the moment a stimulus is recognized to the person's verbal or motor response. This is clearly a more dynamic view of intelligence compared to the older static theories of mental components. Sometimes, investigators focus on speed of information processing and sometimes on strategies of processing. One of the salient questions is whether there is a central processing mechanism (Gardner, 1983). Also, do the processing elements change as the person develops and are there general problem-solving skills or only skills specific to certain ability areas? While the model here may be more dynamic, the questions seem reminiscent of the competing theories of Spearman and Thorndike.

Sternberg (1985) has proposed a **triarchic theory of intelligence.** He argues that we function intellectually on the basis of three aspects. The **componential** aspect refers to analytical thinking and would characterize the person who is good at taking tests. The **experiential** aspect relates to creative thinking—one who can take separate elements of experience and combine them insightfully. Finally, the **contextual** aspect is seen in one who is "street smart." This is the person who can "play the game" and manipulate the environment. Increasingly, investigators are beginning to zero in on social competence as an important aspect of intelligence (Sternberg and Wagner, 1986). In any case, Sternberg (1985) feels that our performance is governed by these three aspects of intelligence. But his focus is not so much on speed and accuracy of performance as it is on planning and monitoring responses.

Gardner (1983) talks about **multiple intelligences.** He suggests that competence involves sets of problem-solving skills. There is a family of six intelligences: linguistic, musical, logical-mathematical, spatial, bodily-kinesthetic, and personal. Gardner is trying to widen the scope of what is considered to be intelligence.

A passing observation. You may have decided by now that all this business of definitions, prototypes, and theories of intelligence is rather abstract and not tuned into everyday realities. Apparently, many builders of intelligence tests seem to agree. As we shall see in the following pages, constructing intelligence tests has often been a rather pragmatic exercise closely tied to some set of predictive purposes (school grades, teachers' ratings, etc.). It has not often been a procedure in which selection of items or the format of the test has been derived from an explicit theory of intelligence. Most of those who have to make practical decisions about the intelligence of their clients seem to view intelligence as some sort of general factor that can be broken down into several group factors.

MEASUREMENT OF INTELLIGENCE

Intelligence tests have had many applications in clinical, educational, and vocational assessment (Aiken, 1987). But the one event that did the most to shape modern methods of measuring intelligence occurred in 1905. This was the publication of the **Binet-Simon**

Scale. Alfred Binet (see Figure 14-2) was commissioned by the Paris school system to develop a method of identifying children whose intellectual capacity would not permit them to profit from ordinary classroom instruction. What was needed was an objective method since teachers' judgments often seemed subject to a variety of biases. So it was that Binet, with the assistance of Théodore Simon, put together a scale that has served as a model of intelligence tests since then.

Individual tests

In making judgments about a person's intellectual ability, most clinical psychologists prefer to use **individual tests** — tests that are administered to one subject at a time rather than to groups. The one-on-one relationship permits the clinician to integrate observations about the person's motivation, anxiety, or reactivity to the examiner with the formal IQ score. Such observations would not be possible with tests administered in group settings. It is the opportunity for individualized observations that adds meaning to the simple IQ score itself and enhances the utility of the test. Let us now turn to an examination of some of the more widely used individual tests of intelligence.

The Stanford-Binet.

At one time, the Binet test was the preeminent individual measure of intelligence. It underwent revisions in 1916, 1937, 1960, and 1972. The latest version of what has been called since 1937 the Revised **Stanford-Binet** appeared in 1986 (Thorndike, Hagen, and Sattler, 1986).

Until this latest revision, the Stanford-Binet was notable for being an age scale. This means that it was organized into twenty age levels beginning at Year II and proceeding through Superior Adult Level III. There were six items at each age level. Each item passed was converted into one or two months of mental-age credit (depending on whether it was located before or after Year Level V). The number of mental-age units (MA) were added up, divided by one's chronological age (CA), and multiplied by 100 (to avoid decimals). The resulting figure was the **Intelligence Quotient (IQ).** Thus, $(MA/CA) \times 100 = IQ$.

FIGURE 14-2 Alfred Binet
National Library of Medicine

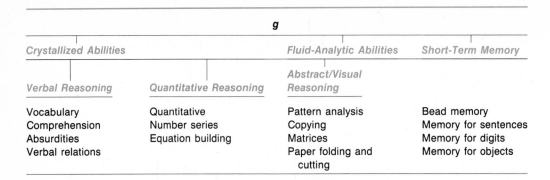

g			
Crystallized Abilities		*Fluid-Analytic Abilities*	*Short-Term Memory*
Verbal Reasoning	*Quantitative Reasoning*	*Abstract/Visual Reasoning*	
Vocabulary	Quantitative	Pattern analysis	Bead memory
Comprehension	Number series	Copying	Memory for sentences
Absurdities	Equation building	Matrices	Memory for digits
Verbal relations		Paper folding and cutting	Memory for objects

FIGURE 14-3   Cognitive-abilities factors appraised in the Stanford-Binet: Fourth Edition. Reprinted with permission of The Riverside Publishing Company from page 4 of *Stanford-Binet Intelligence Scale Guide for Administering and Scoring the Fourth Edition* by R. L. Thorndike, E. P. Hagen, and J. M. Sattler. The Riverside Publishing Company, 8420 W. Bryn Mawr Avenue, Chicago, IL, 60631. Copyright 1986.

The 1986 version of the Stanford-Binet is radically different from the older versions. For one thing, it is based on a hierarchical model of intelligence. That is, a general reasoning factor *(g)* is at the top. There are two additional levels as shown in Figure 14-3. Also shown are the specific kinds of items on the test and the abilities they are supposed to tap. There are, then, a series of subtests each composed of items of the same general type but of varying levels of difficulty suitable for ages two all the way to adulthood.

Another difference from the older versions is the use of an adaptive testing procedure called **multistage testing.** This means that the examiner first gives the vocabulary subtest to determine at which point on each remaining subtest testing should begin for a given person. With this adaptive format, not all examinees of the same age are necessarily given the same items.

Preliminary evidence concerning the reliability and validity of the new Stanford-Binet is promising. However, the test is so new that the complete tale is far from having been written. Studies from other investigators, utilization of a wider range of validity criteria, and reports of the clinical utility of the scale are yet to come (Phares, 1988).

It is important to understand that, in the final analysis, IQs are merely scores based on performance. They are not magic windows into the mind. Furthermore, like any score, an IQ is the product of numerous converging factors. Some of these factors may reflect intellectual potential. But others may involve motivation, health, education, cultural background, and the like. To sort out these factors is a complex job requiring skill, professional training, and sensitivity. Only then can a valid statement be made about someone's intellectual status. There are no shortcuts.

The Wechsler scales.   In 1939, David Wechsler (see Figure 14-4) published the **Wechsler-Bellevue Intelligence Scale.** This was an individual test specifically

FIGURE 14-4 David Wechsler
The Archives of the History of American Psychology, University of Akron

designed to correct some of the deficiencies of the old Stanford-Binet. First, it was a test for adults, with a content more appropriate for them. It also had less of a school flavor and was not so verbally oriented as the old Stanford-Binet. Another difference was that all similar items were grouped together into one subtest whereas the Stanford-Binet's diverse items were arranged in age levels of six items each. For example, in the case of the Wechsler all arithmetic items were grouped into one subtest—and arranged in order of increasing difficulty. The entire test was divided into a Verbal Scale (six subtests) and a Performance Scale (five subtests), and a separate IQ score could be calculated for each of the two scales, in addition to a Full Scale IQ score. The deliberate inclusion of performance items was to rectify the Stanford-Binet's bias in favor of verbal items. Box 14-1 briefly describes the various Wechsler subtests.

Since the original Wechsler-Bellevue appeared, a whole series of related tests and revisions have been published:

■ Wechsler Intelligence Scale for Children (WISC), first published in 1949, and revised in 1974 (WISC-R).

■ Wechsler Preschool and Primary Scale of Intelligence (WPPSI), which first appeared in 1967 and was revised in 1989 (WPPSI-R).

■ Wechsler Adult Intelligence Scale (WAIS), initially published in 1939, and revised in 1955. A further revision, the WAIS-R, was published in 1981.

Although there are obvious differences in difficulty levels among these tests, they all follow the same basic format and philosophy.

Overall, the Wechsler scales have been well standardized on reasonably representative populations and show a high quality of technical construction. Perhaps their weakest feature is a lack of solid construct-validity evidence to help us understand just what aspects of intelligence are being measured.

Box 14-1
A DESCRIPTION OF THE 11 WECHSLER SUBTESTS

1 *Information* — 29 items designed to tap knowledge one acquires in the normal course of living (e.g., "What is the capital of Spain?").

2 *Comprehension* — 16 items requiring the subject to explain certain procedures, interpret proverbs, or decide on a course of action (e.g., "What should you do if you find a child much younger than yourself wandering about lost?").

3 *Arithmetic* — 14 items quite similar to ordinary arithmetic problems in most elementary school texts.

4 *Similarities* — 13 items, each of which names two things. The subject must identify their similarities (e.g., "How are a comb and a brush alike?").

5 *Digit Span* — Two lists of numbers that contain from three to nine digits. Each set of digits is read aloud to the subject. For the first list, the subject must repeat the digits in order. For the second list, the digits must be repeated in reverse order.

6 *Vocabulary* — 35 words that the subject is asked to define.

7 *Digit Symbol* — A code-substitution task (see the figure below).

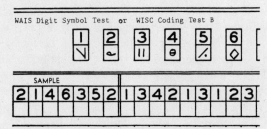

Courtesy of The Psychological Corporation.

8 *Picture Completion* — 20 cards, each with a part missing which the subject must identify (see the figure below).

9 *Block Design* — A series of designs printed on cards. The subject must assemble blocks to reproduce the design on each card.

10 *Picture Arrangement* — Several sets of cartoon drawings presented in a mixed-up sequence. The subject is to arrange each set so that it tells a logical, coherent story.

11 *Object Assembly* — Four puzzles or cut-out objects that the subject must put together correctly.

Courtesy of The Psychological Corporation.

As for the WAIS specifically, Parker, Hanson, and Hunsley (1988) surveyed studies that appeared over a twelve-year period. They found strong evidence for the reliability and validity of the test as shown in Figure 14-5.

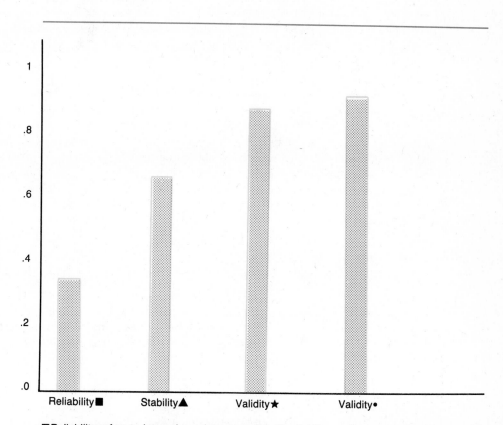

■Reliability refers to internal consistency, split-half reliability, alpha, inter-rater and intra-rater reliability, etc.

▲Stability refers to test-retest reliability.

★Validity based on studies in which there was no theoretical or empirical basis for the predicted outcome.

•Validity based on studies in which there was a theoretical or empirical basis for the predicted outcome.

FIGURE 14-5   Estimated average correlations for reliability, stability, and validity. From "MMPI, Rorschach, and WAIS: A Meta-Analytic Comparison of Reliability, Stability, and Validity" by Kevin C. H. Parker, et al., *Psychological Bulletin,* Vol. 103, No. 3, May 1988. Copyright © 1988 by the American Psychological Association. Reprinted by permission of Kevin C. H. Parker.

Intelligence tests and validity

Binet originally envisioned his test as a diagnostic instrument to help place children in the proper educational setting. Accordingly, he constructed a device that was very school oriented — one that contained items closely related to activities and information important to success in school. This orientation still permeates most of the common intelligence tests in use today. But over the years, laypersons and even some psychologists have come to view them as measures of some global capacity that transcends mere school achievement.

But are intelligence tests valid? That is, do they, in fact, measure intelligence? If by intelligence we mean the capacity for doing well in school or being rated as intelligent by teachers, the answer is probably yes. If we are referring to abilities that society values highly, such as verbal ability, reasoning, reading capacity, information acquisition, or analytical abilities, the answer is also probably yes. But if we are talking about such things as "street smarts," ability to drive a shrewd bargain, common sense or even wisdom, or perhaps the ability to be a "survivor," the answer may just as easily be no. And if by intelligence we mean some innate, inherited intellectual capacity unaffected by environment or cultural opportunity, the answer is most assuredly no. In the final analysis, what intelligence tests measure is defined by those things with which IQs correlate and not by the name or title printed on the test kit. In general, IQ tests sample the knowledge and skills valued by the majority culture.

Major correlates of IQ.   IQs have been shown repeatedly to correlate highly with grades in school and with achievement tests that measure what has been learned in school. It should also not surprise anyone to learn that IQ and occupational status are related. This is true whether occupational status is defined by income or social prestige. However, once one has entered a given occupation, degree of intelligence does not appear to separate the more eminent achievers from the less eminent ones (Matarazzo, 1972; Roe, 1953). Perhaps it is true that entry into each occupation requires some minimal level of ability whereas degree of subsequent success depends upon nonintellectual factors such as motivation, perseverance, and social skill. Overall, however, the relationship between IQ and achievements outside the classroom is an elusive one.

Creativity.   There are certainly many instances in which a high IQ does not result in what we usually think of as creativity. Indeed, Wallach (1971) argues that intelligence and creativity are really separate things. Perhaps this separation is not surprising when we consider what creativity typically involves. Research by Barron (1968) and MacKinnon (1965) suggests that creative individuals such as writers, artists, architects, and the like, are self-confident, highly motivated, and committed to their work. Roe (1953), in a study of eminent scientists, found them to be absorbed in their work, devoting enormous amounts of time over periods of many years. There is an intuitive quality and an openness to experience that likewise characterize creative persons. We may safely assume that most creative people are also quite intelligent (Nicholls, 1972). But even

One of the characteristics of creative people tends to be their strong motivation and commitment to work. Photograph Michal Heron.

here there are exceptions, particularly if we define intelligence narrowly in terms of IQ. At the same time, many highly intelligent people such as lawyers, doctors, business people, and professors never produce much of what is commonly thought of as creative in nature. Similarly, the relationship between IQ and what many would call wisdom is tenuous at best (Holliday and Chandler, 1986).

Aptitude or achievement?

Achievement tests are designed to measure what one has learned prior to taking the test. **Aptitude tests,** on the other hand, are supposed to predict one's performance in the future. What, then, are intelligence tests? Do they measure aptitude or achievement? For people who regard an IQ as an index of one's capacity, intelligence tests are probably thought of as aptitude tests. Yet when we look at intelligence tests of various sorts, we find them to contain items that not only appear in many achievement tests but also seem to reflect what ought to have been learned in school (e.g., "How far is it from Paris to Rome?" or "Define the word *escalate*"). Do such items tap aptitude or capacity or do they tell us what a person has learned? In a real sense, aptitude and achievement tests are distinguished not by the kinds of items they contain but by the purposes for which they are used. A college entrance test can be thought of as a measure of what has been learned in high school. But it can also be used to predict success in college.

Culture-fair tests

If, as just noted, achievement and aptitude get mixed up in our current tests, why not devise a test that separates them? If ability to define the word *escalate* depends upon one's motivation, amount of education, practice in reading, or even how much one trusts the examiner, could we not construct a test that is free of such nonintellectual factors — a test composed of items that relate directly to one's innate ability? It certainly has been tried.

A number of so-called **culture-fair tests** have appeared. These are tests that attempt to rule out the effects of factors that distinguish one culture or subculture from another — that is, to neutralize the operation of nonintellectual variables. Ideally, use of culture-fair tests should prevent individuals from being penalized by factors that reflect cultural background instead of innate capacity. Take the example of language. Administering the Stanford-Binet to a child who does not speak English (or even one who comes from a family whose first language is not English) will most certainly produce results that reflect the language handicap. Speed of reaction is another important factor. Many tests require the person to answer items within a certain time limit or else award point bonuses for quick answers. But some cultures (and even subcultures) are not geared to quick responsiveness — they do not understand that "faster is better."

In the United States, a multiracial and culturally diverse nation, questions have long been raised about the fairness of tests for those who are not from the dominant, white middle or upper class. Are our tests completely fair for inner-city blacks, for Hispanics, or even for rural populations? Probably not. Sometimes it seems that the experiences of the white suburban child are the very things most required for a good performance on the tests. By the same token, little of the black ghetto child's experience seems relevant for the testing situation. Situational variables in the testing interaction can also be important. For example, a number of studies have suggested that black children achieve lower IQ scores when the test is administered by a white examiner than when the examiner is black, although this conclusion has been questioned (Sattler and Gwynne, 1982). Whether all the differences between racial groups or between subcultures and the dominant group are simply attributable to the test or to examiner characteristics is still being debated (Lambert, 1981).

Typically, culture-fair tests adopt one of two strategies: items are employed with which everyone is thought to be equally familiar or else equally unfamiliar. A good example of a culture-fair test is the **Progressive Matrices** developed by Raven in 1938. The subject examines a series of geometric figures, tries to discover the element common in each, and then applies this knowledge to a specific problem involving those figures. Figure 14-6 presents a sample item from this test.

Another approach is through drawing a person. The **Goodenough-Harris Drawing Test** (D.B. Harris, 1963) requires children to draw pictures of a man, a woman, and one of themselves. The assumption is that everyone is equally familiar with the persons being drawn and thus the task is appropriate regardless of culture.

Although sound in theory, culture-fair testing has not worked very well. For some subjects, the whole idea of being tested is a foreign one. The attempt to remove language barriers has not canceled the subtle effects of cultural or familial background.

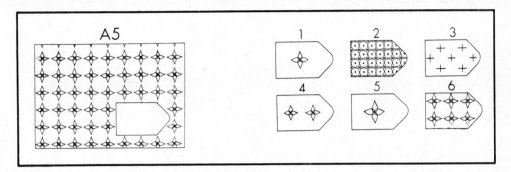

FIGURE 14-6   Sample item from the Raven Progressive Matrices. Subjects must select from the alternatives to the right of the large box the one that fits the blank item.

Item A5 from the *Raven Standard Progressive Matrices*. Reprinted by permission of J. C. Raven Ltd

Minority subjects or those from other cultures continue to show deficiencies on these tests just as they did on tests such as the Stanford-Binet. To provide valid assessments of intelligence, we must continue to apply clinical sensitivity to the evaluation of not just test performance but also of various background, learning, motivational, and emotional factors.

IQ consistency

Were intelligence merely a simple, innate capacity, the IQ would not be expected to change much throughout the course of one's life. There might be some minor fluctuations due to errors in the measurement technology, but that is about all. However, there is a great deal of evidence suggesting that, in fact, IQ scores do change (Anastasi, 1976). Let us examine a bit of that evidence now.

Test performance.   Several things may affect test performance. For example, temporary states may interfere with a person's test performance. There may be illness, motivational or emotional upheavals, and the like. In addition, intelligence tests tend to measure different things at different age levels. For example, infant tests of intelligence require the subject to respond to simple stimuli such as bells and mirrors. Preschool items involve such things as stacking blocks and identifying parts of the body. These items are very different from the highly verbal, abstract, and mathematical items that appear on college entrance examinations and adult intelligence tests. As a result, IQs obtained from very young chiidren do not correlate highly with their IQs obtained in late adolescence. The correlation between IQs measured at age two and at age fourteen is usually only about .30. However, between the ages of fourteen and eighteen, the correlation is commonly about .80. Of course, instability of IQs is hardly rampant. Still, there is enough variability to give pause to those who view the IQ as a straightforward reflection of innate capacity.

Aging.   Aging is another factor that can influence intellectual performance as measured by tests (Botwinick, 1984). Beyond the age of forty or so, there is sometimes a detectable decline in intellectual performance. This does not mean that numerical IQs will decline much, since intelligence tests often utilize the **deviation IQ concept.** This means that the average IQ of each age group is statistically set to be 100. Thus, as Botwinick (1984) points out, to achieve an IQ of 100, someone aged twenty-five to thirty-four must make a score of 114.5, while someone aged seventy to seventy-four must score only 81. As can be seen in Figure 14-7, for the young person the "age debit" is 14.5; for the older person, the "age credit" is 19. But whether the score is 114.5 or 81, the IQs for both age levels are 100. Nevertheless, the absolute level of performance does decline over the years. Why is this? Several factors have been implicated. There may be a general deterioration of health or growing impairments of hearing and eyesight. In addition, aging individuals become increasingly cautious and fearful of making mistakes and this tendency can affect their test performance. In some instances, the testing circumstances themselves may intimidate the elderly person. Interestingly, alterations in testing procedures will sometimes improve performance. For example, giving older persons extra time or allowing them to familiarize themselves with the test procedures will often lead to higher scores.

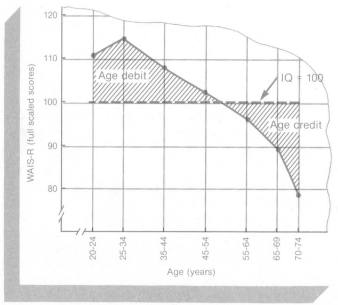

FIGURE 14-7   WAIS-R Full Scale scores as a function of age.

From *Aging and Behavior,* Third Edition by Jack Botwinck. Copyright © 1984 by Springer Publishing Company, Inc. Reprinted by permission of Springer Publishing Company, Inc., 536 Broadway, New York, NY 10012.

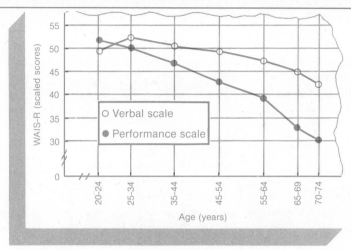

FIGURE 14-8 WAIS-R verbal and performance score as a function of age. From *Aging and Behavior,* Third Edition by Jack Botwinck. Copyright © 1984 by Springer Publishing Company, Inc. Reprinted by permission of Springer Publishing Company, Inc., 536 Broadway, New York, NY 10012.

There is also a pattern of decline on the Verbal and Performance subtests of the WAIS that is so common that it has been called the "classic aging pattern." In general, there is relatively little decline in scores on verbal tasks but a more noticeable decline on performance tasks. This is shown in Figure 14-8. In addition, the amount of intellectual decline with age is affected by factors such as amount of education. People with college backgrounds tend to show noticeably less decline than those who have only an eighth-grade education.

Mental retardation. Can the intellectual level of retarded individuals be raised? This is an important yet very difficult question whose answer may pretty much depend upon how one defines intelligence in the first place (Detterman and Sternberg, 1982). For those who see intelligence as some underlying entity whose nature is determined at conception, it would be difficult to see any possibility for significant increases (Spitz, 1986). For those, however, who focus merely on intelligence as a performance on a test, the answer is likely to be less gloomy. And then there are those like Doll (1941) who many years ago asserted that one of the critical criteria for diagnosing the presence of mental retardation was a decision that the person's intellectual condition was "essentially incurable." Therefore, anyone whose IQ score rose beyond the cutoff point for mental retardation could not have been retarded in the first place!

Head Start. Some preschool programs such as Head Start have been designed to help children develop skills and confidence they might not otherwise secure. Without such skills and confidence they are very likely to encounter virtually insurmountable problems in school. Some studies have concluded that such preschool interventions make little difference in children's success in the first three grades (Westinghouse/Ohio University, 1969). Others, however, have concluded that children do make significant gains in IQ and achievement test scores, but those gains may disappear as the child enters regular public schools (e.g., Weikart, 1972).

A final comment

Tests have become powerful tools in our society. They help determine who gets into college, who is given a job, who is placed in special classes, and so on. Any technology that is potentially so intrusive and important in our lives must be examined closely. How tests are standardized, how they are used, to whom test results are released, and indeed whether someone needs to be assessed at all, are important questions that must be seriously considered in each separate case. Tests by themselves are just paper and cardboard. But they can be used for good or for ill. In the hands of skilled and sensitive people, tests can be of enormous help. In the hands of untrained people or those who have less than noble motives, they can be equally harmful. There is still considerable "art" involved in the "science" of mental testing. In most controversial instances, the problem lies not so much with tests but with the insensitivity or lack of training of those who use them.

The ultimate answers to the controversy over the use of IQ tests will surely not reside in facile bans of intelligence tests. To ignore our testing technology is to return to the sole use of subjective judgments of mental ability. It was the potential biases inherent in such judgments that led to the development of intelligence tests in the first place.

DIFFERENCES IN INTELLIGENCE: INHERITED OR ACQUIRED?

When Binet and Simon developed their objective scale, it seemed we were finally in a position to label everyone neatly with an IQ. Consequently, answers to some age-old questions seemed in the offing. Is intelligence largely inherited or mainly shaped by the environment? Is one race more intelligent than another? Are men superior intellectually to women? Are there intellectual differences among the social classes? These are explosive questions whose answers usually lead to controversy and acrimony. It is interesting to note that the answers have had a tendency to change in rhythm with the social and political climate. This bears out Samelson's (1975) observation that scientific truths are rarely the antiseptic conclusions they are thought to be.

For example, take the first quarter of this century. At that time, it was widely accepted that people from southeastern Europe were the intellectual inferiors of those from northern and western Europe. IQ testing data from World War I seemed to corroborate this belief since the immigrants drafted into the U.S. Army who came from southeastern Europe obtained lower IQ scores than those from Sweden or England. But Brigham's (1923) analysis of these data revealed a curious thing: immigrants who lived in the United States for at least twenty years showed IQs little different from people born in this country. Were we to interpret this finding today, we would likely con-clude that these immigrants, having had time to absorb the language and customs of their adopted country, were better able to demonstrate their ability on the tests. But this was not Brigham's interpretation. Instead, he noted that the immigrants of twenty years earlier were usually from northern and western Europe while the recent arrivals were mainly from southeastern Europe. Thus, he reasoned that the data confirmed the innate superiority of northern and western Europeans! The debate over who is brighter and why has continued to simmer. In the following sections, we shall take a closer look at these issues.

Heritability of intelligence

In any group of people, both genetic and environmental factors contribute to the varia-tions in IQ among the members. But how do we determine the relative importance of each set of factors? To answer this question, geneticists have developed a concept called the **heritability ratio.** This refers to the proportion of variance of IQs in a given popu-lation that is the result of genetic variations among the individuals in the group. Figure 14-9 illustrates this notion.

To further illustrate the concept of heritability, imagine that every Hispanic child born in the United States grew up under exactly the same environmental conditions. Were these individuals tested at age fifteen, we would still observe differences in IQ. All of these differences would be due to genetic factors since the environment was the same for all. In this case, heritability would be 1.00. It is important to understand, however, that heritability applies to groups, not to individuals. If some expert claims that the heritability ratio for intelligence is .80, this does not mean that 80 percent of a person's intelligence is inherited and 20 percent is due to the environment. For the individual, environment is just as important in shaping intelligence as is heredity. But within the large group to which that individual belongs, the expert is asserting that 80 percent of the variation among members is due to genetic factors.

It might be noted that actual heritability estimates for intelligence seem to vary with the dates of the research in question. It seems that methodologies change and with them the resultant heritability estimates. For example, studies published before 1963 produced estimates as high as 80 percent. Those published after 1975 seemed to be closer to 50 percent. Now, the estimates are back up to around 80 percent (Loehlin, Willerman, and Horn, 1988).

Role of heredity

In Chapter 1 it was observed that Galton's investigations of the hereditary basis of ge-nius were flawed because he could not really separate the effects of environment from those of heredity. Studies that compare fraternal and identical twins (e.g., Jensen, 1972) likewise have the problem that identical twins typically have environments that are more alike in both subtle and overt ways than those of fraternal twins.

Use of the **co-twin method** (again, see Chapter 1) should, however, be enlighten-ing since it involves studying identical twins reared apart. But again, we are plagued

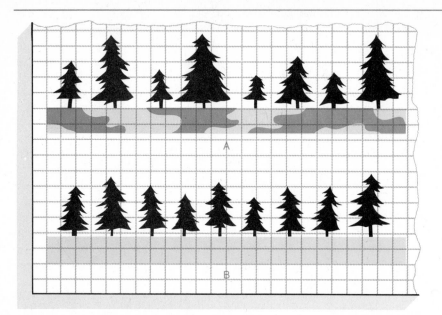

FIGURE 14-9   The concept of heritability. The evergreens in A vary in height. The degree to which they vary from each other is called the variance. What produces this variance? Some is probably due to genetics. To find out how much, we equate environmental conditions such as soil, water, and sunlight (indicated by different shadings of the ground). We now take a random group of seedlings chosen from A. We plant them in this equated environment (B) and wait patiently until they mature. We note that the size variation in B is less than it was in A. This reflects the fact that environmental conditions in B are equal for all the trees so that any environmental sources of variance have been eliminated. The remaining variance in B is entirely produced by genetic factors. Therefore, the heritability of height for A is the variance in B (the variation attributable to genetic factors) divided by the variance in A (the total variation in the population.)

Adapted from *Psychology* by Herny Gleitman, by permission of W. W. Norton & Company, Inc. Copyright © 1981 by W. W. Norton & Company, Inc.

with the same old problems: it is hard to locate such twins; we are not always sure they really are identical; sometimes they are reared apart but only after having spent considerable time together; and sometimes their separate environments were actually rather similar. While such research is very suggestive, it is neither definitive nor precise in spelling out the exact roles of heredity and environment. It does seem, nonetheless, that the closer the relationship between pairs of individuals, the more alike are their IQ scores.

The Burt affair.   Some of the best-known co-twin research was carried out by Sir Cyril Burt, perhaps England's foremost psychologist. His work had long been regarded as staunchly supportive of a genetic position (e.g., Burt, 1966). For example, he had asserted that in the case of fifty-three pairs of identical twins reared apart in totally different kinds of environments, IQ similarities were remarkable. Unfortunately, however, the first knighted psychologist turned out to have "cooked" his data (Dorfman, 1978). In 1973, shortly after Burt's death, Kamin noticed several peculiarities in Burt's reports. For example, although the number of twins included in his research over the years varied, the correlations he reported remained identical—even to the third decimal! The uncovering of other ambiguities and inconsistencies followed. Investigative reporting by Oliver Gillie, a *London Sunday Times* reporter, also revealed information suggesting that two supposed collaborators in Burt's research program never existed. Hearnshaw (1979) has produced evidence to show that after 1950, Burt actually collected no new data at all. In the ensuing furor, several people came to Burt's defense (e.g., Eysenck, 1977). But the evidence of fraud seemed inescapable.

However, it is doubtful that this sad affair has detracted significantly from the body of evidence that supports the genetic position. Many studies besides Burt's work have varied the degree of genetic similarity among individuals. For example, one classic survey summarized fifty-two independent studies from around the globe (Erlenmeyer-Kimling and Jarvik, 1963). The results are shown in Table 14-1. More recent studies and surveys (e.g., Bouchard and McGue, 1981; Henderson, 1982) show relationships that are quite close to those in Table 14-1. Again, the closer the relationship between a pair of individuals, the more alike their IQ scores tend to be.

TABLE 14-1 *Median correlations in IQ scores from individuals who differ in their degree of relationship and genetic similarity.*

Genetic Relationship	Developmental Status	Median Correlation
Unrelated persons	Reared apart	– .01
Unrelated persons	Reared together	.23
Foster-parent-child	Living together	.20
Parent-child	Living together	.50
Siblings	Reared apart	.40
Siblings	Reared together	.49
Dizygotic twins	Reared together	.53
Monozygotic twins	Reared apart	.75
Monozygotic twins	Reared together	.87

Adapted from "Genetics and Intelligence: A Review" by L. Erlenmeyer-Kimling and L. F. Jarvik, *Science*, December 1963, Vol. 142, p. 1478. Copyright © 1963 by the American Association for the Advancement of Science. Reprinted by permission of the AAAS and Dr. L. Erlenmeyer-Kimling.

Studies of adopted children.   Although research on adopted children has provided additional data, definitive answers still elude us. A commonly held belief is that the IQs of adopted children more closely resemble the IQs of their biological parents than those of their adoptive parents. But Skodak and Skeels (1949) reported that adopted children have IQs that clearly surpass those of their biological parents. This may mean that adoptive parents, being carefully screened by adoption authorities, provide superior environments that have beneficial effects. In another project (Horn, Loehlin, and Willerman, 1979), families were identified in which there were both an adopted child and a natural child of the same parents. The correlations between the mother's IQ and each of her two different kinds of children were virtually identical (.20 for mother and biological child, .22 for mother and adopted child). Such results are not very supportive of a strong genetic position. But the picture remains quite unclear. These and other data are subject to a variety of different interpretations. The genetic camp looks at the data and sees evidence of a heritability ratio as high as .80. The environmental camp looks at the same information and concludes the ratio is but .40. Not only is there disagreement but the arguments can become heated, as illustrated in the following exchange (Eysenck and Kamin, 1981). Kamin concludes:

> The data on heredity and IQ are, at best, ambiguous. Though some are consistent with the notion that IQ is heritable, others are not. The data consistent with a genetic interpretation seem equally consistent with an environmental interpretation. The plausible environmental interpretations have been ignored or soft-pedalled by behavior geneticists, which might, I have argued, reflect social and political as well as just plain professional bias. (p. 54)

But then Eysenck argues:

> Kamin is entirely wrong in thinking that there is no evidence to support the view that genetic factors play an important part in producing differences in cognitive ability between people. This notion runs counter to all the available evidence, is contradicted by every expert who has done work in the field, and leaves completely unexplained the quantitative agreement found between many different avenues of approach to the problem of estimating the heritability of intelligence. (p. 171)

Such disagreements only fuel the debate over the social, educational, and political ramifications of the heredity-environment issue.

Gender differences

Little systematic evidence exists that one gender is intellectually superior to the other. However, from time to time throughout the life cycle, gender differences in achievement or problem solving can be observed. Thus, it is not unusual for the grades of elementary school girls to exceed those of boys. But this may be attributable more to personality and conformity differences or to differential needs for competitiveness than to differences in IQ. There also is some evidence that adult and adolescent males do better on tasks involving spatial visualization. But not everyone agrees that this is a sex-linked genetic phenomenon. (DeFries, Johnson, Kuse, McClearn, Polovina, Vandenberg, and Wilson, 1979). With respect to problem solving, Young (1971), has reported that men are superior to women when we consider people in their forties. But by the time we reach our sixties, women are superior to men. This latter difference could be the result of physiological changes related to declining cerebral circulation in men.

But whenever gender differences in intelligence are reported, it is not difficult to find evidence of coexisting differences in cultural expectations, learning experiences, role stereotypes, or other specific variables that could easily have produced these results. Indeed, a further complicating factor in simply comparing IQs of females and males is the manner in which several IQ tests have been developed. For example, Terman and Merrill (1937) assumed that there were no IQ differences between men and women. Therefore, whenever they encountered during the construction of the Stanford-Binet an item that discriminated between men and women, they discarded it. Consequently, it would be difficult for this test to show any gender differences, even if they existed.

Socioeconomic factors

Not surprisingly, IQs are consistently found to be higher as we move higher up the occupational ladder. Similarly, the higher one's social class, the higher the IQ is likely to be. Figure 14-10 illustrates some general findings in this area. While the fact of such differences is hardly a surprise, there has been less agreement on the explanations for these differences. One possibility is simply that IQ is determined principally by the genes. This being so, brighter individuals will rise to the top socioeconomically and pass their genes along to their offspring. Over many generations, this means that the upper classes and the higher occupations are going to be largely populated by genetically superior individuals. The reverse scenario applies to those less well endowed genetically. Such a theory has been propounded for a thousand years and most recently by Herrnstein (1973). Others have argued just as forcefully that higher socioeconomic status confers on the child a greater opportunity for education, social graces, values, connections, and all the things likely to propel one ahead in life. The child's parents have greater verbal skills. It is more likely that reading material will be available, along with the opportunity to take enriching vacations and so on. Again, one must keep in mind the bias that is subtly built into most intelligence tests—bias that favors urban, school-oriented families. Once more, then, we are confronted with the same quandary— nature, nurture, or both. And if both, what are relative weights of each (Scarr, 1981)?

Racial differences

Racial consciousness seems almost an indigenous characteristic of American life. Unfortunately, it appears always to have been so. Psychology became entangled in questions of IQ differences during World War I, as was noted earlier. The Army testing program of that era did reveal distinct IQ differences between blacks and whites. Discussions about the meaning of these differences continued in relatively subdued academic tones for the next fifty years or so. Then in 1969, Arthur Jensen, an educational psychologist, wrote an article in which he asserted that the commonly observed finding that blacks, on the average, have IQs below whites is very likely attributable to hereditary factors. The ensuing controversy was both immediate and vehement and continues to this day. Such a dispute produces few neutral observers. While the facts here are relatively clear, their meaning is less so. Let us try to distinguish fact from inference.

There are significant differences between the IQs of whites and blacks, and these differences have been reported in numerous studies over the past thirty years (again, see Figure 14-10). Often, the mean difference is as much as fifteen points. At the same time, there is tremendous overlap between groups. That is, a very large number of blacks exceed the average IQ for whites, and this overlap is so large that knowing only that a person is black provides almost no basis for predicting his or her IQ. Even Jensen conceded that all degrees of human ability are represented in both races.

That blacks are at a disadvantage in our society hardly needs documentation. The discrimination and deprivation they have endured stretches so far back into American history that it has become part of their cultural heritage. The reality of prejudice, discrimination, and the ensuing inequality of opportunities for blacks makes very unconvincing any simple judgment that they are genetically inferior to whites in intelligence. In fact, until the environments of the two groups are essentially the same, the question of whether IQ differences are genetically determined is unanswerable. Perhaps the environmental gap between blacks and whites is narrowing. Jones (1984) reports that evidence now exists that at ages nine, thirteen, and seventeen, the average relative achievement levels of black students in the U.S.A. rose during the 1970s in reading, mathematics, and in a variety of other learning areas.

Whatever hope there may be of closing the racial gap will require educational, psychological, cultural, and economic programs targeted at both children and their parents. When such programs, coupled with cognitive training, begin early in life and continue through the formative years, change still seems possible (Anghoff, 1988).

Meaning of the IQ difference.

The genetic position, typified by Jensen, asserts that 80 percent of the variance in IQ scores is attributable to genetic influences. Because of this, it is argued that remedial and compensatory programs such as Head Start are doomed to failure. As a result of this heritability factor, the brighter individuals will move up in society and achieve better jobs, seek more education, and generally become socioeconomically advantaged. Others, however, point to evidence they feel refutes Jensen's conclusions. They believe that Jensen's heritability figure of .80 is incorrect. For example, just because the IQ differences among members of a racial group can be said to be determined in part by the genes should not be taken to mean that the IQ differences between groups are also genetically based. Furthermore, until the environmental conditions for blacks and whites are the same, no conclusions can be reached about group differences.

There is certainly a welter of environmental factors that can affect test performances and which may place blacks in a poorer light. Samuda (1975) has reviewed a number of these. For example, much of the early IQ data was gathered before the rise in black self-awareness and identity. When one has a poor self-concept or expects to do poorly, the effect on test performance can be disastrous. These problems are often compounded by schools that make little attempt to recognize the handicaps under which a black child may labor in a system dominated by whites. The nature of IQ tests and the circumstances that surround their use clearly give white middle-class children an advantage.

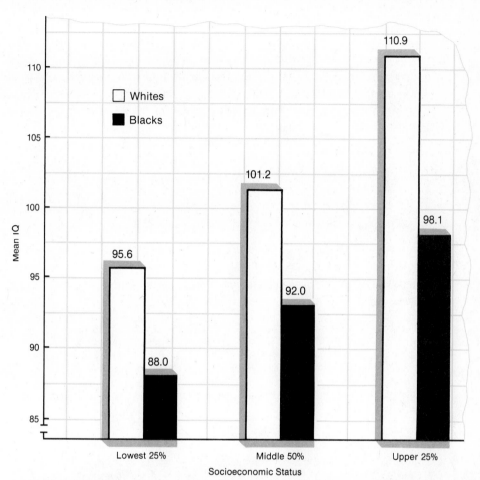

FIGURE 14-10 Mean IQs of 4-year-old children classified by socioeconomic status and race. After Broman, S. H., Nichols, P. L., and Kennedy, W. A. (1975). *Preschool IQ: Prenatal and early developmental correlates,* Hillsdale, NJ: Erlbaum.

The amount of experience with verbal testing situations, to say nothing of the fairness of the test items themselves, can affect the IQ obtained. Box 14-2 shows what might happen when the tables are turned.

Another of Jensen's contentions was that supportive educational programs do not redress the IQ deficits in culturally deprived groups. But more recent evidence (e.g., Zigler and Valentine, 1979) suggests that providing disadvantaged young children the opportunity to develop learning readiness skills prior to entering the formal school sys-

Box 14-2
A BLACK ALTERNATIVE

Many IQ tests contain items that measure, in effect, how much and what kind of information the individual has acquired as a normal part of living. Supposedly, these acquisitions reflect intellectual capacity. But what is "a normal part of living?" Some have vigorously contended that the kind of information elicited by IQ tests depends primarily on the white middle-class experience. To illustrate this point Williams (1972) described a Black Intelligence Test of Cultural Homogeneity (BITCH). A typical item is

>   Running a game means
>   a. writing a bad check
>   b. looking at something
>   c. directing a test
>   d. getting what one wants from another person or thing

The means score on this test for 100 black teenagers was 30 points higher than for 100 comparable whites.

Perhaps Cronbach (1978) placed the contributions of tests such as the BITCH into proper perspective when he remarked:

> To publicize BITCH as an "intelligence" test is a gesture of political propaganda. By not taking the word "intelligence" seriously, BITCH mocks and discredits established instruments and so strikes a blow to gain respect for persons who score low on them. By taking street slang seriously, BITCH dramatizes the concept of cultural pluralism. By showing educated whites an intellectual task on which they do poorly, BITCH challenges whites to defend the functional worth of other tests loaded with culture-specific tasks. (p. 250)

tem has paid rich dividends in the sense of both better academic performance and social responsibility. Other information also suggests that environmental factors rather than genetics are at work. Both Klineburg (1935) and Lee (1951) discovered that the IQs of southern black children increased when the children moved to northern cities such as New York and Philadelphia. Moreover, the extent of that increase was directly linked to the number of years they spent in northern schools. Jensen (1977) himself has reported that IQs of rural blacks in Georgia decline between the ages of five and sixteen whereas the IQs of whites during the same years do not. Similarly, the differences in IQs between young blacks and young whites are minimal, but as the children grow older the differences become quite noticeable (Osborne, 1960). Finally, Scarr and Weinberg (1976) have found that when black children are adopted by white families whose socioeconomic level is solid, these children show both IQ scores and school achievement as good as those of adopted white children.

The most straightforward conclusion to all of this seems to be that despite the considerable effort and breastbeating, there is no scientific basis to the contention that differences in IQ scores between racial groups are due to genetic factors. Those differences observed seem most parsimoniously explained on the basis of different opportunities, values, and environmental exposure characterizing the black and white experiences.

SOME CONCLUDING OBSERVATIONS

Any discussion of personality without attention to intellectual processes must be considered incomplete. Intelligence is closely related to what Mischel (1973) refers to as competence variables. It reflects our ability to generate both cognitions and behaviors. How we act, how we interpret our experience, and how we develop our skills are all influenced by intelligence. No one can argue the fact that the marked individual differences we observe in all these personal areas are affected by intellectual differences. A variety of personality processes are shaped at least in part by intellectual factors. But the reverse is also true. That is, personality affects the manner in which intelligence operates. The relationship, then, between intelligence and personality is a reciprocal one.

In concluding our discussions, the following summary observations seem pertinent.

Lack of theory

We have no really adequate theory of intelligence. All we have are definitions of intelligence, some crude notions about general and specific aspects of it, and some attempts to develop taxonomies of various intellectual factors. If this were not bad enough, our broader theories of personality and behavior do not systematically incorporate intelligence or even competence as an important variable. Whether it be psychoanalysis, self theory, or behavior theory, intelligence does not occupy much space. Of course, we all agree that motivation, prior learning, and adjustment are important contributors to our ability to solve problems or even do well on IQ tests. But there is no systematic theory that tells us exactly how such variables influence (and are influenced by) intellectual factors. When clinical psychologists attempt to determine an IQ, they proceed in a haphazard way. They know they must establish rapport in the testing situation and as much as possible reduce the client's anxiety. But they have no theoretically derived agenda to guide them. They work under a kind of blind hope that if they identify factors that may have interfered with the ability of their clients to express their full intellectual potential, the latter will stand revealed.

We agree that solving a problem (in either a test situation or a real-life setting) involves behavior that has followed certain general laws. For example, imagine a subject being given the Stanford-Binet. The item is "Tell me what is funny about this picture." The child does not know. But why? Perhaps the answer is simply not in the child's repertoire. But, then, maybe the child really knows the answer but fears failure to such an extent that silence seems the better policy. Or is it possible that the child is so un-motivated that he or she is not paying attention? Little in the test or in theories of intel-ligence will help us select the proper explanation. It goes without saying that what is true for one child confronted with a single test item is equally true when it comes to making sense out of group differences in intelligence test scores. What we lack is an overall theory of problem solving or intelligence that will systematically incorporate and weight the contribution of both intellectual and nonintellectual variables (Liverant, 1960).

All of this takes on added force when intelligence is viewed as a simple trait. As we saw in earlier chapters on the trait perspective, a single trait is not a good predictor of behavior. Its role is affected by specific situational conditions and by other person-ality characteristics. Knowing only that a person has an IQ of 115 will not be of much assistance in predicting behavior in one specific situation although it may be of some-what greater value when applied to predicting some average level of behavior in a range of situations. In a sense, all this takes us back to the trait discussions of Chapter 8. Epstein's aggregation research as regards traits is equally applicable here with intelligence.

Intelligence as an abstraction

Chein (1945) has observed that we often fail to realize that intelligence is not observed; rather, intelligent behavior is observed. When we fail to make this distinction, we may lose sight of the fact that we can neither see, touch, nor smell intelligence — that it is only revealed by the inferences we make from behavior. When a person does nothing or even does an unintelligent thing, we are faced with a problem. Is the individual stu-pid, did he or she choose not to do well, or was there some set of factors that com-pelled the unintelligent behavior?

In any event, like an attitude, intelligence is not a thing. It is an abstraction we make based on the individual's behavior. If Mary achieves good grades, is well regarded by her instructors, and is admired by her friends for her achievements, I will likely conclude that she is intelligent. Out of these three instances, I have abstracted the com-mon element — intelligence. Once having made the abstraction, I can then use it to help predict her behavior in the future. But it is critical to understand that it is my abstrac-tion. My abstraction does not make her intelligent nor does it suggest that intelligence is some sort of entity that resides in a specific location in the brain. The concept is not reality; it is only an aid to prediction.

Innate potential

A great deal of confusion stems from the belief that intelligence is some simple, uni-tary potential with which we are endowed at conception. Supposedly this potential is determined by the genes and is basically unmodifiable. When our environment during the formative years is just right (or so goes the belief), we will come close to achieving that potential. But nothing can happen that will allow us to exceed it. Take an analogy from athletics. At conception, it was determined that my upper limit for the high jump is six feet five inches. If I train diligently, receive excellent coaching, eat the right food, and maintain my motivation, perhaps I will come close to achieving that upper limit. But nothing (lest it be springs in my shoes) will enable me to exceed that limit.

But is this a valid assessment of the way intelligence works? Many think not. As Liverant (1960) has pointed out, we may indeed inherit an intellectual potential, but that potential will vary depending upon the environment we encounter during development. Thus, my potential IQ may be 110 if I am raised in a stimulating environment. But were I to be raised in another set of circumstances, that potential IQ might be only

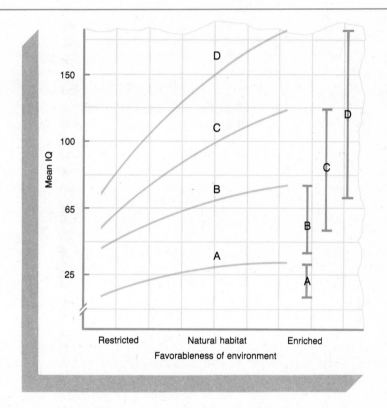

FIGURE 14-11   The interaction between heredity and environment. Each curve represents an individual with a particular intellectual potential depending upon the nature of the environment. The lines on the right indicate the range for each person. For example, Person B will have an IQ of about 25 when raised in an extremely deprived environment but will achieve an IQ of more than 65 when raised in a superior environment.

Adapted from "Genetic Aspects of Intelligent Behavior" by I. I. Gottesman. In *Handbook of Mental Deficiency: Psychological Theory and Research* by N. Ellis [Ed.] [New York: McGraw-Hill], 1963. Copyright 1963 by McGraw-Hill.

87. And who is to say what the ultimate environment is? Take another example. Cretin children are born with a thyroid deficiency. Without early diagnosis and treatment, they will likely be doomed to function at a mentally defective level with an IQ scarcely above 55. But proper treatment with thyroid extract may permit them to escape this fate and function with an IQ of perhaps 95. What, then, is their true potential? It may be that genes set the intellectual limits for a given person within a given environment. But those limits will change as the environment changes. In short, each of us is born with multiple intellectual potentials and for each possible environmental manipulation there is another set of limits. Therefore, it is just as fair to say that the environment sets limits as it is to say that the genes set limits. Figure 14-11 will help clarify this point.

We seem to have moved away from any rigid or exclusive adherence to environmental explanations of intellectual development. In fact, biological, genetic views may even be the preeminent ones these days. But as we conclude this chapter, it is well to recall Plomin's (1989) comments about the current state of affairs:

> As the pendulum swings from environmentalism, it is important that the pendulum be caught in midswing before its momentum carries it to biological determinism. Behavioral genetic research clearly demonstrates that both nature and nurture are important in human development. (p. 110)

SUMMARY

- Intelligence is of such central importance to every facet of human activity that its measurement has become a matter of legislative and public policy debate.

- Most often, intelligence is regarded as a trait. However, numerous diverse definitions have been offered over the years, many of which are too broad or general to have much specific application. However, there is some evidence that experts and laypersons agree that in some fashion intelligence comprises problem-solving ability, verbal facility, social competence, and possibly motivation.

- Theories of intelligence have ranged from Spearman's emphasis on a broad, general underlying factor coupled with a number of specific factors to Thorndike's claim that intelligence can be reduced to numerous specific factors. Thurstone argued for a compromise view that entailed a small number of group factors intermediate between specific and general factors.

- Others have proposed hierarchical models in which a general factor subsumes group factors which, in turn, subsume specific factors. Cattell has postulated that general intelligence can be partitioned into fluid ability (biological capacity) and crystallized ability (culture-based learning). Guilford has classified intelligence along three dimensions—Operations, Contents, and Products—resulting in 120 separate abilities. More recent approaches have emphasized the role of cognitions or information processing.

- Binet, who in collaboration with Simon developed the Binet-Simon Scale, is generally regarded as the father of the intelligence testing movement. Binet regarded mental age as an index of mental performance. By assigning each test item a given number of months' credit and then adding up this credit for all items passed, one's mental age could be determined.

■ Individual tests of intelligence (those administered to one subject at a time) are usually the preferred assessment devices since they permit clinical observations that aid in the interpretation of the IQ score.

■ The Stanford-Binet has been a widely used test for children and is a direct descendent of the Binet-Simon Scale. Several features of the newly standardized version of the Stanford-Binet were described. This test employed the IQ concept: ratio of mental age to chronological age multiplied by 100.

■ Wechsler developed several intelligence tests that are widely employed. They include adult, child, and preschool versions.

■ The validity of intelligence test scores is ultimately described by IQ correlates. The major correlates are school success, occupational status, and the like. IQ scores do not readily reflect innate ability, practical abilities, or even wisdom. They do reflect verbal skills, reasoning ability, analytic skills, and similar school-oriented matters. High intelligence and creativity are not one and the same.

■ Intelligence tests measure achievement in the sense that they involve what one has learned. But they are also measures of aptitude because they allow us to predict performance in the future.

■ To neutralize the effects of nonintellectual variables on IQ scores, some have tried to develop culture-fair tests such as Raven's Progressive Matrices and various drawing tests. These tests consist of items with which everyone is presumed to be equally familiar or equally unfamiliar. While sound in theory, such tests have not been able to eradicate fully the influence of cultural variables on test performance.

■ Were IQs measures of innate capacity, we would not expect a person's IQ to change over time. Yet there is considerable evidence of instability in many cases. Many factors can contribute to this instability, including the nature of the test items, age-related factors, and amount of education. The topics of mental retardation and programs such as Head Start were also discussed in this context. Again, all this suggests that the IQ is not a direct measure of innate potential.

■ Group differences in intelligence have long fascinated and preoccupied psychologists. Usually, the issues involved relate to the heritability of intelligence.

■ The heritability ratio is the proportion of variance of IQs in a given population attributable to genetic variations among the members of that group.

■ Research on the role of heredity in determining intelligence has ranged from Galton's observations about eminent families to more sophisticated comparisons between fraternal and identical twins. Although IQ correlations for identical twins are greater than they are for fraternal twins, the role of the environment cannot be adequately controlled.

■ To remedy this, the co-twin method has been used. Here, identical twins reared apart are studied. Any differences in IQ should be attributable to the role of the environment. However, a variety of methodological problems in such research prevent us from fully ascertaining the heritability of intelligence.

■ Further doubt was cast upon the meaning of co-twin studies by the deplorable Burt affair. Burt's data on the IQs of identical twins reared apart indicated the strong heritability of intelligence. However, much of the data apparently is fraudulent. However, this does not appear to have altered any basic conclusions in this area.

■ Relationships between the IQs of adopted children and both their biological and adoptive parents have also failed to provide definitive answers for the genetic position.

■ Little systematic evidence of gender differences in intelligence exists, although differences in patterns sometimes appear. Again, differences are just as easily attributed to cultural factors as to sex-linked factors.

■ As we move up the socioeconomic ladder, IQs become higher. As with sex differences, questions of nature versus nurture are difficult to resolve.

■ Racial differences in intelligence have occupied investigators for many years. The issue seems indigenous to American life, unfortunately. Although whites, on the average, typically show higher mean IQs than blacks, there is so much overlap that group membership is not a good predictor of IQ.

■ Since blacks as a group have been disadvantaged for so long in our society, IQ differences can be more parsimoniously explained by such disadvantages. Therefore, until blacks and whites are equal in terms of environment and opportunity, any claims of white superiority in IQ are distinctly premature.

■ Many of the issues and controversies about intelligence, group differences, and the like, could be softened were we to consider several things. First, we lack a theory that systematically incorporates both intellectual and nonintellectual variables and that explains how they interact. Second, we often fail to remember that intelligence is not a thing but an abstraction that we invent to assist us in making predictions. Third, it is important to recognize that intelligence does not represent a single, innate potential. Rather, we inherit multiple potentials that will vary depending upon the environment in which we are raised.

CHAPTER 15

ANXIETY, STRESS, AND HEALTH

For many years, everyone talked about neurotic anxiety and how it was produced by repressed sexual or aggressive urges. And when the field of psychosomatic medicine was so popular in the 1940s, everything from gastric ulcers to chronic headaches was said to stem from underlying conflicts specific to each problem (Dunbar, 1947). But psychosomatic medicine was a narrow field inhabited mainly by psychiatrists and physicians who pretty much hewed to the psychoanalytic line.

But then we entered the nuclear age and began to realize that anxieties from within were being joined by stress from without. Being perpetually caught in traffic jams or everlastingly worried about pollution were also important and could lead to high blood pressure or else ultimately blunt our sense of personal control and even culminate in apathy. All of this has been reflected in escalating health-care costs. These costs comprised 4.5 percent of the U.S. gross national product in 1950 but more recently have ballooned to 11 percent with total costs of 400 billion dollars annually (Taylor, 1987).

The topics of anxiety, stress, and health represent a blend of psychodynamic theory, social learning and behaviorism, trait theory, and certain aspects of cognitive psychology. In a sense, this blend has been applied to the understanding of anxiety, stress, and health. That same blend has also been applied to the development of methods designed to control anxiety and stress and to promote behaviors that enhance health.

Therefore, the business of this chapter will be the discussion of anxiety, stress, and health psychology.

ANXIETY

Dictionaries tend to describe *anxiety* as a state of apprehension or uneasiness and *stress* as some sort of emotional tension. In practice, however, the two terms overlap considerably and usage may be dictated more by one's age than by any scientific niceties.

Thus, psychologists over forty or fifty may prefer *anxiety* while their younger counterparts have more likely been imprinted on *stress*. But let us begin our discussion with an examination of anxiety.

Definitions of anxiety

In Part 2, each theory of personality was described as defining anxiety in a particular fashion. For example:

FREUD: (Neurotic) anxiety stems from unconscious conflicts and serves as a signal that unconscious impulses may erupt into consciousness

ROGERS: Anxiety is the outgrowth of a perceived threat to the self-concept

KELLY: Anxiety stems from a realization that one's construct system is not leading to valid predictions

CATTELL: Anxiety is the sum total of our unfulfilled needs and the degree of our confidence in their being satisfied

ROTTER: Anxiety reflects a discrepancy between needs that are strong and expectancies for their satisfaction that are relatively low

The foregoing definitions and those summarized by Epstein (1972) may appear to create a theoretical morass. However, there are some common themes running throughout these and other definitions (Maher, 1966). First, **anxiety** may be regarded as referring to an aroused state of the nervous system that is manifested by cardiovascular, respiratory, and gastrointestinal symptoms (e.g., heart palpitations, breathlessness, nausea). Second, this state often occurs when the person perceives a threat, is unprepared to respond adequately, or both. Third, there is a disruption or breakdown in effective coping and problem solving. Fourth, this state may be labeled neurotic when it occurs in the face of no clearly perceived stimuli or of stimuli that objectively pose little or no danger.

Anxiety: A quick history

Some, like Freud, approached anxiety as a clinical phenomenon. Others, however, tried to grasp its nature by studying it in the laboratory. For example, Pavlov (1927) was able to induce in animals what he regarded as an experimental neurosis. He did this by first conditioning dogs to expect food whenever a circle was presented and to expect electric shock whenever an ellipse was presented. By gradually making the ellipse and the circle more and more alike, the dogs eventually could not differentiate between the stimuli and lapsed into states of howling, barking, and struggling against their restraining harnesses.

However, such work, objective and laboratory controlled as it was, seemed a far cry from what clinicians encountered daily in their patients. Over twenty years of research and study convinced Mowrer (1960) that we learn to be anxious through classical conditioning but that we learn to reduce this anxiety through instrumental acts. Thus, as we saw earlier with Watson and Rayner's (1920) work, Little Albert learned to fear a white rat when its presence was paired with a very loud noise. According to Mowrer, the child would then engage in behaviors designed to reduce or avoid the anxiety. In some cases these would be realistic coping behaviors, but in other instances they could just as easily be neurotic ones. The point is that, whatever worked—that is, reduced anxiety—would be "stamped in." Dollard and Miller (1950) espoused a similar view. As you will recall from Chapter 10, they described anxiety as a painful affective drive state that motivated the learning of behaviors that would reduce the drive.

The Dollard and Miller view of anxiety as a drive state was elaborated by Hull (1943) and Spence (1958). They tried to understand how fear can become attached to a previously neutral stimulus by looking at the number of occasions in which the neutral (conditioned) stimulus and the unconditioned stimulus are paired (i.e., the more often the rat and the loud noise are presented together, the greater is the likelihood that the fear response will occur). Also, a more intense stimulus will be more effective than a relatively weak one. For instance, in developing a fear of elevators, dropping suddenly five floors before the elevator catches would be more effective than a momentary drop of three feet. Then, too, there are individual differences in emotional responsiveness that will affect the conditioning process.

To provide a way of ordering and conceptualizing these and other factors, Hull (1943) proposed that the strength of the relationship between the conditioned response and the conditioned stimulus was dependent on two basic factors: the habit strength associated with the response and the overall drive level of the organism when the stimulus occurs. These two general variables combine multiplicatively to determine the response potential. Thus:

$$E \text{ (response potential)} = D \text{ (drive)} \times H \text{ (habit strength)}$$

This formula suggests that when people become emotionally aroused by some stimulus, they will perform more intensely those responses that have become habitual or overlearned. For example, we all overlearn the responses of putting our hand on the doorknob, twisting it, pulling on the knob, stepping through the open door, and then pulling it shut behind us. All of us go through the sequence repeatedly every day, and habit strength is very high, to say the least. But what happens when I become very angry just before I have to make an exit? According to the Hull-Spence view, under such emotional arousal (high drive) my door-opening responses will be intensified. I yank on the knob, twist it ferociously, and slam the door with abandon. Drive and habit combined to intensify the normal response potential. Of course, there may occasionally be inhibiting factors present that must be subtracted from the $D \times H$ product (e.g., my hand is in a cast, my superior is watching me). As for anxiety specifically, it was Spence's (1958) contention that by knowing a person's anxiety level in a given situation, we could then better predict the manner in which classical conditioning would proceed.

The Manifest Anxiety Scale

To help predict the manner in which classical conditioning proceeds, J. A. Taylor (1953) developed the **Manifest Anxiety Scale** or **MAS** to measure individual differences in chronic levels of anxiety. She built a fifty-item scale from items on the MMPI. Table 15-1 shows several of these items. People who receive high scores on the MAS are regarded as chronically anxious. That is, they are high on the trait of anxiety, and this should manifest itself across a variety of situations over time. There have been hundreds of studies showing how this trait of anxiety affects behavior. From this mass of research, two generalizations can be made:

On simple tasks, subjects high in anxiety perform better than subjects low in anxiety—a finding consistent with the Hull-Spence drive theory. This theory contends that in simple tasks, there are relatively few competing responses that are incorrect. Thus the high anxiety drive strength combines (multiplies) with the higher habit strength of the correct responses to produce a facilitative effect.

On more difficult or complex tasks, subjects high in anxiety perform more poorly than subjects low in anxiety—particularly in the early stages of the task. As learning proceeds, the performance of highly anxious subjects will improve and often surpass that of subjects low in anxiety. On difficult tasks, the correct responses are weaker than the competing incorrect responses. The result is that the high drive level activates a larger number of those incorrect tendencies, creating a poorer performance.

Test anxiety

Test anxiety—a subject dear to the hearts of many students—suggests an alternative way of explaining the effects of anxiety. Instead of drive theory, the role of interfering thoughts and responses is emphasized. This approach was initially proposed by Mandler and S. B. Sarason (1952) and more recently elaborated by I. G. Sarason (1980). It regards anxiety as a response to what is cognitively appraised as a threatening situation. The key here is perception of threat. It is not the objective situation but one's appraisal of it that is crucial. A student who feels she has prepared well for a test is not likely to approach the test with anxiety even though, in fact, her preparation has been inadequate. Another student, expecting to do poorly, will experience stress and will react to it in one of three general ways. The student can try to cope with the stress by studying more, consulting with the instructor, or perhaps practicing on possible test questions. A maladaptive response would be to do nothing and just hope things will

---

TABLE 15-1   Examples of MAS items. The response in parentheses after each item indicates anxiety.

T F   4. I have very few headaches. (false)

T F   7. I worry over money and business. (true)

T F   25. I am easily embarrassed. (true)

T F   32. I am happy most of the time. (false)

T F   36. I have sometimes felt that difficulties were piling up so high that I could not overcome them. (true)

SOURCE: From "A Personality Scale of Manifest Anxiety" by J.A. Taylor, *Journal of Abnormal and Social Psychology*, 1953, *48*, 285–290.

be better on the next test. An anxious response would be simply to worry or to decide that one is stupid or unworthy. Sarason (1980) describes the characteristics of such anxiety as follows:

1 The situation is seen as difficult, challenging, and threatening.

2 The individual sees himself as ineffective, or inadequate, in handling the task at hand.

3 The individual focuses on undesirable consequences of personal inadequacy.

4 Self-deprecatory preoccupations are strong and interfere or compete with task-relevant cognitive activity.

5 The individual expects and anticipates failure and loss of regard by others. (p. 6)

Naturally, there are individual differences in the way anxiety is experienced and the situations that precipitate it. But the interfering thoughts or debilitating self-preoccupations of the anxious person are probably traceable to a history of experiences which have taught the person that successful coping is unlikely. It should be remembered, however, that "successful coping" is an individually defined matter that also depends upon prior experience and the personal standards that have been acquired.

To measure individual differences in test anxiety, the **Test Anxiety Scale (TAS)** (Sarason, 1978) is commonly used. This is a thirty-seven-item scale that measures responses to testing situations. Several illustrative items are shown in Table 15-2. In contrast to the MAS, the TAS measures anxiety as it relates to a specific kind of situation. By focusing on testing situations, it can be considered as a narrow rather than as a broad or generalized measure of chronic anxiety.

Research with the TAS suggests that high levels of anxiety impair our ability both to process task information and to perform well on tasks. More specifically, anxiety

---

TABLE 15-2 *Examples of TAS items. The response in parentheses after each item indicates anxiety.*

T F   2. If I were to take an intelligence test, I would worry a great deal before taking it. (true)

T F   7. During tests, I find myself thinking of the consequences of failing. (true)

T F   15. When taking a test, my emotional feelings do not interfere with my performance. (false)

T F   20. During exams, I sometimes wonder if I'll ever get through college. (true)

T F   25. If examinations could be done away with, I think I would actually learn more. (true)

SOURCE: From "Introduction to the Study of Test Anxiety" by I.G. Sarason. In *Text Anxiety: Theory, Research, and Applications* by I.G. Sarason (Ed.) (Hillsdale, N.J.: Erlbaum), 1980. Copyright 1980 by Lawrence Erlbaum Associates. Reprinted by permission.

negatively influences three basic processes: (1) our ability to utilize correctly task stimuli necessary for us to do well on a given task, (2) our reactions to our own successes or failures during performance on the task, and (3) our interpretation of our own body state during task performance (Geen, 1980). An anxious person is less likely to pay attention to the appropriate cues during the task. Such an individual is also likely to react poorly as failure is encountered in the initial phases of a difficult task. Finally, worry and emotionality will combine to impede performance further (Sarason, 1984).

State vs. trait anxiety

It may have occurred to you that there must be a difference between anxiety as a rather constant condition which is with us everywhere and the anxiety that comes and goes or is tied to certain situations but not to others. Cattell and Scheier (1961) were among the first to try to measure these two separate aspects of anxiety. Spielberger (1966) also differentiated between anxiety as a trait and anxiety as a state. He defines **anxiety as a trait (A-Trait)** as an acquired behavioral tendency predisposing the person to perceive a wide range of objectively nonthreatening situations as dangerous. The resultant responses are disproportionate to the real danger. **Anxiety as a state (A-State)** is a more transitory state of emotional arousal; it varies in intensity and fluctuates over time. There are feelings of tension and apprehension accompanied by activations of the autonomic nervous system. This A-State will arise whenever there is an appraisal of threat in a situation.

To measure A-Trait versus A-State, Spielberger, Gorsuch, and Lushene (1970) have developed a questionnaire called the **State-Trait Anxiety Inventory (STAI).** The STAI A-State scale consists of twenty statements used by subjects to describe how they feel at a certain moment, for example: "I feel tense"; "I am jittery"; or "I am worried." The twenty items on the STAI A-Trait scale include such items as "I lack self-confidence" or "I feel like crying." The A-Trait scale asks people to describe how they generally feel. All items are rated by subjects on a four-point scale. Basically, the A-Trait scale is a measure of individual differences in anxiety proneness. A person high on this scale will respond to psychological stress with a high level of A-State intensity, particularly if the stressful situation involves loss of self-esteem. Anyone, however, will experience an anxiety state if a situation is perceived to be threatening. As a general rule, anxiety as a trait exists in those individuals who respond to a wide range of stimuli as threatening.

A study by Kendall, Finch, Auerbach, Hooke, and Mikulka (1976) illustrates how stress affects changes in A-State for subjects who differ in trait anxiety. The subjects were college students enrolled in an experimental psychology class. Stress was induced by an examination that was worth 100 points and counted for one third of their final grade. The students filled out the STAI several times during the course, including just before the examinations were handed out and just after the collection of the test booklets. The results of this experiment are shown in Figure 15-1. They indicate that on three separate occasions (prior to the examination day, just before the examination, and afterward), the A-State scores were more extreme for subjects high in trait anxiety than they were for subjects low in trait anxiety.

With our general review of anxiety now complete, let us turn to its companion concept, stress.

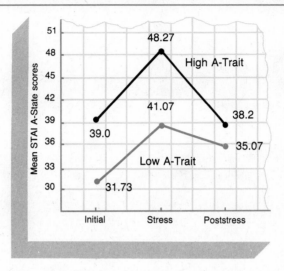

FIGURE 15-1 A-State scores for high- and low-A-Trait groups across three situations.
From "The State-Trait Anxiety Inventory: A Systematic Evaluation" by P. C. Kendall, A. J. Finch, Jr., S. M. Auerbach, J. F. Hooke, and P. J. Mikulka, *Journal of Consulting and Clinical Psychology*, 1976, *44*, 406–412. Copyright 1976 by the American Psychological Association. Reprinted by permission.

STRESS

In the aftermath of Hiroshima, the world soon was faced with the Cold War. Suddenly, the world had become a very dangerous place in which to live. Even worse, modern civilization seemed to be increasing our tensions by its urbanization and all the stresses that accompany it. Everything was getting bigger or worse—cities, armies, bureaucracies, noises, pollution, crowding, alienation, and even debts. As a consequence, investigators began to turn their attention to the environment as the source of this stress. Along with post-World War II events, the 1960s ushered in the distinction between trait and state anxiety. People like Richard Lazarus (1966) began discussing stress and ways to investigate it and cope with it.

Definitions of stress

As has been stated, stress and anxiety are not separate concepts. What is more, there have been many ideas about the nature of stress ranging from the biological to the psychosocial (Fleming, Baum, and Singer, 1984). R. S. Lazarus (1969) regards **stress** as an external circumstance that makes unusual or extraordinary demands upon the person. This could be a flood or a tornado, or it could be failure on a major examination,

Work stress seems to be a very common feature in today's world.
Photograph Chwatsky/Leo DeWys.

a divorce, or facing combat. But stress can also refer to one's responses to the stressful event. For Lazarus, these could be (1) emotional responses such as fear, anxiety, or anger; (2) motor responses such as speech disturbances, tremors, or perspiring; (3) cognitive responses such as failures in concentration, perceptual distortions, and the like; or (4) physiological changes, for example, in heart rate or breathing. On the other hand, some prefer to view stress as a condition of the organism and **stressors** as those things in the world outside the person (or within the person's mind) that precipitate a state of stress (Geen, 1976a).

Appraisal

The latter qualification—"within the person's mind"—introduces the cognitive element. That is, events will only produce stress when individuals perceive the event as a threat to themselves. A tornado is a threat because it threatens my coping strategies. A demanding job induces stress precisely because I view that job as something I may not be able to handle. Thus, it is not the event so much as it is my cognitions about the event. Of course, this notion of cognitions or perceptions brings us back full circle to the idea of predispositions. My job stress may stem less from its objective demands than from childhood experiences in which my father constantly reminded me that I was not living up to the family's standards. Also, there are some stressors that would frighten nearly everyone regardless of their predispositions (natural calamities, nuclear warfare, etc.). But even here, it is not likely that the degree of stress would be identical for everyone.

This interaction between person and situation has led Lazarus and Folkman (1984) to define stress as "a particular relationship between the person and the environment that is appraised by the person as taxing or exceeding his or her resources and endangering his or her well-being" (p. 19).

Several kinds of factors may affect the appraisal process. First, there is the role of familiarity. In general, unfamiliar events are more likely to provoke stress. Second, there is that ubiquitous factor of controllability. Being in control tends to lessen our stress. For example, when I am a passenger in a car, I am much more likely to be nervous than when I am driving. Then there is the predictability factor. Sudden, unexpected events are said to be more stressful than predictable or expected events. Many argue that this is why severe earthquakes leave so many psychological scars on people. In contrast, tornadoes, while hardly a picnic, often are preceded by warnings that allow time for preparation, both psychological and physical.

Types of stress

Stress can result from almost any kind of event depending upon the person and how that person appraises the event. The following are some major types of events that may result in stress.

Frustration. Whenever our progress toward a goal is blocked or impeded, frustration may well be the outcome. In some cases, aggression will result from frustration and we shall have more to say about this in Chapter 17. Another form of frustration that produces stress is personal loss. This could be the death of a loved one, loss of income, and the like. When this loss is extensive and perceived as likely to be permanent, depression may ensue (Phares, 1972). But in all cases of frustration, some degree of stress can be expected.

Recently, the concept of **daily hassles** has emerged (e.g., DeLongis, Folkman, and Lazarus, 1988; Gruen, Folkman, and Lazarus, 1988). These are ordinary, daily kinds of events that create stress in our lives. Lazarus and his colleagues (Kanner, Coyne, Schaefer, and Lazarus, 1981) have developed a scale that measures stress as a product of daily hassles. Ten hassles that were reported most frequently by 100 middle-aged adults are shown in Table 15-3. Also, DeLongis et al. (1988) have found a significant relationship between daily stress and the occurrence of health problems such as the flu, sore throat, headaches, and backaches. Although the final verdict is not in, it may be that small daily hassles act cumulatively over time to produce significant difficulties or stress for the person. An example may be those people who must adapt to the daily chronic hassles of providing in-home care to disabled adults. While there are significant individual differences in how care-givers cope with stress, the degree of stress experienced is mediated by the appraisal process (Stephens and Zarit, 1989).

Natural disasters. Generally speaking, traumatic events such as earthquakes, tornadoes, accidents, riots, and so on are major sources of stress. These are usually powerful, sudden occurrences that often affect large numbers of people. As noted above, their tendency to be unpredictable and to result in loss of personal control makes them especially traumatic.

TABLE 15-3   *The ten most common events that produce daily stress*

Item	Times Checked (%)
1. Concerns about weight	52.4
2. Health of family member	48.1
3. Rising prices of common goods	43.7
4. Home maintenance	42.8
5. Too many things to do	38.6
6. Misplacing or losing things	38.1
7. Yard work or outside maintenance	38.1
8. Property, investment, taxes	37.6
9. Crime	37.1
10. Physical appearance	35.9

From "Comparison of Two Modes of Stress Management: Daily Hassles and Uplifts versus Major Life Events," by Kanner, A.D., et al., *Journal of Behavioral Medicine*, Vol. 4, pp. 1-39 (1981). Reprinted by permission of Plenum Publishing Corporation and the author.

Conflict.   We saw in Chapter 10 that conflict is frequently related to maladjustment. Whenever we experience two or more incompatible motives or behavioral urges, the outcome is going to be stress. Whether we are talking about approach-approach conflicts, avoidance-avoidance conflicts, or approach-avoidance conflicts, stress is a likely companion.

Change.   Life changes can be major sources of stress. In fact, some investigators believe that the *one* element that makes an event stressful is the fact that it entails change (Dohrenwend and Dohrenwend, 1981). Indeed, even positive change such as a promotion or buying a new house can promote stress and even precipitate illness or other bodily symptoms. With change there often comes expectations that we may not be able to successfully handle the new situations. And therein lies the potential for stress.

What kinds of life events are typically associated with the development of stress reactions? Examining the records of about 5,000 medical patients, Holmes and Rahe (1967) identified a list of events that seemed to have occurred about the time of the onset of their medical problems. These events were then rated by 394 judges in terms of the amount of readjustment required. Following the judges' ratings, each event could be assigned a mean value in terms of degree of life-change entailed by experiencing the event. Table 15-4 shows the resulting **Social Readjustment Rating Scale.** When subjects respond to the scale, they usually are asked to indicate which events they have experienced in the last six months to a year. The total of the life-change units for the events checked constitutes the subject's score. Using the scale in this fashion, Rahe

(1972) was able to predict with significantly better than chance accuracy who would develop an illness and who would remain in good health over the subsequent year. Those who remained healthy received an average score of 150 life-change units while those who become ill reported up to 300 life-change units. Although not free of methodological criticisms, the scale has stimulated numerous studies and shows promise in helping us understand the relationship between stress and the onset of illness.

Responses to stress

Our responses to stress are complex and fall into a variety of categories ranging from the emotional to the physiological. Figure 15-2 outlines how these reactions follow from objective events and their appraisal.

Emotional responses.   Emotional reactions of various kinds usually accompany stress and are most commonly experienced as unpleasant. The most likely emotions are: (1) annoyance, anger, and rage; (2) apprehension, fear, and terror; (3) pensiveness, sadness, and grief (Woolfolk and Richardson, 1978). This relationship is illustrated in a study by Caspi, Bolger, and Eckenrode (1987). They had ninety-six women complete diaries each day in which they listed the stresses and moods that occurred during a twenty-eight-day period. It was found that daily fluctuations in mood were significantly correlated with daily fluctuations in stress. In essence, as stress grew, so did the unpleasantness of the moods. Other research has also indicated that negative emotions are associated with a broad range of subjective complaints and physical symptoms (Watson and Pennebaker, 1989; Bolger, DeLongis, Kessler, and Schilling, 1989).

Physiological responses.   Many years ago, Cannon (1932) said that threat leads to physiological responses that enable the autonomic nervous system to prepare the organism to either flee or fight. But it was Hans Selye (1956, 1974), a pioneer along with Cannon in stress research, who voiced concerns over the effects of prolonged physiological arousal. Selye believed that in reaction to any kind of stress, there is a **general adaptation syndrome.** This is a set of physiological responses that occur in three distinct stages. The initial response to stress is *alarm,* during which the sympathetic nervous system is activated (e.g., heartbeat and respiration increase). Assuming that the stress continues, the second stage—*resistance*—begins. This is a period during which the outward signs of emotion actually decline. Breathing and heartbeat slow down, but an analysis of the blood during this stage will reveal the presence of several hormones normally associated with emotional states. Even though outwardly all now appears well, a long interval of stress will deplete the body's defenses and make one susceptible to diseases such as flu and mononucleosis. If the stress continues for a very lengthy time, the person will enter the third stage—*exhaustion.* And this can, in extreme cases, result in death.

Many of Selye's conclusions were based on animal research and, as always, there is some question as to how directly they apply to humans. Lacey (1967) suggests that different kinds of stress will induce different patterns of physiological responses. In short, there appear to be more individual differences and variety than the general adap-

TABLE 15-4　The Social Readjustment Rating Scale

Rank	Life Event	Mean Value (life-change units)
1	Death of spouse	100
2	Divorce	73
3	Marital separation	65
4	Jail term	63
5	Death of close family member	63
6	Personal injury or illness	53
7	Marriage	50
8	Fired at work	47
9	Marital reconciliation	45
10	Retirement	45
11	Change in health of family member	44
12	Pregnancy	40
13	Sex difficulties	39
14	Gain of new family member	39
15	Business re-adjustment	39
16	Change in financial state	38
17	Death of close friend	37
18	Change to different line of work	36
19	Change in number of arguments with spouse	35
20	Mortgage over $10,000	31
21	Foreclosure of mortgage or loan	30
22	Change in responsibilities at work	29
23	Son or daughter leaving home	29
24	Trouble with in-laws	29
25	Outstanding personal achievement	28
26	Wife begins or stops work	26
27	Begin or end school	26
28	Change in living conditions	25
29	Revision of personal habits	24
30	Trouble with boss	23
31	Change in work hours or conditions	20
32	Change in residence	20
33	Change in schools	20
34	Change in recreation	19
35	Change in church activities	19
36	Change in social activities	18
37	Mortgage or loan less than $10,000	17
38	Change in sleeping habits	16
39	Change in number of family get-togethers	15
40	Change in eating habits	15
41	Vacation	13
42	Christmas	12
43	Minor violations of the law	11

SOURCE: From "The Social Readjustment Rating Scale" by T. H. Holmes and R. H. Rahe, *Journal of Psychosomatic Research*, 1967, *11*, 213–218. Copyright 1967 by Pergamon Press. Reproduced by permission.

Potentially stressful objective events A major exam, a big date, trouble with the boss, a financial setback, all of which may create frustration, conflict, and the like	Subjective cognitive appraisal Personalized perception of threat, which is influenced by familiarity with the event, its controllability, and so on	Emotional response Annoyance, anger, anxiety, fear, dejection, grief
		Physiological response Autonomic arousal, hormonal fluctuations, neurochemical changes, and so on
		Behavioral response Coping efforts, such as lashing out at others, blaming oneself, seeking help, solving problems, and releasing emotions

FIGURE 15-2 Outline of the stress process.
From *Psychology: Themes and Variations* by Wayne Weiten. Copyright © 1989 by Wadsworth, Inc. Reprinted by permission of Brooks/Cole Publishing Company.

tation syndrome would suggest. Then, too, Selye did not seem to take into account adequately the cognitive appraisals that play such an important part in determining what will become a stressor (R.S. Lazarus, 1966). However, regardless of the exact details of theories of stress, there can be little doubt that when it becomes chronic it has many harmful effects.

The physiological responses (e.g., increased heart rate, rapid breathing, etc.) that occur in response to stressful events are the result of brain signals to the endocrine system. The path is through the autonomic nervous system (Asterita, 1985). A second path is directly between the brain and the endocrine system. The precise mechanisms responsible for physiological reactions are still unclear, but the effects are pervasive and unmistakable.

Behavioral responses.   A variety of behaviors can follow from the perception of threat and the ensuing stress. For example, the person may respond to frustration with aggression (Dollard et al., 1939) but this is not inevitable; it all depends on several factors (see Chapter 17 for a more complete discussion). In contrast, another person may respond to stress by giving up. This has come to be referred to as "learned helplessness" and will be described in detail in the next chapter. Still others respond defensively. For example, a number of Freudian-like mechanisms such as denial, over-compensation, intellectualization, and the like are possible. Of course, others may employ much more effective coping behaviors in the face of stress and we shall focus on them later in this chapter.

We noted earlier that in the case of anxiety, impaired performance on tasks is a frequent outcome. And we also saw how, for example, test anxiety can interfere with our performance. Similarly, athletes are sometimes said to "choke" in certain games.

Baumeister and Steinhilber (1984) checked statistical performance records from numerous championship baseball and basketball games over the years. Contrary to conventional wisdom, they found that home teams are often at a distinct disadvantage in final championship games. Apparently, this is because the pressure is so great for that final game when everything is on the line. This is shown in Table 15-5.

Another example of impaired performance is reflected in the differences in functioning between older and younger individuals—especially when stress is an element. Bäckman and Molander (1986) studied both younger and older miniature golf players who were skilled at the sport. All the players showed an increased heart rate and also rated themselves as more anxious when they moved from training to actual golf competition. Older players also displayed a dropoff in their performance in the competitive phase. The older players in particular, however, were less proficient in coping with the stress of competition. It seems likely that cognitive impairments were responsible here. That is, poor decisions about the speed of one's backswing or misjudging the proper angle for bank shots were probably involved. The results of this study are shown in Figure 15-3.

When prolonged stress is coupled with preexisting personality characteristics, clear pathology can result. This can range from the so-called burnout which is said to be so prevalent today (so much so that it has become a buzzword) to psychiatric disorders such as posttraumatic stress disorders that are associated with the Vietnam conflict and on to alcoholism, drug addiction, and the like (Davison and Neale, 1990).

Stress and urban society

Without question, a major feature of the twentieth century has been the growing urbanization of our environment. Along with this there seems to have developed an increasing awareness of the stresses and strains such environments thrust upon us. In this section, we shall examine three characteristics of urbanization that may promote

TABLE 15-5   *Outcomes of championship games*

Games	Home	Visitor	Home %
Baseball: World Series Results 1924–1982*			
1 and 2	59	39	.602
last game	20	29	.408
7	10	16	.385

*10 series excluded where same team won all games

Basketball: NBA Championship and Semifinal Results 1967–1982			
1–4	115	49	.701
last game	19	22	.463
7	5	8	.385

Adapted from Roy F. Baumeister and Andrew Steinhilber, "Paradoxical Effects of Supportive Audiences on Performance Under Pressure: The Home Field Disadvantage in Sports Championships," *Journal of Personality and Social Psychology*, Vol. 47, No. 1, July 1984. Copyright © 1984 by the American Psychological Association. Reprinted by permission of Roy F. Baumeister.

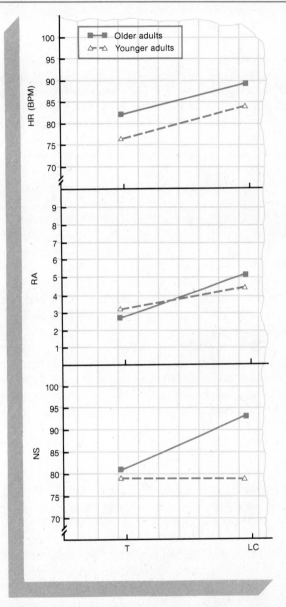

FIGURE 15-3 Mean heart rate (top panel, HR), mean related anxiety (middle panel, RA), and mean number of shots per two rounds (bottom panel, NS) for older and younger adults during training (T), and club championship (LC).

From Bäckman, L., and Molander, B., (1986). Adult differences in the ability to cope with situations of high arousal in a precision sport. *Psychology and Aging, 1,* 133–139.

stress reactions: crowding, noise, and bureaucracy. To some extent, these are extensions of the daily hassles discussed earlier.

Crowding.   We have known for a long time that crowding has a variety of ill effects on animals (Calhoun, 1962). In the case of humans, matters are more complex.
In fact, high density does not always lead to stress and then on to behavioral breakdowns. Animal behavior is heavily dependent on biological factors whereas in humans
culture and expectations play a more dominant role. The crucial thing is probably not
the actual degree of physical density but the extent to which one feels crowded (Stokols,
1972). However, others believe that distinguishing between density and crowding merely
confuses the issue (Freedman, 1975). Whatever the ultimate decision about this question, it is obvious that architects believe strongly that an illusion of space and openness
has many positive benefits for people.

High density has been observed to have several effects on illness, physiological
arousal, and emotions. For example, Baum and Greenberg (1975) compared the reactions of subjects who thought they would be sharing a room with ten others with the
reactions of those who anticipated a group of four. The latter subjects reported less
discomfort. Similarly, Baron, Mandel, Adams, and Griffen (1976) found that students
who perceived themselves as living in crowded dormitories were likely to feel crowded,
to see themselves as having less personal control, and to have more negative interpersonal attitudes.

Density also affects social behavior. Griffitt and Veitch (1971) reported that crowded
and hot conditions result in lower levels of interpersonal attraction toward strangers.
Related to this are the experimental findings of the study by Baum and Greenberg noted
in the preceding paragraph. Their subjects in the high-density room seemed to withdraw from each other (e.g., had less eye contact, turned their heads away from others).

Noise.   One of the most characteristic features of urban living is noise. It is
everywhere—jackhammers, automobile horns, screeching tires, jet engines, and on and
on. To a certain extent, one adapts to this noise. Yet evidence is accumulating from
a variety of sources that urban noise has become a significant source of stress. And
this does not refer just to the obvious negative effects of high-intensity noise on hearing.

Over the years, research has suggested that chronic exposure to noise can result
in cardiovascular changes (Cohen and Weinstein, 1981), problems in attention (Cohen, 1978), and lessened feelings of personal control (Glass and Singer, 1972). However, to answer more definitively questions about the consequences of prolonged
exposure to noise and about whether adaptation ultimately reduces any negative effects, Cohen, Krantz, Evans, and Stokols (1981) undertook a longitudinal study of children. These investigators found a variety of cognitive, motivational, and physiological
effects resulting from aircraft overflights. Children from noise-impacted third-and fourth-
grade classrooms were compared with similar children in quiet schools. All children
were tested on the same measures twice, with a one-year interval between testing
sessions.

What were the effects of serious airplane noise on these children? Children attending noisy schools had higher systolic and diastolic blood pressure than children in quiet

Urban society can be a noisy, crowded place where stress is hard to avoid.
Photograph Donald Dietz/Stock, Boston.

schools (see Figure 15-4). Attendance at the noisy schools resulted in reduced ability to solve puzzles successfully and to persist in trying to solve them during testing sessions. A somewhat surprising finding was that selective inattention apparently does not develop as a means of tuning out distracting noise. As a matter of fact, children from noisy schools displayed greater distractibility, and it increased with length of exposure to noise. In general, these effects were so stable over a one-year period that little basis seems to exist for concluding that people adapt to noise stressors over time. Obviously the message from this study is not a happy one, assuming that later work will replicate the findings.

Bureaucracy.   With bigness comes procedures, red tape, and formalities. These are code words for bureaucracy. Rules, authorities, and stupid regulations seem to become a way of life. For many of us, this way can become a stressful one. Glass and Singer (1972) report a study carried out by Shaban and Welling which demonstrates under controlled conditions what many people have experienced at one time or another in their own lives. College students were assigned to either of two conditions. Some were harassed by having to fill out boring, repetitious questionnaires and then later informed that they had filled them out improperly and must, therefore, do it all over again. The experimenter was rigid and petty and even took personal phone calls during the experiment! A second group was treated much the same way except that the experimenter was quite pleasant during everything. A control group was not hassled at

449

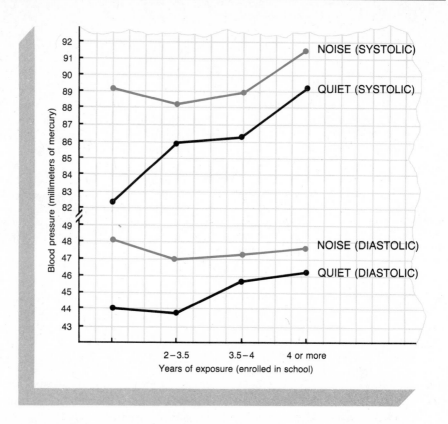

FIGURE 15-4   Blood pressure in school children as related to noise level and duration of exposure.

From "Physiological, Motivational, and Cognitive Effects of Aircraft Noise on Children: Moving from the Laboratory to the Field" by S. Cohen, G. W. Evans, D. S. Krantz, and D. Stokols, *American Psychologist*, 1980, *35*, 231–243. Copyright 1980 by the American Psychological Association. Reprinted by permission.

all. Following all this, subjects were required to perform several tasks. Both experimental groups reported higher levels of irritation and also made more task errors than did the control group. Negativism was shown by those subjects who had been exposed to the rigid, petty experimenter. The subjects in the other experimental group exhibited compliance. In this simulated bureaucratic situation, then, stress was one of the outcomes. But reactions to stress seemed to depend on how much control subjects attributed to themselves. Blaming the experimenter led to negativism. But attributing things to an immutable system led to feelings of lack of control and, eventually, to compliance.

COPING WITH ANXIETY AND STRESS

People whose mental health is shaky or who are under stress tend to use less adaptive coping strategies such as avoidance or escapism (Aldwin and Revenson, 1987). Psychotherapy, behavior modification, and the like are methods devised to deal with anxiety and related problems and to enhance coping strategies. Indeed, the sections on changing behavior that appeared in previous chapters were, in effect, describing techniques of controlling anxiety. Psychotherapy, then, can be an effective means of dealing with chronic forms of anxiety that seem to stem largely from inner conflicts and unresolved or unrecognized problems. When anxieties appear to be the result of more circumscribed problems or are tied specifically to certain situations (e.g., phobias), a variety of behavior modification procedures are useful.

But most people never seek professional help. They must cope with their anxieties and stress in their own ways. A number of possible coping strategies have been identified (Meichenbaum, Price, Phares, McCormick, and Hyde, 1989). Let us take a look at each in turn.

Tension reduction

Many times, just being able to unwind by ventilating feelings or relaxing can be helpful in reducing stress. A variety of methods have been used to unwind (Meichenbaum et al., 1989), for example:

■ Deciding to passively ride out the event

■ Simply ignoring the situation for a while

■ Letting the tension wear off

■ Engaging in unrelated activities

■ Just carrying on as usual

■ Getting out of the situation temporarily and seeking advice from others

■ Talking over the problem with others away from the situation

■ Engaging in such activities as exercise, hobbies, and the like

■ Seeing the humor in the situation

■ Doing relaxation exercises

Problem solving

At some point, more direct action may be necessary to cope with stress. One way to do this is to appraise the events as problems to be solved and then undertaking a step-by-step approach to solve the problems (Goldfried and Davison, 1976; Meichenbaum et al., 1989). Translated into a series of questions that one might ask oneself, this becomes

■ What is really the problem here?

■ What is it that I want?

■ What steps can I take?

■ What will be the outcomes of these steps?

■ Shall I do it?

■ Assuming the action is taken, how did it turn out?

Leon, McNally, and Ben-Porath (1989) studied a North Pole expedition team to identify their methods of coping with stress. It turned out that they displayed an attitude of "planfulness" that was high on the list of successful coping strategies as was a tendency to appraise situations in a positive light.

Distraction

Sometimes denial of the threat that is implicit in stressful situations can be a positive coping strategy (R. S. Lazarus, 1980). Particularly when the person cannot exert personal control or when no great loss will come from not paying attention to stress, denial may be useful. For example, if the chances are one in a thousand that a bad outcome will occur, perhaps it is not wrong to ignore the situation. Even illusion and self-deception can sometimes help reduce stress. But like most principles, this is not a universal truth. Thus, the woman who finds a lump in her breast would surely be ill-advised to ignore it.

Cognitive reappraisal

In a sense, psychotherapy and cognitive behavior-modification procedures are successful because they lead the person to reappraise the nature of what were formerly stressful events. The pressure of a job diminishes when the individual achieves the insight that he is really trying to prove to his wife that he is a worthy person. Speaking in public becomes less threatening when we are armed with a variety of techniques for coping with the situation.

A study by Lazarus and Alfert (1964) illustrates one way in which cognitive appraisal can affect the amount of stress experienced. They showed a film to male college students which depicted part of a coming-of-age rite in a primitive tribe. The film graphically showed a rather painful and bloody operation on the penises of boys being initiated into manhood. The film, however, was presented in three different ways. One group of subjects was shown the film without comment or introduction. In the second condition, a commentator downplayed the painful aspects of the rite and suggested that the procedure was really not physically harmful. Indeed, he indicated that the boys were proud and pleased to be able to participate in this rite of passage. This commentary accompanied the film. A third group received the same commentary but it occurred prior to the showing of the film rather than during it.

Stress was measured by recording both skin conductance and heart rate for each subject. Results indicated that the first condition (no commentary) produced the greatest autonomic arousal, with the second condition (commentary accompanying the film) creating the next largest increase in heart rate and skin conductance. The least amount of anxiety was experienced by those subjects who received the commentary prior to the showing of the film. It was as if the preliminary comments provided the subjects with a way of appraising the film as less harmful and frightening, thereby reducing the experience of stress.

Social support

It was noted earlier that the vast majority of people who experience stress and anxiety never seek out or have available to them professional help. Yet there are many informal care-givers, ranging from bartenders and hairdressers to lawyers and supervisors. Although the success of their efforts is difficult to gauge, there is some minimal evidence that they can be effective in helping others control their anxieties (Cowen, 1982). Phillips and Fischer (1981) also discuss the stress-reducing role of social networks. Especially in the case of the elderly, social support can be a buffer against the negative effects of stress (Cutrona, Russell, and Rose, 1986). Friends, neighbors, relatives, and fellow employees can all be important sources for all of us to draw upon as we confront the stresses of everyday life. Especially in the case of the elderly, social support seems to buffer stress by bolstering self-esteem (Krause, 1987a).

Humor

Perhaps the greatest stress-buffer for many people is their ability to laugh at themselves and to find the humor in otherwise stressful situations. Dixon (1980) has shown that humor can be adaptive and, as Martin and Lefcourt (1983) have discussed, Freud, Allport, and May all considered humor as healthy and adaptive. Also, Nezu, Nezu, and Blissett (1988) have found that humor can help moderate depression. It was such reasoning that led Rotter and Rafferty (1950) to score humor responses on an incomplete sentences blank as an indication of adjustment tendencies.

But all too often, none of these coping strategies just discussed work or else they are not employed. And then the experience of stress becomes chronic. When this happens there can be many implications for health as the succeeding pages will reveal.

HEALTH

A clue that suggests a once-emerging field has finally established itself is the appearance of textbooks and handbooks detailing that field. In the field of health psychology we now have textbooks (e.g., Feuerstein, Labbé, and Kuczmierczyk, 1986; Gatchel, Baum, and Krantz, 1989; Taylor, 1986) as well as handbooks (e.g., Baum and Singer, 1987). The basic message in all of them is that both personality variables and behavioral excesses can significantly increase our risk for chronic diseases, accidents, and injuries (Jeffery, 1989).

The influence of stress

There are a variety of processes by which behavior and personality factors culminate in physical disease. Before identifying them, however, let us look briefly at some historical events which may help bring things into focus.

Historical perspectives.   Suls and Rittenhouse (1987) have pointed out several significant historical points. First, the realization that nonphysiological aspects are critical in disease outcomes goes back even farther than Aristotle. And even in the nineteenth century, people sometimes voiced the belief that tuberculosis was caused by excessive feeling. By the 1940s such crude conceptualizations had coalesced into the field of **psychosomatic medicine.** Now the message was that a variety of physical illnesses were caused by or related to psychological factors. Not only that, but many researchers (e.g., Alexander, 1950) identified several psychosomatic diseases such as peptic ulcers, essential hypertension, and bronchial asthma. Furthermore, it was believed that each psychosomatic illness had a different, specific underlying unconscious conflict that predisposed a person to the disorder. For example, chronic repressed hostility supposedly helped to precipitate rheumatoid arthritis. But ultimately it was decided that such specific psychogenic factors were not very predictive. As a result, more general, nonspecific factors such as stress began to be the focus of research. For example, Engel (1968) proposed that events such as bereavement or personal loss could promote feelings of helplessness or hopelessness which, in turn, led to physiological reactions involving the autonomic nervous system or the immune system. All of this increased one's susceptibility to illness. In Table 15-6 we can see the move from specific to general or nonspecific explanatory factors and their role in precipitating disease.

At about this same time, Holmes and Rahe (1967) suggested that life events that require change in the person's lifestyle can be quite stressful and thereby may increase subsequent risk of illness. Then, beginning in the 1960s, along came the Type A pattern—a complex of personality and behavioral predispositions—said to make one prone to coronary complications. A relatively simple measurement technology came with it and helped propel the whole field of health psychology. These events, along with the other developments noted later in this chapter, have pushed the field into its current position of prominence.

Since we have repeatedly referred to the link between stress and disease, let us now turn to an examination of that link.

Direct influences.   A variety of psychosocial stimuli may generate stress which can directly affect the hormonal system, the autonomic arousal system, and the immune system (Krantz et al., 1985). Even thinking about a future stressful event can produce the physiological responses that are present during the actual event (Mason, 1971). Hormones such as catecholamines, neurotransmitters in the brain that help regulate blood pressure, heart rate, and blood glucose levels are important here. Chronic high levels of catecholamine secretion can even precipitate damage to the cardiovascular system (Frankenhaeuser, 1980).

In other cases, the immune system is adversely affected by stress so that it cannot as effectively play its customary role of destroying viruses, bacteria, tumors, and irregular cells. Stress suppresses the system and can thereby dramatically increase the body's vulnerability to everything from allergies to some forms of cancer. As shown in Figure 15-5, there are many common physical reactions to stress which can heighten one's susceptibility to illness.

TABLE 15-6 The move from specific to nonspecific explanatory factors in the precipitation of disease

---

I. Psychosomatic Medicine in the 1940s

There are *seven psychosomatic* diseases:

1. Peptic ulcer
2. Essential hypertension
3. Bronchial asthma
4. Thyrotoxicosis
5. Rheumatoid arthritis
6. Ulcerative colitis
7. Neurodermatitis

There is a *specific* underlying unconscious conflict for each disease. For example, the chronic conflict over the wish to be fed or cared for leads to increased secretion of stomach acid, which leads to the development of ulcers.

II. Psychiatry in the 1960s

There are *nine psychophysiological* disorders:

1. Skin disorders (e.g., acne, eczema, psoriasis)
2. Musculoskeletal disorders (e.g., backache, tension headache)
3. Respiratory disorders (e.g., bronchial asthma, hyperventilation)
4. Cardiovascular disorders (e.g., essential hypertension, migraine headache, Raynaud's disease)
5. Hemic and lymphatic disorders
6. Gastrointestinal disorders (e.g., gastric ulcers, gastritis, mucous colitis)
7. Genitourinary disorders (e.g., dysmenorrhea, impotence, vaginismus)
8. Endocrine disorders (e.g., goiter, obesity)
9. Disorders of organs of special sense (e.g., Ménière's disease)
10. Other types

III. Psychiatry in the 1980s

There is *one broad* category (but *no specific* ones):

1. Psychological factors affecting physical condition.
   "This category can be used for any physical condition to which psychological factors are judged to be contributory. It can be used to describe disorders that in the past have been referred to as either "psychosomatic" or "psychophysiological."

   "Common examples of physical conditions for which this category may be appropriate include, but are not limited to: obesity, tension headache, migraine headache, angina pectoris, painful menstruation, sacroiliac pain, neurodermatitis, acne, rheumatoid arthritis, asthma, tachycardia, arrhythmia, gastric ulcer, duodenal ulcer, cardiospasm, pylorospasm, nausea and vomiting, regional enteritis, ulcerative colitis, and frequency of micturition." (American Psychiatric Association, 1980, p. 303)

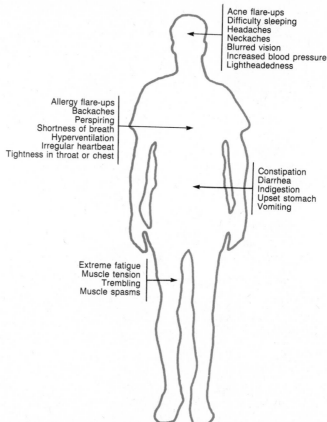

FIGURE 15-5   Common physical reactions to stress

From *Exploring Choices: The Psychology of Adjustment* by Donald Meichenbaum, Richard Price, E. Jerry Phares, Naomi McCormick and Janet Hyde. Copyright © 1989 Scott, Foresman and Company.

Much of the work in this area should most probably be regarded as preliminary or tentative until it is replicated in other studies. Still, this is an exciting field and many of its findings are provocative. For example, Baum, Fleming, and Singer (1982) found that people living near the Three Mile Island nuclear reactor showed high levels of stress after the nuclear accident there. They also showed a high incidence of illness (e.g., high blood pressure, upper respiratory infections). The investigators also found that these people had deficient immune systems relative to those living outside the area.

Others, focusing on recovery from illness, have even speculated that positive emotions can trigger chemicals in the brain that will reduce pain and speed healing (e.g., Cousins, 1976).

Indirect influences. In other cases, behaviors, habits, or lifestyles can culminate in disease. Such behaviors include smoking, poor diet, lack of exercise, excessive alcohol or drug use, and poor hygiene practices. Often, these behaviors are deeply rooted in our culture; other times they are imbedded in the needs and expectations of the individual.

Another influence results from the ways in which people respond to illness. Sometimes they are unwilling or unable to appreciate the severity of their illness and do not seek appropriate medical aid promptly enough. And some are unwilling to comply with medical advice or rehabilitation programs. In too many cases the outcomes are unpleasant indeed. We will have more to say about all this later in this chapter.

Dispositional factors

There are several potential ways in which personality and disease might be linked (Friedman and Booth-Kewley, 1987a): (a) personality features might be the *result* of disease processes; (b) personality features might lead to unhealthy behaviors which then promote disease; (c) personality could directly affect disease through physiological mechanisms; (d) a third underlying biological variable might be related to both personality and disease; and (e) several different causes and feedback loops might affect the relationship between personality and disease.

There have certainly been many personality traits or styles said to relate to disease. But all this gets confusing since we cannot always be sure that supposedly different traits really are different; maybe they are basically the same but with different names (Costa and McCrae, 1987)! Therefore, Friedman and Booth-Kewley (1987a) have argued that there may be a kind of "generic" disease-prone personality, although they admit the evidence for this is not overwhelming.

With the above considerations in mind, we can now examine several of the more prominent personality dispositions that have been associated with disease outcomes.

Type A behavior pattern. In 1892 Sir William Osler described the typical coronary patient as neither delicate nor neurotic but robust, keen, ambitious, and vigorous in mind and body. Many years later, Friedman and Rosenman (1974) pioneered in the identification of what has come to be called the **Type A behavior pattern (TABP).** Their work has loosed a veritable flood of research over the past fifteen years or so.

In tune with Osler's early descriptions, Friedman and Rosenman (1974) depicted TABP as "an action-emotion complex that can be observed in any person who is aggressively involved in a chronic, incessant struggle to achieve more and more in less and less time, and if required to do so, against the opposing efforts of other things or persons" (p. 67). The **Type B pattern** refers to the absence of Type A behaviors. This is an individual differences approach to the development of stress which recognizes the maxim that not every life event, stressful or not, has the same impact on everyone under all circumstances (Matthews and Glass, 1981).

A variety of behaviors are often said to characterize Type A individuals (Glass, 1977). Thus, Type A subjects tend to:

- Perceive time passing rather rapidly

- Show a deteriorating performance on tasks that require delayed responding

- Work near maximum capacity even when there is no time deadline involved

- Arrive earlier for appointments

- Become aggressive and hostile when frustrated

- Report less fatigue and fewer physical symptoms

- Become motivated by intense desires to master their physical and social environments and to maintain control

However, Wright (1988) draws a slightly different picture of TABP in coronary patients. He asserts that the basic ingredients of TABP include a:

- Sense of time urgency—but not over large amounts of time but over seconds (e.g., changing lanes to save a few car lengths)

- Chronic activation level—being keyed up most of the time every day

- Multiphasic quality—the tendency to have many irons in the fire and to do more than one thing at a time

But the search for the "real" nature of TABP goes on. For some, it is merely a set of overt behaviors while for others it is a fixed personality trait (Rodin and Salovey, 1989). Still others regard the Type A-B distinction as a true typology and not a dimensional concept (Strube, 1989).

But how do we identify TABP? Both structured interviews and questionnaires have been used to identify Type A behavior (Matthews and Glass, 1981). The interview contains questions about, for example, how the person responds when waiting for someone who is slow. The interviewer will also try to provoke the person by interrupting or questioning the interviewee's accuracy. Such a strategy is designed to produce Type A behavior (if it is prone to occur) in the interview itself. The most frequent questionnaire employed is the **Jenkins Activity Survey for Health Prediction (JAS)** (Jenkins, Zyzanski, and Rosenman, 1971). It contains fifty-four self-report items similar to those asked in the interview. The problem, however, is that the questionnaire and the interview do not always produce the same results (Matthews, Krantz, Dembroski, and Mac-Dougall, 1982). For example, Suls and Wan (1989) surveyed a large number of studies using either questionnaires or interviews to identify TABP. It was discovered that Type A subjects who reported chronic unpleasant emotional states were identified by questionnaires but not by interview techniques. But then Friedman and Booth-Kewley (1987b) contend that structured interviews are better than questionnaires as predictors of coronary heart disease. The lack of a clearly understood measurement technology here may be responsible for the current uncertainty about the relationship between Type A behavior and risk of coronary heart disease (CHD)—a topic to which we can now turn.

From the very beginning, the major interest in TABP centered on its potential relationship to health. Possible links have been shown often. For example, Kelly and Houston (1985) found that Type A women tend to be in higher, more demanding occupational levels than Type B women. Moreover, they experience more stress and tension. Male Type A individuals who are working on a challenging intellectual task have been shown to become more aroused than Type B individuals. This relationship between arousal and task difficulty is shown in Figure 15-6, where arousal is defined in terms of systolic blood pressure. More recently, Contrada (1989) has shown a modest but reliable relationship between TABP and elevated blood pressure. But this occurred only when TABP was measured by an interview; not when questionnaires were used (that old measurement bugaboo again!).

But the real key to the popularity that the Type A pattern has enjoyed as a research topic lies in its presumed link to CHD. A number of studies over the years have suggested that Type As have at least twice the likelihood of CHD as do Type Bs. Matthews and Glass (1981) have suggested several possible explanations for this heightened risk. For example, the specific Type A characteristics of competitive drive and impatience have been linked with the subsequent onset of CHD. These same features have

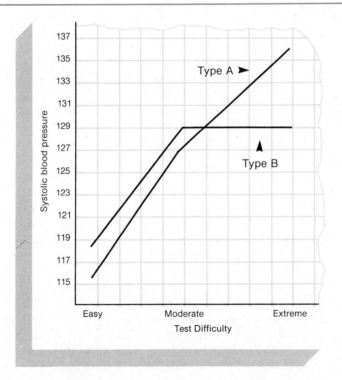

FIGURE 15-6 Systolic blood pressure of Type A and Type B subjects while working on the easy, moderately difficult, and extremely difficult tasks.
From Holmes, D. S., McGilley, B. M. and Houston, B. K., 1984. Task-related arousal of Type A and Type B persons: Levels of challenge and response specificity. *Journal of Personality and Social Psychology, 46,* 1322–1327.

been found to be associated with elevations of systolic blood pressure and heart rate in experimental settings. So it may be that Type As respond to environmental stress with greater physiological reactions than do their Type B counterparts. Another possibility relates to the notion of self-involvement. People who focus a great deal on themselves tend to show higher blood-pressure levels. Since Type A individuals are acutely aware of themselves, this may explain the elevated blood pressure and, ultimately, the development of CHD. A third possibility hinges on the Type A person's need to exert personal control over the environment. Some evidence suggests that in coping with stress and thus maintaining control, sympathetic nervous system activity increases and catecholamine neurotransmitters are released, which may elevate blood pressure, increase the rate of arterial damage, facilitate fatal cardiac arrhythmias, and the like. However, only further study can pin down the precise mechanisms involved. Other research (Humphries, Carver, and Neumann, 1983; Matthews and Brunson, 1979) suggests that Type As may have a tendency to focus on important events to the exclusion of more peripheral events or stimuli. If such events happen to be frustration or anger, autonomic hyperactivity could result and thus increase the risk of CHD.

As a general framework of explanation, it has been suggested that Type As do not just respond to challenges or demands; they seek out and create such an environment by their own thought processes and actions (Smith and Anderson, 1986). This explanation is presented schematically in Figure 15-7.

The trouble with all this, however, is that there is a growing suspicion that the relationship between the Type A pattern and CHD is not as strong as once thought (Matthews, 1984). In recent years, a number of large-scale studies carried out over periods ranging from three to eight years have failed to find the customary Type A— CHD relationship (e.g., the Multiple Risk Factor Intervention Trial Study sponsored by the National Heart, Lung, and Blood Institute).

The anger-hostility component seems to be a highly prominent element of TABP (Moser and Dyck, 1989). Therefore, it may turn out that while global TABP scores do not predict coronary heart disease, the anger-hostility component may do so (Rodin and Salovey, 1989). And, as if things were not complicated enough, it has been reported that among those individuals who survive their first heart attack, the coronary death rate was *higher* among Type B patients than Type As (Ragland and Brand, 1988)!

A key element in the Type A syndrome is thought to be perceived lack of control (Glass, 1977; Strube and Werner, 1985). Type A individuals feel a strong need to exert control. Their active, dynamic style even makes them look as if they are in control of situations regardless of whether or not they are (Strube, Lott, Heilizer, and Gregg, 1986). Much of their Type A behavior may be thought of as a chronic attempt to regain the control that they continually feel is slipping away from them. It is almost as if they have a set to control everything, followed by an inevitable frustration-hostility reaction when events in their lives elude their grandiose plan of control. They constantly feel challenged, experiencing a great deal of stress as a result. This interpretation is highlighted in a study by Brunson and Matthews (1981). Type A and Type B subjects were confronted with a series of insoluble problems (lack of control) and were also asked to verbalize their thoughts as they worked on the task. Eventually the efforts of Type

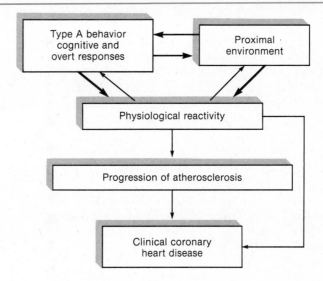

FIGURE 15-7   From Type A to CHD: An interactional model.
From Smith, T. W. and Anderson, N. B., 1986. Models of personality and disease: An interactional approach to Type A behavior and cardiovascular risk, *Journal of Personality and Social Psychology, 50,* 1166–1173.

As deteriorated, and they reported that their failures were due to themselves. They also expressed increasing disappointment with themselves, along with a growing pessimism. All of this suggests that lack of personal control over this situation was especially disruptive for Type As.

Perceived lack of control is a theme that runs persistently through the literature on stress. It is so important that the next chapter will be devoted to a further exploration of its nature and consequences.

Dispositions that strengthen

A whole array of other dispositions has been described over the years. The one thing they all have in common is the tendency to promote optimism, flexibility, persistence, and resiliency in response to stress or threat. For example, there is **hardiness,** which is a stress-buffering characteristic that includes a sense of (a) commitment to self, work, and other values; (b) personal control; and (c) challenge—a recognition that change is normal and that it promotes development. Hardiness helps to inoculate the individual against stress-induced illness (Kobasa, Maddi, and Kahn, 1982). Research has seemed to support the relation between hardiness and the avoidance of illness (e.g., Roth, Wiebe, Fillingim, and Shay, 1989). But there are many contradictions in reported findings. For example, Allred and Smith (1989) found support for the presumed "hardy" cognitive style but not for any linkage between hardiness and health. Currently, the problem seems to be that hardiness is a kind of composite of a variety of qualities (e.g., personal control, optimism, etc.) and it is hard to know exactly what is carrying the predictive freight (Funk and Houston, 1987; Hull, Van Treuren, and Virnelli, 1987).

Others, such as Scheier and Carver (1987) believe that there is a general quality of **optimism** that provides a coping style that helps individuals resist a variety of stress-related illnesses. Peterson and Seligman (1987) echo this line of reasoning as they argue for a dimension of optimism-pessimism that relates to coping effectiveness. Dispositional optimism has also been shown to relate to faster recovery from coronary bypass surgery (Scheier, et al., 1989).

And then there is **self-efficacy.** Although there is no single dispositional measure of self-efficacy (as noted earlier in Chapter 13), several studies suggest that perceived self-efficacy affects physiological systems associated with health. For example, Bandura, Taylor, Williams, Mefford, and Barchas (1985) found that phobic individuals who had doubts about their ability to cope produced significant increases in circulating catecholamines. As the subjects began to gain mastery, the secretions declined. Also, arthritic patients who perceived their own efficacy showed an increase in the number of suppressor T cells. The latter inhibit the production of antibodies. A variety of other studies have shown a relationship between self-efficacy and compliance with health-related regimens such as exercise (e.g., Kaplan, Atkins, and Reinsch, 1984).

Two other traits that are relevant here are ego-control and ego-resiliency. **Ego-control** refers to the ability to control one's impulses by delaying gratification, inhibiting aggression, and making plans (Funder and Block, 1989). The related notion, **ego-resiliency,** involves the ability to adapt to environmental demands by modifying ego-control; a kind of "ego elasticity." One of the correlates of these dispositions is the ability to regroup after experiencing stress (Block and Block, 1980). A related idea suggests that there may be a general personality trait that prompts some individuals to behave in a self-assertive fashion. This, in turn, tends to reduce psychological distress (Towbes, Cohen, and Glyshaw, 1989).

Then there is the work of Holahan and Moos (1986) that identified the following factors that predispose one to resist stress: feelings of self-confidence, an easy-going disposition, a disinclination to use avoidance as a coping technique, and the availability of family support.

Motives.   Recently, McClelland (1989) has reviewed evidence suggesting that motive systems such as power and affiliation are related to physiological systems and ultimately to health and illness. For example, a relaxed or easygoing affiliative syndrome characterizes some types of diabetics and can, if aroused, lead to poorer blood sugar control in those affected individuals. A stressed power motive syndrome is related to sympathetic nervous system activation, release of stress hormones, depressed immune functions, and greater susceptibility to infections. In contrast, affiliative trust and sense of efficacy are associated with better health.

Control.   The most ubiquitous factor is one's belief in personal control (see Chapter 16). In general, the feeling of not being in control of one's life or future can have profound effects upon emotional, cognitive, and physical well-being (Rodin, 1986a).

Many different mechanisms could mediate the effects of control (Rodin, 1986b). These include stress reduction, better awareness of symptoms, direct effects on the immune system and the neuroendocrine system, and more effective attempts at initiating health-promoting behaviors.

But personality traits and dispositions are not alone in their effects. In the next section we shall discuss some additional factors that place individuals at risk.

Additional risk factors

Epidemiology refers to the study of the distribution and determinants of health conditions. Such study has uncovered many risk factors, particularly in the case of coronary heart disease (CHD) (Jenkins, 1988). It is clear that many of these factors have their origins in the behavior of the individual, as we saw earlier in the case of TABP.

Age. Clearly, the risk of many major diseases increases sharply with age. According to Jarvik and Perl (1981), 86 percent of people over the age of sixty-five suffer from at least one chronic disease. And for many of the elderly, these diseases are the culmination of the lifestyles and health practices of their youth (Siegler and Costa, 1985). Also, psychosocial factors such as the death of a spouse can help precipitate illness (Woodruff-Pak, 1988). But it is important to note that, as with everything else, there are wide individual differences.

Gender. Women are significantly less prone than men to encounter life-threatening diseases; particularly in the case of CHD (Jenkins, 1985). One reason for this is that, relative to women, men show a higher incidence of TABP, they tend to exhibit patterns of work overloads, they smoke more frequently, and they manifest a greater willingness to engage in risky behaviors that involve physical danger and illegal activities (Waldron, 1976, 1986). All of this affects health. However, it may be interesting to speculate whether these differences will persist as more and more women ignore traditional roles.

Socioeconomic and ethnic factors. The risk of CHD is 10 to 70 percent higher in the lowest socioeconomic levels. To a large extent this reflects the greater incidence of smoking, obesity, high blood pressure, and hypertensive disease among the less affluent (Jenkins, 1988). Links among socioeconomic status, racial groups, and disease seem largely attributable to related factors such as unstable environments and lack of social support along with poor education and nutrition, inadequate health care, and the like (Rodin and Salovey, 1989).

Other factors. Many, many other factors are also associated with increased risk of CHD and other illness (Jenkins, 1988). These include several of the factors already noted in passing: elevated blood pressure, cigarette smoking, dietary habits, obesity, blood lipids, alcohol, and lack of exercise. All of these factors are, again, at least to some extent, intimately wrapped up in the ways people choose to lead their lives (or else are forced to because of lack of education, lack of money, etc.).

Behavioral medicine

The preceding pages have made clear that psychological and behavioral variables are vital in understanding many forms of illness and in maintaining health. In recent years, the field of **behavioral medicine** has shown a remarkable development. This specialty refers to "the broad interdisciplinary field of scientific investigation, education, and practice which concerns itself with health, illness, and related physiological dysfunctions" (Gatchel, Baum, and Krantz, 1989, p. 10).

A description of the full range of problems to which behavioral medicine has been applied is beyond the scope of this chapter. However, in Table 15-7 a partial list of these problems is provided.

Treatment approaches.   Earlier in this chapter, a variety of coping strategies were noted as methods of warding off the effects of stress. When these strategies are not employed or are otherwise ineffective, *chronic* stress may ensue and problems such as those listed in Table 15-7 may arise. When this happens, an array of treatment approaches are available, depending on the specific nature of the problem (Phares, 1988). Some of these approaches are summarized in Table 15-8.

TABLE 15-7   *A partial list of problems to which behavioral medicine has been applied*

Smoking	Ulcers
Alcohol abuse	Irritable bowel syndrome
Drug abuse	Spasmodic torticollis
Obesity	Tics
Type A pattern	Cerebral palsy
Hypertension	Cerebrovascular accidents
Cardiac arrhythmia	Epilepsy
Raynaud's disease	Asthma
Anorexia nervosa-Bulimia	Neurodermatitis
Chronic vomiting	Urticaria
Encopresis-fecal incontinence	Psoriasis
Prurigo nodularis	Hyperhydrosis
Chronic pain	Headaches
Insomnia	Diabetes
Dysmenorrhea	Dental disorders
Cancer	Spinal cord injuries

TABLE 15-8   A partial list of treatment techniques associated with behavioral medicine

Extinction	Contingency contracting
Counterconditioning	Biofeedback
Relaxation	Cognitive restructuring
Aversion therapies	Covert conditioning
Operant conditioning	Self-management techniques
Modeling	Social support
Assertiveness training	

Prevention.   Treating problems and diseases after they develop is important. But in the long run, programs designed to prevent problems from developing in the first place are more efficient. A few simple but widely practiced behaviors would dramatically reduce the toll of human misery and the flood of dollars that are cascading into the health-care system. Who, for example, would disagree with the following advice:

- Do not begin to smoke and do not use alcohol excessively

- Reduce salt and cholesterol intake

- Drive carefully and fasten your seatbelts

- Exercise regularly

A major thrust of behavioral medicine, then, has been in the direction of prevention.

Several large-scale prevention programs have been launched to cut down on a variety of risk factors such as smoking, fat intake, lack of exercise, and high blood pressure. For example, the Stanford Heart Disease Prevention Project involved three communities (Meyer, Nash, McAlister, Maccoby, and Farquhar, 1980). One community was exposed to a mass media campaign, another to the mass media campaign plus behavior therapy for truly high-risk individuals, and the third community served as a control. At a three-year followup it was determined that a substantial reduction in health-impairing behaviors had occurred when the media campaign was coupled with behavior therapy. Moderate reductions took place with the media campaign alone.

Another example is in the case of obesity. The Stanford Adolescent Obesity Project employed a variety of strategies with adolescents in the hope that control at this period in their lives would lead to prevention in adulthood (Coates and Thoresen, 1981). These strategies were self-observation, elimination of eating cues, and social support.

Coping with medical procedures.   The prospect of surgery or an imminent visit to the dentist can strike fear into the hearts of the strongest. It has long been recognized that many individuals cope with their fears of medical procedures with sheer anxiety or avoidance. The result is far too often deteriorating health and even death in some cases. In other instances, the stress involved interferes with the effectiveness of the medical procedures. Several methods in behavioral medicine have been applied in an attempt to deal with patients' anxiety and stress here. Recently, a special section of the *Journal of Consulting and Clinical Psychology* (June, 1989) was devoted entirely to this topic. Also Ludwick-Rosenthal and Neufeld (1988) have identified a number of successful stress-management techniques that are employed in connection with noxious medical procedures. For example, numerous studies have been devoted to ways of improving psychological preparation for surgery. Successful strategies have included: relaxation, imparting accurate information about the procedures to be used, information about what to expect during the surgery experience, and the provision of cognitive-coping skills (Olson and Elliott, 1983). In the case of children, research suggests that watching a movie that depicts a model successfully coping with the prospect of surgery significantly reduces patients' emotional reactions during their stay in the hospital (Melamed and Siegel, 1975).

Compliance with regimens.   All too often, individuals just do not comply with medical advice or with behavioral instructions—at least for substantial periods of time. This lack of compliance can, of course, be highly dangerous to health. Factors that enhance compliance include the physician's manner and ability to communicate, the extent to which the patient's expectations are met, and the clarity of the diagnosis (Korsch and Negrete, 1972). Similarly, in dealing with alcohol and drug abuse, relapses can be reduced if the patient has been provided with coping strategies designed to deal with high-risk situations that will be encountered after treatment (Marlatt, 1975).

SUMMARY

- There are numerous definitions of anxiety. Most, however, incorporate three elements: a state of physiological arousal, a perception of threat and lack of preparedness, and a disruption of coping behavior. When this pattern occurs in the face of no clearly perceived stimuli, the anxiety is likely to be viewed as neurotic.

- Anxiety as a concept has been identified historically with two broad traditions. The first is the clinical approach. The second tradition springs from the experimental-laboratory perspective, beginning with Pavlov's work on dogs and culminating in the research of Dollard and Miller, who tried to integrate the clinical and experimental traditions.

- The Hull-Spence approach, growing out of the experimental tradition, declared that response potential is determined by drive multiplied by habit strength. This implies that emotional arousal will lead subjects to perform habitual responses more intensely. Thus, by knowing a person's anxiety level we can better predict exactly how classical conditioning will develop.

■ The need to measure level of arousal so as to predict conditioning led to the development of Taylor's Manifest Anxiety Scale (MAS), a fifty-item self-report inventory.

■ Over the years, MAS research has led to the development of two broad generalizations. First, anxiety facilitates learning when the task is easy or when the correct responses are readily available. Second, with complex tasks or in the case of responses with weak habit strength, learning proceeds more slowly for anxious subjects.

■ An alternative approach to drive theory has arisen out of research on test anxiety. The role of interfering thoughts is emphasized here. The subject's appraisal of a situation as one in which failure is likely leads to the perception of threat. These cognitions and preoccupations about failure then interfere or compete with more appropriate problem-solving thoughts and action.

■ To pursue the implications of this approach and to identify individual differences in test anxiety, the Test Anxiety Scale (TAS) was developed. Research with this scale suggests that high levels of test anxiety impair one's ability to process task information and to perform well on the task at hand.

■ Further work has led to the differentiation of anxiety as both a state and a trait. State anxiety is a more transitory phenomenon while anxiety as a trait refers to an acquired behavioral predisposition. The State-Trait Anxiety Inventory (STAI) has been developed to measure individual differences in these dual aspects of anxiety.

■ In the aftermath of World War II, attention shifted to the role of external events in promoting stress. Whether or not one experiences stress is heavily dependent upon how events are appraised. In particular, the elements of familiarity, controllability, and predictability are important.

■ Some major kinds of events that often produce stress include: frustrations and daily hassles, natural disasters, conflict, and change. The Social Readjustment Rating Scale was described as one prominent measure of stressful life events.

■ Our responses to stress are complex but, in general, they include emotional reactions (e.g., anger or fear), physiological reactions (e.g., the general adaptation syndrome), and behavioral reactions (e.g., aggression).

■ Major forms of contemporary stress seem to emanate from the nature of urban societies. Examples of stress-producing urban factors that were discussed included crowding, noise, and bureaucracy.

■ Several methods of reducing anxiety and stress were noted. These include the traditional psychotherapy and behavior-modification techniques. But most people do not seek therapy. For them, methods of tension reduction, problem solving, and distraction can be helpful. Cognitive reappraisal is another method of reducing stress. Social support networks are highly useful as is humor.

■ When coping strategies fail and stress becomes chronic, health problems may follow. Recognition of these consequences goes back to antiquity. But the rise of psychosomatic medicine in the 1940s especially underlined how specific unconscious conflicts could promote illness.

■ Stress operates to produce health problems in several ways. Some effects are direct and occur through the hormonal, autonomic, or immune systems. Other influences are indirect and operate through our behaviors (e.g., smoking, failure to exercise, etc.) and eventually lead to poor health outcomes.

■ Some individuals seem to possess psychological characteristics that make them prone to CHD. They have been described as action-oriented people who are chronically engaged in an aggressive struggle against other persons or things to achieve more and more in less and less time. Both a structured inventory and a questionnaire have been devised to identify these so-called Type A individuals.

■ Research has indicated that Type As have several distinct characteristics. They perceive time as passing rapidly; they perform poorly on tasks requiring patience; they work hard even when it is not necessary; they arrive early for appointments; they react to frustration with aggression and hostility; and they show an intense desire to master their physical and social environments and to maintain personal control.

■ The link between Type A behavior and CHD may well be elevated blood pressure. But whether this link is forged through intense competitive needs, an extreme self-focus, or the chronic desire to control one's environment is still unclear. It certainly appears, however, that the need for personal control over events is a very important element in the Type A pattern.

■ There is a growing suspicion that the relationship between the Type A pattern and CHD is not as strong as was once thought. But it may be that specific elements of the Type A pattern, such as anger or hostility, will predict CHD better than global Type A scores.

■ Other dispositions such as hardiness, optimism, self-efficacy, and ego-control and ego-resiliency may help inoculate some individuals against undue stress. Certain motives and a sense of personal control may likewise be important here.

■ Additional risk factors for stress-related illnesses include: age, gender, socioeconomic and ethnic factors, and a variety of behaviors such as smoking, overeating, excessive alcohol and drug use, lack of exercise, and the like.

■ Behavioral medicine is an interdisciplinary field that is showing rapid growth. It involves the treatment of health-related problems that have arisen in part from chronic stress or faulty behaviors. It also includes programs designed to prevent problems from occurring in the first place. Other features include measures intended to assist people in coping with medical procedures or in following medical or other therapeutic advice.

CHAPTER 16

PERCEIVED CONTROL

A four-year-old struggles to get his jacket zipped. He tries time and time again but is so far from being successful that his efforts border on the ludicrous. Being a kind person, you step in and reach down to help him. He howls in anger and screams, "I can do it myself!"

A seventy-five-year-old widow is so frail and ill that she just cannot continue to live alone; she must move to a senior citizens' enclave. As her son labors to explain this to her, she breaks into sobs and then demands to be allowed to take care of herself.

A passenger in the front seat of a car is on pins and needles. Each time they approach another car, she presses her foot hard against the floorboard. She repeatedly warns the driver about traffic to the left and traffic to the right. After a few minutes of this the driver is ready to throw her out of the car.

An executive works constantly; there is never enough time to get everything done. He comes early for appointments, denies ever being fatigued, and becomes hostile whenever he is thwarted in some activity. If ever there was a Type A personality, it is he.

What do these four people all have in common? They all want to be in control! They react emotionally when blocked in their efforts to remain in control. In the last twenty-five years, this topic has surged to the point where it is one of the leading research areas in personality. As a result of all this research, it has become apparent that lack of perceived control can mediate a host of reactions from depression and apathy to anger and aggression. It can produce an entire litany of stress reactions. To be in control and to maintain mastery over one's circumstances can be regarded as a basic human motive (Rodin, Timko, and Harris, 1986). In this sense, control reflects a need. But it can also be regarded as an expectancy—a belief that one's behavior is or is not responsible for the consequences that follow from it (Phares, 1976). But whether expectancy or need, control is a most powerful variable indeed. This chapter should help make some of the reasons for this clear.

IMPORTANCE OF PERCEIVED CONTROL

There are many practical and theoretical reasons why control is so important for us all. Let us examine some of them now.

Inability to find a job after repeated efforts can lead to a feeling of lack of personal control.

Control of outcomes

Most of us are basically hedonistic organisms. We try to maximize our pleasures and minimize our pain. Of course, we do not blindly engage in orgies of self-gratification because we normally learn that doing so results eventually in punishment, pain, rejection, and the like. Most of us also learn early and quickly that when we are not in control, the chances of achieving valued goals are reduced. An authoritarian government, an overcontrolling set of parents, or a highly unpredictable environment—all threaten our ability to gain satisfactions and avoid pain. We opened this chapter with four examples of lack of control. Consider the following additional examples:

- A subject in an experiment is told that a painful electric shock may be delivered whenever a red light comes on. But the contingency is completely unpredictable.

- After three tests during the first half of the semester, it finally dawns on a student that the instructor's exams are so difficult that nothing he does will enable him to pass the course. He wishes he could drop the course but cannot.

- An unemployed worker tries repeatedly for six months to find work. But nothing she does seems to pay off.

All of these people are trapped in circumstances where the exercise of personal control is minimized. The circumstances also reduce the likelihood that the person will be able to achieve gratification or ward off pain. The subject will be shocked, the student will flunk, and the worker will not be able to support her family. A contingency between behavior and outcomes simply does not exist. Of course, there are those occasional examples where the foregoing reasoning will not apply. If I cannot drive, I will hardly wish control of the car. If I have accepted my extremely severe physical limitations, I will hardly want personal control where it could actually be injurious to my health. When exceptions occur, then, they arise out of the recognition that personal control will actually interfere with the attainment of valued outcomes. Knowing when to exercise control and when to abandon it is difficult and could lead to a paraphrase of the old prayer:

> Please, God, grant me the strength to exercise control when it can be productive, the willingness to abandon control when it will be unproductive, and the wisdom to tell the difference between the two situations.

Theoretical views

Personal control and predictability of events are not the sole concern of laypeople. As we saw in Chapters 6 and 7, Kelly (1955) regarded the use of personal constructs to be one of enhancing our ability to predict, control, and understand our world. Likewise, Robert W. White (1959), in discussing the motivating properties of competence, views personal control as something that will increase our feelings of satisfaction. Lerner (1970) has argued that people become quite uncomfortable when events suggest that the world is either uncontrollable or unpredictable. To avoid such feelings, they will try very hard to view the world as a just place where no one is a victim and people get what they deserve. For example, victims of random violence are seen as somehow at fault. They should have stayed in their own neighborhoods where they belong. To see them as just unlucky threatens us by suggesting that the same event could touch our lives. Finally, in the field of attribution theory, control is viewed as an important key to the ways in which people judge their experience. The point of trying to determine the causes of various events is to allow the perceiver to determine the regularities in the world that make it a predictable, controllable place in which to live (Heider, 1958). Similarly, Harold Kelley (1971) states that we make attributions of causality not for the sheer joy of it but as a way of increasing our knowledge so that we can better manage our environment.

Need for control

In the foregoing instances, control was important because it was seen as enhancing the probability of attaining satisfactions or avoiding punishments through an increased ability to predict our world. As noted earlier, for some, the desire for control is viewed as basic human motive (Rodin et al., 1986). Thus, control becomes an end in and of itself—not just something that leads to "good" outcomes. Whether this desire is inborn, learned, or, to use Allport's term, has merely become functionally autonomous, there it is.

Several studies have illustrated how this desire for control can operate. For example, Burger, Oakman, and Bullard (1983) required subjects to work on tasks in a small, crowded room. Subjects with a strong desire for control perceived the room as especially crowded and seemed to feel their control over the situation was restricted. Also, individuals who are high in desire for control have been shown as less likely to conform to a norm or to respond to information merely by agreeing with others (Burger, 1987). People who desire control have also demonstrated a variety of achievement behaviors (Burger, 1985). This is shown in Table 16-1 along with some of the benefits and liabilities that go along with strong or weak desires for control. Finally, people high in their desire for control also seem to demonstrate their need by controlling the flow of conversations (Burger, 1990).

Others believe that people have a general desire to regard themselves as causal agents—they want to be "origins" of events rather than "pawns" (deCharms, 1968). In the field of social psychology, Brehm (1966) identified what he termed **psychological reactance.** This is a response that can occur when a formerly available choice is eliminated or threatened in some fashion. Many individuals will respond in such circumstances with an increased desire to engage in that very behavior. In short, assail my sense of personal control by telling me I cannot do something and I will want to do it all the more!

CONSEQUENCES OF DIMINISHED CONTROL

There are many gradations of lack of control. The trivial examples are perhaps little more than annoyances. But an utter lack of personal control can lead to a sense of helplessness that is so devastating that it may even end in death (Seligman, 1975). Bruno Bettelheim (1943) recounted some of the unspeakable crimes visited upon prisoners in the Nazi death camps during World War II. He described prisoners who came to believe what their guards said—that release was impossible and death inevitable. They

TABLE 16-1 *Relationship between desire for control and achievement-related behaviors.*

Desire for Control (DC) Status	Aspiration Level	Response to Challenge	Persistence	Attributions for Success and Failure
Theoretical Relationship with High DC as Compared with Low DC	Select harder tasks; Set goals more realistically	React with greater effort	Work at difficult task longer	More likely to attribute success to self and failure to unstable source
High-DC Benefit	Higher goals as achieved	Difficult tasks are completed	Difficult tasks are completed	Motivation level remains high
High-DC Liability	May attempt goals too difficult	May develop performance-inhibiting reactions	May invest too much effort	May develop an illusion of control

SOURCE: From Burger, J. M. (1985). Desire for control and achievement-related behavior. *Journal of Personality and Social Psychology, 48,* 1520–1533.

saw their environment as totally uncontrollable, and so there was no reason to pay attention to anything—even to life itself. It was then that death often bore down upon them. Lefcourt (1982) describes a psychiatric patient whose presumed lessened will to live seemed to bring about her sudden death. Being moved from an open ward back to a ward for chronic patients probably snuffed out the last flame of optimism. The same phenomenon has also been attributed to animals. For example, Richter (1957) discovered that wild rats will show a sudden death syndrome under certain conditions. These rats had been held in the experimenter's hand and also had had their whiskers trimmed. They were then placed in a vat of warm water. Normally, such wild rats would swim about for hours before becoming exhausted. The experimental animals, however, quickly gave up trying to swim and soon drowned. Richter concluded that the restraint and the trimming, along with being placed in the water, combined to produce a feeling of hopelessness in the rats.

The foregoing is but a brief sampling of the extensive observations that have been made on both animals and humans. The next topic, learned helplessness, is a widely investigated current topic that exemplifies some of the dangers of lack of perceived control.

Learned helplessness

In the mid-1960s, a group of experimental psychologists at the University of Pennsylvania was conducting a series of laboratory experiments on fear and conditioning with mongrel dogs (Seligman, 1975). They placed the dogs in a restraining harness and then exposed them to a series of painful though not physically harmful electric shocks. The critical thing, however, was that the shocks were completely uncontrollable. No matter what the dogs did, the shocks would occur—they were totally independent of the dogs' behavior. Next, the dogs were put in what is called a shuttle box, a two-sided chamber designed so that a dog can jump over a barrier or fence from one side to the other and thereby escape from the shock. If the dog jumps before the onset of the shock, no shock will occur. What Seligman and his colleagues observed was unusual and resulted in a series of studies on what has come to be called **learned helplessness.**

> When placed in a shuttle box, an experimentally naive dog, at the onset of the first electric shock, runs frantically about until it accidentally scrambles over the barrier and escapes the shock. On the next trial, the dog, running frantically, crosses the barrier more quickly than on the preceding trial; within a few trials it becomes very efficient at escaping, and soon learns to avoid shock altogether. After about fifty trials the dog becomes nonchalant and stands in front of the barrier; at the onset of the signal for shock it leaps gracefully across and never gets shocked again.
>
> A dog that had first been given inescapable shock showed a strikingly different pattern. This dog's first reactions to shock in the shuttle box were much the same as those of a naive dog: it ran around frantically for about thirty seconds. But then it stopped moving; to our surprise, it lay down and quietly whined. After one minute of this we turned the shock off; the dog had failed to cross the barrier and had not escaped from shock. On the next trial, the dog did it again; at first it struggled a bit, and then, after a few seconds, it seemed to give up and to accept the shock passively. On all succeed-

ing trials, the dog failed to escape. This is the paradigmatic learned-helplessness finding. (Seligman, 1975, p. 22)

This program of research leaves little doubt that in animals, experience with an uncontrollable aversive stimulus leads to the expectation that escape is impossible. This expectation then generalizes to succeeding situations and serves as the basis for learned helplessness. The critical question is whether the learned helplessness model is useful way to look at various aspects of human behavior. Evidence such as that produced by Hiroto and Seligman (1975) suggests that it is. In a complex design, college students were subjected to inescapable, aversive noise and then tested later on a cognitive problem-solving task that was quite distinct from the original learning task. It was found that subjects displayed a definite decrement in performance on the second task as a result of their earlier helplessness training. From these results, Hiroto and Seligman concluded that there is generality to learned helplessness.

To sum up Seligman's (1975) explanation of learned helplessness, there are three major components: (1) experience with uncontrollable events depletes the individual's motivation to behave in a way that might, in certain situations, actually influence events; (2) previous experience with uncontrollable events reduces the individual's ability to learn that many events can, to some degree, be controlled through appropriate behavior; (3) repeated experiences with uncontrollable events lead to depression. More recently, Seligman has added a fourth component. He now argues that individuals may attribute their helplessness to themselves or to the specific nature of the situation (Abramson, Seligman, and Teasdale, 1978). Learned helplessness will result when the attribution is to personal factors rather than to external or situational ones.

Learned helplessness has become a very popular concept. At first it represented a rather direct generalization of animal research to human beings. As a result, the initial formulations of the model were somewhat naive in that they failed to recognize the truly complex, cognitive nature of humans. Then, too, laboratory studies of learned helplessness such as those of Hiroto and Seligman have not always been replicated (e.g., Cole and Coyne, 1977). In addition, some have suggested that the behavioral deficits observed by Seligman and others are not the result of learned helplessness but rather the outcome of frustration and hostility (e.g. Boyd, 1982). Learned helplessness has also been proposed as a major explanation for the depressions observed in clinical samples of neurotic and psychotic patients (Seligman, 1975). Others, however, regard chronic depressions in humans as complexly determined by several different factors (Costello, 1978).

Increasingly, Seligman's formulations of learned helplessness have become more cognitive. For example, some children habitually explain bad things that happen to them in global terms that are not specific to the situation at hand. Their explanations tend to be stable over time and self-oriented. Such children are much more likely to develop depressive symptoms than ones who make causal attributions differently. Thus, the critical thing is not so much events as the style we use to explain them. Table 16-2 illustrates these various kinds of causal attributions.

The cognitive reformulation of the learned helplessness model is an improvement. Yet, it continues to produce confusing results. On the one hand, Alloy, Peterson,

Abramson, and Seligman (1984) have found support for the attributional reformulation. In contrast, Ford and Neale (1985) could not find evidence for expected cognitive deficits in subjects exposed to uncontrollable outcomes. Still others (e.g., Frankel and Snyder, 1978) argue that prolonged failure damages self-esteem so that individuals are less likely to try in the future and again risk failure. Mikulincer (1989) contends that people who habitually focus their attention inward are the ones most susceptible to debilitating reactions after failure. And if all this were not confusing enough, Zuroff (1980) has shown that we can easily reanalyze learned helplessness from the standpoint of Rotter's social learning theory. As is so often the case, then, the phenomenon of learned helplessness seems alive and well. But it is still subject to a variety of explanations.

Personal control and the elderly

People are living longer these days and, as a result, problems of the elderly are gaining in visibility. The elderly are especially vulnerable because so many factors challenge their sense of personal control (Rodin, 1986b). There is retirement, bereavement, and the ever-present decline in strength and vigor. There are also underlying physiological changes (e.g., immune system depression, decline in metabolism of certain hormones, increase in chronic illness) that enhance their vulnerability. Virtually every facet of the aging process relates to health, maintenance of well-being, cognitive functioning, or just plain feeling good about oneself. And attitudes of personal control are implicated in every one of them (Baltes and Baltes, 1986).

E. J. Langer (1981) has suggested that much of what often is regarded as senility in elderly people is really a response to an environment that has robbed them of the

---

TABLE 16-2 *Samples of several types of causal attributions*

	Explanation	
Style	*Internal*	*External*
Stable		
Global	"I'm incapable of doing anything right"	"All institutions chronically make mistakes"
Specific	"I always have trouble figuring my balance"	"This bank has always used antiquated techniques"
Unstable		
Global	"I've had the flu for a few weeks, and I've let everything slide"	"Holiday shopping demands that one throw oneself into it"
Specific	"The one time I didn't enter a check is the one time my account gets overdrawn"	"I'm surprised—my bank has never made an error before"

SOURCE: From "Causal Explanations as a Risk Factor for Depression: Theory and Evidence" by C. Peterson and M. E. P. Seligman, 1984, *Psychological Review, 91,* p. 349. Copyright 1984 by the American Psychological Association. Reprinted by permission.

One of the dangerous aspects of growing old is a growing sense that personal control is waning. Photograph Fusco/Magnum.

opportunity to exert personal control. Take the research by Langer and Rodin (1976), for example. These investigators studies two groups of elderly residents in a New England nursing home. Ages ranged from sixty-five to ninety. Members of the experimental group were shown in some detail how they possessed a great deal of personal responsibility in their day-to-day lives. They could decide on their room arrangement, where they wished to meet visitors, and how they wanted to spend their time (reading, watching TV, visiting, etc.). They were urged to report any complaints about their situation to the staff so that changes could be made. They could also choose whether to attend movies and on which night. Finally, each resident was given a living plant to care for. The comparison group was given instructions covering the same points, but in each case the impression was left that everything was largely a matter of staff responsibility. They were told how eager the staff was to take care of them—even to the extent of caring for their plants.

Two questionnaires were administered. Each was given one week prior to the foregoing communication and again three weeks afterward. The first questionnaire dealt with the residents' feelings of personal control, and how happy and how active they were. The second questionnaire was filled out by the nurses. Items asked for ratings of how happy, alert, dependent, sociable, and active each resident was. Other questions asked in what kind of activities the residents engaged each week and for how long. There were also several behavioral ratings made by the staff, such as how often each resident went to the movies or to the occupational therapy room, joined in group activities, or generally was active. It might also be noted that neither the staff nor the nurses who made the ratings were aware that an experiment was underway.

Virtually all before-after items showed differences in favor of the experimental group. That is, even though the two groups had initially been matched on variables such as health, residents in the experimental group were more alert, happy, and generally felt better three weeks later than did the comparison group. Staff ratings of improvement and activity levels followed a similar pattern.

These results were exceptional in themselves. But also suggestive were the findings of a follow-up study conducted eighteen months later by Rodin and Langer (1977). Only half as many experimental subjects (seven out of forty-seven) had died as had subjects in the comparison group (thirteen out of forty-four). This finding is, however, only marginally significant statistically. In addition, the positive benefits of the original personal control instructions continued to be visible.

While the results of Rodin and Langer illustrate that an intervention designed to heighten a sense of perceived control can produce positive effects that last over an eighteen-month period, there was also some decline in both groups. A certain amount of such decline is to be expected in aging individuals such as these. The important thing, however, is that the rate of decline seems to have been slowed by showing these elderly residents that they do possess control over some important aspects of their lives.

A study by R. Schulz (1976) reinforces these results. He studied several groups of elderly subjects (ages sixty-seven to ninety-six) who were living in a church-affiliated retirement home in North Carolina. The experimental manipulation involved visits by undergraduates. There were four conditions under which the visits took place:

■ The residents had complete control over the duration and frequency of the visits.

■ The residents knew when the visitor would come but could not actually control the timing or duration of the visit.

■ The residents received visits in the same pattern as in the first condition. However, they could not control frequency or duration. The visits appeared to be random.

■ The residents received no visits at all.

Results of this experiment showed that when residents could either control or predict their visits by the undergraduates, their health status, psychological condition, and activity level were all significantly better as compared to residents who were visited randomly or received no visits at all. However, a follow-up to this study raises some important theoretical and ethical issues (see Box 16-1).

On the brighter side, it has been found that even elderly nursing home residents can be taught skills that enhance their sense of personal control (Rodin, 1983). These skills also dramatically increase their problem-solving behavior and at the same time reduce feelings of stress. Even eighteen months later improvements in health are still apparent.

It has long been recognized that financial strain is one of the greatest sources of stress among the elderly. But Krause (1987b) has shown that when elderly individuals

believe that the locus of control resides within them, they are significantly less susceptible to the stress effects of poor finances.

Personal control and health care

The last chapter touched upon topics of stress, control, and health. Therefore, it should
come as no surprise to discover that recent years have seen a growing trend toward
involving patients in their own health care. In the case study on page 482 we can see
a reflection of this movement. Some doctors are authoritarian and try to thrust a passive role upon their patients. Others see to it that their patients are informed and active
participants in their own treatment. For example, Krantz (1980) has argued that providing
information to a cardiac patient can help lessen threat. Also, providing patients with
options in their lives can likewise reduce the threat, as can arranging the environment
to allow patients a measure of personal control.

To illustrate specifically how reduction in threat can work, consider a study by
Johnson and Leventhal (1974). Subjects were hospitalized medical patients who were
required to undergo a very threatening endoscopic examination that involves swallowing a tube. Patients were provided with detailed information that was designed to reduce their emotional reactions and to facilitate behaviors on their part that would reduce
the dangers inherent in the endoscopic procedures. Such information was successful
in facilitating desirable patient reactions and illustrates the importance of involving patients in medical interventions by preparing them cognitively.

Not only can threat be reduced by a sense of personal control, depression can also
be lessened. For example, in the case of newly diagnosed cancer patients, it has been
found that the relationship between severity of illness and degree of depression is weaker
in patients who believe they can personally control their health (Marks, Richardson,
Graham, and Levine, 1986).

Lest you be left with the impression that it is always better to sensitize patients
with information and coping strategies, a reminder is in order. There are individual
differences in the way people characteristically deal with threat. Some use denial, and
will therefore become even more threatened by too much information about their illness. Others are what might be called fatalistic and are not likely to pay attention to
instructions on how to help care for themselves. To ignore these individual differences
in how the causes of illness are categorized or how threat is dealt with is to reduce
the effectiveness of intervention strategies. A great deal more will be said about generalized individual differences in personal control later in this chapter. However, in the
context of health care several scales have been developed to measure these individual
differences. There is, for example, the **Krantz Health Opinion Survey** (Krantz, Baum,
and Wideman, 1980). This scale was designed to measure preferences for (1) self-
treatment and active involvement in one's health care and (2) information about health
care. Similarly, Wallston, Wallston, Kaplan, and Maides (1976) have developed the
Health Locus of Control Scale to better predict health-related behavior. Each of these
instruments is based on the premise that recognition of individual differences is important in recommending effective programs. Table 16-3 (page 485) presents several items
from the Krantz Health Opinion Survey.

Box 16-1
LONG-TERM EFFECTS OF INTERVENTIONS: FINDINGS AND ETHICS

To determine whether the positive effects noted in the R. Schulz (1976) study would persist beyond the conclusion of the experiment, Schulz and Hanusa (1978) conducted a follow-up. They returned to the retirement home used in the first study and reevaluated all forty subjects used in that study. Health and psychological data were collected twenty-four, thirty, and forty-two months after the close of the initial study. The results were both startling and dismaying. For one thing, no positive long-term effects of the control-predictability visitation interventions could be demonstrated. Even more surprising was the finding that the two groups which had initially benefited from the interventions exhibited precipitous *declines* in both health status and "zest for life" once the first study was over (see the figure).

These results raise several important issues. First of all, in trying to increase someone's sense of personal control, we should be careful not to use inherently unstable interventions. That is, visits such as those used in this study cannot go on forever. Thus, personal control is tied to agents who in reality cannot be completely controlled or predicted by the subject. When the visits cease abruptly, the subject must find an explanation. The explanation may be that what was thought to be personal control was really an illusion. And facing an illusion may be a shattering experience that not only wipes out all the gains formerly achieved but pushes the individual even farther toward apathy and gloom. If this is so, then the second issue becomes an ethical one. Does such research actually harm the participants? In the present example, is it responsible research to allow bonds of friendship between visitors and residents to develop only to be terminated in the name of research design? Is it responsible to build a sense of control only to remove it later? These are crucial issues that each experimenter must answer—especially in field settings. Fortunately, Schulz and Hanusa had the presence of mind and the courage to raise these questions about their own work. By doing so, they have provided a service and a reminder to us all.

The fact that Rodin and Langer (1977) did not encounter similar adverse long-term effects in their research is probably explained by the nature of the interventions they used. The sense of control they induced was probably less dependent on another figure (visitor) and more directly related to the residents' own efforts.

Box 16-1 *continued*

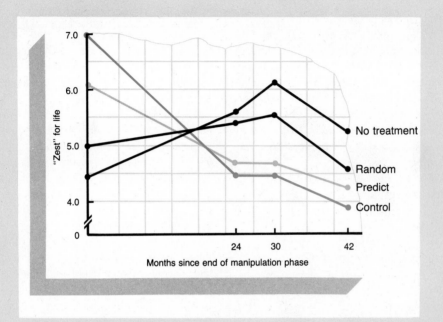

Mean *"zest for life" data at four different points in time.* Patients were rated on zest for life along a 9-point scale. Point 0 along the horizontal axis indicates the status of the residents at the conclusion of the first study. Points 24, 30, and 42 refer to months after the first study, at which time follow-up data were collected. (From "Long-term Effects of Control and Predictability-enhancing Interventions: Findings and Ethical Issues" by R. Schulz and B. H. Hanusa, *Journal of Personality and Social Psychology,* 1978, *36,* 1194–1201. Copyright 1978 by the American Psychological Association. Reprinted by permission.)

CASE STUDY

Personal Responsibility for Treatment

What exactly are the effects of exerting choice or sensing that personal control and responsibility still exist in our lives? Consider the words of Norman Cousins, formerly editor of the *Saturday Review,* whose personal bout with a supposedly irreversible illness led him to campaign for the importance of personal responsibility:

For the past three years I have been studying some forty patients who have recovered from supposedly irreversible illnesses.

A case history from the group may be instructive at this point. It concerns a man, forty-two, married and the father of two children. He had lost his job as an assistant plant manager after sixteen years with the same firm. It was the first time in his life he had been unemployed. He suffered a loss of self-confidence, reflected in increased tensions inside the family. He became morose and found it difficult to approach prospective employers. After three months, he developed a pain in his left hip. It became increasingly severe. Cancer cells were found in the hip. The precise extent of the spread of the cancer could not be determined, but there was no doubt in the mind of the specialist that metastasis had already taken place.

The patient was given an unadorned report. The effect was one of emotional devastation. He knew the cancer was spreading. There was no assurance it could be arrested. The radiation treatment caused his hair to fall out. The chemotherapy produced severe nausea and dizziness. All his savings were rapidly used up by medical and hospital expenses not covered by insurance. He could feel himself falling ever more deeply into a pit.

He decided to find out whether other people recovered under similar circumstances. He read the medical and popular literature. He found his way to a group called "We Can Do," an organization of cancer survivors founded by Barbara Coleman of Los Angeles, herself a cancer sufferer. The most important thing he learned is that members of the group had decided that they wanted to live, that they would not allow themselves to feel defeated, that they were going to experience joy and all the things that made life worth living, and that they were going to prove the experts wrong.

He said he could feel himself breathing more deeply and experiencing a surge of energy just in listening to the "We Can Do" members. He had no difficulty in adopting the same course for himself. This decision had some immediate results. First, when he took the chemotherapy he "programmed" himself for a good result. That is, instead of expecting adverse effects, he visualized the process by which his body would derive maximum benefits from the medication. He was delighted with the reduced nausea and other adverse effects.

He assured his family that he was now on high ground and would come through. He took genuine pleasure in his family life.

Case continued

He knew that money matters, however pressing, were actually secondary. He forced himself to do physical things. His appetite was better. He was able to sleep through the night. After two months, X-rays confirmed the retreat of his cancer. There is still some pain in the hip but it is significantly less than it was at the time of the original diagnosis and it is diminishing all the time. The oncologist now predicts a sustained remission.

What this case and others like it seem to indicate is that treatment for any disease has twin requirements. One is the availability of the best that medical science has to offer. The other is that the patient himself or herself become fully involved in the recovery effort. Brain research is now turning up evidence that attitudes have biochemical effects. Attitudes of defeat or panic will constrict the blood vessels and have a debilitating effect on the entire endocrine system. Attitudes of confidence and determination activate benevolent and therapeutic secretions in the brain.

Obviously, we can't expect to live forever. We can't expect that every disease will be reversed. But we can get the most out of whatever is possible. We can give it our best shot. Not until then do predictions mean anything. (1982, p. 12)

Perception of control

The reality of the control situation is probably not as important as our subjective experience or perception of control. When the individual *believes* that control is lost or that predictability is impossible, a number of important consequences are possible. In the following pages, we will review some of these potential outcomes. But whether we can or cannot actually exert control is not as important as what we think. That is why the title of this chapter is "Perceived Control."

E. J. Langer (1975) has discussed what she calls the "illusion of control." This exists when people believe that they exert control over what is really a chance-determined event. A good example is choosing a lottery number on which to bet. By making this choice, the individual often erroneously comes to believe that control is being exerted over the ultimate outcome of the bet. Burger (1986) has also found that people with a strong desire to control events are more susceptible to the illusion of control. In a sense, the illusion of control is the inverse of learned helplessness. In certain specific cases, it may prove a therapeutic kind of belief. It may be a way of stimulating changes in a person's life and, more specifically, improve the well-being of residents in homes for the elderly as well as patients in hospitals. At the same time, it is important to remember that the illusion of control can backfire. And when it does, a whole new set of problems is generated.

Another facet of perceived control is the tendency for people to exaggerate the degree of control they possess when outcomes are positive. This means that people take more credit for good outcomes than they probably deserve. It is almost as if by so doing they can enhance their self-regard (Wright, Zautra, and Braver, 1985).

Box 16-2
THE LEGACY OF KARL S

This case, first described by Phares (1976), concerned an unmarried male veteran whom we shall call Karl S. He had been referred for psychotherapy by a Veterans Administration official. Therapy was conducted within the general framework of Rotter's (1954) social learning theory (see Chapter 12).

As therapy proceeded, it became evident that Karl's problems were not of the typical neurotic variety. There were no unconscious forces about to burst into consciousness nor were there many of the classical symptoms that fill the pages of psychiatric textbooks. He was sometimes anxious, and a bit distressed. His main problem seemed to be an almost total lack of social and interpersonal skills. He was jobless and living off a small government pension.

Quickly, then, the focus of therapy became the development of techniques to help Karl find employment, enhance his education, and create at least a rudimentary set of social skills. Therapy turned into a teaching process, with the goals of helping him learn how to find a job, keep a job, talk with a woman, interest her, have dates, and so on. But progress was painfully slow. Even in those instances when Karl was successful, there appeared to be little effect on his subsequent behavior. This seemed strange. Normally, we assume that when a behavior is successful or leads to reinforcement, it grows in strength and will be more likely to occur again under similar circumstances. But for Karl, reinforcement seemed to have no effect.

At first, all of this was quite puzzling to the therapist. For example, after much coaching and discussion, Karl applied for a job and got it. But this did not raise his expectancies of being able to get another job should he have to do so. Indeed, he attributed his success entirely to good fortune. He believed that the employer probably was partial to veterans or just happened to be in a good mood that day. After several comparable episodes, it began to dawn upon the therapist that here was a person who believed that the occurrence of reinforcement was outside his own personal control. Once this belief system became clear, the failure of reinforcement to affect his expectancy for future reinforcement also came to make sense. Karl was not responding in defiance of learning theory. Rather, it was the therapist's conception of the learning process that was inadequate. The message in Karl's behavior was simple: reinforcement will "stamp in" a behavior but only when the individual perceives a causal link between the behavior and subsequent reinforcement. But without such a belief, the reinforcement that follows an act becomes an irrelevant piece of information—it carries no implications for the future. The riddle of Karl's behavior seemed to have been solved.

TABLE 16-3 Sample items from a scale measuring preferences regarding health care

---

From the Krantz Health Opinion Survey:

■ I'd rather have doctors and nurses make the decisions about what's best than for them to give me a whole lot of choices.

■ I usually ask the doctor or nurse lots of questions about the procedures during a medical exam.

■ It's always better to seek professional help than try to treat yourself.

■ It is better to rely less on physicians and more on your own common sense when it comes to caring for your body.

SOURCE: From "Assessment of Preferences for Self-Treatment and Information in Health Care" by D. S. Krantz, A. Baum, and M. V. Wideman, *Journal of Personality and Social Psychology,* 1980, *39,* 977–990. Copyright 1980 by the American Psychological Association. Reprinted by permission.

INTERNAL-EXTERNAL CONTROL OF REINFORCEMENT

We turn now to the question of individual differences in perceived control. Not everyone reacts to events with a sense of powerlessness. Instead, many persistently strive to grab events by the tail and twist them to their own purposes. It is as if certain people feel the outcomes of their efforts are controlled by forces and events external to themselves while others are convinced that control is an internal matter related to their own efforts or attributes. This is the so-called internal-external control of reinforcement notion which first emerged from Rotter's social learning theory in the mid-1950s. This has been a highly seminal concept that has led to much of the work in the broad area of perceived control. Interestingly, the initial stimulus for the concept came from a clinical case which is described briefly in Box 16-2.

Definition of I-E

Although a great deal of empirical research had to be done before the message described in Box 16-3 could be judged to have been confirmed, the basis for a very important concept had been uncovered. Referred to as both **internal-external control of reinforcement (I-E)** and **locus of control,** the concept was soon outlined systematically by Rotter (1966), who defined it as follows:

> When a reinforcement is perceived by the subject as following some action of his own but not being entirely contingent upon his action, then, in our culture, it is typically perceived as the result of luck, chance, fate, as under the control of powerful others, or as unpredictable because of the great complexity of the forces surrounding him.

When the event is interpreted in this way by an individual, we have labeled this a be-lief in *external control*. If the person perceived that the event is contingent upon his own behavior or his own relatively permanent characteristics, we have termed this a belief in *internal control*. (p. 1)

With Rotter's definition of the I-E variable, a whole new area of research opened with relevance to many individuals out there in society who, over the years, have been variously described as "powerless," "normless," "alienated," and "fatalistic." While it is easy to use the terms **internals** and **externals,** it should be understood that I-E is not a typology. Rather, it is a continuum and a person can fall anywhere along that continuum.

Since 1966, a truly amazing volume of research has been published on I-E. The studies now number in the thousands. Several books (e.g., Lefcourt, 1981, 1982; Phares, 1976) and chapters (e.g., Phares, 1978; Strickland, 1977) have summarized a good share of this work. A recent paper by Strickland (1989) provides an excellent over-view of the I-E field. Rotter (1990) has also commented on the extremely heuristic value of the I-E concept.

Theoretical foundation

From a social learning perspective, I-E is a generalized expectancy about how best to construe the nature of reinforcement (Rotter, Chance, and Phares, 1972). When faced with a problem situation, internals expect that construing the situation as one in which their efforts will make a difference will help them to resolve it. Externals, on the other hand, will behave on the basis of their expectations that chance or other uncontrollable factors are critical and will behave accordingly. Again, however, it should be recalled that people vary along the I-E dimension so that some are very internal, some quite external, and the majority somewhere in between.

Suppose, for example, that I have the opportunity to buy a new car. I go to Sellin' Sam's agency to check out the new models. What will be my expectancy that buying a car from Sam will lead to the reward of carefree driving for years to come? First of all, there is my specific experience with Sam in the past. Perhaps I bought a car from him earlier that turned out to be a lemon. If so, that experience may become the overriding consideration. But suppose I have no previous experience with Sam. Then, my expectancy that buying a car from him will lead to a happy experience will hinge on other factors. One factor is simply my generalized expectancy that I will be suc-cessful in the transaction. This is like a general self-confidence and operates across a wide band of situations. But also of importance will be a variety of problem-solving generalized expectancies. For example, perhaps I am generally not a very trusting per-son. This will lower my expectancy that dealing with Sam will be a useful experience. Or perhaps I am an externally controlled person, which may also tend to decrease my expectancy that buying a car will lead to a positive outcome. Whether I can trust peo-ple or whether the world is really a very capricious place are just two potential ways of construing the nature of this problem situation. This whole car-buying experience can be expressed by the following equation (Rotter, Chance, and Phares, 1972, p. 41):

$$E_{s_1} = \frac{f(E' \ \& \ GE_r \ \& \ GE_{ps_1} \ \& \ GE_{ps_2} \cdots GE_{ps_n})}{f(N_{s_1})}$$

This formula tells us that in Situation 1 (buying a car from Sam), my expectancy that a given reinforcement will occur (a successful buy) is determined by previous experience in the same situation (E'), experiences generalized from other, related situations (GE_r), and a variety of problem-solving generalized expectancies (GE_{ps_1}, . . . , GE_{ps_n}). The importance of the GE entries is determined by the number of previous experiences the individual has had in the specific situation (N_{s_1}). This latter point suggests that the effects of generalized expectancies are greatest when the person has had little prior experience in a given situation. Therefore, if I have dealt with Sam several times before, this experience will be more important than any generalized I-E beliefs I may have. This formula also reminds us that generalized I-E beliefs are only one factor in a complex set of factors that determine behavior. In fact, in some situations they may not be a very important one. This is why in our quest for successful prediction we must approach the task with a broad theoretical perspective that will systematically incorporate I-E along with other relevant concepts.

Measurement of I-E

Work on I-E began with research by Phares (1957). This was a simple study showing that subjects developed expectancies differently when they believed that success on a task was determined by skill rather than by chance factors. The essence of the results was that changes in expectancies following success or failure were greater under skill conditions than under chance conditions. A variety of other studies showed that the generalization and extinction of expectancies vary depending upon whether skill or chance situations are involved (see Phares, 1976). These studies corroborated in the laboratory what had been observed with Karl S in the clinic.

Laboratory work like the foregoing not only provided important clues as to how perceptions of control influence the role of reinforcement. It also increased our confidence that if specific skill (internal)—chance (external) conditions in the laboratory could produce detectably different outcomes, then the same thing may occur in real-life settings. That is, Karl S was probably not an anomaly at all but represented other chronic externals "out there" who show in their everyday behavior what had been produced by specific laboratory situations.

The **I-E Scale** (Rotter, 1966) was based upon earlier scales developed by Phares (1955) and James (1957). The final version was developed by Julian Rotter with the collaboration of his colleagues Shephard Liverant, Douglas Crowne, and Melvin Seeman. The I-E Scale consists of twenty-three forced-choice items, along with six filler items added to help disguise the purposes of the test. Table 16-4 lists some sample items.

The Rotter I-E Scale has been the most widely employed method of measurement for adults. It conceptualizes I-E as a broad, generalized factor. However, over the years increasing evidence has accumulated that I-E is not a unidimensional concept but is instead a multidimensional one consisting of several elements. It was not long after the publication of the I-E Scale that a variety of other measuring devices began to appear. Some were designed for children, others for adults. In some cases, a distinction was made between I-E beliefs about positive outcomes and those concerning negative outcomes. Some scales continued the tradition of measuring I-E in broad, general terms while others were designed to measure I-E in more specific life areas such as well-being or health. Many developments in measurement technology and research have been reviewed elsewhere (Lefcourt, 1981, 1982, 1984; Phares, 1976; Strickland, 1977).

I-E and behavior

Over the years, internals and externals have been shown to differ in many ways ranging from the ways they seek to gain information to the manner in which they respond to social influence. Consider the following:

Reactions to social influence.   A number of studies have accumulated to indicate that externals are more likely to be compliant and conforming than are internals. They are more persuasible and ready to accept information from others. As representative of the studies in this area we will consider the work of Ritchie and Phares (1969). These researchers asked college students to fill out a survey concerning their attitudes toward the national budget. About two weeks later, the students filled out the survey again. During the two-week interval, half the subjects had been presented arguments about expenditures attributed to a prestigious, nationally known economics authority. The other half received the same arguments attributed to an obscure graduate student in a small college. The two groups were matched in terms of their initial views on national expenditures. The results of the study are shown in Figure 16-1.

As expected, those students who had received external scores on the Rotter I-E Scale changed their attitudes more in response to a high-prestige source than to a low-

---

TABLE 16-4   *Items similar to those on the I-E Scale. These are drawn from unpublished preliminary versions of the 1966 scale.*

I more strongly believe that
1. a. Many people can be described as victims of circumstance.
   b. What happens to other people is pretty much of their own making.

2. a. Much of what happens to me is probably a matter of luck.
   b. I control my own fate.

3. a. The world is so complicated that I just cannot figure things out.
   b. The world is really complicated alright, but I can usually work things out by effort and persistence.

4. a. It is silly to think one can really change another's basic attitudes.
   b. When I am right I can convince others.

5. a. Most students would be amazed at how much grades are determined by capricious events.
   b. The marks I get in class are completely my own responsibility.

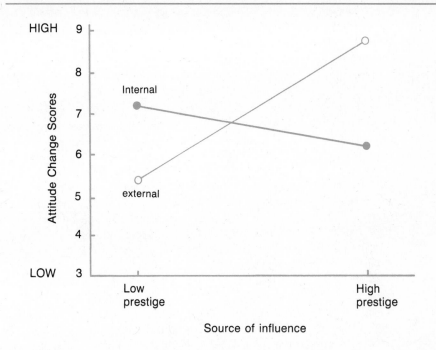

FIGURE 16-1   Attitude change as determined by I-E and prestige of the source of influence. (Adapted from Ritchie and Phares, 1969)

prestige source. They also changed more than internals when both received a high-prestige communication. In contrast, internals did not differ significantly in their responses to high- and low-prestige sources. These results suggest that externals are influenced by the prestige of a message's source whereas internals are more likely swayed by the actual content of the persuasive message regardless of the source.

Information seeking.   Perhaps the most influential difference between internals and externals lies in the ways they seek knowledge about their environment. Feeling that one is in control of the reinforcements that follow behavior should lead to greater efforts to acquire information about one's environment. This seems to be the single most consistent finding running throughout the I-E research literature. Very early, Melvin Seeman (1963) observed that prisoners in a reformatory who expressed internal beliefs were more knowledgeable than externals about reformatory policies and rules, parole regulations, and long-range economic facts that could affect their lives after release. Davis and Phares (1967) also found that when subjects believed they were going to be required to exert influence to change someone's attitudes about the war in Vietnam, internals made greater efforts to seek information about the other person's attitudes than did externals. They did this by asking more questions of the experimenter regarding the person's attitudes. This general finding held for subjects who were told that changing someone's attitudes was a matter of skill and also when no particular instructions were given. When subjects were told that attitude change is largely a matter of luck, there were no differences between internals and externals (although internals did ask fewer questions under this condition). These findings are shown in Figure 16-2. Prociuk and Breen (1977) reached similar conclusions in their work with students in a classroom setting. The same general theme is even apparent in the work of geographers who have observed that internals tend to be more aware of earthquake hazards in certain regions than are externals (Simpson-Housley and Bradshaw, 1978).

Social action.   In the early 1960s, civil rights in the United States had become a central issue in the national consciousness. As might be expected, black internals were found to be significantly more active than their external counterparts in undertaking social action to gain their civil rights. Both Gore and Rotter (1963) and Strickland (1965) found that activities such as taking "freedom rides" across southeastern states and aiding in voter registration were much more characteristic of black internals than black externals. But as time went on, the nature of social action began to change. And the nature of the I-E measuring devices also changed. For example, a distinction was made between personal control and system-blame. Blacks who believed in personal control (internals) were likely to engage in the traditional behaviors that lead to academic achievement and competence (Lao, 1970). But blacks who blamed the system for discrimination and repression (externals) were more likely to be involved in social action to change matters.

Achievement.   Given everything that has been said so far — internals are more likely to seek information, be resistant to social influence — one would certainly expect I-E differences in achievement behavior. A considerable body of research data appears to support this expectation (Lefcourt, 1982; Phares, 1976; Strickland, 1977). It seems fair to say that, on the whole, internality is directly related to achievement behavior. A review of 100 studies of locus of control and achievement revealed several interesting conclusions (Findley and Cooper, 1983):

■More internal beliefs are associated with greater academic achievement.

■The magnitude of the relationship ranges from small to medium

■The relationship is stronger for adolescents than for adults or children

■The relationship is stronger in males than in females

■The relationship is stronger when specific locus of control scales for academic situations are used and standardized tests of achievement are employed rather than teachers' grades

Attributions.   By definition, internals attribute to themselves the responsibility for the outcomes of their own behavior. Externals, in contrast, attribute that responsibility elsewhere. But how do internals and externals regard the behavior of others?

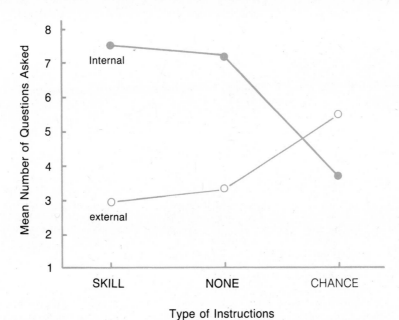

FIGURE 16-2 Number of questions asked as determined by I-E and kind of instructions (Adapted from Davis and Phares, 1967)

This is an important question since the extent to which we either blame or admire others for the consequences of their behavior could thereby be mediated by I-E beliefs. In general, it appears that internals and externals attribute responsibility to others in much the same way they do to themselves. For example, both Phares and Wilson (1972) and Sosis (1974) asked subjects to judge the responsibility for a series of automobile accidents described to them. In both studies, internals attributed more responsibility to the drivers and judged them more harshly. Likewise, Hochreich (1972) asked college students to react to the Vietnam incident at My Lai in which Vietnamese civilians were killed and for which the officer in charge, Lt. Calley, was court-martialed. External males responded by downplaying Lt. Calley's responsibility and, instead, attributing blame to the American government and military establishment. Such results underscore the fact that I-E beliefs not only affect the ways we regard our own behavior. They also help determine the manner in which we regard others. Since our treatment of others is directly influenced by the way we regard them, the importance of I-E beliefs becomes even more pervasive. For example, I-E has been shown to relate to the manner in which people offer help (see Chapter 18).

Health-related behavior.   If the tendency to seek information about one's surroundings and the desire to maintain personal control characterize internals, we would expect them to differ in important ways from externals in the area of health maintenance.

In general, the data bear out these expectations. Internals are more likely to show enhanced efforts to maximize their health and well-being and minimize illness. From a review by Strickland (1979), the following are some of the health-related behaviors or characteristics in which internals have been found to surpass externals (although the evidence is not always completely clear-cut):

▪ Information-seeking about health maintenance

▪ Precautionary health practices

▪ Greater knowledge of their own illnesses when stricken

▪ More positive attitudes about physical exercise

▪ Greater participation in physical activities

▪ Greater likelihood of refraining from smoking or of having given it up

▪ Some tendency to complete more successfully weight reduction programs

▪ Lessened susceptibility to essential hypertension and heart attacks

▪ Better prognoses once heart attacks occur

As was the case in our discussion earlier in this chapter regarding health care and personal control, it is important to recognize individual differences. Advice and treatment have to be tailored to meet the control expectancies of the individual. Lau and Ware (1981) have developed a specific locus of control inventory to measure beliefs about self-control over health. Lau (1982) has investigated how individual differences in these health locus of control beliefs arise. Thus far, it appears that practicing a variety of health habits as a child is important, as is experience with sickness in one's family.

Adjustment and I-E

Research on I-E began in the context of the problems being experienced by a patient in therapy. A major focus of I-E research has continued to be on the relationship between I-E beliefs and adjustment. This research has consistently revealed that internals are better adjusted, less anxious, and less likely to be classified with psychiatric labels than are externals (Phares, 1976, 1978). It is possible that the active, self-reliant qualities of the internal lead to the kind of successes that promote adjustment. Or perhaps simply believing that one's own destiny is under personal control results in a better level of adjustment which then retards the growth of anxiety. Since most of the data in this research area are correlational, it is very difficult to disentangle cause from effect. One can argue that external beliefs promote anxiety, but then perhaps anxiety stimulates a certain amount of externality.

Coping.   Some have contended that an internal orientation is the one disposition that most consistently acts to lessen the effects of stressful events (Cohen and Edwards, 1989). The evidence for this may be a bit equivocal. But if is is, the reason may be because, as suggested by Phares (1976), *extreme* internals may be so racked by guilt over every little failure that their coping efforts are effectively neutralized (Krause and

Stryker, 1984). Less extreme internals are probably more adept at employing effective and diverse schema to solve problems than their extreme internal brethren who are so tuned into their failures.

Parkes (1984) has suggested that the patterns internals use to cope with stress are more adaptive than those employed by externals. This would lead, over the long haul, to the better adjustment on the part of internals noted in so many studies. Some examples of adaptive and maladaptive responses noted by Parkes are shown in Table 16-5.

Internal control—the best orientation? Given the foregoing it must surely be better to operate with an internal orientation. Perhaps not. Wolk and Kurtz (1975) found that in a noninstitutionalized population of elderly individuals, internality was associated with adjustment and feelings of satisfaction. But they wondered how an institutionalized internal individual might feel. That is, being in a place where opportunities for personal control are hard to come by might require an especially difficult adjustment for an internal. Indeed, it could be argued that an external belief system would be more adaptive under such circumstances. And that is exactly what Felton and Kahana (1974) found with an elderly institutionalized population. Therefore, whether it is "good" to be internally or externally oriented will vary with the situation.

As Burger (1989) has observed, sometimes a sense of control brings with it a corresponding sense of responsibility. This can generate a lot of stress and, as noted above by Phares (1976), can interfere with coping efforts. It is bad enough when anyone holds low expectancies that valued goals can be achieved. But when this is accompanied by a strong sense of personal responsibility, the situation can become doubly stressful. In the next section we will see how some in this situation may react to reduce that stress.

TABLE 16-5 *Examples of adaptive and maladaptive coping strategies in the face of stress*

+	1.	Got professional help and did what they recommended.
+	2.	Made a plan of action and followed it.
+	3.	Just took things one step at a time.
+	4.	Rediscovered what is important in life.
−	5.	Hoped a miracle would happen.
−	6.	Wished that the situation would go away, or be over with.
−	7.	Blamed myself.
−	8.	Tried to make myself feel better by eating, drinking, smoking, taking medication, etc.

+ = adaptive

− = maladpative

SOURCE: Adapted from "Locus of Control, Cognitive Appraisal, and Coping in Stressful Episodes" by K. R. Parkes, 1984, *Journal of Personality and Social Psychology, 46,* 655–668.

Role of defensiveness in external beliefs

For a long time there has been speculation that there are, in fact, two kinds of externals (Phares, 1978, 1979; Rotter, 1966). **Congruent externals** are those who for realistic reasons have come to appraise their world as externally controlled. Perhaps they have been raised under deprived socioeconomic conditions with little access to power or upward mobility. Or perhaps their childhood experiences in the family were chaotic and unpredictable. Whatever the reasons, their I-E beliefs tend to square closely with the reality they have experienced. **Defensive externals,** on the other hand, are people who espouse external beliefs as a defense against anticipated failures. They have low expectancies for success and rationalize both their potential and real failures by attributing them to forces beyond their control. To a certain extent, an external orientation lends itself to the adoption of this rationalizing posture, as Phares and Lamiell (1974) have shown. Basgall and Snyder (1988) have noted a similar phenomenon in their study of excuses.

Several methods have been employed in identifying these defensive externals. For example, D. E. Davis (1970) defined them as individuals who receive external scores on the I-E Scale but who, at the same time, indicate a preference for action-taking strategies on a second questionnaire. Thus, on the one hand they express external beliefs but on the other seem to embrace an action orientation as would be expected from an internal. Defensive externals have also been identified as those who score high on externality but low in interpersonal trust (Hochreich, 1974).

Several studies have supported the utility of distinguishing between defensive and congruent externals. For example, Hochreich (1974) found that male defensive externals were less likely than either congruent externals or internals to attribute personal blame to individuals who were described as having failed in achievement situations. Lloyd and Chang (1979) discovered that defensive externals assume responsibility for their own success but not for their failures whereas congruent externals do not vary in their attributions. Like Hochreich's results, this suggests a definite reluctance on the part of defensive externals to take responsibility for own failures. Evans's (1982) work on persistence showed that defensive externals are more like internals than they are congruent externals. Such a finding supports the utility of the congruent-defensive distinction.

Origins of I-E beliefs

A moment ago it was observed that some external beliefs seem to arise out of the need to rationalize real or expected failures. There are, of course, other potential antecedents of I-E beliefs. However, it seems fair to assert that thus far research has, in general, been more successful in identifying the consequences of I-E beliefs than in determining the causes of those same beliefs.

Family antecedents.   In some general fashion, child-rearing practices that can be characterized as warm, protective, positive, and nurturant seem to be related to the subsequent development of an internal locus of control in the child (e.g., Davis and

Phares, 1969; Katkovsky, Crandall, and Good, 1967). But there are exceptions to these findings. Furthermore, the exact manner in which such child-rearing practices produce internality is far from clear even though some general social modeling of I-E beliefs surely occurs (Rotter, 1966). Indeed, there is the likelihood that the child's I-E beliefs may, to some extent, reflect parents' own attitudes about locus of control (Chandler, Wolf, Cook, and Dugovics, 1980).

Consistency of experience. When a child is subjected to inconsistent parental discipline, either by one parent or between parents, a basis might be laid for the perception that the world is capricious and unpredictable. In support of this, Davis and Phares (1969) found that externals tend to report their parents as inconsistent in their discipline more often than do internals. Similarly, Shore (1967) and W. L. Davis (1969) have indicated that externals have experienced a larger discrepancy in child-rearing attitudes between their parents than have internals.

Social antecedents. It would seem entirely plausible that individuals who, for whatever reasons, enjoy little access to power, social mobility, opportunity, or material advantages would be predisposed toward an external belief system. Their cumulative experience would teach them that their own efforts have little to do with their achievement in society. In general, a review of the research (Phares, 1976) is supportive of this expectation. Minority groups and those from lower socioeconomic levels do tend to be more external than white, middle-class individuals. However, as in the case of familial origins, the exact way in which all this is learned is still unclear. Because most of the research is correlational, what is cause and what is effect is not always evident. It is also important to note that while subjects may respond to general I-E measures in an external way, they may still manifest internal beliefs in specific areas of their lives. For example, a young black may learn as he leaves the family and confronts the white-dominated society for the first time exactly how powerless he really is. Nevertheless, he may well have internal beliefs when it comes to holding his own in an athletic contest against his peers.

The aging process. Do people become more external as they grow older? One might think so given that many elderly people must increasingly confront problems over which they have less and less control—health problems, shrinking income, growing cognitive deficits, and the like. But then one could argue that the elderly were raised in a more "internal era" when people felt they really had control over their lives. The young, in contrast, exist in a world marked by stress, bureaucracy, threat of war, and so on. Over the years, the research has sent mixed signals on this question. Recently, however, Lachman (1986) has reviewed this evidence and provided some data of her own. What she found is that on broad, generalized I-E scales such as Rotter's, few age differences in I-E beliefs are found. However, when specific I-E measures that relate to beliefs about intelligence and health are used, older individuals are found to be more external than are younger ones.

Gender differences in I-E

Generally speaking, most studies have reported similar I-E mean scores for male and female populations. On the other hand, Hochreich (1975) asked college students to complete the I-E Scale as if they were a "super male" or a "super female." Both male and female subjects presenting themselves as males showed highly internal scores. In contrast, instructions to respond in the feminine role produced very external scores. To explore further the issue of gender differences in I-E scores, Strickland and Haley (1980) examined patterns of responses on the I-E Scale. They discovered that on certain items, males and females respond differently. Thus, while it may be true that overall I-E scores are little different for males and females, their patterns of responses are not the same. For example, items dealing with attitudes about political influence revealed females to be more internal than males. At the same time, items related to academic achievement showed males to be more internal than females.

Concluding observations

It will do no harm to reiterate two warnings that Rotter (1975) has made regarding the use of the I-E variable in prediction. First, internals can be expected to be more active in seeking information or in generally pursuing their goals. But before an internal does these things, he or she must value the goal involved. Internals, for example, will not sign a petition or march in a protest if they do not believe in the specific cause. Second, the accuracy of our predictions based on I-E scores will depend on the specificity of measurement. Scores on the Rotter scale reflect general I-E beliefs that apply broadly to many situations. Therefore, in using such general scores to predict a specific behavior, one can expect a rather modest level of accuracy. To predict health care behavior, for example, one would be better advised to use I-E scores from a health care I-E scale rather than those from the Rotter scale.

SUMMARY

- Maintaining a sense of personal control is a prime goal for people of all kinds.

- The concept of personal control occupies a central place in theories of many psychologists.

- For many individuals, personal control represents a need and its frustration can lead to reactance.

- Diminished personal control can lead, in extreme cases, to severe distress and even death. A related concept here is learned helplessness, which developed out of research with dogs that were trained in such a way that they came to expect that a painful stimulus could not be avoided regardless of their own behavior. Such an expectancy generalized to other situations, leading to maladaptive behaviors.

- Learned helplessness has also been observed in humans. Experience with uncontrollable events can lead people to become apathetic and will often reduce their ability to learn that control is actually possible in certain situations. Repeated experiences of this kind have sometimes been implicated in depressive reactions.

■ There have been those who regard the learned helplessness model as somewhat naive and too simple to account by itself for clinical depressions. More recent formulations have become increasingly cognitive. However, several issues remain unsettled in this research area.

■ Several studies have shown that physical and mental decline in the elderly is increased by their inability to exercise personal control. Even mortality rates in the elderly may be linked to factors of personal control. However, skills to enhance a sense of control in the elderly can be taught.

■ Recent research has also indicated that involving patients in their own health care maintenance can facilitate their recovery. In particular, providing patients with information about medical procedures can be helpful in reducing stress and enhancing cooperation. At the same time, we must remember that there are individual differences in the desire for control. Thus, patients should not all be treated alike.

■ In some cases, people exhibit what is called the illusion of control—they believe they exert control when they really do not. People are also more likely to exaggerate the control they believe they exert when outcomes are positive.

■ Internal-external control (I-E) has been a widely investigated personality dimension. At one end of this dimension are those who perceive that events are contingent upon their own efforts or characteristics (internals). At the other end are those who perceive the occurrence of reinforcements to be the result of luck, chance, fate, the intervention of powerful others, or the unpredictability of the world (externals).

■ The first outlines of the I-E construct were developed out of clinical work with a patient. The theoretical context of I-E is Rotter's social learning theory, in which it is construed as a problem-solving generalized expectancy.

■ The most prominent measurement technique has been Rotter's I-E Scale—a twenty-three-item, forced-choice device. However, many other I-E scales have been developed which are targeted for specific populations and areas of prediction.

■ Research has revealed a number of behavioral characteristics of internals and externals. For example, externals are more likely than internals to be conforming and compliant. They are also more easily persuasible.

■ A prominent characteristic of internals is their relatively more active role in seeking information about their environment so as to be in a better position to exert control.

■ Internals are more prone to becoming involved in social action (assuming they believe in the cause in question) than are externals. However, in some instances those externals who blame the system for social injustices will become quite active in righting the wrongs.

■ Although the results are somewhat complex, internals seem to be more achievement oriented than externals, especially in the case of academic achievement in adolescents.

■ In general, internals and externals attribute responsibility for the acts of others in much the same ways they do for their own behavior.

■ In the area of health-related behavior, internals are more sensitive to health messages, have greater knowledge about health conditions, and make more attempts to improve their physical status. They seem to experience fewer heart attacks and are less susceptible to hypertension.

■ A great deal of evidence suggests that internals are better adjusted and less anxious than externals. External scores are more likely to be associated with a variety of psychiatric syndromes and reduced ability to cope. However, it would be dangerous to assume that an internal orientation is always the best or most serviceable orientation.

■ Recent evidence suggests that it may be useful to distinguish between two kinds of externals: defensive externals and congruent externals. The former express external beliefs but otherwise often behave like internals. They seem to espouse external beliefs as a way of protecting themselves or rationalizing expected failures. Congruent externals behave in keeping with their expressed I-E beliefs. Those beliefs appear to reflect directly their experiences in life or their learning history.

■ Several possible origins of I-E beliefs were discussed. Families that can be described as warm, protective, positive, and nurturant often produce internally oriented children. Likewise, families in which discipline and overall treatment of the child are consistent and predictable seem to promote the growth of internal beliefs.

■ By and large, individuals who come from groups with little access to power, mobility, opportunity, or material advantages seem to be predisposed toward developing external orientations.

■ Aging individuals tend to be more external than younger persons in the areas of beliefs about intelligence and health.

■ While sex differences are not always apparent in I-E scores, there is some evidence of sex-role stereotyping. In the eyes of many, internality is associated with the male role and externality with the female role. There is also some evidence that males and females show different patterns of responses on the I-E Scale.

■ The chapter closed with two observations. Internals will not always be more active than externals; they must first value the goal toward which the activity is directed. Second, general or broad I-E scores will be only moderately predictive of specific behavior in a given situation.

CHAPTER 17

AGGRESSION

Listen to virtually any nightly TV newscast in virtually any large city (and some not-so-large places as well) and you are bombarded with a litany of reports on the latest robberies, stabbings, shootings, and assaults. According to some sources, 3 percent of all U.S. citizens are victims of violent crime each year (Langan and Innes, 1985). That translates into about six million people. During 1984 there was a violent crime (murder, rape, robbery, or aggravated assault) every twenty-five seconds! And the most common form of violent crime is domestic violence. Nearly 13 percent of all U.S. marriages are marked by chronic violence (Straus, 1977). If this were not bad enough, somewhere between 1.4 and 2.3 million children have been beaten up by a parent sometime during their childhood (Straus, Gelles, and Steinmetz, 1980).

All of this says nothing about the endless wars that have plagued us for centuries upon centuries, the mass murders (as this is being written, the reports continue to come in about the fourteen women in Montreal slain by a lone gunman), or even the everyday, inconsequential (?) uncaring acts we commit in the normal course of interpersonal relations. Perhaps worst of all, it almost seems as if we are beginning to "adjust" to all this.

Obviously, aggression and violence are major problems. So, then, what does this say about the kind of societies we live in? What does it say about the kinds of people we are producing these days? In this chapter, we will examine some of the ways of studying aggression, its determinants, the conditions and personalities that foster it, and some potential ways of reducing it.

DEFINING AGGRESSION

What kinds of behaviors qualify as aggression? Certainly the mugger who attacks an elderly woman who has just cashed her Social Security check is aggressing. And so am I if I repeatedly make sarcastic remarks designed to put certain people in their places. But what about the drunk motorist who inadvertently runs someone off the road? Or what if a shopkeeper fires at a burglar but misses? And is the psychotherapist who encourages a patient to relive anguishing moments really causing psychic pain and thereby being aggressive? The last three examples raise difficulties in defining aggression since they involve the issue of intent. The motorist did not intend harm but certainly created it. The shopkeeper intended to inflict harm but did not actually do so. And does provoking an unpleasant experience for another person count as aggression if the intent is ultimately to help? As Baron (1977) suggests, these kinds of examples definitely muddy the waters. As a result, different investigators have, over the years, defined aggression differently. For example, Zillmann (1978) defines aggression as an attempt to produce bodily or physical harm to another. This definition would exclude psychological injury. Investigators such as Berkowitz (1974) and S. Feshbach (1970) argue that aggression must involve the intent to injure rather than merely inflicting harm. In contrast, for A. H. Buss (1961) aggression is any behavior that harms another regardless of intent. Perhaps a typical definition of human **aggression** is the one offered by Baron (1977): "Aggression is any form of behavior directed toward the goal of harming or injuring another living being who is motivated to avoid such treatment" (p. 7). Lysak, Rule, and Dobbs (1989) have found that subjects (as well as psychologists) tend to judge harmful acts as more aggressive, more typical, and more blameworthy when those acts involve malevolent intent or unacceptable motives.

Obviously, aggression is not some piece of reality waiting out there to be discovered and defined correctly. There are many different ways to conceptualize aggression, and each allows the investigator to pursue its study using different paths. Each can be useful for a given set of purposes.

METHODS OF STUDY

The study of value-laden behaviors is difficult, and aggression is no exception to this rule. Unsystematic observation of aggression can be fraught with all kinds of sampling and interpretational problems. Experimental-laboratory studies also have their share of problems, including ones of sampling and generalization. Aggression is especially hard to investigate because of ethical constraints. We cannot ask people to hurt each other just so we can observe them. Similarly, putting people in laboratory settings and then proceeding to harm them raises justifiable questions of ethics and morality on the part of the investigator.

Observation

The importance of systematic observations of aggressive behavior cannot be overstated. This method has yielded many significant insights. Freud accumulated much of his knowledge of human aggression just by listening to his patients. For generations, philosophers, cultural commentators, and novelists have observed and described human aggression and come to a variety of conclusions regarding its antecedents and consequences. In the final analysis, however, they remain but observations. Although they often appear provocative, insightful, or clever, one can never totally separate the event from the observer and his or her own needs, perceptions, and interpretations.

Laboratory approaches

According to Baron (1977), laboratory studies can be classified as employing one of the following methods: (1) verbal attacks against others; (2) attacks against inanimate objects; (3) attacks against others which cannot, however, actually cause harm because the instruments used are innocuous (e.g., styrofoam swords); (4) attacks that appear capable of being harmful but which, in fact, are not (e.g., administering electric shock from a machine that only "looks real").

In the verbal attack method, subjects are typically frustrated in some fashion and then given the opportunity to respond with verbal aggression. For example, Zillmann and Cantor (1976) studied subjects' responses to an unpleasant experimenter who unfairly accused them of cheating. A subsequent series of questions similar to the following allowed the subjects to retaliate through their verbal responses: "Are you dissatisfied with the way you were treated in this experiment?"; "Should this student be reappointed as a research assistant?" Such methods are attractive since no actual harm is done (especially since the so-called victim is usually a confederate of the experimenter). The aggression is also reasonably representative of what can occur in real-life settings. Furthermore, since some people may be very reluctant to administer physical punishment, verbal aggression may be easier to elicit. However, it is important to note that verbal responses may better be thought of as examples of emotional reactions unless it can be demonstrated that subjects really believe their response can negatively affect the victim in some way.

Under the category of attacks upon inanimate objects, subjects are put in situations that promote varying degrees of aggression and are then observed in terms of the frequency or intensity with which they kick, hit, or otherwise assault some inanimate object. The most widely known example of this method is the Bobo doll procedure used by Bandura and his colleagues, which was described in Chapter 13. The most telling criticism of this method is that what it stimulates may only be a form of play. In addition, since the object is nonhuman, it is very hard to generalize to situations where a "live" human would be the object of attack.

The third set of approaches noted by Baron allows the subject to respond with aggression against a victim (normally a confederate of the experimenter) who does not "fight back" (Diener, 1976). Often, the instrument of aggression is a toy gun that shoots Ping-Pong balls, or perhaps soft bricks or the like. Although subjects will often behave aggressively in such situations, it seems likely that they may sometimes perceive the whole procedure as a game or else realize that their actions are not particularly harmful. On the other hand, there have been a few instances in which a subject got carried away and had to be restrained.

The most widely employed method currently being used to study aggression under laboratory conditions is the so-called **Buss technique** (A. H. Buss, 1961). In general, the procedure runs as follows. Subjects appearing for an experiment are told they will be participating in a study of the effects of punishment on learning. One subject will be the "learner," and another the "teacher." Whenever the learner responds correctly to the material presented, the teacher rewards him or her by illuminating a light informing the learner that a correct response has been made. But when the learner is incorrect, the teacher will press a button that delivers an electric shock to the learner. The teacher is seated before a machine containing an array of buttons labeled from 1 to 10. Button 1 represents a very light shock while Button 10 supposedly delivers a very painful shock. The scenario is always contrived so that actual subjects are always appointed as teachers and a confederate of the investigator who appears for the experiment at the same time as the subject is always designated as the learner. The machine that delivers the shock is a very scientific looking apparatus, but in reality it does not produce electric shocks. But, then, the subject does not know this (see Figure 17-1). The learner always makes a prearranged series of mistakes on the learning task so that the teacher will have the opportunity to press shock buttons of varying intensity. The strength of the teacher's aggressiveness is measured by both the duration and intensity of the button pushes.

In all the laboratory methods discussed, the critical issue is their validity. Do they measure aggression as we understand it, and are the techniques representative of what we regard as aggression situations? Does the ability to control relevant variables in these laboratory situations outweigh the possibility that subjects will see them as contrived? And will subjects respond on the basis of what they think is expected of them or in terms of other personality and situational variables operative at the time?

Field methods

Several field approaches have been used to study aggression. First, there are those very indirect methods which try to link events reported by the media to the subsequent occurrence of aggression. For example, Berkowitz (1971) compiled monthly figures from the FBI on the incidence of crime. Increases in violent crime could then be checked following such dramatic events as the assassination of President Kennedy. This kind of method allows us to study what might be called the "contagion of violence." How-

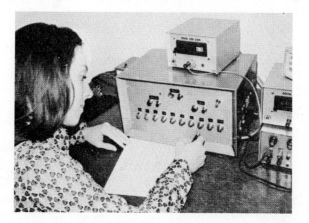

FIGURE 17-1   Apparatus used in teacher-learner (or Buss) paradigm. It provides feedback on the amount of pain supposedly experienced by a confederate.   Photo courtesy of Academic Press and R. A. Baron, 1983, p. 176.

ever, such methods can, at best, only provide a basis for hypothesizing since we may be dealing with relationships that do not involve cause and effect.

Another somewhat indirect method is illustrated in work by Baron (1976). This study involved an indirect confrontation in traffic between a male confederate driving a car and another driver. The confederate waited fifteen seconds after a traffic signal turned green before moving his car forward. Two observers in a car parked nearby recorded the reactions of the drivers behind the confederate each time. Tape recordings were made of horns honking so that the frequency, duration, and latency of such behavior could be studied. Also noted were the verbal comments, gestures, and facial expressions of the other drivers.

More direct field methods have also been employed. Typically, the settings for these studies are airports, shopping malls, restaurants, and the like. In one particular study (M. B. Harris, 1973), a confederate of the experimenter bumped into a second confederate in a crowded situation while a random, unsuspecting subject-to-be was watching. This second confederate responded with either verbal aggression or politeness, depending upon the experimental condition. A bit later, a third member of the research team followed the subject and jostled the latter from behind. It was found that subjects who had witnessed the verbally aggressive responses earlier tended to respond more often with verbal aggression of their own as compared to subjects who had earlier observed polite responses.

This kind of research does have its problems, however. Although there is little question about the representativeness of the settings producing the aggression, there are a few unsettling ethical issues to be considered. First of all, there is no way of obtaining in advance a subject's consent to be in the experiment. This could be regarded as a form of exploitation, which raises both legal and ethical problems for the experimenter. Then, too, there is the possibility that by inciting others to aggression (e.g., by jostling them, delaying at a traffic light), one puts them at risk. A scene could develop which might draw other people into a web of aggression. Or the subject might actually assault one of the confederates (which, by the way, has happened). When research in such a potentially volatile area as aggression is conducted, reactions can be uncorked which are hard to put back in the bottle. Before embroiling themselves in such scenarios, no matter how cleverly contrived, investigators must carefully weigh the potential risks and benefits to all involved.

Now that we have discussed what aggression is and how it may be studied, we can consider a number of potential causes.

BIOLOGICAL-GENETIC DETERMINANTS OF AGGRESSION

Debates over the instinctual and biological origins of aggression in human beings have raged for years. In this section, then, we will briefly examine psychoanalytic, sociobiological, genetic, and physiological approaches.

A Freudian view

Freud was convinced that innate aggressive urges constantly seek expression and are a fundamental part of human nature. **Thanatos,** the **death instinct** described in Chapter 3, pushes us toward self-destructive and aggressive behavior. He saw many human reactions, from sarcasm, suicide, and wars, as reflections of this basic urge to harm self and others. His rather pessimistic conclusion was that aggression is inevitable. This aggression builds up inside us and requires some manner of release—a **catharsis** perhaps. Such release could find expression in physical violence, verbal attacks, or it could even be vicarious—watching a violent movie, for example. We will return to this latter topic a bit later in this chapter.

Sociobiology

The study of relationships between biological factors and social behavior describes the field of **sociobiology** (see Chapter 1). Thus, aggression could be an evolutionary product of the way the human brain and nervous system are structured.

A prominent advocate of the instinctual origins of human aggression was the Nobel Prize winner Konrad Lorenz. He believed that there is a fighting instinct in both animals and humans that is directed toward members of their own species (Lorenz, 1974). This aggressive energy, if not regularly dissipated through various forms of behavior, will accumulate and then be expressed even when appropriate environmental stimuli are not present. A major implication of Lorenz's thesis is that lethal outbursts of aggression in humans can be prevented by allowing the individual to engage in frequent episodes of minor hostility and aggression.

Lorenz also contended that we humans continue to have problems with aggression because our ancestors never really evolved an innate reluctance to kill their own. Other species, according to Lorenz, almost never escalate their aggression against others in the species to the point of killing. Researchers such as E. O. Wilson (1975) have countered by asserting that there is evidence that other animals (e.g., lions, hyenas) do occasionally kill within their own species.

Another unique quality in humans was also said by Lorenz to promote aggression. We constantly strive to suppress our instinct for fighting, whereas other members of the animal kingdom do not. As noted a moment ago, this suppression results in an accumulation of aggressive energy, which can then burst forth in terrible ways. This would explain the overcontrolled person who for years is regarded as a paragon of virtue and who suddenly, without warning or provocation, kills his entire family.

Basically, however, Lorenz's arguments are deficient in three important ways. First, as mentioned earlier, there is a dearth of solid experimental evidence to support his theories. Second his ideas do not easily account for why there is so much variation among human cultures in the expression of violence and aggression. Whereas members of some cultures seem constantly at odds with each other, members of other cultures almost never fight. Third, his instinct theories cannot readily account for why there is so much variation in aggression among individuals within a given culture.

Sociobiologists seek to understand human aggression by studying it in animals where the mechanisms may be simpler and more easily understood. However, as Berkowitz (1983) has observed, while there are many parallels between human and animal aggression, there are many differences as well, especially in the realm of thought processes. More recently, however, sociobiologists have turned to the study of a variety of current human problems such as rape, family violence, and reproductive strategies in men and women (e.g., Crawford, Smith, and Krebs, 1987). Their conclusions are often highly provocative.

Genetics

Rushton and his colleagues had monozygotic and dizygotic pairs of twins fill out questionnaires measuring aggression and assertiveness (Rushton, Fulker, Neale, Nias, and Eysenck, 1986). Their conclusions are that very little of the twins' aggressive tendencies are due to their common, shared environments. As we shall see later, however, many other investigators look to environmental, learned explanations.

A more experimental tack has been taken by others studying the role of heredity in aggression. Plomin and Foch (1981) employed the old standby, the Bobo doll, to study aggression in children. Using a genetic analysis of the responses of 108 pairs of twin children (aged five to eleven), they could find no evidence of hereditary influences in aggression. It must be noted, however, that such a study does not address the question of whether people are innately aggressive, but only whether genetic differences among people relate to observed differences in aggressive behavior.

A specific hypothesis about the role of genetics in aggression has emerged from research on the XYY chromosomal anomaly. While it is fair to say that all of us have the potential for violence, it has been found that males with an extra Y chromosome seem to be represented more frequently in prison populations than one would expect on the basis of chance alone (Jarvik, Klodin, and Matsuyama, 1973). Thus, when the Y chromosome (which ordains at conception that the offspring will be a male) is accidentally joined by a second Y chromosome, some claim that this not only produces a taller individual but also an increased propensity for violence. Yet the frequency of this XYY occurrence is very unusual (only about one in a thousand births). Besides that, most XYY males lead quite normal lives (Kessler, 1975). In addition, those criminals showing this chromosomal anomaly do not seem especially prone to commit crimes of violence.

Physiological mechanisms

It is tempting to conclude that biological abnormalities cause aggression. After all, there was Charles Whitman, the man who killed his wife and mother and then proceeded to shoot at dozens of people on the University of Texas campus, killing fourteen of them. He was finally shot and an autopsy revealed a walnut-sized tumor in the temporal lobe of the brain near the amygdala. In the case of Paul M (Mark and Ervin, 1970), evidence of brain damage was found after Paul had admitted himself to the hospital because of his inability to control his own violence. Antiseizure drugs put an end to his violent rages. But in both of these cases, strong evidence that psychosocial factors were implicated turned up in the case histories.

Certainly, neural mechanisms play a role in aggression (as they do in all human behavior). And animal studies have revealed that damage to certain areas of the brain can increase or decrease aggressiveness, depending on the specific area involved (Smith, King, and Hoebel, 1970). It may be that the oldest, most primitive areas of the brain are involved in violent behavior. The hypothalamus and other temporal lobe structures

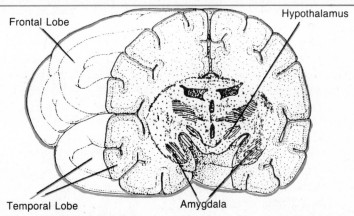

FIGURE 17-2   Areas of the brain said to mediate aggressive behavior
Adapted from *Human Aggression and Conflict* by K. R. Scherer, R. P. Abeles, and C. S. Fisher (Englewood Cliffs, NJ: Prentice-Hall, 1975). Reprinted by permission.

help mediate aggressive behavior, and, in some cases, surgical removal of the hypothalamus and amygdala has caused loss of emotional reactivity (see Figure 17-2). However, translating this rudimentary knowledge into practical and successful efforts to control aggression through surgery have rarely been observed. At the present time, the more immediate route to understanding and control appears to reside in psychosocial factors, to which we can now turn.

PSYCHOSOCIAL DETERMINANTS OF AGGRESSION

There are many ways in which psychosocial factors can influence the expression of aggression. The possibilities include everything from frustration to watching TV. Let us start with frustration as we catalog some of these possibilities.

The frustration-aggression hypothesis

Intuitively, we all seem to recognize that frustration is an important instigator of aggression. The door will not open; I become frustrated and kick it viciously. One child will not share; the other becomes angry and strikes out in retaliation. In fact, from the tiniest corners of interpersonal relations to those massive confrontations between nations, frustration is a potent mediator of aggression. A systematic psychological theory of the relationship between frustration and aggression was first formulated by Dollard, Doob, Miller, Mowrer, and Sears (1939). Their initial statement of the theory was rather extreme in that they proposed that frustration always leads to aggression and that aggression is always the result of frustration. By frustration they meant any interference with a person's goal-directed behavior. While aggression may be disguised, delayed, or even displaced to other persons or objects, it is never dissolved.

It did not take long for the shortcomings of this simple frustration-aggression hypothesis to become evident. Not everyone, it was pointed out, shows aggression in the face of frustration, nor does the same person react to every frustration with aggression. Frustration is sometimes followed by depression and withdrawal. Furthermore, aggression can often be shown to occur in the absence of frustration. Observational learning studies have shown that children will increase their level of violence toward a Bobo doll in imitation of a model even though they themselves have not been frustrated. Drill sergeants have been known to behave aggressively toward recruits just to toughen them up a bit. Thus, to twist every instance of aggression into the frustration mold does not seem reasonable or useful. Miller (1941) recognized this and suggested a modified form of the frustration-aggression hypothesis. He proposed that frustration can produce any number of responses, only one of which is aggression. Many different conditions can affect the connection between frustration and aggression, including what the individual has learned during the process of becoming socialized. The task then became the identification of these various conditions and the development of ways to detect aggression in its more disguised forms. However, there still seemed to be the implication that aggression is the first or natural response to frustration—an unlearned reaction, if you will, that can be modified subsequently by experience.

While recognizing the intrinsic possibilities of the frustration-aggression hypothesis, most investigators were put off for many years by the difficulties in pursuing it experimentally. However, in the 1960s a program of research was begun by Berkowitz (1969), who viewed aggression as but one of several possible responses to frustration. His contention was that frustration initially generates anger, not aggression. But if there are appropriate cues in the situation, then aggression will ensue. Recently, Berkowitz (1989) has argued for the core validity of the Dollard et al. formulation. However, the modification that Berkowitz would make is as follows: frustration is aversive and will produce the potential for aggression, but only when it generates unpleasant emotions in the individual.

Research has identified a number of links between frustration and aggression (Geen, 1976b). Many studies have used the "shock machines" described earlier in this chapter. For example, Berkowitz and LePage (1967) instructed a confederate to make the subject angry and frustrated. Subjects were then put in a situation where there was an opportunity to express aggression (i.e., deliver electric shock to another confederate). It was found that when aggressive cues were present in the room, such as a shotgun and a revolver lying on a nearby table, the subject was much more likely to give supposedly powerful shocks to the second confederate. The link between frustration and aggression was based on environmental cues. In a similar vein, A. H. Buss (1963) prevented subjects from reaching a goal. Subjects were then placed in the "learning-shock machine" situation and instructed to do as good a job as possible in teaching the confederate. It was found that the aggression exhibited by three experimental groups differed little from that expressed by a control group. Also, three forms of frustration produced few differences in aggression. Such work does not especially support the original frustration-aggression hypothesis and seems to reinforce the Berkowitz thesis that aggression in the face of frustration is not inevitable. However, when the frustration experienced is seen as arbitrary, the connection between frustration and aggression can be direct (Zillmann and Cantor, 1976). Likewise, when frustration robs the person of the freedom to act, strong aggression can follow (Worchel, 1974). Such findings suggest a link between the concept of personal control (discussed in the previous chapter) and aggression.

Of course, not everyone reacts to or experiences frustration in the same way. Many years ago, Rosenzweig (1944) developed a picture completion test **(Rosenzweig Picture Frustration Study)** to measure these individual differences. The ways in which subjects responded to a series of cartoons depicting one person frustrating another yielded clues as to the direction of expressed aggression and also as to the type of reaction to frustration (see Table 17-1). The test is not widely used today but it does remind us of the possibilities for an individual differences approach to the study of frustration and aggression.

SOCIAL LEARNING AND AGGRESSION

It is generally conceded that neither instinct theories nor the frustration-aggression hypothesis is by itself adequate in accounting for human aggression. The missing ingredient is learning. Social learning theorists argue that, quite simply, we learn to be aggressive both by observing models who are aggressive and by being reinforced for our own aggressive behavior (Bandura, 1976).

Observational learning

Bandura's work on modeling and observational learning was presented in Chapters 12 and 13. In the area of aggression, the classical demonstration of the effects of imitation is a study by Bandura, Ross, and Ross (1961). Children in a nursery school watched either of two adult models: one who ignored an inflated, five-foot-tall Bobo doll and

---

TABLE 17-1 *Examples of individual differences in direction and type of reaction to frustration*

Direction

Situation: A passing car splashes me with mud as I stand on a corner.
  Direction of response
    Extrapunitive: I hurl a rock after the car in retaliation.
    Intropunitive: "I am so dumb; one should never stand so close to the curb in this weather."
    Impunitive: "That's ok, these slacks were dirty anyway."

Type

Situation: I receive a low grade on a midterm exam.
  Type of reaction
    Ego defensive: "I didn't put in much time studying."
    Need persistence: I request that the exam be rescored.
    Obstacle dominance: I decide to "get even" by criticizing the instructor to all my friends.

---

instead played with a set of Tinker Toys, or one who violently abused the doll both verbally and physically. The violent model punched the doll in the face repeatedly, beat it about the head with a mallet, threw it angrily into the air, and kicked it, all the while shouting such things as "Kick him," or "Sock him in the nose." Later, when these same children were exposed to the doll after being frustrated, they reacted according to their previous experience with the adult models. Those children who had been exposed to the violent model reacted to the frustration more aggressively than did those who had observed the quiet model or else no model at all. They shouted, punched, and hit the doll in a way that indicated both that they had learned something from the model and that their inhibitions had been effectively diminished by the model's behavior (see Figure 17-3 for an example of this paradigm). Also, Bandura (1965) has produced evidence indicating that when children observe a model who is punished for being aggressive, they are much less likely to imitate the model than a model who is rewarded for aggression. Even a relatively brief exposure to an unaggressive model can inhibit the expression of aggression (Baron, 1971). Evidence such as the foregoing seems to support clearly the general thesis that aggression is often a direct outcome of the opportunity to observe it.

Bandura's contention that the expression of aggression is enhanced when it leads to reward probably does not require much in the way of proof. However, Geen and Stonner (1971) employed the shock machine method and verbally reinforced subjects ("You're doing fine") for delivering electric shocks to another person each time a light went on. Another group was not reinforced at all. Findings indicated that reinforced subjects increased the intensity of the shocks they administered over a long series of trials more sharply than did nonreinforced subjects.

Observational learning is probably responsible in part for the plague of airline hijackings over the past two decades. Seeing hijackings on TV or reading about them in the newspapers undoubtedly increases their potential for repetition by others (see Figure 17-4). Even TV news stories on teenage suicides over a six-year period have been shown to increase the very phenomenon being covered (Philips and Carstensen, 1986).

Childhood experiences

Hardly anyone disputes the idea that much of what we become in the way of adults is determined by early childhood experiences in the family. Unfortunately, this is where the agreement usually ends. There sometimes seem to be as many explanations of the effects of childhood experience on adult behavior as there are experts to propound them. And the methodological problems in doing research in this area are formidable. Nevertheless, Sears, Maccoby, and Levin (1957) conducted a now-classic large-scale interview study of several hundred mothers. With respect to the child-rearing antecedents of aggression, they correlated mothers' reports of their child-rearing practices with the behavioral outcomes in the child. Although most of the mothers accepted the notion that control of aggression in the child is very important, they endorsed many different ways of achieving this goal. For example, one mother remarked:

> I just told them in no uncertain terms that it was something that was never done, and I have never had any trouble with it; and if I did, I don't know just how I would cope with it, because I wouldn't stand for it. (Sears, Maccoby, and Levin, 1957, p. 235)

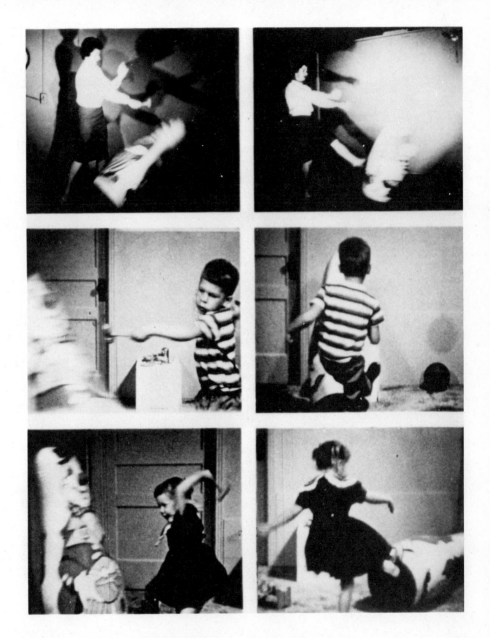

FIGURE 17-3 Photographs of children reproducing the aggressive responses of a female model they had observed in a film.

From Bandura, A., and Walters, R. (1963). *Social learning and personality development*, New York: Holt, Rinehart and Winston.

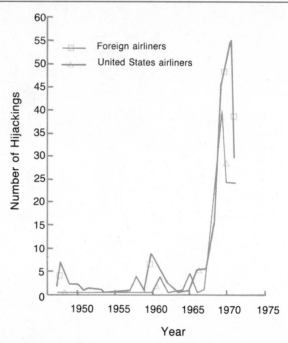

FIGURE 17-4   Incidence of airline hijackings from 1950 to 1975 (sharp decline reflects countermeasures)

Adapted from *Aggression: A Social Learning Analysis* by Albert Bandura. Copyright © 1973 by Prentice-Hall, Inc. Reprinted by permission.

On the more permissive side, take this mother:

> If I saw it was a habit, I'd certainly make provisions to prevent it, but in Susan's case every once in a while she gets so furious with me, that she does strike out, and I sort of overlook it a little bit because I think it's very natural. (Sears, Maccoby, and Levin, 1957, p. 236)

In general, the work of Sears, Maccoby, and Levin seems to suggest that when parents are very permissive in their relations with the child, a higher level of aggression is the result. As Bandura has contended, the child's aggressiveness seems to be reinforced by such parents.

Violence begets violence

The work of Sears et al. (1957) also showed that parents who vigorously applied physical punishment for aggressive acts produced aggressive children. Such parents probably induced frustration and anger in their children and also provided aggressive models for them.

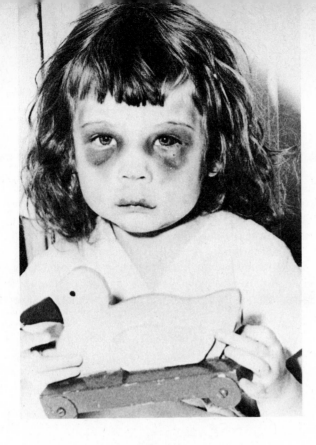

Child abuse—a devastating social problem that has been ignored for too long.
Photograph UPI/Bettmann News Photos.

Child abuse has surely been going on since the beginning of time. But only recently has it been receiving extensive media coverage. One thing we have learned is that it is not confined to any particular socioeconomic group (Gil, 1973). Furthermore, in a recent survey Widom (1989) examined the hypothesis that "violence breeds violence." She suggests that research indicates that there is a greater likelihood of abuse by parents if the parents themselves were abused as children. But among adults who abuse their children, the majority were not abused in their own childhood.

Unfortunately, the role of modeling seems alive and well here. Too often, in the attempts of parents to discipline their children, they display a lack of control that is exceedingly harmful. The child cries too long and uncontrolled parental anger culminates in anything from a fractured skull or scalding to chronic rejection and neglect. In any case, the growing substantiation of child abuse and neglect is a problem that will not go away on its own (Eckenrode, Powers, Doris, Munsch, and Bolger, 1988).

TV AND THE MOVIES: MODEL OR PRESSURE VALVE?

What do children see on TV and in the movies these days? They see blood spurting everywhere. They see eyes being gouged out. They see cars engulfed in flames. They see limbs being severed. This is not the "gentle" aggressions of Daffy Duck that so many adults seem to remember.

Children spend a large amount of time viewing TV each day (Liebert and Sprafkin, 1988). Some say the average child has seen 18,000 murders on TV (Brody, 1975). What is more, amount of TV-viewing is a stable behavioral pattern that persists over substantial periods of time (Tangney and Feshbach, 1988).

For many people, the point of all this is simple—children imitate what they see (as do many adults). This means that children will learn new ways of behaving violently. And maybe it also means that children will learn that people often get away with violence; they are not always caught and punished. Then, too, after seeing countless murders and other forms of mayhem, we may all become desensitized. The outrageous or bizarre becomes the norm and aggression no longer seems so awful.

Others, however, say not to worry. After all, it is mainly aggressive people who are drawn to violent programs and movies in the first place; they would be aggressive anyway. Still others claim that TV and movie violence can have a cathartic effect. By living vicariously through others we drain off some of our potential for violence. But what is the evidence?

General evidence

There is considerable evidence from laboratory studies that connects violence on film with the expression of aggression by its viewers. One example is the work by Bandura,

"Let's wait. Maybe he kills her or something."

Drawing by Weber, copyright 1966, The New Yorker Magazine, Inc.

Ross, and Ross (1961). Using real, filmed, and cartoon models of aggressive behavior, they studied the reactions of nursery school children. As usual, the object against which the children could aggress was a Bobo doll. The children watched the models and were then mildly frustrated. Children in all three experimental groups showed a higher level of aggression toward the doll (hitting, kicking, yelling, etc.) than did children in a control group who had not observed a model.

In another study, Josephson (1987) studied boys in Grades 2 and 3. They watched violent or nonviolent TV in groups of six. Half of these groups were later exposed to a cue associated with the violent TV program. Either before or after viewing TV, they were frustrated. By observing the children, ratings of aggression were made while the boys played floor hockey. It was discovered that violent television did increase aggressive behavior but mainly among groups who had been earlier rated as disposed toward aggressiveness. The same boys were also more likely to become aggressive when the violence-related cue was present as compared to being exposed to the violent content only. Leyens, Camino, Parke, and Berkowitz (1975) first observed the behavior of a group of boys living at a private school. The boys were then divided into two groups and exposed either to five violent movies or five nonviolent movies. These were shown one per evening for five consecutive evenings. The boys' behavior after viewing the five films was compared to their behavior prior to the films. The boys exposed to violent films did increase their level of aggression, although not in every behavioral aspect under study. However, subjects who had viewed nonviolent films showed no consistent changes in their behavior. Other research outside the laboratory has produced comparable results implicating the role of viewing filmed violence in aggressive behavior (e.g., Greenberg, 1975; Parke, Berkowitz, Leyens, West, and Sebastian, 1977).

More recently, Eron and Huesmann (1984) have reported a strong relationship between TV viewing at an early age and subsequent crime, as is shown in Figure 17-5. Also Eron (1982) has described the results of two large-scale longitudinal studies. One involved 875 children eight years old from a semirural upstate New York county, and the other 750 children who were eight to ten years old and came from suburban and inner-city Chicago. In summarizing the research, Eron (1982) had this to say:

> One persistent and ubiquitous finding deserves special consideration, and that is the relation between the continued observation of television violence and aggressive behavior. It is now apparent that the relation does not just go in one direction. Although we have demonstrated that television violence is one cause of aggressive behavior, it is also probable that aggressive children prefer to watch more and more violent television. The process is very likely circular. . . . Aggressive children are unpopular, and because their relations with their peers tend to be unsatisfying, they spend more time watching television than their popular peers. The violence they see on television reassures them that their own behavior is appropriate while teaching them new coercive techniques that they then attempt to use in their interactions with others, which in turn makes them more unpopular and drives them back to television, and the circle continues. (p. 210)

Eron goes on to observe that aggression is also related to low school achievement and that these low achievers spend a great deal of time watching TV, thereby getting more opportunity to observe and identify with aggressive models. This idea is compat-

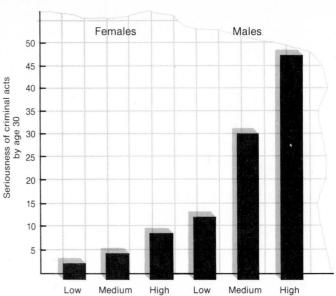

FIGURE 17-5   Relation of TV viewing frequency at age 8 to seriousness of crimes committed by age 30.

From Eron, L. D. and Huesmann, L. R., "The control of aggressive behavior by changes in attitudes, values, and the conditions of learning" in R. J. Blanchard and D. C. Blanchard, eds., *Advances in the Study of Aggression,* Vol. 1, 1984. Copyright © 1984 by Academic Press, Inc. Reprinted by permission.

ible with research that has shown that aggression in childhood interferes with the development of intellectual functioning and is even associated with poorer intellectual achievement in adulthood (Huesmann, Eron, and Yarmel, 1987).

However, it should be noted that not everyone regards the link between viewing violence on the screen and subsequent aggression to be a firmly established one (Kaplan and Singer, 1976; Sawin, 1981). One study that failed to establish this connection was conducted by Feshbach and Singer (1971). These investigators were given complete control over the TV-viewing habits of two samples of preadolescent and adolescent boys. One group was fed a steady diet of violent shows (westerns, wrestling, crime shows, etc.) while another group saw nothing but nonviolent programs (comedies, nonaggressive cartoons, talk shows, etc.). Quite unexpectedly, the results revealed that boys seeing only bland shows subsequently manifested a higher level of aggressive behavior than those who watched the aggressive shows. The latter group, in fact, reduced their aggression over what it had been prior to their TV viewing. These findings were especially apparent for boys from lower socioeconomic levels. Feshbach and Singer comment that it is quite likely that children have, by the age of ten or so, already learned to distinguish between fictional violence and real violence. They further suggest that aggressive TV themes may actually purge one's aggressive impulses. They also warn that we should be careful about removing all violence from children's shows since this might paradoxically raise their levels of aggression. They argue for better quality of programming rather than total censorship of violence.

Aggression as catharsis

Both Freud's instinct theory of aggression and the Dollard et al. (1939) frustration-aggression hypothesis have suggested that release of aggressive impulses in "safe" ways will help reduce future possibilities of the expression of aggression. Freud, however, was not especially optimistic about how effective such catharsis really is. The afore-mentioned work by Feshbach and Singer (1971) could also be interpreted as suppor-tive of the catharsis position.

In a study by Hokanson and Burgess (1962), subjects were frustrated and made angry. To determine whether their anger or arousal would be lessened by the opportu-nity to aggress against their frustrator, three conditions were studied: (1) opportunity to express aggression physically by delivering electric shock, (2) chance to aggress verbally through ratings of the experimenter, and (3) production of fantasy responses to a set of pictures. There was also a control group which had no opportunity to ag-gress. Both physical and verbal aggression reduced subjects' arousal as compared to both the fantasy and no-opportunity conditions.

However, it is important to note that just because a person may feel better after expressing aggression, there is no guarantee that aggression in the future will be diminished. In fact, feeling better could serve as a reinforcement that will actually pro-mote aggression later. Even kicking the furniture or breaking a plate, far from reduc-ing impulses, may only serve to strengthen such outbursts in the future (Mallick and McCandless, 1966). These and other such acts of aggression are only somewhat be-nign, and it is a bit odd to argue that we must aggress in order not to aggress! As Baron (1977) remarks, "While participation in certain cathartic activities may sometimes suc-ceed in reducing later aggression, the potential benefits of such procedures have in the past been greatly overstated" (pp. 248-249). Some have argued that engaging in ag-gressive competitive sports drains off aggression in both the players and the spectators in ways that are socially acceptable. While the vocal advocates of aggressive sports claim they have redeeming social value because of their cathartic effects, research more often indicates they enhance aggression (Zillmann, Bryant, and Sapolsky, 1978). Hu-mor, sarcasm, and the like, have also been suggested as acceptable outlets for aggres-sion. But others contend that, in reality, such humor can be punishing and demeaning and thus it only promotes aggression (Zillmann, 1978).

A conclusion

So, what do we conclude? Although not completely consistent, the evidence seems to be mounting that heavy doses of TV violence do lead to increased aggression by young viewers (NIMH, 1982). Television provides models of aggression or scripts that can be triggered by events or cues in the environment (see Huesmann and Eron, 1986). Some evidence suggests that children who are more prone to aggression in the first place prefer to watch violent TV programs. Most investigators, though, have found, simply, that increased viewing of violent TV leads to greater aggression, regardless of initial disposition (Roberts and Maccoby, 1985). Theorizing by Berkowitz (1990) as well as empirical research by Bushman and Geen (1990) indicate that violent media presentations promote violent cognitions and emotions. These could be precursors of later behavior. The debate over whether aggression observed on TV or elsewhere catalyzes further aggression or serves as a means of catharsis for our otherwise unacceptable aggressive impulses rages on. However, neither the scientific evidence nor the evidence provided by crowd behavior at professional football games would offer much hope for the catharsis hypothesis.

CONDITIONS THAT ENHANCE AGGRESSION

It goes without saying that many specific conditions can affect the expression of aggression. Observational learning efforts are mediated by the nature of the models and by what happens to them. Intentional harm is more likely to provoke retaliation than inadvertent harm (Dyck and Rule, 1978). Fictionally portrayed violence on TV may have lesser effects than violence explicitly portrayed as a slice of life (Geen, 1975). The variety of such factors makes it very difficult to arrive at a single conclusion about violence that will apply to everyone under all circumstances. Nevertheless, we shall discuss a few situational factors to illustrate how they may operate.

Temperature

Since antiquity, people have associated heat with aggression—and for good reasons. We all sense that tempers flare during those long, hot summers. The U.S. Riot Commission suggested that the riots that dotted the urban landscape of the 1960s and 1970s were encouraged by the heat of summer. Laboratory studies such as those by Griffitt (1970) and Griffitt and Veitch (1971) further reinforced the notion that heat leads to irritability, to negative reactions to others, and on to aggression. Although laboratory studies have not always been consistent, field studies seem unequivocal in their support (Anderson, 1989). Hot weather produces increases in aggressive motives and tendencies. The hotter parts of the world produce more aggression. Hotter years, seasons, months, and even days yield more aggression in the form of murders, rapes, assaults, riots, wife beatings, and the like. As Anderson (1989) concludes, temperature effects operate at the level of individuals and they are important in influencing virtually every form of antisocial behavior imaginable. Some of these relationships are shown in Figure 17-6.

Drugs

There seems little doubt that alcohol consumption is related to the expression of aggression (Taylor and Leonard, 1983). The conventional wisdom is that the mildly inebriated person is amicable and happy—more friendly than aggressive. In contrast, progressive levels of intoxication lead to a belligerent attitude and even aggression, especially in the face of frustration and arousal. Marijuana, however, is thought to ac-

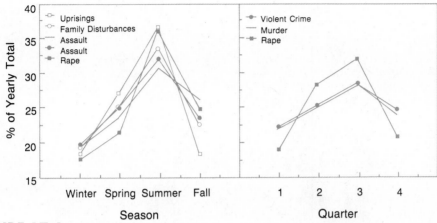

FIGURE 17-6 **Seasonal and quarterly occurrence of aggressive behavior**

Adapted from "Temperature and Aggression: Ubiquitous Effects of Heat on Occurrence of Human Violence" by Craig A. Anderson, *Psychological Bulletin*, Vol. 106, No. 1, July 1989. Copyright © 1989 by the American Psychological Association. Reprinted by permission of the author.

tually inhibit aggression because of its relaxing properties. Work by S. P. Taylor and his colleagues largely supports these observations. In a study by Taylor, Vardaris, Rawitch, Gammon, Cranston, and Lubetkin (1976), groups of subjects were given "cocktails" containing either no alcohol, alcohol, or THC (the active chemical ingredient in marijuana). Using the shock method in a competitive experimental setting, it was found that small amounts of alcohol tended to inhibit aggression (delivering electric shock to a competitor) whereas larger amounts facilitated aggression. However, it is necessary to qualify this latter observation by noting that large quantities of alcohol promoted aggression only if the drinker was provoked or frustrated in some fashion. In the case of marijuana, Taylor et al. found that small doses had little effect on aggression while larger doses seemed to actually inhibit it. The results of the Taylor and Leonard study are shown in Figure 17-7. Research by Myerscough and Taylor (1985) is also consistent with the conclusion that marijuana does not instigate or enhance aggression. However, we know little as yet about the effects of marijuana on individuals with preexisting aggressive or antisocial tendencies.

Other research indicates also that the relationship between the ingestion of amphetamines and subsequent aggression is relatively weak (Beezley, Gantner, Bailey, and Taylor, 1987). This research hardly proves that amphetamines never stimulate aggression because drug-behavior relationships are highly complex. Still, the current evidence does not support any strong cause-effect relationship. In contrast, diazepam (the most widely prescribed drug for the treatment of anxiety) has been shown to promote aggressive behavior (Gantner and Taylor, 1988).

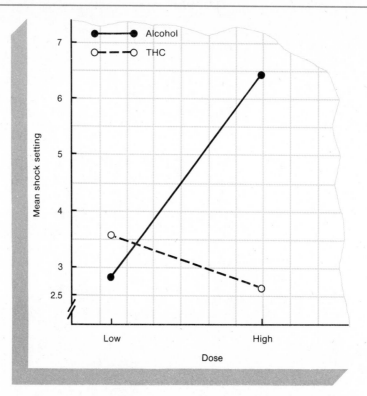

FIGURE 17-7 Mean shock settings as a function of high and low doses of alcohol and THC.

From Taylor, S. P. and Leonard, K. E., "Alcohol and human physical aggression" in R. G. Geen and E. I. Donnerstein, eds., *Aggression: Theoretical and Empirical Reviews*, Vol. 2, 1983. Copyright © 1983 by Academic Press, Inc. Reprinted by permission.

It is important to consider the role of cognitive variables in this complex area of research. For example, some evidence is compatible with the notion that if people believe they have ingested a drug, they will sometimes react to provocation with aggression and then attribute their behavior to the effects of the drug (e.g., Ferguson, Rule, and Lindsay, 1982). Thus, thinking can be a more powerful agent than the chemicals themselves. However, intoxicated individuals and sober individuals alike tend to inhibit their aggression when they are made self-aware. That is, aggression decreases when they are in front of a mirror and video camera and when the opportunity to aggress against another person arises (Bailey, Leonard, Cranston, and Taylor, 1983).

Clearly, the effects of alcohol and other drugs on aggression are complex and depend greatly on preexisting personality dispositions, situational cues (e.g., Leonard, 1989), the nature of the specific drug, and level of intoxication.

Diffusion of responsibility

People in groups are often prompted to behave in ways they would not were they alone. Presumably, the presence of others leads them to feel a lessened sense of personal responsibility for their actions. Such appears to be the case with aggressive behavior as well. As an illustration of this phenomenon, Mathes and Kahn (1975) exposed subjects, either alone or in threes, to insult. Similar groups were not insulted at all. Results showed that subjects desiring revenge and who were in groups of three responded more aggressively to the insult than did subjects who were alone or were in groups but had no reason for seeking revenge. What is more, subjects in groups did not feel as responsible for their aggression as those who were alone. All of this may be related to what Zimbardo (1969) refers to as **deindividuation** – the loss of self-awareness, self-observation, and self-evaluation with a loss in sensitivity to social norms. Urbanization, for example, has led to a kind of anonymity in which people become faceless. Such a sense of anonymity may, in turn, increase the likelihood of mob violence and aggression.

The dehumanized victim

A pervasive human propensity seems to be the tendency to justify our aggression toward others by diminishing or dehumanizing them. We call them names, portray them in lurid or animalistic terms, and otherwise try to make them less than they really are. By so labeling them, we can better justify our aggression toward them. A look at movies from World War II era provides many examples of this. These films now seem amusing since we are so far removed from the stresses of the time. German and Japanese soldiers, for example, seemed always to be raging beasts lusting after American women or sadistically torturing victims all over the place. While not totally outside the pale of reality, their very exaggeration probably served to heighten the country's level of arousal and patriotism. Bandura, Underwood, and Fromson (1975) produced this same phenomenon in the laboratory. By describing potential victims as either perceptive and understanding or animalistic and rotten, these investigators succeeded in influencing the amount of punishment delivered by subjects to those potential victims.

Obedience to authority

The Holocaust, in which the Nazi regime exterminated thousands upon thousands of Jewish victims, provides mute evidence of the power of situations in turning otherwise sane individuals into savage aggressors (Kren and Rappoport, 1980). Terror on such a monstrous scale seems nearly incomprehensible to those who would try to explain it. Yet Stanley Milgram (1963) was able to induce subjects in the laboratory to deliver what they thought were highly painful shocks to a hapless victim. Whenever subjects wavered in their willingness to shock the victim, the experimenter would in effect, command them to continue. And these were not college students participating in a study for class credit. They were adult males in occupations ranging from unskilled laborers to professional engineers. Even when their supposed victims screamed and pounded on the wall for the shock to stop,most subjects were little deterred in their rush to obey the experimenter. Fully 65 percent of the subjects obeyed the experimenter's commands.

Box 17-1
BLACK UNIFORMS AND AGGRESSION IN PROFESSIONAL SPORTS

In almost every culture, black is seen as the color denoting evil and death. Bearing this in mind, Frank and Gilovich (1988) speculated that black uniforms might somehow have an impact on the wearer's behavior. More specifically, are professional football and ice hockey teams that wear black uniforms more aggressive than those wearing nonblack uniforms? To answer this question, the investigators examined the penalty records in the National Football League (NFL) and the National Hockey League (NHL) from 1970 to 1986. Also, subjects were asked to rate the uniforms of the various teams as presented via color slides. The rating scales were: good/bad; timid/aggressive; nice/mean; active/passive; and weak/strong. The results were referred to as "malevolence" ratings. In the case of football, the malevolence ratings and yards penalized are shown in the accompanying tables.

Mean Number of Yards Penalized (in z Scores) for National Football League Teams From 1970 to 1986

Football Team	z
LA RAIDERS	1.19
Buffalo	0.63
PITTSBURGH	0.48
Cleveland	0.44
Houston	0.38
Atlanta	0.30
CHICAGO[a]	0.29
CINCINNATI	0.27
San Diego	0.27
Denver	0.24
Dallas	0.23
NEW ORLEANS	0.10
San Francisco	0.09
Detroit	0.04
Seattle[b]	0.02
NY Jets	0.01
St. Louis	-0.01
Washington	-0.07
LA Rams	-0.09
New England	-0.18
Kansas City	-0.19
Indianapolis	-0.19
NY Giants	-0.32
Tampa Bay[b]	-0.41
Philadelphia	-0.49
Green Bay	-0.73
Minnesota	-0.81
Miami	-1.60

Malevolence Ratings of the Uniforms of Professional Football Teams

Football Team	Rating
LA RAIDERS	5.10
PITTSBURGH	5.00
CINCINNATI	4.97
NEW ORLEANS	4.83
CHICAGO	4.68
Kansas City	4.58
Washington	4.40
St. Louis	4.27
NY Jets	4.12
LA Rams	4.10
Cleveland	4.05
San Diego	4.05
Green Bay	4.00
Philadelphia	3.97
Minnesota	3.90
Atlanta	3.87
San Francisco	3.83
Indianapolis	3.83
Seattle	3.82
Denver	3.80
Tampa Bay	3.77
New England	3.60
Buffalo	3.53
Detroit	3.38
NY Giants	3.27
Dallas	3.15
Houston	2.88
Miami	2.80

Note. Teams in boldface capitals are those with black uniforms.
[a]Chicago's uniform is often thought to be black but is in fact a dark navy blue.
[b]These teams have only been in the National Football League since the 1976 season

Note. Teams in boldface capitals are those with black uniforms. The malevolence ratings represent the average rating of three semantic differential scales: good/bad, timid/aggressive, and nice/mean.

Adapted from "The Dark Side of Self-and Social Perception: Black Uniforms and Aggression in Professional Sports" by Mark G. Frank and Thomas Gilovich, Journal of Personality and Social Psychology, Vol. 54, No. 1, January 1988. Copyright © 1988 by the American Psychological Association. Reprinted by permission of Thomas Gilovich.

As can be seen, NFL teams wearing black were penalized significantly more often than their rivals wearing nonblack. Subjects' ratings suggest that teams wearing black are judged more harshly. It was also found in the research that when teams switched from nonblack uniforms to black ones, there was an immediate increase in penalties. All these results were also true of NHL teams. Thus, even a seemingly trivial environmental factor can become associated with aggression.

Professional teams that wear black uniforms are often thought to be more aggressive and thus incur more frequent penalties. Photograph Mike Powell/Allsport, U.S.A.

While many complex factors were undoubtedly implicated in producing this obedience, the fact that an authority figure could induce otherwise responsible individuals to become highly aggressive should give everyone pause for thought.

In passing, it should be noted that Milgram's work has been harshly criticized on ethical grounds. His critics argue that without any forewarning, subjects were exposed to extreme stress and were not screened in advance for psychological health. Others claim that Milgram should have canceled the experiment once the degree of stress became obvious. Baumrind (1964) suggested that many of the participants may have suffered lasting effects from the experiment. Perhaps just the realization that one became so obedient in such circumstances was enough to alter the self-concept. Or maybe the experience led to a heightened distrust of authority figures. Milgram (1964, 1974) rejected such arguments. He claimed that steps were taken after the experiment to reduce the possibility of such reactions. He also noted that questionnaires sent later to participants showed no signs of such reactions and that, indeed, subjects were pleased to have been able to participate.

Ironically, others have criticized Milgram's research as having been fakery; that his subjects were merely pretending to believe that their victims were in peril. Of course, critics cannot have it both ways. They cannot say that the research is quackery then turn round and say it was unethically dangerous. An excellent and evenhanded review of all these points has been provided by Miller (1986).

Sexual arousal

Philosophers, not to mention lovers, have long remarked about the close kinship between aggression and sexuality. Freudians likewise are prone to view sexual and aggressive behavior as intimately connected and mutually enhancing. But experimental evidence is conflicting on this issue. For example, Zillmann (1971) showed three kinds of movies to groups of male subjects: (1) erotic (a couple engaging in explicit foreplay), (2) aggressive (a violent boxing match), or (3) neutral (a journey through China). Afterward, subjects were placed in the familiar teacher-learner shock paradigm, which allowed them to vent their aggression. It was found that the erotic movie led to greater expressions of aggression than did the aggressive movie. Baron (1974) found just the opposite. Following an anger-producing experience, male subjects were shown erotic stimuli (pictures of nude females), pictures of fully clothed females, or neutral stimuli (scenery, etc.). When later placed in the shock machine situation, subjects who had earlier seen either nude or clothed females were less aggressive than those who had viewed the neutral stimuli. To resolve such incompatible sets of findings, Donnerstein, Donnerstein, and Evans (1975) have proposed that mildly erotic stimuli (e.g., nude females) are pleasant and distracting and serve to divert the subject's attention from previous aggression or frustration. And explicitly erotic stimuli (e.g., couples having intercourse) significantly heighten arousal so that the anger previously experienced is not inhibited. Others have suggested that what is really important is the quality of the subject's reactions to erotic stimuli (L. A. White, 1979). Some individuals are more likely to react to mild stimuli (e.g., "cheesecake") with positive feelings whereas they respond to very strong stimuli (e.g., sadomasochistic sex, oral sex) with repugnance. When the latter happens, aggression is likely to be enhanced if the subject has been frustrated or made angry earlier. Erotic stimuli and aggression are likely related, but in a complex way that involves many variables.

VIOLENCE AGAINST WOMEN

With the women's movement has come increased awareness of a problem long ignored by societies all over the world—violence directed against women. While new statistics on the prevalence of the problem are coming out nearly every day, it is likely that upwards of two million wives in the United States suffer battering from their husbands every year. Often, what begins as "psychological" aggression culminates in physical aggression (Murphy and O'Leary, 1989). Because violence in the home is so prevalent (see Kazdin, 1988), many battered women are forced to leave home and seek shelter elsewhere. Recent evidence suggests that battered women may have difficulty in assuming personal responsibility for their own goal-direction to solve their predicament and will display a general sense of helplessness (Cheney and Bleker, 1982). Aggression in the home also generates problems in those children who are witnesses to it (Jouriles, Murphy, and O'Leary, 1989).

But the battered woman is only a part of the violence syndrome directed against women. There is the violence of rape which affects women of all ages, races, and social strata. More recently, incest directed against young females has emerged as a problem of critical magnitude that occurs everywhere in society. Even lesser instances of violence such as sexual harassment, obscene phone calls, and the like, are emerging from the shadows as women become increasingly unwilling to tolerate them. All of these acts, from the most violent to the mildly harassing, represent what Leidig (1981) refers to as "tip of the iceberg" phenomena. That is, women tend not to report many acts of violence (Clark and Lewis, 1977; L. Schulz, 1976; Walker, 1979), and so their actual prevalence is probably severely underestimated.

For many years, violence against women was largely excused or else ignored. Everyone "knew" that rape victims had probably behaved in sexually provocative ways. And wives who failed to obey their husbands or keep their place in the family "had it coming." There was even the myth that women enjoy being humiliated. Other excuses engaged the idea that it cannot be helped—after all, men are just by nature more sexual and aggressive and these things will happen. Clearly, such reasoning has found great support in our male-dominated culture.

Also of special concern is the presence of so many R- and X-rated films that are violent and degrading to women. Large numbers of men view pornography every year and a significant number of them view violent pornography as well (Demaré, Briere, and Lips, 1988). Pornography usually subordinates women to men, as if they exist solely for the sexual satisfaction of the male. They are portrayed as willing and even eager to accommodate every male sexual whim. Many of these films contain highly aggressive erotic material (e.g., beating, maiming, raping). Some argue that males who are repeatedly exposed to such films may increase their antisocial attitudes and behaviors toward women (e.g., Donnerstein, 1983). Furthermore, sexually violent material that begins by provoking anxiety or depression in the male viewer seems to decline in that ability with prolonged exposure (Linz, Donnerstein, and Penrod, 1988). Whatever the reasons, sexual assaults against women are common and are associated with increased risk for later depression, drug abuse, and anxiety in those women (Burnam et al., 1988). In any given situation, specific factors can be identified—everything from alcohol and finances to summer heat and sexual arousal. But taken as a whole, these instances coalesce into a kind of dehumanization of the woman. When there is a complete equality between men and women, aggression will certainly decline. By derogating her role, dignity, or individuality, one can then rationalize aggression against her in the "finest spirit" of dehumanization of the victim. In the final analysis, it is socially transmitted attitudes toward women that foster the release of sexual aggression against them (Briere and Malamuth, 1983). There will be violence against women as long as men continue to be socialized into believing they are entitled to control the lives of women, even violently (Walker, 1989). There will only be real changes when sexism is reduced or eliminated and men's socially sanctioned hatred of women disappears (Leidig, 1981).

PERSONALITY AND AGGRESSION

Although we mentioned earlier some research on individual differences in reactions to frustration, there has not been a lot of research devoted to the topic of generalized aggressive dispositions. Yet, it would be surprising were personality not somehow linked to aggressive behavior.

Stability

We know that children, especially boys, are highly consistent in their expression of aggression over periods of several months (Deluty, 1985). And, as Widom (1989) notes, aggressiveness is such a stable trait that early aggressiveness (even in eight- to twelve-year olds) is predictive of later antisocial behavior. What is more, research carried out over a twenty-two-year period suggests that aggression is a reasonably stable phenomenon and that it even perpetuates itself across generations (Huesmann, Eron, and Yarmel, 1987). We noted earlier a similar situation in the case of child abuse; those abused as children often seem to become abusers themselves as adults. Unfortunately, too, longitudinal research reveals that aggressiveness in children is associated with low levels of academic achievement and high rates of psychiatric treatment (Moskowitz and Schwartzman, 1989). All of this tends to support a dispositional view of aggressiveness. Furthermore, specific measures of aggression often intercorrelate positively when the same subjects aggress in several ways (Carlson, Marcus-Newhall, and Miller, 1989).

Other personality variables

Personality variables other than aggressiveness have sometimes been linked with aggressive behavior. For example, in a competitive reaction-time task, anxious subjects did not press the shock button as long as did nonanxious subjects (Taylor, 1953). Need for approval has been suggested as a trait that reduces the likelihood of aggression (Dengerink, 1976). Similarly, guilt can impede the expression of aggression (Knott, Lasater, and Shuman, 1974). Even the I-E variable (Rotter, 1966) has been shown to relate to aggressive behavior. For example, Dengerink, O'Leary, and Kasner (1975) have observed that internals, in a competitive reaction-time situation, are more likely than externals to aggress in tune with their opponent's level of aggression.

Psychopathology

The field of abnormal psychology is littered with so many examples of aggressiveness that we can mention just a very few. In the case of children, there is the **socialized conduct disorder** (Quay, 1964). Such children are prone to a variety of antisocial or delinquent behaviors including truancy, running away, serious lying, and stealing. Obviously, many adults are characterized by repeated offenses such as vandalism, breaking and entering, fire setting, assault, mugging, extortion, purse snatching, armed robbery, and rape. When these occur in children, the category is referred to as **undersocialized conduct disorder** and may portend similar problems when the child reaches adulthood (Robins, 1966).

Another example is the so-called **passive-aggressive personality.** Here, the person "passively" resists the demands of others in interpersonal and work situations (Davison and Neale, 1990). This is a kind of disguised aggression that often appears as stubbornness or even incompetence. Such people are chronically late, procrastinate, and do a lot of "forgetting." Another subtle manifestation of aggression is in the case of some psychosomatic or psychophysiological disorders such as essential hypertension. Hostile impulses are dammed up and eventually may lead to illness. Similarly, in some cases of alcoholism, hostility seems to be a factor. The alcoholic may hurt others (such as family) by embarrassing public displays of intoxication. In some cases of depression the analysis involves a kind of turning of hostility inward. And, of course, from a psychoanalytic perspective, suicide becomes the ultimate form of aggression against the self (Davison and Neale, 1990)!

CONTROLLING AGGRESSION

To some extent, earlier sections have touched on the control of violence. Topics such as frustration, catharsis, social learning, television, situational factors, diffusion of responsibility, dehumanization, sexual arousal, and violence toward women all contained either implicit or explicit suggestions about reducing aggression. But the control of aggression is terribly difficult. Were it not, the problem would have been solved generations ago. This is also a controversial topic because there are so many conflicting values. Furthermore, when aggression encompasses such a wide diversity of areas (e.g., child and spouse abuse, violence in the schools, juvenile delinquency, television, terrorism, etc.), the approaches to controlling it will of necessity be equally diverse (Center for Research on Aggression, 1983).

Improving quality of life

In trying to summarize the utility of various methods of curbing aggression, Zillmann (1978) offers several generalizations. First, we must find better ways of providing access to goods and services for people who do not now have them. Clearly, this involves social and economic programs of great magnitude about which there is little consensus in the world today. By reducing frustration and deprivation and improving the quality of life on a large scale, the hope is that provocation to aggression will decrease accordingly.

Punishment

A second method of curbing aggression involves the even and consistent application of punishment that is not physical and will not lead to injury. The use of force too often seems to breed greater frustration and hence more aggression. In addition, making it clear that aggression will lead to social reprisal and condemnation will tend to dampen it (R. W. Rogers, 1980). Indeed, Blanchard and Blanchard (1986) argue for a reexamination of the role of punishment as a deterrent for aggression. They suggest that appropriate punishment from parents, educators, and the like can be effective. However, individuals must understand clearly and quickly that aggression leads to unacceptable outcomes for them.

Treatment of children

Antisocial behavior in children is a pervasive social and clinical problem. A variety of behavioral methods of intervention with overly aggressive children have been offered recently (Goldstein and Keller, 1987). These include such methods as relaxation training, anger control, cognitive restructuring, and so on. Also important are instilling prosocial skills that will replace aggression. However, there are still few effective interventions that have been empirically established. Several techniques do seem promising, such as parent management training, family therapy, and wider community-based interventions (Kazdin, 1987).

Empathy

At an interpersonal level, Baron (1983) has suggested that aggression can be prevented or controlled by inducing responses that are incompatible with aggression. One example is humor. Also, there is empathy. Specifically, when a victim's pain or suffering can be shown to an aggressor, empathy may be aroused which, in turn, may retard further aggression (assuming the aggressor is not extremely angry). It seems clear that empathic/sympathetic responding is negatively related to aggression and is something that deserves an important role in controlling antisocial behavior (Miller and Eisenberg, 1988). Again, however, these are steps rather than panaceas.

Changing attitudes and values

Eron and Huesmann (1984) feel that the control of many forms of aggression lies in changing attitudes, values, and the conditions of learning. For example, TV networks should be pressured to reduce violence on television. Given the reluctance of TV executives to do this, Eron and Huesmann go on to suggest that children be specifically taught that television is not a realistic portrayal of the world and that aggressive behaviors are not as universally accepted as television programming might suggest. Eron and Huesmann also suggest that nonaggressive habits be taught to children. They even go to the extent of recommending that boys be socialized more in the ways girls in our society have been in the past. Finally, they urge that we love and nurture our children if we want to reduce their potential for antisocial behavior. Admittedly, these recommendations are tall orders indeed given the heterogeneity of our values, personal and psychological resources, and prior learning. We must also try to curb impulsive aggression by teaching people habits or predispositions that will prevent aggression from becoming the prepotent response when they become annoyed or frustrated (Zillmann, 1978).

SUMMARY

■ Some define aggression as the attempt to inflict bodily harm on another. Others suggest that psychological harm be included as well, or that the intent to do harm be present. Still others claim that outcome and not intent is the critical element.

- A major technique for studying aggression is observation. This can be a very useful, insightful method. However, there are problems of bias and reliability.

- Several laboratory methods have been used to study aggression. Sometimes, a subject is frustrated and then allowed to retaliate with verbal aggression. Another method involves the opportunity to aggress against inanimate objects—for example, against a Bobo doll. In other cases, one is allowed to aggress with toy weapons. There are, of course, problems with each method, especially in the sense of how closely it imitates reality.

- The most common laboratory methods are a series of techniques in which a teacher-learner situation is contrived. The teacher (subject) has the opportunity to deliver what he or she thinks is electric shock to the learner. Aggression is then defined as the intensity or duration of shock delivered in response to some behavior on the part of the learner. A critical issue here is also how similar such methods are to real-life settings.

- Field methods are also sometimes used. For example, number of reported aggressive incidents may be correlated with ongoing conditions in society. Disentangling cause from effect can be difficult, however. In other cases, subjects are actually frustrated in public settings, and their reactions are recorded. Such methods can raise legal questions and the possibility that someone may be hurt. General ethical issues exist as well.

- A number of biological-genetic determinants of aggression have been offered. The Freudian view involves the death instinct or Thanatos.

- Sociobiologists see aggression as an evolutionary product of the way the nervous system is structured. While investigators such as Lorenz stoutly maintain that human aggression has a biological and instinctual foundation, there is little empirical research support for this thesis. Nor does there appear to be much solid evidence that males with the XYY chromosomal anomaly are more prone to violence. The debate over the relative contributions of heredity and environment continues. While the temporal lobe and hypothalamus may mediate aggression, our understanding here is still rudimentary.

- Early on, Dollard and his colleagues suggested the frustration-aggression hypothesis—that frustration always leads to aggression and that aggression is always the product of frustration. This hypothesis was soon modified in recognition of the fact that frustration can produce a variety of responses in addition to aggression. Others suggested that the first response to frustration is anger and that if the proper cues are present in such a situation, aggression will ensue.

- People differ both in their characteristic levels of frustration tolerance and in the ways they typically respond to frustration. Rosenzweig developed a test to identify these individual differences.

■ Social learning theorists suggest that we learn to be aggressive by observing aggressive models and by being reinforced for our aggressive behavior. Bandura and his colleagues have produced considerable evidence for this view.

■ Much of our social learning of aggression occurs within the family and is related to child-rearing practices. A particularly unfortunate example of this is child abuse.

■ A controversial question is the extent to which aggression is enhanced by movies and TV. Many fear that by seeing so much violence on the screen, children learn new ways of behaving aggressively, tend to lose their inhibitions over expressing aggression, and generally become desensitized to violence.

■ Laboratory studies, work in natural settings, and longitudinal research all seem to point to the role of filmed violence as a contributor to aggression in those who view it. Yet, there are studies that have not shown this link. Thus, the controversy continues.

■ It has been argued that release of violence in "safe" ways enables us to purge ourselves of aggressive tendencies—the catharsis effect. However, the evidence for this effect is not strong, and many contend that catharsis through TV or otherwise is just another way of enhancing our potential for aggressiveness.

■ Several examples of how situational conditions can promote the expression of aggression were described. They were the effects of heat, the role of drugs, situations that diffuse the responsibility for aggression or dehumanize the potential victim, situations that promote obedience, and circumstances that lead to sexual arousal.

■ A major social problem is violence against women. While many complex reasons undoubtedly exist for this phenomenon, the feminist explanation is that such violence is just one more example of pervasive sexism in our society.

■ Aggressiveness is a stable phenomenon in individuals and thus can be viewed in personality terms. A number of pathological expressions of aggression relate to personality features. Several personality variables were also cited as sometimes related to aggressive behavior under certain conditions.

■ This chapter closed with a brief outline of several methods of controlling aggression. These included better access to goods and services, the even-handed and consistent application of punishment, the teaching of predispositions to avoid violence as a solution, treatment interventions with children, and promotion of empathy. Ultimately, controlling aggression may reside in changing attitudes, values, and the conditions of learning. Inducing responses that are incompatible with aggression would be useful as well. Clearly, however, these methods are enormously difficult to implement given the complexity of societies.

CHAPTER 18

ALTRUISM, EMPATHY, AND MORAL JUDGMENT

The last chapter taught us that people have the capacity for violence. In this chapter we will see that they have a corresponding capacity for helpfulness and kindness. Of course, we cannot begin this chapter (as we did the last) with statistics setting forth the frequency of altruistic acts. Nobody compiles such figures. Perhaps it is in our nature to be fascinated with negative stories so that we scarcely notice the selflessness about us. But occasionally stories do creep into the nightly news. A fire fighter rescues a child at considerable risk to himself. A woman foregoes her own comfort to provide meals for the homeless on Thanksgiving. And it has always been thus. How many soldiers have crawled across bloody fields to rescue a fallen comrade, oblivious to the artillery shells bursting everywhere? And those brave women and men who sheltered slaves escaping from the South during the Civil War were hardly thinking of themselves, nor were those in France who aided Jews in their flight to neutral countries to evade their Nazi tormentors. What is it that makes people perform acts of heroism or generosity rather than taking the easier road? Where does altruism come from? Is it in the genes, is it learned, do the demands of the situation extract help from us, or does some set of internal dispositions ordain our acts of generosity? Is it a product of empathy or some kind of moral force? And what about individual differences in altruism? These are some of the questions that we shall confront in this chapter.

A FEW DISTINCTIONS

The subject matter of this chapter has been variously labeled as *helping, altruism,* and *prosocial behavior* (Rushton and Sorrentino, 1981). Many investigators use these terms interchangeably. They apply them to myriad behaviors ranging from contributing to charities to donating time to a senior citizens home; from defusing a bomb to helping a friend study for an exam; from responding to a request for directions to returning a lost credit card. But in some instances, distinctions among these terms are made.

For example, Staub (1978) means by **altruism** an act that is intended solely to benefit another person or group and which provides no material benefit to the person who commits it. **Prosocial behavior,** in contrast, could result in benefit to another person without there being any real intent to help. Or there could even be some material gain expected by the initiator of the behavior. A person might donate a considerable sum of money to a charitable foundation knowing full well that a significant tax break is in the offing. This would qualify as prosocial behavior but not as altruism. Altruism would be exemplified by the person who plunges into an icy river to rescue a mongrel dog stranded on an ice floe and has nothing material to gain by the act.

Altruism also provides an interesting dilemma for those who believe that all behavior is determined by the expectations of reinforcement (Rosenhan, 1972). If an act is truly selfless, where is the reinforcement? If there is no reward and, instead, the potential even for personal injury or loss, how do we account for such behavior? The easy answer is that the person gains a feeling of well-being or is motivated by internal, intangible goals that cannot be defined in material terms. This explanation is, perhaps, acceptable if we are able to specify in advance that certain people do carry about within them such tendencies. But to resort to these kinds of explanations because we are having trouble locating the external gains that are motivating the person is not acceptable.

In the present chapter, we shall take the broader view of altruistic, prosocial behavior while keeping in mind the foregoing qualifications about intent and material gain. We shall, as Pervin (1978) has done, increasingly regard assistance as noble or altruistic the more it is given without the expectation of external rewards and the more costly it is to the helper. But the reader must realize that the ambiguities in using the two terms in this chapter reflect the confusion that exists in this research area today.

THE BIOLOGICAL PERSPECTIVE

Both learning and biological explanations of prosocial behavior have been offered over the years and each point of view has its staunch supporters. Let us begin this section with a brief look at animal prosocial behavior.

Animal prosocial behavior

Prosocial behavior is by no means the exclusive property of human beings (Cunningham, 1981; E. O. Wilson, 1975). There are certainly numerous examples of prosocial behavior in the animal kingdom. When interlopers invade their hive, bees attack and in the process destroy themselves. Birds sometimes protect their young by feigning injury and thus luring predators away from the nest and toward themselves. Other birds accomplish the same goal by emitting whistles to attract predators toward themselves and away from the nest. Chimpanzees will respond to the entreaties of other chimps and allow them to share their food. According to Wilson, this kind of behavior promotes what is called **kin selection.** That is, by behaving selflessly, these animals increase the likelihood that their closely related brethren will live to procreate. Since these relatives share their genes, they will be passed along to succeeding generations.

Some investigators also claim that prosocial tendencies are not only passed along by the genes but that an animal's behavior may serve to stimulate prosocial acts by the beneficiary sometime in the future.

Conscious intent

But can observations and inferences from lower animals be generalized to human beings? They can if we define altruism solely in terms of its effects since many animals and insects behave in ways that protect other members of the species while putting themselves in considerable danger (Hinde, 1974). But many social scientists suggest that altruism is not altruism at all if there is neither intent to help nor consciousness of the self-sacrifice and costs involved. And intent is hard enough to measure in humans let alone in animals. In fact, many claim that altruism is a uniquely human characteristic. The argument is also made that with animals, we are dealing with acts that are species-specific and built into the biological fiber of the organism. There is no intent or motivation in the human sense, only a blind response to a specific set of stimuli.

Biology and heredity

Whether altruism is a part of human nature is probably more a philosophical question than a psychological one (Darley and Latané, 1970). On the other hand, Hoffman (1981) clearly leans toward a biological explanation of altruism. He bases his conclusion on two major points. First, there is the evidence from the field of evolutionary biology and the fact that humans have the necessary underlying neural structures for empathy, which is thought by many to be an important mediator of altruism. Second, many individuals who have been socialized in a self-oriented society behave altruistically. Such behaviors often seem impulsive—almost unlearned, if you will—and do not appear to be hedonistic attempts to gain approval from others.

As noted a moment ago, a number of investigators believe that prosocial behavior is stimulated by an empathic concern for others. **Empathy** is typically defined as a vicarious affective response to another's feelings (Stotland, 1969), and we shall talk more about it a bit later. But for the moment, it might be noted that some researchers are beginning to suggest that empathy has a genetic basis (Batson, Darley, and Coke, 1978; Hoffman, 1981; Krebs, 1975). Matthews, Batson, Horn, and Rosenman (1981) have presented preliminary evidence that empathic concern for others does, indeed, have a genetic component. Their evidence is based upon responses of monozygotic and dizygotic twins to empathylike self-report items. Rushton and his colleagues (Rushton et al., 1986) have likewise administered self-report questionnaires on empathy and altruism to monozygotic and dizygotic pairs of twins. They found evidence for the heritability of both empathy and altruism. In interpreting all these results, however, one must recognize that the data come from self-reports rather than objective observations of actual behavior in real-life settings. Furthermore, the question of the greater similarity of the environments of monozygotic twins as compared to their dizygotic counterparts cannot be totally ruled out.

More recently, Rushton (1989) has also hypothesized that individuals who mate together are genetically more alike than those who do not. This will, then, tend to perpetuate the genetic basis for altruism. While hardly a settled issue, this is an intriguing hypothesis.

A learning rejoinder

The ambiguities inherent in genetic research on altruism have persuaded most social scientists that the most logical explanation of altruism in humans is one based upon learning. Gould (1976) uses the classic story of the aged Eskimo who effectively commits suicide by remaining behind on an ice floe while the remainder of the family group moves on in search of food. To do otherwise might endanger the survival of the entire family by slowing them down or else consuming scarce food supplies. A sociobiologist might contend that family groups without altruistic genes have already disappeared through natural selection since the old and sick hindered migrations and thus led to the death of whole family units. The aged with altruistic genes ensured the survival of their family when they passed those genes along. Gould states that we could just as easily argue, however, that there are no altruistic genes. While the sacrifices of the aged are adaptive and certainly prosocial, it is not genetics at work but tradition. Families without such a culturally learned tradition do not survive. With such a tradition, Eskimo children very early learn to celebrate as heroes those old people who put the clan above their own life. Such an attitude helps ensure that when these children in turn become old and weary, they too will seek out that final ice floe. The cultural-learning explanation of altruism is at least as plausible as the genetic one.

DEVELOPMENT OF MORAL JUDGMENT

Very often when we behave altruistically we do so because we have arrived at a moral judgment. Thus, the connection between altruism and moral judgment is an intimate one. But how is it that we develop a sense of morality, acquire a conscience, or reach these moral judgments? In this section, we shall examine several possibilities.

The Freudian perspective

As we saw in Chapter 3, Freud linked the development of a superego or conscience to the process of identification. Prosocial behavior emanates from the demands of the superego that we live up to our internalized standards. Ideally, the child incorporates the features of the appropriate parent and assumes his or her behaviors, values, and standards. The adoption of these values and standards gains the child acceptance into the larger culture. Through these processes, the child eventually comes to embrace the moral standards of society. The bases of the socialization of the child lie in the specific quality of early parent-child interactions. Of course, to the extent that these interactions are unusual, the socialization and moral standards of the child may depart from the norm. Once the superego has developed appropriately, however, morality and altruism are upheld by the unpleasantness of the guilt experienced when the individual behaves immorally or selfishly.

At a general level, then, we can account for altruistic behavior in part by regarding it as a product of identification with an altruistic figure—a warm, nurturing mother who gives of herself or a father who repeatedly sacrifices to help others. But sometimes there can be malignant overtones even to altruistic behavior. In some instances, the psychoanalyst may even regard altruism as part of a neurotic process. For example, a person may try to compensate for feelings of early deprivation by repeatedly sending gifts to other people. Charity becomes a way of denying one's own persistent feelings of powerlessness and deprivation. Or the person who is really selfish may attempt to disguise this by a reaction formation—giving to others in order to hide the wish to take from them. For the psychoanalyst, then, the complete understanding of altruistic acts can only come from examining the underlying unconscious motive.

Two studies are especially informative in suggesting the dynamic interplay of the motives that sometimes underlie prosocial behavior. The first is the well-known study of people who helped Jews evade the Nazis during World War II (London, 1970). This was an intensive investigation of twenty-seven individuals who rescued Jews, often at the risk of great personal harm. What was striking about the results of the study was the complexity of the motives that were identified in the rescuers. Some were motivated by financial gain, others by sympathy. Some did not even particularly like the people they were rescuing. In some cases, a rescuer initially became involved quite by accident. But continued involvement could only be explained by deeper personality determinants. For some, it was probably the spirit of adventurousness that sustained their involvement. But for others, there seemed to be a strong element of parental identification. That is, rescuers were behaving as they felt a parent would have wanted them to. In a similar study of 682 rescuers, nonrescuers, and Jewish survivors, Oliner and Oliner (1988) distinguish among four kinds of rescuers: the religiously motivated, the socially connected, the socially committed, and the egalitarians.

A study by Rosenhan (1970) also supports the notion of the complexity of the motives that drive people to act altruistically. Rosenhan found that there were at least three major types of individuals who supported the civil rights movement in the United States during the 1950s and 1960s. There were **Passive Supporters,** who gave money but little else; their personal sacrifice was minimal. Their response seemed stimulated mainly by requests from friends, and their activity was brief and not sustained. If anything, their behavior was supported by the social approval they received from their friends. **Partially Committed** individuals were those who, for example, participated in a few freedom rides across portions of the South. They were more committed than the first group but not as involved as the **Fully Committed** group. The latter individuals sustained their efforts over time and also were involved in a variety of different activities including donating money, participating in freedom rides, and assisting in voter registration. What was especially interesting was the differing attitudes toward parents that characterized two of the groups. The Partially Committed seemed conflicted about their parents. They were ambivalent toward them, perhaps because their parents seemed concerned about morality but did not always act in accord with their beliefs. Half of the group had been or was in psychotherapy. In contrast, the members of the Fully Committed group expressed warm, positive feelings about their parents, and only rarely was a member of this group found to have undergone any therapy. Again, we see the identification process at work in altruism as the quality and quantity of altruism vary with the nature of the parent-child relationship.

A cognitive view

Whereas psychoanalytically oriented investigators might search for the roots of altruism in the individual's emotional relationships, others would look to cognitive development. Jean Piaget (1932) wanted to know how children reach moral judgments as they mature, and also the explanations they give for their decisions. To do this, he asked children from six to twelve years of age to listen to pairs of stories such as the following:

> John was in his room when his mother called him to dinner. John goes down and opens the door to the dining room. But behind the door was a chair, and on the chair was a tray with fifteen cups on it. Johnny did not know the cups were behind the door. He opens the door, the door hits the tray, bang goes the fifteen cups, and they all get broken.

> One day when Henry's mother was out, Henry tried to get some cookies out of the cupboard. He climbed up on a chair, but the cookie jar was still too high, and he couldn't reach it. But while he was trying to get the cookie jar, he knocked over a cup. The cup fell down and broke. (p. 122)

In this case, Piaget's question to the children was, "Which boy was naughtier and why?" From his analysis of children's responses to such questions about the various stories to which they had listened, Piaget was able to identify two chief orientations. Children younger than ten seemed to have an **objective orientation.** That is, Johnny was naughtier because he broke more cups than Henry. But as the child became older (above ten), a **subjective orientation** emerged. What was important was not the number of cups broken but the intentions involved. Henry was naughtier because he was doing something wrong when he accidentally broke a single cup. From the viewpoint of Piaget's structural-cognitive model, the young child takes things literally and often misses the subleties of intentions and purposes. As the child matures, moral judgments become relative to the circumstances and intentions of the person involved. It might be noted that Bandura disputes the need to consider stages in the development of moral reasoning. Bandura and MacDonald (1963) have provided evidence that the judicious use of models can readily influence the child's objective-subjective judgments. Others, such as E. J. Langer (1975), claim that while one can, via modeling, alter the child's statements that seem to imply subjective or objective orientations, it is less easy through modeling procedures to change his or her real judgments or reasoning.

Another cognitive point of view has been offered by Lawrence Kohlberg (1969). Like Piaget, Kohlberg was not particularly interested in overt behavior. Whether a person steals a bracelet in a department store or cheats on a tax return is of less concern than the person's reasoning as the moral dilemma involved is confronted. Kohlberg typically posed a moral dilemma to subjects and then asked them how the main character should act and why. He did not claim that the behavior chosen is what the subject would really do were the situation a real one. He used a subject's responses to infer that person's level of moral reasoning. Of the ten stories Kohlberg used to assess moral reasoning, the following is the most widely quoted:

In Europe a woman was near death from cancer. One drug might save her, a form of radium that a druggist in the same town had recently discovered. The druggist was charging $2000, ten times what the drug cost him to make. The sick woman's husband, Heinz, went to everyone he knew to borrow money, but he could only get together about half of what it cost. He told the druggist that his wife was dying and asked him to sell it cheaper or let him pay later. But the druggist said "No." The husband got desperate and broke into the man's store to steal the drug for his wife. Should the husband have done that? Why? (1969, p. 376)

Kohlberg analyzed the responses of thousands of subjects in all walks of life, intellectual levels, and so on. From this mass of data he determined that there are three broad levels of moral development and that each of these, in turn, consists of two stages, as shown in Table 18-1. He asserted that these stages are universal and apply regardless of culture. To reach each stage, one must have passed through all lower stages. Over the years, a considerable volume of research has accumulated in support of Kohlberg's position (Lickona, 1975).

TABLE 18-1 Kohlberg's six stages of moral reasoning

Level I—Preconventional (Young Children)

Child is influenced by the consequences of a behavior and does not analyze society's standards.

Stage 1—Punishment and Obedience Orientation. Actions are good or bad depending upon whether one is punished or not punished.

Stage 2—Instrumental Relativist Orientation. Actions are oriented around satisfying one's own needs and wishes. Pragmatism is dominant.

Level II—Conventional (Middle Childhood)

Child is influenced by the ideals of upholding the standards of family, group, or country.

Stage 3—"Good or Nice" Child Orientation. Actions that are altruistic rather than selfish are desirable. Striving for approval of others is paramount.

Stage 4—"Law and Order" Orientation. One must act in accordance with authority and maintain the social order.

Level III—Postconventional (Adolescence to Adulthood)

Person's sense of right and wrong becomes separate from identity with the group.

Stage 5—Social Contract Orientation. General sense of rightness and wrongness: awareness that there are different values; importance of consensus; realization that intent is critical; growth of empathy.

Stage 6—Universal Orientation. Evolution of one's own ethical position over the years. Principles are abstract and comprehensive.

SOURCE: Adapted from "From Is to Ought: How to Commit the Naturalistic Fallacy and Get Away with It in the Study of Moral Development" by L. Kohlberg. In *Cognitive Psychology and Genetic Epistemology* by T. Mischel (Ed.) (New York: Academic Press), 1971. Copyright 1971 by Academic Press. Used with permission.

Kohlberg himself showed little interest in correlating stages of development with overt behavior. Yet there are studies that point to such relationships. For example, when subjects were put into a situation where an authority figure urged them to deliver increasingly severe shocks to another person, an interesting thing happened (Kohlberg, 1971). Subjects who were determined to be in Stage 6 and viewed human rights as taking precedence over any contractual agreements with the experimenter refused to follow orders and shock their victim. In fact, 75 percent of Stage 6 subjects refused while only 13 percent in lower stages declined. Similar kinds of results have been reported by Haan, Smith, and Block (1968) in their studies of students at Berkeley during the civil disobedience period of the 1960s. Of those students who were at Stage 6, 80 percent were involved in acts of civil disobedience, and 50 percent of those at Stage 5 were involved. In contrast, only 10 percent of the students at Stages 3 and 4 were participants.

These kinds of results led Erkut, Jaquette, and Staub (1981) to reason that cognitive development affects behavior by changing a person's definition of a given situation. They contrived a situation where an "ailing" confederate of the experimenter needed help. The experiment contained several conditions which varied how permissible it was for subjects to interrupt their work on a task to help the confederate. Stage 5 subjects in the permission condition were more likely to help than Stage 5 subjects in the other conditions (prohibition and no information). Stage 3 and 4 subjects would not help under any circumstances. As a result of such work, Erkut, Jaquette, and Staub (1981) and Kurtines (1986) conclude that the critical issue seems to be the interaction between situation and moral judgment.

In closing this section, it might be noted that Kohlberg does have his critics. Simpson (1974) has argued that his scheme contains significant bias. Others (e.g., Hogan, 1973) have mentioned the almost cultish nature of Kohlberg's work, which makes it difficult to understand and score responses by subjects and thus assign them to the proper stages. Finally, Alston (1971) has suggested that Kohlberg's separation of behavior and reasoning is artificial and inappropriate. Still, a dedicated group of Kohlberg's collaborators contend that the six moral stages are universal, invariant, occur in an irreversible sequence, and can be measured reliably (see Colby, Kohlberg, and collaborators, 1987; Colby et al., 1987).

A final issue has to do with the proper application of Kohlberg's scheme to women. Gilligan (1982) believes that men and women differ in terms of how they define themselves. Men are attracted to success and autonomy while women often value themselves in roles that are caring and nurturant or involve close relationships with others. Too often, Gilligan asserts, moral theories relegate that same care, nurturance, and closeness to a lower stage. However, neither Thoma (1986) nor Mednick (1989) seem to feel that women do, in fact, score lower on Kohlberg's measure.

ROLE OF EMPATHY

Empathy has long been implicated as a factor in the expression of altruism or in the inhibition of aggression and recently has come of age as a research area (Eisenberg and Strayer, 1987). But empathy has been defined differently by different investigators. Flavell, Botkin, Fry, Wright, and Jarvis (1968) define it as the ability to infer accurately the feelings of other people. Thus, empathy becomes primarily a cognitive skill. For others, however, empathy is more than that. It is also the tendency to experience vicariously the emotions others are feeling (N. D. Feshbach, 1978; Hoffman, 1975a). This latter definition accords a more important role to empathy in promoting altruism since it implies that an empathic person would be motivated to help another person in need. If I experience distress, I would certainly be motivated to reduce it. Likewise, if I have empathy for someone else's distress, then I will vicariously experience that distress to some extent and thereby wish to relieve it—hence, an altruistic response. When pleading for contributions, charitable organizations work hard to play upon our emotions. They do not just remind us that there are starving children; they show us pictures of those starving children and try to arouse an empathic response that will enhance our need to make a contribution. The teenager who wants to extract a few more dollars from an unsympathetic parent asks, "Didn't you ever need money like this when you were my age?" After a moment's reflection, how could one refuse?

Empathy-based helping: Altruistic or egoistic?

Mussen and Eisenberg-Berg (1977) have stated not only that empathy is a critical factor mediating prosocial actions but that the relationship has been amply supported in research. Much of this support is in the form of research in which empathy is aroused in subjects through some situational manipulation and the incidence of any ensuing altruism is observed. However, in the beginning of this chapter the question was raised as to whether pure altruism in humans really exists. Some have argued that seeing another person in difficulty leads to an empathic reaction of sadness which, in turn, propels one to reduce this unpleasant reaction. If so, it would seem that empathy-based helping is selfishly rather than selflessly motivated. A study by Batson, Duncan, Ackerman, Buckley, and Birch (1981) reinforces the idea that empathy leads to altruistic rather than to egoistic motivation to help. Here, subjects watched another subject receive electric shocks and were then given the opportunity to help by taking the remainder of the shocks themselves. The experimenters induced both high and low levels of empathy in the observing subjects and also made it either easy or difficult for them to escape from the situation. As predicted, empathic subjects were as ready to help when avoidance of the situation was easy as when it was difficult. When empathy was low, subjects were ready to help, but mainly when avoidance was difficult. This and other evidence leads Batson (1990) to believe that more than a self-centered kind of motivation is involved in helping. Indeed, empathic motivation may turn out to be what some would regard as an intrinsic kind of motivation. That is, regardless of whether avoiding the person in need is easy or difficult, the empathic person is persistently altruistic.

Krebs (1975) measured the psychophysiological responses of adult subjects as they watched another person play a roulette game. Some subjects were led to believe that they were quite similar to the other person, and others that they were really rather dissimilar. Some subjects also were told that the other person was experiencing either pleasure or pain depending on whether it was a win or a loss. Other subjects were made to think that the performer was merely participating in a motor skills task. Several interesting results emerged from this study. First, subjects who believed the performer was alternately experiencing pain and pleasure showed greater evidence of emotional arousal, and this reaction was stronger for those subjects who believed they were similar to the performer. As part of the experimental procedure, subjects could choose to help themselves at the expense of the performer or help the performer at some cost to themselves. Interestingly those subjects who had earlier given evidence of empathic responses were more likely to help than those who had shown little in the way of empathy.

Thus far, we have considered only research involving adult subjects. But the role of empathy in promoting altruism is not restricted to adults. Barnett, King, and Howard (1979) were able to demonstrate similar effects in children. They asked children between the ages of seven and twelve to discuss happy (positive), sad (negative), or neutral incidents that either they or another child had experienced. For participating in the study, the children were awarded chips which could later be exchanged for prizes. They were also told that some children similar to themselves could not be in the study and would not, therefore, be able to receive any prizes. They were further informed that they could, if they wished, donate some of their prize chips to these other children. However, it was made clear that they did not have to do so. The investigators found that children who had described sad experiences encountered by another child shared significantly more than children who had described sad incidents they themselves had experienced (see Figure 18-1). These results suggest that induction of a mood normally characteristic of empathy enhances generosity in children.

Additional research by Batson and his colleagues (e.g., Batson et al., 1981; Toi and Batson, 1982) also seems to demonstrate that when helping is stimulated by empathy, the critical factor is selflessness. Yet work by Cialdini, Schaller, Houlihan, Arps, Fultz, and Beaman (1987) suggests the role of egoism or selfishness. They appear to have been successful in experimentally separating empathic emotion from sadness. When that happened (i.e., subjects were sad but not empathically so), amount of helping was predicted by level of sadness but not by empathy. Furthermore, when empathic individuals do not expect feedback on their altruistic efforts, they are less likely to help (Smith, Keating, and Stotland, 1989). It is doubtful, however, that we have heard the last of this debate; especially since Batson and colleagues (e.g., Batson et al., 1988; Batson, Batson, Griffitt, Barrientos, Brandt, Sprengelmeyer, and Bayly, 1989) continue to produce results supportive of the high empathy-altruism hypothesis.

Empathy training

Since there seems to be a relationship between empathy and subsequent helping, it seems logical that if we could raise empathy levels through training, we could increase the incidence of altruism. Based upon this rationale, Staub (1971) trained kindergarten children through role playing to understand and to express the feelings of people in need and also to assume the role of helper. A day later, these children were observed as they heard cries of distress coming from an adjacent room. The children's reactions were viewed from a one-way mirror. Girls who had had role-playing experience responded to the distress cries more often than did those without training. Although

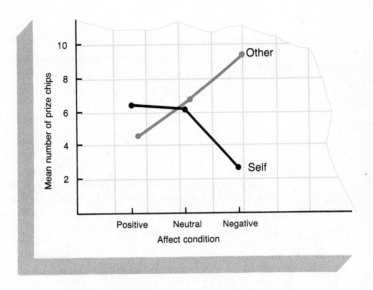

FIGURE 18-1 Mean number of prize chips donated by children according to self-other experience and affect.
From "Inducing Affect about Self or Other: Effects on Generosity in Children" by M. A. Barnett, L. M. King, and J. A. Howard, *Developmental Psychology*, 1979, *15*, 164–167. Copyright 1979 by the American Psychological Association. Reprinted by permission.

it is unclear how long-lasting such effects really are, in this study at least, they persisted for one week after the experiment concluded.

Dispositional empathy

It seems generally clear that by inducing empathy in a specific situation, we can increase the likelihood that altruistic behavior will follow. But matters are less clear when we consider altruism as a disposition or trait. A common method of measuring this disposition in children is the **Feshbach Affective Situations Test for Empathy (FASTE)** (N. D. Feshbach, 1978). It consists of a series of slide sequences that are shown with the object of eliciting the emotional reactions of happiness, sadness, anger, and fear. Typically, the results with the FASTE and other picture/story methods have been so inconsistent that Eisenberg and Miller (1987) were led to conclude that scores on these tests are unrelated to prosocial behavior. One of the problems may be that dispositional measures of empathy in children depend too heavily upon the child's verbal facility and thus empathic responses on the measure are masked.

When dealing with adults, however, the picture is somewhat brighter. For example, Mehrabian and Epstein (1972) have developed a generalized measure of empathy **(QMEE).** In two experiments, scores on this scale correlated with independent measures of altruism. In the first study, highly empathic subjects aggressed less toward another person than did less empathic subjects. The situation employed was the teacher-learner shock paradigm described in Chapter 17. In a second study, empathic subjects were more likely to help another subject in the experiment than were those low in empathy. Examples of some of the Mehrabian-Epstein items are presented in Table 18-2. Likewise, the **Hogan Empathy Scale** or **EM Scale** (Hogan, 1969) has also shown good validity. In fact, it has been suggested that, together, the QMEE and EM Scales do measure empathy but that each taps a different facet of it (Chlopan, McCain, Carbonell, and Hagen, 1985). The scales together seem to define empathy as a capacity to become emotionally aroused over another's plight and to take that other person's point of view.

Davis (1983) has described the development of another individual differences measure of empathy in adults. With it, he found that people who have a tendency to experience sympathy and concern for others are more likely to contribute to the annual Muscular Dystrophy Telethon.

LEARNING TO BE ALTRUISTIC

The social learning model of altruism has been summarized by Batson, Fultz, Schoenrade, and Paduano (1987) as one in which helping is promoted by a sequence of rewards. In the young child, prosocial behavior is elicited by material rewards (e.g., a piece of candy). A few years later, praise by a significant adult will usually increase the child's helpfulness. As adults, though, we are stimulated to prosocial behavior by the self-rewards involved in seeing ourselves as caring, kind persons.

TABLE 18-2 *Some Mehrabian-Epstein items measuring empathic tendencies*

---

1. It makes me sad to see a lonely stranger in a group. (+)

3. I often find public displays of affection annoying. (−)

14. I like to watch people open presents. (+)

27. I am very upset when I see an animal in pain. (+)

33. Little children sometimes cry for no apparent reason. (−)

From Albert Mehrabian and Norman Epstein, "A measure of emotional empathy," *Journal of Personality* 40:4, p. 528, 1972. Copyright © 1972 by Duke University Press. Reprinted by permission.

NOTE: Subjects may respond from "Very strongly agree" (+4) to "Very strongly disagree" (−4). A positive sign after an item means that agreement indicates empathy; a negative sign means that disagreement indicates empathy.

The essence of altruism is caring for others and like so much else, this is heavily influenced by learning experiences. Photograph Charles Gupton/TSW Click/Chicago.

If altruism is like so many other human behaviors, we would expect that many of its origins can be traced to the learning experiences to which the person is exposed. In short, we can look to the socialization process for the wellsprings of altruism. We know that there are differences among cultures in the frequency of expressions of altruism. This implies that people learn different things in different cultures. But even within a given culture, not everyone behaves alike. Some are more generous or cooperative than others. Therefore, we must consider something beyond broad differences among cultures as an explanation for altruism. The family models to which one is exposed, the kinds of peers one grows up with, the adults, teachers, and religious figures one encounters—all combine to produce individual differences in many characteristics, including altruism. Since not everyone within a given culture is exposed to exactly the same kinds of models, the door is opened for differences in learning. Let us take a look at some of the modeling and identification processes thought to be important in the learning of altruism.

Research on observational learning

A number of experiments on the imitation of prosocial behavior have been carried out with children. This research suggests that if children can learn altruistic behaviors in experimental settings, they can just as easily do so in natural settings where the cues may be even more compelling. As an example, Rushton (1975) studied children aged seven to eleven years from a largely working-class area in London. The children played an electronic bowling game in which they rewarded themselves with tokens, which could be exchanged later for prizes. Nearby was a bowl beneath a "Save the Children Fund" poster. The experimenter explained that children could, if they wished, donate tokens won to Bobby, the poster child. A man was then introduced as a possible future teacher in the school. This model played the game first while the subjects watched. The model, depending on the experimental condition, either donated some of his winnings to Bobby or pocketed them all for himself. As it turned out, modeling did occur. Subjects observing the generous model donated more tokens than those observing the selfish model. In addition, similar results were obtained in a follow-up two months later and in a situation somewhat different from the original one. Thus, the imitation effects showed both durability and generality. Rice and Grusec (1975) were also able to show the positive effects of modeling on sharing, and in some cases they noted that simply hearing a model talk about sharing is effective. After reviewing studies such as these, Rushton (1976) was led to conclude that even brief exposures to significant models can result in increased prosocial behavior on the part of children. It is not true, of course, that children will imitate just any model. They will tend to follow models who have reinforcing properties. As Mussen and Eisenberg-Berg (1977) observe, this translates mainly into power and nurturance. Models who are in a position of power and authority over the child will likely have more influence than those who are not. Similarly, the model who is warm, interested in the child, and generally nurturant will also likely be influential. And it goes without saying that models who not only preach but also practice altruism will have more of an effect.

An example of how parental values and the child's level of altruism may be linked is shown in a study by Hoffman (1975b). This researcher identified altruistic children by asking children who knew one another to each nominate three same-sexed peers who (1) were most likely to care about the feelings of others and (2) would stick up for another child who was the object of name-calling or jokes. The parents of these children ranked eighteen values in terms of their importance to themselves. Included were such items as concern for others' feelings and trying to help others. As it happened, fathers of the more altruistic boys and mothers of the more altruistic girls tended to place altruism high in their personal value scheme.

After an analysis of socialization processes in the family, Mussen and Eisenberg-Berg (1977) have concluded that modeling and identification are forceful determinants of the acquisition and development of prosocial behavior.

Religious orientation

Presumably, one learns to be religious or nonreligious. Furthermore, many of us tend to believe that religious people are more likely to be altruistic than those not religiously involved. This belief probably prevails even though some of us have encountered evidence to the contrary. Batson and Gray (1981) decided to test the hypothesis that being religious will lead a person to be more responsive to the needs of others. They defined two kinds of religiousness. First, there is the person who sees religion as an end in and of itself—a person who has the need to be helpful. Second, there is the quest-oriented person whose religious beliefs are focused on the desire to help those who are in need of help. In a sense, the difference here is that people in the first group focus on their own needs while those in the latter group focus on the needs of the victim. To test their hypothesis, Batson and Gray confronted female undergraduates with a female undergraduate confederate who was described as lonely. This confederate indicated that she either wanted help or did not want it, preferring to work through her problem herself. The subjects had previously filled out a questionnaire designed to separate people into one of the two religious orientations described. As predicted, those subjects whose religious beliefs centered on the need to help were as likely to offer help when it was wanted as when it was not. On the other hand, having a religious orientation that focused on the needs of the other person was correlated positively with offers of help when it was wanted but negatively when help was not desired. More recent work has also supported the relation between altruism and a quest orientation (Batson, Oleson, Weeks, Healy, Reeves, Jennings, and Brown, 1989). Perhaps, then, the way in which one is religious is a better predictor of prosocial behavior than merely the description of oneself as religious.

SITUATIONAL DETERMINANTS OF HELPING

A number of years ago, Kitty Genovese was brutally attacked outside her apartment in Queens, a borough of New York City. She was on her way from work; the time was 3:00 a.m., and her apartment was in a middle-class neighborhood. Her screams for help aroused at least thirty neighbors who came to their windows to look. The attackers kept at their savage task for half an hour. No one tried to help. No one called the police. Kitty Genovese died of multiple stab wounds.

One survey has shown that helping behavior is more likely to occur in rural environments than in urban ones (Steblay, 1987). So, is the Genovese tragedy just another example of the uncaring big city? Not exactly. The press covered the episode in great detail. People were outraged—but still, no one had helped. Why? Kitty's neighbors were far from indifferent since they stood transfixed for thirty minutes watching the whole thing. To try to answer some of these questions, a number of psychologists embarked on a series of studies. Indeed, over the past fifteen years or so, much of the research on helping has concentrated on the characteristics of situations that affect helping. To a large extent, this research implies that there is the potential for prosocial behavior in all of us. By investigating the nature of various situations, the idea is that we can determine how powerful the elements in them are in activating this potential. Staub (1980) has organized what is now a considerable volume of research on these situational determinants along several dimensions. Let us now consider some of them.

Ambiguity of situations

Situations that clearly reveal someone in need of help are more likely to prompt people to step forward with assistance than are those situations that are ambiguous. An experimental demonstration of this phenomenon has been provided by Clark and Word

TABLE 18-3   Mean reaction times (in seconds) and percentage of helping in several experimental conditions

Condition	Low Ambiguity	High Ambiguity
Alone	6.97 (100%)	55.67 (30%)
Two-person group	7.74 (100%)	61.59 (20%)
Five-person group	10.39 (100%)	52.18 (40%)

SOURCE: From "Why don't Bystanders Help? Because of Ambiguity?" by R. D. Clark, III and L. E. Word, 1972, *Journal of Personality and Social Psychology, 24,* p. 397. Copyright 1972 by the American Psychological Association. Reprinted by permission.

(1972). Subjects overheard a maintenance man in an adjoining room fall from a ladder. In the ambiguous condition, they heard just the sounds of the ladder hitting the wall and some blinds falling. In the nonambiguous condition, subjects also heard him cry out in pain. The likelihood of subjects offering help was significantly lower in the ambiguous situation. Table 18-3 shows these dramatic results. In a series of studies, Solomon, Solomon, and Stone (1978) showed that when bystanders heard just the sounds of a victim in the midst of an emergency, they were less likely to proffer help than when they both heard and saw the emergency situation. The investigators were able to demonstrate these results in both laboratory and field settings.

On the basis of common sense, we would certainly expect that people actually seeing someone in serious distress would be especially likely to offer help. In one sense, several of the studies on ambiguity could be viewed as relevant here, since nonambiguous situations are often characterized by numerous obvious cues that may lead the observer to infer a more serious state of affairs. To investigate this serious-nonserious dimension, Staub and Baer (1974) had a confederate feign a physical problem out on the street. In one condition, the confederate clutched his heart while collapsing to the ground. In the other situation, he grabbed his knee and fell. Observers noted that subjects (passersby) were much more likely to offer help to the apparent heart attack victim than to the victim of a knee problem.

Diffusion of responsibility

In 1970, Latané and Darley published a monograph on bystander intervention in emergencies. Their prime thesis was that the presence of other people at an emergency tends to inhibit one's impulse to help. A great deal of research has now been completed on this **diffusion of responsibility** effect. Latané and Nida (1981) have concluded that, "despite the great diversity of styles, settings, and techniques among studies, the social inhibition of helping is a remarkably consistent phenomenon" (p. 308). Latané and Darley (1970) suggest that three processes must be overcome before a decision to help another person in need will be made:

■ *Avoidance Inhibition* – The risk of being embarrassed if the situation is misinterpreted.

When others are present, this possibility of misinterpreting the situation can be avoided simply by leaving it to others.

- *Social Influence*—Most helping situations are a bit ambiguous. By looking to others (who are probably also looking to others) and not seeing anyone act, a definition of the situation as a no-help one is confirmed. Sometimes, the presence of others encourages us to "let someone else do it." Sometimes, being alone allows us to get away with not helping (see the accompanying cartoon).

- *Diffusion of Responsibility*—Knowing that others are available to help permits one to shift some of the responsibility for helping to them, even if those others cannot actually be seen or heard.

Numerous studies illustrate the operation of these processes. For example, Smith, Smythe, and Lien (1972) constructed a situation in which a female experimenter in the presence of the subject(s) appeared to become ill. She covered her face, groaned, and staggered to an adjoining room where she bumped into a filing cabinet and collapsed into a chair. Subjects were exposed to this little drama under one of three conditions: (1) alone, (2) in the presence of a confederate similar to themselves who did not react, or (3) in the presence of a nonreactive confederate who was dissimilar. Under the alone condition, 65 percent of the subjects intervened. But in the dissimilar other condition, only 35 percent attempted to help. And in the similar other condition, only 5 percent of the subjects made an effort.

Situational definition of the help needed

It was noted earlier that help is more likely to be offered when the situation clearly calls for intervention. But there is another aspect of this ambiguity-clarity factor. Even situations in which help is obviously needed differ in how explicitly they define the kind of help required. Research has shown that people are more likely to help when they know just what kind of help to provide. In part, it is because of this principle that public service advertising campaigns have been mounted to encourage people to learn cardiopulmonary resuscitation techniques. When a person recognizes the nature of the emergency and also possesses the needed skills, the likelihood of helping is significantly enhanced. A simple demonstration of this principle comes from the work of Schwartz and Clausen (1970). When a distressed person asked for help in retrieving a pill from his coat pocket, help was forthcoming more often than when it was not clear what a potential helper could do to assist.

Cost of helping

In nearly every helping situation, there is some potential cost to the helper. Coming to the aid of someone being mugged raises the possibility that you yourself may be attacked. Helping a stranded cat out of a tree means that you may get your coat dirty or tear your shirt. Assisting a confused elderly couple to find the right subway train results in your being late for an important appointment. Everything has some cost. In a sense, the individual in all these examples is torn between two goals—

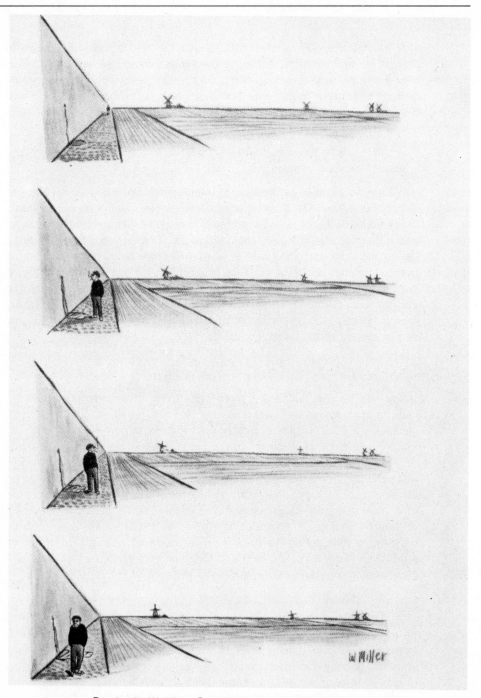

Drawing by W. Miller; © 1966 The New Yorker Magazine, Inc.

self-interest and altruism. This conflict has been demonstrated repeatedly. For example, Tims, Swart, and Kidd (1976) contacted male college students by phone and asked them to answer an attitude questionnaire. This questionnaire was variously described to them as requiring from twenty minutes to three hours to complete. Not surprisingly, the rate of refusals increased as the described length of the questionnaire increased. This is why telephone solicitors begin their pitch with, "This will only take a minute."

State of the potential helper

Everyone has good days and bad days. A feeling that all is right with the world can increase the potential that we will help someone in need. Intuitively, we recognize this when we attempt to put someone in a good mood before asking them for a favor. Even rather transient mood states can help or hinder help-giving depending upon the positive or negative nature of the mood. Cunningham, Steinberg, and Grev (1980) demonstrated how these temporary mood states can influence helping. They induced a positive mood by contriving a situation so that a subject would find a free dime in a telephone booth coin-return slot. In another condition, subjects were approached and asked to take a picture. The experimenters induced the subjects to feel guilty by intimating to them after the camera had failed that perhaps they had done something to break it. In both cases, a confederate shortly thereafter walked near the subject and dropped a file of papers on the ground. The measure of helping behavior consisted of whether the subject helped the confederate pick up the papers. It was found that both a positive mood (finding a dime) and the induction of guilt served to increase helping in comparison to control groups. Research by Kidd and Marshall (1982) has, on the other hand, shown that inducing subjects to feel bad about themselves will reduce their helpfulness. Such apparent contradictions have been analyzed by Miller and Carlson (1990). They suggest that when people see themselves as the cause of a negative event, helpfulness is actually increased. But when people see themselves as the target of a negative event, helpfulness is decreased. However, Cialdini and Fultz (1990) are not confident of the latter analysis.

A model of intervention

The foregoing situational factors are only a few of the many situational determinants of helping. In most instances, a person confronted by an emergency will find more than one of these dimensions present. Ambiguity, diffusion of responsibility, cost-benefit elements, and the like are all operative in varying degrees. The task of predicting whether a specific person will help under those specific circumstances becomes a very difficult one indeed. To clarify this situation, Latané and Darley (1970) have proposed a model of the intervention process. According to this model, there are five stages to be negotiated before the person will intervene. The individual must (1) notice that something is happening, (2) interpret the situation as an emergency, (3) conclude that it is his or her responsibility to act, (4) decide what form of assistance is required, and (5) engage in the helping required.

Suppose you are in your apartment late at night. You hear a loud bang. This means you have noticed something. Had the same noise occurred in the middle of the day, it might not have been noticed—just part of the usual backdrop of noise. But since you did notice something, you now move into the next stage. What is your interpretation? If you decide it is just the neighborhood hotrod backfiring again, you will do nothing. But if you interpret it as a gunshot, you are likely to perceive that an emergency of some sort exists. You are now moving to the responsibility stage. You must decide whether it is your responsibility to intervene. You might decide that someone else in the apartment building surely must have heard the shot and will have already called the police. Or maybe you will conclude that it is not your floor so somebody else should worry about it. If so, you will take no further action. But perhaps it is between school terms and few people are in the building. Therefore, you decide it is your responsibility, and the decision about what form of assistance to give is the next step. You must decide whether to shout for help, phone the police, run up and down the hall checking for unlocked doors, or whatever. Finally, you must decide exactly how to implement your decision. Suppose you have decided to phone for help. All that remains is to engage in the phoning behavior. In some instances, this last stage is easier said than done. You might be so nervous or distraught that you cannot remember the 911 emergency phone number. Or if you do not have a phone, you may not recall whether the pay phone is on the second floor or the fifth floor. Maybe you are out of change. All of these choices are shown schematically in Figure 18-2.

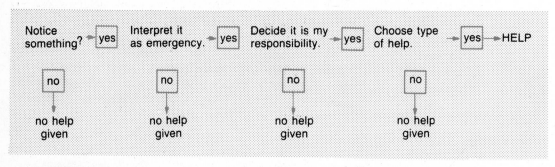

FIGURE 18-2   Five stages of the helping process according to Latané and Darley (1970)

PERSONALITY DETERMINANTS OF HELPING

From the previous discussion, it is clear that the specific characteristics of situations play a major role in determining how people react to others in need. But what about the personality characteristics of those people who are in a position to lend aid? We have already discussed the roles of moral judgment and empathy in the helping process. But in addition to these factors, people surely bring with them to potential help-ing situations a variety of other personal characteristics which may also influence their decisions to help or not to help. In fact, however, most social psychologists who have studied prosocial behavior have been primarily interested in the situational determinants of helping. A number of these investigators are quite skeptical about the role of per-sonality variables. Some have offered reasons why personality factors might not be as closely related to prosocial behavior as we might expect (Latané and Darley, 1970). For example, the impact of the situation may be so strong and so immediate that the individual does not have time to debate. Personality dispositions such as self-confidence, needs, and the like are swallowed up in the demands of a pressure-packed now. Also, there may be opposing personality characteristics operative at the same time. For ex-ample, a person may be quite sympathetic or empathic and want very much to donate money at a crowded shopping mall during a telethon for some worthy cause. But that person may be so shy and inhibited that stepping forward with a contribution is just not possible.

This latter example raises another point. All helping situations are not alike. Some are emergencies—such as a bleeding person on a sidewalk. But helping can also be a quiet, contemplative process that takes place in, say, the privacy of one's own home—for instance, donating money to a university, the United Way, and so on. Because of these differences among situations, it becomes very difficult to assert that personality characteristics X, Y, and Z are related to altruism whereas R, S, and T are not. Some people are chronically generous with their money but not with their time. Others give their skills away but not their money. Similarly, what is important in one emergency situation may not be relevant in other situations. For these reasons, it is difficult to generate any "laws" of altruism that apply equally in every situation or for every kind of person. It may be recalled that a similar conclusion was reached for aggression in the previous chapter.

It is also true that sometimes our offers of help are spurned. When this happens, negative emotions are felt and the potential recipient of help is evaluated less favorably (Rosen, Mickler, and Collins, 1987). How does this relate to personality and situa-tional interactions?

Personality traits

Given the foregoing disclaimers, we might nevertheless ask whether certain personal-ity traits are likely to prompt altruistic responses. Well, it depends. In the emergency or unusual situations that Latané and Darley (1970) studied, personality variables such as authoritarianism, Machiavellianism, need for approval, and social responsibility showed little relationship to prosocial behavior. But in other situations, relationships with some traits have been reported. For example, Rutherford and Mussen (1968) found that nursery school boys who exhibited generosity tended to be rated by others as kinder, less hostile, and less competitive.

Studies by Midlarsky (1971) and Midlarsky and Midlarsky (1973) have shown that an internal locus of control facilitates helping behavior. In the first study, Midlarsky told male subjects that they were participating in an armed forces research project to develop tests for selecting pilots. Each subject worked with someone who was really a confederate of the experimenter. Each pair was told that in the event one finished the task before the other, it was all right for him to help his partner. A motor coordination task was used, and each time an item in the task was manipulated, electric shock was experienced--even when helping a partner. In essence, Midlarsky found that internally oriented subjects were more likely to help their partners than were external subjects. This occurred even though subjects had nothing to gain by helping their partner and, indeed, experienced some discomfort as the result of their assistance.

In contrast, Phares and Lamiell (1975) found something quite different. Internal and external college students examined brief case histories of an ex-convict, a welfare recipient, and a war veteran. All subjects were asked to judge each case in several ways. These judgments revealed first of all that internals were significantly less prone than externals to regard other people in need as deserving. In addition, help, money, understanding, and sympathy were more likely to be offered by externals—at least to the extent that we can generalize from paper-and-pencil ratings to overt behavior in real settings. The fact that these results are different from the Midlarsky findings underscores the necessity for examining carefully the role of personality factors in each situation. The Midlarsky studies involved helping in face-to-face settings and factors of competence and stress. In contrast, the Phares and Lamiell study was one in which deservedness was attributed to others. How one regards others in the abstract may be quite different from the actual behavior one will choose when confronted with a flesh-and-blood person in need of help.

Could need for social approval also relate to helping? Deutsch and Lamberti (1986) thought so and devised a method of testing their hypothesis. Subjects who were either high or low in need for social approval observed a confederate of the experimenters drop books and papers all over a hallway. Shortly before this event, subjects had been either rewarded or not rewarded with social approval for filling out some forms. Interestingly, subjects high in need for approval were likely to help pick up the books only if they had been previously rewarded with approval. Subjects with a low need for approval were unaffected in their helping behavior by prior reward or lack of it.

Prosocial orientation

Staub (1974) has constructed what he calls a "composite prosocial orientation" index. This index is derived from scores on several scales: a test of the tendency to ascribe responsibility to the self for others' welfare, a test of social responsibility, a test of Machiavellianism, a measure of beliefs about human nature, a short written test of moral reasoning, and a test of values. Using these combined measures, Staub was able to predict altruism in a situation where subjects heard what seemed to be moans and groans coming from an adjacent room. Such a study takes us beyond the notion that there may be some specific personality traits related to helping. It implies that people may possess a generalized prosocial orientation that motivates them to perform altruistic acts. Specifically, Staub (1974) argues that this orientation "probably represents, primarily, a way of looking at, of thinking about, other people's welfare, and one's own responsibility toward other people" (p. 335).

The altruistic personality

Rushton, Chrisjohn, and Fekken (1981) have, like Staub, argued that there is a *broad* personality trait of altruism. They state that "such people are consistently more generous, helping, and kind than others" (p. 296). Rushton (1980) has also concluded that several studies have successfully demonstrated that individual differences in paper-and-pencil measures of empathy, moral reasoning, and social responsibility can predict altruistic behavior in specific situations. To buttress these conclusions, Rushton, Chrisjohn, and Fekken (1981) have developed the **Self-Report Altruism Scale (SRA).** It is a twenty-item scale in which subjects indicate the frequency with which they have engaged in several altruistic acts (see Table 18-4). To assess the validity of the SRA, Rushton and his colleagues compared subjects' scores on the scale with peer ratings of altruistic behavior. They found highly significant relationships. They also found that the SRA correlates with a variety of other self-reported acts of altruism. It was also noted that those with high scores on the SRA were more likely to have completed the medical organ-donor card attached to all Ontario, Canada, drivers' licenses.

Other research has also shown that personality variables involving self-esteem, responsibility, and empathic concern are related to helping behavior (Batson, Bolen, Cross, and Neuringer-Benefiel, 1986). Yet the same research suggests that the underlying motivation is really egoistic, leading the investigators to ask. "Where is the altruism in the altruistic personality?" Still, Eisenberg et al. (1989) on the basis of their research have concluded that altruistic, other-oriented personality dispositions enhance prosocial behavior; at least in some situations. What is more, the intention to help seems affected by one's sympathetic reactions to the other person.

Although the underlying motives of those said to have altruistic personalities may

---

TABLE 18-4   *Several items from the Self-Report Altruism Scale*

	Never	Once	More Than Once	Often	Very Often
1. I have helped push a stranger's car out of the snow.					
6. I have donated clothes to a charity.					
8. I have donated blood.					
16. I have offered to help a handicapped or elderly stranger across a street.					
20. I have helped an acquaintance to move households.					

Reprinted with permission from *Personality and Individual Differences*, 2, J. P. Rushton, R. D. Chrisjohn, and G. C. Fekken, "The Altruistic Personality and the Self-Report Altruism Scale." Copyright © 1981 Pergamon Press plc.

be in question, it does seem that certain people, over a range of situations and time periods, are more likely to offer help than are others. The exact way in which such individual differences will manifest themselves will be defined by the nature of each specific situation. Even altruistic people cannot donate money if they have none. And even kind and generous people may be slow to react at an accident scene if they become ill at the sight of blood. As has been noted so often throughout this book, definitive answers will more likely emerge from those views that consider behavior to be a joint product of situational and personality characteristics.

SUMMARY

- As in the case of aggression, people seem to have a corresponding capacity for spectacular as well as simple acts of altruism.

- Some investigators do not distinguish between altruistic and prosocial behavior. Others, however, suggest that altruism involves the intention to help while prosocial behavior simply results in benefit to another person regardless of any intent.

- An interesting question involves the motivation for selfless acts. Do they truly occur without any personal gain? If so, they raise a curious dilemma for those who claim that all behavior is driven by the expectation of reinforcement.

- Numerous examples of prosocial behavior in animals have been noted. The question, however, is whether this implies a biological basis for altruism in humans. Many argue that since altruism must involve intent, it is not appropriate to generalize from animal behavior which cannot be shown to involve any such intent.

- Nevertheless, biologically oriented investigators claim that not only is altruism genetically based, but empathy as well. However, most social scientists are persuaded that altruism in humans is rooted in the learning process.

- The question of how people develop a sense of morality has long fascinated investigators. Dynamic views such as psychoanalysis seek the origins in the identification process that evolves out of the psychosexual stages. The dynamic interplay of motives that underlie altruism is shown, for example, by those who helped Jews escape the Nazi net and by people who supported in varying degrees the civil rights movement in the United States.

- Others, such as Piaget, have adopted a more cognitive framework. Piaget viewed moral judgment as evolving out of a maturing cognitive-developmental process.

- Kohlberg, in a similar vein, believed that moral judgment arises out of the individual's passage through several stages that are universal across all cultures. Several studies have shown a relationship between the individual's stage of moral development and the incidence of altruism. Kohlberg was not without his critics, however.

■ Empathy—the ability to infer accurately the feelings of others—is regarded by many as an important factor in promoting altruism. It has been viewed both as a cognitive skill and as a kind of vicarious experience.

■ Many argue that empathy is a critical factor in mediating prosocial behavior. Some see empathy as an egoistic kind of motivation that impels us to do something that will make us feel better. Others, however, regard empathy as an altruistic, selfless factor.

■ Training children to be more empathic seems to be possible in certain instances.

■ Some work has also indicated that people vary in terms of a general disposition to be empathic. In the case of children this evidence is inconsistent; with adults it is stronger. Some research also shows that training will enhance empathic responses in children. Current research is also addressing the question of whether helping based on empathy is selflessly or selfishly motivated.

■ The social learning process is where many look for the origins of altruism. In particular, modeling is regarded as a major factor in the acquisition of prosocial behaviors. Various aspects of religious orientations have also been investigated as determinants of prosocial behavior.

■ There seem to be many characteristics of situations themselves that affect prosocial behavior. For example, when situations are ambiguous in that they do not clearly indicate that someone needs help, altruism is inhibited.

■ The presence of others sometimes will also inhibit prosocial behavior since there is a diffusion of responsibility regarding who should really help. The volume of research on this phenomenon is large and indicates that the effect is both stable and pronounced.

■ When people know the specific kind of help needed, they are more likely to respond. The costs to the helper will also directly affect the likelihood that help will be given.

■ Another factor is the state of the potential helper. This includes even transient mood states. In general, positive moods increase and negative moods decrease the incidence of helping responses, but relationships here are complex.

■ Latané and Darley have proposed a cognitive decision-making model of the intervention process. Briefly, before helping, one must notice that something is happening, interpret the situation as an emergency, conclude that there is a responsibility to act, decide what form of help to give, and then provide that help.

■ Although most of the research on helping has been directed toward identifying its situational determinants, it would be surprising were there not to be personality determinants as well. Both moral reasoning and empathy could be viewed as personality determinants.

■ However, it is important to note that some situations are so compelling that personality determinants will take a backseat. Similarly, in some cases opposing personality characteristics may operate to obscure one's predisposition to help. It is also important to recognize that not all helping situations are alike. Therefore, a disposition to help in one situation may not carry over to another situation.

■ Several studies involving such personality traits as generosity, locus of control, nurturance, and need for social approval were noted as they relate to prosocial behavior.

■ Some work has suggested that a generalized altruistic or prosocial predisposition can be identified which promotes helping responses in specific situations.

CHAPTER 19

SEX ROLES AND GENDER DIFFERENCES

If anything characterizes modern society, it is our rapidly changing ideas about the roles of men and women. The differences between men and women and the roles these differences dictated once seemed wide and clear. Now, those differences are blurred to the point of invisibility in many instances. A generation ago women on the police force or working in construction crews were rare. But, then, lest the traditionalists out there despair, we still have Miss America pageants. So, while our stereotypes about sex roles have crumbled a bit, they have far from disappeared. In the past, sex roles were more often prescribed than debated. Little boys were supposed to grow up to be masculine, dominant, and aggressive and little girls to be feminine, submissive, and passive. Everybody knew that anatomy was destiny. A few might chafe under the restrictions this so-called law of nature imposed. But ultimately, aspirations would have to yield to the inevitability of biology and the cultural expectations that followed closely on its heels.

But if everyone felt that biology were nothing more than a genetic-hormonal clock ticking off the inexorable march into preordained sex roles, there would probably be little current discussion about sex differences. But there have always been those who have refused to accept the prevailing notions of sex roles and the traditional explanations for them. It is not that these individuals have disputed the importance of being born male or female. Quite the contrary. In fact, sex may be the most important factor in the overall determination of behavior, thoughts, and emotional reactions. How your parents react to you, your choice of friends, the way you dress, the courses in school you are encouraged to take—all this and more is directly affected by your sex. This may seem to confirm the anatomy-is-destiny viewpoint. But we shall see later that biology, hormones, or whatever will not always prevail over psychosocial experiences. Although one's **sex** (biological heritage) is important, it is **gender** (psychosexual identity) that really is critical. Increasingly, the words *gender* and *sex* are being used interchangeably; they will be used in this way in this chapter.

Our discussion of gender will begin with the subject of sex-role stereotyping.

SEX-ROLE STEREOTYPES

While it is all well and good to say that our conceptions about sex roles are changing or that hormones do not inevitably prevail over socialization experiences, the fact remains that sex-role stereotypes still exist to a significant degree. What exactly is a **sex-role stereotype**? Unger (1979) defines it as "an attitudinal or behavioral bias against individuals in identical situations engaged in identical behaviors because of their membership in some specific sexual group" (p. 27). Stereotyping begins at a very early age. A good example of it comes from a study by Rubin, Provenzano, and Luria (1974) in which parents were interviewed within one day of the birth of their first child. Male and female infants showed no differences in terms of body length, weight, or activity scores. Yet daughters were more likely to be described as cute, little, beautiful, or pretty and boys to be characterized as firmer, more alert, or stronger. As the child grows older, these stereotypes persist. A great deal of what we know about sex stereotyping comes from work with college students carried out by I. K. Broverman and her colleagues (e.g., Broverman, Vogel, Broverman, Clarkson, and Rosenkrantz, 1972). In most of these studies by Broverman and others, students are asked to list the personality characteristics they feel differentiate between men and women. Items from such lists are then presented to other students, who are requested to indicate which items would likely apply to a person about whom they know nothing except that he is a male. The students perform the same task for a hypothetical female as well. Results show that there is general agreement between male and female subjects about what typical men and women are like. Furthermore, the masculine traits are rated as more socially desirable than the feminine ones, and it also appears that a greater number of male traits are positively valued than are female traits. Positive stereotypic traits that distinguish between men and women are shown in Table 19-1.

Cross-cultural research indicates that degree of stereotyping is not invariant, however. Zammuner (1987) reports that Dutch children differentiate between the sexes less than do Italian children. This suggests that learning to stereotype is mediated by a number of cultural and familial factors. It is also probably mediated by a desire to sort people into social roles; stereotyping then becomes a way of rationalizing our biases (Hoffman and Hurst, 1990).

Extent of stereotyping

Sex stereotyping is, then, a pervasive phenomenon in society. It begins in infancy and persists throughout the life cycle (Del Boca and Ashmore, 1980). We have known for a long time that stereotyping was rampant among psychoanalysts who only recently have begun systematically revising their ideas about gender (Alpert, 1986). But analysts have not been alone in their tendencies toward stereotyping. A study by Broverman, Broverman, Clarkson, Rosenkrantz, and Vogel (1970) included subjects who were psychologists with clinical training, psychiatrists, and social workers. They were asked to alternately describe a man, a woman, and an adult (sex unspecified) who were all healthy, mature, and socially competent. The subjects' descriptions differed along sex lines. There was agreement that competence characterized the healthy male more than it did the healthy female. Healthy women in comparison to healthy males were also depicted as

---

TABLE 19-1 Positive stereotypic traits for men and women

Positive Traits for Men

- Aggressive
- Independent
- Unemotional
- Hides emotions
- Objective
- Easily influenced
- Dominant
- Likes math and science
- Not excitable in a minor crisis
- Active
- Competitive
- Logical
- Worldly
- Skilled in business
- Direct

- Knows the way of the world
- Feelings not easily hurt
- Adventurous
- Makes decisions easily
- Never cries
- Acts as a leader
- Self-confident
- Not uncomfortable about being aggressive
- Ambitious
- Able to separate feelings from ideas
- Not dependent
- Not conceited about appearance
- Thinks men are superior to women
- Talks freely about sex with men

Positive Traits for Women

- Does not use harsh language
- Talkative
- Tactful
- Gentle
- Aware of feelings of others
- Religious

- Interested in own appearance
- Neat in habits
- Quiet
- Strong need for security
- Appreciates art and literature
- Expresses tender feelings

SOURCE: From ''Sex-Role Stereotypes and Self-Concepts in College Students'' by P. Rosenkrantz, S. Vogel, H. Bee, I. Broverman, and D. M. Broverman, *Journal of Consulting and Clinical Psychology*, 1968, *32*, 287–295. Copyright 1968 by the American Psychological Association. Reprinted by permission.

---

being more submissive, less independent and adventuresome, less objective and more easily influenced, less aggressive and competitive, more easily excitable in minor crises, more conceited about their appearance, and more prone to having their feelings hurt. These results are not unlike the ratings of college students shown in Table 19-1. Whether it is called sex stereotyping or simply the assertion of a double standard for women, the fact remains that women are being put in the position of having to choose between being adult and being feminine. Curiously, this negative view of women was shared by male and female professionals alike! What this tells us is that these mental health professionals had failed to immunize themselves against the biases of stereotyping. It also suggests that stereotyping is a deeply rooted phenomenon in our society although we are becoming more sensitized to stereotyping issues. Sex-role stereotyping is so firmly etched into the design of our culture that it appears everywhere. As Graham (1975) has shown, our language itself tends to reinforce sex-role stereotypes. For example, the use of qualifiers such as *woman* doctor or *career* woman implies exceptions to what are normally male activities. Words such as *poetess* and *suffragette* provide what amounts to an unnecessary qualification or even trivialization of roles. And children get an early start in developing sex-role stereotypes through the books they are given to read. The textbooks they study all too often misrepresent the possibilities and varieties of activities open to women. By presenting examples that describe only the norm in society rather than a range of possibilities, stereotypes are reinforced. A monograph, "Dick and Jane as Victims," was published in 1972 by the National Organization for Women. Examining 2,760 stories in 134 children's books, it was found that the ratio of boy-centered to girl-centered stories was 5 to 2. Male adults were three times more likely to appear as characters, and male biographies were six times more frequent than female ones. Boys were described as clever 131 times, but girls only 33 times. Subtle but probably quite effective. Sternglanz and Serbin (1974) found much the same thing in their analysis of male and female role models on ten popular children's TV programs. Not only were there twice as many male roles as female roles, but the frequency of various kinds of behavior was characteristically different for males and females.

Between the years 1972 and 1976 research suggested that in the case of both students and adults, there were large and significant shifts of attitudes in the direction of equality between the sexes (Helmreich, Spence, and Gibson, 1982). However, between 1976 and 1980 male students showed no overall change in attitudes while female students showed a small but significant shift in the conservative or traditional direction. Helmreich, Spence, and Gibson suggest that these data may signal a leveling off in the trend toward acceptance of sex-role equality.

However, in conclusion it should be noted that Eagly and Mladinic (1989) have collected data that challenge the widely accepted idea that people hold negative stereotypes about women. They found that women were perceived as inferior to men in their ability to successfully execute instrumental acts but superior in their expressive abilities. They were also judged as "good" people while being seen as lesser individuals in terms of power and privilege. We shall note again, in a moment, that stereotyping is a complex reaction.

Some consequences of stereotyping

Because sex-role stereotyping is such a pervasive phenomenon, it is not possible to disentangle completely the web of cause and effect. However, in some instances these matters are relatively clear.

Success and failure.
There seem to be differences in the ways men and women view the causes of their own successes and failures. Women are more likely than men to attribute their success on a task to luck and their failure to lack of ability (Nicholls,

1975). This pattern almost ensures expectations that will inhibit women's striving persistently for achievement. If luck accounts for success, there is little point in developing the skills normally thought of as contributing to success. Nor will success raise one's expectations for success in the future, since it is all a matter of luck. Consistent with this analysis, it has been found that males, given a choice of activities, are more likely to attempt activities involving skill than are women. In addition, they persist at such tasks longer than do women. True to their role stereotype, women account for their successes and failures in a manner almost guaranteed to discourage achievement in the future. It is as if the stereotyped views of society about women's achievements encourage them to accept the blame for failure but attribute success to factors outside themselves.

One sex-role stereotype is that success and achievement are associated with masculinity. But in the case of women, success — no matter how professionally desirable — often leaves them with a sense of personal failure at the same time. Somehow, in the process of attaining success, the woman's sense of femininity has been lost. Therefore, in our culture women sometimes develop a "fear of success." Horner (1972) decided to investigate this motive that some women have to avoid success. She asked male and female college students to write a story about "John" or "Anne" — a student at the top of his or her class in medical school. Female subjects wrote about Anne, and male subjects wrote about John. Of the stories written about Anne, 65 percent suggested that she was unhappy or that her grades brought her a variety of negative consequences. But in the case of male subjects, only 9 percent of their stories indicated negative outcomes because of John's success. Since Horner's original work, numerous studies in this area have appeared. The percentages of men and women who seem to exhibit a fear of success vary, however, from study to study (Schaffer, 1981; Unger, 1979). Indeed, Zuckerman and Wheeler (1975) urge caution in any wide acceptance of fear of success as a motive that differentiates men from women. And Mednick (1989) has speculated on the bandwagon effect of the fear-of-success notion. Nevertheless, it does appear clear that success and failure are very often responded to in different ways by men and women even though there are several hypotheses to account for all this (Hyland, 1989).

Do women stereotype women?   Stereotypes can easily distort one's perceptions about the nature of certain events. For example, Goldberg (1968) showed that women were more likely to rate male authors more favorably than female authors. Similarly, Pheterson, Kiesler, and Goldberg (1971) asked female college students to evaluate some paintings. Half the subjects thought the artist was female, and half thought the artist was male. Also, half thought the painting was an entry in a contest whereas the other half thought it was a winner. The data showed that paintings thought to be the work of a male were judged as better than identical paintings believed to be by a female. However, the paintings thought to be winners were judged the same regardless of the presumed sex of the artist. Such findings imply that when a situation is a bit vague, stereotypes will come to life and affect perceptions. But when a situation is clearly structured (in this case, winning paintings done by a female artist), stereotypes and biases are less likely to operate. This suggests the complexity of gender stereo-

While sex-role stereotyping is still common, there are signs that it is receding.
Photograph courtesy AT&T.

types and the manner in which they operate. Indeed, Swim, Borgida, Maruyama, and Meyers (1989) could find little evidence that gender stereotypes bias evaluation of people. Evaluative stereotypes are out there alright, but they occur differently in different contexts.

Another manifestation of women being unfair to themselves involves the world of work. Major, MacFarlin, and Gagnon (1984) asked male and female college students to perform two tasks. In one, they were asked to pay themselves and, in another, to do as much work as they thought fair for a fixed amount of money. The result was that women paid themselves less than did men (except when an objective comparison was available) and they worked longer and completed more work than their male counterparts as well.

Stress and health. Adjustment to stress is another consequence of stereotyping. For example, it has been found that women who identify with the feminine role are especially vulnerable to helplessness symptoms when they confront tasks that are defined to them as appropriate for men (Baucom and Danker-Brown, 1984). In a similar vein, it has also been shown that when faced with strong life stress, sex-typed in-

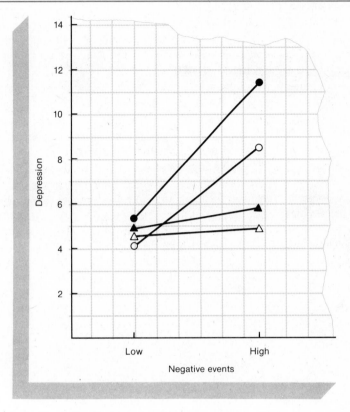

FIGURE 19-1 Prediction of depression by negative events (life stress), masculinity, and femininity.

After Roos, P. E. and Cohen, L. H. (1987). Sex roles and social support as moderators of life stress adjustment *Journal of Personality and Social Psychology, 52,* 576–585.

dividuals (either masculine or feminine) respond with relatively greater depression (Roos and Cohen, 1987). In contrast, individuals whose gender identification is undifferentiated or else who show both feminine and masculine traits (called *androgynous*—see the section later in this chapter), manifest lower levels of depression. This is shown in Figure 19-1.

It is interesting to note that the life expectancy of men is shorter and that they experience higher rates of life-threatening illness as compared to women. In contrast,
women express more frequent physical complaints and affective dysfunctions. Perhaps
men react more physiologically to stress while women react more psychologically (Barnett, Biener, and Baruch, 1987).

In today's world, the working woman has become the norm (Matthews and Rodin,
1989). We can see in Figure 19-2 the increase of women in the labor force. Given
this fact, we might speculate that the stress involved in employment would have a negative impact on women's health. In general, this does not appear to be the case. Rather,
employment appears to improve the health of unmarried women and those married
women who have positive attitudes toward working (Reppeti, Matthews, and Waldron,
1989). Perhaps the social support received from co-workers and supervisors is partly
responsible. Similarly, for mothers who work, the fact of their employment does not
seem critical for the quality of their marital relations, child development, or their own
personal reactions. Instead, the truly important factors are attitudes and expectations
about maternal employment in both partners, the circumstances of the family, and the
sharing of household tasks (Scarr, Phillips, and McCartney, 1989).

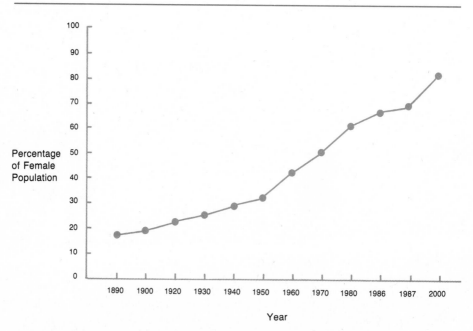

FIGURE 19-2   Percentage of women aged 20 to 64 years in the labor force from
1890 to 2000   Adapted from Foster, Siegel, and Jacobs (1988)

GENDER DIFFERENCES IN PERSONALITY

Women are gentle and men are aggressive. Women are quite talkative while men are more taciturn. Women make good nurses because they are nurturant. Men are more likely to succeed in engineering because of their superior mathematical-spatial abilities. Having just discussed sex-role stereotypes, it is not unreasonable to ask whether the foregoing descriptions of men and women reflect real differences or simply stereotypes. There has been a great deal of research on gender differences (Hyde and Linn, 1986), and interest in them has existed since the beginning of recorded history. But many of the differences that have been cataloged are often more apparent than real, more variable than one might think, and of a lesser magnitude than many believe. Indeed, Maccoby (1990) argues that behavioral differences in the sexes are minimal, especially when we test or observe children individually. Let us examine some of these differences.

Aggression

Few would disagree that males, on the average, are more aggressive than females. Whether we measure aggressiveness through observation, by means of ratings by parents, teachers, or peers, or with self-ratings, fantasy measures, or laboratory measures, the answer usually emerges that, yes, males are more aggressive (e.g., Maccoby and Jacklin, 1974). An example of such research is a study by Reinisch and Sanders (1986). They asked male and female college students to make estimates of their own verbal and physical aggression when they were thirteen-year-olds. Although the two groups did not differ in self-reported verbal aggression, males were much more likely to report having resorted to physical aggression (see Figure 19-3).

These differences in aggression occur as early as age three and exist at every subsequent age level (Rushton et al., 1986). The fact that they appear in so many different cultures could suggest a biological foundation (Whiting and Edwards, 1973). Hormonal levels also have been offered as explanations for these differences (Hines, 1982; Joslyn, 1973). But given all the variables that can contribute to differential aggression in men and women, biological-hormonal factors are probably relatively weak in their effects. The role of social learning must be recognized as a potent contributor to these differences regardless of whether they occur in the bedroom, on the playground, at the office, or on the freeway (Bandura, 1977).

The research is rather clear-cut in showing that overt, physical aggression is more characteristic of males than of females. However, if we include subtler, even passive, forms of aggression, the picture immediately becomes less clear (Eagly and Steffen, 1986). For example, some work has shown that girls will "indirectly" aggress against another person even more than boys by rejecting or excluding a newcomer to their group (N. D. Feshbach, 1969; Feshbach and Sones, 1971). It may be important, then, to distinguish between intent or motives and overt behavior. In this sense, the roughhouse play exhibited by boys may not be symptomatic of underlying aggressiveness so much as it is of a learned style of relating to peers. From this point of view, verbal remarks could be regarded as really more aggressive than punching a friend in the arm

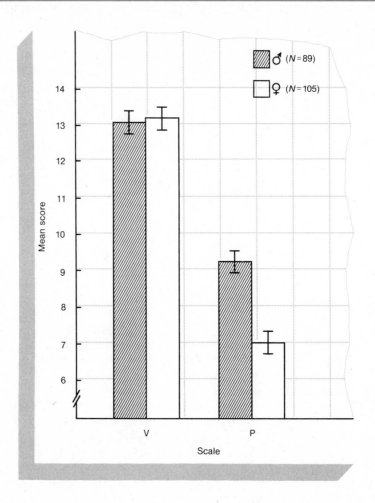

FIGURE 19-3   Mean scores for verbal aggression (V) and physical aggression (P) for men and women.

From Reinisch, J. M. and Saunders, S. A. (1986). A test of sex differences in aggressive response to hypothetical conflict situations. *Journal of Personality and Social Psychology, 50,* 1045–1049.

since they contain a stronger intent to harm. Other evidence suggests that aggressive behavior certainly exists in the female's repertoire but that learned restraints such as guilt or role expectations inhibit its expression. As an example, the study by Bandura, Ross, and Ross (1961) noted in Chapter 17 showed that girls will produce as many aggressive responses as boys when rewarded for doing so but in the absence of such reward will exhibit fewer aggressive responses. Some experimental literature indicates that women are often as openly hostile and aggressive as men (e.g., Frodi, Macauley, and Thorne, 1977). It could be that this narrowing of gender differences is itself a cultural phenomenon that reflects the changes in sex roles and stereotypes occurring of late. So, in a deeper sense, the magnitude of sex differences in aggression depends upon how we define aggression and what kinds of gender-typed responses a given situation calls forth (Frieze, Parsons, Johnson, Ruble, and Zellman, 1978).

Altruism

As was noted in Chapter 18, altruistic behaviors are heavily influenced by the presence of situational cues. This is no less true as we confront gender differences in helping.

When data from self-report measures of helping are examined, it seems clear that women are more altruistic than men all across the age span from nineteen to sixty (Rushton et al., 1986). But once we move into more realistic situations, the picture becomes increasingly murky. For example, Senneker and Hendrick (1983) studied subjects who were either sex-typed as masculine or feminine or else possessed a mixture of masculine and feminine traits (so-called androgynous individuals described later in this chapter). They were in a situation in which a "victim" supposedly began to choke on some food. Speed of helping and the proportion of subjects helping revealed that (1) more help was given by males than by females, and (2) more help was given by androgynous than sex-typed subjects. Data from a subsequent questionnaire suggested that females felt less competent in the situation and thus offered less help. In addition, subjects who were strongly sex-typed as feminine were less likely to help.

In contrast to the foregoing work, a very similar situation contrived by Tice and Baumeister (1985) produced very different results. Highly masculine subjects were less likely to help the choking victim than were other subjects. One possible explanation for these results is that masculine individuals have a greater fear of personal embarrassment and loss of poise so they are reluctant to intervene. Since the Senneker and Hendrick victim was a female and the Tice and Baumeister victim a male, the embarrassment effect may have operated more strongly in the second experiment. It might be noted that a more recent experiment has shown results that are supportive of those of the second study above (Siem and Spence, 1986). It may well be that masculine-typed individuals generally are more afraid of appearing foolish and thus avoid helping. But each situation must be analyzed to discover whether there are cues that will activate tendencies such as embarrassment on the one hand or felt lack of competence on the other. What is certain is that there is no clear relationship between gender and helping independent of the situation and the expectancies that it generates.

As we turn to empathy, a component that is often said to underlie helping, things are hardly much clearer. After an extensive review and evaluation of the research, Eisenberg and Lennon (1983) decided that several conclusions were warranted. First, large gender differences favoring women exist when the measure of empathy is self-report. Second, moderate differences favoring women occur in laboratory research settings. Third, when the measure of empathy is either physiological or else unobtrusive, no gender differences are apparent. Perhaps self-report measures lead to the activation of personal stereotypes.

Dependency and dominance

While greater overt aggression in males is common at all age levels, the same does not hold for dependency. For example, in nursery school children little in the way of gender differences in dependency has been observed (Maccoby and Jacklin, 1974). But when we shift to studies in which behavior is rated by teachers or parents in terms of dependency, then girls are often seen as more dependent. Thus, what is observed does not always correspond to what is rated. The different results from the two research strategies may reflect that familiar phenomenon—sex-role stereotyping. This possibility is reinforced by the findings that as girls become older, both their self-reported dependency and their trait ratings of dependency by others become increasingly apparent. However, observers of the contemporary cultural scene believe they are now witnessing a growing surge of independence in the modern woman. While definitive comparisons between this modern woman and her earlier counterpart have yet to be reported, it would be surprising were dependency in women not found to have diminished.

Additional complications for a simple view that women are more dependent than men arise when we shift our attention to the related trait of dominance. Much research indicates that women are less dominant in interpersonal situations than men. However, when we also consider the variable of race, results are much less clear-cut. For example, Adams (1980) found that in a task requiring pairs of subjects to come to a joint decision, white females were rather compliant. In contrast, black females were more dominant than either black males or white females. Earlier, in the case of aggression, it was noted that it is important to define what we mean by aggressive acts. The same holds true for dominance. Men and women express their dominance in different ways. For example, D. M. Buss (1981) examined sex differences in the acts through which dominant men and women express their dominance. Table 19-2 shows those acts that correlated with trait ratings of dominance in the case of men and women. It can be seen that some acts relate only to dominance in males while others relate only to dominance in females.

Emotionality

Everyone "knows" that females are more emotional than males. They are moody one day and happy the next. They cry one moment, then they laugh. But is this what really happens or is it merely another stereotype? The most consistent data on gender differences in emotional reactions come from studies involving stereotypes and especially from those depending upon self-reports, interviews, and self-attribution behaviors (Brody, 1985). For example, if one accepts the self-reports of females on rating scales, then the answer would appear to be, yes, it really happens (Spiegler and Liebert, 1970). But when actual observations are made of the reactions of males and females, the results are not nearly so clear (Maccoby and Jacklin, 1974). Of course, one of the troubles with self-report measures is that males tend to be defensive on them while females are considerably more open. Perhaps males feel a need to protect their masculine image. Females, believing they are expected to be emotional and fearful, have nothing to lose by expressing their real feelings. Furthermore, as Frieze et al. (1978) suggest, some

---

TABLE 19-2   *Acts of dominance that characterize separately men and women who are high on the trait of dominance*

Acts Characteristic of Dominant Men

■ I told others to perform menial tasks, instead of doing them myself.

■ I managed to get my own way.

■ I argued vigorously on behalf of my personal beliefs.

■ I solicited funds for a cause in which I was interested.

■ I refused to compromise despite considerable group pressure.

■ I assigned roles and got the game going.

■ I voiced my opinions in a large class.

■ I spoke with a loud, firm voice.

■ I made a final decision.

■ I was able to get the other person to do what I wished.

■ I set goals for the group.

■ I readily used the authority of my position.

■ I told him which of the two jobs he should take.

■ I managed to control the outcome of the meeting without others being aware of it.

■ I demanded that he run an errand.

Acts Characteristic of Dominant Women

■ I settled a dispute among members of the group.

■ I took the lead in organizing a project.

■ I challenged someone to discuss her position.

■ I took the initiative in a sexual encounter.

■ I introduced the speaker at the meeting.

■ I made a bold sexual advance.

■ I chose to sit at the head of the table.

■ I refused to have sexual relations with my partner.

■ I initiated a conversation with a stranger.

SOURCE: Adapted from "Sex Differences in the Evaluation and Performance of Dominant Acts" by D. M. Buss, *Journal of Personality and Social Psychology*, 1981, *40*, 147–154. Copyright 1981 by the American Psychological Association. Used with permission.

---

questionnaires are gender biased. That is, they contain fewer items that relate directly to the important concerns of males such as anxiety over money or business. Again, then, gender differences in this area appear most often on questionnaires or self-ratings. However, these measures may be subject to a variety of sex-role biases and stereotypes which obscure rather than enlighten.

There well may be an emotional double standard. As Shields (1987) has concluded, observers may be more likely to look for and note the presence of emotionality in women as compared to men. And even in identical situations, there may be different standards for what are "appropriate" emotional displays for men and women.

GENDER AND INTELLECTUAL-COGNITIVE ABILITIES

It has long been assumed that men and women differ significantly in their intellectual-cognitive abilities, which could then account for their subsequent differences in achievement. In particular, the trinity of spatial ability (men are better), mathematical ability (men are better), and verbal ability (women are better) has interested most investigators (see Halpern, 1986). Similarly, differential suitability for careers has been said to depend upon these intellectual-cognitive factors thought to separate men from women. But, as before, things are not always as they seem, as we shall see in the following sections. Even more interesting, whatever gender differences may have existed in the past, they seem to be disappearing (Feingold, 1988).

Verbal abilities

In general, there is a tendency for girls to begin talking sooner than boys and to show greater word fluency, a stronger vocabulary, and better grammar and spelling (Gesell et al., 1940). However, consistent gender differences in verbal ability do not emerge until around the age of eleven, when girls begin to show superiority over boys (Maccoby and Jacklin, 1974). This superiority encompasses such things as use of vocabulary, ability to name objects, grammar and fluency, ability to write creatively, reading ability, comprehension, and language reasoning. There is, however, great variability, and we would be frequently incorrect if gender were the only basis upon which predictions of verbal ability were made.

More recently, however, Hyde and Linn (1988) have surveyed 165 studies that reported on gender differences in verbal ability. What they found contradicts all our conventional wisdom. They discovered gender differences so small that they can be considered to be nonexistent. Neither vocabulary, reading comprehension, nor analogies yielded substantial evidence of differences. Only in the area of speech production was there a difference in favor of women. Nor were there detectable age or developmental trends in verbal abilities. Perhaps, as Hyde and Linn conclude, we do need to rewrite the textbooks.

Mathematical abilities

Much evidence suggests that males surpass females in mathematical skills. Such skills confer real advantages to males since college aptitude tests as well as entry to such fields as engineering and science depend heavily upon mathematical abilities. How do we account for such a difference between the sexes? Before becoming too expansive in our hypotheses, it should be noted that we are talking about *small* differences based on large populations. This means that such differences cannot be used to argue that certain professions or activities should be limited to men (Kagan, 1975). In fact, Hyde, Fennema, and Lamon (1990) analyzed one hundred studies and found that females out-performed males by a negligible amount.

Some investigators (e.g., Leder, 1974) suggest that women do poorly on certain mathematical problems because the content does not engage their interests or because examples in mathematics classes are too often sex-typed for males. Others suggest that the problem resides in the fact that mathematical ability is dependent upon visual-spatial aptitude, in which males are superior to females. Still others, such as Tobias (1976), contend that women are especially susceptible to "mathematics anxiety." Women too often accept the cultural stereotype that decrees they are supposed to be poor in things mathematical—cannot figure interest rates, grow panicky when trying to balance the checkbook, and so on. Osen (1974) has coined the term *feminine mathique* to describe this conditioned anxiety about arithmetic and the like.

Before leaving this section we should mention a little noted gender difference here. In contrast to scores on mathematics achievement tests, girls receive *better* math grades than do boys. The reasons for this are still not clear (Kimball, 1989). Maybe boys have more math experience outside the classroom and take more math-related courses than girls. Hence, this gives them an advantage on standardized tests that include items not always covered in regular math classes. Or maybe boys take a more autonomous approach to learning math while girls rely more on a rote learning approach that does not work as well when confronting novel or unfamiliar questions on standardized tests. Finally, perhaps girls are better when dealing with familiar achievement situations such as classroom exams. In any case, given girls' superior classroom performance it is too bad they are not more often encouraged to take advanced math classes and are later underrepresented in science and engineering careers.

Spatial abilities

In the case of both adolescents and adults, males seem to perform better on tasks requiring spatial skills. They appear better able to manipulate visually and to judge objects and their relationship to one another. For example, when the task is for subjects to form designs out of blocks that are shown in relationships to each other different from what the final designs require, males often do better than females. Another example would be a problem that requires subjects to visualize a design upside down from the way it is presented to them. Male superiority on such tasks seems to be a reliable finding (Maccoby and Jacklin, 1974), although it is not apparent in young children. By high school, it is clearly discernible. This pattern of differences may indicate that girls and boys differ in their experience with various kinds of tasks (Sherman, 1974). Girls and boys are given different kinds of toys with which to play (e.g., boys are given blocks and erector sets; girls get dolls and toy makeup kits). Such speculation gains credence from research indicating there is little in the way of gender differences in certain nonindustrialized societies (Berry, 1971). Furthermore, Goldstein and Chance (1965) have shown that when extended practice is given on specific spatial tasks, gender differences disappear for all practical purposes. The role of the self-concept may also be implicated here in gender differences. For example, Signorella and Jamison

(1986) discovered that when the masculinity and femininity in subjects' self-concepts is consistent with the gender stereotyping of mathematical and spatial tasks, performance will be superior.

In conclusion, although it is still widely accepted that males are superior to females when they perform on spatial tasks, not everyone is sure (Caplan, MacPherson, and Tobin, 1985). The inconsistency of research results, the small differences between men and women that we often obtain, and even the difficulties in defining exactly what we mean by spatial tasks should lead us to be very cautious in our conclusions.

Cognitive style

Many people believe that men and women think differently. That is, when a man and a woman are each given the same information, they will not process it in the same fashion. Gutmann (1970), for example, has described men as more analytical in their approach to problems. They do not identify with a problem so much as they try to analyze and then solve it. In contrast, women are more likely to have difficulty separating themselves from the problem and to imitate others' problem-solving efforts. Very frequently, gender differences in thinking styles involve what is called "analytic" or "field-independent" approaches versus "global" or "field-dependent" approaches (Witkin, Dyk, Faterson, Goodenough, and Karp, 1962). The **Embedded Figures Test** and the **Rod and Frame Test** are most often used to identify these two cognitive styles. The first test requires subjects to locate a simple hidden figure embedded in a complex stimulus pattern. This can also be construed as a spatial task, as noted previously. In the second test, a rod inside a frame is projected on the wall in a dark room. As the frame is tilted, the subject must adjust the rod so that the frame will remain vertical. As in the case of spatial performance, gender differences are not consistent until the age of seventeen or so (Witkin et al., 1962). From that age on, women perform at a level inferior to that of men.

Most of the research that reveals men to be more analytic than women is based on visual-spatial tasks. Thus, it is probably a mistake to conclude that men are better at analytic tasks than women. When tasks to measure analytic ability do not involve spatial ability, gender differences are found much less frequently (Sherman, 1967). As in most cases, when we closely examine so-called gender differences, they begin to disappear into a cloud of socialization and sex-stereotyping factors.

Implications

Frieze et al. (1978) observe that people are often interested in gender differences for quite practical reasons. Since engineering tasks or piloting a plane requires spatial skills, and since men are often believed to possess a higher level of such skills, should men be counseled into such activities and women not? Since many women seem to be more nurturant than the average man, should all child care be turned over to women? But differences such as the foregoing are not consistent, nor do average differences tell us much about a specific person. Many women have superior spatial abilities, and any number of men are highly nurturant. One cannot look at relatively small average differences and then decide what is best for all men or all women.

ORIGINS OF SEX ROLES

So far, we have discussed a variety of gender differences along with sex-role stereotyping. But how is it that these differences and stereotypes arise in the first place? How does a person acquire and come to value behaviors that are thought to be appropriate for one gender rather than the other?

Sex-role stereotypes are not something that appeared yesterday. Schaffer (1981) makes clear that the origins of these stereotypes go back at least as far as the Greek and Roman civilizations. She observes that in early Greece, women were regarded as inferior and excluded from social and political life. They were burdens to be tolerated for their reproductive capacities. Although the lot of women in ancient Rome was better in that they were educated and allowed to own property, they were often blamed for causing misery and suffering and regarded as basically unworthy of men's love. The primacy of men is also apparent in religion—God created man and only later woman. Women were property to be owned first by their fathers and then by their husbands. Rape of a virgin was punished by requiring reimbursement to the father for damage to his property. With Christ came a more enlightened view of women, but then one must remember that all the disciples were male. Later, the relationship between sex and sin became important, and women often came to be seen as evil and a source of temptation for men. Their intellectual, spiritual, and moral inferiority to men was accepted. Later, in the fifteenth and sixteenth centuries, thousands upon thousands of women were burned as witches in the name of God. Throughout the Judeo-Christian tradition, the male has been regarded as dominant, the female inferior. With the coming of industrialization, sex-role matters became exaggerated. Men's work began to move from the home to factories; women were to stay home and supervise the household. The role of homemaker had become a vital part of the woman's image, starting the stereotype that has, up to now, hounded those women who have wanted to move beyond the confines of the home. Even today, expectations that women should have a major role in the home limit their ability to compete on an equal basis with men in the industrial-professional world. However, while history can give us some sense of the panorama of women's roles throughout the ages, we must look elsewhere to learn how a specific man and woman in a specific era are led to adopt their characteristic roles. Let us now turn to an examination of some major explanations for the development of sex roles.

Biological determinants

Freud's contention that anatomy is destiny typifies the extreme biological position, in which gender differences in personality and temperament are believed to be inevitably related to anatomical differences between the sexes. Genes and hormones along with anatomical sex differences are viewed as the major factors in one's ultimate sex-role identification. The battle lines are firmly drawn by those who claim that, other than differences in reproductive capacities, women and men are essentially the same, and therefore if there are differences in sex roles, the culprit must be differential socialization experiences. As in most cases, the truth will likely turn out to be somewhere in between. To the extent, however, that biological and socialization factors operate in concert, it is difficult to evaluate the relative contributions of each (a point made in some detail earlier in the discussion of the relative contributions to intelligence of culture and genetics; see Chapter 14).

Differences in infants.   One way of approaching this problem is to search for gender differences in infants—before they have had a chance to be systematically trained according to sex stereotypes. In this connection, it has been found that infant girls vocalize more than infant boys (Lewis, 1969). They also smile more and show greater variety in expressions to facial stimuli. For some, these findings suggest a biological basis for subsequent gender differences in tendencies to socialize. Likewise, it is not unusual to find studies that report greater evidence of irritability (crying, fussiness) in male infants than in female infants (e.g., Moss, 1967).

Although it is logical to do research on gender differences in infants before the culture has had a crack at them, in practice it is not easy. In most cases, we are dealing with newly emerging behaviors that are highly unreliable and unstable. For example, a variety of vocalizations may occur one day but not the next. Thus, getting a proper index of vocalization so that gender differences in that behavior can be assessed may be quite difficult. In addition, it is not at all clear what certain behaviors in the infant will translate into later in life. It is doubtful that just because an infant moves his or her legs rapidly, a career as a world-class sprinter will follow. This is the same kind of problem we have in testing for infant intelligence. The behaviors from which we must infer intellectual levels in infants are so different from those behaviors from which we make IQ inferences in the adult that it is virtually impossible to predict later IQs from infant IQs. Finally, in many studies the observers of infants cannot help but know the sex of the infants they are watching. As a result, it can be all too easy for them subconsciously to apply gender stereotypes to the behaviors they see. What is seen as sociability in the female infant may be scored as aggressiveness in the male. For all these reasons—and more—research on sex differences in infants has not provided any crystal-clear insights into the biological origins of adult gender differences in behavior. While behavioral differences between male and female infants are of considerable interest, they must be interpreted with caution.

Furthermore, not all gender differences would be expected to reveal themselves as early as infancy. For example, hormones are often used to account for behavioral differences in adulthood. But the hormone system undergoes many changes during puberty. As a result, differences in such things as aggressiveness or nurturance might be more directly traceable to this stage of maturation. However, by this time the socialization process has been at work so long that it would be extremely difficult to separate out the effects of biology from those of learning, stereotyping, and socialization. By the beginning of adolescence, an entire pattern of parent-child interactions has had its chance to work. How infants' behavioral characteristics and parental responses might combine to produce distinctly different response patterns later is shown in Box 19-1.

The case of animals.   In the case of animals, there is considerable evidence that sex hormones affect behavior, especially sexual behavior. Sexual responsiveness

Box 19-1
THE PRODUCTION OF DIFFERENTIAL RESPONSE PATTERNS IN BOYS AND GIRLS

Infant A (More characteristic of a girl)	Infant B (More characteristic of a boy)

Infant's Characteristics

■ Physically mature ■ Sleeps a lot ■ Vocalizes to faces ■ Smiles at faces	■ Physically less mature ■ Cries a lot ■ More active

Parents' Responses to Above

■ Affectionate ■ Responsive when child does cry ■ Talks to child	■ Irritable ■ Less responsive to child's frequent cries ■ Uses physical restraints and punishment

Child's Responses to Parents' Responses

■ Affiliative—comes to like people and expects them to satisfy needs ■ Early vocalization	■ Aggressive ■ Expects to satisfy needs through own efforts

SOURCE: Adapted from *Women and Sex Roles* (p. 78) by I. H. Frieze, J. E. Parsons, P. B Johnson, D. N. Ruble, and G. L. Zellman, 1978, New York: Norton.

in male animals is closely linked to high levels of testosterone while for females high estrogen and progesterone levels are important. Altering hormone levels experimentally or changing the levels in young animals can significantly affect sexual behavior. For example, when young female rats are injected with testosterone right after birth, they will subsequently exhibit a much greater incidence of mounting behaviors (normally characteristic of males) than is usual (Levine, 1966). In essence, exposing young rats to altered hormone levels has a direct effect on subsequent sexual behavior. Similar results have been shown for aggression. For instance, introducing androgen neonatally to female rhesus monkeys results in their showing patterns of aggressiveness normally characteristic of males (Young, Goy, and Phoenix, 1964). While it seems clear that testosterone in particular affects aggressiveness and sexual responses, it is less clear how directly applicable these findings are to humans. However, Hines (1982) seems optimistic. She suggests that much animal research is relevant and that even in humans prenatal hormone levels may turn out to be specifically related to gender differences in behavior. But as a rule of thumb, the higher a species is in the evolutionary hierarchy, the less hormones seem to affect behavior directly and the more important learning becomes.

External versus chromosomal sex.

This rule of thumb may be seen to operate in cases of humans whose external genital development is inconsistent with their chromosomal sex. For example, the newly born infant may have external male genitals but its internal sex organs are female. Is the infant a male or female? Perhaps the critical variable is how such individuals are raised. Hampson (1965) investigated nineteen such cases who were reared on the basis of their external sex characteristics. That is, their sexual and gender socialization was the opposite of their biological sex. In every instance, their gender-role orientation was in tune with the manner in which they had been regarded by their parents and peers. This conclusion is also reinforced by the work of Money and his colleagues (Money, 1965, 1975; Money and Ehrhardt, 1972). An individual with male hormones who has been reared as a girl (clothes, values, outlook, etc.) will grow up to function as a woman. Therefore, important as hormones are, their role cannot be understood without considering the person's experience. The joint influence of hormones and learning is also shown in research by Money and Ehrhardt (1972) in which females who were "androgenized" before birth were compared to a control group. The experimental group showed a higher level of masculine tendencies (toy and clothing preferences) and little interest in feminine things such as infant care. They were more career oriented than most girls of their age, although they still thought about romance, marriage, and having a family.

Biology and cognition.

Some investigators contend that even cognitive abilities in men and women are affected by biological factors (Broverman, Klaiber, Kobayashi, and Vogel, 1968). They conclude that hormone levels are implicated in gender differences in cognitive processes. Similarly, geneticists have sometimes discussed the possibility that a recessive gene may be responsible for the apparently superior spatial abilities in males, noted earlier in this chapter. However, more recent work has not corroborated this hypothesis (e.g., T. Williams, 1975). Another possibility involves brain lateralization. The brain consists of two hemispheres. The right hemisphere is more involved in spatial perception, and the left specializes in verbal abilities. Lateralization culminates eventually in one hemisphere becoming dominant (most often the left). It has been argued that somehow the manner in which this lateralization proceeds results in girls performing better on verbal tasks, and boys on spatial tasks. In particular, it has been noted that lateralization begins later in males and that perhaps this gives them an advantage on spatial activities (see Springer and Deutsch, 1981, for a general discussion of sex differences in laterality). Not everyone accepts these findings of delayed lateralization in males (e.g., Maccoby and Jacklin, 1974). Indeed, the whole research area of gender differences in spatial and verbal abilities as they are determined by lateralization processes is a controversial one. However, although the exact biological processes involved here are unclear, there does appear to be some evidence for their effects.

Role of identification

Psychoanalytic notions about identification have been discussed throughout this book. While there is little consistent research that strongly supports the general theory of identification, this theory continues to play a major role in the field of personality. Despite these research shortcomings, the theory is intriguing enough to lead many to use it as an explanation for the development of sex roles.

As we have observed several times previously, the identification process works differently for boys and girls. In order for identification to occur, the child must be dependent upon the parent—and this is true for girls and boys alike. The difference for boys and girls lies in the form of identification. Identification in females is usually what is called **anaclitic.** This means that the child identifies with a given parent in order to avoid loss of love. In the case of males, identification is more often **defensive** in that it occurs as a way of avoiding punishment from an all-powerful parent.

Psychoanalysis.   For Freud, the differential identification processes in males and females were biologically determined. The reason for this is supposedly quite simple—boys have a penis and girls do not. And when children discover this bare fact, different mechanisms of identification are set off. However, before their discovery of their anatomical differences, boys and girls alike form an anaclitic identification with their mothers. Since mother is most responsible for comforting them, feeding them, and generally providing for their satisfactions, they value her highly. They feel better when they think about her, and in order to become as close to her as they can, they assume some of her characteristics and values. This helps guard against her potential loss. But things change during the Oedipal phase and the growing awareness of anatomical differences. The boy wants his mother but fears his father. He also assumes that if he does not heed his father's implicit or explicit admonitions to stop competing for his mother's favors, his penis will be cut off. This becomes a real threat when he observes that girls have no penis. He assumes they were "bad" and that their penises were removed as a result. To avoid this horrible outcome, the boy engages in defensive identification with his father. In the case of the girl, things are a bit different. She cannot fear castration since she has no penis. But she notices this deficiency and, as a result, develops feelings of personal inferiority as well as a sense of the inferiority of women generally. She also becomes jealous of the male and his penis. She then decides that having a baby will be a good substitute for the missing penis. This desire reinforces her earlier anaclitic identification with the mother by encouraging her to adopt the female sex role and thus ensure that she becomes a mother just like her own mother. Basically, then, little boys adopt the male sex role out of the defensive identification process. They identify with the aggressor (father), avoid retaliation, and at the same time vicariously enjoy the mother. Girls, in contrast, have no reason to employ defensive identification. Their identification remains anaclitic and their self-image one of inferiority.

Learning.   Of course, learning is important. A little girl learns to enjoy music like her mother, or she learns to be self-effacing. Maybe she chooses the role of homemaker like her mother rather than a career (or if she does choose a career, experiences guilt via anaclitic identification). The little boy likes sports as his father does. He wants to do things and affect the world—become a mover and shaker like Dad rather than a passive responder like Mom. The particular quality of each child's learning can be predicted from his or her identifications. Identification, then, mediates the learning process. In addition, the environment is not viewed as terribly important in shaping sex-role development. Because of one's specific identification, there is an internal desire to become like father or mother, as the case may be. A child does not casually respond to any cue in the environment, nor is the child shaped willy-nilly by just any reinforcement in the environment. Because of the identification process, the child is motivated to select certain aspects of the environment and respond to them. Those aspects will be compatible with the evolving identifications—anaclitic or female for girls and defensive or male for boys. All of this generates what might be called emotional bonds between the child and the same-sexed parent. Once developed, these bonds provide another reason to be like that parent.

A useful concept?   Many investigators, such as Uri Bronfenbrenner (1960), feel there is little concrete evidence that identification is a useful concept at all. Other explanations for sex-role development have certainly been offered, as we shall see in a moment. Nevertheless, identification notions persist. In some cases, what is said to be valued and thus serve as the basis of identification is not the penis so much as status (e.g., Whiting, 1960). Others (e.g., Kagan, 1958) feel that each child observes the same-sexed parent's experience, notes the parent's reactions, and, almost on the basis of empathy, comes to share those reactions (both pleasant and unpleasant ones). Eventually, the child has internalized that parent's reactions to such a degree that it is not necessary to actually observe the parent any longer. Whatever the specific version of identification may be, the concept has proved to be an attractive one for psychologists over the years. While it is certainly not without its conceptual and empirical shortcomings, it seems to contain enough kernels of utility or truth that many find it difficult to discard entirely.

The social learning perspective

From our earlier discussion of social learning, you might predict that identification is regarded by more behaviorally oriented investigators as surplus baggage. They argue that with notions such as observation and imitation, it is not necessary to invoke such mediating concepts as identification. The processes by which a boy learns the acts of cleaning and oiling a rifle (observation and imitation) are not fundamentally different from those involved in learning to take pleasure in stalking an elk or trailing a deer (Bandura, 1969b). Specific behaviors as well as emotional reactions and feeling states can be accounted for by observation and imitation.

Consistency.   Also true to the behavioral tradition, social learning theorists are likely to play down consistency in sex-role behavior. If there is any traitlike consistency, it occurs because the person is repeatedly reinforced for one particular sex role. Again, the focus shifts from internal states to external reinforcers. Perhaps, argues the social learning theorist, this is why we are now seeing women both engage in and be proud of their accomplishments in what were formerly considered masculine activities (jogging, truck driving, police work, etc.). As they are permitted to be reinforced by the culture for success in such roles, they will continue in them. Such examples also imply the social learning view that sex-role learning is not something on which the person is imprinted at an early age. Sex roles are not inflexible, nor is the learning that underlies them. As the environmental rewards change, so do the behaviors and roles. For example, the elderly woman who has worn dresses or pants suits all her life cannot imagine wearing a jogging outfit—it is not, she thinks, appropriate. Finally, she yields and then receives many compliments about how good she looks. Compliments are such potent reinforcers that our elderly friend goes out and buys three more outfits.

This latter example also suggests that sex-role learning is not the inevitable province of parent-child interactions. The elderly woman hardly learned the possibilities of jogging outfits from her parents. She learned about them from watching others, and from TV, magazines, and the like. Similarly, children do not learn their sex-typed behaviors from just a same-sexed parent. They learn from peers, teachers, the movies, and on and on. Obviously, parents play an important role in this learning. After all they control the lives of their children and have sustained contact with them. All that is being said is that a parent is not the exclusive source of a child's learning.

Reinforcement.   From a social learning point of view, the acquisition of sex-typed behaviors is determined by a very simple principle—reinforcement. We do what we are reinforced for doing. The idea is that girls and boys are differentially reinforced by their parents and others. This may be reflected in the fact that mothers' femininity and fathers' masculinity are strongly associated with their children's sex stereotyping of occupations and toys (Repetti, 1984). Very early, girls are dressed in pink, boys in blue. This little girl gets a doll and is praised when she plays with it "correctly." When she expresses the desire to climb trees like the little boy next door, frowns and displeasure may be forthcoming from the traditional mother. The use of the word *traditional,* of course, implies that things are beginning to change. For example, in one study, female college students, their mothers, and their grandmothers were all administered a questionnaire on sex roles (Dambrot, Papp, and Whitmore, 1984). Students were the most liberal and their grandmothers the least liberal, with their mothers in the middle. But though what is regarded as an appropriate sex-typed behavior may change, the role of reinforcement does not. It is certainly true that parents feel they treat their sons differently from their daughters and, indeed, the children themselves

Imitation is behind much sex-role behavior.

echo this feeling (Maccoby and Jacklin, 1974). But there is some dissenting evidence. For example, Sears, Rau, and Alpert (1965) note that the greater observed aggressiveness in boys would suggest that they have been more frequently reinforced for such behavior. In fact, boys are reported as being punished relatively more often for their aggressiveness than are girls (Rothbart and Maccoby, 1966; Sears, Rau, and Alpert, 1965). Yet, in other ways—through games and sports, for example—it seems likely that even here there is a rather strong cultural sanction for greater aggressiveness in males. Therefore, all things considered, it is probable that a great deal of sex-typing occurs via the medium of parental, peer, and general cultural reinforcement differentially applied to males and females almost from the moment of birth.

Imitation. In addition to reinforcement, imitation is assumed by social learning theory to be important in sex-role learning. The concept of imitation was discussed at some length in Chapters 12 and 13. As it applies to sex-role matters, imitation is assumed to occur when the child is more often exposed to same-sexed models than to opposite-sexed ones. Actually, this is a dubious assumption in early childhood since both boys and girls spend more time with their mothers or other females than with their fathers. But, then, it could be that even under these conditions, the child will pay more attention to same-sexed than opposite-sexed models. An example of this comes from a study by Maccoby and Wilson (1957). Seventh-grade children watched two films. One film presented two boys; the other film involved an interaction between a male and a female adolescent. A week later, all subjects returned and an assessment was made of various aspects of their recall. Subjects of both gender revealed that they identified more with the same-sexed leading character. Also, their memories of the actions and verbalizations of the same-sexed character were greater. Their memories also had a sex-linked quality. Aggressive content was better remembered by boys than by girls, and the girls recalled more male-female interactions involving the leading female character than did the boys. Such results do suggest differential attentional processes with respect to potential models on the part of boys and girls. Of course, in later childhood the importance of differential attending is not so important since the child has the opportunity to spend more time with same-sexed peers, parents, and other adults. But if it is true that children pay differential attention to potential male and female models depending upon their own gender, the next question is why this should be true. It may simply be that they learn that they are rewarded for doing so. Boys are overtly and subtly rewarded by both their mothers and fathers for paying attention to things masculine; the opposite scenario applies to girls. Of course, this learning does not have to be direct. It can also occur vicariously by watching others.

Another possible answer is that, having already gleaned some idea of their gender, boys and girls attend differentially to males and females in order to learn what is appropriate for that identity. Thus, we are back to the identification process. As was noted earlier, more behaviorally oriented social learning theorists would not be comfortable with such an explanation.

Cognitive approaches

Kohlberg (1966) took a distinctly cognitive-developmental view of sex-role behavior. Very early, the child comes to a decision about his or her own "maleness" or "femaleness." Anatomical sexual identity reinforces this early judgment such that, as Kohlberg maintained, sexual self-categorization remains rather stable. The child has now arrived at a crucial self-judgment. Consequently, that judgment about sexual identity begins to serve as a highly potent organizer of the child's values. Almost without thinking, a boy now values those objects and activities he associates with the masculine role. The child is, in effect, motivated to accommodate to his or her own physical sexual identity by acquiring, maintaining, and enhancing the appropriate self-image—femininity for females, masculinity for males. In Kohlberg's (1966) own words, "I am a boy, therefore I want to do boy things (and to gain approval for doing them)" (p. 89). All of this suggests a drive for cognitive consistency. Children make their early judgments about their physical sexual identity. They will then strive to arrange their values and behavior so that the latter are viewed as consistent with their physical characteristics.

Differential attention. There is certainly evidence that boys and girls attend differentially to events in their environment associated with sex roles. The research by Maccoby and Wilson (1957) described a moment ago is one example. In a similar vein, Perry and Perry (1975) demonstrated that when children view a videotape of an interaction between an adult male and an adult female, children of either sex who have a masculine orientation will recall more about the behavior of the male character than about that of the female.

Other evidence is supportive of Kohlberg's contention that children strive to behave in ways consistent with their sex-role judgments about themselves. For example, take the research of Hartup, Moore, and Sager (1963). They found that boys in particular were resistant to playing with "feminine" toys. What is more, this resistance increased with age. Such a study bears out the everyday observation that many boys find even the thought of playing with "girl" toys a horrid one indeed. Since these researchers found no effects for girls, it may be that girls' sex-typing is not so rigid as that of boys.

Differential reinforcement.

It is important to note that not all boys are alike in their preferences for particular sex-typed behaviors; nor are girls. This means that within a vast array of appropriate possibilities, the child picks and chooses. These choices will be affected by parental reinforcements. Similarly, research by Hetherington (1965) indicates that the child's preference for his or her own sex role is affected by the nature of the parent-child relationship. The point is that, while cognitive consistency may exert strong effects, there is no reason to rule out the operation of reinforcement from parents and peers in accounting for the occurrence of sex-typed behaviors. Differential reinforcement can affect the child's choice of one sex role over another, and also the choice of specific behaviors within any given sex role. Thus, a comprehensive view of sex-role acquisition will probably have to consider both cognitive consistency and social learning.

However, it is true that Kohlberg's analysis places the emphasis not on reinforcements delivered by key environmental figures or models but on the child. In effect, Kohlberg argued that the child figures out his or her own gender and then goes about the task of identifying with one parent or the other. The cognitive commitment, then, precedes paying attention to one kind of model rather than another and the preference for one kind of activity instead of others. The emergence of gender preferences can be attributed to the child's cognitive categorization of the self as male or female.

Role of expectancies

The causes of gender differences have been approached from many perspectives. Some of these causes are remote in time; for example, the role of heredity or early socialization of the child that affects the acquisition of gender-related behaviors. Such causes stress the stability of behaviors that differentiate men and women. Yet many of these differences seem ephemeral—they swell and recede in importance depending upon the nature of particular situations or the personalities of interacting individuals. Deaux and Major (1987) have chosen to focus on the flexibility and variability of gender-related behaviors. They emphasize the importance of social interaction, where the expectations of those interacting are so critical. Thus, in addition to heredity or social learning or identification, there is the nature of specific interactions. For example, how I react to my spouse is determined in part by my preexisting gender beliefs, by situational factors that trigger such beliefs, and by the self-perceptions of my spouse. Although a bit forbidding in appearance, these ideas are represented in the model shown in Figure 19-4.

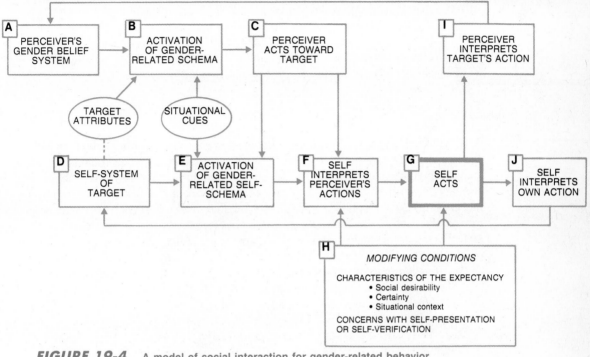

FIGURE 19-4 A model of social interaction for gender-related behavior
Adapted from "Putting Gender Into Context: An Interactive Model of Gender-Related Behavior" by Kay Deaux and Brenda Major, *Psychological Review*, Vol. 94, No. 3, July 1987. Copyright © 1987 by the American Psychological Association. Reprinted by permission of the authors.

ANDROGYNY

The words *masculine* and *feminine* have been used repeatedly throughout this chapter. Perhaps inadvertently, we have polarized masculinity and femininity by implying that they are extremes of a single dimension. There is an ideal masculine role and an ideal feminine role and never the twain shall meet. Unhappy with the traditional stereotyping and polarizing that seem to occur in this context, Sandra Bem (1975) suggested that we look at things from a fresh point of view. She offered the possibility that some people may be androgynous. That is, a person could exhibit both masculine and feminine behaviors and traits. This concept of **androgyny** has found a wide and sympathetic audience among many investigators, and there has been a rapidly burgeoning body of literature associated with it. Androgyny has most often been assessed by either the **Bem Sex Role Inventory (BSRI)** (Bem, 1974) or the **Personal Attributes Questionnaire**

(PAQ) (Spence, Helmreich, and Stapp, 1975). While a welcome relief from the sex-role stereotyping that has often been reinforced by the research literature, androgyny has been criticized both as a concept (Locksley and Colten, 1979) and in terms of the approaches to its measurement (Pedhazur and Tetenbaum, 1979). The validity of the BSRI has likewise been questioned (Myers and Gonda, 1982).

Tenor of the times

Quite obviously, androgyny is a topic in tune with the rising sentiment that women should behave in ways that are compatible with their abilities and aspirations rather than accepting the constraints of stereotypes so often thrust upon them. According to Bem (1975), androgynous individuals tend to behave in an effective masculine or feminine way depending upon the demand characteristics of the situation. This flexibility, then, confers upon such persons a greater potential for effective problem solving, satisfactions, and psychological adjustment (Wiggins and Holzmuller, 1981). A number of investigations have reported relationships between androgyny and adjustment. Several of these relationships are summarized in Table 19-3. However, others report that the evidence does not, on balance, support the idea that androgynous individuals are healthier than sex-typed individuals (Hall and Taylor, 1985).

The androgynous woman is a common phenomenon these days.
Photograph courtesy Delta Airlines.

TABLE 19-3 A summary of relationships between androgyny and adjustment

---

Androgyny Is Associated With

■ Higher levels of psychosocial development (Waterman and Whitbourne, 1982)

■ Happiness; tendency to regard stressful experiences as less undesirable (Shaw, 1982)

■ Psychological well-being (hypothesis partially supported) (Lubinski, Tellegen, and Butcher, 1981)

■ Being perceived by others as adjusted (Major, Carnevale, and Deaux, 1981)

■ Higher self-esteem and perceptions by others as competent (for females only) (Heilbrun, 1981)

■ Adjustment and perceived homeostatic balance with the environment (Flaherty and Dusek, 1980)

■ General self-esteem in children (Alpert-Gillis and Connell, 1989)

Some research has outlined the characteristics and background of androgynous individuals. Work by Janet Spence and colleagues (1975) reveals that androgynous men and women date more, receive more awards during their school years, and are sick less frequently. Parents of androgynous children have been described as warm, competent, encouraging, and considerate (Kelly and Worell, 1976). It may well be that such results are typical and, indeed, will become even more prevalent as sex roles in our society continue to evolve. Only time will tell. As Olds and Shaver (1980) conclude, in the final analysis "traditional sex roles may be easier to transcend if we talk directly about universal standards of competence and health rather than tie these standards to outmoded conceptions of masculinity, femininity, or even androgyny" (p. 340).

Language and values

While it may be fair to regard androgynous persons as possessing greater potential flexibility in their behavior, how one regards all this is another matter. The whole notion of adjustment and flexibility is entangled with personal and social values. Often, a language that is heavily loaded with value judgments creeps into discussions of androgyny. For example, Bem (1975) often refers to nonandrogynous subjects as showing behavioral deficits and to androgynous subjects as doing well. She describes feminine subjects as having "flunked" critical tasks. All of this subtly implies that androgynous individuals are better adjusted. For one committed to the values of androgyny, there will likely be agreement with these descriptions. But the nonandrogynous reader may think otherwise. The controversy over the unidimensional nature of devices designed to measure androgyny, exactly what they measure, and other conceptual and psychometric questions goes on (e.g., Bem, 1981; Spence and Helmreich, 1981). The sex of an individual plays a pervasive role in our society. To the extent that androgyny suggests that social and biological factors associated with sex roles can be ignored in developing behavior repertoires, the concept seems a bit out of touch with the real world. Our sexual state is an unavoidable influence on our perceptions of ourselves as well as on others' perceptions of us.

Two processes

Taylor and Hall (1982) have contended that androgyny should not be viewed as some independent characteristic that certain people have within them. All androgyny signifies is that masculinity and femininity operate simultaneously to influence behavior in some people. Most importantly, this implies that androgyny is not a thing; it is merely two processes—masculinity and femininity—operating in concert within the same person. In this sense, the androgyny hypothesis really refers to the avoidance of a sex-typed self-definition—an avoidance that constitutes a distinctive kind of psychological functioning with a variety of positive consequences. Nevertheless, the mere existence of the concept of androgyny reminds us that sex biases and sex-role stereotypes are rampant in our society (Schaffer, 1981).

The idea that people are *either* masculine or feminine seems a bit quaint now. Especially when we examine old scales that contained items that referred to masculine activities such as spitting on the sidewalk. While the motives that earlier impelled some to embrace androgyny as a concept may not have been exactly quaint, they may have been personally driven (Morawski, 1987). Thus, androgyny remains controversial and unclear both as it is measured and defined.

CONCLUDING OBSERVATIONS

One thing seems clear: there are many fewer sex differences than either psychology or the lay public has come to believe. As Unger (1979) has observed, we tend to conceptualize gender as a dichotomy. We use biology to divide the world into two genders and then view the psychology of what are now two worlds in separate ways. Our attention focuses on mean differences rather than on the variability between the two genders. It is a fact that, behaviorally, females and males overlap tremendously—and this overlap is much greater than the differences between them (see Figure 19-5). In recent years, the study of gender differences and sex-role development has become much more than just a stale compilation of dry facts. It has become politicized and has now assumed a consciousness-raising role. It has become a field tilled alternately by those who would maintain the status quo and by those who wish to change radically the nature of traditional sex roles. Objectivity can be a rare commodity under such conditions. It is an area in which investigators must constantly grapple with their own subtle stereotyping tendencies as well as their visions of what should be. Both biology and psychology can become victimized as accessories after the fact in such circumstances if we are not careful.

Within discussions of sex roles, gender differences, and feminism there often lurks a very basic contradiction (Grady, 1989). There is often a demand for equality and a parallel demand that differences be respected. Both demands are valid and we can only hope that a third demand will also be honored: that both positions be allowed to coexist without ill feelings.

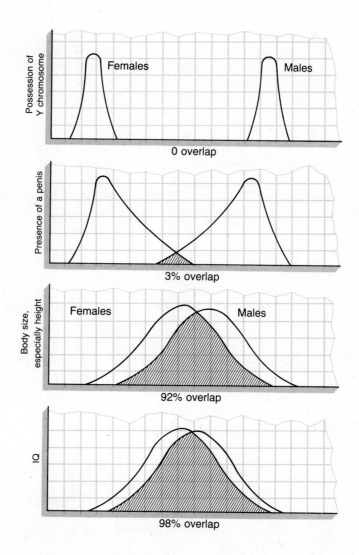

FIGURE 19-5 Frequency distributions of selected characteristics related to sex. Frequencies are idealized to illustrate the range of possible overlap in characteristics supposedly dichotomized by sex.
From *Female and Male: Psychological Perspectives* by Rhoda K. Unger. (New York: HarperCollins, 1979). Reprinted by permission of the author.

SUMMARY

- Conceptions about sex roles are changing rapidly. Although for many years sex roles were assigned on the basis of biological sexual characteristics, evidence existed that learning and cultural expectations were critical factors.

- Sex-role stereotypes still exist. They begin almost at the moment of birth and persist throughout the life cycle. They even exist in the minds of some professional mental health workers. There is no doubt that sex stereotyping is a deeply embedded social phenomenon. However, stereotyping does not always occur in connection with women.

- There are numerous consequences of sex stereotyping. For example, women are more likely to attribute their successes to luck and their failures to personal shortcomings. Some women even seem to harbor a fear of success since to attain success is, at the same time, to lose one's femininity.

- Sometimes, women even have a tendency to negatively stereotype other women. In addition, women sex-typed as feminine seem to be especially prone toward helplessness symptoms. Furthermore, individuals sex-typed as either masculine or feminine tend to be more subject to depression.

- Women sometimes seem to respond to stress psychologically while the response of men tends to be more physiological in nature. Interestingly, however, the increasingly visible role of women in the workforce does not seem to have had a negative impact on their health.

- A number of gender differences in behavior have been cataloged. Early research indicated that males were more aggressive than females largely as a result of the socialization process. However, biological and hormonal factors have also been suggested as contributors, although the strength of their contribution is debatable. More recently, studies have shown that when females are exposed to strong provocation, they react as aggressively as males. This may be related to recent changes in our culture regarding what is acceptable behavior in women.

- In the case of altruism, both genders tend to respond largely in terms of the specific situation. Females tend to be more dependent and less dominant.

- Women are said to be more emotional than men. Often, however, this conclusion is based on findings from research methods that have sex-role biases built into them.

- By late childhood, girls tend to surpass boys in verbal abilities, although there is great variability. However, recent research tends to question any real gender differences in verbal abilities.

■ In both mathematical and spatial abilities, males show greater skill than females (although in the classroom, girls receive better grades in math). Again, however, the differences are small and the variability is great, which suggests that career assignments should not be made along lines of gender. It is likely that these differences as well as supposed differences in cognitive style depend heavily upon cultural factors.

■ Sex-role stereotypes have existed throughout history. For some observers, this is further evidence for the role of biology. But since culture and biology operate simultaneously, it is difficult to separate the influence of one from that of the other.

■ There is some evidence that sex differences in behavior (e.g., smiling, irritability) occur even in infants. But the methodological pitfalls in such research make it difficult to assert that the results are unequivocal support for the role of biology. It is also difficult to generalize to humans the results of animal research on the effects of hormones upon sex differences in behavior.

■ Research with individuals whose external genitalia are inconsistent with their chromosomal sex has revealed that sex-role identity is more closely allied to how one is perceived by others than it is to one's internal, genetic sex characteristics.

■ Some evidence suggests that certain differences in cognitive abilities in men and women are influenced by differential brain lateralization in the two genders. However, the findings here are still controversial.

■ Sex-role development is explained by many in terms of the process of identification. How one resolves the Oedipus conflict during psychosexual development is said to determine one's sex-role choices. Particularly important are anaclitic versus defensive identification processes. Some feel, however, that little research evidence for the importance of identification exists. Others have reinterpreted Freud's ideas about identification.

■ The social learning perspective emphasizes the roles of observation and imitation in the development of sex roles. Reinforcement is likewise seen as a powerful agent. Furthermore, sex-role learning is viewed as more than a product of parent-child interactions; it is a process that occurs throughout the life cycle and is affected by numerous cultural agents.

■ The more cognitively oriented approach of Kohlberg suggests that a sense of gender identity stems from the child's discovery that there are two genders and the subsequent categorization of self into one of them. Gender, then, becomes an organizer for information about the social world.

■ It is important to note the role of expectancies in influencing gender differences in specific social interaction situations. The remote effects of heredity or socialization do not always take precedence over immediate factors.

■ Androgyny has become a popular research topic. The concept suggests that a given person may exhibit both masculine and feminine behaviors. Some hold that such behavioral flexibility confers upon individuals a greater potential for adjustment.

■ Androgyny is a value-laden concept that has a number of conceptual and methodological problems associated with it. Nevertheless the concept serves to remind us that there are alternatives to the traditional sex-role stereotypes that have been with us for so long.

■ In conclusion, it was noted again that the overlap in behavior between the genders is greater than the differences between them. Beyond that, it is important that investigators not get caught up in either consciousness-raising or stereotyping and, instead, strive to maintain their objectivity.

GLOSSARY

Ability traits For Cattell, traits that determine our effectiveness in the pursuit of goals.

Absurdity For existentialists, a characterization of many human beliefs. The very absurdity of these beliefs lends credence to them.

Achievement test Test designed to measure what one has learned in a given area prior to taking the test.

Acquiescence Tendency to respond "true" to each true-false item.

Acquired motives Motives whose value is learned as is the means of satisfying them and which, therefore, vary from person to person.

Act frequency approach Method of studying consistency of dispositions by determining the relative frequency of acts that we agree are characteristic of a given dispositional category.

Aggression Attempt to harm another. Some would restrict this to physical harm whereas others would include psychological harm. Still others would argue that intent to do harm must also be present. For Kelly, an attempt to extend one's construct system.

Ahistorical approach Behavior is explained as a product of one's current perceptions and not as an outcome resulting from the past.

Aim In Freudian theory, a characteristic of instincts referring to their goal of removing a state of excitation.

Alienation State in which people feel separated or detached from their experience.

Alpha press For Murray, an environmental force that is real in its effects on the person.

Altruism Pertaining to an act intended solely to benefit another person or group and which provides no benefit to the person engaging in the act.

Anaclitic identification Situation in which a child identifies with a given parent in order to avoid loss of love.

Anal expulsive In Freudian theory, a period of psychosexual development (from 6 months to 3 years) when an important source of pleasure is the expulsion of feces.

Anal retentive In Freudian theory, a period of psychosexual development (from 12 months to 4 years) when an important source of pleasure is the retention of feces.

Anal stage In Freudian theory, the second psychosexual stage, in which pleasure and attention are focused on bowel control along with retention and expulsion of feces.

Analytical psychology Term used to describe Jung's personality theory.

Androgyny The state of being able to perform both "masculine" and "feminine" behaviors.

Anger-anxiety conflicts According to Dollard and Miller, conflicts produced in the child when parents punish that child's anger responses.

Anima-animus For Jung, archetypes representing the feminine side of men (anima) and the masculine side of women (animus).

Anxiety Unpleasant state of emotional arousal characterized by diffuse fears, physiological arousal, and bodily symptoms such as rapid breathing, accelerated heartbeat, etc. Specific personality theorists each define the concept somewhat differently. For existentialists, an emotion resulting from the failure to be authentic. For Kelly, an awareness that events cannot be construed within one's construct system.

Anxiety as a state (A-State) Level of anxiety experienced momentarily in a specific situation; varies in level from time to time and situation to situation.

Anxiety as a trait (A-Trait) Person's chronic or stable level of anxiety.

Approach-approach conflict Conflict between two positive motives.

Approach-avoidance conflict Conflict that results from the desire to satisfy a motive in whose very satisfaction may reside other negative consequences.

Aptitude test Test designed to predict one's performance on a task in the future.

Archetypes For Jung, the structural elements of the collective unconscious.

Asthenic According to Kretschmer, a body type describing slight, long-boned, slender persons who are predisposed toward a schizophrenic personality type.

Athletic According to Kretschmer, a body type describing strong, muscular, broad-shouldered individuals with a tendency more toward a schizophrenic than a manic-depressive adjustment.

Attentional processes In observational learning, those processes of attention to the model's behavior that permit learning.

Attitudes For Cattell, overt expressions of interest marked by a particular level of intensity.

Authenticity State of expressing who one really is through behavior and emotions.

Autonomous ego Term used by ego psychologists to refer to an ego that grew not out of the id but in accordance with its own predispositions.

Autonomous self Kohut's ideal type characterized by self-esteem and self-confidence, ambition, and talents and skills.

Aversion therapy Induction of negative feelings or reactions to a stimulus regarded as attractive by the person but viewed as negative by the larger culture (e.g., pairing alcohol with a nausea-inducing drug).

Avoidance-avoidance conflict Conflict between two negative motives.

Bad-me For Sullivan, the result of negative reactions from the mother and others; helps the child develop a conscience.

Basic anxiety For Horney, the singular motive that impels behavior to cope with threat.

Behavior potential In Rotter's theory, the potential for a behavior to occur in a given situation as a way of achieving a particular goal.

Behavioral Coding System (BCS) A system developed by Patterson and colleagues to record behavioral observations in the homes of predelinquent boys.

Behavioral deficit Situation in which the quantity or quality of a given behavior is lacking in the person's behavioral repertoire.

Behavioral medicine The broad, interdisciplinary field of research, education, and practice that involves health, illness, and related physiological dysfunctions.

Behaviorism (behavioral tradition) Movement begun by Watson that emphasizes behavior as the only appropriate subject for study in psychology.

Being values (metamotives) According to Maslow, growth motives whose purpose is to extend our experience and enrich our lives.

Bem Sex Role Inventory (BSRI) Measure of androgyny.

Beta press For Murray, an environmental force that is significant only because the person views it so.

Binet-Simon Scale Early intelligence scale developed in France by Binet and Simon. Forerunner of the present Stanford-Binet.

Biofeedback Feedback provided to the person from various autonomic or somatic systems by means of special equipment; often used to treat headache, hypertension, etc.

Bivariate research strategy Research method in which only two variables are considered at a time.

Blacky Pictures Projective test developed from a psychoanalytic framework composed of pictures depicting the adventures of a dog named Blacky.

Buss technique Laboratory method of studying aggression. A confederate is presumably electrically shocked by a subject who presses buttons to deliver the desired level of shock (aggression).

Cardinal trait For Allport, a master motive or ruling passion that affects virtually every aspect of our existence.

Catharsis Release of pent-up energy; tendency for the verbal or fantasy expression of an impulse to reduce its likelihood of actual expression; prominent notion in psychoanalytic therapy and theory.

Central trait For Allport, a trait that is less important than a cardinal trait but that still exerts widespread influence.

Cerebrotonic According to Sheldon, a restrained, inhibited, somewhat withdrawn temperament most often characteristic of ectomorphs.

Chaining Pairing of a secondary reinforcer with a neutral event which, in turn, becomes a secondary reinforcer.

Characterology Method of personality analysis going back to ancient times in which categories are constructed and then people are described as fitting one or another of the categories.

Classical conditioning Form of conditioning or learning emphasized initially by Pavlov in which the response to an unconditioned stimulus (e.g., food) is conditioned to a formerly neutral stimulus (e.g., a noise) by repeated pairings of the two stimuli.

Cleanliness training According to Dollard and Miller, the period during which the child learns to control the processes of urination and defecation.

Client-centered Term used to describe Rogers's brand of therapy; synonymous with *nondirective* and *person-centered*.

Clinical method For Cattell, a research method akin to the multivariate strategy in which the observer notes how variables move in concert.

Coercion to the biosocial mean For Cattell, the exertion of pressure by society for people to conform to a kind of social mean.

Cognitive restructuring Broad set of techniques designed to change one's cognitive processes or thoughts and thereby change undesirable behaviors.

Cognitive social learning person variables Person variables described by Mischel that result from cognitive development and social learning. They include competencies, encoding strategies and personal constructs, expectancies, subjective values, and self-regulatory systems and plans.

Collective unconscious According to Jung, the seat of memory traces from our ancestral past including even prehuman ancestry.

Common trait For Allport and Cattell, a trait that is common to many people.

Compensation For Adler, the development of physical or mental abilities to overcome feelings of inferiority.

Competence motivation For White, the need to deal effectively with our environment.

Componential aspect In Sternberg's theory of intelligence, the analytical aspect.

Concurrent validity Extent to which a test correlates with an existing criterion.

Conditions of worth Conditions or rules in the family that serve as the bases on which the child will receive love, approval, and attention.

Confession For Jung, an initial period in therapy similar to catharsis.

Conflict-free sphere Term used by ego psychologists to refer to a part of the ego, the processes of which are not in conflict with the id, superego, or real world.

Congruent externals Persons who, for realistic reasons, appraise the environment and the occurrence of reinforcements as controlled by forces beyond their control.

Conscience In Freudian theory, that part of the superego incorporating moral values and ideals.

Conscious area Those sensations, perceptions, experiences, and memories of which one is aware at any given moment.

Constellatory construct In Kelly's system, a construct that has wide connections throughout a person's construct system.

Constitutional trait For Cattell, a source trait with a constitutional origin.

Construct Term in personality theory commonly regarded as synonymous with *concept*.

Construct validity General pattern of relationships between a test and relevant behaviors as defined by a particular theory.

Content validity Extent to which test items constitute an adequate sample of the events being measured.

Contents In Guilford's model of intelligence, the dimension that refers to the material or information to which the person reacts.

Contextual aspect In Sternberg's theory of intelligence, the "street smart" aspect.

Continuous reinforcement Reinforcement of an organism's response 100% of the time.

Control group Subjects in an experiment who undergo the same conditions as the experimental subjects except for the key factor being studied.

Correlate Statistical method to compare two sets of observations on a group of people to determine the relationship, if any, between those observations.

Correlation coefficient Numerical value indicating the strength and direction of the relationship between two variables.

Correlation matrix An array of correlations between all possible pairs of scores.

Correlational method Method used to determine the extent to which two or more variables are related.

Co-twin method Research method involving the study of identical twins reared apart.

Counterconditioning Conditioning of a desirable response that is incompatible with an undesirable one.

Countertransference In psychoanalysis, the tendency of the therapist to react to the patient on the basis of the therapist's own needs and conflicts.

Crisis In Erikson's system, one of eight critical stages influenced by both biological and psychological factors. Either positive or negative outcomes are possible.

Criterion analysis Eysenck's method of testing hypotheses through factor analysis.

Criterion contamination Situation in which, for example, judgments about a subject's standing on a given variable are influenced by preexisting related information.

Criterion validity Extent to which test scores relate to some agreed-upon behavioral criterion.

Crystallized ability According to Cattell, a broad kind of intelligence that reflects one's experiences in the culture.

Cue-producing responses Production of similarity or differences among situations by virtue of the cues residing in the language.

Cues Stimuli that determine the particular response a person will make.

Culture-fair test Test designed to measure intelligence free from the influence of cultural factors.

Daily hassles A form of stress that emerges from the ordinary, daily events in our lives.

Daseinsanalysis In existential psychology, the analysis of the immediate experience of the individual.

Death instincts In Freudian theory, those instincts (or Thanatos) responsible for the destructive aspects of human behavior.

Decoding In information processing, interpreting meaning or information by comparing and combining it with previously stored information.

Defensive externals Persons who express beliefs in external control as a way of warding off the harmful effects of anticipated failures.

Defensive identification Situation in which a child identifies with a given parent in order to avoid punishment from that parent.

Deindividuation General loss of self-awareness; a reduced ability to observe oneself or to evaluate oneself, coupled with a loss in sensitivity to social norms.

Delay of gratification Ability to defer immediate, smaller rewards in favor of larger but delayed ones.

Dependent variable Factor in an experiment that may or may not change as a result of manipulation of the independent variable.

Deviation IQ concept IQ is derived by comparing the individual's performance to that of his or her age peers.

Diagnostic council A strategy used by Murray in which several observers come together to synthesize their separate observations and come to a final conclusion about the subject.

Diathesis-stress Viewpoint suggesting that in order for a given mental disorder to appear, both a neural defect and a characteristic set of environmental stresses must be present.

Dichotomous construct Either-or nature of constructs, according to Kelly.

Differential R-technique Statistical method of comparing scores received on two occasions and then correlating the changes between them; these changes are then factor-analyzed. Often associated with Cattell.

Diffusion of responsibility General notion that when in groups, individuals will often behave in a manner indicating a lessened sense of personal responsibility.

Discrimination of cues Process in which the individual pays appropriate attention to those environmental signals relevant to achieving reinforcement.

Discriminative stimulus Stimulus that indicates one response rather than another is likely to be rewarded.

Displacement In psychoanalytic theory, the defense mechanism in which an impulse is deflected from its true target to a less threatening one.

Dispositions Those inclinations or tendencies that help direct and energize our behavior.

Distance For Adler, the tendency (often psychological) to establish distance between the self and goals in order to avoid failure.

Dread and despair For existentialists, emotions resulting from the person's failure to be authentic.

Drive activation method Method of studying the unconscious by activating it through subliminal perception.

Drives According to Dollard and Miller, strong internal stimuli that impel on organism to action.

Dynamic lattice For Cattell, the relationships among dynamic traits, ergs, sentiments, and attitudes.

Dynamic self-concept A view of the self-concept as dynamic, forceful, and changing.

Dynamic trait For Cattell, a trait that initiates a person's response in a given situation.

Dysplastic According to Kretschmer, a body type characterized by disproportionate physical development or features of several body types.

Early sex training According to Dollard and Miller, a source of conflict that can produce chronic anxiety in the child.

Ecological validity Extent to which a test or observation is a representative sample of a subject's behavior.

Ectomorphy According to Sheldon, a body type characterized by a delicate, fragile, poorly muscled frame; said to have cerebrotonic temperament.

Education For Jung, a period in therapy when the therapist promotes new learning.

Edwards Personal Preference Schedule Self-report test designed to assess 15 needs.

Ego In Freudian theory, the reality-oriented portion of the personality; utilizes learning, perception, and reasoning to satisfy id impulses in the light of real-world constraints. Jung used a similar concept in referring to an "I" feeling.

Ego-control Ability to control one's impulses by self-delay, inhibition of aggression, and making plans.

Ego defenses (defense mechanisms) Methods employed by the ego to protect the individual against threats from the id; involve the distortion and falsification of experience.

Ego-ideal In Freudian theory, that part of the superego consisting of standards of perfection which, if realized, bring a sense of pride and self-esteem.

Ego identity In Erikson's system, all those self-perceptions that give one a sense of uniqueness and stability over time.

Ego-resiliency Ability to adapt to environmental demands by modifying ego-control.

Electra complex In Freudian theory, the counterpart in girls of the Oedipus complex in boys.

Elucidation For Jung, a stage in therapy in which the patient attempts to explain problems being experienced.

Embedded Figures Test A test to determine cognitive style.

Empathy Vicarious affective response to another's feelings.

Empirical Method in which observations of the events in question are taken.

Enactive attainment One's performance in a dreaded situation that has an effect on self-efficacy.

Encoding In information processing, entering information into the system and then storing it in symbolic form.

Endomorphy According to Sheldon, a body type characterized by a highly developed visceral structure; said to have a viscerotonic temperament.

Environmental-mold trait For Cattell, a source trait developed out of experience with the environment.

Epidemiology Study of the distribution and determinants of health conditions.

Epigenetic principle According to Erikson, the developing personality follows a blueprint which guides it toward broader and broader social interactions.

Episodic memory Memory for events or episodes.

Erg For Cattell, a dynamic constitutional source trait, which is innate, motivates the person, and determines numerous surface traits.

Erotogenic zones In Freudian theory, those parts of the body which, if manipulated, produce pleasurable sensations.

Existentialism Theory emphasizing freedom of choice, taking responsibility for one's own life, and the achievement of one's full potential.

Expectancy In Rotter's theory, a subjectively held probability that a particular reinforcement will occur as the result of a specific behavior.

Experiential aspect In Sternberg's theory of intelligence, the creative aspect.

Experimental hypothesis Hypothesis to be tested by means of an experimental procedure.

External control In Rotter's theory, the belief or expectancy that attaining or failing to attain reinforcements is due to luck, chance, fate, or powerful others; contrasts with internal control.

Extinction Elimination of a learned response following repeated nonoccurrence of reward.

Extraversion For Jung, an orientation toward the outer world; sociability and friendliness are usually prominent. Contrasts with introversion. Term also widely used by Eysenck.

Face validity Extent to which a test is composed of items that appear logically related to the variable being measured.

Factor analysis Mathematical technique of arranging traits or responses into homogeneous groupings within a matrix of intercorrelations.

Factors The basic dimensions to which data are reduced by means of factor analysis.

Fear Survey Schedule Self-report test widely used by behaviorally oriented clinicians; designed to reveal the stimuli that provoke anxiety in the client.

Feeding situation According to Dollard and Miller, the early situation in which the groundwork is laid for many subsequent emotional reactions.

Feminine protest According to Adler, the tendency of a child to equate feminine behavior with superiority. Occurs when the child learns that a female is the dominant family member.

Feshbach Affective Situations Test for Empathy (FASTE) Series of slides designed to elicit various emotions in children and thereby serve as a measure of dispositional empathy.

Fixation In Freudian theory, a tendency to remain at or regress to a particular psychosexual stage as the result of earlier under- or overgratification at that stage.

Fixed-role therapy Form of therapy associated with Kelly in which clients play roles for a specified time period.

Fluid ability According to Cattell, the ability determined by one's biological capacity.

Focus of convenience Term often used by Kelly to indicate that each theory is best applied to a particular universe of situations or events.

Free association In psychoanalytic therapy, the method whereby the patient verbalizes every thought no matter how irrational, trivial, or threatening it may appear.

Freedom of movement In Rotter's theory, the mean subjective probability that a group of related behaviors will lead to a particular set of goals.

Frustration Reaction occurring when our progress toward a goal is blocked.

Fully Committed In a study of altruism and civil rights, those who showed sustained efforts over time and who committed both time and money.

Fully functioning person According to Rogers, an individual who fully utilizes his or her potential.

Functional analysis Analysis of behavior designed to show how a behavior covaries with the environmental conditions that control it.

Functional autonomy Allport's idea that adult motives are often independent of their early beginnings (e.g., a man no longer fishes because of the desire for food but because he simply enjoys fishing).

G analysis of projective data method Method of studying the unconscious through projective tests.

Gender One's psychosexual identity.

General adaptation syndrome Selye's notion that in response to stress, there is a set of physiological responses that involve several distinct stages, the last of which could be death.

General factor (g) According to Spearman, the broad factor underlying all intellectual activity.

Generalized expectancies In Rotter's theory, expectancies based upon experiences accumulated over a variety of related situations.

Generalized reinforcer Reinforcer whose value does not depend solely on one drive state.

Generativity In Erikson's system, the concern in middle age for the well-being of the next generation.

Genital stage In Freudian theory, the final psychosexual stage, in which the mature development of heterosexual impulses and behavior occurs.

Goodenough-Harris Drawing Test Test of intelligence requiring children to draw pictures of a man, a woman, and themselves.

Good-me For Sullivan, the result of positive reactions received from the mother and others by the child. The result is high self-esteem.

Group factors According to Thurstone, factors intermediate between g and s factors that affect intellectual performance.

Guided participation Method by which a patient or subject is helped by assistants to perform a desired behavior.

Guilford-Zimmerman Temperament Survey Test developed through factor analysis designed to reveal a person's standing on 10 traits.

Guilt For Kelly, awareness that one is not behaving in the manner dictated by one's core constructs.

Habits Associations between stimuli and responses that develop as a result of rewards.

Habitual responses For Eysenck, large numbers of repeatedly performed behaviors which comprise a trait.

Hardiness Stress-buffering characteristics such as commitment, control, and challenge said to make individuals resistant to stress-induced illness.

Health Locus of Control Scale Scale designed to measure individual differences in the desire for personal control in health care.

Heritability ratio Proportion of variance of IQs in a given population that is the result of genetic variation among the individuals in the group.

Hierarchical models Models of intelligence that often emphasize the superior role of g factors which, in turn, affect s factors.

Hogan Empathy Scale (EM) A generalized measure of empathy.

Hostility For Kelly, the person's attempt to extort validation for a construct that is failing in its task of prediction.

Humanism Point of view emphasizing the essential goodness of human beings and the optimistic belief in their potential for growth.

Id In Freudian theory, the deep, unconscious part of the personality composed of the biological, instinctual drives; its goal is the immediate gratification of impulses.

Ideal-self That which the person would like to feel, be, or experience.

Identification with the aggressor During the Oedipal period, a process by which the son resolves his conflict by identifying with his father.

Identity crisis According to Erikson, the period of life during which the young person struggles to define the "real me."

Idiographic Approach emphasizing the intensive study of one individual; contrasts with the nomothetic approach, which focuses on the search for general laws by combining data from many individuals.

Implicit personality theory Notion that everyone develops a theory to account for the way another person's traits fit together to form the personality.

Inappropriate set of responses Responses that appear to the observer as not suited to the nature of the situation.

Incomplete Sentences Blank (ISB) Test developed by Rotter in which subjects complete 40 sentence stems.

Independent variable Factor deliberately manipulated by the investigator to determine its effect on the dependent variable.

Individual psychology Term used to describe Adler's personality theory.

Individual tests Tests administered to subjects one at a time; contrasts with group tests.

Individuation For Jung, the process that culminates in the attainment of selfhood.

Inferiority complex For Adler, strong feelings that one is inferior to others.

Initial (innate) hierarchy According to Dollard and Miller, the order in which an organism's responses can be arranged in terms of their likelihood of occurrence; this order is innate.

Innate motives Biological motives that relate directly to the survival of the individual and species (e.g., food and water).

Instincts In Freudian theory, collections of unconscious wishes that have a source, an aim, and an object; usually divided into the life instincts and the death instincts.

Institutional neurosis Erosion of the personality, overdependence, and loss of interest in the outside world occurring in connection with institutionalization.

Instrumental conditioning Learning to perform a given response as the result of having it reinforced or rewarded; sometimes called *operant conditioning.*

Integration learning Term often used by Cattell, referring to our tendency to repress, suppress, or sublimate certain ergs in order to satisfy other ergs.

Intelligence Many definitions have been offered but most involve the ability to adjust to the environment, the capacity for learning or education, or the ability to employ abstract concepts.

Intelligence quotient (IQ) At first, defined as one's mental age divided by one's chronological age and multiplied by 100; now refers to one's test performance in relation to age peers.

Intentions For Allport, one's hopes, aspirations, plans, and wishes.

Interjudge reliability Extent to which different observers who are observing the same event make similar judgments about that event.

Internalization In object relations theory, representations of important environmental objects.

Internal control In Rotter's theory, the belief or expectancy that attaining or failing to attain reinforcements is due to one's own efforts or lack of them; contrasts with external control.

Internal-External Control Scale (I-E Scale) Test developed by Rotter to measure generalized expectancies for internal-external control (sometimes called *locus of control*).

Internal standards For Bandura, self-regulated internal standards that influence our thoughts, actions, and emotions.

Interpersonal trust In Rotter's theory, a problem-solving generalized expectancy regarding how trusting one should be of others.

Interpersonal Trust Scale Test developed by Rotter to measure the generalized problem-solving expectancy of interpersonal trust.

Intropunitive Aggressive response directed toward oneself.

Introversion For Jung, a reserved, withdrawn orientation; interest in ideas rather than sociability. Contrasts with extraversion. Term also widely used by Eysenck.

Jenkins Activity Survey for Health Prediction (JAS) Method of identifying Type A individuals.

Kin selection By behaving selflessly, animals increase the likelihood that relatives will live to procreate and thus pass along their genes to succeeding generations.

Krantz Health Opinion Survey Scale designed to measure preferences for self-treatment and active participation in one's health care along with information about health care.

Latency period In Freudian theory, period following the phallic state, in which instinctual sexual urges lie dormant.

L-data Data drawn from life records; often associated with Cattell's methods.

Learned helplessness Condition resulting from exposure to painful, inescapable stimuli or failure in which passive helplessness behavior or diminished effort endures even in later situations when escape or success is possible.

Libido In Freudian theory, the energy responsible for the life instincts.

Life instincts In Freudian theory, those instincts (or Eros) responsible for the positive or constructive portions of behavior.

Loading In factor analysis, the extent to which a given measure correlates with a given factor.

Locus of control In Rotter's theory, a generalized problem-solving expectancy regarding the extent to which reinforcement is controlled by self or other factors. Synonomous with *internal-external control of reinforcement.*

Manifest Anxiety Scale (MAS) Developed by Taylor, an objective true-false test for the measurement of anxiety levels.

Masculine protest According to Adler, masculinity is often equated with power. Thus, individuals, particularly females, often strive for superiority by becoming assertive and dominant.

Mediated stimulus generalization Tendency for a response learned in one situation to generalize to other situations labeled as similar to the first; similarity is based not on physical similarity but on labeling.

Mental age (MA) Score on an intelligence test that has been converted into months and years.

Mesomorphy According to Sheldon, a body characterized by a predominance of musculature; said to have a somatotonic temperament.

Minimal goal level In Rotter's theory, the lowest goal in a hierarchy of goals that is perceived by the individual as reinforcing.

Minnesota Multiphasic Personality Inventory (MMPI) Widely used objective test originally designed to determine appropriate psychiatric diagnosis.

Moral anxiety In Freudian theory, an awareness experienced as guilt stemming from the threat of punishment by the superego.

Motivation The forces within us that activate and direct our behavior toward certain goals rather than others (e.g., hunger, achievement, power).

Motivational processes In observational learning, those motivational processes that determine whether we actually perform behaviors we have learned through observation.

Motive Goal or outcome of a given behavior as it relates to a particular motivational state (e.g., money, food).

Motor reproduction processes In observational learning, production of those behaviors exhibited by the model.

Multiple abstract variance analysis (MAVA) Statistical tool used by Cattell to study the role of heredity-environment factors in personality.

Multiple intelligences For Gardner, the theory that intelligence is formed out of six sets of problem-solving skills: linguistic, musical, logical-mathematical, spatial, bodily kinesthetic, and personal.

Multistage testing An adaptive testing procedure used in the 1986 Stanford-Binet. Involves giving the vocabulary subtest to determine the entry point for other subtests.

Multivariate research strategy Variety of measurements on the same person taken at one time; there is no experimental manipulation of variables.

Myers-Briggs Type Indicator Test Test used to measure Jung's four functions of the mind: thinking, feeling, sensing, and intuiting.

National character The idea that there are distinct behavioral differences among people of different nationalities.

Need for Achievement According to McClelland, the learned desire to perform well and to strive to attain a standard of excellence.

Need for Affiliation The desire to seek the company of others, and to achieve their friendship.

Need for Power The desire to exert control over the events that affect our lives.

Need potential In Rotter's theory, the mean potential for a group of related behaviors to occur as a way of achieving a particular set of goals.

Need value In Rotter's theory, the value of a group of related reinforcements composing a given need.

Needs In Murray's system, forces that organize and give direction to feelings, thoughts, and behaviors so that an unsatisfying state of affairs can be overcome.

Neo-Freudians Group of psychoanalysts who revised Freudian theory to give it a more social context; the most prominent members are usually considered to be Horney, Fromm, and Sullivan.

Neurotic anxiety In Freudian theory, an awareness of a threat that unconscious id impulses are seeking expression.

Nomothetic Approach focusing on the search for general laws by combining data from many individuals; contrasts with the idiographic approach, which emphasizes the intensive study of one individual.

Nondirective Term used to describe Rogers's brand of therapy; synonymous with *client-centered* and *person-centered*.

Not-me For Sullivan, the result of strong disapproval from the mother or others. Experienced as strong anxiety by the child.

Object In Freudian theory, a characteristic of instincts which refers to that which will remove the state of excitation.

Object representation One's internalized image of a significant other object.

Objective orientation For Piaget, the cognitive orientation in children younger than 10.

Objective test Self-report test in which the subject provides responses to questions about feelings, thoughts, and behavior.

Oblique method In factor analysis, an approach that specifies that obtained factors may be correlated.

Observational learning Term often associated with Bandura, referring to learning by means of observing a live or symbolic model; also called *vicarious learning*.

Oedipus complex In Freudian theory, sexual longing for the parent of the opposite sex; occurs in the phallic stage.

Operant behavior Behavior acquired on the basis of instrumental conditioning.

Operations In Guilford's model of intelligence, the dimension that refers to what the person does.

Optimism A general quality said by some to help make people resistant to stress-related illnesses.

Oral biting In Freudian theory, a period of psychosexual development (from eight to eighteen months) when a chief mode of pleasure is biting.

Oral stage In Freudian theory, the first psychosexual stage, in which the mouth is the prime area of pleasure.

Oral sucking In Freudian theory, a period of psychosexual development (from birth to eight months) when the chief mode of pleasure is sucking.

Organ inferiority For Adler, a congenital weakness in a body organ that stimulates feelings of inferiority in the person.

Orthogonal In factor analysis, an approach that specifies that obtained factors must be uncorrelated.

Output In information processing, the product of the processing operations that results in some action or solution.

Partial reinforcement Less than 100% reinforcement of a response; usually increases that response's resistance to extinction. Sometimes called *intermittent reinforcement*.

Partially Committed In a study of altruism and civil rights, those who, for example, participated in a few freedom rides.

Passive-aggressive personality One who "passively" resists the demands of others.

Passive Supporters In a study of altruism and civil rights, those who donated money but little else.

Peak experience For Maslow, an experience that is intensely fulfilling; often characteristic of self-actualizers.

Peak performance For Maslow, a superior performance by the individual.

Pearson product moment correlation coefficient Particular method of calculating a correlation coefficient.

Penis envy In Freudian theory, the girl's desire to have a penis; persists throughout life and is responsible for the wish (in symbolic terms) to have a child, achieve power, etc.

Percept-genetics method Method of studying the unconscious, using tachistoscopic exposure of varying levels of illumination or exposure lengths.

Permeable construct In Kelly's system, a construct that can be applied to new events not yet a part of the construct system.

Persona For Jung, the archetype representing the public face we put on in response to social demands.

Personal Attributes Questionnaire (PAQ) Measure of androgyny.

Personal constructs theory Term applied to the personality theory of George Kelly; represents a person's interpretations of life or experiences.

Personal Orientation Inventory (POI) Test developed by Shostrom often used to measure self-actualization.

Personal self-concept Part of the self containing physical, behavioral, and psychological characteristics.

Personal trait For Allport, a trait unique to a given person.

Personal unconscious Jung's concept which is roughly equivalent to the preconscious of Freud.

Personality Pattern of characteristic thoughts, feelings, and behaviors that persists over time and situations and distinguishes one person from another.

Person-centered Most recent term used to describe Rogers's brand of therapy; synonymous with *client-centered* and *nondirective*.

Phallic stage In Freudian theory, the third psychosexual stage, in which the genitals become the focus of attention and pleasure.

Phenomenal field Everything experienced by the person at a given moment.

Phenomenal self That part of the phenomenal field designated as the "I" or "me."

Phenomenology Personality approach emphasizing the idea that behavior, emotions, and thoughts are determined by the person's subjective experience or perceptions.

Physiognomy Method of personality analysis by which personality characteristics are inferred from appearance—especially from the expression and shape of the face.

Pleasure principle In Freudian theory, the principle by which the id operates; seeking of immediate gratification of impulses.

Positive regard For Rogers, a strong need to be well-regarded by others. It motivates a vast array of human behavior.

Positive self-regard For Rogers, a strong need to think well of oneself.

Preconscious area Those contents of the mind that, although not presently conscious, may be made so by a little effort.

Predictive validity Extent to which a test can predict to some criterion in the future.

Preemptive construct In Kelly's system, a construct that does not permit its elements to belong to any other category.

Press In Murray's theory, environmental factors that aid or hinder goal attainment.

Primary drive Basic, innate drive such as hunger or thirst.

Primary (viscerogenic) needs For Murray, physiological needs.

Primary process In Freudian theory, the id process whereby tension is reduced by forming a mental image of an object that will satisfy a drive.

Primary reinforcers Reinforcements such as food, water, and so on.

Problem-solving generalized expectancies In Rotter's theory, expectancies that construing situations in a given fashion will help solve the problems presented by those situations.

Products In Guilford's model of intelligence, the dimension that refers to the form in which information is processed.

Progressive Matrices A so-called culture-fair test developed by Raven which consists of a series of geometric designs.

Projection In psychoanalytic theory, the defensive attribution of one's own unacceptable impulses or thoughts to others.

Projective test Test in which personality factors are revealed by the way a subject responds to ambiguous test stimuli; a familiar example is the Rorschach test.

Proprium According to Allport, everything in the personality regarded by the person as his or her own.

Prosocial behavior Behavior that results in helping another person or group; the intent to help or an expected gain may or may not be present.

Psychic determinism Belief of Freud that every behavior, thought, and emotion has meaning and purpose.

Psychobiography The study of individuals, usually from a psychoanalytic standpoint, that seeks both to validate the theory and to understand the individuals in question.

Psychohistory Method of inquiry especially associated with Erikson in which major themes in a person's life are related to certain historical events.

Psychological reactance The tendency to show an increased desire to engage in a given behavior when someone threatens your choice of that same behavior.

Psychosomatic medicine A field in which certain illnesses are regarded as caused by or related to psychological factors.

Psychoticism Dimension or type used by Eysenck; at the extreme end, a person would be solitary, without loyalties, uncaring of others, and insensitive.

P-technique Statistical technique by which a single person's scores on a number of measures are compared from one time to another; often associated with Cattell.

Pyknic According to Kretschmer, the body type of round, stocky, heavy individuals who are predisposed to manic-depressive reactions.

Q-data Self-rating questionnaire data; often associated with Cattell's methods.

QMEE A generalized measure of empathy.

Q-sort technique Method of obtaining trait ratings. The subject sorts cards containing traits or other information into a series of piles; these piles are labeled from "Very characteristic" to "Not at all characteristic."

Q-technique Statistical method in which people's scores on several measures are correlated, with the resulting index revealing the similarity among individuals; often associated with Cattell.

Rationalization In psychoanalytic theory, the defense mechanism whereby people offer reasonable (although incorrect) explanations for their shortcomings.

Reaction formation In psychoanalytic theory, the defense mechanism in which an anxiety-provoking impulse is replaced by its opposite (e.g., hate for another is experienced as love).

Reality anxiety In Freudian theory, an awareness of a threat from the environment which has a rational basis.

Reality principle In Freudian theory, the principle used by the ego whereby immediate gratification is postponed until appropriate objects or conditions are identified.

Reciprocal determinism Term usually associated with Bandura referring to the reciprocal influence on one another of the situation, the person, and behavior.

Recoding In information processing, internal revision of information to better prepare it for further processing.

Regression In psychoanalytic theory, the defense mechanism in which threatening events are evaded by returning to behavior characteristic of an earlier stage of development.

Reinforcement value In Rotter's theory, the degree of preference for one reinforcement rather than others given the possibility that all are equally likely to occur.

Reinforcer According to Skinner, an event or stimulus that follows a response and is then determined to have increased the likelihood of that response.

Reliability Consistency with which a test or observational method yields comparable results under the same conditions.

Repression In psychoanalytic theory, an unconsciously determined defense mechanism in which ego-threatening thoughts and impulses are involuntarily banished to the unconscious. For Dollard and Miller, it refers to "stopping thinking."

Resistance Important point in psychotherapy when the patient becomes anxious over the eruption of unconscious material and responds by attempting to impede therapy in various ways.

Respondent behavior Behavior emitted in response to stimulation.

Response An act prompted by an internal or external stimulus.

Response style Tendency for a subject to respond to an item in a particular way (e.g., agree or disagree) regardless of the item's content.

Retention processes In observational learning, those processes of retention that permit learning through forming mental images and verbal codings of the model's behavior.

Reward According to Dollard and Miller, anything that increases the likelihood of a given response being elicited by a particular stimulus.

Rod and Frame Test A test to determine cognitive style.

Role Construct Repertory Test (REP Test) Test devised by Kelly to identify and measure important constructs in a person's construct system.

Role playing An assessment or therapeutic technique in which individuals act out parts given them.

Roles For Cattell, roles characterize the nature of a person's situation (e.g., doctor, politician, etc.) so as to affect his or her perceptions of an event.

Rosenzweig Picture-Frustration Study Completion test for the measurement of individual differences in responses to frustration.

R-technique Traditional correlation method in which the scores from a large number of tests administered to many subjects are correlated; often associated with Cattell.

Schedule of reinforcement Rate and frequency of reinforcement and associated time elements.

Schemas Structures of knowledge that reside in memory.

Schizophrenia Severe form of mental illness characterized by withdrawal, apathy, thought disorder, general emotional disturbance, and delusions and hallucinations.

Schizotaxia Neurological impairment, possibly inherited, that results in a tendency toward a schizophrenic-like adjustment, a predisposition to schizophrenia.

Scripts Organized representations of familiar activities used to perceive and understand events.

Secondary drive Learned drive such as fear, guilt, or need for approval.

Secondary (psychogenic) needs For Murray, needs that arise out of primary needs but are not connected with organic processes.

Secondary process In Freudian theory, the principle employed by the ego whereby cognitive and perceptual skills help prevent the individual from being endangered by the gratification of instinctual needs.

Secondary reinforcers Reinforcers that, by having been paired with primary reinforcers, come to serve as reinforcers in their own right (e.g., money, smiles).

Secondary trait For Allport, a trait that exerts a relatively narrow or specific influence on behavior.

Self According to Rogers, the perception of oneself and its associated values; the "I" or "me." For Jung, an archetype that promotes search for unity. For Sullivan, the reflected appraisals of others.

Self-actualization Term associated with both Maslow and Rogers; a tendency or desire to be all that one can become.

Self-efficacy Bandura's concept referring to a person's belief that a given behavior can be successfully executed.

Self-handicapping Defensive strategy in which the person acquires an impediment to successful performance which, in turn, provides an excuse for potential failure.

Self-ideals Aspects of the self as one would like them to be.

Selfism Scale Scale designed to measure the generalized problem-solving expectancy of selfism.

Self-monitoring Method of assessment in which subjects monitor their own behavior by keeping records such as diaries.

Self-regulation The continuous and conscious evaluation and monitoring of progress toward some goal.

Self-Report Altruism Scale Objective scale on which subjects indicate the frequency with which they have engaged in several altruistic acts.

Self-schemata (self-schemas) Cognitive generalizations about the self, derived from past experience, that organize and guide the processing of self-related information.

Semantic differential Method of studying the meanings of concepts. The subject rates a series of concepts or words along 7-point scales, each of which is defined by polar adjectives (e.g., weak-strong).

Semantic memory An organized store of information about concepts and meaning.

Sentiment For Cattell, a dynamic source trait arising out of experiences in the culture.

Sex One's biological male-female heritage.

Sex-role stereotype Bias against individuals in similar situations engaged in similar behaviors because of their membership in a specific sexual group.

Shadow For Jung, the archetype incorporating the dark, evil side of human nature.

Shaping In operant conditioning, the gradual molding of behavior into the desired behavior through reward; sometimes called *method of successive approximation.*

Sign versus sample Contrasting approaches that deal with test data as signs of underlying processes or as a sample of a larger pool of observations that could be made in other situations.

Sixteen Personality Factor Questionnaire (16 P-F Questionnaire) Test designed by Cattell to reveal the basic personality profile.

Social breakdown reaction Illustrated by the scenario in which elderly persons come to see themselves as useless and helpless.

Social desirability Response style characterized by a tendency to give socially acceptable responses to items.

Social interest For Adler, a predisposition, nurtured by experience, to contribute to society.

Social learning theories Theories that emphasize learning in the social context and the role of cognitive processes.

Social Readjustment Rating Scale Scale listing potential stressful life events that may be implicated in the production of illness.

Social self-concepts Those parts of the self referring to how you believe others see you.

Socialized conduct disorder Refers to children who commit frequent antisocial acts such as truancy, running away, stealing, and the like.

Sociobiology Field that studies the relationships between biological factors and social behavior.

Somatotonic According to Sheldon, an active, assertive, vigorous temperament most often characteristic of mesomorphs.

SORC Signifies the behavioral clinician's interest in assessing four kinds of variables: stimuli, organismic variables, responses, and the consequences of behavior.

Source In Freudian theory, a characteristic of instincts referring to the location of a state of excitation within the body.

Source traits For Cattell, underlying structures that cause behavior (surface traits); constitute the core of the personality.

Specific expectancies In Rotter's theory, expectancies based on experience in a specific situation.

Specific factor *(s)* According to Spearman, a factor underlying performance on specific tasks that require intellect.

Specific reflexes Reflexes with which the infant is endowed at birth and which make it responsive to a very narrow range of stimuli.

Specific responses For Eysenck, the behavioral elements of habits.

Specification equation For Cattell, the formula combining all information about traits to predict a person's behavior in a specific situation.

Stability-instability Type or dimension used by Eysenck that refers to level of adjustment.

Stanford-Binet Intelligence test developed by Terman and based upon Binet's early work.

State anxiety (A-State) Level of anxiety experienced momentarily in a specific situation; varies in level from time to time and situation to situation.

States For Cattell, temporary conditions such as fatigue or anxiety which characterize individuals.

State-Trait Anxiety Inventory (STAI) Test that measures both state and trait anxiety.

Stimulus generalization Tendency for a response learned in connection with one stimulus to occur in relation to other, physically similar stimuli.

Stress Psychological and physiological state produced by a wide variety of unpleasant and sometimes dangerous events.

Stress inoculation Method of therapy in which patients are cognitively prepared and then taught to acquire and rehearse the skills necessary to deal with their problems.

Stressors Those events in the environment that precipitate a state of stress in the person.

Striving for superiority For Adler, the desire to overcome feelings of inferiority and to reach the limits of one's abilities.

Structure of the intellect (SOI) Model employed by Guilford that classifies intelligence along three dimensions: Operations, Contents, and Products.

Study of Values Test originally designed by Allport and Vernon which assesses the person's theoretical, economic, aesthetic, social, and political values.

Style of life For Adler, the unique pattern of characteristics that distinguishes the behavior of one person from that of another.

Subjective orientation For Piaget, the cognitive orientation of children older than 10.

Sublimation In psychoanalytic theory, the defense mechanism involving the diversion of instinctual impulses to socially desirable goals.

Successive approximation A method of producing a response in the organism by reinforcing those responses that bring it closer and closer to the desired behavior.

Superego In Freudian theory, the conscience representing the ideals and values of society as acquired from the parents.

Superordinate construct In Kelly's system, a construct that exercises an overriding influence in a person's construct system.

Surface traits For Cattell, clusters of observable responses, the elements of which all seem to belong together.

Symbiosis Primitive period in which the infant does not differentiate between self and, for example, mother.

Symbols For Jung, objects that represent complex ideas that cannot otherwise be defined completely (e.g., a cross). Especially prominent in dreams.

Syntality For Cattell, the dimensions along which groups of people can be described.

Systematic desensitization Behavior-therapy technique based upon counterconditioning principles in which an incompatible response (often relaxation) is paired with progressively more anxiety-provoking stimuli until the person is able to imagine or be in the presence of such stimuli without anxiety.

T-data Objective test data; often associated with Cattell's methods.

Temperament trait For Cattell, a constitutional source trait affecting the person's level of emotionality.

Tennessee Self Concept Scale Self-report test designed by Fitts to measure several aspects of the self.

Test Anxiety Scale (TAS) Developed by Sarason, a true-false test of the extent to which a person responds to testing situations with anxiety.

Test-retest reliability Extent to which a test yields, under the same conditions, similar scores at different times.

Thema In Murray's theory, a combination of needs and presses that results in a given outcome.

Thematic Apperception Test (TAT) Widely used projective test in which subjects make up stories in response to pictures.

Third force Descriptive term sometimes applied to humanistic approaches in personality.

Threat For Kelly, an awareness of an imminent change in one's construct system.

Time-out Behavior-therapy method in which the individual is briefly removed from situations where positive reinforcement of unwanted behavior is possible.

Token economy Operant conditioning approach in which a given behavior earns tokens, which can then be exchanged for specific reinforcements; often used in institutional settings.

Trait Enduring personality characteristic that describes some and not others. For Allport, a neuropsychic structure that influences perception of stimuli and gives consistency to modes of response.

Trait anxiety (A-Trait) Person's chronic or stable level of anxiety.

Transference Essential element of psychoanalytic therapy in which the patient responds to the therapist as if the therapist were a parent or some other significant figure from childhood. When issues of transference become paramount in therapy, the term *transference neurosis* is used.

Transformation For Jung, a therapy stage in which the patient begins to achieve self-realization.

Transient variables For Cattell, temporary states in the individual (e.g., hunger) or roles people play in specific circumstances.

Transitional objects Objects (e.g., blankets, diapers) that enable the child to tolerate separation from significant others.

Triarchic theory of intelligence Sternberg's theory that intelligence consists of three basic aspects: componential, experiential, and contextual.

Type In early characterology, a category to which people with certain characteristics in common were assigned. For Eysenck, types are dimensions along which people differ.

Type A behavior pattern (TABP) Pattern related to coronary proneness that is characterized by competitiveness, aggressiveness, and a desire to do more in less time.

Type B behavior pattern Absence of Type A behaviors.

Unconditional positive regard According to Rogers, total and genuine love and respect given without conditions or strings attached.

Unconscious In psychoanalytic theory, that portion of the mind that is largely inaccessible to the ego or conscious thought.

Unconscious motivation In Freudian theory, drives which motivate individuals without their being aware of the source.

Undersocialized conduct disorder In children, antisocial acts characteristic of adults (e.g., rape, assault, fire-setting, etc.).

Unique traits For Cattell, traits not possessed in common with other people.

Unities Synonym for factors identified by factor analysis.

Unobtrusive measures Methods, often conducted in the field, that do not require the subject's cooperation or knowledge that assessment is being conducted (e.g., examination of life records).

Validity Extent to which a test measures what it purports to measure.

Vicarious conditioning Observation of another person being conditioned that increases the likelihood the observer will become similarly conditioned.

Vicarious experience In observational learning, watching the performance of others.

Vicarious reinforcement Being reinforced (although less intensely so) by observing a model receive reinforcement.

Viscerotonic According to Sheldon, a relaxed, comfort-loving, sociable temperament most often characteristic of endomorphs.

Wechsler intelligence scales Series of scales designed by Wechsler to measure intelligence in different age groups (Wechsler-Bellevue, Wechsler Intelligence Scale for Children, Wechsler Preschool and Primary Scale of Intelligence, and Wechsler Adult Intelligence Scale).

REFERENCES

Abramson, L. Y., Seligman, M. E. P., and Teasdale, J. D. (1978). Learned helplessness in humans: Critique and reformulation. *Journal of Abnormal Psychology, 87,* 49–74.

Adams, K. A. (1980). Who has the final word? Sex, race, and dominance behavior. *Journal of Personality and Social Psychology, 38,* 1–8.

Adams-Webber, J. R. (1979). *Personal construct theory: Concepts and applications.* Chichester, England: Wiley.

Adler, A. (1924). *The practice and theory of individual psychology.* New York: Harcourt, Brace.

Adler, A. (1939). *Social interest: A challenge to mankind.* New York: Putnam.

Aiken, L. R. (1987). *Assessment of intellectual functioning.* Boston: Allyn and Bacon.

Aldwin, C. M., and Revenson, T. A. (1987). Does coping help? A reexamination of the relation between coping and mental health. *Journal of Personality and Social Psychology, 53,* 337–348.

Alexander, F. (1950). *Psychosomatic medicine.* New York: Norton.

Alker, H. A. (1972). Is personality situationally specific or intrapsychically consistent? *Journal of Personality, 40,* 1–16.

Allen, K. E., Hart, B., Buell, J. S., Harris, F. R., and Wolf, M. M. (1964). Effects of social reinforcement on isolate behavior of a nursery school child. *Child Development, 35,* 511–518.

Alloy, L. B., Peterson, C., Abramson, L. Y., and Seligman, M. E. P. (1984). Attributional style and the generality of learned helplessness. *Journal of Personality and Social Psychology, 46,* 681–687.

Allport, G. W. (1937). *Personality: A psychological interpretation.* New York: Holt.

Allport, G. W. (1955). *Becoming: Basic considerations for a psychology of personality.* New Haven, CT: Yale University Press.

Allport, G. W. (1961). *Pattern and growth in personality.* New York: Holt, Rinehart and Winston.

Allport, G. W. (1965). *Letters from Jenny.* New York: Harcourt, Brace and World.

Allport, G. W. (1966). Traits revisited. *American Psychologist, 21,* 1–10.

Allport, G. W. (1967). Autobiography. In E. G. Boring and G. Lindzey (Eds.), *A history of psychology in autobiography* (Vol. 5). New York: Appleton-Century-Crofts.

Allport, G. W. (1968). *The person in psychology: Selected essays.* Boston: Beacon Press.

Allport, G. W., and Odbert, H. S. (1936). Trait-names: A psycholexical study. *Psychological Monographs, 47*(1, Whole No. 211).

Allport, G. W., and Vernon, P. E. (1933). *Studies in expressive movement.* New York: Macmillan.

Allport, G. W., Vernon, P. E., and Lindzey, G. (1960). *A study of values* (3rd ed.). Boston: Houghton Mifflin.

Allred, K. D., and Smith, T. W. (1989). The hardy personality: Cognitive and physiological responses to evaluative threat. *Journal of Personality and Social Psychology, 56,* 257–266.

Alpert, J. L. (Ed.). (1986). *Psychoanalysis and women: Contemporary reappraisals.* Hillsdale, NJ: Analytic Press.

Alpert-Gillis, L. J., and Connell, J. P. (1989). Gender and sex-role influences on children's self-esteem. *Journal of Personality, 57,* 97–114.

Alston, W. P. (1971). Comments on Kohlberg's "From is to ought." In T. Mischel (Ed.), *Cognitive development and genetic epistemology.* New York: Academic Press.

American Psychiatric Association. (1980). *Diagnostic and statistical manual of mental disorders* (3rd ed.). Washington, DC: American Psychiatric Association.

American Psychological Association. (1977). *Ethical standards of psychologists.* Washington, D.C.: American Psychological Association.

American Psychological Association. (1981a). Ethical principles of psychologists. *American Psychologist, 36,* 633–638.

American Psychological Association. (1981b). Specialty guidelines for the delivery of services. *American Psychologist, 36,* 639–685.

American Psychological Association (1990). Ethical principles of psychologists (Amended June 2, 1990). *American Psychologist, 45,* 390–395.

Anastasi, A. (1976). *Psychological testing* (4th ed.). New York: Macmillan.

Anderson, C. A. (1989). Temperature and aggression: Ubiquitous effects of heat on occurrence of human violence. *Psychological Bulletin, 106,* 74–96.

Angoff, W. H. (1988). The nature-nurture debate, aptitudes, and group differences. *American Psychologist, 43,* 713–720.

Ansbacher, H. L. (1977). Individual psychology. In R. J. Corsini (Ed.), *Current personality theories.* Itasca, IL: Peacock.

Ansbacher, H. L., and Ansbacher, R. R. (Eds.). (1956). *The individual psychology of Alfred Adler.* New York: Basic Books.

Aronoff, J. (1985). *Personality in the social process.* Hillsdale, NJ: Erlbaum.

Asterita, M. F. (1985). *The physiology of stress.* New York: Human Sciences Press.

Atkinson, J. W. (1957). Motivational determinants of risk-taking behavior. *Psychological Review, 64,* 359–372.

Atkinson, J. W. (1964). *An introduction to motivation.* Princeton, NJ: Van Nostrand.

Ayllon, T., and Azrin, N. H. (1964). Reinforcement and instructions with mental patients. *Journal of the Experimental Analysis of Behavior, 7,* 327–331.

Ayllon, T., and Azrin, N. H. (1968). *The token economy: A motivational system for therapy and rehabilitation.* New York: Appleton-Century-Crofts.

Ayllon, T., and Michael, J. (1959). The psychiatric nurse as a behavioral engineer. *Journal of the Experimental Analysis of Behavior, 2,* 323–334.

Azrin, N. H., and Lindsley, O. R. (1956). The reinforcement of cooperation between children. *Journal of Abnormal and Social Psychology, 52,* 100–102.

Babledelis, G. (1984). *The study of personality.* New York: Holt, Rinehart and Winston.

Bäckman, L., and Molander, B. (1986). Adult differences in the ability to cope with situations of high arousal in a precision sport. *Psychology and Aging, 1,* 133–139.

Baer, J. S., Holt, C. S., and Lichtenstein, E. (1986). Self-efficacy and smoking reexamined: Construct validity and clinical utility. *Journal of Consulting and Clinical Psychology, 54,* 846–852.

Bailey, D. S., Leonard, K. E., Cranston, J. W., and Taylor, S. P. (1983). Effects of alcohol and self-awareness on human physical aggression. *Personality and Social Psychology Bulletin, 9,* 289–295.

Baldwin, A. (1942). Personal structure analysis: A statistical method for investigating the single personality. *Journal of Abnormal and Social Psychology, 37,* 163–183.

Baltes, M. M., and Baltes, P. B. (Eds.). (1986). *The psychology of control and aging.* Hillsdale, NJ: Erlbaum.

Bandura, A. (1965). Influence of models' reinforcement contingencies on the acquisition of imitative responses. *Journal of Personality and Social Psychology, 1,* 589–595.

Bandura, A. (1969a). *Principles of behavior modification.* New York: Holt, Rinehart and Winston.

Bandura, A. (1969b). Social-learning theory of identificatory processes. In D. A. Goslin (Ed.), *Handbook of socialization theory and research.* Chicago: Rand McNally.

Bandura, A. (1973). *Aggression: A social learning analysis.* Englewood Cliffs, NJ: Prentice-Hall.

Bandura, A. (1974). Behavior theories and the models of man. *American Psychologist, 29,* 859–869.

Bandura, A. (1976). Social learning analysis of aggression. In E. Ribes-Inesta and A. Bandura (Eds.), *Analysis of delinquency and aggression.* Hillsdale, NJ: Erlbaum.

Bandura, A. (1977). *Social learning theory.* Englewood Cliffs, NJ: Prentice-Hall.

Bandura, A. (1978). The self system in reciprocal determinism. *American Psychologist, 33,* 344–358.

Bandura, A. (1982). Self-efficacy mechanism in human agency. *American Psychologist, 37,* 122–147.

Bandura, A. (1986). *Social foundations of thought and action: A social cognitive theory.* Englewood Cliffs, NJ: Prentice-Hall.

Bandura, A. (1989). Human agency in social cognitive theory. *American Psychologist, 44,* 1175–1184.

Bandura, A., Adams, N. E., and Beyer, J. (1977). Cognitive processes mediating behavioral change. *Journal of Personality and Social Psychology, 35,* 125–139.

Bandura, A., Adams, N. E., Hardy, A. B., and Howells, G. N. (1980). Tests of the generality of self-efficacy theory. *Cognitive Therapy and Research, 4,* 39–66.

Bandura, A., Blanchard, E. B., and Ritter, B. (1969). Relative efficacy of desensitization and modeling approaches for inducing behavioral, affective, and attitudinal changes. *Journal of Personality and Social Psychology, 13,* 173–199.

Bandura, A., Cioffi, D., Taylor, C. B., and Brouillard, M. E. (1988). Perceived self-efficacy in coping with cognitive stressors and opioid activation. *Journal of Personality and Social Psychology, 55,* 479–488.

Bandura, A., and Kupers, C. J. (1964). The transmission of patterns of self-reinforcement through modeling. *Journal of Abnormal and Social Psychology, 69,* 1–9.

Bandura, A., and MacDonald, F. J. (1963). Influence of social reinforcement and the behavior of models in shaping children's moral judgments. *Journal of Abnormal and Social Psychology, 67,* 274–281.

Bandura, A., and Mischel, W. (1965). Modification of self-imposed delay of reward through exposure to live and symbolic models. *Journal of Personality and Social Psychology, 2,* 698–705.

Bandura, A., O'Leary, A., Taylor, C. B., Gauthier, J., and Gossard, D. (1987). Perceived self-efficacy and pain control: Opioid and nonopioid mechanisms. *Journal of Personality and Social Psychology, 53,* 563–571.

Bandura, A., and Rosenthal, T. L. (1966). Vicarious classical conditioning as a function of arousal level. *Journal of Personality and Social Psychology, 3,* 54–62.

Bandura, A., Ross, D., and Ross, S. (1961). Transmission of aggression through imitation of aggressive models. *Journal of Abnormal and Social Psychology, 63,* 575–582.

Bandura, A., and Schunk, D. H. (1981). Cultivating competence, self-efficacy, and intrinsic interest through proximal self-motivation. *Journal of Personality and Social Psychology, 41,* 586–598.

Bandura, A., Taylor, C. B., Williams, S. L., Mefford, I. N., and Barchas, J. D. (1985). Catecholamine secretion as a function of perceived coping self-efficacy. *Journal of Consulting and Clinical Psychology, 53,* 406–414.

Bandura, A., Underwood, B., and Fromson, M. E. (1975). Disinhibition of aggression through diffusion of responsibility and dehumanization of victims. *Journal of Research in Personality, 9,* 253–269.

Bandura, A., and Walters, R. (1959). *Adolescent aggression.* New York: Ronald.

Bandura, A., and Walters, R. (1963). *Social learning and personality development.* New York: Holt, Rinehart and Winston.

Bandura, A., and Wood, R. (1989). Effect of perceived controllability and performance standards on self-regulation of complex decision making. *Journal of Personality and Social Psychology, 56,* 805–814.

Bannister, D. (Ed.). (1970). *Perspectives in personal construct theory.* New York: Academic Press.

Bannister, D. (Ed.). (1985). *Issues and approaches in personal construct theory.* Orlando, FL: Academic Press.

Barker, R. G., and Wright, H. F. (1951). *One boy's day.* New York: Harper and Row.

Barnett, M. A., King, L. M., and Howard, J. A. (1979). Inducing affect about self or other: Effects on generosity in children. *Developmental Psychology, 15,* 164–167.

Barnett, R. C., Biener, L., and Baruch, G. K. (Eds.). (1987). *Gender and stress.* New York: Free Press/Macmillan.

Baron, R. A. (1971). Reducing the influence of an aggressive model: The restraining effects of discrepant modeling cues. *Journal of Personality and Social Psychology, 20,* 240–245.

Baron, R. A. (1974). The aggression-inhibiting influence of heightened sexual arousal. *Journal of Personality and Social Psychology, 30,* 318–320.

Baron, R. A. (1976). The reduction of human aggression: A field study of the influence of incompatible reactions. *Journal of Applied Social Psychology, 6,* 260–274.

Baron, R. A. (1977). *Human aggression.* New York: Plenum.

Baron, R. A. (1983). The control of human aggression: A strategy based on incompatible responses. In R. G. Geen and E. I. Donnerstein (Eds.), *Aggression: Theoretical and empirical reviews: Vol. 2. Issues in research.* New York: Academic Press.

Baron, R. M., Mandel, D. R., Adams, C. A., and Griffen, L. M. (1976). Effects of social density in university residential environments. *Journal of Personality and Social Psychology, 34,* 434–446.

Barraclough, G. (1973, March 3). Psycho-history is bunk. *Guardian,* p. 23.

Barron, F. H. (1968). *Creativity and personal freedom.* New York: Van Nostrand Reinhold.

Barry, H., Child, I., and Bacon, M. (1959). Relation of child training to subsistence economy. *American Anthropologist, 61,* 51–63.

Bartlett, F. C. (1932). *Remembering.* London: Cambridge University Press.

Basgall, J. A., and Snyder, C. R. (1988). Excuses in waiting: External locus of control and reactions to success-failure feedback. *Journal of Personality and Social Psychology, 54,* 656–662.

Batson, C. D. (1990). How social an animal? The human capacity for caring. *American Psychologist, 45,* 336–346.

Batson, C. D., Batson, J. G., Griffitt, C. A., Barrientos, S., Brandt, J. R., Sprengelmeyer, P., and Bayly, M. J. (1989). Negative-state relief and the empathy-altruism hypothesis. *Journal of Personality and Social Psychology, 56,* 922–933.

Batson, C. D., Bolen, M. H., Cross, J. A., and Neuringer-Benefiel, H. E. (1986). Where is the altruism in the altruistic personality? *Journal of Personality and Social Psychology, 50,* 212–220.

Batson, C. D., Darley, J. M., and Coke, J. S. (1978). Altruism and human kindness: Internal and external determinants of helping behavior. In L. Pervin and M. Lewis (Eds.), *Perspectives in interactional psychology.* New York: Plenum.

Batson, C. D., Duncan, B. D., Ackerman, P., Buckley, T., and Birch, K. (1981). Is empathic emotion a source of altruistic motivation? *Journal of Personality and Social Psychology, 40,* 290–302.

Batson, C. D., Dyck, J. L., Brandt, J. R., Batson, J. G., Powell, A. L., McMaster, M. R., and Griffitt, C. (1988). Five studies testing two new egoistic alternatives to the empathy-altruism hypothesis. *Journal of Personality and Social Psychology, 55,* 52–77.

Batson, C. D., Fultz, J., Schoenrade, P. A., and Paduano, A. (1987). Critical self-reflection and self-perceived altruism: When self-reward fails. *Journal of Personality and Social Psychology, 53,* 594–602.

Batson, C. D., and Gray, R. A. (1981). Religious orientation and helping behavior: Responding to one's own or to the victim's needs? *Journal of Personality and Social Psychology, 40,* 511–520.

Batson, C. D., Oleson, K. C., Weeks, J. L., Healy, S. P., Reeves, P. J., Jennings, P., and Brown, T. (1989). Religious prosocial motivation: Is it altruistic or egoistic? *Journal of Personality and Social Psychology, 57,* 873–884.

Baucom, D. H., and Danker-Brown, P. (1984). Sex role identity and sex-stereotyped tasks in the development of learned helplessness. *Journal of Personality and Social Psychology, 46,* 422–430.

Baum, A., Fleming, R., and Singer, J. (1982). Stress at Three Mile Island: Applying psychological impact analysis. In C. Beckman (Ed.), *Applied social psychology annual* (Vol. 3). Beverly Hills, CA: Sage.

Baum, A., and Greenberg, C. I. (1975). Waiting for a crowd: The behavioral and perceptual effects of anticipated crowding. *Journal of Personality and Social Psychology, 32,* 671–679.

Baum, A., and Singer, J. E. (Eds.). (1987). *Handbook of psychology and health, Vol. 5: Stress.* Hillsdale, NJ: Erlbaum.

Baumeister, R. F., and Steinhilber, A. (1984). Paradoxical effects of supportive audiences on performance under pressure: The home field disadvantage in sports championships. *Journal of Personality and Social Psychology, 47,* 85–93.

Baumrind, D. (1964). Some thoughts on the ethics of research: After reading Milgram's "Behavioral study of obedience." *American Psychologist, 19,* 421–423.

Baumrind, D. (1975). *Early socialization and the discipline controvery.* Morristown, NJ: General Learning Press.

Beach, F. (1975). Behavioral endocrinology: An emerging discipline. *American Scientist, 63,* 178–187.

Beezley, D. A., Gantner, A. B., Bailey, D. S., and Taylor, S. P. (1987). Amphetamines and human physical aggression. *Journal of Research in Personality, 21,* 52–60.

Bell, P. A., Fisher, J. D., and Loomis, R. J. (1978). *Environmental psychology.* Philadelphia: Saunders.

Bellak, L. (1954). *The Thematic Apperception Test and the Children's Apperception Test.* New York: Grune and Stratton.

Bem, D. J., and Allen, A. (1974). On predicting some of the people some of the time: The search for cross-situational consistencies in behavior. *Psychological Review, 81,* 506–520.

Bem, S. L. (1974). The measurement of psychological androgyny. *Journal of Consulting and Clinical Psychology, 42,* 155–162.

Bem, S. L. (1975). Sex-role adaptability: One consequence of psychological androgyny. *Journal of Personality and Social Psychology, 31,* 634–643.

Bem, S. L. (1981). Gender schema theory: A cognitive account of sex typing. *Psychological Review, 88,* 354–364.

Bendig, A. W. (1956). The development of a short form of the Manifest Anxiety Scale. *Journal of Consulting Psychology, 20,* 384.

Berkowitz, L. (Ed.). (1969). *Roots of aggression: A reexamination of the frustration-aggression hypothesis.* New York: Atherton.

Berkowitz, L. (1971). The contagion of violence: An S-R mediational analysis of some effects of observed aggression. In W. J. Arnold and M. M. Page (Eds.), *Nebraska Symposium on Motivation* (Vol. 18). Lincoln: University of Nebraska Press.

Berkowitz, L. (1974). Some determinants of impulsive aggression: The role of mediated associations with reinforcements for aggression. *Psychological Bulletin, 81,* 165–176.

Berkowitz, L. (1983). Aversively stimulated aggression: Some parallels and differences in research with animals and humans. *American Psychologist, 38,* 1135–1144.

Berkowitz, L. (1989). Frustration-aggression hypothesis: Examination and reformulation. *Psychological Bulletin, 106,* 59–73.

Berkowitz, L. (1990). On the formation and regulation of anger and aggression: A cognitive-neoassociationistic analysis. *American Psychologist, 45,* 494–503.

Berkowitz, L., and LePage, A. (1967). Weapons as aggression-eliciting stimuli. *Journal of Personality and Social Psychology, 7,* 202–207.

Berry, J. W. (1967). Independence and conformity in subsistence-level societies. *Journal of Personality and Social Psychology, 7,* 415–418.

Berry, J. W. (1971). Ecological and cultural factors in spatial perceptual development. *Canadian Journal of Behavioral Science, 3,* 324–336.

Bettelheim, B. (1943). Individual and mass behavior in extreme situations. *Journal of Abnormal and Social Psychology, 38,* 417–452.

Bettelheim, B. (1976). *The uses of enchantment: The meaning and importance of fairy tales.* New York: Knopf.

Binswanger, L. (1963). *Being-in-the-world* (trans. and with a critical introduction by J. Needleman). New York: Basic Books.

Blanchard, R. J., and Blanchard, D. C. (Eds.). (1986). *Advances in the study of aggression, Vol. 2.* Orlando, FL: Academic Press.

Block, J. (1989). Critique of the act frequency approach to personality. *Journal of Personality and Social Psychology, 56,* 234–245.

Block, J. H., and Block, J. (1980). The role of ego-control and ego-resiliency in the organization of behavior. In W. A. Collins (Ed.), *The Minnesota symposium on child psychology, Vol. 13.* Hillsdale, NJ: Erlbaum.

Blum, G. S. (1968). Assessment of psychodynamic variables by the Blacky Pictures. In P. McReynolds (Ed.), *Advances in psychological assessment* (Vol. 1). Palo Alto, CA: Science and Behavior Books.

Bolger, N., DeLongis, A., Kessler, R. C., and Schilling, E. A. (1989). Effects of daily stress on negative mood. *Journal of Personality and Social Psychology, 57,* 808–818.

Bonarius, J. C. J. (1965). Research in the personal construct theory of George A. Kelly: Role construct repertory test and basic theory. In B. A. Maher (Ed.), *Progress in experimental personality research.* New York: Academic Press.

Bootzin, R. R., and Acocella, J. R. (1988). *Abnormal psychology: Current perspectives* (5th ed.). New York: Random House.

Boss, M. (1963). *Psychoanalysis and Daseinsanalysis.* New York: Basic Books.

Boss, M. (1977). *Existential foundations of medicine and psychology.* New York: Aronson.

Bottome, P. (1957). *Alfred Adler.* New York: Vanguard.

Botwin, M. D., and Buss, D. M. (1989). Structure of act-report data: Is the five-factor model of personality recaptured? *Journal of Personality and Social Psychology, 56,* 988–1001.

Botwinick, J. (1984). *Aging and human behavior: A comprehensive integration of research findings* (3rd ed.). New York: Springer.

Bouchard, T. J., Jr., Heston, L., Eckert, E., Keyes, M., and Resnick, S. (1981). The Minnesota study of twins reared apart: Project description and sample results in the developmental domain. *Twin research 3: Intelligence, personality and development.* New York: Alan R. Liss.

Bouchard, T. J., Jr., and McGue, M. (1981). Familial studies of intelligence: A review. *Science, 212,* 1055–1059.

Bowers, K. S. (1973). Situationism in psychology: An analysis and a critique. *Psychological Review, 80,* 307–336.

Boyd, T. L. (1982). Learned helplessness in humans: A frustration-produced response pattern. *Journal of Personality and Social Psychology, 42,* 738–752.

Bowlby, J. (1969). *Attachment and love* (Vol. 1). New York: Basic Books.

Bray, D. W. (1982). The assessment center and the study of lives. *American Psychologist, 37,* 180–189.

Breger, L., and McGaugh, J. L. (1965). Critique and reformulation of "learning theory" approaches to psychotherapy and neurosis. *Psychological Bulletin, 63,* 338–358.

Brehm, J. W. (1966). *A theory of psychological reactance.* New York: Academic Press.

Breuer, J., and Freud, S. (1955). *Studies on hysteria.* In *Standard edition* (Vol. 2). London: Hogarth Press. (First German edition, 1895)

Briere, J., and Malamuth, N. M. (1983). Self-reported likelihood of sexually aggressive behavior: Attitudinal versus sexual explanations. *Journal of Research in Personality, 17,* 315–323.

Brigham, C. C. (1923). *A study of American intelligence.* Princeton, NJ: Princeton University Press.

Brody, E. B., and Brody, N. (1976). *Intelligence: Nature, determinants, and consequences.* New York: Academic Press.

Brody, J. E. (1975, December 17). TV violence cited as bad influence. *New York Times,* p. 20.

Brody, L. R. (1985). Gender differences in emotional development: A review of theories and research. *Journal of Personality, 53,* 102–149.

Broman, S. H., Nichols, P. L., and Kennedy, W. A. (1975). *Preschool IQ: Prenatal and early developmental correlates.* Hillsdale, NJ: Erlbaum.

Bronfenbrenner, U. (1960). Freudian theories of identification and their derivatives. *Child Development, 31,* 15–40.

Broverman, D. M., Klaiber, E. L., Kobayashi, Y., and Vogel, W. (1968). Roles of activation and inhibition in sex differences in cognitive abilities. *Psychological Review, 75,* 23–50.

Broverman, I. K., Broverman, D. M., Clarkson, F. E., Rosenkrantz, P. S., and Vogel, S. R. (1970). Sex-role stereotypes and clinical judgments of mental health. *Journal of Consulting and Clinical Psychology, 34,* 1–7.

Broverman, I. K., Vogel, S. R., Broverman, D. M., Clarkson, F. E., and Rosenkrantz, P. S. (1972). Sex-role stereotypes: A current appraisal. *Journal of Social Issues, 28,* 59–78.

Brown, J. F. (1940). *The psychodynamics of abnormal behavior.* New York: McGraw-Hill.

Brown, J. S. (1965). A behavioral analysis of masochism. *Journal of Experimental Research in Personality, 1,* 65–70.

Bruch, M. A., Kaflowitz, N. G., and Berger, P. (1988). Self-schema for assertiveness: Extending the validity of the self-schema construct. *Journal of Research in Personality, 22,* 424–444.

Bruner, J. S. (1956). You are your constructs. *Contemporary Psychology, 1,* 355–357.

Bruner, J. S., and Tagiuri, R. (1954). The perception of people. In G. Lindzey (Ed.), *Handbook of social psychology* (2 vols.). Cambridge, MA: Addison-Wesley.

Brunson, B. I., and Matthews, K. A. (1981). The Type A coronary-prone behavior pattern and reactions to uncontrollable stress: An analysis of performance strategies, affect, and attributions during failure. *Journal of Personality and Social Psychology, 40,* 906–918.

Brunswik, E. (1943). Organismic achievement and environmental probability. *Psychological Review, 50,* 255–272.

Bugental, J. F. T. (1989). Guru for the 1960s; Moses for the 1990s. *Contemporary Psychology, 34,* 893–894.

Burger, J. M. (1985). Desire for control and achievement-related behavior. *Journal of Personality and Social Psychology, 48,* 1520–1533.

Burger, J. M. (1986). Desire for control and the illusion of control: The effects of familiarity and sequence of outcomes. *Journal of Research in Personality, 20,* 66–76.

Burger, J. M. (1987). Desire for control and conformity to a perceived norm. *Journal of Personality and Social Psychology, 53,* 355–360.

Burger, J. M. (1989). Negative reactions to increases in perceived control. *Journal of Personality and Social Psychology, 56,* 246–256.

Burger, J. M. (1990). Desire for control and interpersonal interaction style. *Journal of Research in Personality, 24,* 32–44.

Burger, J. M., Oakman, J. A., and Bullard, N. G. (1983). Desire for control and the perception of crowding. *Personality and Social Psychology Bulletin, 9,* 475–479.

Burnam, M. A., Stein, J. A., Golding, J. M., Siegel, J. M., Sorenson, S. B., Forsythe, A. B., and Telles, C. A. (1988). Sexual assault and mental disorders in a community population. *Journal of Consulting and Clinical Psychology, 56,* 843–850.

Burnham, J. C. (1968). Historical background for the study of personality. In E. F. Borgatta and W. W. Lambert (Eds.), *Handbook of personality theory and research.* Chicago: Rand McNally.

Burnstein, M. H. (1981). Child abandonment: Historical, sociological, and psychological perspectives. *Child Psychiatry and Human Development, 11,* 213–221.

Burt, C. (1966). The genetic determination of differences in intelligence: A study of monozygotic twins reared together and apart. *British Journal of Psychology, 57,* 137–153.

Bushman, B. J., and Geen, R. G. (1990). Role of cognitive-emotional mediators and individual differences in the effects of media violence on aggression. *Journal of Personality and Social Psychology, 58,* 156–163.

Buss, A. H. (1961). *The psychology of aggression.* New York: Wiley.

Buss, A. H. (1963). Physical aggression in relation to different frustrations. *Journal of Abnormal and Social Psychology, 67,* 1–7.

Buss, A. H. (1989). Personality as traits. *American Psychologist, 44,* 1378–1388.

Buss, D. M. (1981). Sex differences in the evaluation and performance of dominant acts. *Journal of Personality and Social Psychology, 40,* 147–154.

Buss, D. M., and Craik, K. H. (1983). The act frequency approach to personality. *Psychological Review, 90,* 105–126.

Butler, J. M., and Haigh, G. V. (1954). Changes in the relation between self-concepts and ideal concepts consequent upon client-centered counseling. In C. R. Rogers and R. F. Dymond (Eds.), *Psychotherapy and personality change: Coordinated studies in the client-centered approach.* Chicago: University of Chicago Press.

Butler, R. N., and Lewis, M. I. (1982). *Aging and mental health* (3rd ed.). St. Louis, MO: Mosby.

Button, E. (Ed.). (1985). *Personal construct theory and mental health: Theory, research, and practice.* Cambridge, MA: Brookline Books.

Byrne, D., and Kelley, K. (1981). *An introduction to personality* (3rd ed.). Englewood Cliffs, NJ: Prentice-Hall.

Calhoun, J. B. (1962). Population density and social pathology. *Scientific American, 206*(2), 139–148.

Cann, D. R., and Donderi, D. C. (1986). Jungian personality typology and the recall of everyday and archetypal dreams. *Journal of Personality and Social Psychology, 50,* 1021– 1030.

Cannon, W. B. (1932). *The wisdom of the body.* New York: Norton.

Caplan, P. J. (1984). The myth of women's masochism. *American Psychologist, 39,* 130–139.

Caplan, P. J., MacPherson, G. M., and Tobin, P. (1985). Do sex-related differences in spatial abilities exist? A multilevel critique with new data. *American Psychologist, 40,* 786–799.

Carlson, M., Marcus-Newhall, A., and Miller, N. (1989). Evidence for a general construct of aggression. *Personality and Social Psychology Bulletin, 15,* 377–389.

Carlson, R. (1975). Personality. In M. R. Rosenzweig and L. W. Porter (Eds.), *Annual review of psychology.* Palo Alto, CA: Annual Reviews.

Carlson, R. (1980). Studies of Jungian typology: II. Representations of the personal world. *Journal of Personality and Social Psychology, 38,* 801–810.

Carlson, R., and Levy, N. (1973). Studies of Jungian typology: I. Memory, social perception, and social action. *Journal of Personality, 41,* 559–576.

Carr, A. C. (1949). An evaluation of nine nondirective psychotherapy cases by means of the Rorschach. *Journal of Consulting Psychology, 13,* 196–205.

Carson, R. C. (1989). Personality. In M. R. Rosenzweig and L. W. Porter (Eds.), *Annual review of psychology.* Palo Alto, CA: Annual Reviews.

Carson, R. C., Butcher, J. N., and Coleman, J. C. (1988). *Abnormal psychology and modern life* (8th ed.). Glenview, IL: Scott, Foresman.

Carver, C. S., and Scheier, M. F. (1981). *Attention and self-regulation: A control-theory approach to human behavior.* New York: Springer-Verlag.

Carver, C. S., and Scheier, M. F. (1988). *Perspectives on personality.* Boston: Allyn and Bacon.

Caspi, A., Bolger, N., and Eckenrode, J. (1987). Linking person and context in the daily stress process. *Journal of Personality and Social Psychology, 52,* 184–195.

Cattell, R. B. (1946). *Description and measurement of personality.* New York: World Book.

Cattell, R. B. (1950). *Personality: A systematic, theoretical, and factual study.* New York: McGraw-Hill.

Cattell, R. B. (1957). *Personality and motivation structure and measurement.* New York: Harcourt Brace Jovanovich.

Cattell, R. B. (1963). Theory of fluid and crystallized intelligence: A critical experiment. *Journal of Educational Psychology, 54,* 1–22.

Cattell, R. B. (1965). *The scientific analysis of personality.* Baltimore, MD: Penguin.

Cattell, R. B. (1971). *Abilities: Their structure, growth, and action.* Boston: Houghton Mifflin.

Cattell, R. B. (1980). *Personality and learning theory: Vol.2. A systems theory of maturation and structured learning.* New York: Springer.

Cattell, R. B., and Scheier, I. H. (1961). *The meaning and measurement of neuroticism and anxiety.* New York: Ronald Press.

Center for Research on Aggression. (1983). *Prevention and control of aggression.* New York: Pergamon Press.

Chance, J. E. (1959). Generalization of expectancies among functionally related behaviors. *Journal of Personality, 27,* 228–238.

Chandler, T. A., Wolf, F. M., Cook, B., and Dugovics, D. A. (1980). Parental correlates of locus control in fifth graders: An attempt at experimentation in the home. *Merrill-Palmer Quarterly, 26,* 183–195.

Chein, I. (1945). On the nature of intelligence. *Journal of General Psychology, 32,* 111–126.

Cheney, A. B., and Bleker, E. G. (1982, August). *Internal-external locus of control and repression-sensitization in battered women.* Paper presented at the annual meetings of the American Psychological Association, Washington, D. C.

Chlopan, B. E., McCain, M. L., Carbonell, J. L., and Hagen, R. L. (1985). Empathy: A review of available measures. *Journal of Personality and Social Psychology, 48,* 635–653.

Chodorow, N. (1978). *The reproduction of mothering: Psychoanalysis and the sociology of gender.* Berkeley, CA: University of California Press.

Cialdini, R. B., and Fultz, J. (1990). Interpreting the negative mood-helping literature via "mega"-analysis: A contrary view. *Psychological Bulletin, 107,* 210–214.

Cialdini, R. B., Schaller, M., Houlihan, D., Arps, K., Fultz, J., and Beaman, A. L. (1987). Empathy-based helping: Is it selflessly or selfishly motivated? *Journal of Personality and Social Psychology, 52,* 749–758.

Clark, L., and Lewis, D. (1977). *Rape: The price of coercive sexuality.* Toronto: Women's Press.

Clark, R. D., III, and Word, L. E. (1972). Why don't bystanders help? Because of ambiguity? *Journal of Personality and Social Psychology, 24,* 392–400.

Cleary, A. T., Humphreys, L. G., Kendrick, S. A., and Wesman, A. (1975). Educational uses of tests with disadvantaged students. *American Psychologist, 30,* 15–41.

Coates, T. J., and Thoresen, C. E. (1981). Treating obesity in children and adolescents: Is there any hope? In J. M. Ferguson and C. B. Taylor (Eds.), *The comprehensive handbook of behavioral medicine* (Vol. 2). New York: Spectrum.

Cohen, S. (1978). Environmental load and the allocation of attention. In A. Baum, J. E. Singer, and S. Valins (Eds.), *Advances in environmental psychology* (Vol. 1). Hillsdale, NJ: Erlbaum.

Cohen, S., and Edwards, J. R. (1989). Personality characteristics as moderators of the relationship between stress and disorder. In R. W. J. Neufeld (Ed.), *Advances in the investigation of psychological distress.* New York: Wiley.

Cohen, S., Evans, G. W., Krantz, D. S., and Stokols, D. (1980). Physiological, motivational, and cognitive effects of aircraft noise on children: Moving from the laboratory to the field. *American Psychologist, 35,* 231–243.

Cohen, S., Krantz, D. S., Evans, G. W., and Stokols, D. (1981). Cardiovascular and behavioral effects of community noise. *American Scientist, 69,* 528–535.

Cohen, S., and Weinstein, N. (1981). Nonauditory effects of noise on behavior and health. *Journal of Social Issues, 37,* 36–70.

Colby, A., Kohlberg, L., and collaborators. (1987). *The measurement of moral judgment, Vol. 1: Theoretical foundations and research validation.* Cambridge, England: Cambridge University Press.

Colby, A., Kohlberg, L., Speicher, B., Hewer, A., Candee, D., Gibbs, J., and Power, C. (1987). *The measurement of moral judgment, Vol. 2: Standard issue scoring manual.* Cambridge, England: Cambridge University Press.

Cole, C. S., and Coyne, J. C. (1977). Situational specificity of laboratory-induced learned helplessness. *Journal of Abnormal Psychology, 86,* 615–623.

Coles, R. (1970). *Erik Erikson: The growth of his work.* Boston: Little, Brown.

Comrey, A. L. (1973). *A first course in factor analysis.* New York: Academic Press.

Condrey, J. (1977). Enemies of exploration: Self-initiated versus other-initiated learning. *American Psychologist, 35,* 459–477.

Contrada, R. J. (1989). Type A behavior, personality hardiness, and cardiovascular response to stress. *Journal of Personality and Social Psychology, 57,* 895–903.

Cooley, C. H. (1902). *Human nature and the social order.* New York: Scribner's.

Coopersmith, S. (1967). *The antecedents of self-esteem.* San Francisco: Freeman.

Corcoran, D. W. J. (1964). The relation between introversion and salivation. *American Journal of Psychology, 77,* 298–300.

Costa, P. T., Jr., and McCrae, R. R. (1987). Personality assessment in psychosomatic medicine: Value of a trait taxonomy. In T. N. Wise (Ed.), *Advances in psychosomatic medicine.* Switzerland: Karger.

Costa, P. T., Jr., and McCrae, R. R. (1988). From catalog to classification: Murray's needs and the five-factor model. *Journal of Personality and Social Psychology, 55,* 258–265.

Costello, C. G. (1978). A critical review of Seligman's laboratory experiments on learned helplessness and depression in humans. *Journal of Abnormal Psychology, 87,* 21–31.

Cousins, N. (1976). Anatomy of an illness (as perceived by the patient). *New England Journal of Medicine, 195,* 1458–1463.

Cousins, N. (1982, May 12). Maximizing the possible. *Saturday Review.*

Cowen, E. L. (1982). Help is where you find it: Four informal helping groups. *American Psychologist, 37,* 385–395.

Cox, M. W. (1978). Frequent citations in the *Journal of Consulting and Clinical Psychology* during the 1970s. *Journal of Consulting and Clinical Psychology, 46,* 204–205.

Craik, K. H. (1986). Personality research methods: An historical perspective. *Journal of Personality, 54,* 18–51.

Crain, W. C. (1980). *Theories of development: Concepts and applications.* Englewood Cliffs, NJ: Prentice-Hall.

Cramer, P. (1987). The development of defense mechanisms. *Journal of Personality, 55,* 597–614.

Crandall, J. E. (1980). Adler's concept of social interest. Theory, measurement, and implications for adjustment. *Journal of Personality and Social Psychology, 39,* 481–495.

Crandall, J. E. (1982). Social interest, extreme response style, and implications for adjustment. *Journal of Research in Personality, 16,* 82–89.

Crandall, V. C., Good, S., and Crandall, V. J. (1964). Reinforcement effects of adult reactions and nonreactions on children's achievement expectations: A replication study. *Child Development, 35,* 485–497.

Crandall, V. J. (1955). An investigation of the specificity of reinforcement of induced frustration. *Journal of Social Psychology, 41,* 311–318.

Crawford, C., Smith, M., and Krebs, D. (Eds.). (1987). *Sociobiology and psychology: Ideas, issues, and applications.* Hillsdale, NJ: Erlbaum.

Cronbach, L. (1978). Review of the BITCH test. In O. K. Buros (Ed.), *The eighth mental measurements yearbook* (Vol. 1). Highland Park, NJ: Gryphon Press.

Crowne, D. P., and Liverant, S. (1963). Conformity under varying conditions of personal commitment. *Journal of Abnormal and Social Psychology, 66,* 547–555.

Crowne, D. P., and Marlowe, D. (1964). *The approval motive: Studies in evaluative dependence.* New York: Wiley.

Crumbaugh, J. D., and Maholic, L. T. (1964). An experimental study in existentialism: The psychometric approach to Frankl's concept of noogenic neurosis. *Journal of Clinical Psychology, 20,* 200–207.

Cunningham, M. R. (1981). Sociobiology as a supplementary paradigm for social psychological research. In L. Wheeler (Ed.), *Review of personality and social psychology* (Vol. 2). Beverly Hills, CA: Sage Publications.

Cunningham, M. R., Steinberg, J., and Grev, R. (1980). Wanting to help and having to help: Separate motivations for positive mood and guilt-induced helping. *Journal of Personality and Social Psychology, 38,* 181–192.

Cutrona, C., Russell, D., and Rose, J. (1986). Social support and adaptation to stress by the elderly. *Psychology and Aging, 1,* 47–54.

Dambrot, F. H., Papp, M. E., and Whitmore, C. (1984). The sex-role attitudes of three generations of women. *Personality and Social Psychology Bulletin, 10,* 469–473.

Darley, J. M., and Latané, B. (1970). Norms and normative behavior: Field studies of social interdependence. In J. Macaulay and L. Berkowitz (Eds.), *Altruism and helping behavior.* New York: Academic Press.

Davis, D. E. (1970). *Internal-external control and defensiveness.* Unpublished doctoral dissertation, Kansas State University.

Davis, M. H. (1983). Empathic concern and the Muscular Dystrophy Telethon: Empathy as a multidimensional construct. *Personality and Social Psychology Bulletin, 9,* 223–229.

Davis, P. J. (1987). Repression and the inaccessibility of affective memories. *Journal of Personality and Social Psychology, 53,* 585–593.

Davis, W. L. (1969). *Parental antecedents of children's locus of control.* Unpublished doctoral dissertation, Kansas State University.

Davis, W. L., and Phares, E. J. (1967). Internal-external control as a determinant of information-seeking in a social influence situation. *Journal of Personality, 35,* 547–561.

Davis, W. L., and Phares, E. J. (1969). Parental antecedents of internal-external control of reinforcement. *Psychological Reports, 24,* 427–436.

Davison, G. C., and Neale, J. M. (1990). *Abnormal psychology* (5th ed.). New York: Wiley.

Deaux, K., and Major, B. (1987). Putting gender into context: An interactive model of gender-related behavior. *Psychological Review, 94,* 369–389.

deCharms, R. (1968). *Personal causation: The internal affective determinants of behavior.* New York: Academic Press.

DeFries, J. C., Johnson, R. C., Kuse, A. R., McClearn, G. E., Polovina, J., Vandenberg, S. G., and Wilson, J. B. (1979). Familial resemblance for specific cognitive abilities. *Behavior Genetics, 9,* 23–43.

Del Boca, F. K., and Ashmore, R. D. (1980). Sex stereotypes through the life cycle. In L. Wheeler (Ed.), *Review of personality and social psychology* (Vol. 1). Beverly Hills, CA: Sage Publications.

DeLongis, A., Folkman, S., and Lazarus, R. S. (1988). The impact of daily stress on health and mood: Psychological and social resources as mediators. *Journal of Personality and Social Psychology, 54,* 486–495.

Deluty, R. H. (1985). Consistency of assertive, aggressive, and submissive behavior in children. *Journal of Personality and Social Psychology, 49,* 1054–1065.

Demaré, D., Briere, J., and Lips, H. M. (1988). Violent pornography and self-reported likelihood of sexual aggression. *Journal of Research in Personality, 22,* 140–153.

Dengerink, H. A. (1976). Personality variables as mediators of attack-instigated aggression. In R. G. Geen and E. C. O'Neal (Eds.), *Perspectives on aggression.* New York: Academic Press.

Dengerink, H. A., O'Leary, M. R., and Kasner, K. H. (1975). Individual differences in aggressive responses to attack: Internal-external locus of control and field dependence-independence. *Journal of Research in Personality, 9,* 191–199.

Derry, P. A., and Kuiper, N. A. (1981). Schematic processing and self-reference in clinical depression. *Journal of Abnormal Psychology, 90,* 286–297.

Detterman, D. K., and Sternberg, R. J. (1982). *How and how much can intelligence be increased?* Norwood, NJ: Ablex.

Deur, J. I., and Parke, R. D. (1970). Effects of inconsistent punishment in aggression in children. *Developmental Psychology, 2,* 403–411.

Deutsch, F. M., and Lamberti, D. M. (1986). Does social approval increase helping? *Personality and Social Psychology Bulletin, 12,* 149–157.

Diener, E. (1976). Effects of prior destructive behavior, anonymity, and group presence on deindividuation and aggression. *Journal of Personality and Social Psychology, 33,* 497–507.

Digman, J. M. (1990). Personality structure: Emergence of the five-factor model. In M. R. Rosenzweig and L. W. Porter (Eds.), *Annual review of psychology.* Palo Alto, CA: Annual Reviews.

Disher, D. R. (1959). Improvement without fundamental change. In K. A. Adler and D. Deutsch (Eds.), *Essays in individual psychology: Contemporary application of Alfred Adler's theories.* New York: Grove Press.

Dixon, N. F. (1980). Humor: A cognitive alternative to stress? In I. G. Sarason and C. D. Spielberger (Eds.), *Stress and anxiety* (Vol. 7). Washington, DC: Hemisphere.

Dohrenwend, B. S., and Dohrenwend, B. F. (1981). Life stress and illness: Formulation of the issues. In B. S. Dohrenwend and B. F. Dohrenwend (Eds.), *Stressful life events and their contexts.* New York: Prodist.

Doll, E. A. (1941). The essentials of an inclusive concept of mental deficiency. *American Journal of Mental Deficiency, 46,* 214–219.

Dollard, J., Doob, L. W., Miller, N. E., Mowrer, O. H., and Sears, R. R. (1939). *Frustration and aggression.* New Haven, CT: Yale University Press.

Dollard, J., and Miller, N. E. (1950). *Personality and psychotherapy: An analysis in terms of learning, thinking, and culture.* New York: McGraw-Hill.

Donnerstein, E. I. (1983). Erotica and human aggression. In R. G. Geen and E. I. Donnerstein (Eds.), *Aggression: Theoretical and empirical reviews,* Vol. 2: *Issues in research.* New York: Academic Press.

Donnerstein, E. I., Donnerstein, M., and Evans, R. (1975). Erotic stimuli and aggression: Facilitation or inhibition? *Journal of Personality and Social Psychology, 32,* 237–244.

Dorfman, D. D. (1978). The Cyril Burt question: New findings. *Science, 201,* 1177–1186.

Duke, M., and Nowicki, S., Jr. (1979). *Abnormal psychology: Perspectives on being different.* Monterey, CA: Brooks/Cole.

Dunbar, H. F. (1947). *Mind and body: Psychosomatic medicine.* New York: Random House.

Dunlap, R. L. (1953). *Changes in children's preferences for goal objects as a function of differences in expected social reinforcement.* Unpublished doctoral dissertation, Ohio State University.

Dweck, C. S. (1975). The role of expectation and attribution in the alleviation of learned helplessness. *Journal of Personality and Social Psychology, 31,* 674–685.

Dyck, R. J., and Rule, B. G. (1978). Effect on retaliation of causal attributions concerning attack. *Journal of Personality and Social Psychology, 36,* 521–529.

Eagly, A. H., and Mladinic, A. (1989). Gender stereotypes and attitudes toward women and men. *Personality and Social Psychology Bulletin, 15,* 543–558.

Eagly, A. H., and Steffen, V. J. (1986). Gender and aggressive behavior: A meta-analytic review of the social psychological literature. *Psychological Bulletin, 100,* 309–330.

Eckenrode, J., Powers, J., Doris, J., Munsch, J., and Bolger, N. (1988). Substantiation of child abuse and neglect reports. *Journal of Consulting and Clinical Psychology, 56,* 9–16.

Edwards, A. L. (1959). *Personal Preference Schedule* (rev.). New York: Psychological Corporation.

Efran, J. S., and Broughton, A. (1966). Effects of expectancies for social approval on visual behavior. *Journal of Personality and Social Psychology, 4,* 103–107.

Eisenberg, N., and Lennon, R. (1983). Sex differences in empathy and related capacities. *Psychological Bulletin, 94,* 100–131.

Eisenberg, N., and Miller, P. A. (1987). The relation of empathy to prosocial and related behavior. *Psychological Bulletin, 101,* 91–119.

Eisenberg, N., Miller, P. A., Schaller, M., Fabes, R. A., Fultz, J., Shell, R., and Shea, C. L. (1989). The role of sympathy and altruistic personality traits in helping: A reexamination. *Journal of Personality, 57,* 41–67.

Eisenberg, N., and Strayer, J. (Eds.). (1987). *Empathy and its development.* New York: Cambridge University Press.

Ekehammer, B. (1974). Interactionism in personality from a historical perspective. *Psychological Bulletin, 81,* 1026–1048.

Elliott, R. (1987). *Litigating intelligence: IQ tests, special education, and social science.* Dover, MA: Auburn House.

Ellis, A. (1962). *Reason and emotion in psychotherapy.* New York: Lyle Stuart.

Emmons, R. A. (1987). Narcissism: Theory and measurement. *Journal of Personality and Social Psychology, 52,* 11–17.

Engel, G. L. (1968). A life setting conducive to illness: The giving-up-given-up complex. *Bulletin of the Menninger Clinic, 32,* 355–365.

Entwisle, D. R. (1972). To dispel fantasies about fantasy-based motivation. *Psychological Bulletin, 77,* 377–391.

Epstein, S. (1972). The nature of anxiety with emphasis upon its relationship to expectancy. In C. D. Spielberger (Ed.), *Anxiety: Current trends in theory and research* (Vol. 2). New York: Academic Press.

Epstein, S. (1979a). The stability of behavior: I. On predicting most people much of the time. *Journal of Personality and Social Psychology, 37,* 1097–1126.

Epstein, S. (1979b). Explorations in personality today and tomorrow: A tribute to Henry A. Murray. *American Psychologist, 34,* 649–653.

Epstein, S. (1980). The self-concept: A review and the proposal of an integrated theory of personality. In E. Staub (Ed.), *Personality: Basic aspects and current research.* Englewood Cliffs, NJ: Prentice-Hall.

Epstein, S., and Feist, G. J. (1988). Relation between self- and other-acceptance and its moderation by identification. *Journal of Personality and Social Psychology, 54,* 309–315.

Epstein, S., and O'Brien, E. J. (1985). The person-situation debate in historical perspective. *Psychological Bulletin, 98,* 513–537.

Epting, F. R. (1984). *Personal construct counseling and psychotherapy.* Chichester, England: Wiley.

Erikson, E. H. (1945). Childhood and tradition in two American Indian tribes. In *The psychoanalytic study of the child* (Vol. 1). New York: International Universities Press.

Erikson, E. H. (1958). *Young man Luther.* New York: Norton.

Erikson, E. H. (1963). *Childhood and society* (2nd ed.). New York: Norton.

Erikson, E. H. (1964). *Insight and responsibility.* New York: Norton.

Erikson, E. H. (1969). *Gandhi's truth.* New York: Norton.

Erkut, S., Jaquette, D. S., and Staub, E. (1981). Moral judgment-situation interaction as a basis for predicting prosocial behavior. *Journal of Personality, 49,* 1–14.

Erlenmeyer-Kimling, L., and Jarvik, L. F. (1963). Genetics and intelligence: A review. *Science, 142,* 1477–1479.

Eron, L. D. (1982). Parent-child interaction, television violence, and aggression of children. *American Psychologist, 37,* 197–211.

Eron, L. D., and Huesmann, L. R. (1984). The control of aggressive behavior by changes in attitudes, values, and the conditions of learning. In R. J. Blanchard and D. C. Blanchard (Eds.), *Advances in the study of aggression,* Vol. 1. New York: Academic Press.

Eron, L. D., and Peterson, R. A. (1982). Abnormal behavior: Social approaches. In M. R. Rosenzweig and L. W. Porter (Eds.), *Annual review of psychology.* Palo Alto, CA: Annual Reviews.

Erskine, N. J. (1981). *An investigation into the construct validity of the Selfism Scale.* Unpublished master's thesis, Kansas State University.

Etzioni, A. (1969). Social-psychological aspects of international relations. In G. Lindzey and E. Aronson (Eds.), *The handbook of social psychology* (2nd ed.). Reading, MA: Addison-Wesley.

Evans, R. G. (1982). Skill versus chance tasks: Comparison of locus of control, defensive externality, and persistence. *Personality and Social Psychology Bulletin, 8,* 129–133.

Eysenck, H. J. (1947). *Dimensions of personality.* London: Routledge and Kegan Paul.

Eysenck, H. J. (1950). Criterion analysis: An application of the hypothetico-deductive method to factor analysis. *Psychological Review, 57,* 38–53.

Eysenck, H. J. (1952). *The scientific study of personality.* London: Routledge and Kegan Paul.

Eysenck, H. J. (1953). *The structure of human personality.* New York: Wiley.

Eysenck, H. J. (1957). *Sense and nonsense in psychology.* Baltimore, MD: Penguin.

Eysenck, H. J. (1967). *The biological basis of personality.* Springfield, IL: Charles C Thomas.

Eysenck, H. J. (1970). *The structure of human personality* (3rd ed.). London: Methuen.

Eysenck, H. J. (1975). *The inequality of man.* San Diego, CA: Edits.

Eysenck, H. J. (1977). The case of Sir Cyril Burt. *Encounter, 48,* 19–24.

Eysenck, H. J., and Eysenck, M. W. (1985). *Personality and individual differences: A natural science approach.* New York: Plenum.

Eysenck, H. J. and Kamin, L. (1981). *The intelligence controversy: H. J. Eysenck vs. Leon Kamin.* New York: Wiley-Interscience.

Eysenck, H. J. and Rachman, S. (1965). *The causes and cures of neurosis.* San Diego, CA: Robert L. Knapp.

Falbo, T. (1981). Relationships between birth category, achievement, and interpersonal orientation. *Journal of Personality and Social Psychology, 41,* 121–131.

Feingold, A. (1988). Cognitive gender differences are disappearing. *American Psychologist, 43,* 95–103.

Felson, R. B. (1989). Parents and the reflected appraisal process: A longitudinal analysis. *Journal of Personality and Social Psychology, 56,* 965–971.

Felton, B., and Kahana, E. (1974). Adjustment and situationally bound locus of control among institutionalized aged. *Journal of Gerontology, 29,* 295–301.

Fenigstein, A., Scheier, M. F., and Buss, A. H. (1975). Public and private self-consciousness: Assessment and theory. *Journal of Consulting and Clinical Psychology, 43,* 522–527.

Ferguson, T. L., Rule, B. G., and Lindsay, R. C. L. (1982). The effects of caffeine and provocation on aggression. *Journal of Research in Personality, 16,* 60–71.

Ferster, C. B., and Skinner, B. F. (1957). *Schedules of reinforcement.* Englewood Cliffs, NJ: Prentice-Hall.

Feshbach, N. D. (1969). Sex differences in children's modes of aggressive responses toward outsiders. *Merrill-Palmer Quarterly, 15,* 249–258.

Feshbach, N. D. (1973). Cross-cultural studies of teaching styles in four-year-olds and their mothers. In A. E. Pick (Ed.), *Minnesota Symposium on Child Psychology* (Vol. 7). Minneapolis, MN: University of Minnesota Press.

Feshbach, N. D. (1978). Studies of empathic behavior in children. In B. A. Maher (Ed.), *Progress in experimental personality research* (Vol. 8). New York: Academic Press.

Feshbach, N. D. and Sones, G. (1971). Sex differences in adolescent reactions toward newcomers. *Developmental Psychology, 4,* 381–386.

Feshbach, S. (1970). Aggression. In P. H. Mussen (Ed.), *Carmichael's manual of child psychology.* New York: Wiley.

Feshbach, S., and Singer, R. (1971). *Television and aggression.* San Francisco: Jossey-Bass.

Feuerstein, M., Labbé, E. E., and Kuczmierczyk, A. R. (1986). *Health psychology: A psychobiological perspective.* New York: Plenum Press.

Findley, M. J., and Cooper, H. M. (1983). Locus of control and academic achievement: A literature review. *Journal of Personality and Social Psychology, 44,* 419–427.

Fischer, W. F. (1978). An empirical-phenomenological investigation of being anxious: An example of the meanings of being-emotional. In R. S. Valle and M. King (Eds.), *Existential-phenomenological alternatives for psychology.* New York: Oxford University Press.

Fisher, S., and Greenberg, R. P. (1977). *The scientific credibility of Freud's theories and therapy.* New York: Basic Books.

Fitts, W. H. (1965). *Manual for the Tennessee Self Concept Scale.* Los Angeles: Western Psychological Services.

Flaherty, J. F., and Dusek, J. B. (1980). An investigation of the relationship between psychological androgyny and components of self-concept. *Journal of Personality and Social Psychology, 38,* 984–992.

Flavell, J. H., Botkin, P. T., Fry, C. L., Jr., Wright, J. W., and Jarvis, P. E. (1968). *The development of role-taking and communication skills in young children.* New York: Wiley.

Fleming, R., Baum, A., and Singer, J. E. (1984). Toward an integrative approach to the study of stress. *Journal of Personality and Social Psychology, 46,* 939–949.

Ford, C. E., and Neale, J. M. (1985). Learned helplessness and judgments of control. *Journal of Personality and Social Psychology, 49,* 1330–1336.

Foster, C. D., Siegel, M. A., and Jacobs, N. R. (Eds.). (1988). *Women's changing roles.* Wylie, TX: Information Aids.

Frank, M. G., and Gilovich, T. (1988). The dark side of self- and social perception: Black uniforms and aggression in professional sports. *Journal of Personality and Social Psychology, 54,* 74–85.

Frankel, A., and Snyder, M. L. (1978). Poor performances following unsolvable problems: Learned helplessness or egotism? *Journal of Personality and Social Psychology, 36,* 1415–1423.

Frankenhaeuser, M. (1980). Psychobiological aspects of life stress. In S. Levine and H. Ursin (Eds.), *Coping and health.* New York: Plenum Press.

Freedman, J. L. (1975). *Crowding and behavior.* San Francisco: W. H. Freeman.

Freud, S. (1938). *The basic writings of Sigmund Freud.* New York: Modern Library.

Freud, S. (1953). *The interpretation of dreams* (Vols. 4 and 5). London: Hogarth Press. (Originally published, 1900)

Freud, S. (1955). Analysis of a phobia in a five-year-old boy. In *Standard edition* (Vol. 10). London: Hogarth Press. (Originally published 1909)

Freud, S. (1957). Leonardo da Vinci and a memory of his childhood. In *Standard edition* (Vol. 11). London: Hogarth Press. (Originally published 1910)

Freud, S. (1961). Dostoevsky and patricide. In *Standard edition* (Vol. 21). London: Hogarth Press. (Originally published 1928)

Freud, S. (1964). Moses and monotheism. In *Standard edition* (Vol. 23). London: Hogarth Press. (Originally published 1939)

Friedman, H. S., and Booth-Kewley, S. (1987a). The "disease-prone personality": A meta-analytic view of the construct. *American Psychologist, 42,* 539–555.

Friedman, H. S., and Booth-Kewley, S. (1987b). Personality, Type A behavior, and coronary heart disease: The role of emotional expression. *Journal of Personality and Social Psychology, 53,* 783–792.

Friedman, M., and Rosenman, R. H. (1974). *Type A behavior and your heart.* New York: Knopf.

Frieze, I. H., Parsons, J. E., Johnson, P. B., Ruble, D. N., and Zellman, G. L. (1978). *Women and sex roles.* New York: Norton.

Frodi, A., Macaulay, J., and Thorne, P. R. (1977). Are women always less aggressive than men? A review of the experimental literature. *Psychological Bulletin, 84,* 634–660.

Fromm, E. (1941). *Escape from freedom.* New York: Rinehart.

Fromm, E., and Maccoby, M. (1970). *Social character in a Mexican village.* Englewood Cliffs, NJ: Prentice-Hall.

Frosh, S. (1987). *The politics of psychoanalysis: An introduction to Freudian and post-Freudian theory.* New Haven, CT: Yale University Press.

Funder, D. C., and Block, J. (1989). The role of ego-control, ego-resiliency, and IQ in delay of gratification in adolescence. *Journal of Personality and Social Psychology, 57,* 1041–1050.

Funder, D. C., Block, J. H., and Block, J. (1983). Delay of gratification: Some longitudinal personality correlates. *Journal of Personality and Social Psychology, 44,* 1198–1213.

Funk, S. C., and Houston, B. K. (1987). A critical analysis of the Hardiness Scale's validity and utility. *Journal of Personality and Social Psychology, 53,* 572–578.

Gagnon, J. H., and Davison, G. C. (1976). Asylums, the token economy, and the metrics of mental life. *Behavior Therapy, 7,* 528–534.

Galton, F. (1869). *Hereditary genius.* London: Macmillan.

Gantner, A. B., and Taylor, S. P. (1988). Human physical aggression as a function of diazepam. *Personality and Social Psychology Bulletin, 14,* 479–484.

Gardner, H. (1983). *Frames of mind: The theory of multiple intelligences.* New York: Basic Books.

Gatchel, R. J., Baum, A., and Krantz, D. S. (1989). *An introduction to health psychology* (2nd ed.). New York: Random House.

Geen, R. G. (1975). The meaning of observed violence: Real vs. fictional violence and consequent effects on aggression and emotional arousal. *Journal of Research in Personality, 9,* 270–281.

Geen, R. G. (1976a). *Personality: The skein of behavior.* St. Louis, MO: Mosby.

Geen, R. G. (1976b). Observing violence in the mass media: Implications of basic research. In R. G. Geen and E. C. O'Neal (Eds.), *Perspectives on aggression.* New York: Academic Press.

Geen, R. G. (1980). Test anxiety and cue utilization. In I. G. Sarason (Ed.), *Test anxiety: Theory, research, and applications.* Hillsdale, NJ: Erlbaum.

Geen, R. G. (1984). Preferred stimulation levels in introverts and extraverts: Effects on arousal and performance. *Journal of Personality and Social Psychology, 46,* 1303–1312.

Geen, R. G., and Stonner, D. (1971). Effects of aggressiveness habit strength on behavior in the presence of aggression-related stimuli. *Journal of Personality and Social Psychology, 17,* 149–153.

Geer, J. H. (1965). The development of a scale to measure fear. *Behavior Research and Therapy, 3,* 45–53.

Geiwitz, J., and Moursund, J. (1979). *Approaches to personality: An introduction to people.* Monterey, CA: Brooks/Cole.

Gendlin, E. T. (1988). Carl Rogers (1902–1987). *American Psychologist, 43,* 127–128.

Gesell, A., et al. (1940). *The first five years of life.* New York: Harper and Row.

Gil, D. G. (1973). *Violence against children: Physical abuse in the United States.* Cambridge, MA: Harvard University Press.

Gilligan, C. (1982). *In a different voice.* Cambridge, MA: Harvard University Press.

Ginsburg, H., and Opper, S. (1988). *Piaget's theory of intellectual development.* Englewood Cliffs, NJ: Prentice-Hall.

Glass, D. C. (1977). *Behavior patterns, stress, and coronary disease.* Hillsdale, NJ: Erlbaum.

Glass, D. C., and Singer, J. E. (1972). *Urban stress: Experiments on noise and social stressors.* New York: Academic Press.

Gleitman, H. (1981). *Psychology.* New York: Norton.

Goldberg, P. (1968). Are women prejudiced against women? *Transaction, 5,* 28–30.

Goldfried, M. R. (1976). Behavioral assessment. In I. B. Weiner (Ed.), *Clinical methods in psychology.* New York: Wiley-Interscience.

Goldfried, M. R., and Davison, G. C. (1976). *Clinical behavior therapy.* New York: Holt, Rinehart and Winston.

Goldstein, A. G., and Chance, J. E. (1965). Effects of practice on sex-related differences in performance on embedded figures. *Psychonomic Science, 3,* 361–362.

Goldstein, A. P., and Keller, H. R. (1987). *Aggressive behavior: Assessment and intervention.* Oxford, England: Pergamon Press.

Goodenough, F. L. (1949). *Mental testing.* New York: Rinehart.

Gore, P. M., and Rotter, J. B. (1963). A personality correlate of social action. *Journal of Personality, 31,* 58–64.

Gottesman, I. I. (1963). Genetic aspects of intelligent behavior. In N. Ellis (Ed.), *Handbook of mental deficiency: Psychological theory and research.* New York: McGraw-Hill.

Gould, S. J. (1976). Biological potential vs. biological determinism. *Natural History, 85,* 12–22.

Gourlay, N. (1979). Heredity versus environment: An integrative analysis. *Psychological Bulletin, 86,* 596–615.

Grady, K. E. (1989). Romanticism and rationalism in the study of sex and gender. *Contemporary Psychology, 34,* 337–338.

Graham, A. (1975). The making of a nonsexist dictionary. In B. Thorne and N. Henley (Eds.), *Language and sex: Difference and dominance.* Rowley, MA: Newbury House.

Graham, W., and Balloun, J. (1973). An empirical test of Maslow's need hierarchy theory. *Journal of Humanistic Psychology, 13,* 97–108.

Greenberg, B. S. (1975). British children and televised violence. *Public Opinion Quarterly, 38,* 531–547.

Griffitt, W. (1970). Environmental effects on interpersonal affective behavior: Ambient effective temperature and attraction. *Journal of Personality and Social Psychology, 15,* 240–244.

Griffitt, W., and Veitch, R. (1971). Hot and crowded: Influences of population density and temperature on interpersonal affective behavior. *Journal of Personality and Social Psychology, 17,* 92–98.

Gruen, R. J., Folkman, S., and Lazarus, R. S. (1988). Centrality and individual differences in the meaning of daily hassles. *Journal of Personality, 56,* 743–762.

Gruenberg, E. M. (1967). The social breakdown—Some origins. *American Journal of Psychiatry, 123,* 481–489.

Guilford, J. P. (1959). *Personality.* New York: McGraw-Hill.

Guilford, J. P. (1967). *The nature of human intelligence.* New York: McGraw-Hill.

Gurtman, M. B., and Lion, C. (1982). Interpersonal trust and perceptual vigilance for trustworthiness descriptors. *Journal of Research in Personality, 16,* 108–117.

Gutmann, D. (1970). Female ego styles and generational conflict. In J. Bardwick, E. Douvan, M. Horner, and D. Gutmann (Eds.), *Feminine personality and conflicts.* Monterey, CA: Brooks/Cole.

Haan, N., Smith, N. B., and Block, J. (1968). The moral reasoning of young adults: Political-social behavior, family background, and personality correlates. *Journal of Personality and Social Psychology, 3,* 183–202.

Hall, C. S. (1954). *A primer of Freudian psychology.* New York: New American Library.

Hall, C. S., and Lindzey, G. (1978). *Theories of personality* (3rd ed.). New York: Wiley.

Hall, C. S., and Van de Castle, R. (1965). An empirical investigation of the castration complex in dreams. *Journal of Personality, 33,* 20–29.

Hall, J. A., and Taylor, M. C. (1985). Psychological androgyny and the masculinity × femininity interaction. *Journal of Personality and Social Psychology, 49,* 429–435.

Hall, R. V., Lund, D., and Jackson, D. (1968). Effects of teacher attention on study behavior. *Journal of Applied Behavior Analysis, 1,* 1–12.

Halpern, D. F. (1986). *Sex differences in cognitive abilities.* Hillsdale, NJ: Erlbaum.

Hampson, J. L. (1965). Determinants of psychosexual orientation. In F. A. Beach (Ed.), *Sex and behavior.* New York: Wiley.

Harman, H. H. (1960). *Modern factor analysis.* Chicago: University of Chicago Press.

Harris, B. (1979). What ever happened to Little Albert? *American Psychologist, 34,* 151–160.

Harris, D. B. (1963). *Children's drawings as measures of intellectual maturity: A revision and extension of the Goodenough Draw-a-Man Test.* New York: Harcourt, Brace and World.

Harris, M. B. (1973). Field studies of modeled aggression. *Journal of Social Psychology, 89,* 131–139.

Hartman, D. P., Roper, B. L., and Bradford, D. C. (1979). Some relationships between behavioral and traditional assessment. *Journal of Behavioral Assessment, 1,* 4.

Hartmann, H. (1958). *Ego psychology and the problem of adaptation.* New York: International Universities Press.

Hartmann, H. (1964). *Essays on ego psychology: Selected problems in psychoanalytic theory.* New York: International Universities Press.

Hartup, W. W., Moore, S. G., and Sager, G. (1963). Avoidance of inappropriate sex-typing by young children. *Journal of Consulting Psychology, 27,* 467–473

Hayden, B. (1979). The self and possibilities for change. *Journal of Personality, 47,* 546–556.

Healy, W., Bronner, A. F., and Bowers, A. M. (1930). *The structure and meaning of psychoanalysis.* New York: Knopf.

Hearnshaw, L. S. (1979). *Cyril Burt, psychologist.* Ithaca, NY: Cornell University Press.

Heckhausen, H., and Beckmann, J. (1990). Intentional action and action slips. *Psychological Review, 97,* 36–48.

Heider, F. (1958). *The psychology of interpersonal relations.* New York: Wiley.

Heilbrun, A. B., Jr. (1981). Gender differences in the functional linkage between androgyny, social cognition, and competence. *Journal of Personality and Social Psychology, 41,* 1106–1118.

Helmreich, R. L., and Spence, J. T. (1978). The work and family orientation questionnaire: An objective instrument to assess components of achievement motivation and attitudes toward family and career. *JSAS catalog of selected documents in psychology, 8,* 35.

Helmreich, R. L., Spence, J. T., and Gibson, R. H. (1982). Sex-role attitudes: 1972–1980. *Personality and Social Psychology Bulletin, 8,* 656–663.

Henderson, N. D. (1982). Human behavior genetics. In M. R. Rosenzweig and L. W. Porter (Eds.), *Annual review of psychology.* Palo Alto, CA: Annual Reviews.

Hergenhahn, B. R. (1972). *Shaping your child's personality.* Englewood Cliffs, NJ: Prentice-Hall.

Herrnstein, R. J. (1973). *IQ in the meritocracy.* Boston: Atlantic Monthly Press.

Hermans, H. J. (1988). On the integration of nomothetic and idiographic research methods in the study of personal meaning. *Journal of Personality, 56,* 785–812.

Hetherington, E. M. (1965). A developmental study of the effects of sex of the dominant parent on sex-role preference, identification, and imitation in children. *Journal of Personality and Social Psychology, 2,* 188–194.

Hilgard, E. R. (1952). Experimental approaches to psychoanalysis. In E. Pumpian-Mindlin (Ed.), *Psychoanalysis as science.* New York: Basic Books.

Hilgard, E. R. (1978). Hypnosis and consciousness. *Human Nature, 1,* 42–49.

Hinde, R. A. (1974). *Biological bases of human social behavior.* New York: McGraw-Hill.

Hines, M. (1982). Prenatal gonadal hormones and sex differences in human behavior. *Psychological Bulletin, 92,* 56–80.

Hinkle, D. (1965). *The change of personal constructs from the viewpoint of a theory of implications.* Unpublished doctoral dissertation, Ohio State University.

Hiroto, D. S., and Seligman, M. E. P. (1975). Generality of learned helplessness in man. *Journal of Personality and Social Psychology, 31,* 311–327.

Hjelle, L. A., and Ziegler, D. J. (1981). *Personality theories: Basic assumptions, research, and applications* (2nd ed.). New York: McGraw-Hill.

Hochreich, D. J. (1972). Internal-external control and reaction to the My Lai court martials. *Journal of Applied Social Psychology, 2,* 319–325.

Hochreich, D. J. (1974). Defensive externality and attribution of responsibility. *Journal of Personality, 42,* 543–557.

Hochreich, D. J. (1975). Sex-role stereotypes for internal-external control and interpersonal trust. *Journal of Consulting and Clinical Psychology, 43,* 273.

Hochreich, D. J., and Rotter, J. B. (1970). Have college students become less trusting? *Journal of Personality and Social Psychology, 15,* 211–214.

Hoffman, C., and Hurst, N. (1990). Gender stereotypes: Perception or rationalization? *Journal of Personality and Social Psychology, 58,* 197–208.

Hoffman, E. (1988). *The right to be human: A biography of Abraham Maslow.* Los Angeles: Tarcher.

Hoffman, M. L. (1975a). Developmental synthesis of affect and cognition and its implications for altruistic motivation. *Developmental Psychology, 11,* 607–622.

Hoffman, M. L. (1975b). Altruistic behavior and the parent-child relationship. *Journal of Personality and Social Psychology, 31,* 937–943.

Hoffman, M. L. (1981). Is altruism part of human nature? *Journal of Personality and Social Psychology, 40,* 121–137.

Hogan, R. (1969). Development of an empathy scale. *Journal of Consulting and Clinical Psychology, 33,* 307–316.

Hogan, R. (1973). Moral conduct and moral character: A psychological perspective. *Psychological Bulletin, 79,* 217–232.

Hokanson, J. E., and Burgess, M. (1962). The effects of three types of aggression on vascular processes. *Journal of Abnormal and Social Psychology, 64,* 446–449.

Holahan, C. J., and Moos, R. H. (1986). Personality, coping, and family resources in stress resistance: A longitudinal analysis. *Journal of Personality and Social Psychology, 51,* 389–395.

Holden, C. (1987). The genetics of personality. *Science, 237,* 598–601.

Holliday, S. G., and Chandler, M. J. (1986). *Wisdom: Explorations in adult competence.* Basel, Switzerland: Karger.

Holmes, D. S. (1974). Investigations of repression: Differential recall of material experimentally or naturally associated with ego threat. *Psychological Bulletin, 81,* 632–653.

Holmes, D. S., McGilley, B. M., and Houston, B. K. (1984). Task-related arousal of Type A and Type B persons: Level of challenge and response specificity. *Journal of Personality and Social Psychology, 46,* 1322–1327.

Holmes, T. H., and Rahe, R. H. (1967). The Social Readjustment Rating Scale. *Journal of Psychosomatic Research, 11,* 213–218.

Horn, J. L. (1968). Organization of abilities and the development of intelligence. *Psychological Review, 75,* 242–259.

Horn, J. M., Loehlin, J. C., and Willerman, L. (1979). Intellectual resemblance among adoptive and biological relatives: The Texas Adoption Project. *Behavior Genetics, 9,* 177–208.

Horner, M. S. (1972). Toward an understanding of achievement related conflicts in women. *Journal of Social Issues, 28,* 157–176.

Horney, K. (1937). *Neurotic personality of our times.* New York: Norton.

Horney, K. (1945). *Our inner conflicts.* New York: Norton.

Horney, K. (1967). *Feminine psychology.* New York: Norton.

Howes, D. H., and Solomon, R. L. (1951). Visual duration threshold as a function of word-probability. *Journal of Experimental Psychology, 41,* 401–410.

Huesmann, L. R., and Eron, L. D. (Eds.). (1986). *Television and the aggressive child: A cross-cultural comparison.* Hillsdale, NJ: Erlbaum.

Huesmann, L. R., Eron, L. D., and Yarmel, P. W. (1987). Intellectual functioning and aggression. *Journal of Personality and Social Psychology, 52,* 232–240.

Hull, C. L. (1943). *Principles of behavior.* New York: Appleton-Century-Crofts.

Hull, J. G., Van Treuren, R. R., and Virnelli, S. (1987). Hardiness and health: A critique and alternative approach. *Journal of Personality and Social Psychology, 53,* 518–530.

Humphreys, L. G. (1957). Characteristics of type concepts with special reference to Sheldon's typology. *Psychological Bulletin, 54,* 218–228.

Humphries, C., Carver, C. S., and Neumann, P. G. (1983). Cognitive characteristics of the Type A coronary-prone behavior pattern. *Journal of Personality and Social Psychology, 44,* 177–187.

Huntington, E. (1945). *Mainsprings of civilization.* New York: Wiley.

Huntley, C. W., and Davis, F. (1983). Undergraduate Study of Values scores as predictors of occupation 25 years later. *Journal of Personality and Social Psychology, 45,* 1148–1155.

Hyde, J. S., Fennema, E., and Lamon, S. J. (1990). Gender differences in mathematics performance: A meta-analysis. *Psychological Bulletin, 107,* 139–155.

Hyde, J. S., and Linn, M. C. (Eds.). (1986). *The psychology of gender: Advances through meta-analysis.* Baltimore, MD: Johns Hopkins University Press.

Hyde, J. S., and Linn, M. C. (1988). Gender differences in verbal ability: A meta-analysis. *Psychological Bulletin, 104,* 53–69.

Hyland, M. E. (1989). There is no motive to avoid success: The compromise explanation for success-avoiding behavior. *Journal of Personality, 57,* 665–693.

Ihilevich, D., and Gleser, G. C. (1986). *Defense mechanisms: Their classification, correlates, and measurement with the Defense Mechanisms Inventory.* Owosso, MI: DMI Associates.

Insel, P. M., and Moos, R. H. (1974). Psychological environments: Expanding the scope of human ecology. *American Psychologist, 29,* 179–188.

Jackson, D. N., and Messick, S. (1958). Content and style in personality assessment. *Psychological Bulletin, 55,* 243–252.

James, W. (1890). *The principles of psychology* (Vol. 1). New York: Holt.

James, W. H. (1957). *Internal versus external control of reinforcement as a basic variable in learning theory.* Unpublished doctoral dissertation, Ohio State University.

Janis, I. L. (1958). *Psychological stress.* New York: Wiley.

Jarvik, L. F., Klodin, V., and Matsuyama, S. S. (1973). Human aggression and the extra Y chromosome: Fact or fantasy? *American Psychologist, 28,* 674–682.

Jarvik, L. F., and Perl, M. (1981). Overview of physiologic dysfunction related to psychiatric problems in the elderly. In A. J. Levenson and R. C. W. Hall (Eds.), *Manifestations of physical disease in the elderly.* New York: Raven.

Jeffery, R. W. (1989). Risk behaviors and health: Contrasting individual and population perspectives. *American Psychologist, 44,* 1194–1202.

Jenkins, C. D. (1985). The epidemiology of sudden cardiac death: Incidence, clinical features, biomedical and psychological risk factors. In R. E. Beamish, P. K. Singal, and N. S. Dhalla (Eds.), *Stress and heart disease.* Boston: Nijhoff.

Jenkins, C. D. (1988). Epidemiology of cardiovascular diseases. *Journal of Consulting and Clinical Psychology, 56,* 324–332.

Jenkins, C. D., Zyzanski, S. J., and Rosenman, R. H. (1971). Progress toward validation of a computer-scored test for the Type A coronary-prone behavior pattern. *Psychosomatic Medicine, 33,* 193–201.

Jenkins, R. L. (1968). The varieties of children's behavioral problems and family dynamics. *American Journal of Psychiatry, 124,* 134–139.

Jensen, A. R. (1969). How much can we boost IQ and scholastic achievement? *Harvard Educational Review, 39,* 1–123.

Jensen, A. R. (1972). *Genetics and education.* New York: Harper and Row.

Jensen, A. R. (1977). Cumulative deficit in IQ of blacks in the rural South. *Developmental Psychology, 13,* 184–191.

Jessor, R., Carman, R. S., and Grossman, P. H. (1968). Expectations of need satisfaction and drinking patterns in college students. *Quarterly Journal of Studies in Alcohol, 29,* 101–116.

Johnson, J. E., and Leventhal, H. (1974). Effects of accurate expectations and behavioral instructions on reactions during a noxious medical examination. *Journal of Personality and Social Psychology, 29,* 710–718.

Jones, E. (1953, 1955, 1977). *The life and work of Sigmund Freud: Vol. 1 (1856–1900). The formative years and the great discoveries,* 1953; *Vol. 2 (1901–1919). Years of maturity,* 1955; *Vol. 3 (1919–1939). The last phase,* 1957. New York: Basic Books.

Jones, L. V. (1984). White-black achievement differences: The narrowing gap. *American Psychologist, 39,* 1207–1213.

Jones, M. C. (1924). The elimination of children's fears. *Journal of Experimental Psychology, 7,* 383–390.

Jones, R. R., Reid, J. B., and Patterson, G. R. (1975). Naturalistic observation in clinical assessment. In P. McReynolds (Ed.), *Advances in psychological assessment,* Vol. 3. San Francisco: Jossey-Bass.

Josephson, W. L. (1987). Television violence and children's aggression: Testing the priming, social script, and disinhibition predictions. *Journal of Personality and Social Psychology, 53,* 882–890.

Joslyn, W. D. (1973). Androgen induced social dominance in infant female rhesus monkeys. *Journal of Child Psychology and Psychiatry, 14,* 137–145.

Jourard, S. M., and Landsman, T. (1980). *Healthy personality: An approach from the viewpoint of humanistic psychology* (4th ed.). New York: Macmillan.

Jouriles, E. N., Murphy, C. M., and O'Leary, K. D. (1989). Interpersonal aggression, marital discord, and child problems. *Journal of Consulting and Clinical Psychology, 57,* 453–455.

Jung, C. G. (1910). The association method. *American Journal of Psychology, 21,* 219–269.

Jung, C. G. (1928). *Contributions to analytical psychology.* New York: Harcourt, Brace.

Jung, C. G. (1961). *Memories, dreams, reflections.* New York: Random House.

Jung, C. G. (1970). *Four archetypes: Mother, rebirth, spirit, and trickster.* Princeton, NJ: Princeton University Press.

Kagan, J. (1958). The concept of identification. *Psychological Review, 65,* 296–305.

Kagan, J. (1975). The emergence of sex differences. In F. Rebelsky (Ed.), *Life: The continuous process.* New York: Knopf.

Kallmann, F. J. (1953). *Heredity in health and mental disorder.* New York: Norton.

Kamin, L. J. (1980). Inbreeding depression and IQ. *Psychological Bulletin, 87,* 469–478.

Kanfer, F. H., and Phillips, J. S. (1970). *Learning foundations of behavior therapy.* New York: Wiley.

Kanner, A. D., Coyne, J. C., Schaefer, C., and Lazarus, R. S. (1981). Comparison of two modes of stress management: Daily hassles and uplifts versus major life events. *Journal of Behavioral Medicine, 4,* 1–39.

Kantor, J. R. (1924). *Principles of psychology* (2 vols.). New York: Knopf.

Kaplan, R. M., Atkins, C. J., and Reinsch, S. (1984). Specific efficacy expectations mediate exercise compliance in patients with COPD. *Health Psychology, 3,* 223–242.

Kaplan, R. M., and Singer, R. D. (1976). Television violence and viewer aggression: A reexamination of the evidence. *Journal of Social Issues, 32,* 35–70.

Katkovsky, W. (1976). Social-learning theory analyses of maladjusted behavior. In W. Katkovsky and L. Gorlow (Eds.), *The psychology of adjustment: Current concepts and applications* (3rd ed.). New York: McGraw-Hill.

Katkovsky, W., Crandall, V. C., and Good, S. (1967). Parental antecedents of children's beliefs in internal-external control of reinforcements in intellectual achievement situations. *Child Development, 38,* 765–776.

Kazdin, A. E. (1987). Treatment of antisocial behavior in children: Current status and future directions. *Psychological Bulletin, 102,* 187–203.

Kazdin, A. E. (1988). Introduction to the special series. *Journal of Consulting and Clinical Psychology, 56,* 3–4.

Kelley, H. H. (1971). *Attribution in social interaction.* Morristown, NJ: General Learning Press.

Kelly, G. A. (1955). *The psychology of personal constructs: A theory of personality* (2 vols.). New York: Norton.

Kelly, J., and Worell, L. (1976). Parent behaviors related to masculine, feminine, and androgynous sex role orientations. *Journal of Consulting and Clinical Psychology, 44,* 843–851.

Kelly, K. E., and Houston, B. K. (1985). Type A behavior in employed women: Relation to work, marital, and leisure variables, social support, stress, tension, and health. *Journal of Personality and Social Psychology, 48,* 1067–1079.

Kendall, P. C., Finch, A. J., Jr., Auerbach, S. M., Hooke, J. F., and Mikulka, P. J. (1976). The State-Trait Anxiety Inventory: A systematic evaluation. *Journal of Consulting and Clinical Psychology, 44,* 406–412.

Kenrick, D. T., and Funder, D. C. (1988). Profiting from controversy: Lessons from the person-situation debate. *American Psychologist, 43,* 23–34.

Kermis, M. D. (1984). *The psychology of human aging: Theory, research, and practice.* Boston: Allyn and Bacon.

Kessler, S. (1975). Extra chromosomes and criminality. In R. R. Fieve, D. Rosenthal, and H. Brill (Eds.), *Genetic research in psychiatry.* Baltimore, MD: Johns Hopkins University Press.

Kidd, R. F., and Marshall, . (1982). Self-reflection, mood, and helpful behavior. *Journal of Research in Personality, 16,* 319–334.

Kihlstrom, J. F. (1987). Introduction to the special issue: Integrating personality and social psychology. *Journal of Personality and Social Psychology, 53,* 989–992.

Kimball, M. M. (1989). A new perspective on women's math achievement. *Psychological Bulletin, 105,* 198–214.

Kirsch, I. (1985). Self-efficacy and expectancy: Old wine with new labels. *Journal of Personality and Social Psychology, 49,* 824–830.

Kissinger, H. (1979). *White House years.* Boston: Little, Brown.

Klein, M. (1937). *The psycho-analysis of children* (2nd ed.). London: Hogarth.

Klein, P. (1987). The experimental study of the psychoanalytic unconscious. *Personality and Social Psychology Bulletin, 13,* 363–378.

Kline, P. (1981). *Fact and fantasy in Freudian theory* (2nd ed.). London: Methuen.

Klineberg, O. (1935). *Negro intelligence and selective migration.* New York: Columbia University Press.

Klotz, M. L., and Alicke, M. D. (1989). The effects of schema appropriateness on recall. *Journal of Research in Personality, 23,* 225–234.

Knott, P. D., Lasater, L., and Shuman, R. (1974). Aggression-guilt and conditionability for aggressiveness. *Journal of Personality, 42,* 332–344.

Kobasa, S. C., Maddi, S. R., and Kahn, S. (1982). Hardiness and health: A prospective study. *Journal of Personality and Social Psychology, 42,* 168–177.

Kohlberg, L. (1966). A cognitive-developmental analysis of children's sex-role concepts and attitudes. In E. E. Maccoby (Ed.), *The development of sex differences.* Stanford, CA: Stanford University Press.

Kohlberg, L. (1969). Stage and sequence: The cognitive-developmental approach to socialization. In D. Goslin (Ed.), *Handbook of socialization theory and research.* Chicago: Rand McNally.

Kohlberg, L. (1971). From is to ought: How to commit the naturalistic fallacy and get away with it in the study of moral development. In T. Mischel (Ed.), *Cognitive psychology and genetic epistemology.* New York: Academic Press.

Kohn, M. L. (1973). Social class and schizophrenia: A critical review and a reformulation. *Schizophrenia Bulletin, No. 7,* 60–79.

Kohut, H. (1971). *The analysis of the self.* New York: International Universities Press.

Kohut, H. (1977). *The restoration of the self.* New York: International Universities Press.

Kolb, D. A. (1965). Achievement motivation for underachieving high-school boys. *Journal of Personality and Social Psychology, 2,* 783–792.

Korsch, B., and Negrete, V. (1972). Doctor-patient communication. *Scientific American, 227,* 66–78.

Krantz, D. S. (1980). Cognitive processes and recovery from heart attack: A review and theoretical analysis. *Journal of Human Stress, 6,* 27–38.

Krantz, D. S., Baum, A., and Wideman, M. V. (1980). Assessment of preferences for self-treatment and information in health care. *Journal of Personality and Social Psychology, 39,* 977–990.

Krantz, D. S., Grunberg, N. E., and Baum, A. (1985). Health psychology. In M. R. Rosenzweig and L. W. Porter (Eds.), *Annual review of psychology.* Palo Alto, CA: Annual Reviews.

Krause N. (1987a). Life stress, social support, and self-esteem in an elderly population. *Psychology and Aging, 2,* 349–356.

Krause, N. (1987b). Chronic strain, locus of control, and distress in older adults. *Psychology and Aging, 2,* 375–382.

Krause, N., and Stryker, S. (1984). Stress and well-being: The buffering role of locus of control beliefs. *Social Science and Medicine, 18,* 783–790.

Krebs, D. (1975). Empathy and altruism. *Journal of Personality and Social Psychology, 32,* 1134–1146.

Kren, G., and Rappoport, L. (1976). Introduction: Values, methods, and the utility of psychohistory. In G. Kren and L. Rappoport (Eds.), *Varieties of psychohistory.* New York: Springer.

Kren, G., and Rappoport, L. (1980). *The Holocaust and the crisis of human behavior.* New York: Holmes and Meier.

Kretschmer, E. (1925). *Physique and character.* New York: Harcourt, Brace.

Kris, E. (1952). *Psychoanalytic exploration in art.* New York: International Universities Press.

Kurtines, W. M. (1986). Moral behavior as rule governed behavior: Person and situation effects on moral decision making. *Journal of Personality and Social Psychology, 50,* 784–791.

Lacey, J. I. (1967). Somatic response patterning and stress: Some revisions of activation theory. In M. H. Appley and R. Trumbull (Eds.), *Psychological stress.* New York: Appleton-Century-Crofts.

Lachman, M. E. (1986). Locus of control in aging research: A case for multidimensional and domain-specific assessment. *Psychology and Aging, 1,* 34–40.

Lambert, N. (1981). Psychological evidence in *Larry P. v. Wilson Riles:* An evaluation by the witness for the defense. *American Psychologist, 36,* 937–952.

Lamiell, J. T. (1981). Toward an idiothetic psychology of personality. *American Psychologist, 36,* 276–289.

Lamiell, J. T. (1987). *The psychology of personality: An epistemological inquiry.* New York: Columbia University Press.

Landfield, A. W., Stern, M., and Fjeld, S. (1961). Serial conceptual processes and change in students undergoing psychotherapy. *Psychological Reports, 8,* 63–68.

Langan, P. A., and Innes, C. A. (1985). *The risk of violent crime* (Bureau of Justice Statistics Special Report, NCJ-97119). Washington, DC: U.S. Government Printing Office.

Langer, E. J. (1975). The illusion of control. *Journal of Personality and Social Psychology, 32,* 311–328.

Langer, E. J. (1981). Old age: An artifact? In J. McGaugh and S. Kiesler (Eds.), *Aging: Biology and behavior.* New York: Academic Press.

Langer, E. J., and Rodin, J. (1976). The effects of choice and enhanced personal responsibility for the aged: A field experiment in an institutional setting. *Journal of Personality and Social Psychology, 34,* 191–198.

Lanyon, R. I., and Goodstein, L. D. (1971). *Personality assessment.* New York: Wiley.

Lao, R. C. (1970). Internal-external control and competent and innovative behavior among Negro college students. *Journal of Personality and Social Psychology, 14,* 263–270.

Lasch, C. (1979). *The culture of narcissism: American life in an age of diminishing expectations.* New York: Norton.

Latané, B., and Darley, J. M. (1970). *The unresponsive bystander: Why doesn't he help?* New York: Appleton-Century-Crofts.

Latané, B., and Nida, S. (1981). Ten years of research on group size and helping. *Psychological Bulletin, 89,* 308–324.

Lau, R. R. (1982). Origins of health locus of control beliefs. *Journal of Personality and Social Psychology, 42,* 322–334.

Lau, R. R., and Ware, J. F., Jr. (1981). Refinements in the measurement of health-specific locus-of-control beliefs. *Medical Care, 19,* 1147–1158.

Lawton, M. P. (1980). Psychosocial and environmental approaches to the care of senile dementia patients. In J. O. Cole and J. E. Barrett (Eds.), *Psychopathology in the aged.* New York: Raven Press.

Lazarus, A. A. (1961). Group therapy of phobic disorders by systematic desensitization. *Journal of Abnormal and Social Psychology, 63,* 504–510.

Lazarus, A. A. (1971). Where do behavior therapists take their troubles? *Psychological Reports, 28,* 349–350.

Lazarus, A. A., and Wilson, G. T. (1976). Behavior modification: Clinical and experimental perspectives. In B. B. Wolman (Ed.), *The therapist's handbook.* New York: Van Nostrand Reinhold.

Lazarus, R. S. (1966). *Psychological stress and the coping process.* New York: McGraw-Hill.

Lazarus, R. S. (1969). *Patterns of adjustment and human effectiveness.* New York: McGraw-Hill.

Lazarus, R. S. (1980). The costs and benefits of denial. In S. Breznitz (Ed.), *Denial and stress.* New York: International Universities Press.

Lazarus, R. S., and Alfert, E. (1964). Short circuiting of threat by experimentally altering cognitive appraisal. *Journal of Abnormal and Social Psychology, 69,* 195–205.

Lazarus, R. S., and Folkman, S. (1984). *Stress, appraisal, and coping.* New York: Springer.

Leahey, T. H. (1984). *A history of psychology: Main currents in psychological thought* (2nd ed.). Englewood Cliffs, NJ: Prentice-Hall.

Lecky, P. (1969). *Self-consistency: A theory of personality.* Hamden, CT: Shoe String Press.

Leder, G. C. (1974). Sex differences in mathematics problem appeal as a function of problem context. *Journal of Educational Research, 67,* 351–353.

Lee, E. S. (1951). Negro intelligence and selective migration: A Philadelphia test of Klineberg's hypothesis. *American Sociological Review, 61,* 227–233.

Lefcourt, H. M. (Ed.). (1981). *Research with the locus of control construct: Vol. 1. Assessment methods.* New York: Academic Press.

Lefcourt, H. M. (1982). *Locus of control: Current trends in theory and research* (2nd ed.). Hillsdale, NJ: Erlbaum.

Lefcourt, H. M. (Ed.). (1984). *Research with the locus of control construct: Vol. 3. Extensions and limitations.* Orlando, FL: Academic Press.

Leidig, M. W. (1981). Violence against women: A feminist-psychological analysis. In S. Cox (Ed.), *Female psychology: The emerging self.* New York: St. Martin's Press.

Leith, G. O. M. (1972). The relationships between intelligence, personality, and creativity under two conditions of stress. *British Journal of Educational Psychology, 42,* 240–247.

Leon, G. R., McNally, C., and Ben-Porath, Y. S. (1989). Personality characteristics, mood, and coping patterns in a successful North Pole expedition team. *Journal of Research in Personality, 23,* 162–179.

Leonard, K. E. (1989). The impact of explicit aggressive and implicit nonaggressive cues on aggression in intoxicated and sober males. *Personality and Social Psychology Bulletin, 15,* 390–400.

Lerner, B. (1988). Judge's questions versus specialist's questions. *Contemporary Psychology, 33,* 887–889.

Lerner, M. J. (1970). The desire for justice and reaction to victims. In J. R. Macaulay and L. Berkowitz (Eds.), *Altruism and helping behavior.* New York: Academic Press.

Levine, S. (1966). Sex differences in the brain. *Scientific American, 214*(4), 84–90.

Levinson, D., Darrow, C., Klein, M., Levinson, M., and McKee, B. (1978). *The seasons of a man's life.* New York: Knopf.

Levy, L. H. (1954). *A study of relative information value in personal construct theory.* Unpublished doctoral dissertation, Ohio State University.

Levy, L. H. (1970). *Conceptions of personality.* New York: Random House.

Lewin, K. (1935). *A dynamic theory of personality.* New York: McGraw-Hill.

Lewinsohn, P. M., and Shaffer, M. (1971). Use of home observations as an integral part of the treatment of depression: Preliminary report and case studies. *Journal of Consulting and Clinical Psychology, 37,* 87–94.

Lewis, M. (1969). Infants' responses to facial stimuli during the first year of life. *Developmental Psychology, 1,* 75–86.

Leyens, J. P., Camino, L., Parke, R., and Berkowitz, L. (1975). Effects of movie violence on aggression in a field setting as a function of group dominance and cohesion. *Journal of Personality and Social Psychology, 32,* 346–360.

Lickona, T. (Ed.). (1975). *Morality: Theory, research, and social issues.* New York: Holt, Rinehart and Winston.

Liebert, R. M., and Sprafkin, J. (1988). *The early window: Effects of television on children and youth* (3rd ed.). Oxford, England: Pergamon Press.

Liebert, R. S. (1983). *Michelangelo: A psychoanalytic study of his life and images.* New Haven, CT: Yale University Press.

Lifton, R. (Ed.). (1974). *Explorations in psychohistory.* New York: Simon and Schuster.

Linz, D. G., Donnerstein, E., and Penrod, S. (1988). Effects of long-term exposure to violent and sexually degrading depictions of women. *Journal of Personality and Social Psychology, 55,* 758–768.

Lipinski, D. P., Black, J. L., Nelson, R. O., and Ciminero, A. R. (1975). Influence of motivational variables on the reactivity and reliability of self-recording. *Journal of Consulting and Clinical Psychology, 43,* 637–646.

Liverant, S. (1958). The use of Rotter's social learning theory in developing a personality inventory. *Psychological Monographs, 72*(2, Whole No. 455).

Liverant, S. (1960). Intelligence: A concept in need of re-examination. *Journal of Consulting Psychology, 24,* 101–110.

Lloyd, C., and Chang, A. F. (1979). The usefulness of distinguishing between a defensive and nondefensive external locus of control. *Journal of Research in Personality, 13,* 316–325.

Locke, E. A. (1971). Is "behavior therapy" behavioristic? An analysis of Wolpe's psychotherapeutic methods. *Psychological Bulletin, 76,* 318–327.

Locksley, A., and Colten, M. E. (1979). Psychological androgyny: A case of mistaken identity? *Journal of Personality and Social Psychology, 37,* 1017–1031.

Loehlin, J. C., Willerman, L., and Horn, J. M. (1985). Personality resemblances in adoptive families when the children are late-adolescent or adult. *Journal of Personality and Social Psychology, 48,* 376–392.

Loehlin, J. C., Willerman, L., and Horn, J. M. (1987). Personality resemblance in adoptive families: A 10-year follow-up. *Journal of Personality and Social Psychology, 53,* 961–969.

Loehlin, J. C., Willerman, L., and Horn, J. M. (1988). Human behavior genetics. In M. R. Rosenzweig and L. W. Porter (Eds.), *Annual review of psychology.* Palo Alto, CA: Annual Reviews.

London, P. (1964). *The modes and morals of psychotherapy.* New York: Holt, Rinehart and Winston.

London, P. (1970). The rescuers: Motivational hypotheses about Christians who saved Jews from the Nazis. In J. Macaulay and L. Berkowitz (Eds.), *Altruism and helping behavior.* New York: Academic Press.

Lorenz, K. (1974). *The eight deadly sins of civilized man.* New York: Harcourt Brace Jovanovich.

Lubinski, D., Tellegen, A., and Butcher, J. N. (1981). The relationship between androgyny and subjective indicators of emotional well-being. *Journal of Personality and Social Psychology, 40,* 722–730.

Ludwick-Rosenthal, R., and Neufeld, R. W. J. (1988). Stress management during noxious medical procedures: An evaluative review of outcome studies. *Psychological Bulletin, 104,* 326–342.

Lysak, H., Rule, B. G., and Dobbs, A. R. (1989). Conceptions of aggression: Prototype or defining features? *Personality and Social Psychology Bulletin, 15,* 233–243.

Maccoby, E. E. (1990). Gender and relationships: A developmental account. *American Psychologist, 45,* 513–520.

Maccoby, E. E., and Jacklin, C. N. (1974). *The psychology of sex differences.* Stanford, CA: Stanford University Press.

Maccoby, E. E., and Wilson, W. C. (1957). Identification and observational learning from films. *Journal of Abnormal and Social Psychology, 55,* 76–87.

MacKinnon, D. W. (1965). Personality and the realization of creative potential. *American Psychologist, 20,* 273–281.

Maddi, S. R. (1989). *Personality theories: A comparative analysis* (5th ed.). Chicago: Dorsey Press.

Maddi, S. R., Kobasa, S. C., and Hoover, M. (1979). An alienation test. *Journal of Humanistic Psychology, 19,* 72–76.

Maddux, J. E., Norton, L. W., and Stoltenberg, C. D. (1986). Self-efficacy expectancy, outcome expectancy, and outcome value: Relative effects on behavioral intentions. *Journal of Personality and Social Psychology, 51,* 783–789.

Magnusson, D., and Endler, N. S. (Eds.). (1977). *Personality at the crossroads: Current issues in interactional psychology.* Hillsdale, NJ: Erlbaum.

Maher, B. A. (1966). *Principles of psychopathology: An experimental approach.* New York: McGraw-Hill.

Maher, B. (Ed.). (1969). *Clinical psychology and personality: The selected papers of George Kelly.* New York: Wiley.

Mahler, M. S. (1968). *On human symbiosis and the vicissitudes of individuation.* New York: International Universities Press.

Mahony, P. J. (1986). *Freud and the Rat Man.* New Haven, CT: Yale University Press.

Mahrer, A. R. (1956). The role of expectancy in delayed reinforcement. *Journal of Experimental Psychology, 52,* 101–106.

Major, B., Carnevale, P. J. D., and Deaux, K. (1981). A different perspective on androgyny: Evaluations of masculine and feminine personality characteristics. *Journal of Personality and Social Psychology, 41,* 988–1001.

Major, B., McFarlin, D. B., and Gagnon, D. (1984). Overworked and underpaid: On the nature of gender differences in personal entitlement. *Journal of Personality and Social Psychology, 47,* 1399–1412.

Mallick, S. K., and McCandless, B. R. (1966). A study of catharsis of aggression. *Journal of Personality and Social Psychology, 4,* 591–596.

Maloney, M. P., and Ward, M. P. (1976). *Psychological assessment: A conceptual approach.* New York: Oxford University Press.

Manaster, G. J., and Corsini, R. J. (1982). *Individual Psychology.* Itasca, IL: Peacock.

Mandler, G., and Sarason, S. B. (1952). A study of anxiety and learning. *Journal of Abnormal and Social Psychology, 47,* 166–173.

Marin, P. (1975, October). The new narcissism. *Harper's.*

Mark, V. H., and Ervin, F. R. (1970). *Violence and the brain.* Harper and Row.

Marks, G., Richardson, J. L., Graham, J. W., and Levine, A. (1986). Role of health locus of control beliefs and expectations of treatment efficacy in adjustment to cancer. *Journal of Personality and Social Psychology, 51,* 443–450.

Markus, H. (1977). Self-schemata and processing information about the self. *Journal of Personality and Social Psychology, 35,* 63–78.

Markus, H. (1983). Self-knowledge: An expanded view. *Journal of Personality, 51,* 543–565.

Markus, H., and Kunda, Z. (1986). Stability and malleability of the self-concept. *Journal of Personality and Social Psychology, 51,* 858–866.

Markus, H., and Wurf, E. (1987). The dynamic self-concept: A social psychological perspective. In M. R. Rosenzweig and L. W. Porter (Eds.), *Annual review of psychology.* Palo Alto, CA: Annual Reviews.

Marlatt, G. A. (1975). *Addictions: A cognitive behavioral treatment approach* (Casette recording). New York: Guilford Press, BMA Audio Casettes.

Marsden, G. (1971). Content-analysis studies of psychotherapy: 1954 through 1968. In A. E. Bergin and S. L. Garfield (Eds.), *Handbook of psychotherapy and behavior change: An empirical analysis.* New York: Wiley.

Marsh, H. W., and Richards, G. E. (1988). Tennessee Self Concept Scale: Reliability, internal structure, and construct validity. *Journal of Personality and Social Psychology, 55,* 612–624.

Martin, C. L., and Halverson, C. F., Jr. (1981). A schematic processing model of sex typing and stereotyping in children. *Child Development, 52,* 1119–1134.

Martin, R. A., and Lefcourt, H. M. (1983). Sense of humor as a moderator of the relation between stressors and moods. *Journal of Personality and Social Psychology, 45,* 1313–1324.

Masling, J. (Ed.). (1983). *Empirical studies of psycho-analytical theories,* Vol. I. Hillsdale, NJ: Erlbaum.

Masling, J. (Ed.). (1986). *Empirical studies of psychoanalytic theories,* Vol. II. Hillsdale, NJ: Analytic Press.

ABRAHAM H. MASLOW: A MEMORIAL VOLUME. (1972). Monterey, CA: Brooks/Cole.

Maslow, A. H. (1950). *Self-actualizing people: A study of psychological health. Personality symposia: Symposium #1 on values.* New York: Grune and Stratton.

Maslow, A. H. (1962). *Toward a psychology of being.* Princeton, NJ: Van Nostrand.

Maslow, A. H. (1964). *Religions, values, and peak experiences.* Columbus, OH: Ohio State University Press.

Maslow, A. H. (1970). *Motivation and personality* (2nd ed.). New York: Harper and Row.

Maslow, A. H. (1987). *Motivation and personality* (3rd ed.). New York: Harper and Row. (revised by R. Frager, J. Fadiman, C. McReynolds, and R. Cox).

Mason, J. (1971). A re-evaluation of the concept of "nonspecificity" in stress theory. *Journal of Psychiatric Research, 8,* 325–333.

Masson, J. M. (1985). *The assault on truth: Freud's suppression of the seduction theory.* New York: Penguin Books.

Matarazzo, J. D. (1972). *Wechsler's measurement and appraisal of adult intelligence* (5th and enlarged ed.). Baltimore, MD: Williams and Wilkins.

Mathes, E. W., and Kahn, A. (1975). Diffusion of responsibility and extreme behavior. *Journal of Personality and Social Psychology, 31,* 881–886.

Mathews, K. E., Jr., and Canon, L. K. (1975). Environmental noise level as a determinant of helping behavior. *Journal of Personality and Social Psychology, 32,* 571–577.

Matthews, K. A. (1984). Assessment of Type A, anger, and hostility in epidemiological studies of cardiovascular disease. In A. Ostfield and E. Eaker (Eds.), *Measuring psychosocial variables in epidemiological studies of cardiovascular disease.* Bethesda, MD: National Institute of Health.

Matthews, K. A., Batson, C. D., Horn, J., and Rosenman, R. H. (1981). "Principles in his nature which interest him in the fortune of others . . .": The heritability of empathic concern for others. *Journal of Personality, 49,* 237–247.

Matthews, K. A., and Brunson, B. I. (1979). Allocation of attention and the Type A coronary-prone behavior pattern. *Journal of Personality and Social Psychology, 37,* 2081–2090.

Matthews, K. A., and Glass, D. C. (1981). Type A behavior, stressful life events, and coronary heart disease. In B. S. Dohrenwend and B. P. Dohrenwend (Eds.), *Stressful life events and their contexts.* New York: Prodist.

Matthews, K. A., Krantz, D. S., Dembroski, T. M., and MacDougall, J. M. (1982). Unique and common variance in structured interview and Jenkins Activity Survey measures of the Type A behavior pattern. *Journal of Personality and Social Psychology, 42,* 303–313.

Matthews, K. A., and Rodin, J. (1989). Women's changing work roles: Impact on health, family, and public policy. *American Psychologist, 44,* 1389–1393.

McAdams, D. P. (1988). Biography, narrative, and lives: An introduction. *Journal of Personality, 56,* 1–18.

McCartney, K., Harris, M. J., and Bernieri, F. (1990). Growing up and growing apart: A developmental meta-analysis of twin studies. *Psychological Bulletin, 107,* 226–237.

McClelland, D. C. (1951). *Personality.* New York: Dryden Press.

McClelland, D. C. (1961). *The achieving society.* Princeton, NJ: Van Nostrand.

McClelland, D. C. (1972). Opinions predict opinions: So what else is new? *Journal of Consulting and Clinical Psychology, 38,* 325–326.

McClelland, D. C. (1975). *Power: The inner experience.* New York: Irvington.

McClelland, D. C. (1980). Motive dispositions: The merits of operant and respondent measures. In L. Wheeler (Ed.), *Review of personality and social psychology,* 1. Beverly Hills, CA: Sage Publications.

McClelland, D. C. (1981). Is personality consistent? In A. I. Rabin, J. Aronoff, A. M. Barclay, and R. A. Zucker (Eds.), *Further explorations in personality.* New York: Wiley.

McClelland, D. C. (1982). The need for power, sympathetic activation, and illness. *Motivation and Emotion, 6,* 31–41.

McClelland, D. C. (1985). *Human motivation.* Glenview, IL: Scott, Foresman.

McClelland, D. C. (1989). Motivational factors in health and disease. *American Psychologist, 44,* 675–683.

McClelland, D. C., Atkinson, J. W., Clark, R. W., and Lowell, E. L. (1953). *The achievement motive.* New York: Appleton-Century-Crofts.

McClelland, D. C., Clark, R. A., Roby, T. B., and Atkinson, J. W. (1949). The effect of the need for achievement on thematic apperception. *Journal of Experimental Psychology, 37,* 242–255.

McClelland, D. C., Koestner, R., and Weinberger, J. (1989). How do self-attributed and implicit motives differ? *Psychological Review, 96,* 690–702.

McCrae, R. R., and Costa, P. T., Jr. (1986). Clinical assessment can benefit from recent advances in personality psychology. *American Psychologist, 41,* 1001–1002.

McCrae, R. R., and Costa, P. T., Jr. (1989). Reinterpreting the Myers-Briggs Type Indicator from the perspective of the five-factor model of personality. *Journal of Personality, 57,* 17–40.

McFarlin, D. B., and Blascovich, J. (1981). Effects of self-esteem and performance feedback on future affective preferences and cognitive expectations. *Journal of Personality and Social Psychology, 40,* 521–531.

McGinnies, E. (1949). Emotionality and perceptual defense. *Psychological Review, 56,* 244–251.

Mead, G. H. (1934). *Mind, self, and society.* Chicago: University of Chicago Press.

Mead, M. (1949). *Male and female.* New York: Morrow.

Mednick, M. T. (1989). On the politics of psychological constructs: Stop the bandwagon, I want to get off. *American Psychologist, 44,* 1118–1123.

Meehl, P. E. (1962). Schizotaxia, schizotypy, and schizophrenia. *American Psychologist, 17,* 827–838.

Mehrabian, A. (1968). Male and female scales of the tendency to achieve. *Educational and Psychological Measurement, 28,* 493–502.

Mehrabian, A., and Epstein, N. (1972). A measure of emotional empathy. *Journal of Personality, 40,* 525–543.

Mehrabian, A., and Ksionzky, S. (1974). *A theory of affiliation.* Lexington, MA: Heath.

Meichenbaum, D. (1977). *Cognitive-behavior modification.* New York: Plenum.

Meichenbaum, D., Price, R., Phares, E. J., McCormick, N., and Hyde, J. (1989). *Exploring choices: The psychology of adjustment.* Glenview, IL: Scott, Foresman.

Meier, C. A. (1984). *The psychology of C. G. Jung: Vol. 1. The unconscious in its empirical manifestations: With special reference to the association experiment of C. G. Jung.* Boston: Sigor Press.

Melamed, B. G., and Siegel, L. J. (1975). Reduction of anxiety in children facing hospitalization and surgery by use of filmed modeling. *Journal of Consulting and Clinical Psychology, 43,* 511–521.

Meyer, A. J., Nash, J. D., McAlister, A. L., Maccoby, N., and Farquhar, J. W. (1980). Skills training in a cardiovascular education campaign. *Journal of Consulting and Clinical Psychology, 48,* 129–142.

Midlarsky, E. (1971). Aiding under stress: The effects of competence, dependency, visibility, and fatalism. *Journal of Personality, 39,* 132–149.

Midlarsky, E., and Midlarsky, M. (1973). Some determinants of aiding under experimentally induced stress. *Journal of Personality, 41,* 305–327.

Mikulincer, M. (1989). Cognitive interference and learned helplessness: The effects of off-task cognitions on performance following unsolvable problems. *Journal of Personality and Social Psychology, 57,* 129–135.

Milgram, S. (1963). Behavioral study of obedience. *Journal of Abnormal and Social Psychology, 67,* 371–378.

Milgram, S. (1964). Issues in the study of obedience: A reply to Baumrind. *American Psychologist, 19,* 848–852.

Milgram, S. (1974). *Obedience to authority.* New York: Harper and Row.

Miller, A. G. (1986). *The obedience experiments: A case study of controversy in social science*. New York: Praeger.

Miller, N., and Carlson, M. (1990). Valid theory-testing meta-analyses further question the negative state relief model of helping. *Psychological Bulletin, 107*, 215–225.

Miller, N. E. (1941). The frustration-aggression hypothesis. *Psychological Review, 48*, 337–342.

Miller, N. E. (1948). Theory and experiment relating psychoanalytic displacement to stimulus-response generalization. *Journal of Abnormal and Social Psychology, 43*, 155–178.

Miller, N. E., and Dollard, J. (1941). *Social learning and imitation*. New Haven, CT: Yale University Press.

Miller, P. A., and Eisenberg, N. (1988). The relation of empathy to aggressive and externalizing/antisocial behavior. *Psychological Bulletin, 103*, 324–344.

Mills, C. A. (1942). *Climate makes the man*. New York: Harper.

Mischel, W. (1966). Theory and research on the antecedents of self-imposed delay of reward. In B. A. Maher (Ed.), *Progress in experimental personality research* (Vol. 3). New York: Academic Press.

Mischel, W. (1968). *Personality and assessment*. New York: Wiley.

Mischel, W. (1972). Direct versus indirect personality assessment: Evidence and implications. *Journal of Consulting and Clinical Psychology, 38*, 319–324.

Mischel, W. (1973). Toward a cognitive social learning reconceptualization of personality. *Psychological Review, 80*, 252–283.

Mischel, W. (1979). On the interface of cognition and personality: Beyond the person-situation debate. *American Psychologist, 34*, 740–754.

Mischel, W., and Masters, J. C. (1966). Effects of probability of reward attainment on responses to frustration. *Journal of Personality and Social Psychology, 3*, 390–396.

Mischel, W., Shoda, Y, and Peake, P. K. (1988). The nature of adolescent competencies predicted by preschool delay of gratification. *Journal of Personality and Social Psychology, 54*, 687–696.

Mitchell, C., and Stuart, R. B. (1984). Effect of self-efficacy on dropout from obesity treatment. *Journal of Consulting and Clinical Psychology, 52*, 1100–1101.

Money, J. (1965). Psychosexual differentiation. In J. Money (Ed.), *Sex research: New developments*. New York: Holt, Rinehart and Winston.

Money, J. (1975). Ablatiopenis: Normal male infant-sex reassigned as a girl. *Archives of Sexual Behavior, 4*, 65–72.

Money, J., and Ehrhardt, A. (1972). *Man and woman, boy and girl*. Baltimore, MD: Johns Hopkins University Press.

Morawski, J. G. (1987). The troubled quest for masculinity, femininity, and androgyny. In P. Shaver and C. Hendrick (Eds.), *Sex and gender: Review of Personality and Social Psychology, 7.* Beverly Hills, CA: Sage Publications.

Morgan, C. D., and Murray, H. A. (1935). A method for investigating fantasies: The Thematic Apperception Test. *Archives of Neurology and Psychiatry, 34*, 289–306.

Moser, C. G., and Dyck, D. G. (1989). Type A behavior, uncontrollability, and the activation of hostile self-schema responding. *Journal of Research in Personality, 23*, 248–267.

Moskowitz, D. S., and Schwartzman, E. E. (1989). Painting group portraits: Studying life outcomes for aggressive and withdrawn children. *Journal of Personality, 57*, 723–746.

Moss, H. A. (1967). Sex, age, and state as determinants of mother-infant interaction. *Merrill-Palmer Quarterly, 13*, 19–36.

Mowrer, O. H. (1960). *Learning theory and behavior.* New York: Wiley.

Munroe, R. L. (1955). *Schools of psychoanalytic thought.* New York: Dryden Press.

Murphy, C. M., and O'Leary, K. D. (1989). Psychological aggression predicts physical aggression in early marriage. *Journal of Consulting and Clinical Psychology, 57,* 579–582.

Murray, H. A. (and collaborators). (1938). *Explorations in personality.* New York: Oxford University Press.

Murray, H. A. (1951). Uses of the Thematic Apperception Test. *American Journal of Psychiatry, 10,* 577–581.

Mussen, P., and Eichorn, D. (1988). Mary Cover Jones (1896–1987). *American Psychologist, 43,* 818.

Mussen, P., and Eisenberg-Berg, N. (1977). *Roots of caring, sharing, and helping.* San Francisco: W. H. Freeman.

Myers, A. M., and Gonda, G. (1982). Empirical validation of the Bem Sex-Role Inventory. *Journal of Personality and Social Psychology, 43,* 304–318.

Myers, I. B. (1980). *Introduction to type* (3rd ed.). Palo Alto, CA: Consulting Psychologists Press.

Myerscough, R., and Taylor, S. (1985). The effects of marijuana on human physical aggression. *Journal of Personality and Social Psychology, 49,* 1541–1546.

National Institute of Mental Health (NIMH). (1982). *Television and behavior: Ten years of scientific progress and implications for the eighties* (Vols. 1 and 2). D. Pearl, L. Bouthilet, and J. Lazar (Eds.). Washington, DC: U.S. Government Printing Office.

Neisser, U. (1979). The concept of intelligence. In R. J. Sternberg and D. K. Detterman (Eds.), *Human intelligence: Perspectives on its theory and measurement.* Norwood, NJ: Ablex.

Neisser, U. (1980). On "social knowing." *Personality and Social Psychology Bulletin, 6,* 601–605.

Nezu, A. M., Nezu, C. M., and Blissett, S. E. (1988). Sense of humor as a moderator of the relation between stressful events and psychological distress: A prospective analysis. *Journal of Personality and Social Psychology, 54,* 520–525.

Nicholls, J. G. (1972). Creativity in the person who will never produce anything original and useful: The concept of creativity as a normally distributed trait. *American Psychologist, 27,* 717–727.

Nicholls, J. G. (1975). Causal attributions and other achievement-related cognitions: Effects of task outcome, attainment value, and sex. *Journal of Personality and Social Psychology, 31,* 379–389.

Noller, P., Law, H., and Comrey, A. L. (1987). Cattell, Comrey, and Eysenck personality factors compared: More evidence for the robust five factors? *Journal of Personality and Social Psychology, 53,* 775–782.

Novaco, R. W. (1977). Stress inoculation: A cognitive therapy for anger and its application to a case of depression. *Journal of Consulting and Clinical Psychology, 45,* 600–608.

Olds, D. E., and Shaver, P. (1980). Masculinity, femininity, academic performance, and health: Further evidence concerning the androgyny controversy. *Journal of Personality, 48,* 323–341.

O'Leary, K. D., and Becker, W. C. (1967). Behavior modification of an adjustment class: A token reinforcement program. *Exceptional Children, 33,* 637–642.

Oliner, S. P., and Oliner, P. M. (1988). *The altruistic personality: Rescuers of Jews in Nazi Europe.* New York: Free Press.

Olson, R. A., and Elliott, C. H. (1983). Behavioral medicine: Assessment, patient management, and treatment interventions. In C. E. Walker (Ed.), *The handbook of clinical psychology: Theory, research, and practice* (Vol. 2). Chicago: Dorsey Press.

Osborne, R. T. (1960). Racial differences in mental growth and school achievement: A longitudinal study. *Psychological Reports, 7,* 233–239.

Osen, L. (1974). *Women in mathematics.* Cambridge, MA: M.I.T. Press.

Osgood, C. E., Suci, G. J., and Tannenbaum, P. H. (1957). *The measurement of meaning.* Urbana, IL: University of Illinois Press.

Osler, W. (1892). *Lectures on angina pectoris and allied states.* New York: Appleton.

OSS Assessment Staff. (1948). *Assessment of men: Selection of personnel for the Office of Strategic Services.* New York: Rinehart.

Paige, J. (1966). Letters from Jenny: An approach to the clinical analysis of personality structure by computer. In P. Stone (Ed.), *The general inquirer: A computer approach to content analysis.* Cambridge, MA: M.I.T. Press.

Parke, R., Berkowitz, L., Leyens, P., West, S., and Sebastian, R. (1977). Some effects of violent and nonviolent movies on the behavior of juvenile delinquents. In L. Berkowitz (Ed.), *Advances in experimental social psychology* (Vol. 10). New York: Academic Press.

Parker, K. C., Hanson, R. K., and Hunsley, J. (1988). MMPI, Rorschach, and WAIS: A meta-analytic comparison of reliability, stability, and validity. *Psychological Bulletin, 103,* 367–373.

Parkes, K. R. (1984). Locus of control, cognitive appraisal, and coping in stressful episodes. *Journal of Personality and Social Psychology, 46,* 655–668.

Patterson, G. R. (1977). Naturalistic observation in clinical assessment. *Journal of Abnormal Child Psychology, 5,* 307–322.

Patterson, G. R. (1979). Treatment for children with conduct problems: A review of outcome studies. In S. Feshbach and A. Fraczek (Eds.), *Aggression and behavior change: Biological and social processes.* New York: Praeger.

Pavlov, I. P. (1927). *Conditioned reflexes.* London: Oxford University Press.

Peabody, D., and Goldberg, L. R. (1989). Some determinants of factor structures from personality-trait descriptors. *Journal of Personality and Social Psychology, 57,* 552–567.

Pederson, F. A. (1958). *Consistency data on the role construct repertory test.* Unpublished master's thesis, Ohio State University.

Pederson, N. L., Plomin, R., McClearn, G. E., and Friberg, L. (1988). Neuroticism, extraversion, and related traits in adult twins reared apart and reared together. *Journal of Personality and Social Psychology, 55,* 950–957.

Pedhazur, E. J., and Tetenbaum, T. J. (1979). Bem Sex Role Inventory: A theoretical and methodological critique. *Journal of Personality and Social Psychology, 37,* 996–1016.

Perry, D. G., and Perry, L. C. (1975). Observational learning in children: Effects of sex of model and subject's sex role behavior. *Journal of Personality and Social Psychology, 31,* 1083–1088.

Pervin, L. A. (1978). *Current controversies and issues in personality.* New York: Wiley.

Pervin, L. A. (1985). Personality: Current controversies, issues, and directions. In M. R. Rosenzweig and L. W. Porter (Eds.), *Annual review of psychology.* Palo Alto, CA: Annual Reviews.

Pervin, L. A. (1989). *Personality: Theory and research* (5th ed.). New York: Wiley.

Peterson, C., and Seligman, M. E. P. (1984). Causal explanations as a risk factor for depression: Theory and evidence. *Psychological Review, 91,* 347–374.

Peterson, C., and Seligman, M. E. P. (1987). Explanatory style and illness. *Journal of Personality, 55,* 237–265.

Peterson, D. R. (1965). Scope and generality of verbally defined personality factors. *Psychological Review, 72,* 48–59.

Phares, E. J. (1955). *Changes in expectancy in skill and chance situations.* Unpublished doctoral dissertation, Ohio State University.

Phares, E. J. (1957). Expectancy changes in skill and chance situations. *Journal of Abnormal and Social Psychology, 54,* 339–342.

Phares, E. J. (1962). Perceptual threshold decrements as a function of skill and chance expectancies. *Journal of Psychology, 53,* 399–407.

Phares, E. J. (1972). A social learning theory approach to psychopathology. In J. B. Rotter, J. E. Chance, and E. J. Phares (Eds.), *Applications of a social learning theory of personality.* New York: Holt, Rinehart and Winston.

Phares, E. J. (1976). *Locus of control in personality.* Morristown, NJ: General Learning Press.

Phares, E. J. (1978). Locus of control. In H. London and J. E. Exner (Eds.), *Dimensions of personality.* New York: Wiley-Interscience.

Phares, E. J. (1979). Defensiveness and perceived control. In L. C. Perlmuter and R. A. Monty (Eds.), *Choice and perceived control.* Hillsdale, NJ: Erlbaum.

Phares, E. J. (1980). Rotter's social learning theory. In G. M. Gazda and R. J. Corsini (Eds.), *Theories of learning: A comparative approach.* Itasca, IL: Peacock.

Phares, E. J. (1988). *Clinical psychology: Concepts, methods, and profession* (3rd ed.). Chicago: Dorsey Press.

Phares, E. J., and Erskine, N. (1984). The measurement of selfism. *Educational and Psychological Measurement, 44,* 597–608.

Phares, E. J., and Lamiell, J. T. (1974). Relationship of internal-external control to defensive preferences. *Journal of Consulting and Clinical Psychology, 42,* 872–878.

Phares, E. J., and Lamiell, J. T. (1975). Internal-external control, interpersonal judgments of others in need, and attribution of responsibility. *Journal of Personality, 43,* 23–38.

Phares, E. J., and Lamiell, J. T. (1977). Personality. In M. R. Rosenzweig and L. W. Porter (Eds.), *Annual review of psychology.* Palo Alto, CA: Annual Reviews.

Phares, E. J., and Rotter, J. B. (1956). An effect of the situation on psychological testing. *Journal of Consulting Psychology, 20,* 291–293.

Phares, E. J., and Wilson, K. G. (1972). Role of outcome severity, situational ambiguity, and internal-external control. *Journal of Personality, 40,* 392–406.

Pheterson, G. I., Kiesler, S. B., and Goldberg, P. A. (1971). Evaluation of the performance of women as a function of their sex, achievement, and personal history. *Journal of Personality and Social Psychology, 19,* 114–118.

Philips, D. P., and Carstensen, L. L. (1986). Clustering of teenage suicides after television news stories about suicide. *New England Journal of Medicine, 315,* 685–689.

Phillips, S. L., and Fischer, C. S. (1981). Measuring social support networks in general populations. In B. S. Dohrenwend and B. P. Dohrenwend (Eds.), *Stressful life events and their contexts.* New York: Prodist.

Piaget, J. (1932). *The moral judgment of the child.* New York: Harcourt, Brace.

Piaget, J. (1951). *The child's conception of the world.* New York: Humanities Press.

Piper, W. E., Wogan, M., and Getter, H. (1972). Social learning theory predictors of termination in psychotherapy. In J. B. Rotter, J. E. Chance, and E. J. Phares (Eds.), *Applications of a social learning theory of personality.* New York: Holt, Rinehart and Winston.

Plomin, R. (1987). *Nature, nurture, and human development.* Washington, DC: Federation of Behavioral, Psychological, Cognitive Sciences.

Plomin, R. (1989). Environment and genes: Determinants of behavior. *American Psychologist, 44,* 105–111.

Plomin, R., and Foch, T. T. (1980). A twin study of objectively assessed personality in childhood. *Journal of Personality and Social Psychology, 39,* 680–688.

Plomin, R., and Foch, T. T. (1981). A twin study of objectively assessed personality in childhood. *Journal of Personality and Social Psychology, 39,* 680–688.

Poch, S. (1952). *Study of changes in personal constructs as related to interpersonal prediction and its outcomes.* Unpublished doctoral dissertation, Ohio State University.

Powers, W. T. (1973). *Behavior: The control of perception.* Chicago: Aldine.

Privette, G. (1983). Peak experience, peak performance, and flow: A comparative analysis of positive human experience. *Journal of Personality and Social Psychology, 45,* 1361–1368.

Prociuk, T. J., and Breen, L. J. (1977). Internal-external locus of control and information-seeking in a college academic situation. *Journal of Social Psychology, 101,* 309–310.

Provence, S., and Lipton, R. C. (1962). *Infants in institutions.* New York: International Universities Press.

Quay, H. C. (1964). Personality dimensions in delinquent males as inferred from the factor analysis of behavior ratings. *Journal of Research in Crime and Delinquency, 1,* 33–37.

Quinn, S. (1987). *A mind of her own: The life of Karen Horney.* New York: Summit Books.

Rabin, A. I., Aronoff, J., Barclay, A. M., and Zucker, R. A. (Eds.). (1981). *Further explorations in personality.* New York: Wiley-Interscience.

Ragland, D. R., and Brand, R. J. (1988). Type A behavior and mortality from coronary heart disease. *New England Journal of Medicine, 318,* 65–69.

Rahe, R. H. (1972). Subjects' recent life changes and their near-future illness susceptibility. In Z. J. Lipowski (Ed.), *Advances in psychosomatic medicine: Vol. 8. Psychosocial aspects of physical illness.* Basel, Switzerland: S. Karger.

Raimy, V. C. (1948). Self-reference in counseling interviews. *Journal of Consulting Psychology, 12,* 153–163.

Rapaport, D. (1959). The structure of psychoanalytic theory: A systematizing attempt. In S. Koch (Ed.), *Psychology: A study of a science* (Vol. 3). New York: McGraw-Hill.

Raven, J. C. (1938). *Progressive matrices.* London: Lewis.

Reinisch, J. M., and Sanders, S. A. (1986). A test of sex differences in aggressive response to hypothetical conflict situations. *Journal of Personality and Social Psychology, 50,* 1045–1049.

Repetti, R. L. (1984). Determinants of children's sex stereotyping: Parental sex-role traits and television viewing. *Personality and Social Psychology Bulletin, 10,* 457–468.

Repetti, R. L., Matthews, K. A., and Waldron, I. (1989). Employment and women's health: Effects of paid employment on women's mental and physical health. *American Psychologist, 44,* 1394–1401.

Rescorla, R. A. (1988). Pavlovian conditioning: It's not what you think it is. *American Psychologist, 43,* 151–160.

Ribble, M. A. (1944). Infantile experience in relation to personality development. In J. McV. Hunt (Ed.), *Personality and the behavior disorders* (Vol. 2). New York: Ronald Press.

Rice, M. E., and Grusec, J. E. (1975). Saying and doing: Effects on observer performance. *Journal of Personality and Social Psychology, 32,* 584–593.

Richter, C. P. (1957). On the phenomenon of sudden death in animals and man. *Psychosomatic Medicine, 19,* 191–198.

Riggio, R. E., Lippa, R., and Salinas, C. (1990). The display of personality in expressive movement. *Journal of Research in Personality, 24,* 16–31.

Ritchie, E., and Phares, E. J. (1969). Attitude change as a function of internal-external control and communication status. *Journal of Personality, 37,* 429–443.

Roberts, A. A. (1985). Biofeedback: Research, training, and clinical roles. *American Psychologist, 40,* 938–941.

Roberts, D. F., and Maccoby, N. (1985). Effects of mass communication. In G. Lindzey and E. Aronson (Eds.), *Handbook of social psychology* (3rd ed.). Reading, MA: Addison-Wesley.

Robins, L. N. (1966). *Deviant children grown up.* Baltimore, MD: Wilkins.

Rodin, J. (1983). Behavioral medicine: Beneficial effects of self-control training in aging. *International Review of Applied Psychology, 32,* 153–181.

Rodin, J. (1986a). Aging and health: Effects of the sense of control. *Science, 233,* 1271–1276.

Rodin, J. (1986b). Health, control, and aging. In M. Baltes and P. Baltes (Eds.), *Aging and control.* Hillsdale, NJ: Erlbaum.

Rodin, J., and Langer, E. J. (1977). Long-term effects of a control-relevant intervention with the institutionalized aged. *Journal of Personality and Social Psychology, 35,* 897–902.

Rodin, J., and Salovey, P. (1989). Health psychology. In M. R. Rosenzweig and L. W. Porter (Eds.), *Annual Review of Psychology.* Palo Alto, CA: Annual Reviews.

Rodin, J., Timko, C., and Harris, S. (1986). The construct of control: Biological and psychological correlates. In C. Eisdorfer, M. P. Lawson, and G. L. Maddox (Eds.), *Annual review of gerontology and geriatrics.* New York: Springer.

Rodriguez, M. L., Mischel, W., and Shoda, Y. (1989). Cognitive person variables in the delay of gratification of older children at risk. *Journal of Personality and Social Psychology, 57,* 358–367.

Roe, A. (1953). A psychological study of eminent psychologists and anthropologists, and a comparison with biological and physical scientists. *Psychological Monographs General and Applied, 67*(2, Whole No. 352).

Rogers, C. R. (1951). *Client-centered therapy.* Boston: Houghton Mifflin.

Rogers, C. R. (1956). Intellectualized psychotherapy. *Contemporary Psychology, 1,* 357–358.

Rogers, C. R. (1959). A theory of therapy, personality, and interpersonal relationships, as developed in the client-centered framework. In S. Koch (Ed.), *Psychology: A study of a science* (Vol. 3). New York: McGraw-Hill.

Rogers, C. R. (1961). *On becoming a person: A therapist's view of psychotherapy.* Boston: Houghton Mifflin.

Rogers, C. R. (1967a). Autobiography. In E. G. Boring and G. Lindzey (Eds.), *A history of psychology in autobiography* (Vol. 5). New York: Appleton-Century-Crofts.

Rogers, C. R. (Ed.). (1967b). *The therapeutic relationship and its impact: A study of psychotherapy with schizophrenics.* Madison: University of Wisconsin Press.

Rogers, C. R. (1974). In retrospect: Forty-six years. *American Psychologist, 29,* 115–123.

Rogers, C. R. (1977). *Carl Rogers on personal power.* New York: Delacorte Press.

Rogers, C. R. (1980). *A way of being.* Boston: Houghton Mifflin.

Rogers, R. W. (1980). Expressions of aggression: Aggression-inhibiting effects of anonymity to authority and threatened retaliation. *Personality and Social Psychology Bulletin, 6,* 315–320.

Roos, P. E., and Cohen, L. H. (1987). Sex roles and social support as moderators of life stress adjustment. *Journal of Personality and Social Psychology, 52,* 576–585.

Rose, R. J., Koskenvuo, M., Kaprio, J., Sarna, S., and Langinvainio, H. (1988). Shared genes, shared experiences, and similarity of personality: Data from 14,288 adult Finnish co-twins. *Journal of Personality and Social Psychology, 54,* 161–171.

Rosen, B. C., and D'Andrade, R. (1959). The psychosocial origins of achievement motivation. *Sociometry, 22,* 185–218.

Rosen, S., Mickler, S. E., and Collins, J. E., II. (1987). Reactions of would-be helpers whose offer of help is spurned. *Journal of Personality and Social Psychology, 53,* 288–297.

Rosenberg, S. (1989). A study of personality in literary autobiography: An analysis of Thomas Wolfe's *Look Homeward Angel. Journal of Personality and Social Psychology, 56,* 416–430.

Rosenhan, D. L. (1970). The natural socialization of altruistic autonomy. In J. Macaulay and L. Berkowitz (Eds.), *Altruism and helping behavior.* New York: Academic Press.

Rosenhan, D. L. (1972). Learning theory and prosocial behavior. *Journal of Social Issues, 28,* 151–164.

Rosenkrantz, P., Vogel, S., Bee, H., Broverman, I., and Broverman, D. M. (1968). Sex-role stereotypes and self-concepts in college students. *Journal of Consulting and Clinical Psychology, 32,* 287–295.

Rosenzweig, S. (1941). Need-persistive and ego-defensive reactions to frustration as demonstrated by an experiment on repression. *Psychological Review, 48,* 347–349.

Rosenzweig, S. (1944). An outline of frustration theory. In J. McV. Hunt (Ed.), *Personality and the behavior disorders.* New York: Ronald Press.

Roth, D. L., Wiebe, D. J., Fillingim, R. B., and Shay, K. A. (1989). Life events, fitness, hardiness, and health: A simultaneous analysis of proposed stress-resistance effects. *Journal of Personality and Social Psychology, 57,* 136–142.

Rothbart, M. K., and Maccoby, E. E. (1966). Parents' differential reactions to sons and daughters. *Journal of Personality and Social Psychology, 4,* 237–243.

Rotter, J. B. (1954). *Social learning and clinical psychology.* Englewood Cliffs, NJ: Prentice-Hall.

Rotter, J. B. (1966). Generalized expectancies for internal versus external control of reinforcement. *Psychological Monographs, 80*(1, Whole No. 609).

Rotter, J. B. (1967a). A new scale for the measurement of interpersonal trust. *Journal of Personality, 35,* 651–665.

Rotter, J. B. (1967b). Personality theory. In H. Helson and W. Bevan (Eds.), *Contemporary approaches to psychology.* Princeton, NJ: Van Nostrand.

Rotter, J. B. (1970). Some implications of a social learning theory for the practice of psychotherapy. In D. J. Levis (Ed.), *Learning approaches to therapeutic behavior change.* Chicago: Aldine.

Rotter, J. B. (1971a). Generalized expectancies for interpersonal trust. *American Psychologist, 26,* 443–452.

Rotter, J. B. (1971b). *Clinical Psychology* (2nd ed.). Englewood Cliffs, NJ: Prentice-Hall.

Rotter, J. B. (1990). Internal versus external control of reinforcement: A case history of a variable. *American Psychologist, 45,* 489–493.

Rotter, J. B. (1975). Some problems and misconceptions related to the construct of internal versus external control of reinforcement. *Journal of Consulting and Clinical Psychology, 43,* 56–67.

Rotter, J. B. (1978). Generalized expectancies for problem solving and psychotherapy. *Cognitive Therapy and Research, 2,* 1–10.

Rotter, J. B. (1980). Interpersonal trust, trustworthiness, and gullibility. *American Psychologist, 35,* 1–7.

Rotter, J. B. (1981). The psychological situation in social learning theory. In D. Magnusson (Ed.), *Toward a psychology of situations: An interactional perspective.* Hillsdale, NJ: Erlbaum.

Rotter, J. B. (1982). *The development and application of social learning theory: Selected papers.* New York: Praeger.

Rotter, J. B., Chance, J. E., and Phares, E. J. (Eds.). (1972). *Applications of a social learning theory of personality.* New York: Holt, Rinehart and Winston.

Rotter, J. B., and Hochreich, D. J. (1975). *Personality.* Glenview, IL: Scott, Foresman.

Rotter, J. B., Liverant, S., and Crowne, D. P. (1961). The growth and extinction of expectancies in chance controlled and skill tasks. *Journal of Psychology, 52,* 161–177.

Rotter, J. B., and Rafferty, J. E. (1950). *Manual for the Rotter Incomplete Sentences Blank, college form.* New York: Psychological Corporation.

Rotter, J. B., and Wickens, D. D. (1948). The consistency and generality of ratings of "social aggressiveness" made from observations of role playing situations. *Journal of Consulting Psychology, 12,* 234–239.

Rubin, J. Z., Provenzano, F. J., and Luria, Z. (1974). The eye of the beholder: Parents' views on sex of newborns. *American Journal of Orthopsychiatry, 44,* 512–519.

Runyan, W. M. (1982). *Life histories and psychobiography: Explorations in theory and method.* New York: Oxford University Press.

Rushton, J. P. (1975). Generosity in children: Immediate and long-term effects of modeling, preaching, and moral judgment. *Journal of Personality and Social Psychology, 31,* 459–466.

Rushton, J. P. (1976). Socialization and the altruistic behavior of children. *Psychological Bulletin, 83,* 898–913.

Rushton, J. P. (1980). *Altruism, socialization, and society.* Englewood Cliffs, NJ: Prentice-Hall.

Rushton, J. P. (1989). Genetic similarity, human altruism, and group selection. *Behavioral and Brain Sciences, 12,* 503–559.

Rushton, J. P., Chrisjohn, R. D., and Fekken, G. C. (1981). The altruistic personality and the Self-Report Altruism Scale. *Personality and Individual Differences, 2,* 293–302.

Rushton, J. P., Fulker, D. W., Neale, M. C., Nias, D. K. B., and Eysenck, H. J. (1986). Altruism and aggression: The heritability of individual differences. *Journal of Personality and Social Psychology, 50,* 1192–1198.

Rushton, J. P., and Sorrentino, R. M. (Eds.). (1981). *Altruism and helping behavior: Social, personality, and developmental perspectives.* Hillsdale, NJ: Erlbaum.

Rutherford, E., and Mussen, P. (1968). Generosity in nursery school boys. *Child Development, 39,* 755–765.

Rychlak, J. F. (1981). *Introduction to personality and psychotherapy* (2nd ed.). Boston: Houghton Mifflin.

Ryckman, R. M., Robbins, M. A., Thornton, B., and Cantrell, P. (1982). Development and validation of a physical self-efficacy scale. *Journal of Personality and Social Psychology, 42,* 891–900.

Samelson, F. (1975). On the science and politics of the IQ. *Social Research, 42,* 467–488.

Samelson, F. (1980). J. B. Watson's Little Albert, Cyril Burt's twins, and the need for a critical science. *American Psychologist, 35,* 619–625.

Samuda, R. J. (1975). *Psychological testing of American minorities: Issues and consequences.* New York: Harper and Row.

Sarason, I. G. (1978). The Test Anxiety Scale: Concept and research. In C. D. Spielberger and I. G. Sarason (Eds.), *Stress and anxiety* (Vol. 5). Washington, D.C.: Hemisphere.

Sarason, I. G. (1980). Introduction to the study of test anxiety. In I. G. Sarason (Ed.), *Test anxiety: Theory, research, and applications.* Hillsdale, NJ: Erlbaum.

Sarason, I. G. (1984). Stress, anxiety, and cognitive interference: Reactions to tests. *Journal of Personality and Social Psychology, 46,* 929–938.

Sarbin, T. R., and Coe, W. C. (1972). *Hypnosis: A social psychological analysis of influence communication.* New York: Holt, Rinehart and Winston.

Sattler, J. M., and Gwynne, J. (1982). White examiners generally do not impede the intelligence test performance of black children: To debunk a myth. *Journal of Consulting and Clinical Psychology, 50,* 196–208.

Sawin, D. B. (1981). The fantasy-reality distinction in televised violence: Modifying influences on children's aggression. *Journal of Research in Personality, 15,* 323–330.

Scarr, S. (1981). *Race, social class, and individual differences in I.Q.* Hillsdale, NJ: Erlbaum.

Scarr, S., and McCartney, K. (1983). How people make their own environments: A theory of genotype → environment effects. *Child Development, 54,* 424–435.

Scarr, S., Phillips, D., and McCartney, K. (1989). Working mothers and their families. *American Psychologist, 44,* 1402–1409.

Scarr, S., Webber, P. L., Weinberg, R. A., and Wittig, M. A. (1981). Personality resemblance among adolescents and their parents in biologically related and adoptive families. *Journal of Personality and Social Psychology, 40,* 885–898.

Scarr, S., and Weinberg, R. A. (1976). I.Q. test performance of black children adopted by white families. *American Psychologist, 31,* 726–739.

Schachter, S. (1959). *The psychology of affiliation.* Stanford, CA: Stanford University Press.

Schachter, S., and Singer, S. E. (1962). Cognitive, social, and physiological determinants of emotional state. *Psychological Review, 69,* 379–399.

Schaefer, E. S., and Bayley, N. (1964). Maternal behavior, child behavior, and their intercorrelations from infancy through adolescence. *Monographs of the Society for Research in Child Development, 28*(3, Serial No. 94).

Schaffer, K. F. (1981). *Sex roles and human behavior.* Cambridge, MA: Winthrop.

Schank, R. C., and Abelson, R. P. (1977). *Scripts, plans, goals, and understanding.* Hillsdale, NJ: Erlbaum.

Scheier, M. F., and Carver, C. S. (1987). Dispositional optimism and physical well-being: The influence of generalized outcome expectancies on health. *Journal of Personality, 55,* 169–210.

Scheier, M. F., Matthews, K. A., Owens, J. F., Magovern, G. J., Sr., Lefebvre, R. C., Abbott, R. A., and Carver, C. S. (1989). Dispositional optimism and recovery from coronary artery bypass surgery: The beneficial effects on physical and psychological well-being. *Journal of Personality and Social Psychology, 57,* 1024–1040.

Scherer, K. R., Abeles, R. P., and Fischer, C. S. (1975). *Human aggression and conflict.* Englewood Cliffs, NJ: Prentice-Hall.

Schulz, L. (1976). *Rape victimology.* Springfield, IL: Charles C Thomas.

Schulz, R. (1976). Effects of control and predictability on the physical and psychological well-being of the institutionalized aged. *Journal of Personality and Social Psychology, 33,* 563–573.

Schulz, R., and Hanusa, B. H. (1978). Long-term effects of control and predictability-enhancing interventions: Findings and ethical issues. *Journal of Personality and Social Psychology, 36,* 1194–1201.

Schwartz, S. H., and Clausen, G. T. (1970). Responsibility, norms, and helping in an emergency. *Journal of Personality and Social Psychology, 16,* 299–310.

Scott, W. A., and Johnson, R. C. (1972). Comparative validities of direct and indirect personality tests. *Journal of Consulting and Clinical Psychology, 38,* 301–318.

Scroggs, J. R. (1985). *Key ideas in personality theory.* St. Paul, MN: West.

Sears, R. R., Maccoby, E. E., and Levin, H. (1957). *Patterns of child rearing.* Evanston, IL: Row, Peterson.

Sears, R. R., Rau, L., and Alpert, R. (1965). *Identification and child rearing.* Stanford, CA: Stanford University Press.

Sechrest, L. (1977). Personal constructs theory. In R. J. Corsini (Ed.), *Current personality theories.* Itasca, IL: F. E. Peacock Publishers, Inc.

Sechrest, L. (1984). Review of J. B. Rotter, *The development and application of social learning theory: Selected papers. Journal of the History of the Behavioral Sciences, 20,* 228–230.

Seeman, J. (1949). A study of the process of non-directive therapy. *Journal of Consulting Psychology, 13,* 157–168.

Seeman, M. (1963). Alienation and social learning in a reformatory. *American Journal of Sociology, 69,* 270–284.

Seligman, M. E. P. (1975). *Helplessness: On depression, development, and death.* San Francisco: W. H. Freeman.

Selye, H. (1956). *The stress of life.* New York: McGraw-Hill.

Selye, H. (1974). *Stress without distress.* Philadelphia: J. B. Lippincott.

Senneker, P., and Hendrick, C. (1983). Androgyny and helping behavior. *Journal of Personality and Social Psychology, 45,* 916–925.

Shaw, J. S. (1982). Psychological androgyny and stressful life events. *Journal of Personality and Social Psychology, 43,* 145–153.

Sheldon, W. H. (1940). *The varieties of human physique.* New York: Harper and Bros.

Sheldon, W. H. (1942). *The varieties of temperament.* New York: Harper and Bros.

Shepperd, J. A., and Arkin, R. M. (1989). Self-handicapping: The moderating roles of public self-consciousness and task performance. *Personality and Social Psychology Bulletin, 15,* 252–265.

Sherman, J. (1967). Problem of sex differences in space perception and aspects of intellectual functioning. *Psychological Review, 74,* 290–299.

Sherman, J. (1974). Field articulation, sex, spatial visualization, dependency, practice, laterality of the brain, and birth order. *Perceptual and Motor Skills, 38,* 1223–1235.

Shields, S. A. (1987). Women, men, and the dilemma of emotion. In P. Shaver and C. Hendrick (Eds.), *Sex and gender: Review of Personality and Social Psychology,* Vol. 7. Beverly Hills, CA: Sage.

Shiffrin, R. M., and Atkinson, R. C. (1969). Storage and retrieval processes in long-term memory. *Psychological Review, 76,* 179–193.

Shoben, E. J. (1954). Theoretical frames of reference in clinical psychology. In L. A. Pennington and I. A. Berg (Eds.), *An introduction to clinical psychology* (2nd ed.). New York: Ronald Press.

Shore, R. E. (1967). *Parental determinants of boys' internal-external control.* Unpublished doctoral dissertation, Syracuse University.

Shostrom, E. (1965). An inventory for the measurement of self-actualization. *Educational and Psychological Measurement, 24,* 207–218.

Shostrom, E. (1966). *Manual for the Personal Orientation Inventory (POI): An inventory for the measurement of self-actualization.* San Diego, CA: Educational and Industrial Testing Service.

Siegler, I. C., and Costa, P. (1985). Health-behavior relationships. In J. E. Birren and K. W. Schaie (Eds.), *Handbook of the psychology of aging* (2nd ed.). New York: Van Nostrand Reinhold.

Siegler, R. (1983). Information processing approaches to development. In P. H. Mussen (Ed.), *Handbook of child psychology* (4th ed., Vol. 2, No. 1). New York: Wiley.

Siem, F. M., and Spence, J. T. (1986). Gender-related traits and helping behaviors. *Journal of Personality and Social Psychology, 51,* 615–621.

Signorella, M. L., and Jamison, W. (1986). Masculinity, femininity, androgyny and cognitive performance: A meta-analysis. *Psychological Bulletin, 100,* 207–228.

Siipola, E. M. (1984). Thematic Apperception Test. In R. J. Corsini (Ed.)., *Encyclopedia of psychology.* New York: Wiley-Interscience.

Silverman, L. H. (1976). Psychoanalytic theory: The reports of my death are greatly exaggerated. *American Psychologist, 31,* 621–637.

Silverman, L. H., and Weinberger, J. (1985). Mommy and I are one: Implications for psychotherapy. *American Psychologist, 40,* 1296–1308.

Simpson, E. E. L. (1974). Moral development research: A case study of scientific cultural bias. *Human Development, 17,* 81–106.

Simpson, M. T., Olewine, D. A., Jenkins, F. H., Ramsey, S. J., Zyzanski, S. J., Thomas, G., and Hames, C. G. (1974). Exercise-induced catecholamines and platelet aggregation in the coronary-prone behavior pattern. *Psychosomatic Medicine, 36,* 476–487.

Simpson-Housley, P., and Bradshaw, P. (1978). Personality and the perception of earthquake hazard. *Australian Geographical Studies, 16,* 65–72.

Skinner, B. F. (1938). *The behavior of organisms.* New York: Appleton-Century-Crofts.

Skinner, B. F. (1948). *Walden two.* New York: Macmillan.

Skinner, B. F. (1953). *Science and human behavior.* New York: Macmillan.

Skinner, B. F. (1957). *Verbal behavior.* New York: Appleton-Century-Crofts.

Skinner, B. F. (1967). Autobiography. In E. G. Boring and G. Lindzey (Eds.), *A history of psychology in autobiography* (Vol. 5). New York: Appleton-Century-Crofts.

Skinner, B. F. (1969). *Contingencies of reinforcement: A theoretical analysis.* New York: Appleton-Century-Crofts.

Skinner, B. F. (1971). *Beyond freedom and dignity.* New York: Knopf.

Skinner, B. F. (1974). *About behaviorism.* New York: Knopf.

Skinner, B. F. (1976). *Particulars of my life.* New York: Knopf.

Skinner, B. F. (1987). *Upon further reflection.* Englewood Cliffs, NJ: Prentice-Hall.

Skodak, M., and Skeels, H. M. (1949). A final follow-up of one hundred adopted children. *Journal of Genetic Psychology, 75,* 85–125.

Smith, D. E., King, M. B., and Hoebel, B. C. (1970). Lateral hypothalamic control of killing: Evidence for a cholinoceptive mechanism. *Science, 167,* 900–901.

Smith, K. D., Keating, J. P., and Stotland, E. (1989). Altruism reconsidered: The effect of denying feedback on a victim's status to empathic witnesses. *Journal of Personality and Social Psychology, 57,* 641–650.

Smith, M. B. (1989). Henry A. Murray (1893–1988). *American Psychologist, 44,* 1153–1154.

Smith, R. E., Smythe, L., and Lien, D. (1972). Inhibition of helping behavior by a similar or dissimilar nonreactive fellow bystander. *Journal of Personality and Social Psychology, 23,* 414–419.

Smith, T. W., and Anderson, N. B. (1986). Models of personality and disease: An interactional approach to Type A behavior and cardiovascular risk. *Journal of Personality and Social Psychology, 50,* 1166–1173.

Snyder, M., and Kendzierski, D. (1982). Choosing social situations: Investigating the origins of correspondence between attitudes and behavior. *Journal of Personality, 50,* 280–295.

Solomon, L. Z., Solomon, H., and Stone, R. (1978). Helping as a function of number of bystanders and ambiguity of emergency. *Personality and Social Psychology Bulletin, 4,* 318–321.

Sosis, R. H. (1974). Internal-external control and the perception of responsibility of another for an accident. *Journal of Personality and Social Psychology, 30,* 393–399.

Spearman, C. (1923). *The nature of "intelligence" and the principle of cognition.* London: Macmillan.

Spearman, C. (1927). *The abilities of man.* New York: Macmillan.

Spence, J. T., and Helmreich, R. L. (1981). Androgyny versus gender schema: A comment on Bem's gender schema theory. *Psychological Review, 88,* 365–368.

Spence, J. T., Helmreich, R. L., and Stapp, J. (1975). Ratings of self and peers on sex-role attributes and their relation to self-esteem and conceptions of masculinity and femininity. *Journal of Personality and Social Psychology, 32,* 29–39.

Spence, K. W. (1958). A theory of emotionally based drive (D) and its relation to performance in simple learning situations. *American Psychologist, 31,* 131–141.

Spiegler, M. D., and Liebert, R. M. (1970). Some correlates of self-reported fear. *Psychological Reports, 26,* 691–695.

Spielberger, C. D. (1966). *Anxiety and behavior.* New York: Academic Press.

Spielberger, C. D., Gorsuch, R. L., and Lushene, R. E. (1970). *The State-Trait Anxiety Inventory (STAI) Test Manual for Form X.* Palo Alto, CA: Consulting Psychologists Press.

Spitz, H. H. (1986). *The raising of intelligence: A selected history of attempts to raise retarded intelligence.* Hillsdale, NJ: Erlbaum.

Springer, S. P., and Deutsch, G. (1981). *Left brain, right brain.* San Francisco: W. H. Freeman.

Staats, A. W. (1975). *Social behaviorism.* Chicago, IL: Dorsey.

Staats, A. W., and Staats, C. K. (1963). *Complex human behavior.* New York: Holt, Rinehart and Winston.

Staub, E. (1971). Use of role-playing and induction in training for prosocial behavior. *Child Development, 41,* 805–816.

Staub, E. (1974). Helping a distressed person: Social, personality, and stimulus determinants. In L. Berkowitz (Ed.), *Advances in experimental social psychology* (Vol. 7). New York: Academic Press.

Staub, E. (1978). *Positive social behavior and morality: Vol. 1. Social and personal influences.* New York: Academic Press.

Staub, E. (1980). Social and prosocial behavior: Personal and situational influences and their interactions. In E. Staub (Ed.), *Personality: Basic aspects and current research.* Englewood Cliffs, NJ: Prentice-Hall.

Staub, E., and Baer, R. S., Jr. (1974). Stimulus characteristics of a sufferer and difficulty of escape as determinants of helping. *Journal of Personality and Social Psychology, 30,* 279–284.

Steblay, N. M. (1987). Helping behavior in rural and urban environments: A meta-analysis. *Psychological Bulletin, 102,* 346–356.

Stephens, M. A. P., and Zarit, S. H. (1989). Symposium: Family caregiving to dependent older adults: Stress, appraisal, and coping. *Psychology and Aging, 4,* 387–388.

Stephenson, W. (1953). *The study of behavior.* Chicago: University of Chicago Press.

Sternberg, R. J. (1985). *Beyond the IQ: A triarchic theory of human intelligence.* Cambridge, England: Cambridge University Press.

Sternberg, R. J., Conway, B. E., Ketron, J. L., and Bernstein, M. (1981). People's conceptions of intelligence. *Journal of Personality and Social Psychology, 41,* 37–55.

Sternberg, R. J., and Detterman, D. K. (Eds.). (1986). *What is intelligence? Contemporary viewpoints on its nature and definition.* Norwood, NJ: Ablex.

Sternberg, R. J., and Salter, W. (1982). Conceptions of intelligence. In R. J. Sternberg (Ed.), *Handbook of human intelligence.* New York: Cambridge University Press.

Sternberg, R. J., and Wagner, R. K. (Eds.). (1986). *Practical intelligence: Nature and origins of competence in the everyday world.* New York: Cambridge University Press.

Sternglanz, S. H., and Serbin, L. A. (1974). Sex role stereotyping in children's television programs. *Developmental Psychology, 10,* 710–715.

Stock, D. (1949). An investigation into interrelations between self-concept and feelings directed toward other persons and groups. *Journal of Consulting Psychology, 13,* 176–180.

Stokols, D. (1972). On the distinction between density and crowding: Some implications for future research. *Psychological Review, 79,* 275–278.

Stoler, N. (1963). Client likability: A variable in the study of psychotherapy. *Journal of Consulting Psychology, 27,* 175–178.

Stolorow, R. D., Bandcraft, B., and Atwood, G. E. (1987). *Psychosomatic treatment: An intersubjective approach.* Hillsdale, NJ: Analytic Press.

Stotland, E. (1969). Exploratory investigations of empathy. In L. Berkowitz (Ed.), *Advances in experimental social psychology* (Vol. 4.). New York: Academic Press.

Straus, M. (1977, March 12). *Normative and behavioral aspects of violence between spouses: Preliminary data on a nationally representative USA sample.* Paper presented to Symposium on Violence in Canadian Society, Simon Fraser University, Burnaby, British Columbia, Canada.

Straus, M., Gelles, R., and Steinmetz, S. K. (1980). *Behind closed doors: Violence in the American family.* Garden City, NY: Anchor Press.

Strickland, B. R. (1965). The prediction of social action from a dimension of internal-external control. *Journal of Social Psychology, 66,* 353–358.

Strickland, B. R. (1977). Internal-external control of reinforcement. In T. Bass (Ed.), *Personality variables in social behavior.* Hillsdale, NJ: Erlbaum.

Strickland, B. R. (1979). Internal-external expectancies and cardiovascular functioning. In L. C. Perlmuter and R. A. Monty (Eds.), *Choice and perceived control.* Hillsdale, NJ: Erlbaum.

Strickland, B. R. (1989). Internal-external control expectancies: From contingency to creativity. *American Psychologist, 44,* 1–12.

Strickland, B. R., and Haley, W. E. (1980). Sex differences on the Rotter I-E Scale. *Journal of Personality and Social Psychology, 39,* 930–939.

Strube, M. J. (1989). Evidence for the *type* in Type A behavior: A taxometric analysis. *Journal of Personality and Social Psychology, 56,* 972–987.

Strube, M. J., Lott, C. L., Heilizer, R., and Gregg, B. (1986). Type A behavior pattern and the judgment of control. *Journal of Personality and Social Psychology, 50,* 403–412.

Strube, M. J., and Werner, C. (1985). Relinquishment of control and the Type A behavior pattern. *Journal of Personality and Social Psychology, 48,* 688–701.

Sullivan, H. S. (1953). *The interpersonal theory of psychiatry.* New York: Norton.

Sullivan, H. S. (1964). *The fusion of psychiatry and social science.* New York: Norton.

Suls, J., and Rittenhouse, J. D. (1987). Personality and physical health: An introduction. *Journal of Personality, 55,* 155–167.

Suls, J., and Wan, C. K. (1989). The relation between Type A behavior and chronic emotional distress: A meta-analysis. *Journal of Personality and Social Psychology, 57,* 503–512.

Sundberg, N. D., Snowden, L. R., and Reynolds, W. M. (1978). Toward assessment of personal competence and incompetence in life situations. In M. R. Rosenzweig and L. W. Porter (Eds.), *Annual review of psychology* (Vol. 29). Palo Alto, CA: Annual Reviews.

Swede, S. W., and Tetlock, P. E. (1986). Henry Kissinger's implicit theory of personality: A quantitative case study. *Journal of Personality, 54,* 617–646.

Swim, J., Borgida, E., Maruyama, G., and Meyers, D. G. (1989). Joan McKay versus J. McKay: Do gender stereotypes bias evaluations? *Psychological Bulletin, 105,* 409–429.

Symonds, P. M. (1949). *The dynamics of parent-child relationships.* New York: Teachers College, Columbia University.

Tangney, J. P., and Feshbach, S. (1988). Children's television-viewing frequency: Individual differences and demographic correlates. *Personality and Social Psychology Bulletin, 14,* 145–158.

Taylor, J. A. (1953). A personality scale of manifest anxiety. *Journal of Abnormal and Social Psychology, 48,* 285–290.

Taylor, M. C., and Hall, J. A. (1982). Psychological androgyny: Theories, methods, and conclusions. *Psychological Bulletin, 92,* 347–366.

Taylor, S. E. (1986). *Health psychology.* New York: Random House.

Taylor, S. E. (1987). The progress and prospects of health psychology: Tasks of a maturing discipline. *Health Psychology, 6,* 73–87.

Taylor, S. P., and Leonard, K. E. (1983). Alcohol and human physical aggression. In R. G. Geen and E. I. Donnerstein (Eds.), *Aggression: Theoretical and empirical reviews: Vol. 2. Issues in research.* New York: Academic Press.

Taylor, S. P., Vardaris, R. M., Rawitch, A. B., Gammon, C. B., Cranston, J. W., and Lubetkin, A. I. (1976). The effects of alcohol and delta-9-tetrahydrocannabinol on human physical aggression. *Aggressive Behavior, 2,* 153–161.

Tellegen, A., Lykken, D. T., Bouchard, T. J., Jr., Wilcox, K. J., Segal, N. L., and Rich, S. (1988). Personality similarity in twins reared apart and together. *Journal of Personality and Social Psychology, 54,* 1031–1039.

Terman, L. M., and Merrill, M. A. (1937). *Measuring intelligence.* Boston: Houghton Mifflin.

Thoma, S. (1986). Estimating gender differences in the comprehension and preferences of moral issues. *Developmental Review, 6,* 165–180.

Thomas, A., Chess, S., and Birch, H. G. (1970). The origin of personality. *Scientific American, 223*(2), 102–109.

Thomas, A., and Chess, S. (1977). *Temperament and development.* New York: Bruner/Mazel.

Thorndike, E. L. (1905). *The elements of psychology.* New York: A. G. Seiler.

Thorndike, E. L., Bregman, E. O., Cobb, M. V., and Woodyard, E. (1926). *The measurement of intelligence.* New York: Teachers College, Columbia University.

Thorndike, R. L., Hagen, E. P., and Sattler, J. M. (1986). *Guide for administering and scoring the fourth edition of the Stanford-Binet Intelligence Scale.* Chicago: Riverside Publishing Co.

Thorne, F. C. (1973). The Existential Study: A measure of existential status. *Journal of Clinical Psychology, 29,* 387–392.

Thurstone, L. L. (1938). Primary mental abilities. *Psychometric Monographs,* No. 1.

Tice, D. M., and Baumeister, R. F. (1985). Masculinity inhibits helping in emergencies; Personality does predict the bystander effect. *Journal of Personality and Social Psychology, 49,* 420–428.

Tims, A. R., Jr., Swart, C., and Kidd, R. F. (1976). Factors affecting predecisional communication behavior after helping requests. *Human Communication Research, 2,* 271–280.

Tobias, S. (1976, September). Math anxiety: Why is a smart girl like you counting on her fingers? *Ms,* pp. 56–59.

Toi, M., and Batson, C. D. (1982). More evidence that empathy is a source of altruistic motivation. *Journal of Personality and Social Psychology, 43,* 281–292.

Tomlinson, T. M., and Hart, J. T., Jr. (1962). A validation study of the Process Scale. *Journal of Consulting Psychology, 26,* 74–78.

Towbes, L. C., Cohen, L. H., and Glyshaw, K. (1989). Instrumentality as a life-stress moderator for early versus middle adolescents. *Journal of Personality and Social Psychology, 57,* 109–119.

Truax, C. B. (1966). Reinforcement and nonreinforcement in Rogerian psychotherapy. *Journal of Abnormal Psychology, 71,* 1–9.

Turner, J. H. (1970). Entrepreneurial environments and the emergence of achievement motivation in adolescent males. *Sociometry, 33,* 147–165.

Tyler, L. E. (1978). *Individuality: Human possibilities and personal choice in the psychological development of men and women.* San Francisco: Jossey-Bass.

Ullmann, L. P., and Krasner, L. (1975). *A psychological approach to abnormal behavior.* Englewood Cliffs, NJ: Prentice-Hall.

Unger, R. K. (1979). *Female and male: Psychological perspectives.* New York: Harper and Row.

Van De Water, D. A., and McAdams, D. P. (1989). Generativity in Erikson's "belief in the species." *Journal of Research in Personality, 23,* 435–449.

van Kaam, A. (1966). *Existential foundations of psychology.* Pittsburgh, PA: Duquesne University Press.

Vernon, P. E. (1960). *The structure of human abilities* (rev. ed.). London: Methuen.

Vitiello, M. V., Carlin, A. S., Becker, J., Barris, B. P., and Dutton, J. (1989). The effect of subliminal oedipal and competitive stimulation on dart throwing: Another miss. *Journal of Abnormal Psychology, 98,* 54–56.

Vockell, E. L., Felker, D. W., and Miley, C. H. (1973). Birth order literature 1967–1972. *Journal of Individual Psychology, 29,* 39–53.

Wachtel, P. L. (1973). Psychodynamics, behavior therapy, and the implacable experimenter: An inquiry into the consistency of personality. *Journal of Abnormal Psychology, 82,* 324–334.

Wade, T. C., and Baker, T. B. (1977). Opinions and use of psychological tests: A survey of clinical psychologists. *American Psychologist, 32,* 874–882.

Wagner, K. D., Lorion, R. P., and Shipley, T. E. (1983). Insomnia and psychological crisis: Two studies of Erikson's developmental theory. *Journal of Consulting and Clinical Psychology, 51,* 595–603.

Waldron, I. (1976). Why do women live longer than men? Part I. *Journal of Human Stress, 2,* 2–13.

Waldron, I. (1986). The contribution of smoking to sex differences in mortality. *Public Health Reports, 101,* 163–173.

Walker, L. (1979). *The battered woman.* New York: Harper and Row.

Walker, L. E. A. (1989). Psychology and violence against women. *American Psychologist, 44,* 695–702.

Wallach, M. A. (1971). *The intelligence/creativity distinction.* Morristown, NJ: General Learning Press.

Wallach, M. A., and Wallach, L. (1983). *Psychology's sanction for selfishness: The error of egoism in theory and therapy.* San Francisco: W. H. Freeman.

Waller, N. G., and Ben-Porath, Y. S. (1987). Is it time for clinical psychology to embrace the five-factor model of personality? *American Psychologist, 42,* 887–889.

Waller, N. G., Kojetin, B. A., Bouchard, T. J., Jr., Lykken, D. T., and Tellegen, A. (1990). Genetic and environmental influences on religious interests, attitudes, and values: A study of twins reared apart and together. *Psychological Science, 1,* 138–142.

Wallston, B. S., Wallston, K. A., Kaplan, G. D., and Maides, S. A. (1976). Development and validation of the Health Locus of Control (HLC) Scale. *Journal of Consulting and Clinical Psychology, 44,* 580–585.

Waterman, A. S., and Whitbourne, S. K. (1982). Androgyny and psychosocial development among college students and adults. *Journal of Personality, 50,* 121–133.

Waters, E., and Crandall, V. J. (1964). Social class and observed maternal behaviors from 1940 to 1960. *Child Development, 35,* 1021–1032.

Watson, D., and Pennebaker, J. W. (1989). Health complaints, stress, and distress: Exploring the central role of negative affectivity. *Psychological Review, 96,* 234–254.

Watson, J. B. (1919). *Psychology from the standpoint of a behaviorist.* Philadelphia: Lippincott.

Watson, J. B. (1930). *Behaviorism* (2nd ed.). Chicago: University of Chicago Press.

Watson, J. B., and Rayner, R. (1920). Conditional emotional reactions. *Journal of Experimental Psychology, 3,* 1–14.

Webb, E. J., Campbell, D. T., Schwartz, R. D., and Sechrest, L. (1966). *Unobtrusive measures: Nonreactive research in the social sciences.* Chicago: Rand McNally.

Wechsler, D. (1939). *The measurement of adult intelligence.* Baltimore, MD: Williams and Wilkins.

Wechsler, D. (1949). *Wechsler Intelligence Scale for Children.* New York: Psychological Corporation.

Wechsler, D. (1955). *Manual for the Wechsler Adult Intelligence Scale.* New York: Psychological Corporation.

Wechsler, D. (1967). *Manual for the Wechsler Preschool and Primary Scale of Intelligence.* New York: Psychological Corporation.

Wechsler, D. (1974). *Manual: Wechsler Intelligence Scale for Children* (rev.). New York: Psychological Corporation.

Wechsler, D. (1981). *Manual for the Wechsler Adult Intelligence Scale* (rev.). New York: Psychological Corporation.

Weikart, D. P. (1972). Relationship of curriculum, teaching, and learning in preschool education. In J. C. Stanley (Ed.), *Preschool for the disadvantaged.* Baltimore, MD: The Johns Hopkins University.

Weinberg, R. A. (1989). Intelligence and IQ: Landmark issues and great debates. *American Psychologist, 44,* 98–104.

Weiner, B. (1978). Achievement strivings. In H. London and J. E. Exner, Jr. (Eds.), *Dimensions of personality.* New York: Wiley-Interscience.

Weitan, W. (1989). *Psychology: Themes and variations.* Pacific Grove, CA: Brooks/Cole.

Wells, A. J. (1988). Variations in mothers' self-esteem in daily life. *Journal of Personality and Social Psychology, 55,* 661–668.

Westcott, M. (1986). *The feminist legacy of Karen Horney.* New Haven, CT: Yale University Press.

Westinghouse Corporation/Ohio University. (1969). *The impact of Head Start* (Vols. I and II). Springfield, VA: U.S. Department of Commerce.

White, L. A. (1979). Erotica and aggression: The influence of sexual arousal, positive affect, and negative affect on aggressive behavior. *Journal of Personality and Social Psychology, 37,* 591–601.

White, R. W. (1959). Motivation reconsidered: The concept of competence. *Psychological Review, 66,* 279–333.

White, R. W. (1976). *The enterprise of living: A view of personal growth* (2nd ed.). New York: Holt, Rinehart and Winston.

White, R. W. (1981). Exploring personality the long way: The study of lives. In A. I. Rabin, J. Aronoff, A. M. Barclay, and R. A. Zucker (Eds.), *Further explorations in personality.* New York: Wiley-Interscience.

Whiting, B., and Edwards, C. P. (1973). A cross-cultural analysis of sex differences in the behavior of children aged three through eleven. *Journal of Social Psychology, 91,* 171–188.

Whiting, J. W. M. (1960). Resource mediation and learning by identification. In I. Iscoe and H. W. Stevenson (Eds.), *Personality development in children.* Austin: University of Texas Press.

Wicklund, R. A., and Gollwitzer, P. M. (1987). The fallacy of the private-public self-focus distinction. *Journal of Personality, 55,* 491–523.

Widom, C. S. (1989). Does violence beget violence? A critical examination of the literature. *Psychological Bulletin, 106,* 3–28.

Wiggins, J. S. (1968). Personality structure. In P. R. Farnsworth (Ed.), *Annual review of psychology.* Palo Alto, CA: Annual Reviews.

Wiggins, J. S. (1984). Cattell's system from the perspective of mainstream personality theory. *Multivariate Behavioral Research, 19,* 176–190.

Wiggins, J. S., and Holzmuller, A. (1981). Further evidence on androgyny and interpersonal flexibility. *Journal of Research in Personality, 15,* 67–80.

Williams, D. E., and Page, M. M. (1989). A multi-dimensional measure of Maslow's hierarchy of needs. *Journal of Research in Personality, 23,* 192–213.

Williams, R. L. (1972, September). *The BITCH-100: A culture-specific test.* Paper presented at the meetings of the American Psychological Association, Honolulu.

Williams, T. (1975). Family resemblance in abilities: The Wechsler scales. *Behavior Genetics, 5,* 405–409.

Wilson, E. O. (1975). *Sociobiology: The new synthesis.* Cambridge, MA: Harvard University Press.

Wilson, E. O. (1978). *On human nature.* Cambridge, MA: Harvard University Press.

Wilson, R. S. (1972). Twins: Early mental development. *Science, 175,* 914–917.

Winnicott, D. W. (1953). Transitional objects and transitional phenomena. *International Journal of Psychoanalysis, 34,* 89–97.

Winter, D. G. (1973). *The power motive.* New York: Free Press.

Winter, D. G., and Carlson, L. A. (1988). Using motive scores in the psychobiographical study of an individual: The case of Richard Nixon. *Journal of Personality, 56,* 75–103.

Winter, D. G., and Stewart, A. J. (1978). The power motive. In H. London and J. E. Exner, Jr. (Eds.), *Dimensions of personality.* New York: Wiley-Interscience.

Witkin, H. A., Dyk, R. B., Faterson, H. F., Goodenough, D. R., and Karp, S. A. (1962). *Psychological differentiation.* New York: Wiley.

Wogan, M., and Norcross, J. C. (1982). Sauce for the goose: A response to Wolpe. *American Psychologist, 37,* 100–102. (Comment)

Wolberg, L. R. (1948). *Medical hypnosis: The principles of hypnotherapy* (Vol. 1). New York: Grune and Stratton.

Wolf, M., Risley, T., and Mees, H. (1964). Application of operant conditioning procedures to the behavior problems of an autistic child. *Behavior Research and Therapy, 1,* 305–312.

Wolk, S., and Kurtz, J. (1975). Positive adjustment and involvement during aging and expectancy for internal control. *Journal of Consulting and Clinical Psychology, 43,* 173–178.

Wolpe, J. (1958). *Psychotherapy by reciprocal inhibition.* Stanford, CA: Stanford University Press.

Wolpe, J. (1973). *The practice of behavior therapy* (2nd ed.). New York: Pergamon Press.

Wolpe, J. (1981). Behavior therapy versus psychoanalysis: Therapeutic and social implications. *American Psychologist, 36,* 159–164.

Wolpe, J., and Lang, P. J. (1964). A fear survey schedule for use in behavior therapy. *Behavior Research and Therapy, 2,* 27–30.

Wolpe, J., and Lazarus, A. A. (1966). *Behavior therapy techniques.* New York: Pergamon Press.

Woodruff-Pak, D. (1988). *Psychology and aging.* Englewood Cliffs, NJ: Prentice-Hall.

Woodward, W. R. (1982). The "discovery" of social behaviorism and social learning theory, 1870–1980. *American Psychologist, 37,* 396–410.

Woolfolk, R. L., and Richardson, F. C. (1978). *Stress, sanity, and survival.* New York: Sovereign/Monarch.

Worchel, S. (1974). The effect of three types of arbitrary thwarting on the instigation of aggression. *Journal of Personality, 42,* 300–318.

Wright, L. (1988). The Type A behavior pattern and coronary artery disease: Quest for the active ingredients and the elusive mechanism. *American Psychologist, 43,* 2–14.

Wright, M. H., Zautra, A. J., and Braver, S. L. (1985). Distortion in control attributions for real life events. *Journal of Research in Personality, 19,* 54–71.

Wright, T. L., Maggied, P., and Palmer, M. L. (1975). An unobtrusive study of interpersonal trust. *Journal of Personality and Social Psychology, 32,* 446–448.

Wrightsman, L. S. (1981). Personal documents as data in conceptualizing adult personality development. *Personality and Social Psychology Bulletin, 7,* 367–385.

Wylie, R. (1984). Self-concept. In R. Corsini (Ed.), *Encyclopedia of psychology* (Vol. 3). New York: Wiley-Interscience.

Yates, A. (1981). Narcissistic traits in certain abused children. *American Journal of Orthopsychiatry, 51,* 55–62.

Young, M. L. (1971). Age and sex differences in problem solving. *Journal of Gerontology, 26,* 300–336.

Young, W. C., Goy, R. W., and Phoenix, C. H. (1964). Hormones and sexual behavior. *Science, 143,* 212–218.

Zammuner, V. L. (1987). Children's sex-role stereotypes: A cross-cultural analysis. In P. Shaver and C. Hendrick (Eds.), *Sex and gender: Review of Personality and Social Psychology* (Vol. 7). Beverly Hills, CA: Sage.

Zeller, A. (1950). An experimental analogue of repression: II. The effect of individual failure and success on memory measured by relearning. *Journal of Experimental Psychology, 40,* 411–422.

Zigler, E., and Valentine, J. (Eds.) (1979). *Project Head Start: A legacy of the War on Poverty.* New York: Free Press.

Zillmann, D. (1971). Excitation transfer in communication-mediated aggressive behavior. *Journal of Experimental Social Psychology, 7,* 419–434.

Zillmann, D. (1978). *Hostility and aggression.* Hillsdale, NJ: Erlbaum.

Zillmann, D., Bryant, J., and Sapolsky, B. S. (1978). The enjoyment of watching sport contests. In H. Goldstein (Ed.), *Sports, games, and play.* Hillsdale, NJ: Erlbaum.

Zillmann, D., and Cantor, J. R. (1976). Effect of timing of information about mitigating circumstances on emotional responses to provocation and retaliatory behavior. *Journal of Experimental Social Psychology, 12,* 38–55.

Zimbardo, P. G. (1969). The human choice: Individuation, reason, and order, versus deindividuation, impulse, and chaos. In W. J. Arnold and D. Levine (Eds.), *Nebraska Symposium on Motivation* (Vol. 17). Lincoln: University of Nebraska Press.

Zuckerman, D. M. (1980). Self-esteem, self-concept, and the life goals and sex-role attitudes of college students. *Journal of Personality, 48,* 149–162.

Zuckerman, M. (1978). Sensation seeking. In H. London and J. Exner (Eds.), *Dimensions of personality.* New York: Wiley.

Zuckerman, M., Buchsbaum, M. S., and Murphy, D. L. (1980). Sensation seeking and its biological correlates. *Psychological Bulletin, 88,* 187–214.

Zuckerman, M., Kuhlman, M., and Camac, K. (1988). What lies beyond E and N? Factor analysis of scales believed to measure basic dimensions of personality. *Journal of Personality and Social Psychology, 54,* 96–107.

Zuckerman, M., and Wheeler, L. (1975). To dispel fantasies about the fantasy-based measure of fear of success. *Psychological Bulletin, 82,* 932–946.

Zuroff, D. C. (1980). Learned helplessness in humans: An analysis of learning processes and the roles of individual and situational differences. *Journal of Personality and Social Psychology, 39,* 130–146.

Zuroff, D. C. (1986). Was Gordon Allport a trait theorist? *Journal of Personality and Social Psychology, 51,* 993–1000.

Zuroff, D. C., and Rotter, J. B. (1985). A history of the expectancy construct in psychology. In J. Dusek (Ed.), *Teacher expectancies.* Hillsdale, NJ: Erlbaum.

AUTHOR INDEX

SUBJECT INDEX